W9-AOZ-869

AIDS AND THE LAW

AIDS AND THE LAW
A Guide for the Public

Edited by
Harlon L. Dalton
Scott Burris
and the
Yale AIDS Law Project

Yale University Press
New Haven and London

The Yale AIDS Law Project is composed of members of the Yale Law School community formed specifically to produce this book. The Project is not a formal part or program of the university and has not been endorsed by it. Opinions expressed by authors of the various chapters are their own and do not necessarily reflect the opinions of members of the Project.

Chapter 1, The AIDS Epidemic: The Discovery of a New Disease, is adapted from an article entitled The AIDS Epidemic: An Overview of the Science that appeared in Issues in Science and Technology, 1986, and is published here with permission.

Designed by Nancy Ovedovitz and set in Times Roman Type by Rainsford Type. Printed in the United States of America by Maple-Vail, York, Penn.

Library of Congress Catalogue Card Number: 87–50492
International Standard Book Number: 0–300–04077–6 (cloth)
0–300–04078–4 (pbk)

The paper in this book meets the guidelines for permanence and durability of the Committee on Production Guidelines for Book Longevity of the Council on Library Resources.

10 9 8 7 6 5 4 3 2 1

The Yale AIDS Law Project

Editors-in-Chief

Scott Burris
Harlon L. Dalton

Managing Editors

John L. Steiner
Lee M. Weinberg

Executive Editor

Donna I. Dennis

Editorial Consultant

Catherine Iino

Project Coordinator

Jill A. Zarnetske

Editors

Paul S. Bird
Rosann Bocciarelli
Rhonda Brown
Sabina Brukner
Mark Emerson Collins
Geoffrey B. Dryvynsyde
Ruth E. Harlow
David Huebner
Alexander Kaplen
Elizabeth A. Leiman

Sandra E. Lundy
Julia Mahoney
Louise Melling
Andrea M. Mercado
Nina Morais
Tanina Rostain
Malcolm Stewart
Anthony Thomas
Catherine Weiss
Judith B. White

Faculty Supporters

Robert A. Burt
Bernard J. Dushman
Lucinda M. Finley

Owen M. Fiss
Michael J. Graetz
Jamienne S. Studley

Contents

PART SIX
CONFRONTING AIDS: THE PROBLEMS
OF SPECIAL GROUPS

Preface

HARLON L. DALTON

This book is about *law*. It is not, however, aimed exclusively (or even primarily) at those who are steeped in the law. Rather, it is meant for whoever has a professional need to come to grips with the legal issues spawned by the AIDS epidemic—for educators, counselors, legislators, policy makers, law enforcement and corrections officials, public health officials, health care providers, social service providers, research scientists, employers, employee representatives, insurers, providers of goods and services, social workers, social scientists, social activists, representatives of interest groups, the staffs of drug treatment programs, members of AIDS support groups, and, of course, lawyers for any and all of the above.

Ever since its spontaneous generation eighteen months ago when several law students and faculty expressed to each other the desire to "do something" about AIDS, the Yale AIDS Law Project has had one overriding goal: to sift through the law as it relates to AIDS and to communicate what we find to the people who most need to understand the law's sweep. To that end, we have abandoned, in large measure, the private language that serves to separate us legal types from the great unwashed. Figuring out how to speak plain English, without sacrificing precision or sophistication, has not, however, been easy. It is therefore not surprising that talking about how to talk about law quickly became a major focus of the semester-long AIDS law seminar that sprang up as an adjunct to the project. (We also focused on the difficulties inherent in writing about issues that are contemporaneous, ever-changing, and deeply political.) To ease our "translation" burden, we intentionally solicited authors who, in addition to expertise, had demonstrated the ability to communicate effectively with non-lawyers. Even so, throughout the editorial process, the student editors engaged the authors in a continuing dialogue regarding whether the contours of the law, and its shadings as well, had been conveyed in a way that was accessible to our target audience.

Taken as a whole, *AIDS and the Law* reflects the unique challenge the AIDS epidemic poses for our legal system. In general, the law presupposes that we are rational, self-regarding beings. Its frequent invocation of the "reasonable person" standard suggests, at a minimum, a reluctance to reward or accommodate irrationality. Efforts to regulate conduct through incentives presuppose that people and organizations rationally calculate their self-interest. And even though the law occasionally recognizes (in, for example, statutes permitting consumers to rescind door-to-door sales transactions within a set number of days) that in some circumstances our rational will can be overborne, such enactments look rather like the exceptions that prove the rule.

AIDS stands all that on its head; or, if not AIDS, then the secondary epidemic of fear sometimes labeled AfrAIDS. Increasingly, the law is asked to mediate or resolve conflicts in which at least some of the parties are so consumed by fear as to be incapable of exercising rational judgment. Not infrequently, those tormented by fear disavow any obligation to be rational. "I don't care if the odds are a million to one, I don't want to take the chance." "I know it's crazy, but . . . ." Equally unreachable are people who dispose of that which is fearful by simply denying its existence. "If I'm gonna get it I'm gonna get it and there is nothing I can do about it."

Not only do the fears engendered by AIDS strip people of their capacity to be rational; the fears themselves have a deeply irrational element. No matter how rooted they are in common sense and informed opinion, they inevitably tap into other fears that are deep-seated and largely pre-rational: fear of sex; fear of the unclean; fear of the uncontrollable; and fear of death. In the first category, I would include both the scariness of our own sexuality and the equally scary fact that we are surrounded by sexual beings, whichever way we turn. In thinking about the second, I am struck by our particular culture's discomfort with disease and, more broadly, with physical abnormality. And of course, for many, attitudes toward sex and toward the unclean overlap.

Third, AIDS anxiety taps into our previously stilled suspicions that, despite our fervent wishes, science cannot save us from random and arbitrary pain and dissolution. In a sense, AIDS stands as a surrogate for all the risks and uncertainties that attend living in a technologically advanced and spiritually desolate society. We can remove asbestos, ignore acid rain or radon, and keep switching from one artificial sweetener to another. But we can't seem to make AIDS go away, either through mental gymnastics or the magic of science. And then there is death.

Given this psychic assault, the AIDS epidemic challenges the law to face up to our irrational as well as our rational selves; to structure procedures and fashion rules that, simultaneously, give vent to our fears and life to our aspirations. If the law is to be effective in dealing with the conflicts and turmoil generated by this dread disease, we must learn to console the inconsolate and convince the incredulous. We cannot pretend that we are any less complicated or any more Mr. Spock-like than we truly are.

Now for the good news. In putting together this book, I have become convinced (much to my surprise) that our legal system is uniquely suited to the task at hand. My optimism springs from two rather curious, and somewhat contradictory, features of the system: its tendency to reduce to a formula the most passionate of concerns; and its tendency to promote confrontation. The first feature is familiar to anyone who has turned to the courts for vindication on a matter of some importance and been forced to transmogrify her concerns into a stylized "cause of action" with preset "elements" that may resemble only faintly the precipitating real-world event. The second is familiar to anyone who has experienced the adversarial side of the adversary system. Despite their drawbacks when viewed from any number of perspectives, these features in tandem hold out the promise of a sane and sensitive response to the fallout from AIDS.

The law's formulaic quality means, among other things, that we need not reinvent the wheel to deal with AIDS-related legal issues. As chapter after chapter makes clear, the institutional and conceptual framework for dealing with such issues already exists; the principles and procedures that will guide decision-making are, for the most part, already in place. Analogous situations abound, from cases involving sexual transmission of genital herpes to attempts to quarantine persons with bubonic plague; from cases involving schoolchildren infected with the hepatitis B virus to efforts to round up prostitutes to stem the spread of syphilis. Perhaps the most important guiding light is the explosion of statutes and cases addressing discrimination against the disabled and against people who are perceived as disabled. The tools are there.

Despite its enormous benefits, reasoning from the old to the new has a major downside, especially as respects AIDS issues. For no matter what the analogy, AIDS is viewed by most people as significantly different. The practical differences—difficulty of transmission, prospects for treatment and cure, available safeguards, for example—can be apprehended and taken account of by the law with relative ease. The *emotional* differences are much trickier. In rounding off the edges, in rendering the unique ordinary so as to achieve predictability and order, our legal system can sometimes be deaf to the true anguish that propels people to turn to it in the first place. We cannot let that happen.

Deafness, silence, and denial, by people and by institutions, can lead only to greater pain for all concerned. In other areas, we can count on anger dissipating and fear subsiding as people get drawn along through the legal process. That simply won't happen with AIDS. Fears left unattended will erupt eventually, in settings we can't control and with a fury beyond any we anticipate. We must therefore use the law to promote recognition rather than denial; to encourage people to air their fears and to defend them if possible; to give the fearful the courtesy of responding to their fears, if only by laying out what we find compelling on the other side.

This is where the second peculiar feature of our legal system comes into play—the centrality of confrontation. So long as one "combatant" desires to engage, the silence will be broken. Whether we envision a seropositive employee suing an employer bent on dismissal or a fearful co-worker suing to protect the workplace, the law provides a mechanism for all voices to be heard. Confrontation can be and often is wounding; it can also be healing. Our task is clear. We must think creatively about ways of using confrontation to promote reconciliation.

Finally, we should remember that just as the law frames society's response to the AIDS epidemic, the society as a whole shapes the law. Like it or not, we must decide what kind of society we will be: mean-spirited, shortsighted, and judgmental; or compassionate, clearheaded, and accepting. In the end, society will determine where the burdens of AIDS—social, financial, and emotional—will fall. We can make the choice consciously and purposely, or we can make it by indirection or default, but make it we will. We can refashion our legal rules—reporting requirements, antibody-screening provisions, confidentiality laws, antidiscrimination laws, definitions of terms such as "handicap," insurance regulations, quarantine measures, and the like—to isolate and segregate the people most likely to contract and spread AIDS. Or we can work to ensure that they remain among us, for as long as they are able, free of the weight of *our* anxieties and fears.

If instead of choosing we simply let matters drift, we will trend, inevitably, in the direction of isolation, segregation, and repression. After all, the pressure to contain AIDS is enormous, and though we can't quite get at the disease, we *can* get at the people we think are most likely to spread it. Gay and bisexual men and intravenous drug users are the targets of massive societal disapproval quite apart from AIDS and are thus in a uniquely poor position to hold off the fearful majority. Moreover, homophobia, racism, and the current climate of antidrug mindlessness put those who speak on behalf of such persons at considerable political and social risk. Without a massive, purposeful, and broadly supported effort by the larger society to rein in its worst impulses, the law will surely come to rest heavily upon those who already suffer most.

Such an effort requires healthy doses of what my former colleague Charles Black has labeled "humane imagination," the ability to comprehend, however dimly, how life is lived by people very different from ourselves. We must struggle to see through the eyes and feel with the hearts of those whom AIDS is most likely to fell. We must strive to appreciate how dreadful it is to wait for the disease to make its awful appearance, thinking constantly of the disintegration it promises; and how more dreadful still when the nightmare becomes a waking reality. If only we could imagine how crushing it is to the spirit to be held at arms length when what it desires most is society's embrace.

Connecting up with the experiences of others is never easy, especially when they engender fear or loathing in us. I sometimes despair when I realize that many of his neighbors have not been able to bridge the gap to Ryan White, a sweet-faced Midwestern boy with a ready smile and a winning way. What hope is there, then, that the fearful majority will empathize with Ryan's black and brown big-city counterparts, with adults who stick needles in their arms, or with men who engage in sodomy with other men? The prospects are grim, until and unless we, as a people, take fear and loathing seriously, lance it where possible, and where not, express openly our reasons for siding with those who are dreaded. Admittedly, this is a prescription for short-term pain, but if we want the society that emerges from the AIDS epidemic to be one we can be proud of, we have little choice in the matter.

At a meeting of the Yale AIDS Law Project, called to recruit new blood for the final push toward publication of this book, I rather proudly began to tick off the incredible array of areas the book would cover. One newcomer interjected, quite innocently, "Do you have a chapter on the licensing of new drugs?" It was an excellent question, one that should have gladdened the Mr. Chips in me. In truth, my initial reaction was mild embarrassment that in soliciting manuscripts fifteen months earlier, we had not anticipated how important the issue would become, with the advent of potentially ameliorative drugs such as AZT and DDC. Such are the trials of trying to produce a book about an epidemic when its collateral consequences continue to multiply.

Quite apart from the difficulties of foresight, we doubtless have failed to address issues that even we, upon reflection, may agree are as important as the ones we covered. I am particularly chagrined at not having included a chapter on the impact of AIDS on this nation's Latino communities. I suspect that it, like the chapter we did include on blacks and AIDS, would have significantly enriched the overall enterprise. As time goes on, I know that I will experience other regrets.

Even so, I think you will agree that the scope and reach of this book is remarkable. Some of the topics we cover ("Traditional Public Health Strategies," "AIDS in the Workplace," and "Insurance," for example) are addressed elsewhere, but usually in less depth and with a specialized audience in mind. Other chapters ("Prostitution as a Public Health Issue," "The Military," "Prisons," and "Intravenous Drug Abusers," for example) stand alone in the field and would by themselves justify this book. Some chapters ("Schoolchildren with AIDS," "Housing Issues," and "Torts," for example) grapple directly with legal issues—with cases, statutes, and administrative regulations. Other chapters provide much-needed context: historical ("A Historical Perspective"), cultural ("Physicians versus Lawyers: A Conflict of Cultures") and social ("The Black Community," The Lesbian and Gay Community"). Finally, some who have previewed the book report that the opening two chapters, taken together, are among the most comprehensive, and comprehensible, treatments of *medical* issues available anywhere. If I sound like a "proud papa," at least it is with good reason.

Acknowledgments

The members of the Yale AIDS Law Project are grateful to the many people and institutions that have provided intellectual, financial, spiritual, and physical support during the production of this book and without whom its completion would have been impossible. We are greatly indebted to the Yale Law School and to its administration, especially Deans Guido Calabresi, John Simon, and Stephen Yandle, who encouraged the Project from its inception.

Many members of the Yale community deserve special mention. Richard Green was a steady source of wisdom and information as we moved toward publication. Fred Kass, who produced the glossary in addition to his chapter, lent a hand at virtually every juncture. Bradley Clements, Melinda Cuthbert, Liz Oberle, Michael Rabson, and Patrick Woolley contributed their editing and research skills to the production of a finished manuscript. As deadlines neared, Cathy Briganti, Donna Frandy, and Carmelita Morales helped with crucial typing and Gwen Mathewson and Sally Peterson provided additional, and invaluable, assistance. Richard Pershan supplied encouragement and elbow grease as we converted a law school junk room into a respectable office.

We thank John Beckerman, Gene Harrington, Ben Schatz, and all the other people who helped us find our topics and our authors. We also wish to thank Patricia Cain for her extremely helpful comments on the manuscript, Charles Munnel, Marianne Neal, Carol Peirano, and Bruce Smith for their assistance with the chapter on the military, and the Legal Action Center for its production and editing assistance.

Finally, we are grateful to an anonymous foundation for funding the preparation of an index for the book; and to the law firms of Cahill Gordon & Reindel; Cravath, Swaine & Moore; Morrison & Foerster, and Sullivan & Cromwell, each of which volunteered its phone, mail, and duplicating facilities to the Project during the summer of 1986.

A Little Law
for Non-lawyers

SCOTT BURRIS

We, the People, are the source of law in this democracy. In the Constitution, we have organized our form of government. Through our elected representatives, we make the law. We elect the judges (or elect the people who select the judges) who interpret the law. But when this theory becomes practice, law can seem just as unfamiliar as our sick bodies or our nonstarting cars. If the legal system embodies many fine ideas about how we should live together—ideas we can all understand—it is also a Byzantine tangle of rules giving other people power over our lives.

This book is an attempt to explain how the law deals with the many social conflicts generated by AIDS (the acronym for Acquired Immune Deficiency Syndrome). The epidemic poses challenges to our ideals of fairness, challenges that are being played out according to legal rules most of us don't know, in a legal system most of us don't understand. The legal system cannot be made simple, but we have the right to demand of lawyers, just as we demand of mechanics or doctors or anyone else in whom we place our trust, that they apply their special knowledge in conformity with our values and desires. This book will not teach you how to be the mechanic; we commend it to you rather as a kind of consumer report, a guide to the right questions.

Within the first day or two of law school, the new student is introduced to the *hypothetical*, a teaching tool best analogized to the medical student's cadaver. A hypothetical is a story (or, as lawyers say, *fact pattern*) under whose flaccid skin the legal novice is challenged to discover a world of elaborate legal relations. I will adopt that device here, to illustrate several of the most important rules and practices of our legal system.

The hypothetical: Sally is ten years old. Three years ago, she was injured in a car accident. Through an emergency blood transfusion, she was infected with HIV (Human Immunodeficiency Virus, the virus associated with AIDS) and, last year, was diagnosed as having AIDS. First because of her injuries,

and then because of various illnesses related to her AIDS, she has not attended school since the accident. Recently, however, she has been doing
better, and her doctors found her healthy enough to enroll. Following
guidelines developed by the federal Centers for Disease Control (CDC)
and adopted by the state Department of Health, the principal of Sally's
public school appointed a panel of local doctors and educators to assess
her placement.

The guidelines were premised on the medical judgment that AIDS may be
spread only by intimate transmission of infected bodily fluid, especially blood
and semen, into a healthy person's bloodstream—exceedingly unlikely to
occur in the kind of casual interaction among school children. The panel's
job was to make sure that Sally had no physical or behavioral problems—
such as open sores, or a tendency to biting or incontinence—that would
create an unusual risk that her fluids would infect another child. The panel
found Sally to be well adjusted and well behaved, with an understanding of
her disease and the precautions necessary to avoid its transmission. Since
she presented no meaningful danger to other children according to the
guidelines, it approved her placement in a regular fifth-grade class. The
principal ordered her enrolled.

The guidelines stressed the need for confidentiality, recommending that
only the principal and the child's teacher be informed of her AIDS. Unfortunately, Sally's teacher did not take the news well, and immediately called
his union representative and several friends. Word spread, and within a few
days, the entire community was upset and divided. A large minority of
parents claimed Sally had no right to be in school and threatened a boycott if she attended. After a painful public meeting, the school board
voted to overrule the principal. It ordered Sally to be taught, by telephone,
at home.

At this point, Sally and her parents have several choices, only one of
which is to get involved in a legal battle. Besides simply accepting the school
board's decision and devoting their energies to finding other ways to make
Sally happy, they might seek to enroll her in a private school, or a special
school for handicapped children, or a public school in a district following a
different policy. They might play the system—call their senator, tell their
story to sympathetic reporters, try to enlist the support of local organizations.
People are often prepared to give up quite a bit to avoid getting involved
in the expense and publicity of a controversial lawsuit.

GETTING A LAWYER

Sally's parents decide to fight the decision head on, which they probably
cannot do without a lawyer. Unless the board quickly changes its mind, the
legal bills in a case like Sally's could quickly run into thousands of dollars.
In this hypothetical, Sally's parents are of modest means. Sometimes, es-

pecially in personal injury cases where high money damages may be awarded, attorneys will work on a "contingency" basis—that is, for a percentage of whatever the plaintiff eventually wins in lieu of an hourly fee. But Sally's victory would be getting into school, not getting money, so a contingency arrangement is out. Fortunately, Congress has recognized that inability to pay for counsel may prevent people who have a valid reason to sue from doing so, and some federal laws allow courts to award attorney's fees to the plaintiff if she prevails. (The Education for All Handicapped Children Act, a law that may cover Sally's problem, has such a fee provision.)

If Sally cannot pay for a lawyer or find a private attorney willing to bet on her prevailing, she may seek the help of a public interest legal organization. Groups such as the American Civil Liberties Union (ACLU) and the Lambda Legal Defense and Education Fund provide legal services in cases that fall within their areas of concern. Such groups are generally underwritten by foundations and private donors, although they also may receive attorney's fee awards authorized by statute. Because they have only limited resources for achieving their legal goals, they prefer to take cases with the potential to make major legal points.

Finally, if Sally is unable to afford or find any other help, she might qualify for legal services for the poor provided by government-funded agencies, bar associations, and even a few law schools. (Some private law firms also commit a certain percentage of their time to cases taken, at no charge, *pro bono publico*—for the public's benefit.) In recent years, however, legal aid has suffered serious budget cutbacks, and demand outstrips supply. To a legal aid office without the staff to handle every case that comes in, Sally's problem might seem less compelling than the problem of a poor family about to be evicted from its home or a social security recipient about to lose his benefits. On the other hand, Sally's case may be quite attractive to a *pro bono* lawyer: at least it will be exciting and rewarding, and it may even be good advertising.

Sally is lucky: because of its importance, Lee, a local attorney, is willing to take on her case without pay. The ACLU volunteers to help. This does not necessarily mean that Sally will sue the board. Most legal disputes never go that far. For better or for worse, the mere prospect of protracted and expensive litigation is often sufficient to put even a person confident of the justice of her position into a mood for compromise. (Even after a suit is filed, settlement remains high on the agenda; much of the legal maneuvering before trial is aimed as much at bolstering a negotiating position as preparing to win a trial, and two parties can settle a case at any time up until, and sometimes even after, the moment the jury renders its verdict.) The school board, however, lets Lee know that it is dead set against allowing Sally into school at any time, under any circumstances. It appears that a lawsuit may be needed to get Sally past the schoolhouse door, and her attorney sets about exploring how it should look.

GETTING INTO COURT

Case or Controversy

Courts in this country do not give advice. The board could not simply send a note over to the courthouse asking whether children with AIDS must be allowed into schools. To get before a court, a dispute must present a "case or controversy," a concrete disagreement between two parties who can present it in an adversarial fashion. Sally's case certainly qualifies. But the case must also be *ripe* and it cannot be *moot*. Ripeness and mootness are both concepts having to do with the practical necessity of deciding a case. If Sally's parents were to enroll her in a private school, a court might see no reason to decide the now theoretical question of whether she should be allowed into a public school she no longer wishes to attend, and might dismiss her case as *moot*. Conversely, if the board were attempting to formulate a policy that, upon its completion, might result in Sally's admission, a court could deem her case *unripe*, refusing to hear it unless and until the board had finally barred Sally.

Standing

A real case or controversy is not enough. The person who brings the case to court must herself have a concrete stake in the outcome, providing her a powerful incentive to bring strong, pertinent arguments before the court. A local law professor might be interested in Sally's case for the precedent it would create, but neither mere interest nor even profound concern is enough to confer standing. In this case, Sally (and her parents acting on her behalf) are the only people who have standing to bring her claim.

Cause of Action

Sally and the board clearly have a case or controversy, and Sally has standing to bring it to court. This doesn't mean that Sally has a lawsuit. The law protects us from some things—such as breaking of contracts, the reckless behavior of others, and monopolistic practices by our competitors—and it guarantees us some things—such as freedom of speech or fair trials. But not every right we believe we have is a legal right, and not every wrong done us is a legal wrong. To get into court, Lee must be able to place Sally's problem into a *cause of action*—a legal wrong or right.

Sally's parents believe she has a right to go to school, but that is not strictly true in law. Sally has a right to receive the same educational benefits as other children, *unless* the board has an important reason for treating her differently. Similarly, a classmate's father feels strongly that it is wrong of Sally's parents to expose other children to AIDS by sending her to school, but he has no legal grounds for suing them for damages. Often a lawyer can translate a client's view of right or wrong into a cause of action, but not always. (Indeed, the frequent gap between what large segments of the population perceive to be their rights or protections and what the law decides they are is one of the most troubling features of our legal system. Why, one may well ask, *doesn't* a child have a right to education?) In looking for a suitable cause of action, Sally's lawyer considers constitutions, statutes, and the common law.

State and Federal Constitutions

In addition to the U.S. Constitution, each state has its own constitution. These documents set forth the fundamental rights of citizens and lay out the powers and structure of government. The U.S. Constitution is the supreme law of the land, and any law in conflict with it (including a state constitutional provision) is invalid. State constitutions enjoy a similar preeminence vis-à-vis state laws. People whose constitutional rights have been violated often have a cause of action. In Sally's case, Lee believes that her right to equal protection of laws (guaranteed in the Fourteenth Amendment to the U.S. Constitution as well as in her state's constitution) has been abridged because she has been arbitrarily singled out for special treatment. But Lee does not stop here; for reasons that will become clear, constitutional causes of action can be problematic, and it is quite normal in any case for there to be more than one cause of action.

State and Federal Statutes

A *statute* is a law passed by a legislative body (local statutes are commonly referred to as *ordinances*). The term is used to distinguish this legislative law from "the common law," legal rules created by courts in the absence of statutes. As with constitutions, there are also distinctions of rank within the realm of statutes. In general, federal statutes trump conflicting state statutes, just as state statutes trump conflicting city and county ordinances.

There are some statutes whose primary purpose is to create a cause of action. For example, an important federal statute granting jurisdiction (see below) over civil rights cases to the federal district courts establishes a cause of action for people whose constitutional rights have been deprived "under color of any State law, statute, ordinance, regulation, custom or usage." More typical statutes, those that themselves confer rights or create obligations, often explicitly provide the right to sue to enforce their provisions. On occasion, the right to sue is reserved to the government, which does so on behalf of aggrieved individuals. And some statutes say nothing at all about how they are to be enforced, which may leave a party with an unprotected right. Courts, observing the legal maxim that there is no right without a remedy if the right is abridged, will sometimes provide one by interpreting the statute to include an "implied cause of action."

The implied cause of action is just one illustration of why a lawyer who reads only the statute is leaving half the job undone. To understand what a statute really means, one must see how it has been interpreted by judges in lawsuits. Statutes and constitutions typically are written in general terms; it is hardly possible to imagine in advance all the situations in which a law will be applied. It is up to the judge to decide whether a statute's general terms apply to a case's specific facts; whether a situation that is not covered, but is like those that are, would have been covered had the legislature thought about it; or how social or technological changes since the statute's passage should affect its application.

Sally's case provides an example (and allows one more digression, onto the subject of how lawyers think through a problem by analogy). Lee is considering a cause of action under the Education for All Handicapped Children Act (EHA), a federal law requiring schools receiving federal funds (virtually all public schools) to place handicapped children into regular class-room settings whenever possible. The law defines "handicap" broadly, but the judge in Sally's case will have to decide whether the definition encompasses AIDS, a disease that was unknown when the EHA was passed. In addition to this question of interpretation, the judge might also be asked by the board to fill a perceived gap in the law: the EHA does not distinguish between handicaps that are the result of contagious diseases and those that are not; since Congress could hardly have intended to require local schools to enroll dangerous students, should the law be read to include some kind of exception to its presumption of admission where the handicap is a contagious disease?

Lee turns to an *annotated code*, a collection of statutes that includes summaries of court decisions interpreting each provision. He finds that there has been no definitive court decision that AIDS is a handicap according to the definition in the EHA. But he also finds a very important case in which hepatitis B, a disease more readily transmitted than AIDS, was found to be covered. Arguing, as lawyers do, by analogy, Lee will say that the judge is bound by the previous decision to treat AIDS as a handicap; the board will argue that any similarity in transmission is outweighed by the differences in effect—AIDS, unlike hepatitis, is always fatal—and therefore the analogy is flawed. Whichever way Sally's court eventually rules, however, she can at least credibly *argue* that the law protects her, and therefore she may take advantage of the cause of action the EHA provides.

The Common Law
The common law of England preceded the advent of the modern legislature; judges, not Parliament, provided most of the basic rules of social and economic organization. Gradually, legislatures asserted themselves. Today, they not only make most laws, but also have the power to repeal or replace the laws made by judges. Even torts and contracts,* the legal realms tra-

---

*The law of contract sets forth the rules for making binding agreements (like the *Mailbox Rule*, which provided that an offered contract was accepted the moment the person accepting

ditionally governed exclusively by the common law, are now substantially run according to statutory rules. (For example, a significant portion of the law of contracts has been incorporated into the Uniform Commercial Code, a model statute adopted by all but one of the fifty states.) The shift in power from courts to legislatures is not, however, quite as great as might appear: the power courts lose to make the rules is offset by that they retain to interpret the rules made by the legislatures. Furthermore, they retain the authority to make rules where the legislature has not acted.

There are many practical differences between statutory and judge-made law. Unlike statutes, which apply to the future behavior of everybody, judicial decisions apply first and foremost to the past acts of the parties who fought the case. Future impact comes in part from the weight the decision will have with other judges deciding similar cases and in part from a general moral imperative to respect judicial pronouncements of law. Whereas a statute is passed all at once, judicial rules are fashioned incrementally, emerging from lines of cases dealing with similar issues. The incremental and case-specific nature of the common law is often said to make it more responsive than statutory law to social and technological changes; it is often easier, for example, to get a judge to update a common-law rule than it is to get a legislature to amend a dated statute.

Lee is considering a tort claim against the school board as part of Sally's suit. The teacher who spread the news of Sally's disease told his friends that Sally was involved in a Communist germ-warfare conspiracy. Lee believes that this may constitute slander (an injurious and untrue statement) and that the board can be sued under the doctrine that the employer is responsible for the torts of its employee (*respondeat superior*). Lawyers sometimes find themselves with more causes of action than they can use, however, and Lee makes the strategic decision that a slander action would be difficult to win and would divert the court's attention from Sally's more important claims to a normal education.

CHOOSING A COURT

Armed with his causes of action, Lee must select a court to bring them in. The United States has a dual system of national (federal) and state courts, which may hear many, but not all, of the same causes of action.

---

the offer put his acceptance in the mailbox, not when the person offering the contract actually received the news). The common, and not very helpful, definition of a tort is a legal wrong, other than a breach of contract, for which money damages are appropriate. In general, a tort involves an injury of some kind, caused by the defendant, or which the defendant had a legal duty to prevent. There are many kinds of tort, ranging from battery, an injury to the body, to products liability, the responsibility of a manufacturer for injuries caused by a product it has introduced into the marketplace.

Jurisdiction

Jurisdiction is the authority of a court to hear a case. State courts have what is known as general jurisdiction—authority over virtually all cases pertaining to people, property, or events in their territory. Sally could have sued the loquacious teacher for slander even if the slander had taken place in a neighboring state or if the teacher were a resident of another state. Further, Sally could bring her case to a state court even if her cause of action were based solely on the U.S. Constitution or federal law (except in the rare instances—antitrust cases, for example—where Congress has reserved jurisdiction for federal courts alone).

Federal courts, by contrast, are courts of limited jurisdiction: they may hear cases only if the authority to do so has been conferred by the Constitution or a federal statute. Principally, federal courts deal with two categories of cases: those involving causes of action based on federal laws or the Constitution (*federal question* or *subject matter* jurisdiction) and those in which all the parties reside in different states (*diversity* jurisdiction). Sally's EHA cause of action brings her within the subject matter jurisdiction of the federal courts. However, since her slander action would have been based on state tort law, she could not have brought it in federal court unless she and the teacher lived in different states.

Tactics

Lee also weighs important qualitative differences between the two court systems. Experienced attorneys know the judges in their area and will choose a court for a particular case with judges' preferences and predilections in mind. In Sally's case, Lee wants a judge who is sympathetic to civil rights claims in general and disabled people in particular. He does not want a judge known to believe that the federal government should stay out of local affairs. He is particularly concerned to find a judge who will not be swayed by the politicized status of the case. Most of the state judges to which his case might be assigned were politicians before going on the bench—they are still politicians, in the sense that, like judges in most other states, they are elected (or, periodically put before the voters in a yes-or-no reelection). Federal judges, on the other hand, are appointed for life, insulating them, in theory, from political pressure. In this case, Lee decides he has a better chance for a calm trial in federal court.

THE TRIAL

Sally's case begins, like all cases, in a trial court. In the federal system, the *district court* tries cases. Each of the fifty states has at least one federal court district.

Causes of Action and Preliminary Injunction

Sally claims, first, that she is entitled to regular school placement under the EHA, and second, that her constitutional right to equal protection of law was violated by the school's action. She also seeks a preliminary injunction ordering the school to admit her while the case is proceeding. Normally, courts do not give plaintiffs what they are suing for until after a case has been tried and won, but Sally's trial might not take place for months and even if she wins, the judge may postpone (*stay*) his decision to admit her while the board appeals. Lee's argument to the court is that such delay will make Sally the loser even if she wins, because her goal is to be admitted to school during the brief time she has left to lead a normal life.

Situations analogous to Sally's are common, and the preliminary injunction was designed to deal with them. The standard for granting an injunction turns on whether either party will be irreparably harmed if the status quo is not disturbed. (Often, an injunction is used to prevent a case from becoming moot, as, for example, where preservationists sue to prevent a developer from demolishing a landmark building; once the building is gone, there is nothing to sue about.) If money damages at the end of the trial will sufficiently compensate the victim, a preliminary injunction will not be granted even if harm will continue to occur while the suit goes on.

The judge in Sally's case denies the injunction. While Sally has a strong argument, the board does as well. If the board is right, and Sally is likely to spread HIV, the court would, in ordering her enrollment, have exposed dozens of children to a fatal disease.

Issues of Law and Issues of Fact

The district court is where the trial takes place. The two sides present their legal arguments, their witnesses, and their physical evidence. There is, of course, a judge, and, depending on the nature of the claim and the parties' wishes, a jury (there is no general right to a jury in noncriminal cases). Sally's case, like any other case, is said to present two kinds of issues: issues of fact and issues of law. Roughly, issues of law have to do with which laws apply and how they are to be interpreted. Whether Congress intended to protect children with contagious diseases when it passed the EHA is an issue of law. Issues of fact have to do with the events disputed in the particular case, such as whether, if admitted to school, Sally would really pose a threat to other children.

The distinction is not perfect—some questions are mixed— and can be difficult to apply, but it largely determines who in the system will make which decisions. Questions of law are decided by the judge; questions of fact are decided by the jury (if there is one). If the verdict is appealed, the focus in the court of appeal will be on whether the judge correctly interpreted the law: there will be no witness testimony or other evidence—only lawyers arguing the legal points in written briefs and short oral presentations. The findings of fact of the jury at trial (or judge in the absence of a jury) will be presumed complete and correct and will not be overturned unless they are, on their face, "clearly erroneous."

In Sally's case, the board does not dispute her account of the events leading up to her expulsion; the only real issue of fact disputed by the board is whether Sally would endanger other children in a regular classroom. In law, the board challenges Sally's claim that AIDS is a handicap under the EHA, and argues that her removal did not violate the Constitution because it served an important state interest. The case is tried without a jury.

Burden of Proof

Both sides call several medical experts to testify concerning Sally's dangerousness. As the plaintiff, Sally bears the burden of proof (sometimes called the risk of nonpersuasion). Most people are familiar with the prosecutor's burden in a criminal trial to prove the defendant's guilt "beyond a reasonable doubt." In Sally's case, as is the norm in civil cases, she must show that "it is more likely than not" that she will not present a danger to other children.

In this hypothetical, the judge finds that Sally has satisfied this burden. The overwhelming weight of the testimony and the evidence of the policy of the CDC show that Sally would not pose a danger in the classroom.

Interpreting the Law

The legal decision is more complicated. To begin with, the judge has to decide which legal issues to decide. Judges, for reasons of principle and practicality, try to decide cases on the narrowest possible grounds. Because every case makes rules for later cases, there is reluctance to make a sweeping decision when a narrow and conservative one is possible (though, of course, for the same reason, judges sometimes decide broadly in order to increase the impact of an important case). A broad decision in Sally's case might conclude that the Constitution's equal protection clause prohibits a school from keeping any nondangerous sick child home unless it is prepared to exclude every child with any illness. In this case, the judge finds instead that all the issues in Sally's case can and should be decided under the EHA, and that there is no need to reach the constitutional issue. (This does not mean that Sally could not have won on the constitutional issue; only that the case can be resolved without deciding that.)

To determine whether the EHA applies, the judge first looks to the language of the statute. AIDS had not yet been identified when the law was passed, but it probably would not have been mentioned anyway. In the EHA, Congress sought to secure as normal a public education as possible for every handicapped child; this is clear from both the broad language of the statute and statements the judge finds in the legislative history (speeches by members of Congress or reports or declarations of committees that worked on the bill). But it left the details to the Department of Health, Education, and Welfare (now the Department of Health and Human Services), which was charged with promulgating regulations to implement the general principles set forth in the EHA. Looking at the "regs," the judge notes a broad definition of handicap that seems to encompass AIDS.

The judge next consults other court decisions. In the classic view of courts, judges do little more than identify the past rule that covers the case at hand—the "precedent"—and apply it. This is a little too simple. To begin with, Sally's judge is formally bound to follow only the rulings of the Supreme Court, the U.S. court of appeals for her circuit, and other federal courts in her district. She *may* follow the decisions of other courts as well, but that is discretionary. (The same holds true for state court systems, where decisions of federal or other states' courts are not binding on matters of state law.)

In practice, the nature of legal argument itself weakens the bonds of precedent. Looking over the prior cases, the judge finds one case in her circuit applying the EHA to a contagious disease, the hepatitis B case relied on by Lee; one case in a neighboring state's court ruling that AIDS is not covered; and one in another federal district saying that it is. She is not bound to follow either of the cases directly dealing with Sally's disease; and, while the decision of the circuit court seems to suggest strongly that the EHA covers AIDS, there is an out. The judge can read the case narrowly—it deals only with hepatitis B and has no implications for AIDS; or distinguish it on the facts—AIDS, unlike hepatitis B, is uniformly fatal; or distinguish it on the law—the case was actually decided under the Constitution, not the EHA. In practice, a judge so inclined can nearly always find a way to avoid applying an unwanted precedent. Nevertheless, it is probably fair to say that most judges try hard to figure out what rules emerge from previous cases and to apply them properly in the cases before them.

Of course, judges do not work in a vacuum. Even federal judges, free from direct political pressure, are aware of the broader implications of individual rulings, and most make their decisions with an eye to something like the greatest good for the greatest number. Lee and the attorney for the board have both larded their legal positions with arguments designed to focus the judge's attention on the larger "policy issues" (How should a humane society deal with sick children? What is the most economically efficient way to distribute the costs of education for the handicapped? What do they do in Sweden?). Many of these considerations naturally arise as part of the process of interpreting the statute, but the personal values and interests of the judge are inevitably an important factor in a decision. Finally, even a judge who does not need to worry about reelection may be concerned about the well-being of the court as an institution. Judges tend to be rather careful about using their power to go against the strongly held views of the community.

The Judge's Decision

There is often quite a bit more than meets the eye in a judicial decision, which, after all, is essentially a political document. Some decisions are painfully honest, revealing how difficult it can be to decide a hard case justly. Other opinions are devoted to obfuscating the issues and hiding the traces of whatever reasoning process the judge used. It never hurts to be skeptical, and this is true in Sally's case.

The judge begins by proclaiming the importance of fair treatment and a normal education for handicapped children. She claims to be "compelled" to follow the precedent of the hepatitis case and rules that the EHA does apply to AIDS. She does not, however, order Sally into school. Instead, Sally must start over. Under the law and regulations, children with a school placement dispute under EHA are not allowed to sue in federal court until they have appealed the school's decision administratively. Although a federal district court can eventually decide the case, Sally must first go through a four-tiered process of administrative hearings set up by the state Department of Education. Lee is a little put out about this, because the hepatitis case that "compelled" this decision also ruled that the district court could short-circuit the administrative hearing process and immediately order the child into school.

APPEALING A VERDICT

If no one is entirely happy with the decision, no one is unhappy enough to exercise their right to appeal. Sally's parents would rather not go softly into that good night of bureaucracy, but, on balance, it is her fastest and least expensive chance of getting into school. For its part, the board is satisfied that her entrance will at least be delayed; the hepatitis case suggests to its lawyer that the court of appeals might reverse the district judge and order her admitted. A brief description of the appellate process is nevertheless in order.

Decision of the district court may be appealed to the *circuit court of appeals*. The nation is geographically divided into twelve circuits, each of which takes appeals from several district courts. Appeals from the circuit courts of appeals, when permitted, are taken to the Supreme Court of the United States. About half the states have similar three-tiered systems; a few have an extra intermediate appellate court; and the rest have a two-tiered system composed of trial courts and a single appellate court. The state supreme court has the final say on matters of state law, but its decisions on federal constitutional or statutory issues may be appealed to the U.S. Supreme Court.*

In the United States, there is virtually a universal right to one appeal. Although states with three tiers of courts give litigants the right to appeal unsatisfactory decisions of the intermediate court to the highest court, this right is limited (in most states, severely limited) to particular types of cases. Cases not falling into the right categories may be appealed to the supreme court only with its permission. The federal system is similar: an appeal may be taken "as of right" from the district court to the court of appeal, but most can go on to the Supreme Court only if its gives its permission in the form of a *writ of certiorari.* A denial of "cert" (the most frequent outcome) means that the decision in the next lowest court stands.

THE ADMINISTRATIVE HEARING PROCESS

The EHA's provision of an administrative procedure for deciding placement is not unusual, nor is the fact that the statute left most of the detailed law making to a cabinet-level department. Since the New Deal, large government bureaucracies have played a growing role in the day-to-day making and adjudicating of rules. Not surprisingly, as the job of the federal government has become more complicated, and the amount of money expended has grown, Congress has delegated increasing responsibility to the executive branch of the government. What is perhaps more interesting is the way statutes like the EHA allow the federal government—both Congress and the executive branch—to regulate the behavior of states.

In theory, ours is a federal system, with the national government designated to perform certain national tasks (such as providing for the common defense and regulating interstate commerce) and local affairs (such as public education) left to the states. But the federal government has learned to use its wealth to indirectly regulate affairs nominally outside its authority, principally by attaching strings to the money it gives. Congress, for example, probably could not order states to enforce a speed limit of fifty-five miles per hour. Instead, it simply says that any state that wants federal highway funds (and that is every state) must agree to that speed limit.

The EHA was a similar gambit. Congress felt that education for the handicapped was a national problem and was prepared to spend money to solve it. But it could not act directly: schools are run by the states. So it passed the EHA, with instructions to the Department of Health, Education and Welfare to design a model program in its regulations. In order to get the

---

*A warning on wording: state systems do not necessarily adopt federal nomenclature. New York, for example, calls its trial court the *Supreme Court*, and its supreme court the *Court of Appeals*. The intermediate appellate court—the court of appeals in the federal system—is a happy medium in New York: *Supreme Court, Appellate Division*.

money offered under the act, each state had to pass a law adopting the federal government's program, which explains why Sally, having been told her disease was covered by a *federal* law, is compelled to comply with a *state* administrative procedure.

About two months after the federal judge's verdict, Sally had her first state hearing. The "judge" was an administrator in the state Department of Education. Several doctors testified. Both sides were represented by counsel. The hearing officer ruled in favor of the board. The decision was appealed to a similarly constituted tribunal, and, after a few more months, it was overturned. The board appealed to yet another department official and lost again. At that point, more than a year after she first sought admission, Sally was allowed to start school. Immediately, several other parents went to a state court, seeking to have Sally quarantined. That is another story.

Sally is a hypothetical child, but her story is based on the experience of real children. Legal rules and analogies are ultimately imperfect reflections of complicated problems as they exist in the world. It is a very good idea for all of us to have some acquaintance with the jargon of law, but it is an even better idea to nurse our sense of simple justice. We ought not allow the complexity and formality of law to be the excuse for denying the jurisdiction of humanity and compassion.

PART ONE
THE MEDICAL BACKGROUND

I

The AIDS Epidemic:
Discovery of a New Disease

JUNE E. OSBORN, M.D.

Scientists have argued that it is to the advantage of microorganisms to live in harmony with the hosts on whom they depend for subsistence. As a corollary, they have suggested that pathogenic microbes—agents that cause significant disease—represent recent and unsettled newcomers. In an analysis of the role of epidemic infectious diseases in history, William McNeill hypothesizes that these germs come from pathogens of other animals that suddenly manage to invade humans and maintain person-to-person passage. This happens so rarely that when these microbes first appear they provoke major social upheavals, as measles and smallpox did when they began to infect people.[1]

These provocative concepts about the development of diseases are pertinent to the urgent problems presented by AIDS. For the first time in modern history, a worldwide epidemic of an entirely novel, lethal viral disease has begun, and thus the progress of the disease is taking place under close scientific scrutiny.

Although the number of cases is still small, the epidemic has already taken an appalling toll, and the potential for spread is troubling and difficult to assess. Despite remarkable biomedical advances, we will be sorely tested to gather and apply new knowledge quickly enough to contain the outbreak, because only some of the keys to its solution lie in the realm of natural science. Part of the challenge of the epidemic is the unparalleled diversity of factors intertwined in its development: sociology, psychology, politics, ethics, and law.

Epidemics of lethal infectious diseases are not so very far behind us, although their imprint on our collective memory has faded. The full array of modern vaccines has been developed in just the last few decades. Only thirty years ago Jonas Salk developed the inactivated poliovirus vaccine, and it is instructive to recall the extent to which the announcement of that accomplishment in 1955 calmed a public terrified about paralytic polio-myelitis. Soon a remarkable series of vaccines and a proliferation of anti-biotics allowed affluent societies to relax—for the first time—about uncontrollable, widespread contagious disease. Even the scare of a swine-flu epidemic in 1976 contributed to the sense of calm. When the pathogen (the disease-causing organism) failed to sustain person-to-person passage and the predicted epidemic did not materialize, the general public assumed that health officials had been alarmist rather than prudent.

THE EMERGENCE OF A NEW DISEASE

In 1981, a few alert physicians on both coasts of the United States recognized an entirely new disease in a handful of their patients.[2] Previously healthy men in the prime of life developed a prolonged state of vague ill health, followed after many weeks or months by bizarre and ultimately lethal in-fections. Doctors knew these terminal diseases, but the afflictions had oc-curred previously only in people with genetic immune deficiencies or in individuals immunologically crippled by malignant disease or by powerful drugs administered to facilitate organ transplants. Laboratory testing quickly revealed that critical components of these patients' immune systems had indeed been virtually destroyed, for no apparent reason. In due course medical researchers agreed on the name "acquired immune deficiency syn-drome" to signify this new, complex disease.

The first patients were all participants in a particular male homosexual lifestyle that had already concerned microbiologists. During the late 1970s, even before the appearance of AIDS, scientists became more and more aware of a set of health problems prevalent among gay men who had sexual re-lations with large numbers of partners, many of whom remained mutually anonymous. An early epidemiologic study of risk factors for AIDS established that afflicted patients had averaged over one thousand sexual partners in their lifetimes. Among members in this group, microbial pathogens that were relatively rare in the general U.S. population appeared with alarming frequency. Amoebic dysentery, for instance—normally associated with Third World areas of substandard sanitation—suddenly became widespread among these gay men, as did numerous other exotic gastrointestinal path-ogens and diseases.

In trials of hepatitis-B vaccine, Wolf Szmuness and his colleagues at the New York Blood Center documented a particularly striking example of the risk of unusual infectious diseases in New York's gay community in the late 1970s.[3] Their data established the astonishing fact that the *annual* risk of acquiring hepatitis B for such men was 12 percent; by contrast, the cumu-lative *lifetime* risk for the general U.S. population was close to 1 percent. In retrospect, the situation was clearly propitious for the rapid spread of unusual pathogens and unusual ways to transmit infectious diseases.

Scientists also knew that some infectious agents could temporarily sup-press immune responses. Viruses such as cytomegalovirus have been found to cause little or no disease themselves but to weaken a person's immuno-logical system for a period of days or weeks, during which time other mi-crobes could take advantage of relaxed defenses and cause serious illness. These observations helped to set the intellectual stage for recognition and alarm when the first sufferers of what we now call AIDS were described in the summer of 1981.

Once the new disease was recognized, there was not much time for re-flection. From 1981 on, the number of AIDS cases doubled every six months, concentrated largely but not exclusively in the urban centers of New York, Miami, Los Angeles, and San Francisco. The fact that the number of AIDS cases is now doubling every thirteen months is of little comfort, because in 1986 more new cases of AIDS were diagnosed than in the prior five years. By December 1986, over 28,000 people with AIDS had been reported to the Centers for Disease Control (CDC). More than half of them (15,757) had died, and indeed the mortality rate is almost 80 percent for people in whom AIDS was diagnosed more than two years ago. It is widely assumed that few if any will survive the florid form of the disease.[4]

The clinical illness itself typically starts with vague, debilitating symptoms including drenching night sweats, sustained fevers, chronic diarrhea, and weight loss, sometimes associated with generalized enlargement of lymph nodes (lymphadenopathy). Some, but not all, of the individuals who start with that set of symptoms then experience oral "thrush" (yeast infection of the mouth) or develop the purplish skin lesions of a previously rare kind of malignancy called Kaposi's sarcoma. Alternatively—or as well—strange chronic pneumonias develop, caused by microorganisms rarely seen and resistant to treatment. Over time, some AIDS patients also develop confusion and other signs of progressive neurologic degeneration, which may be caused by additional opportunistic microorganisms or the AIDS virus itself. By which-ever dismal route, full-blown AIDS means a relentlessly downhill clinical course, whose social and psychological consequences have not been expe-rienced on a large scale since the days of polio or, indeed, leprosy.

Early in the epidemic it became evident that while three-quarters of AIDS patients were gay men, other high-risk groups could be identified. The first notable addition to the list was intravenous drug abusers. This suggested the analogy to hepatitis B and sounded the alarm that blood-borne trans-mission might be possible if the syndrome was indeed caused by an infectious agent. Subsequently, the recognition that severe hemophiliacs were at high risk added to concern about blood products. A curious additional risk group consisted of people of Haitian origin, putting Haitians living in the United States into the same fearful social environment that had engulfed the gay communities. The involvement of individuals from Haiti in the epidemic has been one of its most puzzling features. In fact, the CDC at one point removed

Haitians from the high-risk list on the ground that the category was poorly understood, but the category has essentially been restored under a new name. Just recently, the CDC announced that it had found risk factors for most of the people with AIDS who had been unclassified.[5]

Because of the clues implicating blood products as a mode of spreading the disease, the U.S. Public Health Service requested in March 1983 that individuals in the recognized high-risk groups refrain from donating blood or plasma. It was evident by that time that the incubation interval between exposure and disease might be as great as five years; thus, the preventive impact of such a policy might not be apparent for years. In view of this probable lag time, it was not a surprise in late 1983 when CDC scientists confirmed that a small number of AIDS patients had no other recognized risk factor in their background except the receipt of blood transfusions administered since 1978. With an explicit threat to the blood supply, the potential magnitude of the public health problem escalated sharply.

From earliest recognition, the simplest, and therefore the most attractive, hypothesis was that a new virus caused this new medical syndrome. However, features of the high-risk groups—especially the multitude of microbes bombarding the immune systems of the gay population and the large numbers of donors' antigens in hemophiliacs—led some scientists to suggest that AIDS might represent either a collapse of the immune system under siege or a novel outcome of an already known infection. Much thoughtful discourse concerning such hypotheses took place early in the epidemic, and those hypotheses should not be abandoned completely, because for every individual who develops AIDS as a result of infection with the virus, many other people have lesser or no manifestations of the infection.[6] This is not an unusual circumstance; in fact it is a truism to microbiologists—although it comes as a surprise to many others—that even the fiercest microbial pathogens cause disease in only *some* of their hosts. For instance, polioviruses, even in their most virulent state, cause paralysis in only a small percentage of the individuals they infect.

Indeed, researchers quickly noted that other members of high-risk groups were experiencing new syndromes that did not have all the features of fullblown AIDS. These patients might sustain generalized enlargement of lymph nodes but little more (a condition now called the lymphadenopathy syndrome, or LAS). Or they might have some but not all of the more serious manifestations of overt disease, even though their immune systems were demonstrably crippled. Scientists called this condition AIDS-related complex, or ARC. These lesser or different manifestations of infection suggested that if an infectious agent was involved, there would be a sizable proportion of those infected who did not match the formal working definition of AIDS itself and quite possibly lacked any recognizable symptoms, thereby remaining invisible until the causative agent was found.[7] The variation in severity of disease further suggested that the search for cofactors, such as concomitant infection with other microbes or massive immunologic assault, might well continue to be important.

ISOLATION OF THE AIDS VIRUS

Extraordinary scientific effort does not always lead to extraordinarily rapid progress, but in this instance it did. As the first cases of AIDS were being recognized, the sciences of virology, immunology, and molecular biology were reaching advanced levels of sophistication. If the epidemic had begun 20 years earlier, it might have remained an enigma much longer. Fortunately, the 1960s and 1970s were decades of explosive expansion in basic biomedical science, fueled by specific, crucial technological advances that proved indispensable for analyzing AIDS.

Conversely, AIDS research has contributed to our understanding of such phenomena as retroviruses. Until 1980 no human retrovirus had been identified—though not for lack of trying. This was rather puzzling, since retroviruses had been found in most other species where their presence, though often innocuous, sometimes was associated with tumors or with slow, progressive illnesses affecting the blood, lungs, or nervous system. The existence of retroviruses in animals kept alive the hope that analogous human agents might yet be found to help explain the many human chronic diseases of unknown cause.

Retroviruses have an unusual molecular structure. At first they seemed no different from other viruses that have ribonucleic acid (RNA) as their genetic material. Whereas all other organisms have deoxyribonucleic acid (DNA) as their fundamental genetic material (which is then transcribed into RNA and subsequently translated into protein molecules), some viruses carry only RNA. These viruses carry enzymes that allow them to bypass DNA entirely and create new RNA directly from their original molecular message. This is a relatively minor deviation from the usual sequence of genetic reproduction—from DNA to RNA to protein.

In 1969, however, scientists demonstrated that a unique enzyme carried by *some* RNA viruses could transfer genetic information from the viral RNA into DNA—the opposite direction of all known prior reactions. The DNA thus created could then be inserted among the native genes in chromosomes of infected cells, with the result that the viral information was positioned to function as a "new gene" for the infected host. The unique enzyme was called *reverse transcriptase*, and ultimately the group of RNA viruses bearing such enzymes was given the name "retroviruses."

In 1980 the first confirmed isolation of a retrovirus from humans was reported by Robert Gallo and his colleagues at the National Cancer Institute. Soon Gallo's group demonstrated that this new retrovirus had an exclusive predilection for human lymphocytes of the T type, a kind of lymphoid cell that controls cell-mediated immunity.[8] The subsequent discovery of a distinct but very closely related virus from a leukemia patient resulted in the designations HTLV-I and HTLV-II for human T-cell leukemia viruses. By the time these findings were reported and confirmed, the AIDS epidemic in the United States was in full swing, and it was apparent that there might be some relationship. AIDS patients did not as a rule develop leukemia, but the immune incompetence that rendered them so peculiarly susceptible to infection involved loss of the same subset of T-cells that gave rise to the leukemia of HTLV-I.

Researchers hoped to find some correlation between HTLV-I or -II and antibodies in AIDS patients or high-risk individuals. HTLV antibodies were found in a higher percentage, though not a majority, of people in these groups than in people who were neither AIDS patients nor high-risk individuals. This suggested that, like many other more familiar viruses, HTLVI merely had an advantage in these immunologically depleted hosts but did not play a causal role in AIDS.

Progress came quickly in competing laboratories. In France, J.C. Chermann and Luc Montagnier, at the Institut Pasteur, chose to study cells from gay men who had developed the lymphadenopathy syndrome, working on the assumption that AIDS itself was an end stage of which LAS might be the precursor. In 1983 they reported successful isolation of a retrovirus they called LAV—for lymphadenopathy-associated virus—from the lymph nodes of several such men. They demonstrated that this new retrovirus differed significantly from HTLV-I and -II and were further able to show that it had specific affinity for the kinds of human T-cells that are destroyed in AIDS patients.[9]

Gallo's group at the National Cancer Institute was on a similar trail. In May 1984 it reported the isolation from several AIDS patients of a new retrovirus, which it labeled HTLV-III. That laboratory then found a tissue-culture cell line that would allow large-scale production of the new virus, thus opening the way for mass production of viral antigens, a prerequisite for antibody testing.[10] A short while later Jay Levy's group at the University of California-San Francisco independently isolated an agent they called ARV—for AIDS-related virus.[11] After the terminological dust settled and detailed molecular comparisons were made, it became apparent that the three isolates were fundamentally the same and were causally involved in the development of lymphadenopathy syndrome, AIDS-related complex, and AIDS itself. For simplicity's sake the virus will be referred to henceforth as HIV (Human Immunodeficiency Virus—a name recently proposed by the International Committee on the Taxonomy of Viruses).

Once the virus was isolated, tests to determine the presence of virus-induced antibodies were soon developed to assess the scope of the epidemic and to develop control strategies. The interval between recognition of the first few cases of AIDS and the discovery of its cause was less than three years, and the second stage of advance to large-scale antibody testing was accomplished in less than one year. Never before has science moved so swiftly from recognition of a major medical problem to comprehensive understanding of its cause.

The availability of the antibody test for HIV allowed many urgent questions to be answered, creating a fairly coherent but disturbing picture. Although HIV is indeed a new human retrovirus, it is very closely related to certain primate retroviruses that may well have "jumped species" from monkeys to man in Central Africa, possibly as recently as 1960. It is not known how ﹀ infectious agents cross species. Viruses must attach to chemically specific receptor molecules on the surfaces of host cells before they can even get inside those cells. Then they must carry into the cell enough compatible molecular signals to commandeer the cell's metabolic machinery for their own ends. These requirements are sufficiently stringent that most viruses can grow in only a few types of cells, even within the host species to which they have adapted. To make the jump to the cells of a new host species is fraught with hazard from an evolutionary point of view, and the problems of sustaining a chain of transmission—from one human to another, for instance—make widespread epidemics of new diseases rare. Thus, while HIV is a poor spreader as human viral pathogens go, it is unique in recent experience in its ability to survive repeated passages in the human species.

Perhaps because it only recently appeared in humans, HIV is not easy to transmit from one person to another. The most efficient mode of transmission seems to be through semen during sexual intercourse, especially anal receptive intercourse but also in some cases by vaginal intercourse. The only other effective means of transmission are inoculation of infected blood and infection of an infant by an infected mother during the perinatal period of birth. Although the virus has been detected in secretions such as saliva and tears, there is no evidence that contact with those or other bodily fluids can transmit HIV.

GROUPS SUSCEPTIBLE TO HIV INFECTION

The antibody test has greatly facilitated analysis of the epidemic's path. Retrospective testing of stored serum samples has confirmed that the virus first appeared in the United States in 1978. Blood samples drawn then from a large number of men in the San Francisco gay community show that 1 percent or less had antibodies to HIV. The same population was again sampled in 1980 and 1984, and the percentages rose to 25 percent and then to 65 percent.[12] Other studies of high-risk populations have yielded similar results: in general, the acquisition of antibodies (and therefore almost certainly of the virus) has been rapid in gay communities in the United States. We do not know how many infected people will ultimately develop AIDS or ARC, because the interval between infection and the onset of illness can be more than five years. Best estimates at present are that in gay men, once infection occurs, the ultimate risk of developing full-blown AIDS is approximately 20 percent; another 25 percent will probably develop lesser disease states, particularly the lymphadenopathy syndrome. Because of the intimacy and durability with which retroviruses insert their DNA into host chromosomes at the very outset of infection, the remaining, disease-free 50 percent must be presumed to be carriers capable of transmitting the virus. We do not know whether they could become ill at a later date, although we know that 90 percent of infected individuals have laboratory signs of immunologic abnormality one year after infection, even if they are clinically well.

Although the same risk percentages seem to pertain to intravenous-drug abusers, hemophiliacs may have a somewhat brighter outlook. Their likelihood of exposure before 1983 was extremely high, because hemophilia is treated with concentrated clotting factor prepared from hundreds or thousands of donors. Indeed, in some studies, more than 90 percent of hemophiliacs have been found to have antibodies to HIV. The high incidence of HIV infection among hemophiliacs may partly be explained by cofactors; that is, hemophiliacs are more likely to become infected with the virus because they receive clotting factors from many different donors whose blood products carry many different foreign antigens. The percentage of seropositive hemophiliacs who develop AIDS, however, is lower than the general conversion rate. The reasons for this statistic remain unknown. Moreover, fewer hemophiliacs should become infected now that hospitals regularly screen donated blood.

Two other groups of AIDS patients require particular comment. The female sexual partners of infected men may become infected themselves during sexual intercourse, and they appear to play an important role in subsequent transmission both to infants born to them and to other sexual partners. It does not appear that vaginal intercourse is as efficient a mode of transmission as anal intercourse, but in some places many female prostitutes are infected and may serve as an important reservoir for further spread of HIV.[13]

Children are infected in one of two ways: either they have been born to infected mothers or they have received blood transfusions. Infants in the latter group are usually survivors of extreme prematurity, requiring close monitoring after birth, including frequent blood tests. The total blood volume of such babies is so small that they need frequent replacement transfusions of blood. Thus, they may receive donations from a dozen or more individuals over the weeks as they fight their way from one pound to five, and these multiple transfusions in turn put them at risk of blood-transmitted AIDS.

The incidence of AIDS patients who have had no recognizable risk factors other than having received one or more transfusions of blood or blood products within five years before the onset of their AIDS underscores the public-health problem. Approximately three million people each year receive blood or blood products in the United States, usually one or two units per recipient; multiple transfusions are sometimes necessary, especially in unpredictable circumstances such as severe trauma. Most donated blood is divided into two or even three components—red blood cells, plasma, and platelets—that may be given to separate patients for different reasons. In this way, the same donor may benefit (or expose) two or three recipients.

Given the potential threat of a contaminated blood supply, the actual hazard posed by the new virus seems to have been remarkably small. Even seven years into the AIDS epidemic in the United States, only 505 of the 28,000 cases of AIDS can be ascribed to blood transfusion in the absence of other risk factors. Most of those cases occurred in individuals who received multiple transfusions in emergencies. However, public fright about AIDS and transfusions in the early 1980s caused such concern among blood donors as well as recipients that the U.S. Public Health Service issued its March 1983 appeal that members of high-risk groups refrain from giving blood or plasma. The success of that appeal cannot be accurately known, but the frequency of donations dropped in several cities. As of mid-1985, only two transfusion-associated cases of AIDS had been traced to donations made after the self-exclusion appeal. This figure can also be explained, in part, by the increasing use of a new blood test—the enzyme-linked immunosorbent assay (ELISA)—that detects antibodies to HIV. By midsummer 1985 only about 0.2 percent of blood donors were confirmably positive. The detection and exclusion of their blood ensured the integrity of the blood supply.

PROSPECTS FOR A CURE OR VACCINE

The popular response to an epidemic of infectious disease is to call for a cure or, if not a cure, a vaccine. As to a cure, the limited state of our basic knowledge of retroviruses makes quick success unlikely. As the first step in their reproductive strategy, retroviruses copy their RNA into DNA, which is then inserted among normal cell chromosomes. While molecular genetics is advancing rapidly, it is not yet near the stage where specific genes can be found in living cells and excised individually—which is what would be required to undo the outcome of initial infection. Thus, a person with antibodies to HIV can be assumed to be a carrier, if not of the virus itself, then of the genetic information to produce the virus in the future. It is because of this that the question of whether to inform blood donors that they have HIV antibodies has presented such troublesome problems to administrators of blood banks. Even if the potential social stigmatization can be averted, the true meaning of a positive test carries a heavy psychological burden of its own.

As to a vaccine, some progress is being made, but many difficulties remain. Among the scientific barriers that stand in the way of an HIV vaccine, the most ominous appears to be the fact that the virus can evade the immune

response by antigenic variation. This capacity for antigenic change is well recognized in some other retroviruses, and recent studies showing differences among various isolates of HIV suggest that it too may have this property.

If, however, a sound vaccine can be developed, the pragmatic barriers to testing, licensing, and marketing are staggering. Demonstrating the efficacy of the vaccine would require large groups of willing human subjects at high risk of infection. Confirming the safety of the candidate vaccine would have to take into account issues of liability for perceived complications of immunization—problems that are even more complex than those that accompany existing vaccines for familiar infectious diseases. Finally, target groups on whom use of such a vaccine was deemed desirable would have to be defined and then persuaded of its merits. And if public-health authorities decided that universal use was the best strategy for containment of the epidemic, we would be faced afresh with all the problems and issues that made the swine-flu immunization campaign of 1976 so difficult for the public and for health officials alike. Adverse reactions to the vaccine are initially logged by recording any untoward events that occur in immunized individuals within several weeks following immunization. Thus, mass immunization automatically brings to the surface all the ills to which humans are prone, many of which have unknown causes and are therefore ascribed to the vaccine by a litigious public. More than $4 billion in claims were brought against the government before the campaign of mass immunization against swine flu in 1976-1977 was aborted.

Prospects for treatment are not much more promising. Once-touted candidate drugs (such as suramin and HPA-23) are usually inefficacious and unacceptably toxic. More recently, attention has been focused on AZT and DDC, which, like their predecessors, interfere with the virus's reverse transcriptase (and thus are most likely to be efficacious very early in infection). Other candidate drugs are calculated to augment or enhance components of the immune response, but they have not yet stood the test of clinical trials. These strategies may help asymptomatic infected people, but they do not seem to offer much hope for AIDS patients.

Thus, as with many other diseases, prevention is the most attractive way to contain the AIDS epidemic. In simplest terms, breaking the string of transmission would probably contain the virus because HIV is spread through only a few well-known means. High-risk groups are at high risk for reasons that are generally understood: infected intravenous-drug paraphernalia, for example, is known to be dangerous, as are certain sexual practices such as receptive anal intercourse with numerous partners.

It is probably unwise to end on too optimistic a note, because there are genuine obstacles to a preventive solution. In particular, the virus could become easier to transmit and harder to eradicate. If antigenic changes occur, like those in some animal retroviruses, they might blunt the effec-

tiveness or even render useless natural and therapeutic immunological strategies. These considerations make it all the more compelling that the string
of transmission of HIV be broken before such changes can develop and take
hold.

2

The Transmission of AIDS

RICHARD GREEN, M.D.

AIDS is caused by a virus that attacks the body's immune defense system. Studies demonstrate that the AIDS virus, which scientists call Human Immunodeficiency Virus (HIV), is transmitted only through the exchange of semen or cervical or vaginal secretions during sexual contact, from transfusions of blood products that have been contaminated with the virus, by the shared use of hypodermic needles that have been contaminated, and between an infected pregnant woman and her fetus. The virus cannot be spread by casual contact with an infected person. For example, people who share households with AIDS patients but are not their sexual partners do not contract the virus. Moreover, studies of household members and of health care workers who have had extensive contact with AIDS patients or their bodily fluids illustrate that the types of contact experienced in the workplace do not place healthy persons at risk of contracting the virus from infected co-workers.

THE PUBLIC FEAR

In spite of the scientific data collected by the medical community on the ways that HIV can be transmitted, the public treats AIDS as though it were a highly contagious disease spread by a wide range of activities. Consider the following examples of the panic that surrounds AIDS:

- A WNBC-TV television crew walked off the production set rather than tape an interview with two people with AIDS. Another crew resumed taping after it was agreed that microphones used by AIDS patients would be thrown away.[1]
- A man with AIDS went on trial for murder in Stamford, Connecticut. Fourteen prospective jurors asked to be dismissed from the case.[2]

- The Roman Catholic Archdiocese of New York withdrew plans to shelter AIDS patients in a former convent because irate parents threatened to keep their children from attending parochial school next door.[3]
- A resolution by the Queens Community School Board would bar from regular classes any student living with a person who has AIDS.[4] New York City Mayor Koch said that, in his opinion, no child with AIDS should attend city public schools. (He later changed his mind.)[5]
- A man with symptoms of AIDS was ordered to leave Boston City Hospital because workers feared he would infect them.[6]
- A Bronx Municipal Hospital was fined $31,000 for not providing adequate care to a man with AIDS.[7]
- The New York City School Chancellor revealed that three children had been removed from classes by community school-district superintendents because of suspicions that boyfriends of the students' sisters had AIDS.[8]
- A man diagnosed as having AIDS was required to wear a surgical mask while standing trial for murder. Despite a statement by an official from the City Health Commission—who appeared in person to assure court personnel and jurors that AIDS was not transmitted through the air and that they did not have to be concerned about being in the same courtroom with the defendant—half of the prospective jurors asked to be excused and court officers insisted on wearing masks and surgical gloves. The judge denied defense counsel's request that the officers be ordered to remove their protective paraphernalia to avoid prejudicing the jury.[9]
- A September 1985 CBS poll found that 47 percent think it possible to contract AIDS from a drinking glass used by a sick person, 32 percent from a kiss, and 28 percent from a toilet seat.[10]

MEDICAL FACTS OF AIDS

HIV invades and kills the white blood cells, known as T-helper cells, that are primarily responsible for preventing infectious diseases.[11] Consequently, diseases that rarely afflict people with healthy, functioning defense systems prove fatal to people infected with HIV. By December 1986, six years after the first cases of AIDS were reported to the Centers for Disease Control (CDC), more than 28,000 cases had been documented in the United States, almost half of which (15,757) had resulted in death.[12] No treatment permanently reverses the suppression of the immune system; no vaccine prevents infection.

Three distinct conditions after infection with HIV are the seropositive state, AIDS-related complex (ARC), and AIDS. In the seropositive state, blood tests reveal the presence of antibodies to HIV,[13] indicating infection with that virus.[14] Most people become seropositive within two or three months of infection.[15] At least one million people are estimated to be seropositive.[16]

Although a seropositive person does not show symptoms of ARC or AIDS,[17] and may never develop such symptoms, he or she does carry the virus and can transmit it to others.

A person in the seropositive state may develop ARC or AIDS. ARC causes moderate damage to the immune system and is characterized by nonspecific symptoms of illness, such as swelling of the lymph node (a condition called lymphadenopathy syndrome or LAS). Under the CDC's definition for ARC, at least two of the following clinical signs lasting three or more months must be present: fever, weight loss, lymphadenopathy, diarrhea, fatigue, and night sweats. There must be two laboratory findings: a low number of T-helper (white blood) cells and a low ratio of T-helper to T-suppressor (white blood) cells. Additionally, there must be at least one of the following: low white blood cell count, low red-blood cell count (anemia), low platelet (clotting cell) count, and elevated levels of serum globulins (infection-fighting proteins). There are none of the "opportunistic infections" that occur with AIDS, and there is no evidence of the otherwise rare form of cancer known as Kaposi's sarcoma. ARC by itself is not fatal. Furthermore, studies indicate that most people with ARC do not develop AIDS.

AIDS is the most serious of the three conditions caused by HIV. It represents a major collapse of the immune system, which allows infectious diseases (commonly called "opportunistic infections") and Kaposi's sarcoma to invade the body. About half of all patients die from a type of pneumonia (pneumocystis carinii pneumonia)[18] that is extremely rare in persons whose immune systems are working properly. The incubation period for the disease—the time between the initial infection by the virus and the onset of AIDS—has so far been reported to be up to seven years, with the average being four and a half.[19] (Because we have known about the disease for only six years, these figures are obviously provisional.) AIDS is fatal, on average, two years after diagnosis.

The CDC has set these criteria for diagnosing AIDS: (1) a positive blood test for serum antibody to the virus that causes AIDS or a positive cell culture for the virus; (2) a low number of T-helper white blood cells and a low ratio of T-helper white blood cells to T-suppressor white blood cells; and (3) the presence of one or more opportunistic infections that are indicative of underlying cellular immunodeficiency. These infections include diseases caused by protozoa (single-cell, amoeba-like living organisms) or helminthics (worms). The most common are pneumocytis carinii pneuomonia and diseases caused by fungi (molds), such as candidiasis or cryptococcus.[20]

Because AIDS is a new disease, it is unclear how many people who test seropositive will eventually become clinically ill. However, our brief experience with AIDS indicates that the great majority of these people remain clinically well five years after infection. In a study of seventy-eight seropositive men over a three-year period, only ten developed AIDS.[21] In another study, the conversion rate to AIDS over four years was estimated at 10 percent per year.[22] (This estimate does not tell us whether or not all seropositive people will eventually convert.) Finally, out of a group of seventy-five seropositive men under observation for as long as four years, ten developed AIDS.[23]

Seropositive hemophiliac patients are less likely to develop AIDS. Hemophiliacs in the United States first produced the AIDS antibody in 1978, and most of them became seropositive during 1981 and 1982.[24] Of the twenty thousand hemophiliacs in the United States, eighteen thousand—90 percent—are now seropositive.[25] Only about 240 have AIDS.

HOW AIDS IS TRANSMITTED

After extensive research on the epidemiology of AIDS, the CDC has concluded that HIV is transmitted under highly limited circumstances: "through sexual contact (homosexual or heterosexual) and through parenteral (intravenous) exposure to infected blood in blood products." Although the virus has also been found in saliva and tears, there has been no documented transmission of HIV through contact with these bodily fluids.[26]

Because HIV is transmitted almost exclusively in certain narrow circumstances, the CDC has been able to classify almost all people with AIDS into six groups: (1) sexually active homosexual and bisexual men (74 percent); (2) heterosexual intravenous drug abusers who share injection needles (17 percent); (3) heterosexuals who have intercourse with people who are seropositive or at high risk (4 percent); (4) hemophiliacs who have received contaminated blood-clotting factor products (1 percent); (5) other people who have received transfusions of contaminated blood (2 percent); and (6) newborn infants of infected mothers (1 percent).[27]

Transmission through Sexual Intercourse

Sexual interaction is the most common way to transmit HIV. When semen containing white blood cells harboring the virus comes into contact with mucosal tissue in the rectum and vagina, which are rich in superficial blood vessels, the virus can enter the host's blood stream through small tears in the tissue surface. Thus, anal intercourse between a man and a woman or two men can transmit infection, as can vaginal intercourse. No case of transmission of the virus has been documented by oral-genital sexual contact between two men, a man and a woman, or two women.[28]

Since its introduction, the virus has spread exponentially in the male homosexual population in the United States. One study followed more than six hundred men who, in 1978, visited a San Francisco clinic that treats sexually transmitted diseases. When the study began, 4.5 percent tested positive for exposure to HIV. In 1984, the rate was 67.4 percent.[29] In August 1985, it was 73.1 percent, of whom 6.4 percent had developed AIDS and

25.8 percent ARC.[30] Because the lining of the anus tears easily, the risk of infection among homosexual men is borne by the recipient partner in anal intercourse, which allows infected semen to enter the host's blood. Homosexual men with many sexual partners are more likely to be infected, because of the increased probability of their exposure to an infected partner.[31]

Since HIV is transmitted between men by semen it follows logically that men can also transmit the virus to women through both anal and vaginal intercourse. In two small studies, the rates of transmission from seropositive husbands to wives were two of twenty-one women and five of seven.[32] Moreover, in Haiti and some African countries, AIDS is transmitted primarily through heterosexual contact.[33]

Other studies suggest that heterosexual transmission occurs in either direction between men and women. A recent study of forty-five families found that both seropositive men and women transmitted the virus to their spouses, usually through sexual contact.[34] In another report, eight of twenty-two infected heterosexuals transmitted the virus to their sexual partners of at least two years; the spread occurred with equal frequency between the sexes.[35] Indeed, several documented cases of female-to-male transmission have been reported during the past two years. In one instance, one of the few health-care workers to contract AIDS from an infected needle passed the virus to her long-term sexual partner. Another woman, who contracted HIV from her bisexual husband, had sexual intercourse with a male neighbor, who then developed AIDS.[36] Because the AIDS virus has been found in cervical and vaginal secretions of seropositive women,[37] it is believed that women infect men during vaginal intercourse, when secretions harboring the virus reach the urethral lining within the penis.

Transmission through Exchange of Blood

HIV is also spread through a direct exchange of blood or blood products. This mode of transmission occurs most often among intravenous drug abusers who share injection needles, hemophiliacs and other patients who receive blood transfusions, and fetuses whose mothers carry HIV.

Intravenous drug abusers are a high-risk group for AIDS, because they commonly share needles out of economic need, habit, or social custom.[38] Among drug abusers at a New York detoxification center, 87 percent tested seropositive; most of them were male heterosexuals who had transmitted the virus to women through sexual intercourse. This kind of transmission is estimated to be responsible for 90 percent of the cases of AIDS among heterosexuals in New York City.[39]

Hemophiliacs in the United States have been a high-risk group because of their medical reliance on transfusions of blood products. Hemophiliacs are born with an inherited deficiency in blood-clotting mechanisms; the disease affects males nearly exclusively.[40] Factor VIII concentrate, prepared from pooled blood and infused into hemophiliac patients, permits normal blood clotting. Factor VIII is made by processing plasma from between two thousand and twenty thousand donors.[41] Because of this pooling and the former absence of blood screening, HIV found its way undetected into the blood supply. The first cases of AIDS among hemophiliacs were reported in July 1982 among heterosexuals with no history of intravenous drug abuse.[42] Although still well below the general conversion rate for AIDS among people who test seropositive, the incidence of AIDS among the 90 percent of hemophiliacs who test seropositive has risen sharply.[43] It remained at 0.6 cases per 1,000 through 1983, but increased to 5.4 in the first quarter of 1984.[44] It is now 7.5 per 1,000 in some cities.[45]

Another 2 percent of people with AIDS—and approximately 25 percent of all seropositive children—have been infected by medically administered whole-blood transfusions. Current procedures for screening blood donors and donated blood should virtually eliminate this source of infection.[46] The majority of children acquire HIV from their infected mothers in utero.[47]

CASUAL CONTACT DOES NOT TRANSMIT AIDS

In contrast to the high risk from sexual intercourse with an infected person or from injection of AIDS-contaminated blood, people do not increase their chances of contracting the virus by working with or near an infected person. AIDS is not spread by casual contact. This finding has been demonstrated by comprehensive research on people who have been extensively, but not sexually, exposed to people with AIDS—as either hospital workers or members of the same household. Studies show not only that HIV is spread exclusively through blood or semen but also that the virus is fragile and easily killed outside the body. In fact, the virus is destroyed by standard solutions of almost all common disinfectants, such as hydrogen peroxide, bleach, Lysol, or alcohol. Handwashing with a halogenated soap also appears to eradicate the organism.[48]

Several studies collated by the CDC demonstrate that HIV is rarely transmitted to health workers, even with direct, prolonged, nonsexual contact with AIDS patients. During the past five years, more than 1,750 health care workers with intense exposure to AIDS have been studied. Of these workers, 666 had either penetrated their skin with a needle contaminated with blood from a person infected with HIV or splashed body fluid from an infected person on a mucous membrane, such as the lips. Of the 26 who later tested seropositive, only 4 were not in a high-risk group.[49]

Another study, following 150 health care workers with injuries from contaminated needles, has found that as long as four years after exposure none of the subjects is seropositive.[50] Many of these injuries were severe, but the risk of infection, even when there is direct, through-the-skin exposure to bodily fluids from AIDS patients, is extremely low. For example, one nurse penetrated the palm of her hand with a needle used to aspirate bone marrow. Three serum samples, drawn from her at six-month intervals beginning a year after this trauma, were negative.[51]

There have been two documented cases of transmission—other than through needle injuries—from a patient to a person providing health care, but in both cases, the person who became infected did not follow standard precautions. In one report, a child with AIDS transmitted the virus to its mother, who was responsible for the child's medical care. The mother's activities included drawing blood through the child's in-dwelling body tubes at least weekly, removing peripheral intravenous tubes, emptying and changing ostomy (bowel) bags daily for seven months, inserting rectal tubes daily, and changing diapers, surgical dressings, and feeding tubes daily. This woman did *not* follow CDC precautions. She did not wear gloves. On several occasions her hands were contaminated with blood, feces, saliva, and nasal secretions, and she did not wash her hands immediately after such contact. The CDC cautions against generalizing the risk factor from this case.[52] "The contact between the reported mother and child is not typical of the usual contact that could be expected in a family setting."[53] In the other documented case of transmission from a patient to a caretaker, the health care worker also did not follow the CDC recommendation that all health care workers having intimate contact with a patient's bodily fluids wear gloves. She had prolonged contact with the patient's body excretions and secretions, and because of chronic eczema on her hands, her own blood was exposed to the patient's virus-containing fluids.[54]

AIDS is far less contagious than many other diseases. Thus, people infected with HIV and another disease have often communicated only the other disease. For example, a medical student inoculated his hand with a needle contaminated by blood from a patient with a cryptococcal (fungal) infection and HIV. The student contracted cryptococcus yet did not contract HIV.[55] Another health care worker exposed to body excretions contaminated with both hepatitis and HIV contracted only hepatitis.[56] Nor have there been reports of HIV transmission, in either direction, between health care workers and patients during surgery, childbirth, or any dental procedure. Of special interest is the case of a surgeon who died of AIDS after having operated on four hundred patients during the preceding five years. Two years after his death no case of seropositivity has been reported in any of his patients.[57]

Similarly, families and housemates of people with AIDS who are not their sexual partners do not contract the virus. The most comprehensive study of families of people with AIDS reports on 108 nonsexual members of the households of forty-one people with AIDS or ARC. Ninety-four of the 108 lived for at least three months with a clinically ill patient. The sample included 68 children. There was substantial sharing of household items and facilities including toothbrushes, towels, eating utensils, dishes, drinking glasses, beds, toilets, baths, showers, and kitchens. Moreover, 17 percent of the subjects kissed on the lips, and 83 percent kissed on the cheek. Once again, the results confirm that HIV is not spread through casual contact. No adult contracted the virus. One child developed ARC, but the child, age five, appeared to have contracted the virus from her mother during pregnancy and had been sick from infancy.[58]

Indeed, no case of HIV transmission has ever been found among household members except sexual partners or people in some independent high-risk group.[59] A study of hemophiliacs who contracted HIV from the transfusion of infected blood products confirms the finding of safety for household members. Of thirty-five people who shared households with fourteen seropositive hemophiliacs, only one person tested positive for HIV. She had regularly had vaginal and anal intercourse with her housemate during the previous year.[60] Moreover, other housemates who were, in fact, sexual partners of infected hemophiliacs did not contract the virus: in eight other male-female sexual couples, the nonhemophiliac partner remained seronegative.[61]

These studies demonstrate that HIV is difficult to transmit, even with intense, prolonged, and direct contact with HIV and with clinically ill AIDS patients. This is true even under circumstances where people have placed themselves in an especially precarious position, such as by inoculating themselves with bodily fluids from an infected patient. Reassuring data from studies of health care workers prompted the *New England Journal of Medicine* to state in an editorial entitled *Transmission of AIDS: The Case against Casual Contagion*: "Groups whose members are highly unlikely to acquire the virus (i.e., virtually no-risk groups) include health care workers caring for AIDS patients and anyone who had casual contact with a person infected with the AIDS virus." The journal went on to exhort the "members of the medical profession, armed with this knowledge, to take a more active and influential role in quelling the hysteria over the casual transmission of AIDS."[62]

Considerable public concern has been expressed that children who carry the virus will infect healthy children in school or at play. The CDC, however, has not received any reports of a child becoming infected with HIV from another child, either living in the same home or attending the same school. The CDC says that none of the identified cases of HIV infection in the United States has been transmitted in school, day care, or foster care.[63]

Most of the fear has centered on the possibility of an infected child biting a healthy one. The research data, however, do not support this concern. For instance, thirty health care workers were bitten or scratched severely by one brain-damaged hemophiliac with AIDS. Six months after the bite or scratch, all workers were seronegative.[64] Based on data from studies of AIDS, the CDC recommends that HIV-infected children be allowed to attend school with other children. The only exceptions might be children who are physically assaultive or incontinent or have weeping (wet) skin lesions.[65]

Likewise, the removal of HIV-infected people from the workplace is unnecessary because their presence simply does not put co-workers at an increased health risk. The data demonstrating the extremely low likelihood of AIDS transmission between patients and health care workers and between people with AIDS and family household members justify the conclusion that co-workers of people with AIDS or seropositive people are not at risk. The CDC has underscored the lack of risk to co-workers by recommending that people infected with HIV not be restricted from sharing the environment with co-workers on the basis of seropositivity. "Moreover," the CDC advises, "they should be not restricted from using the telephones, office equipment, toilets, showers, eating facilities, and water fountains.[66]

In the six years since the first reports of AIDS in the United States, the CDC has collected an exhaustive body of data on the ways the disease is transmitted. The data document those conditions under which persons have contracted the disease, and those under which they have not. AIDS is a contagious disease because it can be communicated. Despite public misconceptions, however, mere proximity to or casual contact with an infected person creates *no* risk of infection. Co-workers of people harboring HIV are not at increased risk of contracting the disease. Nor are health-care workers who exercise proper medical precautions. Nor are household members who are not sexual partners of an infected person.

3

A Historical Perspective

ALLAN M. BRANDT

Despite philosopher George Santayana's famous injunction that those who do not remember the past are condemned to repeat it, history is not a fable with the moral spelled out at the end. Even if we could agree on a particular construction of past events, it would not necessarily lead to consensus on what is to be done. And yet history provides us with one means of understanding hidden influences and possible courses of action in the present.

The history of medicine and public health can tell us much about contemporary approaches to the very difficult dilemmas raised by AIDS. The way a society responds to problems of disease reveals its deepest cultural, social, and moral values. These core values—patterns of judgment about what is good or bad—shape and guide human perception and action. The AIDS epidemic has been shaped not only by powerful biological forces but by behavioral, social, and cultural factors as well. This essay briefly analyzes the process by which social and cultural forces affect our understanding of disease by examining a telling analogue to the current health crisis.[1]

THE PROGRESSIVE ERA AND THE SOCIAL HYGIENE MOVEMENT

The first two decades of the twentieth century witnessed a general hysteria about venereal infections that parallels today's concern about AIDS.[2] This period, often referred to as the Progressive Era, combined two powerful strains in American social thought: the search for new technical, scientific answers to social problems and the search for a set of unified moral ideals. Both branches of thought were reflected in the "social hygiene" movement— the Progressives' campaign against venereal infection. The social hygiene movement was predicated on a series of major scientific breakthroughs. The specific organism that causes gonorrhea, the gonococcus, and the causative agent for syphilis, the spirochete, were both identified. By the end of the first decade of the twentieth century, diagnostic exams had been established. In 1911, the first major drug effective against the spirochete—Salvarsan— was discovered. These advances reframed the perception of venereal disease in the scientific community: the availability of effective means of diagnosis and treatment led to a more open discussion of the enormous social, cultural, and economic costs of the disease.

Physicians who had been reluctant to discuss and often to treat venereal diseases began to trace the repercussions of syphilis within the family. Doc- tors came to define what they called *venereal insontium*, or venereal disease of the "innocent." Perhaps the best known example of *venereal insontium* was *opthalmia neonatorum*, gonorrheal blindness of the newborn. As late as 1910, up to 25 percent of all the blind in the United States had lost their sight in this way, despite the earlier discovery that silver nitrate solution could prevent infection. Increased public discussion of this form of blindness led many states to require prophylactic treatment.[3]

Doctors stressed the disease's impact on women even more than that on children. In 1906, for example, an American Medical Association symposium on the Duty of the Profession to Womanhood examined the physician's duty to report venereal infection to wives and fiancées.[4] The distinction between venereal disease and *venereal insontium*, of course, had the effect of dividing victims; some deserved attention, sympathy, and medical support, others did not. By determining how infection was obtained, doctors separated victims into the "innocent" and the "guilty."

The train of family tragedy was a frequent cultural theme in these years. In 1913, a hit Broadway play by French playwright Eugene Brieux, *Damaged Goods*, told the story of young George Dupont, who is warned by his physician not to marry because he has syphilis but disregards the advice, only to spread the infection to his wife and, ultimately, to their child. This story was told and retold; it revealed evolving social attitudes about science, social responsibility, and the limits of medicine to cure the moral ailments of humankind.[5]

Intrafamily transmission was not the only fear of Progressive Era phy- sicians. The last years of the nineteenth century and the first of the twentieth were the most intensive periods of immigration to the United States in its entire history; more than 650,000 immigrants came to these shores each year between 1885 and 1910. Many doctors and social critics suggested that these outsiders were bringing venereal disease into the country. Howard Kelly, a leading gynecologist at Johns Hopkins, explained, "The tide [of venereal disease] has been raising [sic] owing to the inpouring of a large foreign population with lower ideals." And he went on to warn, "think of these countless currents flowing daily from the houses of the poorest into those of the richest, and forming a sort of civic circulatory system expressive of the body politic, a circulation which continually tends to equalize the distribution of morality and disease."[6] In fact, examinations at the ports of entry failed to reveal a high incidence of disease. Nevertheless, nativists called for the restriction of immigration.

And how were these immigrants spreading sexually transmitted diseases to native, middle-class, Anglo-Saxon Americans? It was suggested that immigrants constituted the great bulk of prostitutes who inhabited American cities, although data indicated that most prostitutes were native-born.[7]

More importantly, physicians now asserted that syphilis and gonorrhea could be transmitted in any number of ways. Doctors catalogued the various modes of transmission: pens, pencils, toothbrushes, towels, bedding, and medical procedures were all identified as potential means of communication.[8] One woman explained in an anonymous essay in 1912:

> At first it was unbelievable. I knew of the disease only through newspaper advertisements [for patent medicines]. I had understood that it was the result of sin and that it originated and was contracted only in the underworld of the city. I felt sure that my friend was mistaken in diagnosis when he exclaimed, "Another tragedy of the common drinking cup!" I eagerly met his remark with the assurance that I did not use public drinking cups, that I had used my own cup for years. He led me to review my summer. After recalling a number of times when my thirst had forced me to go to the public fountain, I came at last to realize that what he had told me was true.[9]

The diagnosis, of course, had been syphilis. One indication of how seriously these casual modes of transmission were taken is the fact that the Navy removed doorknobs from its battleships during the First World War, claiming—in a remarkable act of denial—that this had been a source of infection for many of its sailors.

We now know, of course, that syphilis and gonorrhea cannot be contracted in these ways. Why, then, did physicians believe they could be? Theories of casual transmission reflected deep cultural fears about disease and sexuality in the early twentieth century. Venereal disease was viewed as a threat to the entire late Victorian social and sexual system, which placed great value on discipline, restraint, and homogeneity. The sexual code of the era sanctioned only sex-in-marriage. But the concerns about venereal disease also reflected a pervasive fear of the urban masses, the growth of the cities, and the changing nature of familial relationships.

In short, venereal disease became a metaphor for the anxieties of the time. Such metaphors are not simply innocuous linguistic constructions; they have powerful sociopolitical implications. And they have been remarkably persistent during the twentieth century.

Beginning in the early 1900s, concerns about sexually transmitted diseases led to a major public health campaign to stop their spread. Many of the public health approaches applied to communicable infections today were developed in these years.

Educational programs formed a major component of the campaign, though, to be sure, when schools first instituted sex education programs in the first decade of the twentieth century, their basic goal was to inculcate fear of sex in order to encourage premarital continence. Indeed, it would be more accurate to call these programs antisexual education.

The new ability to diagnose syphilis and gonorrhea led to other important public health interventions. American cities began to require the reporting of venereal diseases around 1915. Some states used reports to follow contacts and bring individuals in for treatment. By the 1930s, many states had come to require premarital and prenatal screening. Some municipalities mandated compulsory screening of food handlers and barbers, even though it was by then understood that syphilis and gonorrhea could not be spread through casual contact. The rationale offered was that individuals in these professions were at risk for infection anyway and that screening might reveal new cases for treatment.

Perhaps the most dramatic public health intervention devised to combat sexually transmitted diseases was the campaign to close red-light districts. In the first two decades of the twentieth century, vice commissions in almost all American cities had identified prostitutes as a major risk for American health and morals and decided the time had come to remove the sources of infection. During the First World War, more than one hundred red-light districts were closed in an attempt to "drain the swamps" that harbored infection. The crackdown on prostitutes constituted the most concerted attack on civil liberties in the name of public health in American history.

Not surprisingly, in the atmosphere of crisis that the war engendered, public health officials employed radical techniques in their battle against venereal disease. State laws held that anyone "reasonably suspected" of harboring a venereal infection could be tested on a compulsory basis. Prostitutes were also subject to quarantine, detention, and internment.[10] Attorney General T.W. Gregory explained:

> The constitutional right of the community, in the interest of the public health, to ascertain the existence of infections and communicable diseases in its midst and to isolate and quarantine such cases or take steps necessary to prevent the spread of disease is clear.[11]

In July of 1918, Congress allocated more than $1 million for the detention and isolation of venereal disease carriers. During the war, more than 30,000 prostitutes were incarcerated in institutions supported by the federal government. One federal official noted:

> Conditions required the immediate isolation of as many venereally infected persons acting as spreaders of disease as could be quickly apprehended and quarantined. It was not a measure instituted for the punishment of prostitutes on account of infraction of the civil or moral law, but was strictly a public health measure to prevent the spread of dangerous, communicable diseases.[12]

Although many of these interventions were challenged in the courts, most were upheld; the police powers of the state were deemed sufficient to override any constitutional concerns. The program of detention and isolation, it should be noted, had no impact on rates of venereal disease, which increased dramatically during the period. Many of the prostitutes were later found to be free of infection; nevertheless, their incarceration—often in barbed wire-enclosed camps—was justified on the grounds that they were likely, if released, to become infected.

The prostitute had been anathema to generations of American reformers; the exigencies of war effected her banishment from the urban landscape. Issues previously seen to be of a moral nature now achieved the powerful legitimacy of scientific and health concerns. The "cult of the expert" made possible far-ranging policies that conflicted with basic civil liberties.

SOCIAL VALUES AND AIDS

The analogies between reactions to AIDS and reactions, in the early 1900s, to venereal disease are striking: the pervasive fear of contagion, concerns about casual transmission, the stigmatization of victims, the conflicts between protecting public health and ensuring civil liberties. Of course, AIDS is not syphilis, and 1987 is not 1918. Certainly, however, the response to AIDS is no more strictly determined by its biological character than was the Progressive Era response to venereal disease; rather, social policies are powerfully affected by social and cultural understandings of disease and its victims.

As in the early twentieth century, public health measures that require dramatic infringements of civil liberties are being proposed. All too often, these measures can have no positive impact on the public health. This is not to suggest a purely pragmatic measure: if it works it is right. But if a measure does not produce results and yet is supported by officials and the public, one must suspect secondary reasons for that support. Such measures tend to transform protection of the public into punishment of victims of disease. The disease and those who get it are socially disvalued. The punishments, of course, do not fall randomly across society. Existing social disapproval—of drug abusers, for example—may be channeled into medically unsupported "public health" concerns.

How will social and cultural values concerning AIDS influence public policies toward the disease? A series of difficult dilemmas are just off-stage. How can the impact of this disease be mitigated? Can we protect the rights of victims of the disease while avoiding the victimization of the public—and vice versa? What types of policies should be employed? And how will these policies reflect our cultural notions of the disease?

Already, traditional public health policies—screening, testing, reporting, contact tracing, isolation, and quarantine—have been invoked. Will these measures be effective in the case of AIDS, which is complicated by the large number of healthy carriers perhaps infectious for life?. In short, how do we construct a just, humane, and effective policy? How do we protect civil liberties while protecting the public good?

As in the early 1900s, the fear and uncertainty surrounding the epidemic could make us less, rather than more, cautious in seeking solutions. While we know much about AIDS, much lies outside current scientific understanding. Scientists and physicians have experience tolerating such ambiguities, but this level of uncertainty is often avoided or denied by the larger society. Policies relating to AIDS will, of course, be created in this atmosphere of uncertainty. Moreover, the decline of the authority of experts from Three Mile Island, to Love Canal, to the Space Shuttle, to Chernobyl have dramatically lessened the public's faith in experts.

As a society, we have not had to address any epidemics of major infectious diseases since polio. This good fortune means that we lack recent social and political experience in dealing with such problems. And, indeed, we would probably have to go back to the influenza pandemic of 1918 to identify a pathogen as dangerous as the AIDS virus. Thus, we have few models for dealing with public health issues of this magnitude and complexity.

And as a society, we are not good at comparing risks. How does the danger of AIDS compare to other risks? How will the courts, for example, determine the relative risk posed by individuals who carry the AIDS virus? We need to develop better measures for making more sophisticated assessments of the risks we face.

All social policies carry costs, but in our political culture, we tend to reject policies when the costs become explicit, even if they promise significant benefits. For example, as in the early twentieth century, education has been put forward as one of the few positive activities that might slow the spread of AIDS. But some see explicit sexual education as encouraging homosexuality or promiscuity, and many policy makers, from television executives to elected officials, have been unwilling to risk offending those people. Similarly, the idea of providing sterile needles to intravenous drug abusers to prevent the further spread of the disease has been rejected because it is seen as contributing to the drug problem.

On the other hand, policies that have little or no potential for slowing the epidemic could have considerable legal, social, and cultural appeal. What can be done to separate realistic concerns from irrational fears? How can victim-blaming and stigmatization of high-risk groups, already socially devalued, be avoided?

In many respects, the process of dividing victims into the "innocent" and the "guilty"—analogous to the early twentieth century approach to venereal disease—has been activated once again. Take, for example, the following assessment offered by a journalist in the *New York Times Magazine* in 1984:

> The groups most recently found to be at risk for AIDS present a particularly poignant problem. Innocent by-standers caught in the path of a new disease, they can make no behavioral decisions to minimize their risk: hemophiliacs

cannot stop taking bloodclotting medication; surgery patients cannot stop getting transfusions; women cannot control the drug habits of their mates; babies cannot choose their mothers.[13]

In some quarters the misapprehension persists: AIDS is caused by homosexuality rather than by a retrovirus. In this confused logic, the answer to the problem is simple: repress these behaviors. Implicit in this approach to the problem are powerful notions of guilt.

The high mortality associated with AIDS could become the justification for drastic measures. "Better safe than sorry" could become a catch phrase to justify dramatic abuses of basic human rights in the context of an uncertain science. Moreover, the social construction of this disease—its close association in much of the public's eye with violations of the moral code—could contribute to mounting hysteria and anger, which has already led to further victimization of victims, the double jeopardy of lethal disease and social and legal oppression.

The social costs of ineffective draconian public health measures would only augment the crisis. But such measures will be avoided only if we are sophisticated in our medical and cultural understanding of this disease and if we are able to create an atmosphere of social tolerance. Only when we recognize the ways in which social and cultural values shape our responses to this disease will we be able to begin to deal effectively and humanely with AIDS.

PART TWO
GOVERNMENT RESPONSES TO AIDS

4

Traditional Public Health Strategies

LARRY GOSTIN

AIDS is the most serious communicable disease epidemic in contemporary times, and the effort to reduce its spread is the U.S. government's top health priority.[1] AIDS is uniquely problematic: the underlying disease cannot currently be prevented or treated; Human Immunodeficiency Virus (HIV), the virus associated with AIDS, is noted for its propensity to change easily, making the future development of vaccines or treatment difficult; there is no finite incubation period, so carriers of the virus are chronically infectious; and the major risk groups are vulnerable to social prejudice and private discrimination, posing special problems for public health officials seeking to identify persons carrying the virus and capable of transmitting it.

More than 28,000 cases of AIDS as defined by the Centers for Disease Control (CDC) have been reported since 1981, and an estimated 1.5 million people are infected with HIV. The cumulative number of cases and carriers is expected nearly to double by 1988.[2] This predicted geometric increase in the number of carriers has charged the atmosphere of health-policy debate. Public concern is rife, and can itself be viewed as a secondary epidemic of fear. AIDS therefore poses an incomparable challenge for health policymakers, who must seek methods of reducing its spread and of helping ensure the public safety consistent with the protection of individual dignity and autonomy.

The law regulating public health actions is complicated and uncertain. The major cases upon which it was founded arose near the turn of the century, and subsequent advances in medicine and changes in the judicial treatment of individual rights have required revisions in health law that are not yet complete. Many of our public health responses to epidemic disease are decades or even centuries old. The medical basis and appropriate uses of measures like quarantine have changed considerably as twentieth century medicine has developed a better understanding of the cause and transmission

47

of disease. In the same period, American society and its judiciary have become more sophisticated about individual liberties: more rights have been recognized—ranging from privacy in contraception to attendance at non-segregated schools—and protection of all rights has been enhanced.

The AIDS epidemic is an invitation to the court system to fully incorporate these legal and medical developments into the health law. While this is an unfinished process, the general trend may be discerned. Traditionally, judges deferred to health officials and legislatures as long as public health measures were reasonably necessary and not unreasonably oppressive. Deference to elected officials remains a basic judicial value, but the legal and medical changes of the last decades have eroded its practical impact in health cases. The enhancement of individual rights means that more health actions will be seen as infringing rights in a way that requires court intervention and close scrutiny; advances in medicine allow courts to determine precisely how necessary an action is in scientific terms.

This chapter evaluates the application to the AIDS epidemic of classic public health responses to infectious disease. It begins with an introduction to the law governing public health measures. It then examines two measures commonly used to determine the scope of a disease and to provide information to the people most directly affected by it: case finding (the use of screening tests and sexual contact tracing), and case reporting (of infectious individuals to public health officials). If properly designed and tailored, these practices are likely to withstand legal challenge, both because they are justified by current medical knowledge and because they can be accomplished with minimal detrimental impact on individual rights. Nevertheless, these practices raise serious practical and policy problems. The third part of this chapter examines methods used to isolate those believed capable of transmitting the infection: general isolation, modified isolation, criminal law sanctions, and civil law restrictions (such as civil commitment). These measures are very intrusive and minimally effective, and many of them are open to serious legal challenge. The final part of the chapter summarizes my conclusions.

THE LAW GOVERNING PUBLIC HEALTH ACTIONS

The day-to-day protection and promotion of public health has traditionally been a state function. The federal government's role, especially in policy coordination, research, and funding, has grown steadily, but it is the states, through local health departments and school districts, that administer such primary public health measures as school inoculation and disease reporting.[3] States have the authority to carry out health measures under what is traditionally, if confusingly, referred to as their "police power"—the power reserved to the states in the Constitution to take necessary action to promote the public health and welfare, to foster prosperity, and to maintain public order.[4] But while the state's power to enact and administer health laws is unquestionable,[5] the *exercise* of this power is subject to limitations arising from the constitutional protection of individual rights.[6]

Basic individual rights are guaranteed by both the federal Constitution and the constitutions of the several states. Thus, even though this chapter focuses on the U.S. Constitution, it is well to remember that state constitutions may offer the same or even broader protections. The Bill of Rights (the first ten amendments to the Constitution) established basic rights that cannot be infringed by the federal government. These include freedom of speech and religion, freedom from unreasonable searches and seizures, the right to counsel in criminal (and some civil) cases, and, most significant for our purposes, the insistence that life, liberty, and property cannot be abridged without due process of law.[7] The Fourteenth Amendment, enacted after the Civil War, has been deemed to extend many of these protections to the actions of state governments.[8] The Fourteenth Amendment also expressly provides, via its equal protection clause, that laws may not treat in an unequal fashion people who are in relevant respects the same.[9]

Whenever individuals (or classes of persons) assert in litigation that their rights have been abridged by the act of a local, state, or federal government, they are implicitly asking the court to undo the will of the majority as expressed through the executive or the legislature. Given this reality, it is not surprising that rights are rarely regarded as absolute. Some constitutional provisions, by their very terms, invite the exercise of judgment in deciding when the government has overstepped. The Fourth Amendment, for example, prohibits only "unreasonable" searches and seizures. Even rights that are phrased in absolute terms—the First Amendment is a good example[10]—are treated as if they were, of necessity, qualified.[11] Thus, courts find themselves inevitably engaged in a balancing act, with the constitutional rights of the disfavored in one pan and the state's interest in the other. No matter how reluctant a judge is to get involved in deciding whether a challenged health measure is a good idea, if the measure tends to abridge constitutionally protected rights, he or she must inevitably evaluate the measure's propriety, its utility, and its necessity.[12] The principal response of courts to this reality has been the development of formal tests that purport to determine how deeply, and under what circumstances, a challenged measure will be examined.

Most of the important public health cases were decided around the turn of the century. Their hallmark is the deference consistently shown by courts to the will of the legislature. Legislatures were given substantial latitude in determining which measures were necessary, and their handiwork was regarded as presumptively valid.[13] The courts generally took the view that they would not substitute their own judgment for that of the legislature, and that the "manner and mode" of regulatory efforts was wholly within the ambit of the states' police powers.[14]

The major impetus for judicial activity in the public health field was the sporadic occurrence of epidemics of venereal disease,[15] tuberculosis,[16] smallpox,[17] scarlet fever,[18] leprosy,[19] cholera,[20] and bubonic plague.[21] In this context, private rights were subordinated to the public interest and individuals were seen as bound to conform their conduct for society's good.[22] As one court put it, quarantine does not frustrate constitutional rights because there is no liberty to harm others.[23] Even when courts recognized that personal control measures cut deeply into private rights, they would not allow the assertion of those rights to thwart public policy.[24] This preference for social control over individual autonomy emerged as a major characteristic of judicial rulings of the period.[25]

The conceptual underpinning for this deferential approach was what is now known as the rational basis or the means-ends test: a health measure would be upheld if there was a "real or substantial" connection between the measure and the end it was meant to secure.[26] Although this test was used in a notoriously intrusive fashion by the Supreme Court in striking down economic regulations at the start of the New Deal,[27] in general, courts used it to justify a hands-off policy with respect to measures aimed at combatting disease. Courts tended to uphold public health statutes as long as the state did not act in "an arbitrary, unreasonable manner" or go "beyond what was reasonably required for the safety of the public."

In practice, this standard left basic questions unanswered, the most important of which was how "rationality" was to be judged. The "rationality" of a measure quickly came to be seen in terms of whether it was necessary for the protection of public health, but this raised an even more basic question: by what standard was "necessity" itself to be judged?

Many early cases viewed necessity as a general determination to be made by the legislature under such criteria as it judged useful. A New York opinion, quoted with approval in the leading U.S. Supreme Court police power case, left the decision to "the people:"

> While we do not decide, and cannot decide, that vaccination is a preventative of smallpox, we take judicial notice of the fact that this is the common belief of the people of the State, and with this fact as a foundation, we hold that the statute in question is a health law, enacted in a reasonable and proper exercise of the police power.[28]

Nor did the Connecticut court in *State v. Rackowski* require any more stringent evidence than "common knowledge" in deciding that a person exposed to scarlet fever may communicate the disease.[29]

The harm to individual interests that can occur from imposing control measures not clearly supported by scientific evidence is illustrated by *Kirk v. Wyman*, a 1901 South Carolina case. An elderly woman with anaesthetic leprosy was quarantined even though there was "hardly any danger of contagion."[30] She had lived in the community for many years, attended church services, taught in school, and mingled in social life without ever communicating the disease. The South Carolina Supreme Court thought it "manifest that the board were well within their duty in requiring the victim of it to be isolated" when the "distressing nature of the malady is regarded."[31]

In the absence of scientific criteria, spurious factors were often decisive. In *Ex parte Company*, the Ohio Supreme Court upheld a quarantine regulation including a provision that "all known prostitutes and persons associated with them shall be considered as reasonably suspected of having a venereal disease."[32] "Suspect conduct and association" were deemed sufficient to justify imposition of control measures,[33] and the court did not appear concerned with whether the person before the court actually had venereal disease.

In *People v. Strautz*, the Illinois court accepted similarly unfounded assumptions. "Suspected" prostitutes were considered "natural subjects and carriers of venereal disease," making it "logical and natural that suspicion be cast upon them [necessitating] a physical examination of their persons."[34] The court was unclear as to the evidence required to establish a reasonable belief that a person engaged in prostitution.

From the earliest days of major public health litigation, however, some decisions recognized the need for more objective and reliable criteria. Several early cases were much stricter in requiring a demonstration of public health necessity and medical proof that individuals were in fact infectious.[35] *Ex parte Shepard*, a California decision, specifically rejected the proposition that mere suspicion of venereal infection is sufficient to uphold a quarantine order.[36] Similarly, in *Ex parte Arata*, the California court required that reasonable grounds exist to support the claim that a person is afflicted with venereal disease: "Mere suspicion unsupported by facts giving rise to reasonable or probable cause will afford no justification at all for depriving persons of their liberty."[37]

Smith v. Emery, an 1896 New York decision, presents one of the earliest and clearest statements by a court on the need for *medical* evidence to support control measures: "The mere possibility that persons might have been exposed to such disease [smallpox] is not sufficient." They must *in fact* have been exposed to it, the conditions must "actually exist for a communication of the contagion," and all such issues must be determined by "medical science and skill," not "common knowledge."[38]

The highwater mark of the early cases (from the perspective of judicial oversight of public health measures) is *Jew Ho v. Williamson*. There, a federal district court refused to uphold the quarantine for bubonic plague of an entire district of San Francisco containing a population of more than fifteen thousand Chinese persons. Because bubonic plague is most easily communicated in conditions of overcrowding and poor sanitation "[i]t must necessarily follow that, if a large territory is quarantined, intercommunication of the people within that territory will rather tend to spread the disease than to restrict it."[39] The court noted that the form of quarantine applied would therefore enlarge the sphere of the disease and increase its danger and destructive force; that the evidence to show the existence of plague and the circumstances of its transmission was slight; and that the quarantine demonstrated an "evil eye and an unequal hand" because it was made to operate exclusively against the Chinese community. The court's searching scrutiny of the means adopted by the municipal health officials was uncharacteristic of early public health cases but foreshadowed contemporary judicial analysis.

Modern courts have been consistent in requiring a clear public health justification for any personal control measure. In *New York State Association for Retarded Children v. Carey*, the U.S. court of appeals determined that mentally retarded children who were carriers of serum hepatitis could not be excluded from attending regular public school classes. Hepatitis B is transmitted by blood. Although the virus is also found in saliva, transmission via fluids other than blood is relatively inefficient and unlikely. The court found that "the School Board was unable to demonstrate that the health hazard . . . was anything more than a remote possibility." This remote possibility did not justify the action taken, considering "the detrimental effects of isolating the carrier children." The court was sensitive to the fact that segregation of mentally retarded children would "reinforce the stigma to which these children have already been subjected."[40]

Other contemporary public health cases have taken the same critical view of assertions of public health necessity. Discrimination against a teacher with tuberculosis was proscribed by the court of appeals in *Arline v. School Board of Nassau County*: "The Court is obliged . . . [to determine] whether the defendant's justifications reflect a well-informed judgment . . . or whether they are simply conclusory statements used to justify reflexive reactions grounded in ignorance or capitulation to public prejudice."[41] Using similar reasoning, the New York court in *District 27 Community v. the Board of Education of the City of New York* forbade discrimination against a child with AIDS:

> Since "the apparent nonexistent risk of transmission of HTLV-III/LAV" in the school setting finds strong support in the epidemiologic data . . . and because the *automatic* exclusion of children with AIDS . . . would effect a purpose having no adequate connection with the public health, it would usurp the function of the Commissioner of Health if this court adjudged . . . that the non-exclusion policy was arbitrary and capricious simply because in the court of public opinion, that particular policy was . . . not the best choice.[42]

These cases provide important standards that should be applied to all public health responses to AIDS. The exercise of a personal control measure in a particular case requires scientific evidence that the person actually has an infectious condition, that circumstances exist whereby the infection can be communicated, and that the measure would be effective in eliminating or reducing the risk of contagion.[43]

At the same time that the analysis of necessity was becoming more scientific, major changes were occurring in the constitutional law of individual rights. The Supreme Court was recognizing new rights—for example, the right to privacy in matters of procreative choice[44]—and developing a more refined, and more complicated, way of balancing them against governmental interests. The unitary rational basis test, applied without formal regard to the importance of the particular right compromised, has given way to three different tests, with the choice of which one to employ dependent on the nature of the rights infringed or the groups affected by the challenged measure.[45] Most cases continue to be judged under the deferential rational relationship test: A state may justify a measure merely by showing that it has some plausible connection to a legitimate state goal.[46] At the other extreme is the "strict scrutiny" test: measures that infringe upon a fundamental right, or which appear to discriminate against minority groups historically subject to discrimination ("suspect classes") must be proven vital to a compelling state interest; further, even a measure that passes this test may fall if another less restrictive means to the same end is available.[47]

In some cases, the court has applied "intermediate scrutiny," requiring a challenged measure to have a "substantial" (as distinct from merely rational) relationship to an important goal and to be the least restrictive means available. These cases have involved either important rights that have not (or not yet) achieved full fledged constitutional status (such as the right to education), or "quasi-suspect" classifications (notably those based on gender).[48]

The reader who finds this structure confusing is not alone. It has been criticized even from within the Supreme Court;[49] it has been called artificial, mechanical, and even dishonest.[50] One of the most frequent complaints is that the selection of the test determines the outcome: virtually no laws survive strict scrutiny,[51] and virtually none are overturned for lack of a rational relationship.[52] Then, too, the reverse may be true, namely that courts select the test that justifies the desired outcome. Be that as it may, there is no indication that this structure will be abandoned in the near future. Fortunately, the realities of public health law force courts to deal with concrete facts rather than slippery abstractions. In practice, it is only through an examination of medical facts that judges evaluating a particular health measure can decide, for example, how "compelling" a state's interest in the measure is, how "substantially" it is related to the health problem, and whether it is the "least restrictive" alternative.

Finally, it is important not to overestimate the practical importance of constitutional law in the AIDS epidemic. Since the early days of public health law, more has changed than just medicine and constitutional law. In the last fifteen years, legislation aimed at protecting the rights of the disabled has been enacted throughout the nation and now plays a major role in determining both how and under what circumstances public health officials may act.[53] Since then, nearly all the important cases involving public health measures have been decided under these statutes rather than under the Constitution. So, for example, in the *Carey* case, while the trial court found that the exclusion from school of children with hepatitis failed to pass the rational relationship test, on appeal the decision was based on the Rehabilitation Act, not the Constitution. Similarly, the Rehabilitation Act limited the right of a school district to fire a teacher with tuberculosis in an important case recently decided by the Supreme Court.[54] (For a detailed discussion of these statutes, see Chapter 8 and Chapter 5.)

CASE IDENTIFICATION

Epidemiologists require accurate data about the prevalence, distribution (geographic and demographic), and transmission modes of diseases. Consequently, public health authorities traditionally engage in broadscale data collection. To that end, they often screen segments of the population considered to be at risk, trace the "contacts" of persons found to be infected, and collect information on everyone diagnosed as having the relevant disease.

Screening

"Screening" is the systematic use of a medical test on population groups (as distinguished from case-by-case testing of individuals).[55] No one proposes that screening be employed to locate and identify persons who have full-blown AIDS. Given the debilitating nature of the disease, they are likely to seek medical help well before an official AIDS diagnosis could be made. Instead, proposed screening measures focus on identifying persons who, by virtue of their exposure to the virus associated with AIDS, *might* develop the disease or transmit it to others. At present, there is no readily available test for determining whether a person exposed to the virus continues to harbor it, nor is there a test that determines who is infectious. A test does exist, however, for determining whether a person has been exposed to the virus, as evidenced by the presence in the blood of antibodies to it. Caution dictates that such persons be presumed to be infectious.

If administered properly, with appropriate confirmatory tests, AIDS antibody screening has a degree of reliability comparable to other widely used medical tests.[56] (For a more detailed discussion of current tests, see Chapter 9.) At the same time, the psychosocial costs of an erroneous result are extremely high. The test was developed to screen blood, for which purpose it has been successful and uncontroversial. It has also been employed, again uncontroversially, in *voluntary* testing programs, through which persons who fear they have been exposed to the virus can obtain counseling and, if appropriate, take the test under conditions of assured confidentiality. More controversial and problematic is the mandatory screening of military recruits and personnel (see Chapter 16). The most recent screening proposal of similar magnitude came from the CDC, which submitted "for discussion" mandatory HIV antibody testing of all people applying for marriage licenses, entering hospitals, or seeking treatment for venereal disease or pregnancy.[57]

Properly understood, screening is a means, not an end. It provides information, whose value depends on the use to which it is put.[58] In both the legal and the medical arenas, proposals for screening can be evaluated only in terms of how well they accomplish some desirable goal. In theory, HIV antibody screening can do two things: provide a clearer statistical picture of the prevalence of the virus, and identify infected individuals who may benefit from some sort of public health action. On both counts, massive screening is problematic. To begin with, there is, at present, no treatment available for persons who are simply seropositive. New drugs currently being tested, such as AZT and DDC, hold out the prospect of limiting the recurrence of certain infections associated with AIDS. They have not, however, been shown to decrease the likelihood that one who has been exposed to the virus will develop AIDS. Effort is under way to develop drugs that enhance or augment the immune system, but so far with little success.

The principal public health measure available for seropositive people is counseling, designed to reduce their risk of spreading the virus and of developing more serious manifestations of infection. For several reasons, a widespread or mandatory screening program is an inappropriate and counterproductive way of doing this. The hard truth is that antibody status can be a very dangerous piece of information. If their status becomes public knowledge, people who test positively for HIV antibodies may be exposed to discrimination ranging from loss of employment or housing, to denial of insurance, to serious physical abuse. Disclosure aside, the meaning of antibody status is far from clear. A negative result (assuming it is not a false negative) may be of little value if the person tested has engaged in high-risk activity within six months of testing.[59] Moreover, if high-risk behavior has led the person to be tested, he or she should be counseled about how to modify that behavior even if the results are, so far, negative. A positive result (assuming it is not a false positive) does not tell the person tested (or the epidemiologist, for that matter) whether he or she is actually infectious or will ever develop AIDS or ARC. Nor does such a result tell the recipient how to modify behavior so as to reduce the risks of transmission and reinfection. It is precisely for these reasons that confidentiality and individual counseling have been universally recognized as indispensable facets of any screening or testing program.[60]

Of course, no responsible person contests the importance of confidentiality. Strict privacy provisions are included in virtually all public health laws.[61] The problem is that these provisions are far too often breached, not just negligently or irresponsibly,[62] but by officials who sincerely (if misguidedly) regard themselves as serving the public.[63] Even if confidentiality were perfectly preserved, there is a coercive element in any mandatory program that is incompatible with the atmosphere of trust and cooperation that is necessary to foster voluntary behavioral change.

A program aimed at the general population, such as pre-marital screening, would also be a very inefficient way to reach those who need counseling. At present, most people in high-risk groups are readily targeted and can be reached by voluntary programs and public education. Although concern about the spread of AIDS into the heterosexual population is quite appropriate, the scope of the problem is much smaller than the attention being paid it would suggest.[64] Moreover, since most heterosexual cases involve intravenous drug users or their sex partners,[65] it makes sense to focus our resources on drug users in particular rather than on heterosexuals in general. To be sure, any public health program that aims beyond groups at high risk will reach some people—notably the heterosexual contacts of bisexual men— who might not otherwise know they are at risk, but massive screening of low-risk groups requires the investment of considerable time and money testing the many to find the few. It is exactly this needle-in-a-haystack aspect of massive screening that has produced the recent trend among state legislators to repeal pre-marital testing for venereal disease.[66]

Nor should anyone be falsely comforted by the "mandatory" label. The programs in operation today, and those proposed, might better be thought of as "conditional." They impose upon those who give blood, or join the military, or wish to marry, or seek medical treatment, the requirement of being tested. But all of these activities can, to some degree, be avoided. As long as the perceived social costs of being tested are very high, at least some people will, for example, forego military careers, or obtain medical treatment from private doctors. And the people most likely to make this decision are those who know themselves to be at risk. Thus, mandatory screening creates incentives for those most in need of the test not only to avoid screening, but also to avoid medical intervention like venereal disease treatment and prenatal counseling that is independently beneficial to both the individual and society.

All these barriers to participation by those at risk or afraid of disease may also minimize the statistical value of widespread screening. Significant avoidance of the test, especially by those at risk, could lead to false estimates of prevalence. On the other hand, many public health experts feel that the effort against AIDS is now crippled by the lack of data on its impact in the general population. (Current sources of data—blood and military screening—are regarded as inadequately representative.)[67] It should be kept in mind that even the most ambitious programs now under discussion would not involve testing everyone, and it would consequently be wrong to imagine that a massive program of mandatory screening would reveal the actual number of infected people. The issue, instead, is how to improve the data base upon which estimates are built. It is possible that a major testing effort would lead to better estimates, but, the improvement in reliability may not be great enough to justify the costs.

These practical problems with screening might arguably undermine the legality of some programs, but screening by public health officials has traditionally been accepted by the courts as a valid public health measure. While the Supreme Court has recognized the importance of maintaining the confidentiality of medical data, it has also made very clear its faith in the confidentiality protections provided in typical health laws.[68] Current litigation concerning mandatory *drug* screening by the federal government may foreshadow how the courts will treat challenges to governmental HIV antibody screening.[69]

Contact Tracing

Contact tracing is a form of medical surveillance by which public health officials seek to discover the sex partners of an infected person and then inform and, if possible, treat them. Like screening, its legality is probably secure, but its utility depends in large part on what positive action public officials can take once they have found a potentially infected person.

There are several reasons to view contact tracing with caution. First, even more than screening, contact tracing depends on cooperation: there is little a health official can do to force a person to identify truthfully all his or her sexual contacts. The problems are only aggravated if the informant doubts the confidentiality of any disclosure. Second, as in the screening context, the only "treatment" available to those who are traced is counseling—which is already available to those who realize they are at risk—and another round of contact tracing. Finally, contact tracing requires sensitive, trained investigators, and a fair investment of time; it is ill-suited for use on a large scale.[70]

There is much to be said for *voluntary* contact tracing—for counseling "at risk" people and encouraging them either to inform their sex partners themselves or to give public health officials permission to do so. In particular, contact tracing of heterosexual partners of people exposed to HIV may be an efficient way of reaching people who do not know they are at risk. San Francisco has set up such a program,[71] but in general public health officials have not been aggressive in promoting such efforts. *Mandatory* contact tracing aimed at risk-group members, on the other hand, with the attendant threats to confidentiality and the sheer numbers involved, is impractical.

Reporting

Every state requires that specified "listed" or "notifiable" diseases be reported to its public health department. AIDS qualifies as a notifiable disease throughout the country. State reporting requirements can be divided into three categories: rules specifying that CDC-defined AIDS (a precise, consistent, and specific diagnostic classification developed to provide useful data on disease trends) be reported; rules specifying that positive test results for HIV antibodies be reported; and general provisions that do not specify HIV infection as notifiable but require the reporting of any "case," "condition," or "carrier state" relating to listed diseases, including AIDS.[72]

In 1977, in *Whalen v. Roe*, the U.S. Supreme Court concluded that "limited reporting requirements in the medical field are familiar, and are not generally regarded as an invasion of privacy."[73] Thus, current requirements to report AIDS or HIV infection are likely to withstand constitutional challenge so long as the information sought is reasonably related to a valid public health purpose and is limited to public health departments, and so long as statutory confidentiality protections are in place.

Without doubt, the states have a valid public health interest in collecting information about the epidemiological distribution of AIDS within the general population. The vast majority of states require reporting only of CDC-defined AIDS. That approach, if carefully regulated, is a narrowly tailored (and thus constitutional) means of collecting vitally important data: it minimizes the privacy problems associated with other case identification measures, such as mass screening, and is unlikely to deter its targets from seeking medical help, given their advanced stage of illness.

Reporting of HIV antibody status is more problematic. Collecting such information could create a skewed epidemiologic impression of the total infected population. Given that current programs for HIV antibody testing cover quite limited groups in the population and rely, in effect, on self-selection, statistics generated by them probably are an unreliable index of the total infected population. Moreover, statutory requirements to report every positive test result would likely prove a disincentive to voluntary testing by persons who are well but worried, resulting in a further skewing of the sample of infected individuals and creating a barrier to AIDS education and counseling.

PERSONAL CONTROL MEASURES

Traditionally, public health authorities seek not only to identify individuals capable of transmitting infection but also to take positive action to prevent its spread. At present, the U.S. Public Health Service relies solely on voluntary efforts, such as encouraging testing of people in high-risk groups and providing individual counseling and public education.[74] These measures clearly have altered behavior, as evidenced by the substantial reduction in the number of cases of rectal gonorrhea, a disease associated with the same sexual practices that spread AIDS.[75]

Health-policy options, however, extend beyond voluntary efforts. The state has a right to take coercive steps, if necessary, to further the public welfare, and to protect against an epidemic of disease that threatens the safety of its members. At the same time, such steps almost inevitably threaten the right of individuals to autonomy and self-determination. Nowhere is achieving the proper balance between individual and collective rights more difficult or more important than when a state acts to protect the public health.

Types of Personal Control Measures

General Isolation

Infection control measures have long rested on the assumption that disease carriers must be physically separated from the rest of the population to prevent transmission of the infectious agent. Although the terms "isolation" and "quarantine" are often used interchangeably, both in public health statutes and in common parlance, there is a technical distinction between them. Isolation is the separation of infected persons from others during the period of communicability so as to prevent transmission of the infectious agent; "quarantine" is the detention of persons who are healthy but have been exposed to a communicable disease, for a period of time equal to the longest usual incubation period of the disease, to prevent effective contact with persons not exposed.[76] Since proposals for confining persons with AIDS tend to target persons who already exhibit symptoms of the disease or who demonstrably have been exposed to the virus, the term isolation is more appropriate in the AIDS context.

At present, few state public health schemes authorize the isolation of persons with AIDS. Although many states authorize the isolation of persons infected with venereal or sexually transmitted diseases, for the most part AIDS is not so classified.[77] In some states, AIDS is classified as a communicable disease, but that designation does not, alone, provide a legal basis for the imposition of personal control measures.[78] Similarly, the fact that many states require that AIDS cases be reported to public health officials does not, in and of itself, provide legal justification for isolating infected persons.[79]

To be sure, some states have attempted to make AIDS, or even HIV infection, an explicit ground for isolation. A proposal to do so in Texas failed.[80] A similar proposal was considered by the Colorado legislature.[81] A Connecticut statute, amended in 1985, makes no specific mention of AIDS, but would probably justify the detention of at least those persons with AIDS who do not conform their behavior to guidelines established by health officials to minimize risk of transmission.[82]

Isolation is a uniquely serious form of deprivation of liberty because it can be utilized against a competent and unwilling person and is based upon what a person *might* do rather than on what he or she already has done. Even more tellingly, it has no clear temporal limitation; indeed, inasmuch as seropositive people are presumed (given the present state of medical knowledge) to be infectious for the rest of their lives, isolation amounts to a kind of civil life sentence. It is therefore likely to trigger the strictest level of judicial scrutiny; a decision to isolate all persons infected with HIV would withstand judicial challenge only if there were a tight fit between the measure and the attainment of a compelling public health benefit. Such a close relationship between legislative (or administrative) means and ends could not be established in relation to the general isolation of all who are seropositive or even of all who have AIDS. General isolation measures would carry in their sweep persons who are determined to forego the high-risk behavior that makes transmission possible; persons who are no longer infectious because the virus has eliminated its host cells;[83] and persons who are so debilitated or demoralized as to be unable to engage in high-risk behavior.

In addition, general isolation is unwise as a matter of public policy. The number of people capable of transmitting the virus is currently at least one million and is rising geometrically, thus making general isolation unmanageable. Again, since there is no finite period of infectiousness and no known cure, isolation would be permanent, and those whose liberty is infringed would have no way to restore themselves to a "normal" condition in order to rejoin the community. Furthermore, because casual contact does not spread the virus, segregation from society is unnecessary and thus, by definition, overly restrictive. Taken together, these factors set AIDS apart from other communicable diseases that have been the subject of traditional personal control measures and make isolation a singularly inappropriate policy.

Modified Isolation Based upon Behavior, Not Disease Status

The terms "incorrigible" and "recalcitrant" have been used to refer to persons who are aware that they have been exposed to the virus associated with AIDS, yet continue to engage in high-risk activities that expose others to the disease, despite warnings by doctors and health officials to modify their behavior. Recognizing the practical and legal problems with general isolation measures, state health authorities have begun to revise their isolation proposals to encompass only incorrigible cases.

"Modified" isolation suffers from some of the same defects as does general isolation. It does not differentiate between those who are capable of transmitting the AIDS virus and those who are not. If the target is unable to alter his or her behavior, modified isolation is likely to mean permanent confinement. Furthermore, isolation is far more intrusive and restrictive than would be the provision of drug treatment (where appropriate), psychological or medical treatment, and economic assistance designed to alleviate or alter the conditions that lead to "incorrigible" behavior. Despite its defects, modified isolation might escape judicial censure for the following reasons. First, unlike general isolation, it does not focus on a person's health *status* but rather upon his or her *behavior*. Second, it is targeted at a small number of individuals rather than at a sizeable class of persons united by a common characteristic. Third, the most likely targets of modified isolation would be persons engaged in activities that in and of themselves are *criminal*—prostitutes and intravenous drug users. The courts have not been particularly sympathetic to the civil rights of such persons in the past.

Even a well-tailored modified isolation statute would not survive constitutional challenge if it did not create a mechanism for determining, with full due process, that the target of isolation will not or cannot refrain from engaging in conduct likely to spread the AIDS virus. The due process clause of the Fourteenth Amendment guarantees that no one can be deprived of basic rights without a fair and proper hearing. Even when courts accede to the power of state legislatures to protect the public health, they may require procedural safeguards prior to or immediately after the use of control measures. Strict observance of due process in deciding to isolate is necessary because fundamental freedoms are at stake. There is a distinct risk of erroneous fact finding, and there is no state interest in confining nondangerous individuals. The West Virginia Supreme Court, for example, has held that the same procedural safeguards required in contemplation of civil commitment to mental hospitals are applicable in cases of involuntary confinement of infectious patients. These procedures include written notice, representation by counsel, the right to present evidence, cross examination, commitment only if the proof of commitability is "clear and convincing," and a verbatim transcript in the event of an appeal.[84]

Even if modified isolation statutes are constitutional, however, they are likely to be ineffective and, from a public policy perspective, inadvisable. First, the threat of such coercive measures would discourage members of risk groups from seeking testing or treatment and from speaking honestly to counselors about their future behavior. Second, objective statutory criteria and psychological tests could not be framed to determine accurately enough who was "recalcitrant" or to predict future dangerous behavior. Third, those who come to the attention of public health officials as candidates for isolation are likely to be the poorest and least articulate of those harboring the virus. Such a skewed "lottery" would have a negligible impact on the spread of the disease because the vast majority of instances of transmission would continue to go unnoticed and unrestrained. Finally, isolation to prevent sexual activity or drug use would be extremely difficult to monitor and enforce and could be viewed as a license for public health and law enforcement officials to intrude into the most private areas of the lives of people in high-risk groups.

Safe Environment for Isolation

Even if otherwise constitutional, the question arises whether isolation measures may themselves be allowed to pose a health risk to their subjects. Although the court in *Kirk v. Wyman* was quite prepared to uphold an isolation scheme despite the absence of proof that the form of leprosy from which Mary Kirk was suffering was contagious, it nevertheless refused to subject her to an environment it considered unsafe. Public health officials planned to quarantine Kirk in a pesthouse, "a structure of four small rooms in a row, with no piazzas, used heretofore for the isolation of negroes with smallpox, situated within a hundred yards of the place where the trash of the city . . . is collected and burned." The court concluded that "even temporary isolation in such a place would be a serious affliction and peril to an elderly lady, enfeebled by disease, and accustomed to the comforts of life."[85] The public health department was compelled to delay isolating her until it had finished building Kirk a "comfortable cottage" outside the city limits.

A more modern court, however, was less rigorous in reviewing the conditions of isolation. In *Ex parte Martin*, a 1948 California case, county officials had elected to isolate people with venereal disease in a jail, despite uncontested evidence that the jail was overcrowded and had been condemned by a legislative investigating committee. The court supported the attorney general's position that "[w]hile jails, as public institutions, were established for purposes other than confinement of diseased persons, occasions of emergency or lack of other public facilities for quarantine require that jails be used."[86]

The use of the jail as a place of isolation and the absence of any rigorous demonstration that the persons isolated were actually infected with venereal disease suggest that punishment was an underlying purpose in *Martin*. Punishment, however, is not an appropriate public health goal. Public health departments have an obligation not to do unnecessary harm, and that extends to avoiding unsafe or punitive environments for subjects of an isolation. Indeed, those who must forego their individual rights for the collective good should receive the best possible care and conditions. While no recent case tests the issue of a safe environment for isolation, the general trend towards insisting that health-law measures be rooted in medical considerations strongly suggests that courts will reject any isolation scheme which, like that in *Martin*, has punitive overtones.

Criminal Laws Prohibiting Knowing Transmission of the Virus

Public health measures are usually concerned with preventing future behavior. To the extent that criminal law is designed to exact retribution for *past* behavior, it is inappropriate as a means of protecting public health. But criminal law is also forward-looking; it seeks to deter individuals from engaging in future behavior as well. The knowing or reckless transmission of a potentially lethal infection is just as dangerous as many crimes. The use of criminal sanctions is not unfair to people, including gay men and intra-venous drug users, who do not engage in high-risk behavior; indeed, it serves to protect them against the spread of infection. Nor can it be considered unfair to the few whose behavior subjects them to criminal penalties, pro-vided they have been clearly and explicitly warned that certain conduct is unacceptable.

The criminal law has many advantages over the personal control measure most likely to survive judicial scrutiny—modified isolation. Whereas isola-tion statutes employ such general terms as "incorrigibility" and "recalci-trance," criminal statutes must specify clearly and unambiguously the behavior that is prohibited. If its language is vague, a criminal statute fails to forewarn, and is, for that reason, unconstitutional. Whereas isolation statutes arise from predictions about the future, criminal statutes focus on behavior that has already occurred. Whereas "incorrigibility" and "recal-citrance" need only be proved by clear and convincing evidence, each ele-ment of a knowing transmission crime must be proved beyond a reasonable doubt. Whereas the period of isolation is usually indefinite, the period of criminal confinement is usually finite and proportionate to the gravity of the offense. Indeed, given the goal of deterrence, the period of confinement should not last longer than necessary to discourage future reckless behavior, both by the person detained and by others who take note of his or her plight. The longer the period of confinement, the more it smacks of retribution, a goal inconsistent with the mission of public authorities.

Several states—including Texas, New York, California, Pennsylvania, Colorado, and Florida—have public health crime statutes[87] that make it unlawful (usually a misdemeanor) for an individual who knows he or she has an infectious venereal disease to have sexual intercourse with another person. Although these statutes currently apply only to venereal disease and not to AIDS, they are likely to serve as models for new legislation.

AIDS-transmission statutes should be carefully drawn. Their reach should be limited to persons who *know* that they are infectious, who have been repeatedly warned by public health officials to desist from high-risk behavior, and who have nevertheless continued to engage in such behavior. Absent such limitations, overly zealous law enforcement officials could view trans-mission statutes as an invitation to round up prostitutes and others simply because they *might* be infected and *might* engage in unsafe sex or drug use.

In the absence of AIDS-transmission statutes, the creative use of existing criminal statutes is dangerous and should be resisted. Several prosecutors across the country have filed felony assault charges against defendants thought to have AIDS who spit at or bit police officers. A person with AIDS in Flint, Michigan, was recently charged with assault and intent to commit murder after he spat on four police officers,[88] and a person suspected of having AIDS in El Cajon, California, pleaded guilty in December 1985 to a felonious assault charge for biting an officer.[89] In both cases, the prosecutor-

contended that felony charges were warranted because of the risk of spreading AIDS. That contention is insupportable, however, because the likelihood of transmitting HIV by biting or spitting is negligible.

Restricting Incompetent Persons

Criminal AIDS-transmission statutes are aimed at people who are *unwilling* to comply with reasonable guidelines necessary for the public health. Such statutes have no applicability to persons who are incompetent and therefore *unable* to comply with public health requirements.

Incompetence among AIDS patients is an increasingly serious problem. It is estimated that 40 to 50 percent of AIDS patients may experience some loss of higher cerebral function. Indeed, some infected patients whose immune systems remain intact nevertheless suffer from chronic progressive neurologic disease of the brain, variously described as chronic meningitis (inflammation of the membranes of the brain or spinal chord), dementia (marked mental deterioration), and "AIDS encephalopathy" (a general term for disease of the brain caused by HIV).[90] This organic brain syndrome is associated with progressive mental deterioration and disintegration in cognition, emotion, and behavior. It may occasion changes in behavior patterns such as disinhibited sexual activity, aggressiveness, and loss of self-care skills.

If a patient suffering from AIDS encephalopathy cannot refrain from behavior that puts others at risk of exposure to the virus, involuntary civil commitment may be appropriate. Less drastic means are, of course, preferable. Thus, if someone were willing to become the patient's legal guardian, and in that capacity to monitor his or her behavior, the state's interest in limiting the spread of the disease would be satisfied.

Finally, statutory authority exists in many states for the civil confinement of seriously drug-dependent persons who constitute a danger to themselves or others.[91] Such provisions are invoked quite rarely. Most people enter treatment for drug dependence voluntarily, except for criminal offenders diverted to treatment programs in lieu of a criminal sentence. Civil commitment, however, could conceivably be applied to a drug-dependent person who has AIDS or is seropositive, and who persists in exposing other persons to infection through the shared use of contaminated needles. Such continued needle sharing would fulfill the statutory criterion of posing a "danger to others."

Currently, the number of drug treatment centers is inadequate, and most rehabilitation programs have long waiting lists. Compulsion should therefore be used only in those rare cases where a person is unable to control his or her dependency and behavior, where that behavior poses a clear and immediate threat to others, where a suitable treatment program is available, and where there is a reasonable prospect that the person to be committed will derive therapeutic benefit from the program.

There is mounting pressure on public health officials to consider compulsory infection-control strategies to reduce the alarming spread of AIDS. Such measures are unwarranted. Not only do they burden groups who have experienced a long history of social prejudice and unequal treatment, but they are also not, as yet, sufficiently efficacious to justify overriding the rights of the individual to liberty, privacy, and autonomy.

By the foregoing, I do not mean to place a greater emphasis on liberty, autonomy, and privacy than on public health. But public health intervention must focus on modifying the behaviors that transmit AIDS. Compulsory measures are ill-suited to modify the intimate personal behaviors that are at issue. If anything, compulsory legal intervention will deter people vulnerable to HIV infection from being tested, seeking advice and treatment, and cooperating with public health programs.

Public health officials can effectively encourage voluntary behavior modification by disseminating accurate information and offering services such as free counseling and treatment. Thus, substantially greater resources should be devoted to providing highly specific information and counseling to those most vulnerable to AIDS, including information about modes of transmission, safer sexual practices, and safer use of intravenous drugs. Health officials should encourage individuals to take the HIV antibody test on a confidential basis if they believe it relevant to future behavioral choices, and to notify their sex partners of their antibody status.

Public officials must allocate greater resources to treatment programs for sexually transmitted diseases and intravenous drug abuse. The current patient capacity of such programs is drastically insufficient. Clinics dealing with sexually transmitted disease could teach individuals about safer forms of sexual behavior; drug treatment programs could couple their efforts to wean clients from illicit drugs with realistic advice about how to reduce the risk of infection along the way.

A comprehensive public health program that provides education, counseling, treatment, and other health services to vulnerable groups would have a substantial impact on the geometric spread of AIDS. Efforts to encourage voluntary risk reduction are both more respectful of civil liberties and more beneficial to the public health than the imposition of compulsory control policies.

5

Schoolchildren with AIDS

FREDERIC C. KASS, M.D.

In September 1985, the announcement in New York City that a single child with AIDS would enroll in the public schools touched off an angry boycott in two Queens school districts. Parents vowed to "stand in the schoolhouse door" to keep children with AIDS out of school.[1] On the first day of classes, between nine thousand and eleven thousand children stayed home in protest. At the entrance to one school, parents posted a sign saying "Enter at Your Own Risk." Outside another, parents stood by a mock coffin into which they had placed one of their own children. On the coffin they wrote: "Is This the City's Next Idea for Our Kids?"[2]

Against this background of fear and misconception,[3] boards of education and departments of health have struggled to formulate policies that would protect the rights of the few children who were ill as well as the vast majority who were healthy. The issues have been formidable: Do children with AIDS have a right to attend school? Who should decide which children could enroll? What precautions should the schools take?

Largely on the strength of data showing the risk of casual transmission of the disease to be "apparently nonexistent,"[4] many of these children have gained admission to classes. But their presence in school has provoked a new set of questions: To what extent do these children have a right to privacy? Who has a right to know their identities? By what means should these children be protected from harassment and ostracism? Policy makers now struggling with these and other issues are finding the legal and ethical dimensions of the disease in children at least as troubling as the medical questions.

This chapter reviews the characteristics of Human Immunodeficiency Virus (HIV)[5] infection in children. It examines the cases that were initially reported and describes the currently identified patterns of pediatric disease and then reviews the principal legal issues addressed by the courts.

EPIDEMIOLOGY OF PEDIATRIC AIDS

The initial cases of children with AIDS emerged in late 1982.[6] As of December 8, 1986, there were 394 children under the age of 13 among the 28,098 cases of AIDS reported to the Centers for Disease Control (CDC).[7] Of these children with AIDS, about 60 percent have died, a mortality rate comparable to that seen in adults. The mechanisms responsible for the spread of the disease in children, however, are significantly different from those identified in adults. Moreover, the racial, sexual, age, and geographic distribution of childhood cases varies considerably from that observed in adults with the disease.

First, adult AIDS is predominantly a sexually transmitted disease. Two-thirds of adult AIDS patients are homosexual or bisexual men who are not known to use intravenous drugs. In contrast, nearly 80 percent of pediatric AIDS cases are attributable to perinatal transmission of the HIV from infected mothers.[8] Moreover, the incidence of pediatric disease is most closely linked to drug-abuse related AIDS in adults. Of the children with perinatally acquired AIDS, at least 50 percent are born to women who are intravenous drug abusers, and another 10 percent are born to the sexual partners of men who abuse such drugs.[9]

Second, the transfusion of infected blood products is a much more significant cause of AIDS in children than in adults. Recipients of blood (other than hemophiliacs) account for less than 2 percent of adult AIDS cases but 13 percent of childhood cases.[10] Significantly, almost all cases of transfusion-related pediatric disease have been reported in children receiving blood in the first year of life.[11]

Third, adult AIDS has been almost exclusively a disease of men; only 7 percent of adult patients are women. Moreover, 60 percent of adult AIDS patients are non-Hispanic whites. In contrast, childhood AIDS shows only a slight male predominance (55 percent), and only about 20 percent of pediatric cases are white.[12] Because perinatal HIV transmission is responsible for most pediatric disease, the racial composition of childhood cases resembles that of the relatively few infected adult women. About 52 percent of women with AIDS are black, and 20 percent are Hispanic.[13] Similarly, nearly 60 percent of children with AIDS are black, and 22 percent are Hispanic.[14] Furthermore, the racial distribution of pediatric cases reflects the high incidence of intravenous-drug associated AIDS among blacks and Hispanics: 80 percent of adults with drug-associated AIDS are either black or Hispanic.[15]

Fourth, because pediatric HIV infection is so closely linked to intravenous drug abuse, the childhood cases tend to cluster in urban areas such as New York and New Jersey where the incidence of drug-abuse related AIDS is high.[16] New York City alone accounts for 45 percent of all perinatally acquired AIDS.[17] Conversely, in San Francisco, where the vast majority of adult AIDS arises from sexual transmission and the incidence of HIV infection among intravenous drug abusers is relatively low,[18] relatively few pediatric cases occur.[19]

These unique epidemiologic features of pediatric AIDS are of more than academic interest. They highlight the sources of childhood disease and the obstacles to halting its spread. For example, the close linkage between childhood disease and intravenous drug abuse emphasizes the importance of programs directed toward limiting the spread of drug-abuse related disease by altering needle-sharing habits among drug abusers[20] and by interrupting heterosexual transmission between male intravenous drug abusers and their female sexual contacts.[21] Moreover, the significance of transfusions as a cause of pediatric disease highlights the need for and value of universal blood screening procedures.[22] For hemophiliacs, who make up 5 percent of children with AIDS, safer preparations of needed blood factor replacement are now available.[23]

Finally, the racial distribution of childhood cases has important policy implications. At the present time, 75 percent of heterosexual AIDS patients, 73 percent of women with AIDS, and 92 percent of children with perinatally acquired disease are either black or Hispanic.[24] Clearly, education and prevention programs must be designed to reach minority populations.

HIV INFECTION IN CHILDREN

Pediatric AIDS generally becomes manifest early in life. Overall, nearly 90 percent of such children are less than five years of age at the time of diagnosis,[25] and about 50 percent are diagnosed in the first year of life.[26]

The 394 pediatric cases of AIDS that were reported to the CDC by December 1986 consist only of those children with the most severe manifestations of HIV infection. These are the children who meet the relatively rigid diagnostic criteria established by the CDC. They represent an unknown, but probably *small* percentage of the total number of HIV-infected children. They do not include the children with the less severe AIDS-related complex (ARC).[27] Nor do these cases include the asymptomatic children who have been exposed to the HIV and now have detectable blood levels of antibody to the virus.[28] Finally, they do not include infants who have evidence of HIV infection but whose antibody tests are negative.[29]

Thus, AIDS has been called a "tip of the iceberg" phenomenon.[30] In adults, for example, the number of cases meeting the CDC criteria for AIDS may constitute only 1 to 2 percent of those infected.[31] The CDC formulated its definition of AIDS prior to the isolation of the HIV and the development of assays to detect asymptomatic or mildly symptomatic HIV infection. Although the narrow CDC surveillance definition has provided invaluable epidemiologic data, it has tended to obscure from public view the broad spectrum of HIV-related disease.

As a result, the CDC has published a new classification system for HIV infection.[32] All infected patients, even those who are completely asymptomatic, have a place in this new scheme.[33] In publishing the classification system, the CDC emphasized two points: the diagnosis of HIV-related illness should not depend on fulfillment of narrow surveillance criteria; and, more importantly, all patients with positive serum antibody tests "should be considered both infected and infectious."[34]

The risk of perinatal transmission from an infected mother is unknown. Although the risk of transmission is probably high,[35] infected women may give birth to healthy children.[36] At the same time, perinatal HIV transmission may occur in the absence of severe maternal disease. In fact, most perinatally infected children are probably born to asymptomatic mothers.[37]

The precise mechanism of perinatal infection has not yet been elucidated, but the evidence suggests that viral transmission occurs *in utero*.[38] There is a possibility, however, that infants may also become infected through breast feeding.[39] Whatever the mechanism, epidemiologic data have convincingly demonstrated that these children acquired the disease perinatally from their infected mothers and *not* through "casual" intrahousehold contact.[40]

Nevertheless, public anxiety about the possibility of casual transmission has continued to haunt these children, and the scientific data on transmissibility have been at the center of legal battles over their right to attend public school. No one has argued that children with AIDS have forfeited their right to free public education. Rather, at issue has been the right of HIV-infected children to sit in the same classrooms as their healthy peers.

CDC GUIDELINES FOR THE EDUCATION OF CHILDREN WITH AIDS

In August 1985, the CDC released guidelines for the education of children infected with the HIV.[41] These guidelines were formulated following extensive consultation with epidemiologists, state and county health officers, school officials, and representatives of parents' and child welfare organizations. Although these CDC guidelines were merely advisory, they have served as a model for policy makers. For this reason their strengths and weaknesses merit close attention.

First, the guidelines apply to *all* children with evidence of HIV infection. This includes children with ARC and asymptomatic children with detectable antibodies to the HIV.

Second, the guidelines characterize the risk of HIV transmission among school-aged children who were free of neurologic or behavioral impairment as "apparent[ly] nonexistent."

> Based on current evidence, casual person-to-person contact as would occur among school children appears to pose no risk. . . . These [infected] children should be allowed to attend school.[42]

Third, the CDC determined that, for most children with HIV infection, the benefits of an "unrestricted setting" would outweigh their risks of complications from childhood diseases such as chicken pox.

Fourth, the guidelines suggest that the data on contact with younger and neurologically handicapped children "who lack control of their body secretions" are "very limited." The CDC therefore recommended a "more restricted environment" for preschool-aged children, neurologically handicapped children who lack control of their body secretions or who display behavior such as biting, and children who have uncoverable, oozing lesions.

Fifth, the guidelines recommend a case-by-case evaluation of each infected child by a team consisting of the child's physician, public health personnel, the child's parents or guardian, and personnel associated with the proposed educational setting. In each case the team would make decisions regarding the child's educational setting after weighing the "risks and benefits to both the infected child and to others in the setting." According to the CDC, the team's supervisory responsibilities should be ongoing, presumably for the life of the child, with reevaluations to be performed at regular intervals.

Sixth, the CDC emphasized that this team should attempt to respect the child's right to privacy and confidentiality. "The number of personnel who are aware of the child's condition should be kept at a minimum needed to assure proper care of the child and to detect situations where the potential for transmission may increase (*e.g.*, bleeding injury)."[43]

Seventh, the guidelines do not consider mandatory screening of all schoolchildren to be warranted; however, they favor testing all children born to women at increased risk of HIV infection. The CDC also suggests that adoption and foster-care agencies "should consider" screening all high-risk children prior to placement.

Finally, the guidelines propose routine procedures for handling the blood or body fluid of all children, regardless of known health status.

These guidelines represent a major achievement. In the midst of intense controversy, the CDC managed to hammer out a consensus opinion. Moreover, the guidelines take a strong, unequivocal stand on the issue of transmissibility. Finally, the guidelines apply to *all* schoolchildren with HIV infection, including those who are asymptomatic. Although national attention has focused primarily on the few children with AIDS, the guidelines recognize that a child's capacity to transmit the HIV is largely unrelated to his or her clinical condition.

At the same time, four aspects of the guidelines are problematic. First, states which established the evaluation teams recommended by the CDC have generally been left without a mechanism for determining which schoolchildren to review. The vast majority of HIV-infected children are both unidentified and unidentifiable. In New York, for example, the only "list" of infected children consists solely of the relatively few who have been officially reported as meeting the narrow surveillance criteria for AIDS. Moreover, state laws in New York and other jurisdictions guarantee the confidentiality of such reports and in effect prohibit their use by these evaluation teams.

Second, the CDC guidelines permit disclosure of the identities of these children to one or more local school personnel; however, the agency does not answer certain vital questions: Who really needs to know the identity of these children? If the risk of HIV transmission in schools is apparently nonexistent, why is it necessary that these children be identified? Once their identities have been disclosed, how are these children to be protected from harassment and discrimination, both during their education and afterward?

Third, the CDC favors screening all high-risk infants, arguing that routine live virus vaccinations might be hazardous to infected children.[44] Moreover, the agency proposes testing children awaiting placement, so that foster or adoptive parents can "make decisions regarding medical care" and can "consider the possible social and psychological effects on their families."

These are matters of some controversy. How would such screening programs be implemented? What are the rights of these children? Who can give consent on their behalf for such testing? Who is responsible if these children later suffer significant adverse consequences from disclosure of their antibody status? What are the rights and responsibilities of the foster or adoptive parents?

Lastly, the CDC guidelines do not address the possibility of sexual HIV transmission among schoolchildren, an issue that will take on increasing importance as infected children grow older. Moreover, the agency made no mention of the problem of teenage pregnancies among infected schoolgirls, and the likelihood of a second generation of perinatally infected children. In this regard, the U.S. Surgeon General has recommended a nationwide effort to enlighten children about the risk of HIV infection. He has urged that such instruction begin "at the lowest grade possible" in elementary school and be "reinforced at home" by parents.[45] And the New York City Board of Education has financed a videotape entitled "Sex, Drugs and AIDS" for distribution to schools.[46]

Released on the eve of the 1985-1986 school year, the CDC guidelines provoked intense and immediate public debate. The efforts of the CDC and state officials to establish orderly procedures for evaluating infected children were challenged in the courts. As a result, judges rather than medical scientists or school officials decided initially whether children with HIV infection could attend school.

LITIGATION OVER SCHOOLCHILDREN WITH AIDS

Three cases—from New York, Indiana, and New Jersey—illustrate the most important legal issues faced by the courts during litigation over schoolchildren with AIDS. In all three, state health and education officials had established procedures for admitting children with AIDS to the public schools. The admission of these children, however, was challenged in each instance by parents or local school officials, or both. Significantly, all of the children at issue eventually gained entrance to school.

The Queens Case: Decision-Making Authority, Constitutional Issues, and the Rehabilitation Act of 1973

The case that addressed the broadest range of issues arose in New York City in 1985. At that time, the city health department had already recorded over 4,500 cases of AIDS, of whom more than 2,300 had died. Among these cases were 82 children under the age of thirteen, of whom 56 had died.[47]

In April 1985, the New York City Board of Education requested written advice from the city health department concerning the admission of children with AIDS to the public schools. In response, the department drafted regulations permitting full integration of such children into the city school system. However, in late August, the CDC released its guidelines recommending a case-by-case team review of all schoolchildren who had evidence of HIV infection. Although the New York City health commissioner felt such precautions unnecessary, he incorporated similar case review provisions into the New York City procedures. The New York City guidelines, however, applied only to schoolchildren with AIDS; children with ARC or asymptomatic infection were *not* subject to review.[48]

The commissioner then instructed his AIDS Epidemiologic Surveillance Unit to search the New York City AIDS case reports for the names of school-aged children. When that search was completed, he announced the creation of a special panel to review the cases of seven school-aged children, all under eight years of age, who had been reported to have AIDS. The adverse response was immediate; the two community school boards called for a "moratorium" on efforts to consider any infected children for enrollment.[49]

The commissioner's special panel released its findings on September 7, 1985, two days before the beginning of the school year. Of the original seven children, three no longer resided in New York City and two others had been hospitalized. The remaining two were judged physically and emotionally capable of attending school; however, the identity of one had previously been disclosed, and the family was urged to "consider alternate educational opportunities" because of the "potential social discrimination to which the student could be subjected."[50]

The seventh child was recommended for entry into the second grade, having already successfully completed nursery school, kindergarten, and first grade. Infected perinatally, the child had been ill three years before, but apparently had recovered. The child was said to have been fully immunized. According to city officials, he or she had contracted chicken pox and had recovered uneventfully. City officials declined to reveal the name of the child or the school that he or she would attend.

The two community school boards then brought suit against the New York City Board of Education. In *In re District 27 Community School Board v. Board of Education of the City of New York*,[51] they sought either to prevent the second grader from attending school or to force the board of education to reveal his or her identity. A five-week trial ensued, during which eleven medical experts testified. When a decision was announced the following February, the local school boards had lost. In a long and detailed opinion, the court dismissed their petition in all respects.

Three critical aspects of this case warrant comment. First, the child did not actually have AIDS. In the history released by city officials, he or she did not appear to be severely immunocompromised. And a second panel of physicians convened during the trial by the health commissioner concluded that, although the child had indeed been exposed to the HIV, he or she did not meet the CDC surveillance criteria for AIDS.

This was an important finding. The city's school admission regulations apply only to children with AIDS. Others, like this child, with milder or asymptomatic infection, are not subject to review. The misapplication of the city's guidelines in this case arose from the fact that the state reporting requirements apply to all "cases *or suspected* cases"[52] of AIDS. This child was probably reported by a physician as a "suspected case," but was indistinguishable from cases fulfilling AIDS surveillance criteria when the epidemiology data were searched for case review purposes. Arguably, the finding of the second review panel rendered the case moot, and the court could have dismissed the case at this point. However, the judge elected to proceed with a "broad-ranging, aggressive inquiry" into the issues raised by the case because of their public importance.[53]

A second important aspect of this case was: who had the authority to decide initially whether children with AIDS could attend school? In New York City, the health commissioner has broad powers under the city charter to protect the public health and prevent the spread of disease. In particular, he has the authority both to "supervise the reporting and control of communicable . . . diseases" and to "isolate" any person who is "a case or carrier" of such diseases.[54] If he had concluded that the HIV was communicable in a classroom setting, the commissioner could have excluded infected children from public school.[55]

At the state level, the New York Public Health Council has similar powers. The council possesses the statutory authority to "designate [in the state Sanitary Code] the communicable diseases which are dangerous to the public health."[56] Were conflicts to arise with city health rules, the state standards would prevail.[57]

In this instance neither the state Public Health Council nor the city health commissioner designated AIDS as a communicable disease. Both made cases meeting the CDC surveillance criteria reportable to health officials.[58] But neither had exercised their authority to enact regulations requiring the exclusion of children with HIV infection from the public schools.[59]

Third, how much discretion are these agencies afforded? How difficult is it to challenge their actions in court? Briefly, administrative agencies are generally accorded significant discretion; the scope of judicial review is typically quite limited. In New York and other states the courts will overturn agency actions only if (a) they are unconstitutional, (b) they are inconsistent with state or federal statute, (c) they are deemed so unreasonable and irrational as to be "arbitrary and capricious" or an "abuse of discretion" or (d) they are formulated without due regard for the public's right to participate in the rule-making process.

In the New York City case, the local school boards argued that the health agencies had abused their discretion by failing to exclude children with AIDS from the public schools. The court disagreed. In its view, any attempt by these agencies to bar children with AIDS from school would have violated federal statutory and constitutional law.

The constitutional argument arises from the Fourteenth Amendment right to equal protection of the laws. There is no constitutional right to public education;[60] however, under the Fourteenth Amendment, education provided by the states "must be made available on equal terms."[61]

The exclusionary policy advocated by the local school boards in New York City would have applied only to the few school-aged children known to have AIDS. Testimony at the trial, however, estimated that between two hundred and two thousand school-aged children in New York City were then infected with the HIV. The court concluded that a policy excluding *only* students with AIDS would have been discriminatory, since these few children were no more likely to transmit the disease than the far greater number of children with mild or asymptomatic disease.[62]

In reaching this conclusion, the court relied in part upon the precedent established in a 1977 case involving children who were carriers of hepatitis B virus (HBV), a virus with an epidemiology similar to that of the HIV.[63] There, the Board of Education had ordered the removal from schools of fifty formerly institutionalized mentally retarded children who carried HBV. Representatives of these children then brought suit, asserting in part that their right to equal protection had been violated. The courts agreed. They emphasized that the Board of Education had no plans to screen other groups in the public schools for HBV, nor did it propose to exclude HBV carriers who were not retarded. Most importantly, the board failed to demonstrate that the infected children at issue posed any significant health hazard.[64]

Following the reasoning of these cases, school regulations which focus exclusively on children with AIDS would be subject to constitutional attack. Such regulations ignore both the broad spectrum of HIV-related illness and the CDC admonition that *all* patients with positive serum antibody tests should be considered both "infected and infectious." Moreover, regulations which apply to all infected children might still be unconstitutional if the state made no concurrent attempt to identify all of these children but simply excluded those few who met the CDC surveillance criteria for AIDS and whose cases had been officially reported. Finally, it should be noted that regulations which apply only to neurologically handicapped children might be invalid if, as in the hepatitis cases, there is no evidence that these children pose any significant health hazard.

Clearly, the most important element of these cases was the paucity of evidence implicating casual contact as a means of viral transmission. If there were substantial evidence that the children posed a serious threat to their healthy classmates, it is unlikely that the courts would have ordered their admission because other, equally infectious children had not yet been identified.

In addition to the constitutional issues, interpretations of federal statute played an important role in the Queens case. The court ruled that the automatic exclusion of schoolchildren with AIDS would have violated the Rehabilitation Act of 1973. Section 504 of that statute prohibits discrimination against an "otherwise qualified handicapped individual . . . solely by reason of his handicap."[65] It requires that "reasonable accommodations" be made for persons who suffer from handicaps that affect their ability to engage in major life activities.[66] The court found that the act does not mandate the admission of children with AIDS to school; however, it demands that they not be turned away if their presence in school would require only "reasonable accommodations."

The applicability of the Rehabilitation Act to persons with HIV infection was addressed by the U.S. Supreme Court in *School Board of Nassau County v. Arline*.[67] In that case, the school board had dismissed an elementary school teacher when she suffered her third relapse of tuberculosis. In ruling that Arline could not be fired solely because of her handicap, the Court wrote: "Allowing discrimination based on the contagious effects of a physical impairment would be inconsistent with the basic purpose of §504, which is to ensure that handicapped individuals are not denied jobs or other benefits because of the prejudiced attitude or ignorance of others." The Court directed the trial court to determine whether Arline actually posed a health risk to her co-workers or students; her risk of infection will determine whether she is "otherwise qualified" for the job, and so entitled to work.[68]

The *Arline* decision reinforces the case-by-case approach to assessing transmission risk adopted in the Queens case and suggested by the CDC. It means that school districts seeking to exclude infected children will bear the burden of proving that these children pose an unmanageable threat to their healthy peers.

The Ryan White Case: Statutory Issues and the Education of the Handicapped Act

The case in Indiana of thirteen-year-old Ryan White generated enormous national publicity.[69] It also illustrates the applicability of yet another federal statute—the Education of the Handicapped Act—to the admissibility of infected children into the public schools.

Ryan White is a hemophiliac who contracted AIDS through his dependence on transfusions of his missing blood factor. He developed an acute illness in December 1984 that forced him to leave school. On several occasions during the following spring school officials discussed with Ryan's mother the possibility of extended homebound instruction. However, Ryan was recovering from his acute illness, and Mrs. White insisted that Ryan be readmitted to school in the fall.

In Indiana, the *Guidelines for Children with AIDS/ARC Attending School* emphasize that "[n]o evidence exists to support transmission of the disease by casual contact or by the airborne route;" and the state board of health has concluded that "AIDSARC children should be allowed to attend school as long as they behave acceptably (*e.g.*, do not bite, are toilet-trained), and have no uncoverable sores or skin eruptions."[70]

Notwithstanding these provisions, the superintendent of schools denied Ryan entrance into the Western Middle School of Kokomo, Indiana. Ryan and his mother brought suit against the school board, charging that the school board's actions constituted unlawful discrimination.[71] Among the legal bases for their claim was the Education of the Handicapped Act (EHA).[72]

The EHA was an effort to insure that handicapped students receive a "free appropriate public education."[73] The act is implemented in Indiana and other states through panels that review each case and make recommendations to the local school superintendent regarding a child's education. The superintendent's subsequent decision may be appealed to the state board of education, which will in turn conduct a full evidentiary hearing on the matter.

Attorneys for the school board agreed that the case was governed by the EHA; however, they argued that the act required Ryan White to take his case *first* through the state administrative process before asking the courts for assistance. The federal district court agreed. Ryan White's request for relief was denied, and he was directed to take his case to one of the local panels which reviewed the claims of handicapped students.

During the extensive hearings which followed, Ryan's attorneys presented evidence concerning both his educational needs and the means by which AIDS can be spread. At the conclusion of those hearings, Indiana officials ruled that Ryan could attend school with other children. On February 13, 1986, Ryan received a health certificate from the county health officer permitting him to return to school.

Still determined to exclude Ryan White, a group of parents petitioned a local county court for an order barring Ryan from the public schools.[74] They argued that he had a "communicable disease" and was prohibited from attending school by Indiana health regulations.[75] The parents' group won a court order barring Ryan's admission to school. Ryan and his mother then successfully moved the case to a neighboring jurisdiction, where the judge, in April, reversed the order.[76] The court reasoned that the Indiana health regulation barring children with communicable diseases from school had to be read in conjunction with other state regulations that provided for the admission of children with a health certificate. On Monday, August 25, 1986, Ryan White, then fourteen, began classes at Western High School, Howard County, Indiana.

As amply illustrated by this case, disputes over school entry may become protracted and require resources unavailable to most children. Moreover, for children with a shortened life expectancy, the rewards of such extensive efforts may be limited.

The New Jersey Case: Administrative Law Issues

The public has a right to participate in the agency rule-making process, and state laws require agencies to abide by certain procedural formalities. This legal principal formed the basis of a 1985 case arising in New Jersey.

In August 1985, the New Jersey commissioners of health and education jointly announced the adoption of school admission guidelines applicable to all children with "AIDS/ARC or HIV Antibody." As later revised and reissued, these guidelines required the admission of all such children to public school unless "a. The student is not toilet-trained or is incontinent, or otherwise is unable to control drooling. [Or] b. The student is unusually physically aggressive, with a documented history of biting or harming others."[77] Under the guidelines, a school board seeking to exclude an infected child had the burden of proving to a medical review panel that these criteria had been met.

In October and November 1985, such a panel considered the cases of two five-year-old girls—one with AIDS and one with ARC—whose admission had been rejected by their local school boards. The panel found no data to support the exclusion of either child, and the commissioner of education subsequently ordered their admission to school. In a complex series of legal proceedings, a lower state court ordered the local schools to accept these children and the school boards appealed to the state appellate court.[78]

The boards argued that the state guidelines constituted administrative rules adopted without due regard for the New Jersey Administrative Procedure Act.[79] That act requires advance public notice of a proposed rule and an opportunity for interested parties to express their views. The commissioner of education acknowledged that such procedures had not been followed, but asserted that his actions were within the "wide latitude" that administrative agencies are generally accorded. The court disagreed and declared that the regulations could not be enforced. Moreover, the court invalidated the agency's orders to admit the two children, reasoning that the local boards were first entitled to a hearing on the question of whether the two girls should go to public school.

The two children ultimately gained entrance to school. One moved to another school district; the other was admitted pursuant to an out-of-court settlement. The validity of the New Jersey school guidelines was subsequently confirmed by the Supreme Court.

THE IDENTITIES OF CHILDREN WITH HIV INFECTION

From the very beginning, the right of infected children to privacy and confidentiality has been a matter of significant debate. As noted above, the CDC Guidelines imply that state officials should know the identities of these children but do not specify how they should compile the names. Moreover, the guidelines suggest that certain local school personnel should be alerted to the identities of infected children, but do not indicate how the children should be protected from harassment and discrimination. In short, policy makers have wrestled not only with the right of infectious children to attend school, but also with their right to privacy once they get there.

The first aspect of this question—the means by which state agencies should identify infected children for evaluation—was addressed by the court in the Queens case. It ruled that the New York City health commissioner could not use the state's epidemiologic data to compile a list of children for review. According to the court, such action was barred by section 206(1)(j) of the New York Public Health Law, which guarantees that medical case reports "shall be kept confidential and . . . used solely for the purposes of medical or scientific research. . . ."[80] In New York, when state officials utilized the data for determining the fitness of children to attend school, they breached the confidentiality guaranteed by the statute.[81]

There are strong public policy arguments for guarding the confidentiality of reporting data. The ability of the CDC and others to collect epidemiologic data is dependent entirely on the public's willingness to comply with reporting requirements. The disclosure of information collected in confidence would only undermine the atmosphere of trust upon which such data collection depends. Compliance would suffer, and data would become less reliable.[82]

There are additional reasons for barring the use of reporting data to identify infected children. The case reporting requirements vary significantly from state to state. In Florida, the regulations apply to cases of AIDS.[83] In New York, physicians must report suspected cases as well.[84] In New Jersey, recently enacted regulations apply both to ARC and to AIDS.[85] And Colorado has required that all positive antibody tests be reported.[86] When a state's school guidelines do not apply to the same children as its reporting requirements, problems arise. The enormous controversy in Queens emerged from the disparity between these two regulations in New York.

What are the alternatives to surveillance data? In New York City, where the court prohibited further use of epidemiologic records, a system of voluntary reporting by pediatricians is now in place. In August 1986, for example, a four-person panel reviewed the histories of thirteen children whose physicians had referred their cases to the department of health. The panel members were not informed of the names of these children.[87]

This arrangement, of course, raises a whole new set of issues. Does such reporting violate principles of physician-patient confidentiality? By what means should pediatricians obtain informed consent for such voluntary disclosures? If such reporting is not made pursuant to reporting statutes, what rules of confidentiality apply?

The second aspect of confidentiality—the right of local school personnel to know the identities of infectious children in their school—has also been at issue. The CDC guidelines, for example, tacitly acknowledge that such disclosure might be needed "to detect situations where the potential for transmission may increase (*e.g.*, bleeding injury)."[88] In the Queens case, however, the court decided to protect the child's identity. Several medical experts testified that the precautions taken routinely to prevent the transmission of other blood-borne diseases would be sufficient to prevent HIV transmission. Moreover, school officials asserted that disclosure of the child's identity would have made school attendance impossible.[89] In this regard it is worthwhile recalling that *two* infected children had been found physically and emotionally capable of entering the New York City public schools in the fall of 1985; however, the identity of one had been previously disclosed and the family was urged to "consider alternate educational opportunities" in view of the "potential social discrimination to which the student could be subjected."[90]

Finally, it would be unfair to disclose publicly matters with which these children are still struggling privately. In particular, when they are quite young, these children may themselves not appreciate the nature of their illness. The child who was the center of the 1985 New York City protests apparently saw the public demonstrations on television and remarked: "Gee, I feel sorry for the kid."[91]

In one respect, the enormous controversy over admission of children with AIDS to public schools has been one-sided. All of the analyses attempt to balance the rights of these children against the theoretical hazard that they pose. There is little discussion of the benefits that their presence in the classroom offers—benefits to their classmates and to their community.

Traditionally, the nation's public schools have taught values as well as skills. When children with handicaps are admitted to classes, more fortunate children learn important lessons about the value of education and the right to fair and equal treatment. When children with "theoretical" risks are permitted to attend, their classmates gain appreciation for the ways an open society can cope with uncertainty and rationally assess risks. When young victims of AIDS attend school, impressionable youngsters are spared the spectacle of mass demonstrations of prejudice and fear.

Finally, the welfare of the majority of children who are healthy will not be appreciably advanced by the exclusion of the few who are identifiably ill. Only national programs of education and counseling will protect children from this frightening epidemic.

6

Prostitution as a Public Health Issue

JOHN F. DECKER

Although the spread of AIDS has been largely associated with four high-risk groups—homosexual males, intravenous drug users, recipients of blood transfusions, and children born to mothers with AIDS—the frequency of sexual relations among prostitutes has prompted speculation that they, too, could be at high risk of contracting the disease and that their conduct could spread AIDS to others.[1] The recent discovery of what appear to be the first documented cases in the United States of female-to-male transmission of the AIDS virus reinforces this speculation.[2]

Prostitution historically has been the subject of myriad regulatory and criminal control measures.[3] For example, public health alarmists in the sixteenth century managed to force restrictions on prostitution virtually overnight when venereal disease, which was largely blamed on prostitutes, became epidemic in Europe.[4] (For a description of past public health measures against prostitutes in this country, see Chapter 3.) As modern-day legislatures contemplate ways to abate the spread of AIDS, regulation of prostitution is likely once again to attract attention as a possible approach. What is the relationship between what has been described as "the oldest profession"[5] and what some have stated could be a "modern plague?"[6] This chapter will examine existing and proposed legal measures as they relate to the spread of AIDS by prostitution.

Obviously, that which is currently known regarding the spread of AIDS among homosexual males[7] provides cause for serious concern about gay male prostitution. Most prostitution, however, involves the sale of sexual services by a female to a male.[8] The key question, then, is to what extent female prostitutes are likely to spread AIDS. The answer depends both on the evidence regarding the transmission of HIV (Human Immunodeficiency Virus—the virus associated with AIDS) through heterosexual contacts and on the practices and habits of prostitutes as they relate to disease control. I will therefore explore both the public health risks that prostitution poses and the phenomenon of prostitution itself.

In this chapter, the term prostitute refers to any person whose livelihood largely depends on engaging in indiscriminate, unemotional sexual encounters for money with a series of strangers.[9] This definition excludes the "kept woman"[10] and the "amateur prostitute,"[11] since both present a lower risk of spreading AIDS than the traditional prostitute, given their relatively limited number of sexual partners.

THE PRACTICE OF PROSTITUTION AND THE TRANSMISSION OF AIDS

The Centers for Disease Control report that the overwhelming majority of persons with AIDS in the United States are either homosexual or bisexual men not known to have used injected controlled substances (66 percent), heterosexual persons who inject controlled substances (17 percent), homosexual or bisexual men who have used injected controlled substances (8 percent), persons who have had transfusions of blood or blood products (2 percent), hemophiliacs who have been exposed to the AIDS virus through concentrated blood products (1 percent), and newborn children who were infected with the virus by their mothers (1 percent).[12] Thus, in approximately 94 percent of the documented cases of AIDS, the infection is believed to have been transmitted by means *other than* heterosexual contact. In fact, only about 4 percent of patients with AIDS are thought to have contracted the disease by engaging in heterosexual sex.[13] The source of AIDS in the remaining 2 to 3 percent of cases cannot be determined.

Most of the 4 percent who apparently contracted AIDS through heterosexual contacts are the *female* sex partners of intravenous drug users and bisexual men. The *males* in this category are placed there because they report that they have had no homosexual experiences, no intravenous drug use, and no blood transfusions. A significant percentage of them admit a "history of contacts with prostitutes."[14]

Female Prostitutes

The concern about female prostitutes and their possible role in the transmission of the AIDS virus emanates not only from such reports but also from reports on the transmission of AIDS by Central African prostitutes,[15] reports on a significant incidence of AIDS among Haitian females,[16] and reports from American military personnel that they contracted AIDS from West German prostitutes.[17] These claims must be critically evaluated before any public policy is based upon them.

Upon close examination, these reports offer no concrete evidence that contact with a prostitute in the United States poses a serious risk of exposure to the AIDS virus. For several reasons, the Central African findings may not have direct bearing on the spread of AIDS here. Injections are used more often in Central African clinics than here to treat maladies, and the needles typically are reused.[18] Thus, the role of unsterile needles in the spread of HIV to Central African prostitutes and their patrons is, while unknown, potentially large.[19] It is also possible that the patrons of prostitutes risk exposure to the AIDS virus by receiving unsterile intramuscular injections to ward off venereal disease.[20] Similarly, some have suggested that Central African practices involving scarification and tatoos may facilitate HIV transmission.[21] Thus, the relatively equal incidence of AIDS among Central African females and males may suggest shared risk factors in addition to sex.[22] Further, and most important, the infections found among female prostitutes do not alone substantiate female-to-male spread of the virus through prostitution.[23] Controlled studies of Central African men who frequent prostitutes and their incidence of acquiring AIDS are necessary before a causal connection between female prostitution and AIDS can be established.

The charges of American military personnel, who blame West German prostitutes for the presence of the HIV antibodies in their blood, are highly suspect. Since admitting to homosexual behavior and/or intravenous drug use is grounds for a dishonorable discharge from the military, whereas frequenting a female prostitute is not, there are strong incentives to falsely lay the blame on the prostitutes.[24] Furthermore, in a study of 2,000 registered prostitutes in West Germany, where prostitution is legal, only 16 tested positive for HIV; half of the positive group were also identified as intravenous-drug users.[25] This study suggests that in West Germany, prostitutes do not carry (much less transmit) HIV to a degree sufficient to support the American soldiers' assertions.[26] Furthermore, a review of the three hundred cases of AIDS reported within West Germany offers no evidence of any female-to-male transmission.[27]

The theory that prostitutes in the United States are a significant element in the spread of AIDS is likewise not supported by the evidence. Preliminary results of a federal study in seven cities indicate that rates of seropositivity among prostitutes vary widely, ranging from 0 percent in Las Vegas to 57 percent in the Newark area. As in West Germany, intravenous drug abuse among tested prostitutes makes the data harder to interpret, but the federal study does not show that American prostitutes are contracting or spreading HIV in their work.[28] The fact that there are seropositive males who show no AIDS risk factor other than contacts with prostitutes is not hard proof that these men acquired the virus from prostitutes. By conservative estimate, there are more than 200,000 female professional prostitutes in the United States, who engage in more than 300 million acts of prostitution annually.[29] Yet, of the thousands of AIDS cases in the United States, not a single one has been definitively traced to prostitution. In short, although caution is in order, there is no justification for alarmist conclusions in light of current scientific evidence.

Even if one assumes that female-to-male transmissions of AIDS are common,[30] the habits and practices of American prostitutes obviate any major public health concern. The relatively routine insistence by prostitutes that their patrons use condoms during coitus[31] reduces the risk that the AIDS virus could be spread through genital-genital intercourse.[32] Moreover, coitus is not even an issue in many, if not most, transactions with prostitutes. It has been reported that as many as three-fourths of patrons seek only oral sex,[33] a significant consideration given current evidence that the risk of AIDS transmission through oral-genital contact is minimal.[34]

To be sure, if a prostitute suffered from open sores in her mouth, *she* could be at risk of acquiring the AIDS virus during fellatio through the direct transmission of semen-borne HIV into her blood stream. If, in addition, her patron suffered from open lesions on his penis, blood-borne transmission could, in theory, occur in either direction. Even these relatively remote risks are reduced, in practice, by the growing insistence by prostitutes that patrons wear condoms during oral, as well as genital, sex.[35] While cunnilingus (oral-genital sex involving the man's mouth and the woman's genitals) is also common, occurring in as many as 40 percent of encounters,[36] it is unclear that it presents a significant opportunity for the spread of AIDS, and there are no documented cases to date.[37]

Other sex acts are even less likely modes of transmission. Although anal intercourse without a condom could pose a significant danger *to the prostitute* for the same reason that it endangers gay males, anal sex is performed only in approximately 1 percent of encounters with female prostitutes, and condoms are employed routinely.[38] Open-mouthed kissing, practiced in about one-third of encounters,[39] poses even less of a risk since exchange of saliva has not been documented as a way of transmitting the AIDS virus.[40] Finally, transactions that involve only masturbation, or that produce a climax without direct contact between prostitute and patron, present virtually no risk of transmission.

In summary, whatever may be said about male-to-female transmission of AIDS, female-to-male transmission accounts for only a small percentage of reported cases in developed countries.[41] Furthermore, professional prostitutes have incentives to reduce the risk of transmission of the virus. Risk reduction is not just a matter of self-protection; it makes good business sense as well.[42] Prostitutes, individually and as a group, can ill afford to lose customers to the fear of contagion.

Male Prostitutes

Between 5 and 10 percent of professional prostitutes are men who service other men. As to them, there appears to be much cause for concern.[43] Far less is known about male prostitutes than about their female counterparts. Venereal disease appears to be much more prevalent among male prostitutes than female,[44] and it is thought that the patrons of male prostitutes are much more likely to seek anal intercourse.[45] Male prostitution therefore appears to pose a far greater risk of AIDS transmission, especially from the active party (the "pitcher") to the passive one (the "catcher"). Indeed, if a homosexual male prostitute plays the role of both pitcher and catcher, the multiple partners he encounters place him at high risk both of contracting and of spreading AIDS. To be sure, if male prostitutes routinely insist on the use of a condom during anal sex, this risk would be greatly minimized. However, whether they in fact do so has not been documented.

LEGAL CONTROLS ON PROSTITUTION AND PROSTITUTES

Prostitution is a crime virtually everywhere in the United States,[46] except Nevada, where each county retains the option of criminalizing, tolerating, or licensing the activity.[47] Thus, were prostitution thought to contribute to the spread of AIDS, the most obvious response would be to enforce rigorously existing but underenforced anti-prostitution laws.[48] Instead of the customary fine, prostitutes believed to carry HIV might, upon conviction of a prostitution-related offense, receive sentences of incarceration designed to isolate them from the community.[49]

Some states, though not most, also prohibit patronizing a prostitute.[50] States that do not have such laws could decide to enact and enforce them, thus taking aim at the *demand* for commercial sex. Convicted patrons who are seropositive or who for other reasons are thought to harbor the AIDS virus might then be incarcerated as well.

But a major crackdown on prostitutes, their patrons, and their promoters through the use of existing anti-prostitution laws does not appear to be warranted as a way to prevent the spread of AIDS. Similarly, the development of new laws directed at prostitutes and others involved in the profession seems premature and unnecessary, given current scientific data.

Rigorous enforcement of existing anti-prostitution laws will only further distract the law enforcement establishment from more pressing criminal concerns, particularly crimes of violence.[51] There are also direct costs associated with increased enforcement. Fifteen years ago, the San Francisco Committee on Crime determined that the cost of arresting a single prostitute exceeded $175.[52] The estimate can only be higher today because of inflation. Extrapolating from this conservative figure, a single arrest of each of the 200,000 professional prostitutes in America (also a conservative estimate) would cost $35 million. Increased incarceration would push the price even higher and would exacerbate overcrowded conditions in jails and prisons as well.[53]

Furthermore, a major drawback of relying on prostitution-related arrests to prevent the spread of AIDS is that only a small percentage of prostitutes[54] and only a minuscule number of patrons—far fewer than 1 percent[55]—are ever apprehended by law enforcement authorities. The great majority of arrests are the most visible professional prostitutes, the streetwalkers, while call girls, bar girls, massage parlor and brothel prostitutes are seldom apprehended.[56] Male prostitutes are virtually never arrested.[57] Even with more aggressive enforcement techniques, only a small percentage of prostitution is likely to be detected.

Isolation or confinement of prostitutes who have been exposed to the AIDS virus smacks of punishing a person for having a disease, in violation of the Eighth Amendment prohibition against "cruel and unusual punishment." In *Robinson v. California*,[58] the United States Supreme Court held unconstitutional the practice of punishing persons for being addicted to the use of narcotics, and likened the statute under attack to one which would make it "a criminal offense for a person to be mentally ill, or a leper, or to be afflicted with a venereal disease."[59]

At the heart of the *Robinson* ruling is the proposition that it is impermissible under the Eighth Amendment to punish individuals for a *status* or *condition* over which they have very little or no control, as distinct from *conduct* or *behavior* which is a product of their free will. Not surprisingly, the line between status and conduct is not always easy to draw. Consequently, several lower courts have struck down criminal measures directed at a combination of the two, where the conduct at issue was, in other circumstances, perfectly legal.[60] For example, a Chicago municipal ordinance that prohibited loitering in or about premises where alcoholic beverages were sold by any person "known to be a prostitute" was found to unconstitutionally "transform into criminal behavior ordinary conduct of individuals on the basis of . . . status."[61]

Instead of directing their efforts at prostitutes as a class, who *might* (but probably do not) harbor HIV and who *might* (but quite likely will not, for professional as well as physiological reasons) transmit it to others, states might more reasonably prosecute people regardless of their profession who know they have the virus and who knowingly engage in activity that places others at high risk. Some states, including Florida, make it a crime for people who know they have any venereal disease to engage in sexual intercourse.[62] Other states are considering making it an offense for people who know they carry HIV to engage in sexual activity.

There have been efforts to screen arrested prostitutes for HIV antibodies. Different legal standards apply to such testing, depending upon whether it is carried out under the criminal or the public health law. In a jurisdiction that makes it a crime for people who know they have AIDS or the virus to engage in sexual intercourse, HIV antibody testing of an arrested prostitute might be justified as a search for evidence. Of course, this would not be true in a state that did not prohibit knowingly engaging in sexual relations while infectious, since there is no possibility the "search" or test would yield evidence of a *crime*.

The Fourth Amendment governs police searches, generally requiring any search to be reasonable and authorized by a judicial warrant.[63] Blood testing is not considered an unreasonable method of search[64] (as opposed, for example, to surgically "searching" for a bullet in a suspect's body[65]), but the warrant requirement may frustrate any large-scale testing of prostitutes under the criminal law. A warrant may only be issued if there is "probable cause" to believe the search will yield evidence of a crime. Until it is demonstrated that a significant proportion of prostitutes in a given area are infected with HIV, the mere fact that an arrested person is a prostitute would not constitute probable cause to search for infection. Only some evidence that a particular person has HIV and knowingly spread it would suffice.[66]

In addition to criminal prohibitions on knowingly engaging in sex while infectious, some states have public health measures aimed at the transmission of the disease rather than at prostitution *per se*.[67] These afford far greater latitude for HIV testing. In Alabama, for example, a person arrested for prostitution is presumed to have venereal disease, and is therefore subjected to a medical examination.[68] More common are statutes that, without singling out prostitutes, authorize local health officials to require an examination of all people who are "reasonably suspected" of being infected with venereal disease. If those tested are found to be infected, they may be required to report for treatment, or they may even be quarantined.[69] In some jurisdictions, pretrial release[70] or suspended or reduced sentences[71] may be conditioned on the prostitute's submitting to or passing an examination for venereal disease. By simply defining AIDS as a sexually transmitted venereal disease, states could invoke these laws to force arrested prostitutes to submit to HIV testing.

Such public health actions are, however, open to challenge. The trend in public health law is to require a reasonable medical justification for control measures that infringe upon individual rights; mandatory testing, based on an unsupported presumption that prostitutes are likely to harbor HIV, may not measure up to modern standards.[72] Furthermore, to the extent that these civil laws are actually applied as part of the criminal law response to prostitution, they may be subject to Fourth Amendment limitations on searches.

Not surprisingly, concern about the spread of AIDS has prompted some states to consider laws that would achieve the same ends by more direct means. For instance, the Colorado legislature is considering the passage of a statute that would empower state and local health officials to conduct "examinations of persons reasonably suspected of AIDS or the viral infection which causes AIDS and impose restrictions on such persons until the results of such examinations are known," and to "isolate or quarantine" persons with AIDS or HIV where it is "shown to be necessary to protect the public health."[73] Meanwhile, the Michigan legislature is considering legislation allowing judges, magistrates, or local health departments to require that people arrested for prostitution or solicitation be tested for antibodies to HIV.[74] In Florida, a proposed law provides for the testing of all persons convicted of prostitution.[75]

In addition to calls for the mandatory testing of prostitutes, quarantine orders restricting the travel and activities of prostitutes have been implemented. In Jackson, Mississippi, state officials forbade a twenty-eight-year-old male prostitute from having sexual relations without informing his partner of his infection with HIV.[76] Female prostitutes have been quarantined in California, Nevada, and Florida.[77] In one Florida case, a female prostitute with AIDS was confined to her home, and ordered to wear an electronic transmitter that would signal police if she travelled more than 200 feet from her telephone.[78] How this could prevent her from practicing her trade is unclear.

The doubtful utility and legal validity of mandatory antibody testing, quarantine, and isolation, given the present state of medical knowledge, is addressed in Chapter 4 of this volume. When such measures are applied explicitly to prostitutes but not to other groups that are equally (if not more) likely to transmit HIV, they are vulnerable to challenge in court on equal protection grounds.

In addition, states may seek to use involuntary civil commitment procedures to isolate known prostitutes who suffer from AIDS on the ground that they constitute a danger to themselves or the community.[79] Where applicable, civil commitment procedures can be employed without regard for whether the feared danger is punishable as a crime. The difficulties inherent in such an approach are also canvassed in Chapter 4.

RECOMMENDATIONS

First, we urgently need scientific study of persons involved in prostitution-related activity, particularly the prostitutes themselves, similar to that conducted in West Germany to determine what evidence, if any, links prostitution to the spread of AIDS in the United States. A study now under way may prove most helpful in this regard.[80]

Second, no criminal measures should be enacted at this time. AIDS is a disease, not a form of deviance. Strictures that have the potential of labeling sick people as criminal can only foster cynicism and disrespect for law. Criminal laws should be used to control health only as a last resort and only where there exists a compelling need for them—a need not documented by current medical evidence. Criminal law measures will only make it harder to control the disease, for they will prompt people who have been exposed to HIV to attempt to conceal their condition. Further, the specter of jails and prisons filled with people dying of AIDS is completely at odds with contemporary standards of decency.

Third, consideration should be given to changing involuntary civil commitment procedures to reach people who carry HIV and who actually pose a danger to self or to others. Unlike criminal laws that label as deviant everyone in a particular class, civil commitment procedures would allow society to direct its concern on an ad hoc basis to those persons who actually require control.

Finally, attempts to curb prostitution itself are ill-advised and doomed to failure. They merely drive prostitution underground, eliminating the possibility of effective legal, social, and medical control. Moralists, plagues, or criminal laws have never significantly abated the demand for services of those involved in "the oldest profession," nor will AIDS today. Far preferable is a system of licensing, combined with strict criminal measures aimed at unlicensed prostitutes,[81] as exists in much of West Germany and sections of Nevada. Such a system would enable public health officials to examine registered prostitutes, although not their patrons, for evidence of exposure to HIV in circumstances that do not immediately threaten their livelihood and their liberty.

7

Education as Prevention

JANE HARRIS AIKEN

There is now no doubt that public education is the most effective way to stop the spread of AIDS. Yet the amount of education the public now receives is woefully inadequate. The National Academy of Sciences in its 1986 report, *Confronting AIDS*, and the Surgeon General of the United States in his own *Report on AIDS*, both state that education is the most compelling way to significantly reduce the spread of the Human Immunodeficiency Virus (HIV), the virus associated with AIDS. These two reports also urge that much greater efforts be made to educate the public about the effects of HIV. The National Academy of Sciences suggests that educational efforts be expanded and diversified to reach those who are presently infected or at risk of infection, those in a position to influence public opinion, and those who interact with people with AIDS.[1] The Surgeon General endorses education as a necessary step in stopping the spread of AIDS. He stresses that it is the responsibility of all adults to educate the young, pointing out that "the lives of our young people depend on our fulfilling our responsibility."[2] His report calls for AIDS education to begin in "the lowest grade possible."[3]

Education works to prevent the spread of AIDS by altering the behavior through which the virus is transmitted. Because AIDS cannot be contained by medical means such as a vaccine, people must be taught how to contain the spread of the virus through their own activity. The Centers for Disease Control (CDC) argues that behavior can be changed if people are told which of their activities increase the probability of "catching AIDS," and are told of "safe" alternatives.[4] There is evidence that education programs undertaken so far have been successful. One doctor has credited risk-reduction education with the leveling off of the numbers of reported cases of AIDS in San Francisco and New York and with the decreased incidence of other venereal diseases.[5]

Civil rights attorneys have also argued that education is one of the most effective means to stop AIDS-related discrimination.[6] Such evils as employment discrimination[7] and controversy over the attendance of school children with AIDS[8] are the result of unfounded fears about the transmission of AIDS through casual contact. An NBC News poll of November 1985 indicated that some people believe they could catch AIDS by being in the same room as a person with AIDS.[9] Polls have also shown that as much as one third of the general population falsely believes that AIDS can be acquired through blood donation.[10] This misinformation could have a devastating effect on the nation's blood supply. An aggressive educational program aimed at the general public and explaining how AIDS is transmitted will diminish both fear and the animus for discrimination.

Since education has been recognized and advocated by leading experts as the only known way to combat the spread of AIDS[11] and AIDS-related discrimination, one would expect communities across the nation to be instituting education programs for those at risk and for the general public. One would expect to see education campaigns in schools, health facilities, workplaces, and wherever members of high-risk groups could be reached. Unfortunately, efforts to develop and implement educational programs have met with great resistance at all levels of government, while many states have considered more restrictive and less effective alternatives such as mandatory reporting of HIV seropositivity, contact tracing and surveillance, and quarantine.[12] This chapter makes the case for education, and then looks at the resistance to education programs, examines the reasons that have been used to stop or delay aggressive education programs, and analyzes the legal validity of obstacles to education.

THE CASE FOR EDUCATION

Education Prevents the Spread of AIDS

As soon as the medical community began to suspect how AIDS was spread, the gay community attempted to get the word out about possible ways to prevent transmission.[13] Through informal, volunteer efforts, gay organizations—much more than local or state health departments—tried to educate gay men about the disease itself, the symptoms, the prognosis, and safe sexual practices. However, the need for education explaining which sexual practices increase and which sexual practices decrease the chance of transmitting AIDS has only grown.

Medical experts now agree that certain sexual practices are safe: body-to-body rubbing; masturbating alone, or with a partner or a group; massage; hugging; dry kissing; using clean dildos and other sex toys that *are not shared*; watching others; and showing off to others.[14] Safe intravenous drug practices include: avoiding shooting galleries, refraining from shared drugs or equipment, and using only new (not re-bagged) needles. Drug users can also sterilize the "works" with household bleach, alcohol, or boiling water.[15] Unsafe needle use is not confined to users of illicit drugs. AIDS can also be transmitted through needles used for tattooing, ear-piercing or—a widespread practice among weight-lifters and body-builders—injecting steroids.[16] Aggressive and informative educational programs are needed to replace dangerous behavior with AIDS-controlling practices. The CDC has said that "without a vaccine or therapy, the basis for AIDS prevention . . . is a thorough understanding of the risk factors for the [HIV] infection and efforts to change the behavior that contribute to those factors."[17]

Social science research indicates that voluntary adaptation of behaviors conducive to health is more likely to occur when the behavioral recommendations are based on scientific evidence, when the safe and unsafe practices are clearly identified, and when the persons receiving the education are given opportunities to know what practices are likely to increase and decrease their risk.[18] Scientific research also indicates that a new practice will be adopted and continued if it is perceived to be better than the practice that it replaces, is compatible with current values and norms in the target population, and is easy to understand, testable, and observable.[19]

According to the CDC, education about AIDS has taken several forms, from pamphlets about the disease to extensive counseling programs for people with AIDS.[20] Many cities have established telephone hotlines that provide, at low cost, an immediate response to people concerned about AIDS.[21] Telephone hotlines are successful because they allow callers to preserve their anonymity and can be advertised anywhere with low risk of negative public reaction. Some cities conduct AIDS education programs through a speakers bureau that sends volunteers to the community to address the concerns of any group interested in AIDS.[22]

Although everyone is capable of contracting AIDS, and there is concern about the spread of the disease among heterosexuals[23] and women,[24] members of certain groups have a high possibility of contracting the disease and should be the targets of intense education programs. These groups include young people who might experiment with drugs or sex, intravenous drug users, both straight and gay people who acquire multiple sex partners by patronizing bars, gay and bisexual men in sex establishments, and prostitutes. Because blacks and Hispanics comprise a disproportionate number of AIDS cases, there should be special programs in areas having large black or Hispanic populations.

Since educational efforts are most effective if they provide risk-group members with information they can understand and use,[25] several cities have tailored their education efforts to meet the particular needs of these populations. For example, a male prostitute might keep and read a flashy wallet-sized card that provides explicit information. Youth are likely to respond to the use of video educational materials.[26] Since gay men, prostitutes, and intravenous drug users are likely to see the government as a source of persecution and misinformation, workers used in outreach efforts should identify with the community they are serving.

Although assessing the effectiveness of public health measures is difficult, one indicator of changing behavioral patterns is the decrease of sexually transmitted diseases, generally, in the gay community.[27] In New York and San Francisco, two cities with large gay populations, the greatest incidences of AIDS and an acute awareness of the disease and how it is transmitted, cases of rectal gonorrhea, a disease that is transmitted similarly to AIDS, have dropped.[28] This behavioral change is quite significant and appears to indicate that gay men have made appropriate and safe changes in their sexual practices. The increase in reported cases of AIDS is slowing in areas where there are extensive educational programs, although the changes cannot be definitely linked to education.[29] In San Francisco, the number of new cases of AIDS has been constant for the past year, and in New York the rate of increase is slowing. According to one recent epidemiologic survey in San Francisco, only 5 percent of seronegative men showed evidence of exposure during 1984-1985.[30]

Studies on the efficacy of educational programs are almost nonexistent. However, one study (conducted between August 1984 and April 1985) by the San Francisco Health Department reports that gay men made significant changes in their behavior after even a limited educational program that consisted of placing ads discussing safe sex practices in newspapers serving the gay community. The study found that the proportion of gay and bisexual men who reported that they were monogamous, celibate, or performed unsafe sexual practices only with their steady partner increased from 69 percent to 81 percent. Fewer gay and bisexual men reported that they had had more than one sexual partner in the previous thirty days.[31]

Another study, conducted in November 1983 by the San Francisco Department of Health, studied the reactions of four distinct groups of gay men to educational efforts and compared their behavior to that reported in March 1983. The four groups were men who frequented bathhouses, men who frequented bars, men who never went to bars or baths, and men in couples. The study found that educational efforts directed at these groups significantly affected their sexual practices: "Gay men's sexual behavior has changed in a direction that consistently aligns with medical directives."[32]

This study provided useful information about the future direction of AIDS education. It determined that most gay men are aware of the facts about AIDS; in fact, the community had reached the saturation point on information on the disease. What it needed were models of appropriate behavior. The study concluded that communities need more explicit educational materials (such as videotapes) that encourage and shape sexual behavior rather than prohibit or discourage sexual acts. And, as the study put it, "this message would be better presented in the language of sex than in the language of AIDS."[33]

The few studies of the efficacy of AIDS education directed toward intra-venous drug users demonstrate that providing information about safe needle use can promote behavior changes. Forty-seven percent of the respondents in a San Francisco study indicated that they no longer shared needles, or, at least, cleaned the works.[34] A survey of New York City drug users receiving drug treatment in residential programs or clinics found similar changes. While only 19 percent of the clients in methadone programs indicated that the existence of AIDS had influenced them to stop "shooting up" drugs, 50 percent indicated that the threat of the disease had influenced some people to stop sharing needles. Thirty-eight percent of all the respondents said that the threat of AIDS had influenced at least some people who had never used drugs to stay away from drugs.[35]

Information about AIDS and safe needle use has created market pressure on dealers to provide more needles when selling drugs to their customers. A letter to the *New England Journal of Medicine* outlined recent changes in street-drug activity in New York City apparently designed to meet that increased demand. The Street Research Unit of the New York State Division of Abuser Services observed that dealers are selling an extra needle at a very reduced price ("two for one") or are including an extra needle with the purchase of twenty-five to fifty dollar bags of heroin.[36] Eighteen of twenty-two drug vendors in a field study conducted by former addicts re-ported an increase in sales of needles over the past year.[37]

Youth are pinpointed as a potentially high-risk group since they are likely to be exploring their own sexuality and may experiment with illicit drugs.[38] Young people are woefully ill-informed about the existence of the disease and the modes of transmission. The National Academy of Sciences reported that even in San Francisco, an "AIDS epicenter," young people were mis-informed as late as 1986. In a survey of 1,300 high school students, forty percent did not know that AIDS was caused by a virus. One-third of those surveyed believed that a person could contract AIDS by touching a person with AIDS and four in ten students were unaware that the use of condoms during intercourse decreases the risk of contracting the disease.[39] The Sur-geon General recommends that education about AIDS should start in early elementary school and at home. The obstacles that have previously been in the way of effective sex education in the schools should give way to the threat of AIDS.[40]

Education Prevents Discrimination

Education has also been a very effective tool in combatting AIDS-related discrimination. According to Peggy Clarke, public health educator of the New York City Department of Health, "education is the key tool used to allay fears about AIDS by providing accurate information and clarifying mis-conceptions."[41] The Health and Public Policy Committee of the American

College of Physicians has created a position paper encouraging education for the general public, those persons in the health care industry in contact with persons with AIDS, and those persons who are at high risk of contracting the disease. The committee views education as an appropriate way to stem the fear of AIDS and control the epidemic spread of the disease.[42] In an attitude study conducted in San Francisco, New York City, and London, researchers found that the less informed people are about AIDS, the more likely they are to harbor unreasonable fears about the disease. Because many people avoid or discredit gay-associated literature, the researchers concluded that government agencies and non-homosexual health organizations have to play a large role in AIDS education for heterosexuals to combat fear, ignorance, and prejudice.[43]

Community awareness events (such as "AIDS Awareness Week") are particularly useful because they tend to reach a broader spectrum of people than other education efforts.[44] Cities have complemented their events with media campaigns that attempt to educate both the general public and high-risk groups about AIDS by using the press, bus posters, radio announcements, and billboards. Celebrities, political figures, and religious leaders have helped attract the public's attention to the educational message.[45]

The effectiveness of AIDS education in quieting public fear and curbing discrimination has been demonstrated in Canada. There the development of the AIDS epidemic is roughly two years behind the United States. In response to reports of AIDS-related discrimination by police, bus drivers, firemen, undertakers, and even nurses and physicians, the Toronto Department of Public Health began a comprehensive educational policy directed at preventing the spread of both AIDS and "AIDS hysteria." Because it took the initiative to develop an educational program, the Toronto Department of Health developed a strong relationship with community groups and became known as a reliable and credible source of information. According to Bill Mindell, information officer for the Toronto Department of Public Health, the city avoided the panic observed in the United States, and gay men moderated their sexual practices as a result of this government-funded educational program.[46]

OBSTACLES TO EDUCATIONAL PROGRAMS

Disapproval of Homosexuality and Drug Use

The fact that most of the people afflicted with the disease or perceived to be at risk from the disease are homosexual men and drug users has created special problems. Gay men and drug users are disfavored in our society[47] and the attitude that "they get what they deserve" has permeated plans to cope with this epidemic, resulting in an initial failure to take the disease seriously. AIDS education programs in other countries such as the United

Kingdom have met with some resistance,[48] but have been carried out regardless. The British campaign, which has cost $30 million so far, includes television commercials and a royal visit to the nation's first AIDS hospital ward.[49] In this country, Representative William Dannemeyer, advocating restrictive AIDS legislation, stated that "God's plan for man was Adam and Eve, not Adam and Steve."[50] The White House Director of Communications, Patrick Buchanan, publicly stated that gays "have declared war against Nature and Nature is exacting an awful retribution."[51] Provision of effective educational programs has been hampered by the fact that many of the people who need to be reached risk personal stigmatization and even criminal penalties if they are identified. The use of illegal drugs or even syringes without a prescription is a crime everywhere in the United States. Sodomy is a crime in twenty-five states.[52] Obviously, educational programs have to be sensitive to the possible negative ramifications of identification, particularly by agents of the state.

Controversies over the use of frank discussions and slang in educational materials about drugs and sex have delayed use or caused modification of materials in some communities.[53] The distribution of a videotape to New York City high schools was delayed six months because the material did not promote abstinence.[54] Other people find a discussion of gay sex or drug use offensive and "pornographic." As the *New England Journal of Medicine* complained,

> the very message that we must broadcast in order to abort the epidemic and buy time for further scientific advance requires the use of words that are taboo in high places . . . We may not be "explicit," and we may not, in fact, send out messages that even seem to condone sexual and other practices that deviate from a governmentally sanctioned norm. No official document should use the phrase "safe sex," even if it currently appears to be the major promising route to safety for an important segment of the population. Well may the gods laugh![55]

A further barrier to effective AIDS education has been a longstanding ban on condom advertising in the media, based on a perception that it is offensive. In early 1987 the *New York Times*, *Newsweek*, and Time, Inc. (which publishes *Time*, *Life*, *People*, and *Sports Illustrated* among other magazines) all agreed to accept condom advertising as an AIDS education measure, provided the messages focus on disease prevention rather than contraception. As of this writing, however, the major television networks continue to refuse such advertising, despite pleas from Congress and the Surgeon General.[56] The U.K., Denmark, Norway, Italy, and Germany, however, are all conducting aggressive and sometimes explicit education campaigns promoting condoms.[57]

To some degree, well-organized gay communities have been able to compensate for deficiencies in official education efforts by implementing privately funded campaigns. Drug users, on the other hand, are not an organized community, and education about safe needle use is almost entirely dependent upon government funding. Unfortunately, the government at all levels has been reluctant to educate drug users on safe needle use. The National Institute on Drug Abuse put together a pamphlet, *NIDA Capsule*, which informed drug users about AIDS and the dangers of sharing needles. The pamphlet stressed the necessity of sterilizing old needles and equipment before use. Its publication was substantially delayed while it awaited approval by the Reagan administration. According to one White House aide, such information would be released by the federal government "over our collective dead bodies."[58] Los Angeles County and the federal government financed printing a pamphlet on AIDS and needle use. Three county supervisors called for an investigation on the grounds that the literature "gives advice on how to safely inject drugs." The distribution of the pamphlet was stopped.[59]

It is clear that communities cannot afford not to educate drug users about ways to decrease risk of AIDS. Intravenous drug users are the primary source for heterosexual infection to their sexual partners and transmission of AIDS to fetuses. The large differences in seropositivity prevalence among drug users in different parts of the country indicate that a comprehensive education program directed toward this group can substantially decrease the rate of infection.[60] But, as Federico Gonzalez, the Gay Men's Health Crisis Director of Education, says: "Brochures that use scare tactics to get people to stop using drugs won't work any more than brochures that try to get people to stop having sex. We must concentrate on educating people not to share needles. The decision to stop using drugs is a totally separate issue."[61]

Insufficient Funds for AIDS Education

Despite the efficacy of educational programs, very little money has been allocated for such programs, and many communities have resisted putting the available programs in motion.[62] Of the $64.9 million requested for AIDS related activities for 1986,[63] only $15 million is targeted to the states for the development of AIDS education and risk reduction programs.[64] The National Academy of Sciences notes that "AIDS education should be pursued with a sense of urgency and a level of funding that is appropriate for a life-or-death situation." It recommends that the total budget for AIDS education from public and private sources should approximate $1 billion annually by 1990.[65] The Surgeon General estimates that a comprehensive educational program could prevent as many as twelve to fourteen thousand deaths by 1991.[66]

Some people fear that educating people about safe sex and safe needle use may increase or insufficiently discourage sexual activity (in particular, homosexual activity) and drug use. Dr. Ronald Bayer suggests that "[o]ne of the reasons . . . that public dollars have been so scarce [for AIDS education] is that otherwise government would have to fund directly or indirectly educational campaigns which don't make homosexuality taboo."[67] The government is reluctant to face the tension between its criminal laws and the actual behavior of its citizens.

Nevertheless, educational programs are the only effective means that science has suggested to stop the spread of AIDS, and it is ultimately the responsibility of government to protect the health of its citizens. So far most efforts to stop the spread of AIDS have been undertaken by the gay community and have depended on volunteers. But, as the National Academy of Sciences has written, "[t]he most fundamental obligation for AIDS education rests with the federal government, which alone is situated to develop and coordinate a massive campaign. . . ."[68]

Community "Review" of AIDS Education Material

The federal government has placed a number of obstacles in the way of an effective national AIDS educational program. To qualify for federal funds, state and local health departments must comply with numerous conditions, perhaps the most cumbersome of which is the establishment of local review panels to consider the "bounds of explicitness" of risk-reduction literature.[69] These review panels are to be made up of no less than five persons representing a reasonable cross-section of the community and are *not* to be drawn predominately from the target groups. The local panels must approve in writing all educational materials before federal money will be allocated.[70]

The guidelines for the review panel require that any written materials be understood by a broad cross-section of educated adults, but be judged by a reasonable person not to be offensive. Audio-visual materials and pictorials are put to even greater scrutiny. The federal government requires that any visual material communicate by "inference rather than by any display of the anogenital area of the body or overt depiction of performance of 'safer sex' or 'unsafe sex' practices."[71]

The requirement for local review panels is curious and self-defeating, creating a bureaucratic obstacle to the swift production of effective materials. The prohibitions against portraying "the anogenital area" or depicting safe sex go against all the latest evidence on the effectiveness of educational plans directed toward behavior modification. Studies cited by the CDC suggest that educational materials be explicit and written in common terms that are understandable by the at-risk group.[72] The National Academy of Sciences says that "in order to achieve this aim, educators and educational materials must be free to use clear and direct, possibly colloquial, language that will be understood by those being addressed."[73] "Don't let him come in your mouth" tells risk-group members what to do in the language they themselves use to describe such acts. "Mutual exchange of bodily fluids is considered to be an unsafe sexual practice" does not. The slang used in the first example would not pass the scrutiny of a review panel—indeed, it may well have offended some readers of this chapter—but *it is precisely by virtue of its explicitness* that the discussion is educationally effective. The National Academy of Sciences' Committee on the National Strategy for AIDS has expressed concern about the CDC's directive for local review panels. The result of such a process, the committee noted, may be to stop frank, explicit information from getting to the areas where such information is most needed: regions outside those urban areas where there are large concentrations of high-risk groups and already greater awareness of routes of transmission.[74]

The San Francisco Department of Public Health specifically found that sexually explicit videotapes modeling "safe sex" were more likely to result in positive behavioral changes than written materials or inferential visual materials.[75] Gay men respond more favorably to the idea of safe sex when it is presented as pleasurable activity they can enjoy rather than as a drastic limitation on their sexual self-expression. A recent review of pornographic videotapes in *Advocate Men* (the gay male equivalent of *Playboy*) criticized the San Francisco AIDS Foundation's film "Lifeguard" because, "the actors were aware that they [we]re demonstrating techniques rather than truly enjoying the erotic aspects that can and should be a part of any sexual act, safe or not." Another film depicting safe sex, "Inevitable Love," was praised because the actors gave "really good performances" and, "[t]he film avoid[ed] being preachy about safe sex while endeavoring to encourage by example."[76]

The review panel regulations do not explicitly evoke the case law on obscenity but a brief examination of the leading obscenity case is helpful to an understanding of why the review panel requirement is problematic. *Miller v. California* lists three considerations that courts and juries must use to determine whether material is obscene: first, whether the "average person, applying contemporary community standards," would find that the work appeals to prurient interest; second, whether the work depicts or describes, in a patently offensive way, sexual conduct specifically defined by applicable state law; and finally, whether the work, taken as a whole, lacks serious literary, artistic, political, or scientific value. Only if the work violates *all three* criteria will it be considered "obscene." If judged obscene, a work is not protected by the First Amendment.[77]

The idea of using local review boards tracks the Court's belief that obscenity can only be judged against community values, and, consequently, cannot be defined by a national standard.[78] But finding that material offends the community is only one of three necessary elements of an obscenity judgment. Given the inherent scientific and societal value in curbing the spread of AIDS, it is difficult to argue that educational materials, no matter how explicit, lack overall scientific value. Indeed, the Supreme Court chose, as an example of non-obscene graphic material, "medical books for the education of physicians and related personnel."[79] Thus, the review panels, whatever else their justification, are not required to avoid obscenity in any legal sense. When the only known means of curbing an epidemic is education, but effective educational materials offend some members of the public, how should the interests of the public's sensibility and the public's health be balanced? When the cost of not offending someone is someone else's death, the answer to this question should be clear.

THE USE OF THE COURTS IN OBTAINING EFFECTIVE AIDS EDUCATION

The obstacles placed in the way of effective educational programs raise frustrating public policy and legal questions. Because the AIDS issue is so charged with public prejudice and fear, regulations and legislation designed to control AIDS must be analyzed with a critical eye to ensure that they do not reflect irrational and uneducated fears or a veiled attempt to oppress the groups at risk. Unfortunately, while the law may limit the use of the state's power to act irrationally in the name of public health, the law and courts are not very effective means for prompting public health departments to get such educational programs in place. However, at least three legal questions are worth raising. First, are there ways to limit the obstacles to effective education, such as the obscenity review panels? Second, can health departments be required to use educational efforts to curb the spread of AIDS before restrictive means such as quarantine are employed? Third, how can the public prompt public health departments to promote AIDS education when nothing is being done to curb the spread of AIDS in the community?

Challenging the Obstacles to Educational Programs

Although requirements such as community review panels are not mandated by obscenity law and seem to serve no health purpose, legal challenges to such obstacles may be difficult. Yet AIDS education is so important that suits based on several different theories are being considered and may soon be filed.

The First Amendment's mandate that government not interfere with free expression does not entail a governmental obligation to *fund* free expression. Moreover, even if the government does finance a forum for expression— whether a facility, or a medium of communication—the general public does not automatically have a right to use it.[80] The government may dedicate the forum to a specific purpose, opening it only to those whose use will further that purpose. What the government cannot do is bar people from using the forum merely because it disagrees with the ideas they wish to express.[81]

In these terms, the issue of the community review panel may be analogized to the recent case of *American Council of the Blind v. Boorstin*. For some fifteen years, *Playboy* had been one of the most popular offerings in the Library of Congress' braille magazine transcription program. In 1985, under

Congressional pressure to cease "promotion of sex-oriented magazines," the Library removed *Playboy* from its list. A group representing the beneficiaries of the program sued.[82]

In its decision, the U. S. District Court recognized that the government was under no obligation to publish *Playboy* or any other magazine in braille. Indeed, had the Library decided to cancel *Playboy* for reasons of cost, administrative convenience, or subscriber dissatisfaction, there would have been no First Amendment problem. But "[a]lthough individuals have no right to a government subsidy or benefit, once one is conferred, as it is here through the allocation of funds for the [braille magazine] program, the government cannot deny it on a basis that impinges on freedom of speech." Because it was based on official disapproval of *Playboy*'s content, the decision to remove the magazine from the program "was viewpoint-based discrimination impinging on freedom of expression."[83]

The allocation of funds by Congress for AIDS education arguably created a similarly protected forum. Yet the regulations mandating the review panels explicitly require an evaluation of the content of educational material. Given the value of explicitness in effective risk-reduction education, and in light of the underlying controversy over the morality of drug use, and gay and nonmarital sex, review by community panels is neither necessary to promote the government's educational purpose nor politically neutral as to content.

The review panels contemplated by the CDC might also be analogized to the unconstitutional "Book Review Committee" in *Board of Education, Island Trees Free School District No. 26 v. Pico*. In that case, the Supreme Court struck down a school board's decision to remove certain "anti-American, anti-Christian, anti-Sem[i]tic, and just plain filthy" books from the school library (including works by Kurt Vonnegut, Jr. and Richard Wright).[84] A plurality of the Court found that the board's lawful discretion to exclude books may not be exercised in a partisan or political manner.[85] It emphasized that this discretion must be exercised in harmony with the First Amendment, which protects the right to receive (as well as disseminate) information and ideas.[86] The regulation in *Island Trees*, the plurality argued, violated the First Amendment because it unduly burdened the right to receive ideas. It could be similarly argued that the review panels function like the book review committee in *Island Trees*: educational materials are brought to panels, which examine the substance of these materials to determine if they meet guidelines regarding their offensiveness. As in *Island Trees*, the motivation of the review panel should be scrutinized to determine if the panel's decisions are politically neutral, *i.e.*, not based on disagreement with the ideas but rather based on the educational value of the materials. There are, however, many weaknesses in the analogy to *Island Trees*; for example, the Court restricted its holding to the *removal* of school library books, recognizing the board's discretion in the *acquisition* of books and course materials.

A third line of attack is suggested by a recent case in the United States District Court for the Central District of California. In *Bullfrog Films, Inc. v. Wick*, the plaintiffs challenged regulations used to determine if a film was "educational" and therefore exempt from certain customs duties and licensing requirements when distributed internationally. The court found that the conferring of "educational status" was a governmentally-created benefit and could not be withheld on the basis of unconstitutional conditions.[87] The Court then analyzed the regulations and noted that even though it was necessary and appropriate for the government to review the content to determine if the material was "educational," the limited inquiry into content must be neutral as to viewpoint.[88] Since these regulations discriminated on the basis of political beliefs, they violated the First Amendment. A similar argument can be made about the CDC regulations. Review is not based on educational value, since social science literature seems to indicate that explicit materials are likely to be particularly effective. Rather, the restrictions incorporated in the regulations instruct reviewers to assess factors related to political concerns. Because *Bullfrog Films* characterizes the certification of the films as a "government-conferred benefit," it may be precedent for a claim that the review panel "certification process" is in violation of the First Amendment.

A possible nonconstitutional challenge to the review panel is that the Department of Health and Human Services is exceeding its statutory authority by promulgating restrictions not reasonably related to effective health education. Such a challenge would focus on the Public Health Service Act,[89] which authorizes "[t]he Secretary, acting through the Director of the Centers for Disease Control, to make grants to public and nonprofit private entities for information and education programs on, and for the diagnosis, prevention, and control of, acquired immune deficiency syndrome."[90] A court may be persuaded that in light of the urgent need for effective educational materials on AIDS, such unnecessary burdens as review panels should be struck down as outside the scope of the act. The act does not empower public health officials to protect "public decency" or "morality," but only to protect health in ways that are effective and responsive to the need for immediate action. The regulations as promulgated by the Department of Health Services may exceed the scope of the authority delegated by Congress and therefore could be set aside as beyond its power, or *"ultra vires."*[91]

Requiring the Use of Education before More Restrictive Means

The power of state health departments to devise ways to deal with the spread of AIDS is grounded in the police powers reserved to the states by the Constitution. The Supreme Court has recognized that a state has wide discretion in determining what measures are necessary to deal with persons afflicted

with contagious or infectious diseases. Such power is not unrestricted, however, and the limitations of the constitution will be enforced by judicial
review.[92] The power and its extent are discussed in Chapter 4 of this volume,
but one constitutional limitation is especially relevant to public education
on AIDS.

Many public health actions, such as isolation and quarantine, compromise
important constitutional rights to liberty and privacy. The Constitution forbids their application if a "less restrictive alternative" would accomplish the
same result. Many complexities in the application of this principle to health
measures remain unresolved. There is no clear standard, for example, for
comparing the costs and benefits of alternative proposals (to decide, for
instance, whether an alternative that is slightly less effective but significantly
less intrusive should be required). It is clear, however, not only that education is at present both the most effective and least restrictive means of
fighting AIDS' spread but also that courts dealing with public health measures
against the disease will take note of this.

The attempt to prevent unsafe sex by closing San Francisco's bathhouses
illustrates the role of the least restrictive alternative analysis. In late 1984,
following more than a year of trying to stop dangerous bathhouse sex through
unofficial education efforts and essentially voluntary guidelines, the City of
San Francisco closed fourteen bathhouses and bookstores. The health commissioner argued that this was the only way to prevent the unsafe homosexual
behavior. Challenging the closings in court, bathhouse owners argued that
the action implicated constitutional protections of privacy, requiring the city
to choose the least restrictive response. They argued that unsafe sex could
be eliminated by stricter rules enforced by the establishments themselves,
changes in the decor and lighting to discourage public sex, and random
health department checks, rather than by closing. The judge agreed, and
allowed the bathhouses to reopen under a regime similar to that proposed
by the owners.[93] In this case, because there were less restrictive means
available, the regulation that would require closing failed.

Nonetheless, least restrictive alternative analysis remains a *limitation* on
government action that may be invoked only if a particular health action
infringes upon a protected right. In that sense, it is purely reactive. It is not
a general requirement applied to all measures, and is only available after a
fundamental right has been infringed. Health actions such as contact tracing
or reporting of HIV antibody status may not be deemed to infringe a basic
right and so could be invoked despite evidence that education would be a
more cost-effective means of fighting AIDS. Despite this, the concept will be
important in the AIDS crisis. The least restrictive alternative analysis is a
logical component of any consideration of the fairness or necessity of an
action. Long before a health action is reviewed by a judge, the idea of a
least restrictive alternative should play a role in official calculations about

what actions ought to be taken.[94] Public health departments should be encouraged to develop comprehensive AIDS education programs before invoking more intrusive police powers.

Requiring Public Health Departments to Implement AIDS Education

There is no constitutional right to have the government act effectively. However, an argument might be made that state and local health departments have an affirmative statutory obligation to act effectively in the face of a health hazard, on the basis of a statutory grant of authority to the health department. State and local public health departments are authorized to act by legislation that defines their goals and duties. If the department fails to act when required by statute, challenges to that inaction may be brought in the form of mandamus or special actions. These are judicial orders to administrators to perform duties set out in statutes. For example, a Wisconsin statute concerned with public health and venereal disease requires the department to prepare for free distribution upon request from citizens of the state, printed information and instructions concerning venereal diseases.[95] Although this law was not enacted with AIDS in mind, it arguably creates a duty on the part of the health department to provide some AIDS education.

Since the increase in public awareness of the AIDS crisis, legislatures across the country have passed laws that specifically direct their state and local health departments to respond to the epidemic. This has resulted in some laws that create an affirmative duty with respect to AIDS education. California has a very comprehensive statute concerned with AIDS. The statute states as its legislative intent that the state should fund specified pilot AIDS education programs.[96] The programs include education for seropositive individuals, drug users, and the general public.[97] California continues to be the most active state in supporting AIDS education. This legislation makes education a duty of the health department and could be invoked should the health department fail to act consistent with that duty.

Conceivably, too, the government may be required to enforce a statutory obligation on a private party. For example, the Washington State Human Rights Commission has recognized the importance of education in preventing AIDS-related employment discrimination. The commission's *Draft Statement of Policy: AIDS and Employment* states, "when situations arise which threaten the maintenance of a discrimination-free working environment, education is required." Under this policy, an employer could be required to provide AIDS education if the environment in its workplace was discriminatory.[98]

Given our present knowledge concerning AIDS, education promises to be the most effective means to curb the spread of the disease and lessen AIDS-related discrimination. Although authorities such as the Surgeon General and the National Academy of Sciences strongly advocate AIDS education, funding for such education is lacking and substantial obstacles are blocking the swift production and distribution of educational material. Although not much can be done in the legal arena to improve the situation, the arguments in favor of education are compelling and should be useful to community groups in pressuring their local health departments to deal responsibly, compassionately, and effectively with AIDS. And, while courts normally defer to state officials' understanding of what their jobs require, there is precedent for a lawsuit to enforce specific statutory duties.

PART THREE
PRIVATE SECTOR RESPONSES TO AIDS

8

AIDS in the Workplace

ARTHUR S. LEONARD

Many employees in both the private and public sectors are either seropositive for antibodies to Human Immunodeficiency Virus (HIV), have symptoms of AIDS-Related Complex (ARC), or have AIDS as defined by the Centers for Disease Control. These employees do not pose a health threat in the workplace and, with the exception of some persons with acute symptoms, are able to carry out normal job responsibilities. Nevertheless, they may be *perceived* as threatening to co-workers and the business enterprise itself. This conflict between perception and reality poses difficult questions of public policy and practice. This chapter will provide a summary of potentially applicable legal principles and discuss some of their consequences for the rights and responsibilities of employers and employees.

Traditionally, employers had complete discretion to refuse to employ people under the "employment at will" rule. But a relatively new body of law, aimed at discrimination against the disabled, partially limits such discretion. The first part of this chapter discusses the conceptualization of AIDS as a handicap and how this affects the employment relationship.

Several states and cities have passed laws directly prohibiting either AIDS-based discrimination or use of blood tests to "screen" employees for AIDS. In addition, laws governing unemployment, health, and pension benefits may limit an employer's discretion. These laws are discussed in the second part. The third part describes labor laws governing the treatment of employees afraid to work owing to fear of AIDS. The chapter concludes that for reasons of law, public policy, compassion, and common sense, employers should educate themselves and their workforce to avoid AIDS-related discrimination.

AIDS AND LAWS PROHIBITING DISCRIMINATION AGAINST THE DISABLED

At the heart of the legal analysis is the conceptualization of AIDS, ARC, and seropositivity as "handicapping" conditions or "disabilities" within the meaning of laws regulating workplace practices. Since the 1970s, the federal government and almost all of the states have adopted legislation seeking to integrate people with disabilities into the mainstream of society.[1] The principle that an "otherwise qualified handicapped individual"[2] may not be denied the opportunity to participate has been adopted for several purposes, including increasing employment opportunities. If, as appears likely, AIDS is accepted as a handicapping condition, federal, state, and local statutes forbidding discrimination in hiring, termination, or employment conditions against the disabled would affect an employer's discretion in deciding whether to hire or terminate persons affected by AIDS.

The model disability discrimination statute is the federal Rehabilitation Act of 1973.[3] It was not intended to be a comprehensive employment discrimination statute for all sectors of the economy. Its employment provisions govern only federal employees, federal contractors, and programs receiving federal financial assistance. Nevertheless, together these provisions reach millions of workers.

Section 501 requires each "department, agency, and instrumentality" of the executive branch of the federal government to adopt an "affirmative action program" for the employment of "handicapped individuals."[4] (This requirement has been held not to apply to uniformed military personnel.[5]) Section 503 requires that any federal contract in excess of $2,500 contain a provision requiring the contractor to undertake affirmative action to employ "qualified handicapped individuals."[6] Under both sections, government agencies have the primary responsibility to enforce the protections.[7] This means that individuals who believe their rights have been abridged may not go to court but must instead complain to the appropriate agency.

The most broadly applicable part of the Rehabilitation Act may be Section 504.[8] It provides that "otherwise qualified handicapped individuals" may not be excluded from participation in, be denied the benefits of, or be subject to discrimination under "any program or activity" receiving federal financial assistance or conducted by any federal agency or the Postal Service. The Supreme Court has held that this provision applies to the employment policies of programs receiving federal financial assistance.[9] Like Sections 501 and 503, Section 504 may be enforced through complaints to the agency that is the federal funding source. Additionally, several federal courts have ruled that Section 504 gives individuals the right to sue their employers for discrimination.[10]

Despite its apparent breadth, the reach of Section 504 is the subject of debate. The Supreme Court has interpreted the phrase "any program or activity" to mean that within an organization, *only* the particular program receiving federal financing will be subject to the statute. There are, however, Congressional proposals pending to change this. The Supreme Court has also ruled that only *direct* recipients of federal funds are covered by Section 504.[11]

Virtually every state has also adopted some policy concerning the employment rights of the disabled. In more than forty states, the policy is found in a statute (frequently part of a general civil rights or fair employment law), and it is usually applicable to both the private and public sectors.[12] In a handful of states, statutory protection extends only to the public sector.[13] In one state, Delaware, there is no statutory policy, but a gubernatorial order covers public employment.[14] In addition, some municipalities have either by ordinance or executive order extended protection against employment discrimination to disabled persons.[15] Consequently, to determine whether a particular workplace is covered, one must consult state and local laws as well as the Rehabilitation Act.

AIDS as a Handicap

Laws prohibiting discrimination against the disabled will apply to people with AIDS, ARC, or seropositivity only if such conditions meet the legal definition of a handicap. The Rehabilitation Act defines the term "handicapped individual" as "any person who (i) has a physical or mental impairment which substantially limits one or more of such person's major life activities, (ii) has a record of such an impairment, or (iii) is regarded as having such an impairment."[16]

Definitions of terms such as "physical or mental impairment" and "major life activities" are found in regulations adopted by the agencies that administer the Rehabilitation Act. The "model" regulations issued by the Department of Health and Human Services (HHS) define "physical or mental impairment," in pertinent part, as "any physiological disorder or condition . . . affecting one or more of the following body systems: neurological; . . . respiratory . . . ; hemic and lymphatic; skin; . . . ."[17] Since HIV infection involves invasion and destruction of lymphocytes (white blood cells), it is clearly a "disorder or condition . . . affecting . . . [the] hemic and lymphatic [system]." HIV may also cause neurological damage (including dementia and meningitis). Opportunistic infections and other complications associated with AIDS include pneumonia, which affects the respiratory system, and Kaposi's sarcoma, a skin cancer.

HHS describes "major life activities" as functions such as caring for oneself, performing manual tasks, walking, seeing, hearing, speaking, breathing, learning, and working.[18] The medical complications associated with AIDS may impair most of the functions on this list, as may symptoms associated with ARC.

HIV infection that manifests itself as AIDS, therefore, appears to be a "handicap" under federal law, and ARC probably also fits the definition.[19]

Additionally, those who are infected but not experiencing debilitating symptoms would be covered by the third part of the Rehabilitation Act's definition of handicapped—people who "are regarded as having such an impairment"—if they are subject to adverse employer action once their condition is known. Even members of risk groups who are not infected (or not known to be infected) but who suffer adverse employment treatment because of the *perception* that they will present an AIDS-related risk could be protected under the "regarded as" category.[20]

Early uncertainty about the status of AIDS as a handicap centered on the question whether disabilities caused by infectious agents are covered by handicap discrimination laws. Some early decisions by administrative agencies and trial courts indicated an inclination to extend such coverage to AIDS, emphasizing the disease's disabling characteristics and epidemiological evidence against any serious risk of workplace contagion. However, in a controversial legal memorandum, the U.S. Justice Department took the position that Section 504 gives little protection to a person suffering viral infection. The memo argued that discrimination due to fear of contagion was not itself "handicap discrimination."[21] However, shortly after the Justice Department issued its memorandum, HHS issued its first ruling holding that an employer had violated Section 504 by refusing, allegedly due to fear of contagion, to reinstate an employee with AIDS who was able to work.[22] And, in November 1986, a federal judge ruling on the exclusion of a child with AIDS from a public school held that such exclusion could violate Section 504.[23]

On March 3, 1987, the U.S. Supreme Court provided considerable guidance on this question in *School Board of Nassau County v. Arline*.[24] In that case, the court of appeals had decided that tuberculosis, a medical condition caused by an airborne infectious agent, could be considered a handicap, but ordered trial on the issues of risk of infection to others and possible accommodations to the condition of the employee, an elementary school teacher. The Supreme Court affirmed the court of appeals' decision, rejecting the argument that discrimination against a handicapped person could be lawful if it was based on fears deriving from the handicap's contagious nature.[25] However, because Arline suffered from a condition which was actually disabling, the Court refrained from discussing hypothetically whether an individual who was infected but not otherwise physically impaired would be protected from discrimination due to fear of contagion.[26]

The Court sent the case back to the district court for trial on the question whether Arline was "otherwise qualified." The Court adopted a four-part test suggested by the American Medical Association in its *amicus* brief, requiring the trial court to base its decision on

[findings of] facts, based on reasonable medical judgments given the state of medical knowledge, about (a) the nature of the risk (how the disease is transmitted), (b) the duration of the risk (how long is the carrier infectious), (c) the severity of the risk (what is the potential harm to third parties) and (d) the probabilities the disease will be transmitted and will cause varying degrees of harm.[27]

It seems clear from *Arline* that the Supreme Court would consider AIDS or ARC to meet the Rehabilitation Act's definition of handicap. Although the Court refrained from dealing with the issue of asymptomatic carriers of infectious diseases, the opinion suggests that they too should be considered handicapped by approving HHS regulations which extend protection to persons who encounter discrimination because of the attitudes of others[28] and by commenting that "society's accumulated myths and fears about disability and disease are as handicapping as are the physical limitations that flow from actual impairment."[29]

As to the "otherwise qualified" portion of the analysis, the Court's approach contemplates a case-by-case determination of physical ability. The standard for determining whether the infectious nature of the disabling condition presents undue workplace risk is to be applied based on the best available medical evidence, and the Court advises deference to the opinions of public health officials.[30] Presently, the U.S. Public Health Service takes the position that the risk of spreading HIV infection in the workplace is normally nonexistent.[31]

The question whether a person with AIDS, ARC, or seropositivity (or any member of an AIDS risk group) will be considered a "handicapped individual" under state and local disability laws and executive orders depends on the wording of the laws, their legislative histories, and pertinent administrative and judicial interpretations. While the meaning assigned to "handicap" under the Rehabilitation Act may influence how state courts and agencies define it under their laws, states are not bound to follow the federal lead.

Many state laws adopt intact or with only minor variations the federal definitions; others adopt more expansive or restrictive definitions. For example, the New York Human Rights Law definition includes "medical" as well as "physical" and "mental" impairments and appears to provide coverage for such "impairments" even when they do not "prevent the exercise of a normal bodily function," as long as they are "demonstrable by medically accepted clinical or laboratory diagnostic techniques."[32] Washington's law offers perhaps the broadest definition of coverage: "A person will be considered to be handicapped . . . if he or she is discriminated against because of the condition and the condition is abnormal."[33] On the other hand, a few states provide no definition of "handicap" or "disability," leaving the task of definition to administrative agencies and courts,[34] while others provide narrow definitions focusing on particular impairments.[35]

A significant point of variation among the state and local laws is the "regarded as a handicap" category. In places where the statutes lack that category, people who do not actually have disabling symptoms may not find protection under the law, even though they encounter discrimination due to fears on the part of their employer or co-workers. Some state courts, however, have found such protection to be *implied* under the broad policy concerns underlying handicap discrimination law.

As with the federal Rehabilitation Act, the application of state laws to HIV disorders may depend upon whether the laws are read to cover diseases caused by infectious agents. Cases under state disability laws normally begin as complaints to state administrative agencies rather than court suits. As of this writing, charges involving AIDS-related discrimination have been filed with administrative agencies in several states, and so far, the trend appears to be in favor of coverage.[36] National Gay Rights Advocates, a San Francisco public interest law firm, made a survey of state agencies and published the results in September 1986.[37] Two-thirds of the states (thirty-four) had either made formal or informal decisions to interpret their laws to forbid AIDS-based discrimination. With few exceptions, the remainder of the states were either processing charges without expressing an opinion or had not considered the issue. No state had adopted the U.S. Justice Department's reasoning.

Agency determinations are subject to court review, and appeal is a lengthy process beyond the stamina or lifespan of many people with AIDS. Because it is unlikely that many cases will get to the courts, the willingness of agencies to accept and process charges and to pursue conciliation and settlements with employees has provided significant assistance to persons affected by the AIDS epidemic in a legal climate of some ambiguity and uncertainty.[38] If such administrative procedures do not yield a quick settlement, at least one state commission has strongly recommended that the enforcement agency seek interim injunctive relief on behalf of the complainant.[39]

Extent of Protection for Handicapped Individuals

Most handicap discrimination laws protect only *"otherwise qualified* handicapped individuals"[40]—that is, individuals who are physically and mentally capable of participation in the activity covered by the statute.[41] An employer is not obligated to continue employment of an individual whose physical condition makes reasonable job performance impossible.

The Rehabilitation Act and most state laws do require, however, that the employer be flexible in dealing with the disabled.[42] Regulations interpreting Section 504, for example, state that employers "shall make reasonable accommodation" to the employee's handicap unless they can show that accommodation "would impose an undue hardship" on the operation of the program.[43] The determination whether accommodation would impose an "undue hardship" is based on such factors as the overall size and nature of the program and the cost involved. Employers "are not required to find another job for an employee who is not qualified for the job he or she was doing," but otherwise qualified handicapped employees may not be denied "alternative employment opportunities reasonably available under the employer's existing policies."[44]

Major Handicap Law Issues

Issues that arise under federal, state, and local laws include the cost of employee benefits associated with AIDS, reactions of customers and fellow employees to the presence of a person perceived to present an AIDS risk, and the use of the blood tests to screen applicants and employees. Handicap discrimination laws subject employment decisions based on costs or the preferences of customers or other employees to relatively strict scrutiny, because the underlying policy of such laws is to enhance employment opportunities for handicapped people who are capable of working, even when financial and social costs of providing such opportunities may fall on employers, customers, and fellow employees. The large medical expenses generated by AIDS, the disease's unpredictable course, and the public fear of the disease make application of this policy particularly difficult.

The Expense Defense

Employers may claim that persons exposed to HIV might become ill in the future and present a serious drain on employee benefit plans. Courts have generally been skeptical about exclusion of protected persons based on *speculation* about future costs. The highest court in New York recently decided that an employer's fear of incurring future medical expenses due to a job applicant's obesity was not a valid defense to a discrimination charge, even though obese people as a group *are* more likely than others to develop certain health problems.[45]

Despite the high costs associated with AIDS, employer expense claims may often be unfounded. While it is likely that an employee who has actually been diagnosed with AIDS or ARC will incur substantial benefit costs, it is certainly speculative to say that any particular seropositive employee will someday develop AIDS or ARC. (For more information, see Chapter 2.) In addition, these expense arguments may raise issues under the Employee Retirement Income Security Act, discussed below.

These private decisions have broad effects, for a person with AIDS who loses employment may become uninsured and uninsurable, thus throwing substantially all medical and living costs on the public through reliance upon social welfare programs. Does it make sense in evaluating the impact of handicap discrimination laws to say that the employer, who has benefitted from the employee's labor, will now be required to shoulder some of society's burden in meeting these costs?

Under the U.S. system, which leaves primary health care to the private sector, such questions assume a significance they would not have in the other major Western industrial nations, where national health insurance programs theoretically remove the issue of the uninsurable individual.[46] In deciding whether to allow an employer to interpose an expense defense, an agency or court will also necessarily be deciding whether the expenses involved are to be borne directly by the government. Similarly, state insurance regulators deciding whether to grant insurance industry requests to use various devices, including blood tests, to screen out applicants who are "AIDS risks" are also necessarily deciding whether the state will have to assume the costs of benefits for those rendered uninsurable.

Customer and Co-Worker Preferences

Employers may claim that the preferences of customers or other workers justify a refusal to employ persons exposed to HIV. Courts in cases involving race and sex discrimination have generally not accepted such arguments. For example, a federal court ruled that an agency providing social welfare services to a minority clientele could not justify discrimination against a white employee by reference to client preferences.[47] Earlier, another appellate court had decided that alleged preferences of airline customers for service by female flight attendants could not justify the refusal to hire qualified male applicants for those positions.[48] Because of the underlying policy of forbidding discrimination, any argument that the exclusion of a person otherwise protected by civil rights law is necessary for the operation of a business is normally subject to rigorous review by the court.

However, the public's great fear of AIDS makes it appear somewhat harder to apply this strongly articulated public policy against discrimination based on co-worker or customer preference. The argument that a restaurant forced to employ a waiter with AIDS may lose all of its customers seems more serious, despite the medical experts' assurances that HIV will not be transmitted in such a setting, than an assertion that airline travelers prefer to be served by female flight attendants. A public that has been bombarded with mixed messages about a new "plague" may indeed choose to stay away. Should one force the employer to bear the associated financial burden?

A straightforward application of principles from other forms of discrimination law suggests that customer or co-worker preferences should not be given great weight; the question is really one of allocation of costs in connection with employment of the handicapped, rather than one of public health and safety, and the legislative body has made the allocation by providing the statutory protection. But the resolution of this issue is quite difficult and must depend upon the facts of individual cases. An employee who publicizes his seropositivity or illness to co-workers or customers may be less deserving of solicitude (in a job with public contact) than one who makes an effort to accommodate the reasonable business needs of the employer. If the publicity is traceable to the employer, it would seem unfair to make the employee suffer the consequences.

Carrying the co-worker problem a step further, could an employer defend against a discrimination charge by citing a strike threat or refusal to work by fellow employees? The scant precedent on the issue suggests that such co-worker reactions to a protected employee will not normally serve as a defense under employment discrimination statutes. If serious workplace disruption occurs, however, the employer may be able to justify the *temporary* removal of the feared employee while a reasonable attempt to restore order is made.

Testing

Employers worried about AIDS may consider requiring applicants or employees to be tested for exposure to HIV. Such testing presents considerable legal and practical difficulties. Generally, handicap discrimination statutes are interpreted to forbid *discriminatory* use of tests,[49] which means that employees who are members of a protected group may not be singled out for special testing not uniformly given to all employees or applicants. A blood test used to identify infected individuals would be lawful only if it were not used to discriminate against persons protected by law. In fact, since discrimination against seropositive employees may be prohibited by the Rehabilitation Act and most state and local handicap discrimination laws, adoption of antibody screening for purposes of employee selection or retention may be unlawful. However, there seems to be no general prohibition of *nondiscriminatory* medical testing in the private sector. Apart from those few jurisdictions which have specifically banned the use of antibody testing,[50] and the restrictions already noted under the Rehabilitation Act and comparable state and local regulations on the use of test results, it seems that employers are free to test without violating state and local handicap discrimination laws, although some local enforcement agencies have taken a different view of the matter.[51]

What is lawful in this situation may not, however, be what is prudent. The Centers for Disease Control (CDC) has indicated that there is no medical justification for using existing antibody tests for employee screening in virtually any civilian workplace.[52] HIV testing is an issue fraught with emotion and danger for the employer and the employee. Any adverse action against the employee after such testing takes place could expose the employer to serious charges under pertinent federal, state, or local handicap discrimination laws, because the inference of discriminatory intent would be quite strong. An employee who is forced to take a test and upon learning the result suffers severe emotional trauma might also assert a tort claim against the employer for "infliction of emotional distress." There is even the theoretical possibility of an invasion of privacy tort in this circumstance.[53]

Test results in personnel files may create significant confidentiality problems, especially in the health care industry, where there have already been significant instances of breach of confidentiality about AIDS and resultant workplace panic and discrimination charges.[54] Prudence may dictate that employers refrain from testing, even where it is lawful, because the risks involved outweigh the benefits, if any, to be derived from such activity.

OTHER APPLICABLE LAWS

Disability discrimination statutes are the most directly applicable of many laws that may influence employment decisions. Other state and federal statutes aimed primarily at such issues as pension protection and unemployment insurance may also affect employment decisions. Employers' rights to terminate "at will" may also be limited by contracts with labor organizations or under common-law principles modifying the "at will" rule in some jurisdictions. Finally, some states and cities have enacted laws directly prohibiting AIDS-related employment discrimination or testing.

Employee Retirement Income Security Act of 1974

The federal Employee Retirement Income Security Act of 1974 (ERISA),[55] applies generally to all employee benefit plans maintained by employers in the private sector,[56] including pension, life insurance and medical benefit plans.[57] Section 510 of ERISA prohibits an employer from discriminating against or discharging an employee for exercising rights under a benefit plan and from interfering with "the attainment of any right" to which an employee may become entitled under such a plan.[58] Consequently, an employer may not fire an employee with an AIDS-related condition because he has filed a claim for benefits, to prevent him from filing a claim in the future, or to prevent him from achieving eligibility for benefits. Section 510 may be enforced by direct federal court litigation brought by the employee or by the Secretary of Labor on behalf of the employee.[59] While it has rarely been invoked for this purpose, courts that have dealt with the question have held that firing a newly diagnosed employee to prevent future claims for medical benefits is unlawful.[60]

Most Americans' medical benefits are tied to their jobs; losing the latter means losing the former. Use of Section 510 could work a major change in the legal status of employees affected by serious illness. Current interpretations of handicap discrimination laws do not require employers to continue to employ workers who are physically incapable of working up to a reasonable standard. Section 510, however, suggests that an employer cannot automatically terminate such an employee. Advocates for people with AIDS may argue that employees who have earned medical coverage by working for an employer should be entitled to the assistance provided by that benefit plan. The provision might be interpreted to require employers to take a humane approach to the management of an employee disabled by sudden illness. Unpaid disability leave accompanied by continued medical coverage might be a partial solution to the problem, provided that an alternative funding source can be found for the employee's living expenses through disability insurance.

The potentially powerful protection afforded by Section 510 suggests that employers who have employee benefits plans should seriously consider adopting a general policy for dealing with employees who have life-threatening illnesses. The policy should include preservation of earned benefits rights. In addition to being humane, a coherent policy protecting benefits will probably be less costly and disruptive than attempts to avoid payment of legitimate claims.

Amendments to ERISA in 1986 create an additional obligation with respect to employee benefits by requiring the employer to allow an employee who is discharged for reasons other than gross misconduct to continue to participate in the employer's group health plan for up to eighteen months.[61] Although the employer may condition such participation on payment of premiums by the employee, the premiums may not be more than 2 percent above the normal premium for inclusion in the plan by an active employee, the employee has the right to spread out the payments on a monthly basis, and the coverage offered must be the same as that provided active employees.

Unemployment Insurance, Workers Compensation, and Social Security

Employees who are discharged solely because of their medical condition at a time when they are physically able to work are undoubtedly eligible for unemployment insurance benefits, since their discharges could not be said to be for "just cause" or "misbehavior" on the job, the usual bases of disqualification after an involuntary termination of employment. The same should be true of individuals—such as relatives or close friends of persons with AIDS—who are not infected but who lose their jobs because of AIDS panic. Caring for persons with AIDS may also give rise to valid claims. In an unpublished 1985 decision, an administrative judge in California ruled that the life partner of a person with AIDS was eligible for unemployment benefits after he resigned his job in order to take care of his dying partner.[62]

Persons with AIDS are probably not entitled to Workers Compensation benefits. To be eligible, employees would have to prove that this illness resulted from *work-related transmission* of HIV. However, if knowledge about AIDS advances to the point of establishing cofactors for development of medical complications and such cofactors are shown to be work-related, Workers Compensation might enter the picture.

Eligibility for Social Security Disability Insurance benefits for those actually diagnosed with AIDS has been provided for by special regulation, under which AIDS is considered presumptively disabling.[63] In cases falling short of the CDC definition, proof of actual disability is still required of the applicant for benefits. The CDC is working on a surveillance definition for ARC, which may provide a basis for extending presumptive disability coverage further.

Collective Bargaining Agreements

Although less than a fifth of the civilian workforce is covered by collective agreements, such agreements are in effect in many workplaces in states having a high incidence of AIDS cases, including New York and California. Such agreements affect the rights and responsibilities of covered employees and employers. Collective bargaining agreements almost universally require "just cause" for discharge and subject discharge decisions to a grievance arbitration procedure, under which an impartial arbitrator is authorized to make a final and binding determination.

Whether seropositivity is "just cause" for discharge has not yet been faced in any published arbitration award, but, to judge by the work-relatedness standards normally applied by arbitrators,[64] in the absence of any impairment of work performance or demonstrable risk to other employees or customers, seropositivity should not be considered "just cause." Discharge of employees with ARC or AIDS creates more difficult issues. Arbitrators generally recognize the right of employers to establish and maintain reasonable standards of job attendance and productivity and normally decide that employers may discharge employees who do not meet those standards.[65] However, arbitrators are usually sensitive to allegations of discrimination in the enforcement of such rules. If an employer discharges a person with AIDS or ARC on grounds of poor attendance or productivity, an arbitrator would view the justification with suspicion if other employees with attendance or productivity problems have been treated in more accommodating fashion in the past.

In addition to requiring just cause for discharge, some collective bargaining agreements contain substantive and procedural rules for handling issues such as disability leave, sick leave, benefits entitlement, and recall from leave. An employer cannot avoid these rules merely because the illness in question is AIDS-related. In an unpublished arbitration decision, for example, a major airline's grounding of a flight attendant with AIDS was judged to violate contract provisions requiring an individualized medical determination of fitness for duty and danger to the health of co-workers or customers.[66]

AIDS-Specific Laws

Some cities and states have enacted laws that address AIDS-related employment issues directly. In several California cities, including Los Angeles, San Francisco, Oakland, West Hollywood, and Berkeley, and in Austin, Texas, ordinances forbid discrimination against persons with AIDS, ARC, or persons perceived to have AIDS.[67] Because of the publicity these laws have received, they may become models for similar legislation elsewhere. The laws typically recognize the same employer defenses found in handicap discrimination laws, allowing employers to discharge only employees who cannot meet reasonable work standards, and they generally forbid use of HIV testing to screen employees or applicants.

In California, Florida, Massachusetts, and Wisconsin, legislation has been enacted restricting use of antibody testing as an employment screening device,[68] and similar proposals are pending in other jurisdictions. Much AIDS-related employment discrimination since mid-1985 has involved use of these tests, so the restrictions may be the most significant area of AIDS-specific legislation, especially since discrimination on the basis of the disease itself is probably already unlawful under most state handicap discrimination laws. Although these laws are very new, initial experience under them parallels that under handicap discrimination laws: active enforcement results in settlement of virtually all charges of discrimination without protracted and expensive litigation. Enforcement officials in Los Angeles reported that of the first forty-five cases under that city's law, all cases were settled or near settlement.[69]

Common-Law Rights

Several state courts have recognized exceptions to the common-law rules governing "at will" employment, based on theories of implied contract, tort, or public policy. In states where such exceptions exist, the discharge or segregation of an employee with AIDS may give rise to a civil action in contract or tort. In California, for example, it is reported that many persons with AIDS who were discharged in violation of personnel-manual provisions or in an egregiously offensive manner have brought common-law actions and obtained substantial money settlements.[70]

In addition to wrongful-discharge claims, employees who suffer adverse treatment in the workplace due to fear of AIDS may assert tort claims based upon infliction of emotional distress or invasion of privacy, depending upon the circumstances. In Massachusetts, a trial court has recognized a tort action for invasion of privacy under a state privacy statute on behalf of an employee with AIDS whose supervisor failed to keep confidential the nature of the employee's medical condition.[71]

Common-law actions, where appropriate, may provide faster and larger monetary relief to persons with AIDS than administrative or court proceedings under statutes. Because larger damages can be asserted, defendants are more likely to negotiate settlements advantageous to the employees.

Dealing with Frightened Co-workers

Employers frequently ask whether they may take disciplinary steps against employees who refuse to work because of fear of AIDS. In a unionized workplace, the question will probably be subject to a grievance procedure authorized by the collective bargaining agreement. In the absence of such a collective agreement, or in a situation where the union itself is demanding the removal of a worker with AIDS or a modification in job tasks owing to fears of AIDS, various provisions of the Labor Management Relations Act (LMRA)[72] may come into play.

Concerted Action

Collective action by employees holds a special status under the LMRA, Section 7 of which provides that "employees shall have the right . . . to engage in . . . concerted activities for the purpose of . . . mutual aid or protection."[73] The act further protects employees from discharge or discipline that might "interfere with, restrain, or coerce" them in exercising rights guaranteed under Section 7.[74] In *National Labor Relations Board v. Washington Aluminum Co.*, the Supreme Court held that a group of nonunion employees that had refused to work in extreme cold was protected from discharge under these provisions.[75]

The question of whether a group of nonunion employees who refuse to work owing to fears of AIDS will be protected does not have a simple answer, because the National Labor Relations Board (NLRB) has not adopted a precise legal standard for judging employees' claims of danger. Although the board has frequently stated that the good faith rather than the reasonableness of employees' fears is the appropriate test in deciding whether their action is protected,[76] it has never had to confront an issue quite like AIDS before.

It is difficult to compare AIDS with other issues of safety in the workplace. The consensus of opinion among medical experts and public health officials is that HIV is not casually transmitted, but public opinion polls indicate that a large portion of the public believes that it *can* be, despite these assurances. Such a belief is based more on emotion than reason, given the epidemiology of the disease, but there seems no reason to question the good faith of those who hold it. Thus, the stage is set for a difficult decision by the NLRB if an actual case comes before it.

Employers concerned about the situation should be aware that even if a work refusal is protected, the employer is not totally constrained from acting to maintain his business. Employees who refuse to work may lawfully be replaced, if necessary to maintain operations. However, the refusal of employees to work, although protected under the LMRA, will not serve as a defense to a charge of discrimination if the employer seeks to solve the problem at the expense of the employee with AIDS.

Unionized employees working under a collective bargaining agreement may have a more limited right to protest allegedly dangerous conditions. The inclusion of a no-strike provision in the agreement, if coupled with a grievance arbitration provision, will constitute a waiver of the employees' right to engage in concerted work protests during the term of the agreement.

However, the LMRA allows for situations in which a union may be justified in calling a safety-inspired strike, despite such a waiver. Section 502 provides that "quitting of labor" is not to be considered a strike if it is done "in good faith because of abnormally dangerous conditions for work at the place of employment."[77] According to the Supreme Court, a union must have "ascertainable, objective evidence" to support its conclusion that an abnormally dangerous condition exists in order for the employees to come under the protection of Section 502.[78] It seems unlikely that this objective test would be met where AIDS is at issue, given present medical knowledge.

Individual Action

The LMRA is concerned primarily with concerted activity. If an *individual* employee refuses to work, Section 7 is relevant only if the individual is claiming that the union contract protects his refusal, in which case the matter will be resolved through the grievance procedure. In *Minnesota Department of Corrections v. A.F.S.C.M.E. Council 6*,[79] for example, a prison guard discharged for refusing to conduct "pat searches" of prisoners for fear of contracting AIDS won back his job in an arbitration proceeding.

In a nonunion setting, a possible source of statutory protection for an individual employee who refuses to work is a regulation issued by the Occupational Safety and Health Administration (OSHA); the regulation protects an employee who decides not to work "because of a reasonable apprehension of death or serious injury coupled with a reasonable belief that no less drastic alternative is available."[80] However, a work refusal due to fear of "catching AIDS" in the workplace is unlikely to be protected under this regulation, because a reasoned response to the AIDS situation would not result in such an apprehension; furthermore, even in workplaces where exposure to infected blood is possible, safety measures can be taken that would provide a "less drastic alternative" for the employee.

In a recent decision under a state counterpart to OSHA, state occupational safety and health officials in California upheld transfers for rehabilitative training of nurses who refused to carry out their duties for fear of "catching AIDS."[81] As in the Minnesota prison case, the problem centered on a demand by employees to use extra protective gear that the employer believed to be unnecessary.[82]

Employee Education

Like the question of blood testing, the question of how employers can or should react to work refusals connected to fears of AIDS provides an instance where what the law allows is less significant than what makes good labor-relations sense. Discharging employees because of their panic reactions does not seem an effective way to deal with a situation that might settle down with appropriate efforts at employee education.

Of course, employee education must be handled carefully. The Minnesota prison case is instructive. Attempting to avoid workplace problems, the

prison issued written memoranda to prisoners and to guards. The memorandum to inmates summarized the state of medical knowledge about viral
transmission and provided practical advice on how to avoid contagion, concluding that "[n]o one really knows all the ways that AIDS is transmitted,
so be careful." The memorandum to the prison guards took a slightly different tone, describing AIDS as "a rather scary problem." Both memoranda
at least intimated that casual transmission of the virus was possible. While
the memoranda were intended to reassure (and apparently did reassure most
of the inmates and guards), one guard's panic was exacerbated, or so the
arbitrator found in ordering his reinstatement. While acknowledging
that refusal to perform the job would ordinarily justify a discharge, the arbitrator held that the employer had acted unreasonably in refusing to allow the
guard to use gloves for pat searches and had contributed to the guard's
fears by issuing the ambiguous memoranda. Furthermore, the warden's
refusal to deal thoughtfully with the guard's panic made a difficult situation worse.

Recognizing the sincerity of employee fears and attempting to deal with
them effectively makes more sense than inflexibly invoking disciplinary
measures. News reports about successful employee education programs show
that a sensitive and carefully thought-out effort by the employer can make
the question of employee discipline superfluous.[83] Such a program should
be integrated into an overall health and safety education program. If possible, knowledgeable medical professionals should participate so that employees can have their questions answered directly. Company policies for
dealing with the problems presented by serious illnesses should be developed
and communicated to line supervision, so that company policy on a sensitive
matter (that could lead to litigation) is not made on an ad hoc basis by the
line supervisor.

The workplace issue here is *not* a matter of employee protection versus
public health, since employment of persons with AIDS does not appear to
pose any particular threat to the health and well-being of fellow workers or
the general public. Once that is understood, other less dramatic but equally
important policy concerns arise.

AIDS is a catastrophic illness that strikes mainly young and middle-aged
people. Most people with AIDS have not worked long enough to be eligible
for early retirement pensions or old-age disability coverage. An employee
who loses a job will also lose insurance coverage; with loss of the regular
income stream and the relatively low level of public benefits, the individual
is unlikely to be able to afford conversion of employee group coverage to
adequate individual coverage, and may also be unable to afford current
living space or to meet outstanding financial obligations. In major metropolitan areas, the main centers of AIDS, housing tends to be quite expensive,
and there is a housing crisis among people with AIDS who are unemployed.

These economic facts argue strongly in favor of interpreting existing laws to require employers to keep employees with AIDS on their payrolls as long as those people are able to work and want to work. Furthermore, the compassionate response for an employer would be to continue an employee on disability leave if the employee becomes too ill to work. For larger employers with sophisticated personnel staffs, careful case management of the disability coverage for the employee can maximize effectiveness while holding down unnecessary costs. Humane responses to AIDS may not be as expensive as many employers fear and will benefit them in terms of employee morale and peace of mind.

9

Screening Workers for AIDS

MARK A. ROTHSTEIN

Americans have virtually limitless confidence in the ability of new technology to solve problems. In some instances, however, this confidence has been misplaced, either because the new technology was deficient or because it was introduced without a thorough consideration of its legal, ethical, and social consequences. The medical screening of workers for AIDS and AIDS-related conditions presents a case in point of the benefits and dangers of technological responses to new problems.

In part, that is because medical screening of workers brings together two fields—health care and personnel management—each of which has a propensity to apply new technology to problems that have significant nontechnological dimensions. For example, in the health-care field, new technologies such as the artificial heart, in vitro reproductive techniques, and heroic life support systems all raise important social issues. Similarly, many personnel managers have waded into controversy by too casually using polygraphs to combat pilferage, psychological testing to screen out applicants with behavioral problems, and urinalysis to counter drug abuse.

Given these inclinations, it was predictable that one response to the threat of AIDS in the workplace would be a call for massive blood screening of applicants and employees, leading to the rejection or dismissal of all whose test results appear to reveal infection by the Human Immunodeficiency Virus (HIV), the virus associated with AIDS. But while the development of the HIV antibody test was an important step in combatting the spread of AIDS through donated blood, its use in employment screening is both medically and legally problematic. The most widely used test, ELISA, is not reliable when used for large-scale screening of people. Further, because HIV infection in itself neither endangers coworkers nor affects their ability to work, an employer has little need to know a worker's antibody status. Indeed, because antibody status is generally not relevant to employment decisions, its use by employers may violate laws prohibiting discrimination against the handicapped. Finally, even when properly used, the test generates information that must be kept confidential; any careless use could be very damaging to the worker and costly to the employer.

The first part of this chapter presents a framework for analyzing medical screening questions in general and AIDS-related screening in particular. The second section examines the HIV antibody test, explaining what information the test was designed to yield, and how accurately it does so. The third part describes the limitations placed on the screening of employees by local, state, and federal law. Finally, the chapter concludes that use of the test in employment screening, even if legal, creates serious practical and ethical problems that outweigh any possible benefits.

MEDICAL SCREENING OF WORKERS

General Principles

Unlike employee-initiated check-ups, medical screening of workers by employers is usually tied to an actual or potential employment action. For instance, medical screening at the hiring stage determines in part whether an applicant will be employed. Once an employee is on board, screening may be used to determine job assignment. Later, medical screening may be used periodically to determine continuing fitness for the job and, in the event of injury or illness, to find out when or whether the employee is fit to return to work. Thus, it is an integral part of employers' ongoing efforts to maintain a healthy, safe, and productive workforce, and to minimize the costs associated with accidents and illness.[1]

It is helpful to divide medical screening into the assessment of current health status and the assessment of future health status ("predictive screening"). An employer's appraisal of current health status involves determining whether an individual, with reasonable accommodation (such as adding ramps for workers unable to use stairs), can safely and efficiently perform the requirements of the job. Predictive screening, on the other hand, involves determining whether an individual who is currently capable of performing the job has an unacceptably high risk of developing future health problems that would preclude safe and efficient job performance. From a medical standpoint, it is sometimes difficult to distinguish between the two. From a legal standpoint, however, the distinction is often critical, because predictive screening is more likely to run afoul of laws prohibiting discrimination in employment on the basis of handicap.

Medical assessments of workers' *current* physical abilities and limitations have been used widely since the turn of the century and are relatively uncontroversial. Indisputably, certain jobs require good vision, hearing, reflexes, balance, strength, coordination, or other attributes, the presence of which can be determined by means of medical questionnaires, examinations, and laboratory procedures. (There is, of course, inevitable debate about which jobs require which attributes.)

Predictive screening, however, focuses not on current ability or capacity, but on the likelihood that the capacities of particular employees will be substantially diminished in the foreseeable future. This is a highly speculative enterprise because individuals vary markedly in their susceptibility to illness and impairment, for reasons scientists do not fully understand. Increasingly, however, certain genetic, biochemical, physiological, and behavioral factors have been correlated with increased risk of future health problems. The key to predictive screening is identifying these factors.

The list of predictive screening factors is long and varied, ranging from genetic make-up, through ethnic background, to lifestyle and occupational history. For some factors, such as cigarette smoking (especially in combination with certain occupational exposures, such as asbestos), there is overwhelming evidence of an increased risk of serious illness. For other factors, such as psychological make-up, the evidence of increased risk is only suggestive or theoretical.

Numerous considerations play a part in determining whether an employer is legally, medically, and ethically justified in restricting an individual's employment opportunities based on a finding of "increased risk." These considerations include relative risk, absolute risk, severity of consequences, reversibility of illness, latency of illness, risk acceptability, and risk management. For example, the longer the time until the health problem is expected to materialize, the more speculative the prediction is from a scientific standpoint. In turn, the weaker the scientific basis for predictive screening, the more problematic the screening is from a legal, ethical, and policy standpoint.

AIDS Screening

An employer's assessment of the current health status of persons with AIDS or ARC involves several inquiries. The first issue that usually arises is whether an individual with AIDS, ARC, or a related condition is too ill to perform a job safely and efficiently. This is a legitimate area of inquiry, so long as AIDS-related conditions are evaluated in the same manner as are other medical conditions. The employer's focus should not be on the condition itself, but rather on its effects. Exposure to HIV (and the consequent development of antibodies to it) does *not* in itself impair job performance. Persons with AIDS or ARC, however, must be evaluated on a case-by-case basis. Many persons with ARC have only intermittent or mild symptoms. Even individuals with clinical or "full-blown" AIDS may have periods of remission during which they are physically well enough to work and would benefit psychologically and financially from being allowed to do so.

Whenever an employee's or applicant's ability to work is impaired, a second question arises: would a reasonable adjustment in working conditions eliminate the problem? "Reasonable accommodation" to the special needs of workers with AIDS or ARC may be required by laws protecting the handicapped. (Workers who are seropositive and asymptomatic will normally not need special accommodations.) Adjustments that could help a person with AIDS or ARC remain on the job include flexible work schedules (to allow visits to the doctor) and transfers to less strenuous tasks.

A third question that often arises is whether working conditions pose a significant health risk to immunosuppressed employees. It is possible, though unlikely in most settings, that the risk of exposure to infections in the workplace is greater for a person with AIDS or ARC than is the risk elsewhere. Such decisions, however, should be made on an individual basis by a physician familiar with the worker's medical record.

A final question is whether a seropositive person, or one who has AIDS or ARC, poses a health risk to coworkers or the public. According to the Centers for Disease Control, there is no medical justification for refusing to employ health-care, personal-service, food-service, or other workers who have AIDS or ARC, or who have been exposed to the virus. To be sure, in the unlikely event a person with AIDS contracted an opportunistic infection that proved to be readily transmissible, the individual should be excluded from the workplace if less drastic means of protecting against transmission are not available. Such decisions, however, should be made case-by-case, and should be based on sound, first-hand medical opinion.

In contrast to these attempts to assess the current employability of persons with AIDS or ARC, HIV antibody testing of applicants and employees is a form of *predictive screening* that could lead to rejection or firing of currently fit individuals because they are deemed to pose a *future* health risk. As the following discussion will show, this use of the test is not medically justified at the present time. The most commonly used test and test format produce a large number of incorrect results when employed as a general screening tool. Furthermore, even a true positive test result does not tell us whether the tested individual actually has AIDS or ARC or is certain to develop either condition. Even if it were shown that all or substantially all seropositive persons eventually develop clinical AIDS, the inquiry would shift rather than end, and the question would arise whether a given individual was *currently* well enough to perform the job.

HIV TESTING

The Test and What it Measures

In 1982, it was established that AIDS was being spread through the transfusion of blood and Factor VIII, a blood plasma product used by hemophiliacs.

Although only two percent of reported AIDS cases had been traced to trans-fusion,[2] the Public Health Service and the Food and Drug Administration (FDA) issued guidelines on March 4, 1983, designed to ensure the safety of the nation's blood supply.[3] The guidelines asked blood-collection centers: (1) to provide information about AIDS to donors; (2) to ask donors specific questions regarding signs and symptoms of AIDS; and (3) to advise donors in high-risk groups that they should not donate blood.

The discovery of HIV at the end of 1984 paved the way for the development of tests to screen the nation's supply of blood and plasma. The National Cancer Institute (NCI) developed the initial technology, then awarded non-exclusive, royalty-bearing licenses to five private firms to produce commer-cial antibody tests.[4]

On March 2, 1985, after several months of testing, the FDA approved the first of the tests for commercial use.[5] Although the approved tests differ slightly, all use the Enzyme-Linked Immunosorbent Assay (ELISA) technique to detect antibodies to HIV.[6] The test measures the presence of antibodies stimulated by the AIDS virus. (To explain the technique in somewhat more detail: HIV antigens are placed in microtiter wells and exposed to the test serum. Any HIV antibodies present in the serum attach to the HIV. Then another antibody that attaches to human antibodies is introduced. This second antibody is bound to an enzyme that produces a color, the intensity of which is proportional to the amount of human antibody binding to the HIV antigens. The amount of the color is measured spectrophotometrically and is compared with known positive and negative controls.)

The ELISA test is relatively inexpensive, costing between two and three dollars a test.[7] To be accurate, however, an ELISA test with a positive result should be repeated and then confirmed by another test procedure. The most commonly used confirmation test, the Western Blot, is much more expensive (about a hundred dollars), difficult, and time-consuming to perform.[8] (In this technique, HIV antigens are separated by electrophoresis and then blot-ted onto a special paper. The transferred antigens are then exposed to the test serum and any specific antibodies present react with the specific antigen bands.) The Western Blot identifies antibodies to proteins of a specific molecular weight, and therefore helps to eliminate false positives. Of sam-ples that initially show positive on the ELISA test, from 50 to 60 percent do not repeat positive in either the ELISA test or the Western Blot.[9]

It is important to note what the HIV antibody test does and does not measure. First, the test does *not* identify individuals with AIDS. The Centers for Disease Control defines AIDS by its clinical symptoms (such as the pres-ence of opportunistic infections or Kaposi's sarcoma). While a positive an-tibody test may help support a diagnosis, the test is not a primary diagnostic tool.[10] Further, a positive test does not necessarily mean that a person will get AIDS in the future. Although estimates have been revised upward several times, it is projected that only from 25 to 50 percent of seropositive persons will develop AIDS within five to ten years of seroconversion.[11]

Second, the test does not identify individuals with ARC, whose definition is also based on clinical features (for instance, fever, weight loss, lymphadenopathy, diarrhea, fatigue, night sweats) and by laboratory abnormalities indicative of immunodeficiency. The test does not necessarily predict ARC, either. According to most estimates, only a quarter of seropositive persons who do not develop AIDS will develop ARC.[12]

Third, the test does not identify all blood containing the AIDS virus. Since it was designed to detect only nonneutralizing antibodies stimulated by the virus, the test would not identify an individual as positive during the period of time between exposure to the virus and seroconversion—the development of antibodies—which usually takes from six to eight weeks, but may take a year or more.[13] It also would not identify as positive individuals whose immune systems were so severely damaged by the virus that they were not producing antibodies.[14] (To be sure, such seriously ill people are unlikely to be present in the employment setting.) On the other hand, a *false* positive result may be caused by contamination, technician error, or confounding medical conditions.[15]

The Accuracy of the Test

Before discussing the accuracy of AIDS antibody tests, we must address how accuracy in medical tests is measured.[16] The key concepts are "sensitivity" and "specificity." The sensitivity of a test is a measure of its ability to identify persons with the tested-for condition. It is the percentage of persons with the condition who register a positive test result:

$$\frac{\text{true positive test results}}{\text{persons with condition (true positives + false negatives)}} \times 100 \text{ percent}$$

Therefore, if 100 persons have a condition and the test is able to identify ninety of them, the test would be 90 percent sensitive.

The specificity of a test is a measure of its ability to identify persons who do *not* have a condition. It is the percentage of persons free of the condition who register a negative test result:

$$\frac{\text{true negative test results}}{\text{persons free of condition (true negatives + false positives)}} \times 100 \text{ percent}$$

Therefore, if 100 persons are free of a condition and the test is able to identify ninety of them, the test would be 90 percent specific.

The "positive predictive value" of a test refers to the value of a positive test result in identifying the presence of a condition. It is the percentage of persons whose test results are positive who actually have the condition:

$$\frac{\text{persons with condition (true positives)}}{\text{positive test results (true positives + false positives)}} \times 100 \text{ percent}$$

The "negative predictive value" of a test refers to the value of a negative test result in identifying the absence of a condition. It is the percentage of persons whose test results are negative who actually are free of the condition:

$$\frac{\text{persons without condition (true negatives)}}{\text{negative test results (true negatives + false negatives)}} \times 100 \text{ percent}$$

In other words, when a test is negative, the negative predictive value represents the likelihood that the condition is actually absent.[17]

Originally, the HIV antibody test was designed to screen blood, not people. In screening blood, false positives are not a serious problem; the only cost is the precautionary destruction of some healthy blood. False negatives, on the other hand, can be disastrous. A false negative means that blood carrying HIV will slip into the blood supply. Because it is so important to minimize the number of false negatives in testing the blood supply, the key measures of the test's effectiveness in screening blood are sensitivity and negative predictive value. If the sensitivity and negative predictive value are very close to 100 percent, the number of false negatives will be very small, and the blood supply will be quite safe.

When the HIV antibody test is used to screen people, however, false positives, not false negatives, are the serious problem. False positives deceive employers and insurers into labeling healthy people as AIDS risks. As a result healthy people may suffer discrimination as well as anguish from being told, incorrectly, that they have a chance of developing an incurable disease. Because false positives need to be minimized when the test is used to screen people, its specificity and positive predictive value are the most important measures of its accuracy. If the specificity and positive predictive value approach 100 percent, the number of false positives will be very small, and few healthy people will be identified incorrectly as HIV carriers.

There have been only a few studies of the sensitivity and specificity of the various ELISA tests,[18] and the figures vary according to the test used and the way borderline results are counted. The most widely cited figures show a range of sensitivity from 93 to 99 percent and a specificity of about 99 percent.[19] The predictive value of the test, however, varies greatly depending on the prevalence of seropositivity in the tested population. The following tables illustrate how important prevalence is to the predictive value of a test.

The prevalence of seropositivity in high-risk groups may range from 50 to 87 percent.[20] Table 1 looks at a population (for example, intravenous drug users in Newark, New Jersey) in which 50 percent of all individuals have been infected by, and therefore have developed antibodies to, HIV. The table assumes that the sensitivity of the test is 96 percent and that its

TABLE 1
Predictive Value of a Test with a Sensitivity of 96%, Specificity of 99%,
Prevalence of 50%, and 10,000 Subjects

Subjects	True Positive Results (TP)	False Positive Results (FP)	True Negative Results (TN)	False Negative Results (FN)
Persons with condition (5,000)	4,800	N.A.	N.A.	200
Persons free of condition (5,000)	N.A.	50	4,950	N.A.

specificity is 99 percent. The "condition" tested for is exposure to (but not necessarily presence of) HIV. The positive predictive value of the test $\frac{TP}{(TP \text{ and } TP)}$ 4,800/4,850 or 98.969 percent. The negative predictive value of the test $\frac{TN}{(TN \text{ and } FN)}$ is 4,950/5,150 or 96.1 percent.

The total number of seropositive Americans has been estimated at from one to one and a half million people.[21] Table 2 looks at a population of job applicants and assumes that 1 percent of its members are seropositive.

The positive predictive value of the test (TP/TP + FP) in this population is 96/195 or 49.23 percent. The negative predictive value of the test (TN/TN + FN) in this population is 9,801/9,805 or 99.959 percent.

These tables illustrate three important points about the use of HIV tests. First, the test is very accurate in screening blood donations. So long as the prevalence of infection in the donors is very low, the negative predictive

TABLE 2
Predictive Value of a Test with a Sensitivity of 96%, Specificity of 99%,
Prevalence of 1%, and 10,000 Subjects

Subjects	True Positive Results (TP)	False Positive Results (FP)	True Negative Results (TN)	False Negative Results (FN)
Persons with condition (100)	96	N.A.	N.A.	4
Persons free of condition (9,900)	N.A.	88	9,801	N.A.

value is very high. Because high-risk donors are excluded from blood donation,[22] the estimated percentage of seropositive blood donors is from 0.1
to .01 percent.[23] The latter figure computes to a negative predictive value
of 99.99959 percent.[24] Thus, we can be confident that our blood supply is
free of infection.

Second, as Table 1 shows, the test is accurate when used in high-risk
groups in which the prevalence of seropositivity is great. Therefore, high-
risk individuals who elect to be tested can be confident that their result is
accurate.

Third, the test is quite inaccurate when used in the general population,
where the prevalence of HIV antibodies is low. Any test is likely to produce
a large number of false positives whenever the tested-for condition affects
only a tiny percent of the group tested. As Table 2 indicates, when the AIDS
antibody test is used on a general population, such as job applicants, the
positive predictive value of the AIDS antibody test plummets to less than 50
percent. This means, roughly, that for every person with HIV antibodies
detected by the test, one person free of the antibodies would incorrectly be
identified as a carrier—and as a result could be subject to discrimination
and needless psychological trauma.

The large number of false positives generated by initial screening tests
makes it essential to confirm all positives with a second ELISA and a follow-
up Western Blot. But employers may not be willing to incur the considerable
extra expense involved, especially in the case of applicants. At current prices,
for example, the cost of initial and confirmatory testing for a workforce such
as that assumed in Table 2 would be almost forty thousand dollars; and,
because a person who tested negatively could become infected at any time,
employers would have to repeat testing periodically.

The limited data produced by the antibody test and the costliness of
reliable testing make its use as a general screening device problematic.
In addition the test is generally *not* useful as a tool for determining current health status. Employers may legitimately need to know whether
employees or applicants have AIDS or ARC, to the extent that work performance is impaired, but the antibody test does not diagnose those
conditions. Conversely, while the antibody test is the only way to determine infection by the AIDS virus (and the consequent production of antibodies to it), that condition alone does not impair a worker's ability to
perform on the job.

New tests may be developed that detect HIV itself instead of HIV antibodies
or that not only identify seropositivity but also predict whether the individual
is likely to develop AIDS.[25] Although more accurate and predictive tests would
be valuable from a medical standpoint, as discussed below, the key legal
and ethical issue—whether seropositivity alone justifies a refusal to employ—
would remain unchanged.

LEGAL ISSUES

When the HIV antibody test was approved in March 1985, some observers expressed concern that the test might be used not just to screen donated blood but to screen people for employment and insurance.[26] Some of these fears have been borne out. Insurers have shown an increasing interest in the test;[27] private employers generally have not,[28] although AIDS-based employment discrimination reportedly is widespread.[29]

The federal government has sent mixed signals on the issue of testing. The CDC's *Guidelines on AIDS in the Workplace*[30] rejected the use of antibody testing for health-care, personal-service, food-service, and other workers. "Because AIDS is a bloodborne, sexually transmitted disease that is not spread by casual contact, this document does *not* recommend routine HIV antibody screening for the groups addressed."[31] On March 13, 1986, however, the Public Health Service recommended that all individuals in high-risk groups be tested for HIV antibodies.[32] Although this latter recommendation is not directed at the workplace, it may serve inappropriately to focus employers' attention onto the sexual orientation of applicants and employees. Moreover, the federal government itself has extended its testing program to include all military personnel, participants in the Job Corps, and foreign-service employees of the State Department.[33]

The legality of various approaches to testing is no more settled than is their medical necessity. In a few states and municipalities, new laws specifically limit antibody testing and discrimination based on HIV status. In the rest of the country, the principal check on antibody screening is likely to be state and federal laws forbidding discrimination on the basis of handicap. Furthermore, some testing programs could possibly violate race- and sex-discrimination laws. Finally, prudent employers should be aware that the very collection and possession of such sensitive medical data imposes on them a duty of confidentiality and that breaches could result in costly liability.

State and Local AIDS Testing and Discrimination Statutes

California, Florida, Massachusetts, and Wisconsin have enacted laws regulating the use of HIV antibody tests by employers. Wisconsin's law is the most explicit, prohibiting both testing itself and the use of test results. As amended, the law provides that *unless* the state epidemiologist and the Secretary of Health and Social Services declare "that individuals who have HIV] infections may, through employment, provide a significant risk of transmitting HIV] to other individuals," employers are prohibited from: (1) soliciting or requiring as a condition of employment that any employee or applicant take an antibody test; (2) affecting the terms, conditions, or privileges of employment or terminating the employment of any employee who obtains an antibody test; and (3) entering into an agreement with an employee or applicant offering employment or any pay or benefit in return for taking an antibody test.[34] California[35] and Florida[36] prohibit the use of test results in determining suitability for employment. Massachusetts prohibits the requiring of an HIV test as a condition of employment.[37]

A number of California cities, including Los Angeles[38] and San Francisco,[39] as well as Austin[40] and Philadelphia,[41] have enacted ordinances prohibiting discrimination in employment based on AIDS. These laws also extend protection to people who have ARC, carry HIV, or are merely believed to be in a high-risk group. San Francisco specifically prohibits AIDS testing unless the employer can show that the absence of AIDS is a bona fide occupational qualification.

Federal and State Handicap Discrimination Statutes

The federal Vocational Rehabilitation Act and similar laws in virtually every state prohibit discrimination in employment on the basis of handicap. These may provide the best sources of protection against AIDS-based discrimination. In addition to probably prohibiting discrimination (in hiring and firing, and in the terms and conditions of employment) directed against persons having or believed to have AIDS or related medical conditions, handicap-discrimination laws also may prohibit employers from requiring or using the results of HIV antibody tests under most circumstances. The applicability of these laws to AIDS has been the subject of controversy.

On June 25, 1986, the Justice Department issued an opinion that although the clinical manifestations of HIV infection are "handicaps" under the Rehabilitation Act, seropositivity and the ability to transmit the infection to others are not. As discussed at greater length in Chapter 8, this opinion reflects a dubious analysis of the statute and is unlikely to be accepted in court. In *School Board of Nassau County v. Arline*, the Supreme Court reserved this question for another day; but, in deciding that the act covered contagious diseases, the Court stressed that "society's accumulated myths and fears about disability and disease are as handicapping as are the physical limitations that flow from actual impairment."[42] Nevertheless, only a small percentage of employment-discrimination incidents are ever taken to court, and the Justice Department opinion has sent out a pernicious message that wholly irrational exclusion of seropositive individuals does not violate federal law. Consequently, some employers may view the opinion as authorizing the use of HIV antibody testing.

Regardless of the Justice Department's position, each state is free to interpret its own handicap statute as it sees fit, and there is no indication of support for the Justice Department's view at the state level. The following discussion assumes that AIDS and other AIDS-related conditions are handicaps.

[For a full discussion of employment discrimination and the applicability of handicap-discrimination statutes, see Chapter 8.]

The several sections of the Rehabilitation Act regulate different types of employers, ranging from the federal government itself to organizations that receive federal funding. The specific provisions vary in the kinds of testing programs allowed, but the act generally prohibits covered employers from making preemployment inquiries about or testing to determine whether an applicant is handicapped, unless the inquiry or test is relevant to the applicant's ability to perform job-related functions.[43]

Department of Health and Human Services regulations implementing Section 504 of the Rehabilitation Act (the provision that applies to recipients of federal funds) preclude recipients of federal financial assistance from singling out individuals for medical screening:

> Nothing in this section shall prohibit a recipient from conditioning an offer of employment on the results of a medical examination conducted prior to the employee's entrance on duty, *Provided*, That: (1) All entering employees are subjected to such an examination regardless of handicap. . . .[44]

While requiring that medical examinations be given universally or not at all, the regulation quite sensibly does not insist that the medical procedures used on each individual be identical. Obviously, an individual's sex, medical history, and health status might alter the specifics of an examination. Nevertheless, another regulation implementing Section 504 provides that "a recipient may not make use of any employment test or selection criterion that screens out or tends to screen out handicapped persons or any class of handicapped persons" unless the test or criterion is shown to be job-related.[45] "Class of handicapped persons" is not defined but could be interpreted to include individuals who have been exposed to HIV and consequently are perceived to be handicapped. Identical regulations apply to Section 501 (the provision that covers federal agencies in their capacity as employers).[46]

The regulations implementing Section 503 (the provision that governs entities that enter into contracts with the federal government) permit preemployment medical examinations of handicapped applicants even if an examination is not required of the nonhandicapped. The regulations also provide, however, that if such examinations "tend to screen out qualified handicapped individuals," they may not be used unless they are "related to the specific job or jobs for which the individual is being considered and [are] consistent with business necessity and the safe performance of the job."[47]

Many state handicap-discrimination laws are worded quite generally and have not yet been interpreted judicially or administratively. Thus, it is not clear whether testing itself is generally illegal, though it is widely believed that the *use* of antibody test results in employment decision making is illegal absent a showing of job-relatedness.[48] A notable exception to the lack of clarity of state laws on this issue is California's Fair Employment Practice Law.[49] Regulations implementing that law specifically limit preemployment inquiries, medical examinations, and selection practices to job-related criteria.

In general, the standards that apply to job applicants apply to current employees as well. Thus, performing an HIV antibody test or inquiring into test results during a routine periodic medical examination may not violate handicap-discrimination laws, but the *use* of this information to deny employment opportunities (for example, promotions or desirable transfers) or as a basis for dismissal would most likely be prohibited.

For the most part, handicap-discrimination laws were not enacted with much consideration of their effect upon individuals at risk of *future* illness. Although high-risk individuals (as well as persons perceived to be at high risk) are probably covered by the law,[50] the courts are less clear about when the increased risk of illness will justify a refusal to employ. Speculation about future medical conditions will not justify an adverse employment decision,[51] but a *well-founded* concern about an employee's future health may permit an employer to screen out the individual.[52] Among the factors that a court would probably consider in deciding whether an employer may base a hiring decision on risk of future illness are the likelihood the illness will develop, its severity, the probable time period before the onset of the illness, the individual's risk relative to the employee norm, whether the employer has made an individualized determination of fitness, and whether reasonable accommodation is possible.[53]

Employers may, of course, have good-faith concerns about absenteeism, turnover, health-insurance costs, coworker preference, and customer preference. These defenses, however, usually have been rejected in handicap-discrimination cases involving other medical conditions. They are also likely to be rejected in AIDS cases in which the individual is currently able to perform the job. It is clear that these laws impose certain very real costs upon employers. They provide, however, in effect, that the policy in favor of equal employment opportunity for the handicapped takes precedence over productivity.

Other Antidiscrimination Laws

As discussed earlier, a single ELISA test has an acceptable level of accuracy only when performed on selected populations with a high prevalence of seropositivity. Thus, there is a sounder medical basis for testing in high-risk groups than in the general population. Selective testing, however, may raise legal problems. Employers may violate certain employment discrimination laws if they engage in selective AIDS antibody testing. For example, Wisconsin,[54] the District of Columbia,[55] and about fifty cities, including New York[56] and Philadelphia,[57] have laws prohibiting discrimination in employment based on sexual orientation. An employer who tests only known or suspected homosexuals would probably violate these laws.[58]

By engaging in *selective* HIV antibody testing, an employer also might run afoul of Title VII (of the Civil Rights Act of 1964), which prohibits discrimination in employment on the basis of race, color, religion, sex, or national origin. For example, testing only Haitians would probably constitute discrimination on the basis of national origin. Testing only males, or only single males, would probably constitute sex discrimination. Finally, because black and Hispanic Americans are more likely than whites to contract AIDS,[59] it could be argued that use by employers of the HIV antibody test to screen out high-risk persons disproportionately excludes blacks and Hispanics from employment. If a Title VII case were brought, and if the court determined that the claim fell within the scope of the statute, the burden would shift to the employer to prove that seronegativity was a bona fide occupational qualification or was otherwise job-related, or that the HIV antibody test was justified by business necessity. Failure to satisfy this burden would result in victory for the applicant or employee.[60]

Disclosure of Test Results

An individual's HIV antibody test result is extremely personal, and disclosure of it could well lead to embarrassment and discrimination. Therefore, employers who require or otherwise obtain this information may be risking tort liability under a variety of legal theories. For example, actions might be brought for invasion of privacy based on inappropriate publication of the results; for defamation based on inaccurate disclosure of accurate results or accurate disclosure of inaccurate results; for negligence based on negligent maintenance of records, negligent reporting of results, or the failure to maintain the security of records; and for intentional infliction of emotional distress if an individual were subjected to harassment or ridicule by supervisors, coworkers, or customers after test results were disclosed.

Tort actions have already been brought based on the wrongful disclosure of analogous, highly personal information. For instance, in *Houston Belt & Terminal Railway v. Wherry*,[61] a railroad employee was tested for drugs when he fainted following an accident on the job. The initial test result showed a "trace" of methadone, but a follow-up test showed the presence of a normal compound whose characteristics resemble methadone. The employee was later discharged for failure to report his accident in a timely manner. The railroad wrote a letter to the Department of Labor stating that the employee "passed out and fell" and that "traces of methadone" were present in his system. The Texas Court of Civil Appeals affirmed an award of one hundred fifty thousand dollars in compensatory damages and fifty thousand dollars in punitive damages based on the railroad's libelous statements.

In another case, a Texaco employee sued his employer and supervisor for the tort of outrage and invasion of privacy based on his supervisor's alleged disclosure to other refinery employees that the plaintiff was undergoing psychiatric treatment.[62] The Supreme Court of Oklahoma denied the claim, stating that no action for invasion of privacy would lie where *"only a small group* of coworkers were made privy to Eddy's private affairs . . . ."[63] If an employer discloses private facts about an employee to the general public, however, it *would* constitute an invasion of privacy.

The first AIDS-related tort actions have already been filed. According to the complaint in one such case, the county health commissioner in Fayette County, Ohio, received an anonymous note stating that an employee of a local restaurant had AIDS. The commissioner then forwarded the note to the owner of the restaurant, who read it aloud at a meeting of restaurant employees. The employee, with twenty-two years of service, was fired. An action based on wrongful discharge and defamation against the county health commissioner and restaurant owner was brought in March, 1986, seeking $1.5 million in damages.[64] In another case, a Massachusetts court recognized a tort action for invasion of privacy where a supervisor failed to keep an employee's diagnosis of AIDS confidential.[65] Other tort actions undoubtedly loom on the horizon.

SOME FINAL THOUGHTS ON TESTING

Like quarantine, testing has considerable appeal to many people who wish to "do something" about the spread of AIDS. Closer examination shows that worker screening is not a panacea, and, in fact, that its costs may exceed its benefits. Although some components of the situation, such as the accuracy of the test, may be expected to change, universal testing is now an expensive way for employers to generate information that they do not need and may not be allowed to use. Before embarking upon an extensive testing program of doubtful medical efficacy and legality, it is important to inquire into the motivation for the testing.

There are three possible motivations behind an HIV antibody testing program. First, there is a desire to protect the health of coworkers and customers. This does not justify use of the test. The overwhelming weight of medical evidence demonstrates that exclusion of even persons with clinical AIDS is unnecessary to protect the health of other people. Screening is more likely to be used to mollify coworkers and customers or to reduce health insurance and other perceived costs. Most people are in fact terribly afraid of AIDS, but a testing program may increase fear of the illness in the workforce without enhancing understanding; indeed, given the fear, an error-prone testing program could result in considerable resentment and panic.

Second, employers may expect economic benefits from HIV testing. But while some employees who have AIDS or ARC will generate considerable costs in benefit claims and reduced productivity, the test is not an effective way to address this problem. The use of the test in appraising current health status is unnecessary: seropositivity does not substantially affect the current ability to work and does not increase current costs for the employer; AIDS and ARC can be detected by the very symptoms that reduce the ability to perform on the job. Predictive screening might be used as a way to identify those people who at some time in the future may develop AIDS or ARC, but such a use, in addition to being imprecise, is probably illegal. If an employer may not *use* the results, why should employee relations be undermined and tort liability risked in obtaining and retaining such sensitive information?

Third, testing may be seen as a way to further public health generally and specifically the health of seropositive individuals. So far, federal health officials have not called for universal testing or nonvoluntary testing of high-risk individuals. But even if they eventually do, employers are badly suited to play this role. So long as employers can discriminate against persons with AIDS-related conditions, there is a basic conflict between the employer as surrogate public health official and the employer as employer. Furthermore, considerations of medical ethics strongly suggest that a medical test should not be performed unless some useful social purpose could be achieved. For asymptomatic seropositive individuals, however, there is nothing doctors can do. The same medical advice—in particular, avoidance of high-risk activities[66]—should be given to both seropositive and seronegative individuals. Being tested may be beneficial for some people, but it may also be very harmful, and the decision (certainly with regard to employment) should rest with the individual.[67]

New medical screening technology should not be introduced to the workplace setting without a thorough consideration of the relevant medical, legal, and social consequences.[68] This is particularly so when, as with AIDS, the effects of the test results are so crucial and wide-ranging.

10

Housing Issues

DANIEL R. MANDELKER

People with AIDS face difficulties in obtaining and keeping housing. They may have difficulty renting or buying housing and may be evicted from rental housing they occupy. Group homes for people with AIDS may be excluded by local zoning ordinances or restricted to undesirable areas of the community. This chapter reviews the legal protections available to assist people with AIDS in securing and keeping housing.

The first section reviews the legal problems that arise in the private housing market.[1] It considers judicial doctrine that can protect people with AIDS from eviction from rental housing and the legal problems that arise in the sale of housing previously occupied by such persons. The second section considers legislation prohibiting discrimination in the sale or rental of housing. The third section considers zoning restrictions that prevent people with AIDS from living together, either as individuals or in group homes. It reviews the constitutionality of these restrictions and legislation that can protect housing for them from zoning discrimination.

HOUSING IN THE PRIVATE MARKET

Protection from Eviction in Rental Housing

Eviction is a serious problem facing people with AIDS. Tenants may be evicted because they have AIDS, because they have ARC or seropositivity, or because they are thought to be at high risk, even though they have paid their rent. (People with AIDS may also lose rental housing because the cost of medical care has impoverished them and they are unable to pay their rent. Their eviction for nonpayment of rent raises social and humanitarian issues but, in a narrow sense, is not discrimination against them. Therefore, this section does not address this kind of eviction, although the crying need for shelter for people with AIDS is one factor that makes the provision of group homes so important.)

Traditionally, legal rules have given little protection to tenants of rental housing.[2] At common law, the landlord is entitled to possession of rented property at the end of the lease term. There is no limitation on the landlord's right to evict once the lease has expired.[3] A landlord might also claim that a person with AIDS is not permitted to exercise a right of renewal contained in a lease. A clause could even be added allowing eviction if the tenant develops AIDS during the term of the lease. If the lease contains a clause allowing eviction for tenant misconduct, a landlord might attempt to evict a person with AIDS who is a drug user and subject to criminal prosecution on the theory that this constitutes tenant misconduct. If a tenant does not have a formal lease but rents on a month-to-month basis, a landlord can evict at the end of a monthly rental period with proper notice.

Recent developments in landlord and tenant law, however, have substantially increased the landlord's obligations to his tenant.[4] Courts have relied on consumer protection law to infer clauses in leases and tenancies that protect the tenant ("implied clauses"), rather than the property law principles that favored the landlord. In consumer protection law, the courts have inferred a number of clauses in transactions for the sale of consumer goods, such as an implied warranty that the product is fit for its intended use. An implied warranty is a promise courts infer as a matter of law in a transaction even though the parties do not explicitly include it. Courts have similarly read leases to imply that landlords must ensure that the premises are in a habitable condition.[5] Although no appellate court has yet inferred a clause that limits the landlord to eviction for "good cause," the law on the implication of tenant-protective clauses supports the implication of such a clause. A "good-cause" provision would not allow the eviction of a person with AIDS, who does not pose a threat to the property or to neighbors or subsequent tenants.

The rationale for inferring the habitability clause also justifies inferring a clause limiting eviction to good cause. Arbitrary eviction can cause economic and emotional harm and deprives tenants of the basic right to shelter.[6] An implied good-cause eviction clause protects this right by ensuring tenants that their leases will not be broken yet protects landlords by allowing them to evict a tenant when their property interests are threatened. A good-cause eviction clause must be inferred because tenants do not have the bargaining power to demand such a clause in a housing market characterized by shortages (as is the case in such major AIDS-affected cities as New York and San Francisco). Nor are landlords likely to agree to this clause if they understand it prohibits eviction of a person with AIDS.

Some states have eliminated the need to infer such clauses by passing legislation allowing eviction only for good cause. These provisions are commonly included in rent control legislation,[7] and some states have legislation

allowing eviction from mobile home parks only for good cause.[8] Two jurisdictions, New Jersey and the District of Columbia, have such statutes applicable to all housing.[9] Legislation restricting eviction to good cause may
also apply to a refusal to renew a lease.[10]

"Good cause" as defined in this legislation falls into two categories. The
first allows eviction for misconduct by the tenant, such as nonpayment of
rent or destruction of the premises. The second allows eviction for certain
purposes of the landlord, such as a permanent removal of the rental unit
from the housing market or a temporary removal for rehabilitation.[11] A
landlord could evict a person with AIDS if, for example, he claimed the
purpose of the eviction was to rehabilitate the dwelling. Such statutes should
be interpreted to protect the tenant if the landlord's action is a mere pretext
for discriminating against a person with AIDS.

Problems in the Sale of Housing

In the sale of housing previously occupied by people with AIDS, disclosure
of that fact may lower the value of the property. This may, in turn, affect
the future availability of housing to people who have, or are suspected of
having, AIDS. Does the seller have a duty to inform a prospective buyer that
a residence was previously occupied by a person with AIDS? If so, a purchaser
could sue to rescind the sales contract and ask for damages if this disclosure
is not made. If the courts recognize this cause of action, owners would be
discouraged from renting to people with AIDS. The marketability of residences used as group homes for such people also would be affected.

The maxim *caveat emptor* (let the buyer beware) has historically been
applied to contracts for the sale of real estate, but exemptions have recently
been made to this general rule. A seller of a residence in some jurisdictions
is now under a duty to disclose conditions that physically or legally impair
the use of the property, such as a condition that makes the use of the property
unsafe.[12] The California courts have extended this duty to include the duty
to disclose material facts that significantly affect the value of property. In
one recent case, for example, a California court held a seller had a duty to
disclose that multiple murders had occurred in a residence because this fact
could significantly affect the value of the property.[13] This exception could
mean that a seller must disclose whether a person with AIDS has resided in
the dwelling.

This extension of the duty to disclose can be avoided if courts base their
determination of material facts on objective criteria and not the subjective
and personal fears of any particular purchaser, even though that purchaser
would not have bought the residence had she known what the seller did not
disclose. The test should be whether a reasonable purchaser would find the
fact so material that it affects the value of the property. Application of this
objective materiality test should lead a court to conclude that previous

ownership by a person with AIDS is not a material fact a seller has a duty to disclose. Occupation by a person with AIDS does not create risks for subsequent purchasers and so does not affect the value of property.

LEGISLATION PROHIBITING DISCRIMINATION IN HOUSING

Application to People with AIDS

Congress and many states and municipalities have adopted legislation prohibiting discrimination in the sale and rental of housing and in the provision of housing services. The protection afforded by such legislation varies. For example, federal legislation prohibits discrimination in the sale or rental of housing, in the terms and conditions of housing, in housing services, and in advertising.[14] The federal legislation is broad enough to include discrimination through eviction from rental housing,[15] and some state legislation expressly prohibits eviction.[16]

A few municipalities, including San Francisco, have adopted ordinances explicitly prohibiting discrimination against people with AIDS.[17] These ordinances prohibit discrimination in the provision of rental housing and other discriminatory acts prohibited by the federal housing legislation, including eviction from rental housing. Discrimination in the sale of housing is not prohibited.

People with AIDS are not necessarily covered by all legislation against housing discrimination. The federal legislation is at present limited to racial and other minorities and does not protect other groups.[18] State legislation is similar except in states in which it prohibits discrimination against the handicapped.[19] In most states, the definition of a "handicapped" person has been interpreted administratively to include people with AIDS.[20] (For a discussion of handicap antidiscrimination law, see Chapter 8.) This interpretation has not yet been litigated, but if the courts agree with it, state antidiscrimination legislation can provide a valuable legal remedy to prevent housing discrimination against people with AIDS. So far, only local antidiscrimination ordinances expressly prohibit discrimination in housing against them.

Authority to Adopt Local Antidiscrimination Ordinances

While local antidiscrimination ordinances appear to be the swiftest way to protect the housing rights of people with AIDS, not all cities have the authority to pass them. Local governments have only those powers a state confers through express legislative delegation, delegation of authority to regulate for the "general welfare," or constitutional provisions giving "home rule" powers to municipalities. These delegations permit varying degrees of authority to adopt regulatory ordinances such as antidiscrimination ordinances. Local ordinances prohibiting housing discrimination against people with AIDS may be authorized either by statutory general welfare clauses or constitutional home-rule provisions.

A statutory general welfare clause authorizes local governments to adopt ordinances for the "good government" of the municipality or to "preserve the public health, safety, and welfare." Some courts hold that this clause confers only powers granted by specific enabling legislation and so does not confer the authority to adopt ordinances prohibiting discrimination in housing.[21] Other courts hold that a general welfare clause confers additional powers on local governments in matters of local concern.[22] The New Jersey Supreme Court held that a local rent control ordinance was authorized by a general welfare clause as a matter of local concern.[23] This case recognized that housing problems justify local regulation under a statutory general welfare clause and supports the view that an ordinance prohibiting discrimination in housing is authorized by this clause.

Constitutional provisions conferring home rule are of two types.[24] "Classical" constitutional home rule usually grants localities the power to regulate "municipal" affairs. The newer "legislative" home rule delegates all power the legislature has the authority to delegate unless the legislature has "denied" the exercise of a power. Several states have adopted this type of home rule. Under classical home rule, courts allow the exercise of local home rule powers if the local ordinance legislates on a problem that is either a local concern or a shared local and state concern. Courts are likely to hold that housing is at least a matter of shared state and local concern that justifies its regulation by home-rule municipalities as a "municipal" affair.[25] A municipality would be able to adopt an ordinance prohibiting discrimination in housing in most classical home-rule states.[26]

The authority to adopt an ordinance prohibiting discrimination in housing should easily be found under legislative home rule.[27] Legislative home rule is limited only by a power "denied" to municipalities by statute. Problems should arise only if the home-rule provision authorizes an implied statutory denial of local authority to enact a law stricter than the state's. State legislation prohibiting discrimination in housing could be construed as an implied statutory denial. This problem is similar to the problem of legislative preemption, which is discussed in the next section.

Preemption of Local Ordinances by State Legislation

A municipality's authority to prohibit housing discrimination against people with AIDS may be preempted by a state statute that prohibits housing discrimination in general. Whether a state statute prohibiting housing discrimination preempts a local ordinance prohibiting housing discrimination against people with AIDS depends on whether the state statute also prohibits such discrimination. If the state law does not apply to such people, the question is whether a local antidiscrimination ordinance that applies to such people conflicts with the state law. A conflict occurs if the local ordinance prohibits what the state legislation permits; the local ordinance is then preempted. Some may argue that the exclusion of people with AIDS from the state statute is an implicit determination by the state legislature that discrimination against them is permitted.

Whether the exclusion of people with AIDS from a state antidiscrimination statute preempts a local antidiscrimination ordinance depends on how the court interprets the legislature's intent.[28] The courts have not found preemption when they have considered claims that state antidiscrimination statutes preempted similar local civil rights ordinances, but they could find differently in the case of AIDS.[29]

ZONING RESTRICTIONS

Zoning ordinances may restrict housing opportunities for people with AIDS who wish to live together as an unrelated family, in a family residence, or in a group home. Group housing is badly needed because people with AIDS are sometimes financially unable to live alone when not in a hospital and may be physically unable to live alone even when they are too well to need an expensive hospital bed. Many people with AIDS are unnecessarily staying in hospitals, where treatment costs are very high, because they cannot find housing. Group homes are usually much less expensive than hospital treatment.[30]

Zoning ordinances divide a community into districts and designate land uses appropriate to each. Zoning ordinances always include districts limited solely to residential uses. Single family and multifamily residences are usually assigned separate districts. The ordinances define the "family" permitted to live in residential districts, limiting the number of unrelated people who may live together. They may effectively prohibit group homes for people with AIDS because the number of such unrelated people in the group home usually exceeds the number permitted by the zoning ordinance.[31]

Zoning ordinances may provide specifically for group homes by allowing them as a "special use" in residential districts.[32] A special use is allowed in a zoning district only after it has been approved by a local zoning agency or by the municipal governing body. The zoning ordinance always provides criteria for the review and approval of special uses. These criteria vary but generally allow a special use if it is compatible with the area in which it is to be located. Opponents of group homes for people with AIDS may argue that such homes are incompatible with the area.

Zoning ordinances that limit the number of unrelated people who can live together and that require special-use approval of group homes raise constitutional problems. Zoning restrictions based on family type or on living arrangements may not serve a constitutionally acceptable zoning purpose.

These restrictions may also violate the equal protection clause of the Fourteenth Amendment, because they treat unrelated families differently from related families. The cases are divided on whether these restrictions are constitutional.

The Fourteenth Amendment of the Constitution guarantees the equal protection of the laws. A few explanatory words on how this apparently simple idea is applied suggest why courts have divided on its application to zoning. Not all laws that treat people differently violate the equal protection clause—there is probably no law that affects *all* people in *exactly* the same way—and so the Supreme Court has struggled to develop a judicial test to determine when and how closely it may scrutinize a disputed law. Normally, a state may justify a challenged law by showing that it has a "rational relationship" to the fulfillment of a legitimate state goal. If a law impairs a fundamental right (such as the right to vote) or uses an inherently "suspect" classification (such as race, religion, or alienage), the Court will apply "strict scrutiny," requiring the state to demonstrate that the law is necessary to meet a "compelling" need. In a few cases, the Court has charted a course between these two poles. Facing laws classifying people according to gender and illegitimacy (sometimes referred to as "quasi-suspect" classifications), the Court has used an "intermediate scrutiny," generally requiring the law to be "substantially related" to an "important" government interest. Just how this test works is a matter of some dispute among constitutional law scholars and practitioners, and even within the Supreme Court itself. In theory, the test determines only how closely the Court will scrutinize the law, but there is general agreement on the proposition that the level of scrutiny tends to determine the outcome of the case: it is considerably easier for a state to show a law's *rational* relationship to a *legitimate* goal than its *necessary* relationship to a *compelling* one.[33]

A number of states have adopted legislation for some group homes that attempts to avoid these constitutional problems. This legislation may specify the types of zoning regulations municipalities can adopt and the zoning districts in which group homes can locate. Similar legislation could be adopted for group homes for people with AIDS.

Zoning Restrictions on Unrelated Families

The case law on zoning restrictions on unrelated families is dominated by a U.S. Supreme Court case, *Village of Belle Terre v. Borass*.[34] In it, the Court upheld a suburban zoning ordinance that allowed no more than two unrelated people to live together in a single-family residence. Because the ordinance was not directed at a minority group and did not infringe upon a fundamental constitutional right, the Court applied the "rational relationship" test. The Court held that the numerical limitation on unrelated families served the legitimate governmental objective of protecting the integrity of single-family residential areas.

Although state courts are obliged to follow the Supreme Court's reading of the U.S. Constitution, they are free to interpret their own constitutions as they see fit. A number of state courts have followed *Belle Terre* by upholding zoning ordinances restricting the number of unrelated people who can live together,[35] but others have invalidated such restrictions. These courts accepted the rationale of the dissenting opinion in *Belle Terre*, which argued that a zoning restriction on unrelated families invades fundamental constitutional rights to privacy and freedom of association. This approach requires "strict scrutiny" and compelling governmental interests are hard to prove. In *Belle Terre*, the dissenting Justices did not find a compelling justification for the zoning restriction on unrelated families.

The California Supreme Court decision in *City of Santa Barbara v. Adamson*[36] is a leading state case holding a zoning restriction on unrelated families unconstitutional under the rationale of the dissent in *Belle Terre*. The court found that the ordinance infringed the right of privacy guaranteed by the state constitution. An invasion of this right must be justified by a "compelling public need," which the court did not find. The restriction on unrelated families did not protect residential areas because it was not sufficiently related to noise, parking, and other neighborhood problems. Less restrictive alternatives were available to remedy these land-use problems, including regulations limiting population density and parking. Other state courts have also invalidated this type of zoning restriction.[37]

People with AIDS who live together as a family do not present zoning problems different from those presented by any other unrelated family and should be given the same status under zoning ordinances. In states that follow the *Belle Terre* decision, low numerical limits on unrelated families will effectively prevent people with AIDS from living together if they do not organize formally as a group home. State courts that have, under their states' constitutions, invalidated zoning ordinances limiting the number of unrelated people who can live together as a family,[38] should also invalidate family restrictions in zoning ordinances applied to limit the number of people with AIDS who can live together.

Appropriate, nondiscriminatory zoning regulations, such as restrictions on residential density, may still present a problem to people with AIDS. Political pressure may make density limitations so stringent that they place substantial restrictions on the number of unrelated people who can live together.

Zoning Restrictions on Group Homes

State courts have adopted a variety of views on zoning ordinances that restrict the location of group homes. Some avoid constitutional problems by holding that group homes are a permitted family use in residential districts.[39] Several states have followed the reasoning of *Belle Terre* and have held that the exclusion of group homes from residential districts is constitutional,[40] while a few state courts have held such zoning restrictions unconstitutional.[41]

The constitutional doctrine applied to zoning restrictions on group homes was substantially modified by a 1985 United States Supreme Court decision, *City of Cleburne v. Cleburne Living Center.*[42] The zoning ordinance in that case required a special-use permit for a group home for the mentally retarded in an area zoned for "apartment houses." It did not require a special-use permit for similar facilities, such as nursing homes. A special permit for a group home for the mentally retarded was denied. Because similar group homes were treated differently, the special permit denial raised an equal protection problem.

The Court first had to decide which judicial standard for review applied. The owner of the group home conceded that strict scrutiny was not appropriate but argued that the Court should apply "intermediate scrutiny" because, like gender and illegitimacy, retardation had been a basis for unfair discrimination in the past and should be treated as a quasi-suspect classification. The Supreme Court instead chose to apply the rational relationship standard. It reasoned that the mentally retarded were not a quasi-suspect class: although they all are disabled, they are very different from each other in the degree and expression of disability and should not be treated as a homogeneous class. The Court also found that enactment of federal and state legislation to protect them indicated they were not susceptible to legislative prejudice, and expressed fear that legislatures might not adopt any protective legislation at all if such legislation were subject to the more rigorous intermediate standard.

But although the Court did not apply intermediate scrutiny, it invalidated the denial of the special-use permit, a rare instance in which the Court has found a violation of the equal protection clause under the rational relationship standard. The Court rejected the reasons given for denying the special-use permit, such as the fears of neighborhood residents, deciding that "mere negative attitudes" did not justify the denial.[43] The Court did not decide whether the permit requirement itself was unconstitutional.

Cleburne's significance is not entirely clear. The decision was influenced heavily by the arbitrary classification of group homes in the zoning ordinance and the zoning board's unconvincing reasons for denying the special use permit. While it cannot be read to broadly protect group homes regulated under fairer zoning ordinances, *Cleburne* does indicate that the Court will carefully review discrimination against group homes in zoning ordinances, presumably including those for people with AIDS.[44]

Whether the Court would hold that AIDS, like gender and illegitimacy but unlike mental retardation, should be given quasi-suspect status is unclear. People with AIDS, like the mentally retarded, differ in the extent of their disability. Moreover, the Court's refusal in *Cleburne* to extend quasi-suspect status to the mentally retarded may indicate the Court does not intend to add additional classes to the quasi-suspect category.

A court could still invalidate zoning restrictions on group homes for people with AIDS under the rational relationship standard applied in *Cleburne*. "Mere negative attitudes" toward AIDS is no more acceptable a reason for denying a special permit for a group home than the negative attitudes toward the retarded at issue in *Cleburne*. Other restrictions on group homes, such as their total exclusion from residential areas, were not raised in *Cleburne*, but the decision suggests that restrictions of this type may also be unconstitutional.

A number of states have adopted legislation protecting group homes from discrimination in zoning ordinances.[45] The coverage of this legislation varies; it usually does not apply to all types of group homes. The zoning requirements allowed by this legislation also vary. Although municipalities may be required to allow group homes in all residential districts, some statutes allow municipalities to require special-use permits for group homes and to limit the number of group homes in the community. Dispersal standards requiring group homes to be separated by a minimum distance may also be imposed.

Legislation of this type may protect group homes from zoning discrimination, but some of the restrictions in these statutes may still be unconstitutional under the *Cleburne* decision. *Cleburne* clearly implied that any discriminatory treatment of group homes under zoning ordinances may be subject to invalidation as a denial of equal protection.[46] Dispersal requirements for group homes, for example, could be held to violate the equal protection clause because they involve an unconstitutional classification. Certainly, the need to protect residential neighborhoods by dispersing group homes has not been conclusively shown.

Legislation can be adopted protecting group homes for people with AIDS from discriminatory zoning ordinances.[47] This legislation will have to be drafted with care to avoid the legal difficulties raised by the *Cleburne* decision: any restriction or classification must have a rational justification. In addition to dispersal, other special-use permit requirements are constitutionally suspect unless the criteria for approval are based on legitimate zoning purposes, such as the impact of the group home on the adjacent residential neighborhood. For example, group homes with a limited number of residents who do not require extensive outpatient treatment should be allowed without a special-use permit in residential neighborhoods. Larger group homes that require substantial parking for resident staff and visiting medical personnel have a more substantial impact on single-family neighborhoods and might be required to obtain a special-use permit.

STRATEGIES FOR LEGAL REFORM

Legal strategies for protecting people with AIDS in the housing market can to some extent rely on existing statutes or established principles of constitutional law. In some states, for example, the state statute prohibiting discrimination in the housing market applies to the handicapped. Administrative interpretation of this law can extend this protection to people with AIDS. Legislation that prohibits eviction of tenants except for good cause can also protect people with AIDS. Zoning ordinances that discriminate against group homes or that restrictively limit the number of unrelated people who can live together can be challenged in court as unconstitutional under the Supreme Court's *Cleburne* decision.

Other legal reforms may require substantial effort to change legal doctrine or to secure the enactment of new legislation. No appellate court has yet recognized an implied clause in leases limiting eviction to good cause, for example. A case would have to be brought urging the court to recognize this clause. Litigation would be expensive and the outcome doubtful, because the court may be unwilling to increase the legal protection of tenants. If the state law prohibiting discrimination in housing does not apply to people with AIDS, the adoption of a local ordinance prohibiting such discrimination is necessary. The political climate for the adoption of such an ordinance may be improving; several cities have adopted ordinances of this type.

Doubts about the authority of a municipality to adopt a local ordinance on housing discrimination, and the possibility that it may be preempted by state legislation, may argue for the enactment of a state statute, although that may be more difficult than obtaining similar legislation at the local level. More modest reforms may be effective. A local ordinance generally prohibiting discrimination in housing, for example, may provide significant protection from AIDS-related discrimination in the housing market.

Although the reforms discussed in this chapter may be politically difficult to enact, they do not require radical innovations in legal doctrine. Their conceptual legal basis has already been established. They need only to be applied fairly to the problems that arise when people with AIDS seek housing.

11

Torts: Private Lawsuits about AIDS

DONALD H. J. HERMANN

Tort law is the mechanism this society uses to discourage individuals from subjecting others to unreasonable risks, and to compensate those who have been injured by unreasonably risky behavior. We can expect, therefore, that the AIDS epidemic will produce, before it runs its course, a staggering array of tort litigation. That litigation is likely to cover everything from a child's "wrongful life" suit against its mother for transmission of HIV before birth to an adult's libel suit against a newspaper for falsely publishing that he or she has AIDS. Detailed discussion of every kind of tort claim that might arise is beyond the scope of this, or any, book. Instead, this chapter will focus on the areas in which AIDS-related tort litigation is most likely to occur: transmission of the virus through sexual activity, transmission through blood products, and medical malpractice.

INTRODUCTION TO THE LAW OF TORTS

The name *torts* has been used to encompass a variety of harms that one person can inflict on another. We cannot live in our complex, crowded world without bumping into each other, literally and figuratively, in innumerable ways that simply have to be endured as the price of existence. Tort law recognizes, however, that not every injury should be tolerated, and that at some point each of us owes to other persons a "duty of care"; that is, we are obligated to modify our behavior so that we neither intentionally nor negligently inflict certain harms on others. Tort law defines the obligations that the courts (and increasingly legislatures as well) have determined should be judicially enforceable.

The reasons for making such obligations enforceable are several. Foremost is the desire to see to it that those who are wronged are compensated.

In addition, making wrongdoers "liable in tort" discourages behavior that puts others at risk. Tort law can also be used to allocate to injuring parties those costs of doing business that otherwise would be displaced onto others, namely the injured. Increasingly, tort law is also seen as a mechanism for assigning the costs of unavoidable risks to those who can best pay them, or who can best spread the costs as broadly as possible.

Although tort law is something of a grab bag, most torts have a common structure. To prevail, the plaintiff must demonstrate at least that the defendant owed him or her a "duty of care"; that the defendant "breached" that duty; that the breach "caused" the plaintiff injury; and that the injury resulted in losses compensable by money "damages." Breach, causation, injury, and the extent of damages must be proved by a "preponderance of the evidence." That is to say, the plaintiff must prove that it is "more probable than not" that each of these "elements" occurred.

"Due care" is a flexible concept. As situations, surroundings, and hazards vary, so do the requirements of due care. Moreover, the care that is due depends upon such factors as the relationship between the parties, the likelihood that a given formulation will deter undesirable behavior, and the ease with which the risk of injury can be reduced. Each tort has its own duty of care, and the standard of conduct that duty demands is determined by considering the particulars of each case in the light of prior cases of a similar character.

Once the appropriate standard has been identified, it is possible to determine whether a breach has occurred—that is, whether the defendant has failed to act in conformity with that standard. Then the trick is to show that the breach caused the injury in question. For some AIDS-related torts, proving causation may be extremely difficult. This is especially true with respect to suits seeking compensation for the sexual transmission of the virus associated with AIDS. These difficulties are discussed below in the sexual transmission section of this chapter.

Once a breach of a duty of care has been established and its link to the plaintiff's injury shown, the plaintiff may recover damages for injuries that become manifest in the future as well as those that are immediately apparent. However, an injured party ordinarily may maintain only one lawsuit for damages resulting from a single incident, whether the injuries are present or prospective. When a person fails to sue for future damages, he or she will usually be prohibited from suing again when later injuries develop. Moreover, the reluctance of courts to speculate as to future damages may limit the ability of a plaintiff to recover for medical costs and pain and suffering stemming from future opportunistic diseases and infections.

Anyone considering suing in tort must also evaluate his or her chances of collecting any damages that might be awarded by a court. A plaintiff who can win a case on the facts but would recover nothing because the defendant lacks the means to pay does not have a suit economically worth filing.

Attorneys usually accept personal injury cases on a contingency basis, which means that the attorney collects a predetermined portion of any damage award or settlement—generally one-third—rather than payment on an hourly basis. If there is no damage award or settlement, the plaintiff must pay certain expenses, but no fee, to the attorney. Not surprisingly, few attorneys will take on a personal injury case unless they stand to collect enough to pay a reasonable return on the time they spend on the case. And experience indicates that very few injured persons are willing to pay an attorney out of their own pockets to file a suit simply to gain the satisfaction of a judicial ruling pegging blame on someone who is financially judgment-proof.

The defendant's ability to pay damages may be a crucial consideration in the case of an AIDS-related tort. Where the potential defendant has AIDS or may develop AIDS, medical expenses may deplete any assets out of which damages could be paid. Furthermore, if the defendant is an intravenous drug user, it is unlikely that he or she will have sufficient financial resources to justify a suit.

Virtually every state has a survival statute, which permits a personal lawsuit to continue after the death of either the plaintiff or defendant. Most of these statutes permit estates to recover for negligent or intentional injuries. However, some statutes exclude torts such as defamation, which are based on damage to one's intangible interest in reputation. Under most statutes, the cause of death is not the determining factor; a lawsuit will survive whether or not death was the result of the defendant's tort.

In a few states, if death results from a tort, recovery is limited to a "wrongful death" action. Unlike a survival right of action, which can benefit only the injured party, a wrongful death suit can be filed by the decedent's estate or by someone who has suffered a loss because of the victim's death. Under most wrongful death statutes, damages are provided as compensation to the victim's beneficiaries or estate for loss of the economic support that the victim would reasonably have been expected to provide in the form of services and contributions during the remainder of his or her life.

Even if a plaintiff establishes each of the elements of the tort upon which he or she is relying for recovery, the defendant can still avoid liability by establishing (again by a preponderance of the evidence) a legally recognized defense. Some defenses, such as "contributory negligence," apply to particular torts only. Others apply in any tort suit. Two of these are worth outlining in this introduction.

A *statute of limitations* defines a period of time after which a suit cannot be brought. The rationale for such statutes is that potentially disruptive states of affairs should not be allowed to continue indefinitely, that potential defendants have a right to know, at a certain point, that they no longer are exposed to liability, and that unless suits are commenced reasonably soon after operative events occur, witnesses' memories grow stale, evidence disappears, and proof one way or the other becomes difficult.

Often, a crucial question is when the limitations period begins. Typically, the statute begins to run when the injury occurs[1] or when the cause of action (the facts that give a person the right to seek a judicial remedy) accrues.[2] In an AIDS-related suit, neither standard is unambiguous. To take the simpler one, what is the relevant "injury" when HIV is sexually transmitted? Is it the sex act itself, exposure to the virus (which occurs at the time of the sex act), the development of antibodies to the virus, the first signs of the psychic trauma that attends the realization that one carries a deadly virus, the first signs of a suppressed immune system, or the development of ARC or AIDS?

If exposure to HIV triggers the statute, then potential plaintiffs face a serious dilemma. If they file suit a year (or two or three) after exposure, they might not yet know what the full consequences of their infection will be. They might develop ARC or AIDS, but they might not. They might lose their jobs or find themselves uninsurable, but perhaps not. By filing suit right away, they run the risk that their attempt to recover for possible future costs will be rejected by the court as too speculative. Yet, if they delay filing suit, they risk having the statutory limitations period run out.

The position of the potential plaintiff is made all the more complicated if we assume what is probably true in most cases, that the plaintiff does not even know that he or she is infected until well after exposure to the virus. Many, indeed most, people infected with the virus are asymptomatic. Without taking an HIV antibody test, they have no way of knowing whether they are seropositive. A statute of limitations that is interpreted as running from the date of exposure rather than from the plaintiff's discovery that he or she is infected would work substantial unfairness. Fortunately, the courts of most states have determined that where an injury or disease is inherently latent, the statute of limitations does not begin to run until the injured person becomes aware or should have become aware of his or her exposure.[3]

Of course, courts may decide that some event other than exposure to the HIV (or discovery of the fact that one has been exposed) starts the statute running. If so, no doubt that trigger would have its own difficulties. Until these questions are resolved by the courts, the cautious tort plaintiff will consult a lawyer early and file suit within the shortest possible limitations period. Wrestling with the thorny problem of proving future damages is preferable to being shut out altogether.

A second defense that cuts across many AIDS-related tort claims, especially those based on sexual transmission, is the defense of "illegality," since in some states the underlying sexual activity will have violated statutory prohibitions against fornication, sodomy, or adultery. The general rule is that a person cannot maintain a cause of action if, in order to establish it, he or she must rely to any degree on an illegal or immoral act to which he or she is a party.[4] The principle underlying this rule is that the law will not permit a person to take advantage of or acquire the right to make a legal claim through his or her own unlawful act.

The illegality defense in the context of sexual relations has been eroded over the years. Many state legislatures have repealed statutes making consensual sex illegal.[5] Some state courts have concluded that such statutes are invalid under their state constitutions.[6] Some courts have cited the infrequent enforcement of such statutes as grounds for not allowing the illegality defense to be used.[7] Others have limited the defense to situations where the parties are equally culpable, taking into account not only the illegal sex act but also the blameworthiness that attaches to knowingly or negligently transmitting disease. Typical, if somewhat melodramatic, is a Texas case in which the court reasoned, "whatever of either illegality or immorality the two of them together may have indulged in, the woman's deception—induced and unknowing yielding of her clean body to such a union with his disease-carrying one—could not, by any just standard this tribunal knows of, have left her act so culpable as his."[8]

Perhaps most typical of the modern approach are two recent California cases permitting suit to be brought for damages arising out of sexual activity between unmarried persons. In one case, the defendant allegedly misrepresented that he was sterile, leading to an disastrous abnormal pregnancy.[9] In the other, the plaintiff alleged that the defendant had infected her with genital herpes.[10] While neither court expressly considered an illegality defense, both courts implicitly found the legality of the litigants' sexual relationship irrelevant.

Finally, an action seeking a judgment of tort liability for sexual transmission of HIV must overcome the assertion that it violates the constitutional right to privacy. This hurdle is not so much a defense designed to avoid a finding of fault as a claim that public policy, even constitutional principles, argue that the state should not intervene in intimate private affairs. Courts traditionally have been reluctant to sanction state intrusion into private relationships. The question that must be answered in such a case, however, is whether such intrusion is warranted under the particular circumstances at issue.

In 1976, for example, the Arizona Supreme Court upheld a husband's conviction for forcing his wife to perform fellatio on him, rejecting the argument that the Supreme Court cases recognizing a right of privacy in sexual relationships prevented the court from inquiring into such intimate matters.[11] The court reasoned that a state retains an overriding interest in protecting its citizens from violence.

The California Court of Appeal, in 1984, reasoned similarly in finding that the constitutional right to privacy did not preclude an unmarried woman from suing a man in tort for sexually transmitting herpes to her. The defendant maintained that it was not the business of the judiciary to supervise promises or claims made between consenting adults concerning the circumstances of their private sexual conduct. The court acknowledged that the defendant had correctly focused on the constitutional right to privacy as the crux of the litigation, and that courts have recognized that in matters relating to marriage, family, and sex the right of privacy precludes unwarranted governmental intrusion. Nevertheless, the court reasoned that the right of privacy is not absolute, and in some instances it must be subordinated to the state's fundamental right to enact laws that promote public health, welfare, and the safety of its citizens.[12]

The criminal penalties imposed by many jurisdictions for the transmission of venereal disease also suggest that this is an area of significant state concern. This concern should provide an adequate basis for the courts to justify subordinating the privacy rights of persons who knowingly transmit AIDS, endanger the health of the community, and inflict physical injury and suffering on their sexual partners to the right of persons harmed by such conduct to seek a legal remedy.

LIABILITY FOR TRANSMISSION OF THE VIRUS ASSOCIATED WITH AIDS

While tort suits might arise in relation to each of the principal modes of transmission, this chapter focuses on two of the most significant areas of potential transmission liability: sexual encounters and relationships, and the supplying of blood and blood products. Although intravenous needle sharing is a major means of transmission, and, in some localities, the most common, infected drug users are seldom likely to bring suit, and potential defendants are likely to be incapable of paying damages. In addition, needle sharing is almost certain to involve illegal activities that may prevent maintenance of a tort suit.

Liability for Sexual Transmission

In general, each of us has a legally enforceable duty to protect our sexual partners against the transmission of venereal and contagious diseases. Although no court has, as yet, had occasion to recognize this duty in a case involving the transmission of HIV, there is clear precedent in the analogous area of transmission of genital herpes. In the leading herpes case, the California Court of Appeal upheld the plaintiff's right to sue the defendant for "having sexual intercourse with her at a time when he knew, or in the exercise of reasonable care should have known, that he was a carrier of venereal disease."[13] The court was unmoved by the argument that herpes was not among the venereal diseases listed in the applicable health code. "It is a disease that can be propagated by sexual contact. Like AIDS it is now known by the public to be . . . contagious and dreadful."[14]

A sexual partner who transmits such a disease is open to suit for resulting harm under a number of theories of liability. Four of the most common theories or causes of action—negligence, battery, misrepresentation, and statutory violation—are described below. Each has different elements that must be proved for the plaintiff to prevail. A single lawsuit may assert more than one cause of action, and usually does, because one can never be certain which theory is best supported by the facts.

Negligence

To prevail on a negligence theory, a plaintiff must establish four elements: (1) that the defendant had a legal duty to act prudently so as to protect others from the unreasonable risk of harm; (2) that the defendant breached that duty; (3) that there is an adequate causal connection between the defendant's conduct and the injury suffered by the plaintiff; and (4) that the plaintiff suffered damage or loss.[15]

The first element is satisfied only if a court or legislature has decided that a duty of care should be imposed in situations of the type at issue. It is virtually certain that courts will impose such a duty with respect to the sexual transmission of HIV, not simply because the precedent has been set in the herpes cases, but more importantly because requiring infected sexual partners to take reasonable precautions constitutes sound social policy. The state has an undeniable interest in checking the spread of AIDS and in seeing to it that persons who are unwittingly infected are adequately compensated. Although as a theoretical matter the obligation to exercise caution could be placed on either sexual partner, it makes sense to shift the costs of transmission to the party who is in the best position to know whether prophylactic measures are necessary. Moreover, one who knowingly or even negligently infects an unknowing sexual partner is morally culpable.

A duty of care obliges those who are covered by it to act in accordance with a specified standard of care. Under a negligence theory, the applicable standard is set by a hypothetical "reasonable person" who acts with "ordinary prudence." Applying all this to HIV transmission, we can confidently conclude that there exists a duty to take whatever steps a reasonable person of ordinary prudence would take to protect sexual partners from an unreasonable risk of infection.

So much for theory. What can we expect in practice? Ultimately, the courts will apply abstract principles of law to the particular facts of individual cases. Eventually, patterns emerge, and from them solid predictions can be made. For the moment, all we can do is make educated guesses.

At a minimum, the duty to take steps to protect sexual partners will apply to persons who know they are seropositive. The "reasonable person" standard will probably be construed to require that such persons engage in safe sex practices and that, in addition, they disclose their seropositivity to sexual partners. Without such disclosure, sexual partners are in no position to make an informed decision regarding whether to proceed and, if so, with what precautions. In the California herpes case, the plaintiff apparently alleged that the defendant was negligent both in engaging in intercourse while knowingly infectious and in failing to warn her of his condition.[16]

Usually, negligence liability arises not only when a person knows facts that would cause a reasonable person to recognize the existence of an unreasonable risk of harm, but also when he or she *should have known* such facts. How should this standard be applied in the AIDS context? When is it fair to say that a person should have known that he or she was infectious? Some cases are fairly easy. For example, the steady sexual partner of someone who has AIDS probably could not escape liability for transmitting the virus to a third party by claiming that he was unaware of his seropositivity. Similarly, a frequenter of New York's bath houses with a penchant for unprotected anal sex is likely to be found to possess constructive knowledge of his seropositivity in any suit for negligent sexual transmission. At the other end of the scale is the infected but asymptomatic female sex partner of a male she does not know is bisexual. In between these extremes are a host of more troublesome cases.

Consider, for example, the gay male who has been in a monogamous relationship for four years, during which period safe sex has been the rarely broken rule, or the female former drug user who only occasionally shared needles, most recently three years ago, and whose two-year-old child is not infected. Suppose it turns out that they do harbor the virus, and unknowingly (given their asymptomatic condition) transmit it to others who bring suit. Should they be deemed to have been aware of their infectiousness? In such circumstances, although the goal of compensating the unwitting victims could be met by presuming knowledge, it is not obvious that the unwitting victimizers are especially blameworthy, or that they were in a markedly better position than their partners to assay the risks. To be sure, if the consequence of treating the infectiousness of the people in the examples as "foreseeable" is that an incentive is created for people in similar situations to take the HIV antibody test, the state's goal of checking the spread of the virus may be served. This, of course, assumes that the distant threat of tort liability for transmitting the virus to another will create a significantly greater incentive for antibody testing than is created by the fear of AIDS itself.

The suggestion that the sexual partners in these examples are equally positioned to judge the risk of engaging in sex and the desirability of precautionary measures assumes that each partner has certain baseline information about the other. That, of course, may not be true in particular cases. For example, the sex partner of the former intravenous drug user might be unaware of her past, in which event his calculation would be appreciably less informed than hers.

It is possible to control for these disparities of information and at the same time exempt from liability persons who, despite their low to moderate risk of infection, are unknowingly seropositive. Specifically, a court could conclude that a reasonably prudent low-risk person would inform potential sex partners about behavior that makes infection a possibility (e.g., "I used to shoot drugs, but I stopped four years ago.") and would not resist reasonable precautions suggested by the partner in response to that information. As long as a low-risk person acted prudently, the costs of infection would remain where they fall. Such an approach would have the virtue of creating an incentive for both partners to take steps to avoid transmission. This is but one of many ways that courts might choose to balance the considerations that favor the creation of a duty of care to avoid sexually transmitting HIV; I make no attempt to predict what approach a given court (or the majority of courts, for that matter) will follow.

Once the plaintiff has established that a duty of care, however defined, has been or ought to be imposed, the next question is whether the defendant has breached that duty by failing to conform to the standard of conduct entailed in it. In a sexual transmission case, the determination of whether a breach has occurred is fairly straightforward, once the requirements of reasonable prudence have been spelled out. If, for example, a reasonably prudent person infected with HIV would inform sex partners of that fact and would also follow safe-sex guidelines, then the issue of breach reduces to: Did the defendant make the proper disclosure and did he or she take the proper precautions?

Once a duty and breach of duty are established, the plaintiff must convince the judge or jury that his or her injury was caused by the defendant's conduct. In the case of HIV infection, even where other possible means of transmission (such as contaminated blood or dirty needles) can be ruled out, serious problems of proof remain. The virus may lay dormant in a person for years. It is therefore often difficult, if not impossible, to determine how long someone has been infected prior to the discovery of positive antibody status or the onset of AIDS or ARC.

In the ideal case (from the plaintiff's perspective), the plaintiff would be able to prove that he or she was seronegative prior to engaging in sex with the defendant and that he or she did not engage in high-risk sex with anyone else between that encounter and the point that infection became manifest. Few people could clear even the first hurdle; it requires the fortuity of either having had an antibody test close in time to the encounter with the defendant (and no intervening high-risk sex) or having had blood drawn during that same period that somehow remains available for testing. Without this kind of hard data, the plaintiff must rely on evidence of long-term chastity or, at a minimum, low-risk sex, prior to engaging in sex with the defendant.

Alternatively, the plaintiff could offer proof that all of his or her other sex partners (going back perhaps as far as the late 1970s) are seronegative. A single unaccounted-for partner, however, would cloud the issue of whether the defendant was the source of the plaintiff's infection and might even raise the question of who transmitted HIV to whom. Similarly, a single unaccounted for partner *following* the plaintiff's encounter with the defendant would complicate the determination of where the plaintiff's infection originated. At a minimum, subsequent unsafe sex with others would provide grist for the argument that reinfection might have occurred, perhaps break-ing the chain of causation between the defendant's conduct and the plaintiff's present plight. Remember, though, that the plaintiff need not disprove every other possible cause of infection; he or she need only show that it is "more probable than not" that the defendant was the source of the virus.

Even where causation is established, proof of damages may be problematic in some cases. In suits brought by persons who have contracted AIDS or ARC, de-termination of damages will be fairly straightforward; they will include compen-sation for pain and suffering as well as medical expenses, lost wages, necessary support services (such as psychotherapy, nursing care, child care, and the like) and other expenses incurred as a consequence of having AIDS or ARC. Damage awards in suits brought by asymptomatic plaintiffs, by contrast, will be based largely on compensation for emotional trauma—including trauma caused by adjustments in life style undertaken to reduce the risk of transmitting the virus to others—since mere exposure to the virus produces no inevitable effect other than the nearly universal development of antibodies. Some nonpsychic harm must be shown, since courts ordinarily will not allow a recovery for pain and suf-fering without some basis in more tangible injury but HIV infection may itself be deemed such injury.[17] Nevertheless, the uncertainty of whether HIV infection will ultimately lead to AIDS renders considerations of future damages rather speculative.

To the extent that suppression of the immune system can be shown to be "more likely than not," however, an award of damages for that likely consequence is appropriate. As medical understanding of AIDS improves, it may well become possible to make a reasonably reliable prognosis of whether a given person's HIV infection will lead to ARC or full-blown AIDS. Even now, many states allow arguments for damages based on reduced life expect-ancy.

One concrete loss experienced by everyone who is seropositive, whether or not he or she ever develops AIDS or ARC, is a drastic reduction in insur-ability. Even if insurance companies are prohibited by law from excluding applicants from coverage on the basis of HIV antibody status, they are likely to place seropositive policy holders in a separate high-risk—and high-pre-mium—pool. (See Chapter 13.) This increased cost of insurance would be an appropriate element of any damages award. In particular cases, other nonmedical costs or losses may be compensable as well.

Even if the plaintiff has proved every element of a negligence claim, the defendant may still avoid liability if he or she can establish a recognized defense. The negligence defenses most likely to be used in sexual trans-mission cases are contributory (and comparative) negligence and assumption of the risk.

"Contributory negligence" refers to conduct on the part of the plaintiff that is considered a contributing cause of his or her own injuries. It is conduct that falls below the standard of care that one is required to exercise to protect oneself.[18] Until recent decades, contributory negligence completely precluded recovery. Many states, however, have replaced the doctrine of contributory negligence with a system of comparative negligence. Under this system, the plaintiff's lack of care in protecting himself or herself does not bar a recovery; it simply diminishes the awardable damages in proportion to the amount of negligence attributable to the plaintiff.[19]

In a state with strict contributory negligence, courts are likely to be wary of allowing the defense to be asserted in sexual transmission cases, unless the plaintiff actually knew of the defendant's infected condition (a circumstance that, in any event, also gives rise to the "assumption of the risk" defense discussed below). There seems to be little to gain by allowing negligent defendants to escape liability altogether and placing the sole burden of reducing the risk of HIV transmission on their unknowing sex partners.

In comparative negligence states, however, courts may view the defense as a useful means of allocating costs, and responsibility, to both sexual partners in an attempt to maximize tort law's deterrent effect. Perhaps a reasonable person should realize that his or her chances of being exposed to HIV are significantly increased if he or she engages in sex with multiple partners whose sexual history is unknown. A plaintiff engaging in sex with a partner with whom a relationship of trust has not been established might be deemed contributorily negligent for failing to wear a condom (or to ask the partner to wear one) or for engaging in sexual practices that the plaintiff knows, or should know, have been determined by health officials to be unsafe. Whether such a rule would be fair, or effective for that matter, depends in part on the extent to which useful safe sex information has been disseminated to the relevant public.

The defense of "assumption of risk" "has been a subject of much controversy, and has been surrounded by much confusion, because [it] has been used by the courts in several different senses."[20] The thread common to all these uses is that the plaintiff recognized the particular risk at issue, understood its nature and consequences, and voluntarily chose to expose himself or herself to it.[21] When proved, the defense completely precludes recovery in a suit claiming negligence. Thus, when a person infected with HIV informs a sexual partner of his or her condition and the sexual partner understands the risk and voluntarily consents to high-risk sexual activity, that partner has expressly assumed the risk of contracting the virus and cannot prevail in a negligent transmission suit.

Although they are often confused with each other, the defenses of assumption of risk and contributory negligence are quite distinct. "Assumption of risk is a matter of knowledge of the danger and voluntary acquiescence in it, while contributory negligence is a matter of some fault or departure from the standard of conduct of the reasonable person, however unaware, unwilling, or even protesting the plaintiff may be."[22] At the same time, the defenses do overlap. The person who assumes the risk "may be acting quite reasonably, and not be at all negligent in taking the chance, because the advantages of his conduct outweigh the risk. His decision may be the right one, and he may even act with unusual caution because he knows the danger he is to meet. On the other hand, . . . the plaintiff's conduct in encountering a known risk may in itself be unreasonable, because the danger is out of all proportion to the advantage which he is seeking to obtain."[23] In the latter circumstance, assumption of risk and contributory negligence intersect, and the defendant may assert either or both if both are permitted.

A more difficult case is presented when the defendant does not inform the plaintiff of his or her HIV infection, but circumstances are such that the plaintiff has good reason to believe that the defendant is infectious. If the plaintiff voluntarily decides to engage in high-risk sex with the defendant, can the plaintiff be viewed as impliedly having assumed the risk? There are many cases in which plaintiffs have failed to prevail because they are deemed by their conduct to have assumed the risk of injury. The classic example is the baseball spectator who catches a foul ball in the teeth.[24] Nevertheless, implied assumption of risk is not generally favored and is especially inappropriate where, as with HIV transmission, public policy militates against relieving those at fault from liability.

Whenever circumstances are such that the plaintiff should know that the defendant is infected, it is probable that the defendant is even more aware (actually or constructively) of that grim reality. At the same time, for the plaintiff to proceed with unsafe sex is scarcely prudent. Therefore, recognizing a defense of comparative negligence seems to be the optimal way to achieve the noncongruent goals of compensating victims, discouraging unreasonable risk-taking, expressing societal disapproval of advantage-taking, and slowing the spread of AIDS.

Battery

Battery is defined as an intentional, harmful or offensive, and unprivileged contact with the body of another, made without that person's consent.[25] To prove the first element—that the defendant acted intentionally—the plaintiff need not show that the defendant sought purposely to infect him or her. Rather, it is enough to show that the defendant, knowing that he or she was infected with HIV, intended to cause the sexual contact that led to the transmission of the virus. If, on the other hand, the defendant lacked actual knowledge of his or her infected state, the intent element cannot be satisfied. As for the second element, there can be little doubt that a sexual contact that transmits a potentially deadly infection is "harmful or offensive." Even if the sex act, in and of itself, is not offensive, the knowing exposure of one's partner to HIV certainly is.

Battery also requires that the contact between the plaintiff and the defendant be "unprivileged." In some states, a wife may still be deemed to consent to sexual relations with her husband by virtue of having entered into the marital relationship, thus making intramarital sex, in general, "privileged conduct." Nevertheless, even in those states a wife will not be deemed to have consented as a part of the marital relationship to exposure to a sexually transmitted disease.[26] Therefore, where HIV transmission is at issue, lack of consent and lack of privilege will be presumed.

Sexual activity satisfies the contact requirement.[27] Moreover, that contact is sufficient to allow recovery for emotional or psychological distress. Since recovery for negligently induced emotional distress may be limited to the distress that accompanies demonstrable physical injury, where the injury flowing from exposure to HIV is primarily psychological and the defendant acted knowingly, the plaintiff may have a better chance of success if his or her suit is based on battery rather than on negligence. Conversely, where it cannot be proved that the defendant acted knowingly, the plaintiff is more likely to prevail on a negligence claim.

Fraudulent Misrepresentation

One who claims to be free of HIV infection knowing full well that he or she has AIDS or HIV antibodies may be liable in fraud to anyone who becomes infected through sexual activity consented to on the basis of such assurances. A successful case of fraudulent misrepresentation must prove six elements: 1) that the representation by the defendant was false; 2) that the defendant knew the representation was false; 3) that there existed no reason for the defendant to believe that the misrepresentation was true; 4) that the defendant intended and expected the plaintiff to rely upon the misrepresentation; 5) that the plaintiff did rely upon the representation and was justified in doing so; and 6) that damage to the plaintiff resulted from this reliance.[28]

A fairly recent California case illustrates how a claim for fraudulent misrepresentation can arise in a setting involving sexual intimacy. In that case, the defendant allegedly engaged in sexual intercourse with the plaintiff after he falsely assured her that he was sterile. As a result, she suffered an ectopic pregnancy and was forced to undergo surgery to save her life, which left her sterile. The court of appeals held that the plaintiff's allegations created a cause of action for deceit (i.e., fraudulent misrepresentation).[29]

A plaintiff may establish fraud in a case of transmission of HIV by showing that the defendant actually knew of his or her infectious condition and lied about it in order to induce the plaintiff to have sex. The plaintiff must also establish that he or she would have refused sex if the truth had been known, and that he or she was justified in accepting the defendant's false assurances.

Fraudulent misrepresentation may also occur through silence that is meant to lead another person to place himself or herself in a position involving risk or injury. "It has commonly been stated as a general rule, particularly in the older cases, that . . . [a tort claim cannot be based on] tacit nondisclosure. . . . To this general rule, if such it be, the courts have developed a number of exceptions, some of which are as yet very ill defined, and have no very definite boundaries."[30] One exception "is found where the parties stand in some fiduciary or confidential relationship to each other."[31] Such a relationship exists legally between a husband and wife; whether the relationship between unmarried sexual partners would also be considered "confidential" in this sense is unclear. It has been cogently argued that "[p]artners to the sexual intercourse, if only for a brief time, share a trust and intimacy that elevates their relationship from the level of mere friend or acquaintance. Their confidential relationship should invoke a heightened duty, requiring disclosure of specific facts as circumstances dictate: the risk of contracting an incurable disease demands disclosure even to one with whom intimacy has only briefly been shared."[32]

Statutory Violation

In many states, statutes have been enacted making the communication of a venereal disease a crime.[33] Some courts have construed these statutes as also giving rise to a tort action for money damages for a plaintiff who has contracted a sexually transmitted disease.[34] While a court is under no compulsion to do so, many courts have regarded such criminal statutes as reflecting an official determination that certain risks are foreseeable, that certain conduct is prohibited, and that no "reasonable person" would violate the prohibition set down in the criminal statute.

The position of most courts is that conduct that violates a statute created for the protection of the public is negligent per se, which means that it is treated as being conclusively negligent.[35] A minority of courts, however, find a violation of such a statute to be only evidence of negligence,[36] leaving the defendant free to present evidence that he or she in fact exercised due care under the circumstances.

One obstacle to basing tort liability on a statute providing criminal penalties for communicating a venereal disease is that in many jurisdictions AIDS has not yet been officially recognized as a venereal disease. Certain jurisdictions, however, include broad language such as "any other disease which can be sexually transmitted,"[37] which would undoubtedly be construed to include AIDS. The California Court of Appeal, which construed herpes to be a venereal disease, has already indicated a willingness to so categorize AIDS.[38] Some states have adopted more broadly worded statutes providing criminal penalties for transmission of "contagious disease."[39] Where legislation is so broadly worded, the designation of AIDS as a contagious or venereal disease by the Centers for Disease Control may be determinative. A number of states also have legislation pending that would classify AIDS as a contagious disease.[40]

Liability Related to the Provision of Blood and Blood Products

Only 2 percent of the reported cases of AIDS have been caused by transmission of HIV in whole blood and blood products such as Factor VIII, used by hemophiliacs.[41] Despite their small numbers, recipients of HIV-contaminated blood are likely to constitute a disproportionately high percentage of AIDS-related tort plaintiffs, in light of their relative immunity from social opprobrium once the cause of their infection becomes public knowledge, and the fact that hospitals and blood banks have "deeper pockets" (i.e., greater resources, including insurance, from which to pay a sizable tort judgment) than do needle sharers or the average sexual partner. Moreover, since there is little that transfusion patients and hemophiliacs can do to reduce the risk of infection, a powerful argument can be made that the costs of the occasional accidental transmissions of HIV via blood or blood products should be absorbed by the blood supplier (and then spread across all persons who receive blood by charging slightly higher fees to cover the blood supplier's increased insurance) rather than be borne by the luckless individual victim.

At least three legal theories have been advanced by persons seeking compensation as a result of receiving blood contaminated with the hepatitis B virus: breach of implied warranty, strict liability, and negligence. Undoubtedly, the same causes of action will be employed by recipients of HIV-contaminated blood. As explained more fully below, the first two theories are likely to meet with success only in a few states; the latter, negligence, will often present difficult problems of proof.

Breach of Implied Warranty and Strict Liability

An action for a breach of implied warranty is based on statutes that, in effect, read certain warranties into every contract for the sale of products. If such laws apply to the sale of blood, blood suppliers are bound by an implied guarantee that the blood or blood product sold to a patient is fit for transfusion. In hepatitis B cases, most courts considering the matter have held that suppliers of blood cannot be held liable for breach of implied warranties because the supplying of blood constitutes a service rather than the sale of a product.[42] Legislatures in the overwhelming majority of states have adopted statutes to the same effect.[43] Thus, in only a few states can an action against blood suppliers be premised on the theory of breach of implied warranty.

Like breach of implied warranty, a cause of action premised on the theory of strict liability does not require that the injurious act be intentional or the result of negligence. Rather, liability arises simply because certain enterprises or commodities are inherently dangerous and are likely to produce injuries even when reasonable care is exercised. The classic example of an inherently dangerous or ultrahazardous enterprise is the storage of explosives or inflammable liquids. In such situations, courts impose strict liability partly because the defendant is better able than the plaintiff to bear and spread the costs of any injuries, and partly because the defendant is better positioned to take steps to reduce the riskiness of the enterprise.

In recent years, strict liability theory has been applied to the sale of goods as part of the expansion of what has come to be known as products liability.[44] Despite some early indications that courts might hold suppliers of hepatitis B-contaminated blood strictly liable to transfusion recipients,[45] the adoption in most states of statutes declaring that supplying blood constitutes a service rather than a sale has effectively curtailed that approach. In those few states that have no such statutory restrictions, the courts retain the power to decide whether to treat contaminated blood as a defective product. In considering the matter, they may treat differently hospitals (which supply blood only as an incidental function) and blood banks, especially those that are profit-seeking.[46] Similarly, companies that manufacture blood products such as Factor VIII might discover that they are held strictly liable even if hospitals are judged by the lesser negligence standard. Finally, it is at least theoretically possible that courts may impose strict liability upon blood suppliers on the theory that they operate an inherently dangerous enterprise rather than because they sell defective products.

Negligence

Even in states where strict liability and breach of implied warranty are not options, blood and blood product suppliers can still be sued for failing to exercise reasonable care in administering or producing blood.[47] To prevail in a suit for negligence, a plaintiff must show that the blood supplier failed to carry out a duty of care owed to him or her, and that this failure caused the plaintiff injury. Specifically, a recipient of HIV-infected blood would need to establish that donor-screening and blood-screening measures recommended by relevant public health agencies were not employed or, if employed, were carried out negligently.

In considering the potential liability of hospitals, blood banks, and blood products manufacturers for negligently supplying contaminated blood, we must distinguish between cases involving blood and blood products administered prior to the availability of screening tests for HIV antibodies and cases involving blood and blood products administered thereafter. Since the test became available in March 1985, organizations that collect blood and plasma have the capacity to screen subsequent donations. Under guidelines developed by the Centers for Disease Control,[48] blood or plasma that is antibody positive on initial testing may not be transfused or manufactured into other products capable of transmitting the virus. Failure to follow these guidelines might well expose a supplier to negligence suits by the recipients of contaminated blood or blood products. Moreover, even if a blood bank properly tested all donated blood, it conceivably could be found negligent for failing to screen out high-risk donors as well, in accordance with Food and Drug Administration guidelines dating back to 1983. Once the principal means of protecting the blood supply, donor screening could be viewed by courts today as a prudent adjunct to antibody testing.

The duty to exhibit reasonable prudence may also oblige blood suppliers to obtain the "informed consent" of patients before administering blood or blood products, although some courts have refused to recognize such a duty with respect to the hepatitis B virus. Informed consent is a patient's statement that he or she has been made aware of the risks inherent in a given medical procedure. Informed consent may be especially important in relation to HIV infection, inasmuch as some risk remains that blood producing a negative test result nevertheless carries the virus. Studies have reported several asymptomatic individuals infected with HIV for more than six months whose blood did not test positive for the antibody.[49] Therefore, a health care provider administering blood or blood products should inform prospective recipients about the continuing risk of infection. Informed consent would not, however, shield the provider from liability if he or she failed to exercise reasonable care in screening the blood; sound public policy dictates that no one be deemed to have consented to negligent health care.

Moreover, if the blood has been obtained from paid donors, the patient should be informed that he or she may face increased risks by accepting such blood. Intravenous drug users in search of ready cash are likely to be highly overrepresented among those who give blood for payment. For that reason, some states have enacted statutes requiring that blood obtained from paid donors be so labeled.[50]

The question of liability for injury caused by HIV-infected blood or plasma administered prior to the development of the antibody test is more complex. By the end of 1982, evidence had developed associating AIDS with blood transfusions and with Factor VIII. In March 1983, the FDA issued to all blood- and plasma-collecting facilities in the United States specific guidelines for preventing the transmission of AIDS through blood products.[51] These guidelines called upon collection centers to provide information about AIDS to donors so that they would be able to recognize whether they were members of groups at increased risk, to revise standard operating procedures to include specific questions regarding signs and symptoms of AIDS, and to advise donors that members of high-risk groups should voluntarily forgo donating blood. Failure to follow these guidelines might well leave a collection facility open to liability for negligence. Although some commentators have argued that these guidelines were insufficient and that collection facilities should have been required to inquire affirmatively into whether donors were at risk for AIDS, no court is likely to find that a facility that followed the FDA guidelines failed to exercise reasonable care.

MALPRACTICE

A breach of the duty of care a physician owes to his or her patients is called malpractice. As a general rule, physicians and other health care providers are required to act with the level of skill and learning commonly possessed by members of the profession in good standing in their (or similar) communities. Some courts will impose national, rather than local, standards, particularly if the doctor is a nationally certified specialist. Chief among the failings likely to lead to malpractice suits by HIV-infected patients are failures to diagnose, misdiagnoses, and failures to inform patients of the diagnosis.

Errors in Diagnosis

Patients may well believe that a doctor should be held liable whenever a medical error occurs and causes injury. By law, however, a physician is liable only when the error is caused by the doctor's failure to comply with the standards of the profession. In other words, a faulty diagnosis arising from unusual circumstances that would have caused any reasonable physician to err does not give rise to liability for malpractice.

Because AIDS is a syndrome involving multiple symptoms and even other diseases, diagnosis is not a simple matter. The difficulty of diagnosis is compounded by the lack of a simple, reliable test for the disease. HIV-antibody tests merely determine whether the subject has been exposed to the virus. They neither determine whether a person has AIDS nor whether he or she will ever develop it. (See Chapter 9.) But although at present there is no known cure for AIDS, medical researchers agree that an aggressive clinical approach must be taken against the recurrent, severe, multiple opportunistic diseases that mark its course.[52] Moreover, researchers recently have suggested several possible approaches for treating patients with AIDS or ARC. Although they cannot be regarded as cures, these treatments may hold the virus in check and substantially improve and lengthen a patient's life.

A failure to diagnose AIDS properly may lead to a delay in, or failure to obtain, necessary treatment, resulting in an aggravated condition, the hastening of the disease, or premature death.[53] A failure to diagnose properly may also lead to erroneous prescription of a course of treatment harmful to an AIDS patient.[54]

Each of these harms may be compensated for in a suit for malpractice. Thus, the fact that AIDS eventually would have resulted in the plaintiff's death even if an accurate diagnosis had been made earlier does not preclude a sizable award of damages.[55] Moreover, as treatment protocols develop, and particularly as these are directed at early stages of the disease, the physician who fails to diagnose the disease early enough for treatment to be given when it is likely to have its most beneficial effect in restoring the immune system will face greater exposure to damage awards.

A patient whose AIDS or AIDS-related disease has been misdiagnosed or gone undiagnosed may also recover for resultant emotional distress.[56] Where a diagnosis is late in coming, the patient may suffer acute distress upon learning that needed treatment has been delayed. If the diagnosis is timely but erroneous, a patient may have a malpractice claim based on resultant psychological damage even where improper treatment has not ensued and no physical injury has resulted. Damages may be based on such factors as the cost of psychotherapy or counseling, loss of income (if the psychological damage has impaired the patient's ability to work), and pain and suffering.

In a noteworthy case, a doctor was held liable for misinforming a patient that she had tuberculosis, thus causing her to develop "tuberculosis phobia."[57] The similar phenomenon of "AIDS anxiety" is recognized as occurring in a group termed the worried well, and can often be quite debilitating.[58] If an erroneous diagnosis triggers such a response, and if the diagnosis was the result of negligence, the patient could recover damages for his or her anxiety as well as for any losses (such as loss of employment) that are the direct consequence of that anxiety.

Even the unworried well may recover for harms that are the direct consequence of an erroneous diagnosis. In one New Jersey case, the plaintiff was denied employment because his preemployment physical examination produced a diagnosis of active tuberculosis. He then brought a successful malpractice suit after exhaustive tests elsewhere established that he did not have—and had never had—tuberculosis.[59] Similarly, a person diagnosed erroneously as being seropositive or as having AIDS or ARC would have a malpractice claim if his or her employment interests were compromised by the false test results.

Failure to Inform Patient of AIDS Diagnosis

Some physicians may not wish to inform a patient that he or she has AIDS, reasoning that a patient with an untreatable, fatal disease is not benefited by knowing of his or her condition. Others, notably institutional physicians (prison and workplace doctors, for example) who perform examinations at the behest of someone other than their patients, may not think it necessary to communicate diagnoses directly to patients. Once a diagnosis of AIDS has been made, however, failure to inform a patient of that fact or of the nature of the disease will create liability if knowledge of the diagnosis would enable the patient to take measures or obtain treatment that might prolong his or her life.[60] If, as it now appears, persons reinfected with HIV have a worse prognosis than those who avoid multiple infections, then there are indeed life-prolonging measures that a seropositive person can take. As in the case of failure to diagnose, failure to inform a patient of the diagnosis may create liability even though the disease will eventually lead to death in any case.

In a similar situation, a federal court recognized liability based on negligence when a physician failed to inform a patient of the discovery of a suspected tumor during a preemployment examination, even though the plaintiff failed to show that the tumor would have been operable at the time it was discovered by the defendant. The court found that the plaintiff was entitled to damages for being deprived of the benefit of earlier treatment, which might have arrested the tumor's growth or slowed its development and possibly prolonged the patient's life and decreased his suffering.[61]

WHAT TORT LAW CAN AND CANNOT DO

Exposure to HIV has the potential for producing great psychological stress and anxiety. Development of AIDS, with the associated opportunistic infections, most often involves pain, suffering, incapacitation, and death. Some individuals are likely to seek compensation for at least some of these harms through tort litigation.

There are well-established causes of action that may be pursued in various AIDS-related contexts. Nevertheless, many practical problems beset tort plaintiffs. Some of these relate to the difficulty of proving certain of the elements of the various causes of action (such as causation in suits alleging sexual transmission). Other problems stem from uncertainty regarding which defenses are available. Finally, there are procedural obstacles to overcome (such as satisfying the statute of limitations), and evidentiary problems as well (such as proving future damages).

Nevertheless, recognition of tort liability for HIV transmission and for AIDS-related medical malpractice will make it possible for some parties to obtain compensation. Furthermore, tort suits will provide at least a small incentive to others to use proper diagnostic techniques and to alter behavior and procedures so as to limit the likelihood of HIV transmission. But tort suits, especially those directed at the sexual transmission of HIV, are not a very satisfactory means of achieving a third, critically important goal: spreading the costs associated with this dreadful, and dreadfully expensive, disease. That is perhaps best done by society as a whole, using a combination of private-sector insurance and public-sector funding.

PART FOUR
AIDS AND HEALTH CARE

12

The Right to Medical Treatment

TAUNYA LOVELL BANKS

The public's fear of contracting AIDS is escalating as the syndrome spreads. Unfortunately, this fear of AIDS is also high among members of the medical profession and is a special concern of health care workers in hospitals across the nation.[1] The term "medical professionals" includes nurses, doctors, lab technicians, ambulance drivers, paramedics, as well as people in other professions, such as funeral directors and embalmers. Many medical professionals are refusing to treat people with AIDS, even though current medical studies indicate that the occupational risk of transmission of the Human Immunodeficiency Virus (HIV) is minimal.[2] Medical treatment has even been denied to some merely because they are members of AIDS high-risk groups.[3]

Until recently, fear of AIDS within the medical community did not create a serious problem, because most of the early AIDS cases were confined to established, active, urban gay communities. Initially, the primary health care providers for most people with AIDS were physicians close to the gay community. However, many other physicians with highly developed ethical standards feel an obligation to treat patients with AIDS.[4]

As the number of AIDS cases increases, however, the general medical community will be forced to become more involved in the care of people with AIDS. As AIDS spreads beyond large coastal cities, and becomes more commonplace, people with the disease will come into contact not just with sophisticated, cosmopolitan physicians, but with general practitioners and a wide variety of ordinary health care workers. Further, with improved understanding of other illnesses such as AIDS-Related Complex (ARC) and progress in ability to detect the presence of HIV, more demands will be made on the medical community for treatment and counseling of people who have been exposed to the virus but have not developed AIDS.

Several commentators, relying on anecdotal information, suggest that fear of infection has caused the general medical community to be reluctant in treating patient with AIDS and ARC.[5] For example, two paramedics in Los Angeles were sued for allegedly not providing proper medical assistance to a heart attack victim because they believed he had AIDS. In another instance, a nationally known heart surgeon refused to operate on anyone infected with HIV.[6]

Since unlike other terminal illnesses such as cancer, AIDS is contagious, physicians are forced by AIDS to decide how much personal risk they are willing to assume. Two writers recently noted, "[h]istorically, physicians have tacitly accepted an occupational risk of exposure to fatal infectious diseases.... Only the current generation of physicians, trained after the development of effective antibiotics, has never confronted this potential occupational risk."[7] Some physicians choose not to work with AIDS patients, while others elect to care for people with AIDS only when necessary.[8]

As the epidemic grows, these fears of infection are likely to result in an increase in refusals to treat. The problem, then, is to determine what legal obligation, if any, the medical community has to provide care to people who are ill with AIDS or ARC, or infected with HIV.

OBLIGATIONS OF PRIVATE PHYSICIANS AND HEALTH CARE PROVIDERS

While people with AIDS undoubtedly deserve access to adequate medical care, the law does not ensure such access. Because the law views the relationship between a private physician and her patient as consensual, a physician has no legal duty to treat.[9] The reasoning behind this rule is that a private physician is not responsible for a stranger's misfortune she did not cause.

The American Medical Association's Code of Ethics states that "in an emergency [a physician] should render service to the best of his ability." Nevertheless, most courts refuse to impose on physicians a broad legal duty to treat, even in an emergency.[10] A rather limited duty to treat has been recognized and is the subject of the following section.

The Duty to Treat under Common Law and Statute

A physician-patient relationship rests upon an express or implied contract, with most relationships created by implication.[11] Making an appointment with a physician, receiving an examination, and beginning treatment imply the existence of a contract between physician and patient.[12] This contract, however, does not guarantee future care. Even where the physician has previously treated a patient for an illness and may be considered the family physician, she may be under no legal duty to treat a patient for a new illness.[13] A physician may, by notice or by special agreement, limit the extent and scope of her practice, excluding certain diseases or medical conditions.[14] Thus a person with AIDS or ARC may have difficulty obtaining medical care from private physicians, even those with whom she has some preexisting relationship.

A patient affiliated with a health maintenance organization (HMO) may have more rights than a person with a private physician.[15] By paying regular fees for the right of access to the HMO's services, members establish an ongoing contractual relationship with the HMO. Unless the contract specifically excludes treatment for AIDS or ARC, the HMO may be liable if its health care professionals refuse to treat members with those conditions. This liability does not necessarily extend to health care personnel employed by the HMO. Their individual duty to treat may depend upon the terms of their employment contracts with the HMO rather than their relationship with the patient.

Recently, many courts have suggested that a legal duty to treat may be created in another manner. Based on tort rather than contract theory, this duty is commonly referred to as "personal encounters or undertakings." A physician may incur the duty by agreeing to treat a specific, as opposed to an unspecified, illness.[16] Thus, a duty to treat may arise when a patient is referred by one physician to a second physician for treatment of a specific problem and the second physician accepts the referral.[17] However, at least one court has held that no legal duty was created where an associate of the treating doctor was consulted by telephone over a decision to hospitalize a patient.[18] Similarly, where a doctor merely converses with the treating physician about the treatment of a patient, a duty to treat may not exist.

Physicians who contemplate refusing to treat people with AIDS or ARC should be aware that while the courts have not imposed any general duty to treat on private physicians in the absence of some close connection to the patient, whether they will continue to adhere to the traditional "no duty" view is open to question.

Common law obligations fashioned by courts are not the only means by which physicians may be obliged to render care. Statutes may also address the rights and obligations of physicians. Several states, for example, have enacted "good Samaritan laws" that limit the liability of people who provide emergency assistance. These laws do not require physicians to treat all persons in life threatening circumstances,[19] but their purpose is to encourage qualified individuals to provide emergency care by protecting them from lawsuits. Where she chooses to treat, the physician is not legally liable for injuries to the victim unless she is grossly negligent. In the few states that require treatment in emergency situations, the physician is required to treat only if she was at the scene when an accident occurred.[20] Thus even the most demanding good Samaritan law rarely imposes any legal duty to treat.

Duty to Treat under Antidiscrimination Legislation

Of greater potential benefit to persons with AIDS are antidiscrimination statutes. Although a growing number of cities[21] and states[22] have specifically prohibited various kinds of discrimination against people with AIDS, many more cities and states have not acted to prevent such discrimination. However, forty-seven states and many cities have general antidiscrimination laws, many of which prohibit discrimination against the physically disabled.[23] Twenty-one states have formally declared that their handicap-discrimination provisions will be construed to include AIDS as a handicap, and five states have unofficial policies to that effect.[24] Where state antidiscrimination laws prohibit discrimination in public accommodations—places or services representing themselves as open to the general public—they may be interpreted to include the provision of medical and dental care.[25] Washington state, for example, has interpreted its statute concerning discrimination based on handicap in public accommodations to apply to AIDS-based discrimination in dental offices, doctors' offices, hospitals, and nursing homes.[26] Under such a statute, a physician who refused to treat a person with AIDS or ARC would be acting illegally.

Recently, several California cities have enacted laws prohibiting discrimination against people with AIDS. These laws are exemplary and will probably be used as models for future local ordinances. They cover discrimination in medical and dental treatment and clearly include people with ARC, people harboring the virus, and people suspected of having AIDS.[27] Protection for people in the first two categories is also important because they may suffer discrimination when they seek ordinary medical and dental services which are not related to illnesses associated with AIDS. It would also be capricious for a statute to mandate that those who are gravely ill with full-blown AIDS should be treated while those who are mildly ill with ARC and more responsive to treatment can be ignored by physicians.

One state (Wisconsin)[28] and several localities[29] have laws prohibiting discrimination based on sexual preference that can be used to combat discrimination against healthy people in high-risk categories because of the connection, real or imagined, between AIDS and their life style. For example, a dentist who refuses appointments to gay men because she fears AIDS could be charged with discrimination against gay men.[30] Sexual preference laws could not, of course, be used by heterosexual people faced with AIDS-based discrimination.

Termination of the Relationship

A physician often agrees to treat a patient for a specific illness. But as with any consensual relationship, either party is free to end the relationship before treatment is completed. Nevertheless, public policy considerations have led to certain limits on the physician's right to terminate the relationship. The physician may not leave a critically ill patient without making provisions for her care. Such conduct would constitute abandonment, and the physician would be legally liable for any resulting damage.[31]

Unlawful abandonment can take many forms: the outright refusal to treat a patient further; the premature discharge by the physician of a patient from the hospital; the refusal to treat a patient on a timely basis.[32] Even the patient's failure to pay the physician's fee may not be an adequate basis for the abandonment of a patient in need of medical care.[33]

Since liability will attach to a physician who abandons a patient at a critical stage of an illness or disease, and the course of AIDS and ARC is so unpredictable, it might be difficult for a physician treating a person with AIDS or ARC to terminate unilaterally an on-going relationship with the patient without risking legal liability. Therefore, a physician should be careful to ensure that the patient has obtained other competent medical care before ending the relationship.

Hospital Staff

The law treats physicians working in hospitals differently from independent physicians. A physician employed by a hospital is generally required to treat any patient the hospital admits.[34] In agreeing to work for the hospital, the physician waives the right to choose her patients.[35] Likewise, medical students, nurses, and other health care workers affiliated with hospitals or health care organizations are obligated to care for all admitted patients.[36]

Hospital employees' obligation to treat may be modified by hospital regulation or labor agreement, either of which may restore to staff the right to select patients.[37] Furthermore, employees covered by the Occupational Health and Safety Act may refuse to do anything that threatens their safety.[38] As mentioned previously, however, current medical research indicates that the risk of HIV transmission to health care workers in hospitals is negligible. Thus health care workers probably could not successfully assert a threat to their safety as a valid basis for refusing to treat an AIDS patient admitted to the hospital.[39] (For more information on employment law, see Chapter 8.) Some hospitals assign to AIDS patients only those staff members who volunteer to care for them, reasoning that willing professionals are likely to provide better and more sensitive treatment.[40] The use of volunteers also allows hospitals to avoid the problem of firing employees who refuse to care for persons with AIDS.

HOSPITALS' DUTY TO TREAT

The treatment of AIDS patients places greater burdens on hospitals than the treatment of most other patients. People with AIDS tend to be hospitalized frequently, often for long periods.[41] The cost of treating people with AIDS exceeds the average cost of treating many catastrophic illnesses,[42] and many AIDS patients lack full insurance coverage for hospitalization.[43] AIDS patients also require almost twice as much nursing care as patients with other terminal illnesses.[44] As a result, institutional pressures to prohibit or severely limit the hospitalization of people with AIDS are strong. In addition, many private hospitals strive to avoid the "stigma" of being characterized as AIDS hospitals, fearing that other patients will not be referred to them.[45]

Private Hospitals

As a general rule, a private hospital is under no legal duty to admit and treat all who seek care.[46] Even the receipt of federal funds does not substantially affect the discretion of private hospitals in selecting patients.[47] Some jurisdictions recognize an exception to this rule in the case of private hospitals with "well established" emergency facilities,[48] and some states have passed statutes requiring every hospital to admit persons in need of emergency care.[49] And while, in the absence of such requirements, most private hospitals act on what they perceive as a professional obligation to treat people in life threatening circumstances, the provision of emergency care creates no obligation to treat the patient further, and private hospitals may refuse comprehensive treatment without liability.[50] This practice, although legally permissible, is frowned upon by many in the medical profession.

The antidiscrimination laws discussed earlier may apply to private hospitals either directly or indirectly in their capacity as places of public accommodation.[51] If covered by such laws, a hospital that refused to treat a person with, or suspected of having, AIDS or ARC, could be liable for any resulting injury. Liability for discrimination might prove costly, since many of the relevant statutes provide not only for compensatory damages, including emotional injury, but also for punitive damages.[52] Thus antidiscrimination laws will effectively impose greater duties on private hospitals than does the common law, although even under the common law, a court might be persuaded to impose a higher duty on a hospital that was the only accessible facility in the community.

Nonprofit hospitals may be exempt from taxation as charitable organizations.[53] Hospitals that refuse to treat AIDS patients risk losing their tax exempt status. In defining "charitable" in this context, the federal government has suggested that "charitable" hospitals must "provid[e medical care] for all those persons in the community able to pay the cost thereof." One ruling also stressed the importance of a hospital operating an emergency room open to all community members, even those who cannot pay.[54] The force of these rulings may be diminished in practice by the fact that individuals cannot sue to revoke an organization's tax exempt status.[55] The initiative can be taken only by the government.

Public Hospitals

At common law, even a public hospital supported by public tax funds had no duty to accept and treat everyone nor any duty to maintain an emergency room. However, if a public hospital does maintain an emergency room, the hospital cannot refuse to provide emergency treatment to a person because that person has or is suspected of having a specific disease.[56]

Furthermore, courts enforcing federal antidiscrimination laws would most likely forbid a public hospital to refuse nonemergency care to a person solely because she had ARC or AIDS. The equal protection clause of the Fourteenth Amendment requires that any classification by government imposing different benefits or burdens on people must be rationally related to a legitimate government objective. (For a detailed discussion of the equal protection clause, see Chapter 4.) Since AIDS cannot be transmitted through casual contact, neither other patients nor health care personnel are endangered by AIDS patients,[57] so denying care to people with AIDS cannot rationally be related to protecting a hospital's staff and patients from risk of infection. A city, county, or state with a policy denying access to publicly financed health care services by people with or suspected of having AIDS may violate those persons' right to equal treatment, especially in life threatening circumstances. The governmental entity would have to demonstrate that denying people with AIDS equal access to public life-saving facilities was rationally related to some legitimate governmental objective.

OTHER RELATED SERVICES

Ambulance Service

Very little law exists in this area. Most cases involve situations where the ambulance service provided transportation and was sued for operating the ambulance in a negligent manner. In assessing liability the courts look at the ambulance service and determine whether it is gratuitous, operated for a profit, or owned and operated by the city, county, or state.[58]

At least one lawsuit has been filed involving the refusal to provide city ambulance service to a person wrongly suspected of having AIDS.[59] Until September 1985, the District of Columbia permitted posting the names of people with AIDS on the chalkboards of city firehouses, reasoning that it had an obligation to inform ambulance personnel of persons with contagious diseases so that precautionary measures could be taken. Only protest from the local gay community forced the discontinuation of this practice.[60] Whether an ambulance service may refuse to transport a person suspected of having AIDS or ARC depends on whether the service has a legal duty to provide service to all in need. Privately owned and operated services would probably not be found to have a duty to provide services to all who requested them. Like private physicians, they are free to select their customers/ patients.

If the ambulance could be classified as a common carrier, however, a duty to provide services to all might follow. As one court defines them, "[c]ommon carriers of passengers are those who undertake to carry all persons indifferently who apply for passage."[61] The common carrier characterization is important because most antidiscrimination laws cover common carriers.[62] Where antidiscrimination laws prohibit discrimination based on disability, a refusal to transport an AIDS or ARC patient would probably be illegal. Antidiscrimination laws cover private services classified as common carriers as well as ambulance services that provide their services to the general public for no charge.

Some ambulance services provide transportation only to persons who are "members" of the service, that is, those who pay a membership fee entitling them to access to the service. These services are not considered common carriers. Therefore they could refuse to provide service to a nonmember suspected of having AIDS. However, the membership ambulance service would probably be liable for refusing to provide services to a member with AIDS or suspected of having AIDS, on a breach of contract theory. Of course, membership ambulance services could, by contract, restrict the type of cases for which they would provide service, thereby avoiding legal liability for refusing to transport a member who had AIDS.

Many jurisdictions have laws requiring a publicly owned and operated ambulance service to transport any person to or from the hospital in an emergency. These laws may also apply to services that are operated only partly at public expense.[63]

Residential Health Care Facilities

Most residential health care facilities or nursing homes are privately operated and not open to all who request admittance. Many of these facilities have refused to accept people with AIDS.[64] Legally there is not much one can do to force them to admit people with AIDS since the facilities are free to determine what types of medical cases they will admit. This refusal of residential health care facilities to admit people with AIDS creates a problem for hospitals: It means they are unable to discharge people with AIDS who no longer require specialized hospital care but are unable to care for themselves.

Generally hospitals have a duty not to discharge prematurely a patient who has been admitted for treatment. Thus it may be unlawful to discharge involuntarily a person not well enough to care for herself.[65] The absence of alternative residential care makes discharge planning very difficult and also increases the costs for both patient and hospital. Recently, special hospices and residential health care facilities for people with AIDS have been established in cities with a high incidence of AIDS. Most often these centers are small and designed to serve only local AIDS patients. Thus persons from areas with relatively low numbers of AIDS cases may be the most harmed by discriminatory practices of residential health care facilities.

Funeral Homes and Cemeteries

Many funeral homes are reluctant to handle the remains of AIDS patients. A few homes have refused to even accept the bodies of persons who have died from AIDS, but more have discriminated in the provision of services— refusing to embalm and charging extra for handling people with AIDS.[66] Because the embalming process may result in the release of contaminated body fluids, the Centers for Disease Control has issued guidelines for funeral homes that handle the remains of AIDS patients.[67] However, as one embalmer stated, these precautions are no greater than those taken with other bodies.[68]

Since funeral homes are privately operated, they have a measure of discretion in whom they serve, though they are subject to regulation by the state.[69] However, where funeral homes are classified as public accommodations, as they are in several states,[70] and where laws forbid discrimination based on disability, the refusal to provide services might be held illegal, depending on whether the court believes that the antidiscrimination laws apply only to living persons. A New York state court has held that legal protections "are not extinguished with the end of life," in giving the New York City Commission on Human Rights authority to prosecute funeral homes which discriminated on the basis of AIDS.[71]

The right to "decent burial" according to the usual custom in the neighborhood has long been recognized at common law, although the decedent may not necessarily be buried in the plot of her choice.[72] Religious or other institutions can place restrictions on who will be interned in their burial grounds.[73] Advocates for the deceased AIDS patient has several legal arguments to ensure that she is properly buried. A number of cases hold that cemeteries cannot discriminate in the sale of burial plots on the basis of race, since federal law prohibits discrimination based upon race in the sale or rental of property.[74] An analogous claim might be brought by an AIDS patient. Ownership of a lot in a cemetery gives a right to burial therein that, subject to certain religious considerations, the cemetery may not unreasonably abridge.[75] If a plot owner were to develop AIDS after purchasing the plot, her disease may not alter her right to be buried in her plot. Furthermore, courts may give some weight to the deceased's wishes concerning the disposition of her body.[76]

Some AIDS and disability antidiscrimination laws apply to cemeteries directly, or indirectly as public accommodations.[77] Under these laws a privately operated cemetery that was selling burial plots to the general public but refused to sell a plot to a person with AIDS, or to the family of a person who died from AIDS, would be acting illegally. Refusals by public cemeteries owned and operated by some unit of the government to bury a person solely because that person had AIDS would be of doubtful legality since the government would have to show some rational basis for AIDS-based discrimination.

Unfortunately, the law does not automatically require all health care providers to care for people with AIDS. It seems strange that innkeepers and taxicab drivers may owe more of a duty to strangers than physicians, even though the latter provide life-saving and life sustaining services. But the law regarding the physician's duty to treat is unlikely to change in the near future. To require a physician to provide medical care in a nonemergency situation is perceived as akin to requiring involuntary servitude.

Nevertheless, in light of the growing AIDS epidemic, states need to reexamine existing antidiscrimination and good Samaritan laws. These laws should prevent AIDS-based discrimination in medical treatment. No one should be allowed to go without medical treatment simply because she has a terminal illness. To allow this would demonstrate total disregard for the value of human life.

13

Insurance

MARK SCHERZER

Decisions regarding AIDS and insurance are politically highly charged, in part because AIDS primarily affects politically disfavored minorities (gay men and intravenous drug users), but also because of the high costs which treatment for AIDS entails. Without direct legislative attention to the problems of those afflicted and at high risk, insurance regulation will determine how we as a society allocate the costs of an expensive disease among different interests with widely varying degrees of political and economic power. How will insurance companies (including their shareholders), state and local governments, providers of health care and other services, the sick themselves, their families and lovers, their employers, and the broad pool of healthy premium payers divide the financial burden of dealing with AIDS? *Someone* will have to pick up the tab. The question lurking behind most insurance issues is—who?

The government has long intervened in the insurance business, especially when public policy appears to conflict with the strict use of actuarial principles in underwriting decisions, or when industry business practices seem to threaten the public. But the public debate produced by AIDS has not focused on underwriting issues alone. Public concern has also centered on the contractual obligations of insurance companies, on their obligations as holders and transmitters of information, on their impact on the course of medical diagnosis and treatment, and on their role in fostering or impeding social change. This chapter will discuss the difficult issues public officials will confront as they regulate the insurance industry's actions with respect to AIDS.

HOW INSURANCE OPERATES

Insurance involves a contract (embodied in an insurance policy) in which one party, the owner of the policy, pays premiums to another party, the insurer, in return for a promise by the insurer to make payments when certain contingencies occur. The party who is protected by the contract, and to whom or on whose behalf the payments are to be made, is called the insured. The insured is frequently, but not always, the owner of the policy and payer of premiums.

Among the major types of insurance of concern to persons with AIDS are: *health insurance*, an agreement to pay or reimburse the paid medical expenses incurred by the insured under certain defined conditions; *disability insurance*, an agreement to make payments to the insured, usually in set monthly amounts, when the insured is unable to work; and *life insurance*, an agreement to pay money to a person or designated entity upon the death of the insured.[1]

The premium payments made to the insurance company are generally periodic ones. These premiums and the money earned by investing them comprise the funds used to make payments when the contingency covered by the insurance contract comes to pass. Although every insurance contract requires the payment of premiums by the policy owner, the insurer may or may not incur an obligation to pay benefits to the insured or his or her beneficiary. For example, an insured may pay premiums throughout his or her life, and yet never become sick or disabled. Although *death* is inevitable, payment of life insurance proceeds may be contingent upon death coming in a specified manner (*e.g.*, not by suicide) or at the right time (*e.g.*, before expiration of a term policy).

The insurance contract thus bears some resemblance to a gambling contract, in which the bettor must pay money in order to participate in the game, but has no assurance of a return. On the other hand, the insured may collect benefits well in excess of the premiums he or she has paid. Consequently, the insurer—the person running the game—is successful to the degree that it establishes rules favorable to the house. If, in the aggregate, more money is placed in bets (insurance premiums) than is paid out in winnings (policy proceeds), the insurer will profit. Thus, insurers try to strike a favorable balance between broadening the number of people insured (to attract as wide a premium-paying base as possible) and limiting the exposure to claims arising from assumption of those extra risks. The more successful insurance companies have made better judgments about which risks, medical and otherwise, they can profitably assume.

The resemblance between insurance and gambling has at times worried those who regulate the industry. Public officials, including courts called upon to review statutes and regulations, have developed concepts that remove insurance contracts from the realm of gambling contracts. An example is the requirement that the purchaser of insurance have an insurable interest (i.e., an economic interest) in the life of the insured, a rule developed to discourage sales of insurance contracts that would amount to no more than sporting bets on the lives of the insureds.

If insurance were merely a matter of gambling, in which insureds sought to outsmart the companies to reap a bonanza for themselves or their heirs, it would hardly be the focus of the intense political battle that appears to be occurring with respect to AIDS. Insurance, however, is an important social institution, serving essential public functions.

In a society that places an extraordinarily high value on the cure of disease and disability but makes provision of that cure a private business, medical treatment for many conditions costs more than most people can afford. They can obtain adequate treatment for serious illness or injury only through funds provided by others. Although government funds are in some situations available to the indigent and to those struck by catastrophic illness, in most instances the funds come only from health insurance benefits.

Life insurance, too, must be treated as more than a mere gambling contract. It serves useful public functions in maintaining the financial security of people who depend upon a deceased person for support or for fulfillment of mutual financial or business obligations. Those whose assets are severely depleted by caring for a terminally ill person may be made whole to a degree through the proceeds of such insurance. Life insurance thereby may reinforce the stability of "family units."

Our system of health care depends upon solvent insurance companies that can offer an affordable product: in a general way, therefore, the interests of insurers and of the public are in harmony. In particular instances, though, insurance companies' desire to maximize profits may conflict with the public interest in providing the broadest insurance coverage possible. While insurance companies maintain that they are private businesses whose decisions about underwriting risk cannot solely reflect the public interest, there can be no doubt that they deal in a particularly crucial commodity. As such, they are properly subject to extensive government intervention for the public welfare. The regulators' task is to maintain an environment in which insurers can operate profitably while restraining insurers on those occasions when the profit motive threatens important public values.

HOW INSURANCE COMPANIES ARE REGULATED

The state rather than the federal government has traditionally regulated the insurance industry. Thus, more than fifty jurisdictions fix their own sets of rules. For the sake of simplicity, this chapter will focus on insurance issues that are likely to arise frequently in many if not most states.

Governmental regulation of insurance is pervasive. As evidenced by the common requirement that policy holders have a legitimate stake in the fate of their insureds, regulation extends to the very terms on which insurance may be offered or purchased. The operations of insurance companies and agents are also highly regulated, through licensing and other schemes, to make certain that they are financially and ethically responsible. For example, states have developed special mechanisms for dealing with insolvent insurers and have restricted trade practices deemed deceptive or unfair to consumers.[2] In recent years, regulation has focused on mandating insurance coverage for more people and on expanding the insurance benefits available to them.[3]

Governmental regulation is accomplished both through specific legislation and through broad grants of supervisory powers to state insurance commissioners. In New York, for example, the Superintendent of Insurance may determine, after hearings, that insurance company practices constitute unfair trade practices. The superintendent may then issue regulations prohibiting such practices, as he did in 1976 with respect to sex discrimination in insurance, and may fine insurance companies that disobey.[4] Courts will uphold such regulations unless they lack a rational basis or conflict with specific provisions of the Insurance Law.[5]

In some jurisdictions, a concomitant of this broad regulatory authority appears to be a restriction on the ability of individuals to contest unfair trade practices by the insurance companies. In New York, for instance, it remains an open question whether individuals may sue insurance companies for violating the Insurance Law's fair trade provisions, or whether instead they must file administrative complaints with the state insurance commission, which may respond to political pressure more than would courts.[6]

How Insurance Rates are Calculated

Most health insurance in this country is provided through group policies. Policies for large groups typically do not require evidence of individual insurability, so questions as to an individual's health are unlikely to arise. An individual's risk characteristics are most likely to be an issue when the insurance buyer is self-employed or unemployed or the group seeking a policy is so small (generally fewer than ten members) that evidence of individual insurability is required. The issue may also arise if the insurance buyer is a late entrant into a group health plan, who, having initially declined to join, must provide medical information and perhaps submit to a complete physical examination. Some group health care policies provide small amounts of life insurance. Most life insurance in this country, however, is individually underwritten. Rates are based upon an individual applicant's life expectancy.

Most of the controversy concerning AIDS and insurance has focused on individually underwritten policies—a fairly small percentage of the country's health insurance but a great majority of its life insurance. Most American jurisdictions require that insurers set their premiums for individually underwritten policies on the basis of actuarial calculations: that is, the premium charged to an individual must be determined by the expenses which that individual is likely to incur (as determined by statistical evidence regarding individuals who share the identifying characteristics of a prospective buyer). An individual's projected health care costs (in the case of health insurance) or life expectancy (in the case of life insurance) will thus be used in determining insurance rates.

The requirement that insurance rates be based upon actuarial principles has been defended on grounds of fairness: an insurance buyer who seems likely to incur heavy expenses is purchasing a more valuable product, and thus should pay a higher premium, than a customer in a lower-risk group. The practice has also been defended as a means of creating economic incentives for efficient behavior. If individuals are charged premiums based upon the degrees of risk they represent, they may be induced to alter the characteristics which placed them at high risk.[7] For example, discounted premiums for nonsmokers might induce some smokers to give up the habit.

Even if insurers were not required by law to base their rates on actuarial principles, the mechanics of a competitive insurance market would force companies to rely on such principles in setting rates. A company that charged each customer the same premium simply could not survive. Lower-risk consumers would shift their coverage to companies that set rates on an actuarial basis. As these consumers removed themselves from the company's pool, the insurer would be forced to raise its rates for the remaining customers. More people would drop their insurance or switch to other carriers, imposing still greater costs on those who remained. This is the process described by the American Academy of Actuaries as the "spiral of adverse selection."[8]

MAJOR STRATEGIES INSURERS HOPE TO USE TO REDUCE THEIR EXPENSES FROM AIDS-RELATED CLAIMS

The increasing prevalence of AIDS seems likely to impose substantial costs on both life and health insurers. Estimates of the medical costs associated with AIDS have varied widely—from $28,000 to $147,000 per patient over the course of the disease[9]—but by any estimate the potential liability of insurance companies is quite high. Life insurance claims will also be great, especially since some people at risk of developing AIDS may be especially eager to purchase policies.

Insurance companies may attempt to reduce the expenses incurred from AIDS-related claims in several different ways. This section will examine four possible strategies. The first, exclusion of AIDS as a covered condition, could be used in either individually underwritten life or health insurance policies, or in the formulation of new group plans in which individual insurability is not an issue. The other three strategies only apply to the underwriting of individual policies. Since the majority of health insurance is provided by group plans that do not require evidence of individual insurability, the last three strategies would mostly affect the availability of life, not health, insurance.

The Elimination of AIDS from Covered Risks

Insurance companies may seek to exclude AIDS from future coverage on new policies. Blue Cross of Indiana is reported to be studying such an option.[10] In California, in response to requests of employers made through the local Blue Cross organization, the Insurance Department denied the exclusion request.[11] If such a plan were proposed in New York, it might run afoul of state regulations designed to guarantee that policies are of economic benefit to the public and serve its health needs.[12] It remains to be seen whether insurers, particularly those who feel they have lost control of their underwriting, will nevertheless make real efforts to exclude AIDS benefits.

Blanket exclusion of AIDS as a covered condition is unlikely. But much AIDS treatment is experimental and many insurance plans explicitly exclude payment for experimental treatment. The application of that exclusion to AIDS claims may lead to litigation or legislation that will clarify this murky area.

Refusal to Insure People with AIDS

People who have been diagnosed as having AIDS have a very short life expectancy—less than three years. They are also likely to incur significant medical costs. State regulators generally have recognized that requiring insurance companies to assume such risks could affect the companies' willingness to do business in their jurisdictions. I am not aware of any jurisdiction in which insurance companies have been forbidden from asking applicants for insurance whether they have AIDS or have been required to issue policies to persons with AIDS. Regulation in this context generally consists of restrictions on questions that may be asked. In New Jersey, the Commissioner of Insurance issued guidelines to insurance companies[13] permitting them, for example, to ask whether applicants for insurance have been told by their doctors that they have AIDS. However, insurers may not ask whether the applicants have had "any indication" that they have AIDS. The latter is deemed to be a subjective, and therefore unfair, question.

Requiring Tests for Antibodies to HIV as a Condition of Coverage

As long as a significant statistical correlation exists between a positive result in tests for antibodies to HIV and the later development of AIDS—and as long as there is no precise means to determine who will and who will not contract the disease—insurance companies will wish to use the HIV test in assessing their risks of future claims. While it is possible to isolate the actual HIV virus from blood,[14] companies intent on reducing the risks of insuring those likely to develop AIDS have relied primarily on tests that detect the presence of *antibodies* to the virus.[15] These tests, initially designed to screen blood donated to blood banks, are commercially available and far cheaper to perform than culturing of the virus would be. The justification for use of the antibody test is actuarial: a number of longitudinal studies suggest that a significant proportion of those who become "seropositive" will develop AIDS or ARC within a few years thereafter. The insurance industry insists that even less than perfectly accurate tests will protect the economic soundness of the insurance system by screening out, at minimal cost, those most likely to develop AIDS.[16]

The controversy over HIV testing has been especially acute in the case of life insurance. An individual who is seropositive, according to industry calculation, is over twenty times more likely to die within a five-year period than is an applicant of the same age and sex whose test results are negative.[17] Some evidence also indicates that applicants who know that they are at risk attempt to purchase abnormally large amounts of life insurance. The General Reassurance Company, for example, has reported that its average death claim due to AIDS in 1984 was $250,000, while the overall average was $50,000.[18] Since seropositive applicants present a greater risk than do other insurance buyers, since the claims filed with some companies have been unusually large, and since most life insurance is individually underwritten, insurance providers will be particularly eager to use HIV testing in the writing of life insurance policies.

California, the District of Columbia, Maine, and Wisconsin have passed legislation restricting the use of HIV antibody tests for insurance purposes, although the Wisconsin restrictions are almost certain to be abolished through administrative action, and the Maine restrictions expire by the terms of the statute on October 1, 1987.[19] Similar legislation has been proposed but not passed in Massachusetts and in New York.[20] In New York, California, New Jersey, Ohio, and Oregon, administrative complaints have been filed on behalf of individuals whom insurance companies sought to require to take the antibody test.[21] Ohio has yet to act.[22] In New Jersey, the Department of Insurance investigated and determined that the complainant's health history justified the request for a test.[23] As a result the complainant did not pursue his application for insurance. In Oregon, the complaint was also denied.[24] One New York case was resolved when the insurance company withdrew the test requirement and, after giving the applicant a test of immune function, issued the policy to him.[25] Another remains unresolved. New York has established no broad rule, but the Insurance Department has taken the position in individual cases that the test is "unfair" because only a small proportion of those who are seropositive will get sick, and the test does not predict who will contract AIDS.[26] In California, the Insurance Department has required the company to rescind its test requirements.[27]

In Connecticut the right to inquire about testing has been administratively suspended. Massachusetts has administratively determined that requiring antibody testing for insurance is an unfair trade practice.[28] New Jersey and Washington have promulgated guidelines for testing and have prohibited insurance companies from making determinations as to who should take the test on a discriminatory basis.[29] The Insurance Departments of Arizona, Minnesota, and North and South Dakota have also been reported as prohibiting application questionnaires regarding antibody testing.[30]

Events in the District of Columbia demonstrate the severity of the reaction, both economic and political, that may follow efforts to restrict insurers' use of HIV testing. The Prohibition of Discrimination in the Provision of Insurance Act of 1986, passed by the D.C. Council in May of 1986, took effect on August 7 of that year. By August 23, at least twenty insurers had announced that they would no longer underwrite individual life or health insurance policies in the District. It remains to be seen whether other insurers will follow suit, and whether this form of economic pressure will alter the D.C. Council's position. Some insurers will no doubt evade the statute by writing policies through Virginia or Maryland offices, which may itself lead to litigation.

The District's legislation has drawn the attention of Congress as well. Representative Dannemeyer introduced an amendment to a House appropriations bill for the District seeking to limit the use of federal funds in implementing the prohibition on HIV testing. A similar bill subsequently passed the Senate.[31] The amendment was defeated by the full House; although one Congressional opponent expressed strong support for the testing prohibition, Congressional critics of the Dannemeyer amendment generally focused upon the District's right to autonomy and the desirability of local control over insurance regulation.[32] The House vote was preceded by intensive lobbying efforts on the part of groups generally antagonistic to homosexuals.[33]

After the act became effective, the American Council of Life Insurance and the Health Insurance Association of America commenced an action against the District of Columbia in the U.S. District Court for the District of Columbia.[34] They alleged that the legislation was unconstitutional under the Fifth Amendment and sought a declaration that the law had arbitrarily and irrationally deprived insurers of the right to screen applicants and to raise rates to levels commensurate with the insurance risk. On September 19, 1986, District Judge Thomas F. Hogan dismissed the complaint, finding that the legislation was rational and served a legitimate governmental goal, although he expressed grave reservations about the wisdom of the law.

In most of the rest of the country HIV testing by insurers is not restricted. Many states have been awaiting recommendations of the National Association of Insurance Commissioners. However, while the guidelines approved on December 11, 1986, prohibit inquiries into sexual orientation, the committee which drafted them was unable to reach a consensus as to HIV testing.[35]

Since the permissibility of HIV testing is the most crucial AIDS-related issue facing insurance regulators today, it is worth examining in detail the arguments that have been offered both for and against such testing.

Arguments for the Use of HIV Testing by Insurers

Opponents of testing frequently claim that insurers' use of HIV tests constitutes "discrimination." Insurance company spokespersons respond that such testing conforms to traditional industry practices. Each assertion is partly correct and partly misleading. Although insurance underwriting is an inherently "discriminating" process, it is not, for the most part, motivated by desires to discriminate against minority groups. On the other hand, while insurance companies have always used medical tests, rarely in the past have they used tests with the same disregard for broad-based actuarial data.[36]

As noted earlier, the general principle that an insurance buyer's premiums should reflect the expenses he or she is likely to incur seems well-established. A ban on HIV testing would represent an exception to the general rule that insurers may assess the risk of claims and adjust their rates accordingly.

Insurance industry representatives also argue that companies must be allowed to require HIV testing if they are to bargain with prospective consumers on terms of equality. With the increasing availability of the test, customers have access to information about their own antibody status. Some individuals who test positive may be especially anxious to purchase insurance (and to purchase especially large amounts of life insurance). Industry representatives argue that companies will lose control of their underwriting practices if they are denied access to information that their customers already possess.

It has also been argued that there are more democratic means of spreading the costs arising from AIDS. A prohibition on antibody testing could be characterized as a concealed tax by which the expenses of AIDS patients are distributed among other members of the insurance pool. If we as a society believe that the costs of the disease should be spread throughout the entire population, we could allow insurers to use HIV tests and to exclude AIDS-related claims from coverage for those who are seropositive. We could then pay AIDS-related expenses out of the public treasury. Such an approach would give the electorate precise information as to the extent of public spending on AIDS and allow the need for AIDS treatment to be balanced against other pressing needs in allocating scarce public resources. A prohibition on antibody testing might be seen as an end-run, a means of spreading expenditures through part of the population while concealing from the public the true cost of treatment for AIDS.

The insurance industry also contends that a ban on HIV testing would be unfair because the costs of AIDS treatment would fall most heavily on those in the demographic groups in which AIDS is most common. Insurers set their rates on the basis of anticipated claims; if most AIDS patients are males between twenty and forty, then most of the money for AIDS claims would come from increased premiums paid by insurance buyers from this group. If the costs of treatment should be shared by society generally, a ban on HIV testing is an inefficient means to achieve the goal.

Arguments against the Use of HIV Testing by Insurers

Opponents of HIV testing point out that the test, while having some actuarial significance, does not predict who will contract AIDS. They also point out that although rate-setting on an actuarial basis is the general rule, well-recognized exceptions exist. Although separate mortality tables for racial minority and immigrant groups were once in wide use, numerous jurisdictions prohibit consideration of race and national origin in insurance.[37] Some prohibit denial of insurance to people exposed to the carcinogenic drug DES.[38] Others prohibit denial of insurance to people with sickle cell anemia traits.[39]

The arguments for an exception are strongest when actuarial considerations harm a traditionally disfavored minority group. Thus, a prohibition on the use of HIV-antibody test results in setting insurance rates may be justified as a necessary means of keeping insurance available to a minority group—in this case gay men—who would be disproportionately affected by the use of the test. If, as a group, gay men cannot obtain mortgage life insurance, or key person business insurance, they may lose access to significant areas of public and private endeavor. Their insurance disabilities may generate social disabilities and social friction as well.

The spiral of adverse selection is not an argument against *mandated* exceptions to actuarially determined insurance rates. If no insurer may determine who has the antibodies, presumably every insurer will experience increases in health, disability, and death claims related to AIDS, and the increased costs resulting from such claims will be collected from policy holders. If all insurers are legally prohibited from obtaining such information, no company can obtain a competitive advantage, and the adverse selection spiral cannot begin.

It also seems quite doubtful that the use of HIV testing will create incentives for individual risk-minimization. An individual who is already seropositive can do nothing to change that fact, no matter how great the incentive. Could insurers' use of HIV tests deter future high-risk behavior by those who have not yet been infected? Given the well-publicized and widely feared consequences of contracting AIDS, the prospect of increased insurance rates could hardly add a meaningful increment of deterrence where high-risk behavior is concerned.

The prospect of mandatory antibody testing also raises troubling questions as to confidentiality. The release—whether through negligence or through malice—of an individual's positive antibody test could have calamitous results. Insurance industry representatives downplay these fears, pointing out that insurers are frequently privy to medical information that is highly confidential, including information regarding alcoholism and sexually transmitted diseases.[40] Information concerning an individual's seropositivity, however, would seem uniquely sensitive and thus entitled to special safeguards against breaches of confidentiality.

A prohibition on HIV testing might also serve social ends by improving medical care for AIDS patients. Even if public funding for AIDS treatment might in some respects be preferable to a ban on HIV testing, those who regulate the insurance industry cannot ignore political reality. Reaction to the disease thus far has been marked by public ostracism of AIDS patients and minimal public funding for research, education, care, and treatment. State or local proposals to treat AIDS at public expense will face enormous popular resistance, especially if it is perceived that those states and localities that move first may risk an influx of AIDS patients. A federal solution seems preferable but appears highly unlikely in an age of budgetary cutbacks. A ban on HIV testing is an imperfect means of spreading losses associated with the disease, but it may be the most effective means available in the current climate. It makes no sense to reject a ban on antibody testing as a second-best solution if the solution that is theoretically fairer is politically impossible.

If insurers are forbidden to require HIV testing as a condition of coverage, then they should also be forbidden to inquire as to the results of HIV tests taken elsewhere. If companies are allowed to ask about previously administered tests but are forbidden to give their own, then potential insurance buyers—particularly those who fear that they are at high risk—will be deterred from taking the tests. An individual's awareness of his or her positive antibody status may help to prevent the spread of the disease; any disincentive for voluntary test-taking is highly counterproductive.

Regulations If HIV Testing Is Permitted

If HIV testing by insurers is permitted, certain restrictions are essential.[41] First, the test should only be administered when it is medically justified, not on the basis of lifestyle alone. Second, insurers should test only if they obtain informed consent. They should make applicants aware of the meaning of the test they are asked to take and of the circumstances under which those test results may be disclosed to others.[42] Third, the laboratory procedures must be of the highest quality, since initial ELISA tests without thorough confirmatory tests will produce false results for many applicants.

Fourth, insurers should inform applicants about the results of the tests. All too often, denials of insurance applications are explained in vague terms; some insurers refer only to "medical reasons," or "blood test results." If an applicant wishes a more precise explanation of the denial, he or she must make a specific request, and often the information is then communicated only to a physician. While some states, such as Connecticut, have comprehensive statutes guaranteeing access to information in insurance files,[43] and while insurance reports may in some instances be subject to the federal Fair Credit Reporting Act, many applicants may find it difficult to obtain the results of tests performed on them. Blood banks have realized that knowledge of seropositivity places on them a duty, rarely assumed in the past, to counsel those whom they test.[44] The same duty should fall upon the insurance industry if it wishes to use the test.

Fifth, rigorous confidentiality measures must be scrupulously enforced. Employees whose employers discover their seropositivity may find their jobs in jeopardy. People who move to states where the test is prohibited may find that the Medical Information Bureau, Inc., the organization through which insurers cooperate to uncover insurance fraud, has coded their names for seropositivity. They will then be uninsurable in their new homes.

Even if testing is permitted, insurance companies are justified only in charging seropositive applicants premiums that reflect their true risk, not in denying them insurance entirely. Recent information indicates that earlier estimates of the costs of AIDS treatment were highly inflated.[45] Insurers should not be allowed to invoke worst-case scenarios to justify a blanket exclusion of all HIV-positive individuals.

Of course, many seropositive individuals will be unable to afford even premiums that accurately reflect their risks of future claims. Some alternative means, either an assigned risk system or government subsidized pool, must therefore provide insurance to those who cannot obtain it if testing is allowed.[46]

Individuals who go on to develop AIDS are often forced to stop working. Their group health coverage may continue for a limited period of time following termination of employment. In addition, most group health insurance policies contain conversion provisions; these provide that an individual who leaves the group may convert his or her coverage to an individual policy without providing evidence of insurability. This right must be exercised within a short period after the individual leaves the group. Of course, the insured may be paying the premium for the first time, since many group health plans are funded by employers. Not every group health insurance policy provides a right of conversion, and the conversion provisions of some policies have been attacked as inadequate or exorbitantly priced.[47] Since most people who contract AIDS will eventually leave the workplace (and thus the health insurance group), affordable and comprehensive conversion provisions in all group health insurance policies should be a high priority.

As discussed earlier, a government program to pay insurance expenses would make the cost to the public explicit and would spread it more equitably throughout the community. If such a system is not possible for all types of insurance, it should at least be devised for health insurance, which serves the most critical social function.

Refusal to Insure Those in High-Risk Groups without Regard to Their Health

Although the drawbacks of antibody testing are severe, such testing is less offensive and more justifiable (assuming it incorporates the safeguards outlined above) than the wholesale elimination of "high-risk groups" from insurance coverage.

In some localities, where two-thirds or more of the sexually active gay men sampled have been seropositive for HIV,[48] excluding that population from insurance is arguably the functional equivalent of antibody screening. However, any attempt to exclude sexually active gay men from insurance would be fraught with problems. In the District of Columbia, for instance, insurance companies are considered "public accommodations." As such, they are legally barred from discriminating on the basis of sexual orientation.[49] In most states, refusing to write insurance for gay people might constitute an unfair trade practice under the insurance laws.[50] The guidelines issued recently by the National Association of Insurance Commissioners prohibit inquiries into sexual orientation by insurance underwriters.[51]

In addition to these legal problems, any effort to identify sexually active gay men would involve inquiries of a sort that many applicants, no matter what their sexual orientation, would find highly offensive. Moreover, an individual's statement that he was not gay (or was not "sexually active") would be almost impossible to verify, and a subsequent attempt to prove misrepresentation would be difficult. Attempts to exclude gay applicants, therefore, seem likely to take forms other than direct interrogation as to sexual orientation and practice.

For example, several insurance companies (notably major reinsurance companies whose guidelines tend to become public once distributed to the companies whose policies they reinsure) have developed underwriting guidelines based upon apparent "gay lifestyle." This approach is not rational (in the legal sense) because many people who do not lead gay lifestyles are at risk of developing AIDS, and many people who apparently lead gay lifestyles are neither gay nor at risk of developing AIDS.

The markers identified by these insurance companies for determining high-risk applicants are based on social stereotypes that cannot even pretend to the scientific basis on which insurers generally operate. The Great Republic Life Insurance Company, in guidelines challenged in a lawsuit in California, has instructed underwriters to segregate the applications of single males without dependents who are in professions that do not require physical exertion.[52] Explicitly included in this occupational category are florists, interior designers, and people in the fashion business. If an applicant in the segregated pool has gained or lost more than ten pounds in the year prior to application, or has had any sexually transmitted disease, his application will be declined. Similarly, Munich American Reassurance Company, which has since revised its guidelines under pressure from both National Gay Rights Advocates and the California Department of Insurance, instructed underwriters to be wary of single persons in certain cities who name parents or siblings as beneficiaries or who have been exposed to a person capable of transmitting the HIV virus.[53] Lincoln National Life Insurance Company focuses on marital status and geographical location as well.[54]

The irrationality and unfairness of these standards is manifest. If put into practice, they would inevitably lead to skewed inquiries and to the creation of risk classes composed of people presenting many different degrees of risk. They probably cannot withstand scrutiny under the fair trade practices laws of most states, and it is likely that they will be abandoned as AIDS becomes more susceptible of scientific understanding and less the subject of panic and prejudice.

There has been less public debate about the other high-risk groups, although their need for insurance is equally pressing and the likelihood that they will be unable to obtain insurance is at least as great. Although intravenous drug users may for some purposes constitute handicapped persons under public accommodations laws, they have long been denied insurance because they are considered bad risks. They are not organized politically and have no identity as a minority group, and the activity that defines them as a group is precisely the activity that is perceived to put them at risk. Providing quality health services and counseling to intravenous drug users must be a high priority. However, since they are not being removed from the insurance rolls specifically as a result of AIDS, the debate over the insurance industry's reaction to AIDS is unlikely to focus on its treatment of drug users.

Hemophiliacs, perhaps because of the smaller numbers involved, have not been a focus of the insurance debate either. Only in Arizona do they have any explicit statutory protection against insurance discrimination, and there only as respects disability insurance. Even in the absence of protective legislation, however, hemophiliacs can mount a strong defense against blanket exclusion from insurance. Hemophilia, in and of itself, does not put its targets at risk for AIDS. Only past exposure to the viral or other agent that causes AIDS can do that. Moreover, there are ample policy reasons why insurance should not be denied even to those who have been exposed but do not exhibit the symptoms of AIDS.

ADDITIONAL WAYS TO REDUCE COSTS

An applicant for an individual health or life insurance policy is usually required to provide a medical history. In most states, if the applicant materially misrepresents his or her health on the policy application, the policy may be rescinded within two years of the policy issue date or, if the person dies within that two year period, at any time thereafter. At least five lawsuits were pending in New York State alone as of June 1986, in which it was alleged that material misrepresentations were made by people who later died of AIDS.[55] Numerous other claims were in dispute but not yet in litigation.

Such suits are not uncommon in the insurance industry. They constitute a legitimate means by which the industry may avoid paying claims on policies that should not, in all fairness, have been underwritten. However, the concurrent prosecution of so many lawsuits in just one jurisdiction is worrisome. It may demonstrate that the industry is the potential victim of "antiselection" by people who take out insurance expecting that they will soon get sick or die. But it may also demonstrate that the industry is overly suspicious about AIDS claims or is trying to send the public a message about AIDS.

In recent years, there has been a significant move among employers away from third-party insurance and toward self-insurance—a shift which reflects the intense concern of employers about the costs of health care. Self-insurance permits an employer to make interest on its own funds instead of losing their use, to be "flexible" in the benefits it offers, and to escape many insurance regulations. Persons with AIDS, however, may have reasons to fear this trend. Many benefits mandated by state laws, such as mandatory provision for home care in some health policies, are not required of self-insurers, and conversion to an individual insurance policy upon the termination of employment may not be available.

Insurance companies may also seek to avoid paying AIDS-related claims by invoking the "pre-existing condition" rule. Under the terms of some policies, insurance companies are not obligated to pay claims arising from illnesses that pre-dated the issuance of the policy. Several person with AIDS have faced claims by insurance companies that their conditions existed before the effective date of the policy, and that the company should be excused from paying for resultant hospitalization or medical care. At issue, generally, is whether the insured's symptoms were sufficiently manifest prior to the commencement of coverage to give him or her reason to seek medical care. As with the material misrepresentation suits, it is impossible to tell whether the spate of lawsuits about pre-existing conditions reflects deliberate purchases of health insurance by individuals who knew or had good reason to know that they were sick, or whether it reflects overzealous assumptions by insurance companies.

A new means by which insurers may try to reduce the cost of AIDS is to "manage" cases so that they are treated in the most efficient possible manner. Case management has received a great deal of publicity as a way of encouraging out-of-hospital care, providing a more humane environment for the patient, and saving money. In a survey conducted early in 1986, however, only five of thirty-four large employers with employee AIDS cases assigned someone to manage them.[56]

The concept of case management presents delicate legal problems that have yet to be fully considered. In a managed case, for example, what happens when the interests of the patient and the case manager begin to diverge? Does the case manager have a legal right to direct care that is contrary to the patient's wishes? If not, may the insurance company terminate benefits to an insured who refuses to cooperate in the "management" of his or her case? Does the case manager stand in a doctor/patient relationship to the insured, and will the insurer be subject to claims of medical malpractice if the manager misdirects care? As these few questions suggest, the legal parameters of this highly regarded new approach to insurance reimbursement are still uncertain.

The AIDS epidemic presents an enormous challenge to our system of private health, disability, and life insurance. That system serves critical social functions, from the provision of adequate health care to the provision of welfare. Regulators must bear in mind that if the insurance industry does not perform those functions for persons with AIDS, their lovers, and their families, no other institution will. Strategies must be devised to keep full insurance coverage available to the minorities who are the primary victims of AIDS. If necessary, companies must be restricted from applying strict actuarial standards to determinations regarding coverage, unless they are willing to adopt other measures, such as risk pooling, to do their fair share for people with AIDS.

14

Doctors and Patients: Responsibilities in a Confidential Relationship

RICHARD BELITSKY, M.D., AND ROBERT A. SOLOMON

The physician or therapist who diagnoses or treats a patient with AIDS will be faced with important ethical and legal decisions. In particular, he or she will have to deal with the tension between the duty to disclose the diagnosis to protect other parties and the responsibility to safeguard the patient's confidentiality. This is a critical issue for all physicians who care for AIDS patients. Because neuropsychiatric complications are quite frequent and at times the presenting symptom in AIDS, and because substance abusers are a high-risk group, the psychiatrist is frequently involved in the treatment of the AIDS patient and may be the first to confirm the diagnosis. In this chapter, we will address issues relevant to physicians and therapists in general, with special attention to the psychiatrist-patient relationship and the psychiatric hospital.

Physicians have long considered the duty to safeguard a patient's confidences a paramount concern. Indeed, this duty has ethical roots that date back to the Hippocratic oath written during the fourth century BC: "Whatsoever I shall see or hear in the course of my profession . . . if it be what should not be published abroad, I will not disclose, holding such things to be holy secrets." In psychiatry this confidence is considered to be so critical that without it the therapeutic relationship cannot flourish.[1] The privilege is legally protected by statute or judicial precedent in virtually every jurisdiction in the United States.[2] Courts in ten jurisdictions have found physicians civilly liable for improper breach of confidentiality;[3] only Tennessee and Georgia have refused to recognize such claims.[4] Moreover, several courts have recognized the importance of protecting the confidentiality of information collected for medical research.[5]

Nevertheless, the duty to protect confidentiality has been weakened in recent years. State reporting statutes,[6] civil commitment statues based on a diagnosis of dangerousness to self or others,[7] and psychotherapists' civil liability for failure to disclose the dangerousness of a patient who subsequently commits a violent act[8] all impinge on the basic presumption of confidentiality. The therapist or physician is forced to walk a tightrope between the trend toward disclosure when necessary to protect public safety[9] and the threat of civil liability for improper breach of confidentiality.[10]

The dilemma is heightened in the case of a patient with AIDS. The effect on the AIDS patient of disclosure of his or her condition may be catastrophic. Inability to receive medical treatment, loss of employment, eviction, expulsion from schools, segregation from society, and demands to quarantine are all well documented.[11] On the other hand, nondisclosure may result in a third party contracting AIDS, an as yet incurable and ultimately fatal disease. Thus, the physician's decision truly has life-or-death consequences.

As a general principle of medical ethics, a physician who has knowledge of positive test results or even a confirmed diagnosis of AIDS must protect confidentiality and avoid disclosure of this information. There are, however, exceptions. In this chapter we will identify those exceptions in light of current medical knowledge about AIDS as it relates to diagnosis and communicability, and we will review the current state of the law concerning the duty of confidentiality and disclosure to third parties. We will apply this analysis to five sets of individuals or groups likely to be in contact with AIDS patients: known sexual partners; intravenous needle sharers; family members; employers, fellow students, and other known social contacts; and other patients in an inpatient psychiatric unit.

CURRENT MEDICAL KNOWLEDGE

In this section we briefly describe the criteria for confirming infection with the Human Immunodeficiency Virus (HIV) and review the current state of medical knowledge regarding its transmission. (For a detailed discussion, see Chapter 2.) A physician's capacity to foresee contagion is based on this information and is critical in determining liability for failure to disclose and protect potential victims.

The ELISA test, together with the Western Blot technique, indicate an immune-system response to infection with HIV, although they do not alone confirm the diagnosis of AIDS. (For a detailed discussion of these tests, see Chapter 9.) Current medical knowledge indicates that all seropositive individuals, even those who are asymptomatic, may be carrying the virus[12] and are consequently potentially infectious to others.[13] Therefore, despite their clinical differences, for the purposes of this chapter we will consider all persons with AIDS and all seropositive individuals as part of one group who have potential to transmit HIV infection to third parties.

There is no evidence that AIDS is spread through casual contact.[14] Concerns that it might arose mostly from reports that the virus had been isolated from saliva[15] and tears.[16] Despite these findings, studies of family members and household contacts of AIDS patients indicate that there is virtually no risk of contagion through nonsexual contact.[17] In addition, the risk of contagion through occupational exposure, such as occurs among health care workers, is extremely low.[18] There are rare reports of possible contamination through needlestick injury.[19] As a precaution, hospitals, through their infection control guidelines, seek to prevent contact between the body fluids of AIDS patients and the mucous membranes and open lesions of others.[20]

Those means by which the AIDS virus can clearly be transmitted are well-known: sexual intercourse, injection of contaminated blood through the sharing of needles and syringes among intravenous drug users,[21] intrauterine transmission,[22] and possibly breast milk.[23] Contracting AIDS through any other method is extremely unlikely. Persons who are at greatest risk of acquiring HIV infection, and therefore potentially foreseeable victims, include those who engage in sexual intercourse with infected individuals, intravenous drug abusers who share needles or syringes, transfusion recipients, and children born of infected mothers.

THE LAW

Considerations of physician/patient confidentiality have never been absolute. Courts have repeatedly held that a physician's duty of nondisclosure is outweighed in certain circumstances by the need for public safety.[24] The American Medical Association Principles of Medical Ethics recognizes the safeguard of confidences only "within the constraints of the law."[25]

As a general proposition, a physician has a duty to exercise reasonable care to protect others from the dangers emanating from the patient's contagious or infectious illness.[26] Courts in some states have found physicians liable to the patient's family members for failure to disclose that the patient had a contagious disease.[27] Moreover, the duty to warn is not negated by a failure to diagnose the disease correctly.[28]

Some of these decisions are based in part on state statutes requiring physicians and others to report communicable diseases to state or local health authorities.[29] Because AIDS is a contagious disease, such statutes confer a responsibility on the physician to report AIDS to state authorities. In fact, some states are considering even more stringent reporting requirements for AIDS cases.[30] While one could argue that complying with the state reporting statute should relieve physicians from any further duty and that the responsibility to notify others falls on the state authorities receiving the reports, courts have held otherwise, using the statutes as evidence of a legislative intent that the duty to third parties exists.[31] Thus, a physician with knowledge of a diagnosis of AIDS who fails to disclose the information to a foreseeable victim could be found liable.

In *Tarasoff v. Regents of the University of California* (Tarasoff II),[32] the California Supreme Court imposed a duty on psychotherapists to protect third persons from the potentially dangerous acts of their patients. The court held that when a therapist determines—or, pursuant to the standards of the profession, should have determined—that a patient presents a serious danger of violence to another, he or she incurs an obligation to use reasonable care to protect the intended victim against such danger. Discharge of this duty, the court noted, might include warning the intended victim or calling the police. *Tarasoff* was the first case to impose a duty to warn potential victims of injury that might result from a patient's intentional actions. *Tarasoff* is particularly significant in the AIDS context, because the transmission of AIDS can, in some instances, be viewed as the result of intentional action. Moreover, *Tarasoff* reaffirmed a physician's duty to protect third parties from dangers created by a patient's illness.

In adopting the *Tarasoff* reasoning, the New Jersey Supreme Court used broader language, stating that a therapist "may have a duty to take *whatever steps are reasonably necessary* to protect an intended or *potential* victim of his patient" when the therapist determines the probability of danger to that person.[33] The therapist may have the obligation, the court noted, to protect the welfare of the community, an obligation the court saw as analogous to the physician's duty to warn third persons of infectious or contagious diseases.[34]

In *Lipari v. Sears, Roebuck and Co.*,[35] a federal court in Nebraska, accepting the *Tarasoff* rationale, extended the class of potential victims well beyond those persons identifiable to the therapist. In *Lipari*, the patient was receiving outpatient psychiatric care at the Veteran's Administration Hospital. He stopped treatment against the advice of his doctors. Five weeks later, in a department store, he shot two people, killing one and wounding another. In finding the VA liable, the court held that the duty to third persons "requires that the therapist initiate whatever precautions are reasonably necessary to protect potential victims of his patient."[36] Although the victims were not identifiable, the harm was foreseeable.

More recently, the Vermont Supreme Court considered a case in which a patient who wanted to "get back at his father" threatened to burn his father's barn but promised his therapist that he would not do so. The court found that, as a matter of law, the therapist had a duty to his patient's father. The jury had the responsibility to determine whether under the facts of the case the therapist had met that duty.[37]

All of the post-*Tarasoff* decisions considering the issue have followed the reasoning of the *Tarasoff* court and based the therapist's liability on the Restatement (Second) of Torts (1965). (A "Restatement" is a generally accepted explication of the law in a particular area and is often persuasive to courts.) While the general rule is that a person does not have a duty to control the conduct of a third person to prevent harm to another, Section 315(a) of the Restatement sets forth an exception, stating that a person has such a duty if "a special relationship exists between the actor and the third person which imposes a duty upon the actor to control the third person's conduct." Here, the actor is the physician or therapist and the third person is the patient.

Tarasoff is based on the rationale that the therapist-patient relationship is sufficient to place a duty on the therapist for the benefit of other persons, *even though* the therapist does not stand in a special relationship to the injured party. Once that duty is established, the legal impediment to liability has been removed. The remaining questions of breach of the duty and the causal connection between the breached duty and the injury are questions to be answered by a jury (or judge in a bench trial). If the duty exists, the case proceeds on its particular facts.

Few states have yet considered *Tarasoff* questions.[38] In some states, the duty to third persons is controlled by statute.[39] Nevertheless, *Tarasoff* represents a strong trend; the *Tarasoff* rationale has yet to be rejected by the highest court of any state. In contrast, *Lipari*, which established a duty to all potential victims, represents a minority view. Identifiability of a victim has remained an important factor for most courts.[40]

While courts speak of the physicians' duty in terms of protection from communicable or contagious diseases, they have articulated the psychotherapist's duty in terms of protection from intentional torts. Both standards are based on the foreseeability of the risk to third parties. If a physician foresees, based on his or her professional knowledge, that a patient with AIDS presents a reasonable risk of transmission to a third party, the physician has a duty to take reasonable steps to protect the third party. The same duty would seem to apply, under *Tarasoff*, to a therapist who foresees that a patient with AIDS, through his or her intentional actions, runs a reasonable risk of transmission to a third party.[41]

Courts have applied to venereal diseases the general principle that a person negligently exposing another to an infectious disease, which the other subsequently contracts, is civilly liable.[42] A recent case involving the transmission of herpes, *Kathleen K. v. Robert B.*,[43] lends support to the analogy between intentional violent behavior, at issue in *Tarasoff*, and intentional exposure of another person to AIDS. In *Kathleen K. v. Robert B.*, a party contracting herpes sued her partner. A California court found liability against the defendant on the grounds that his misrepresentation that he was disease-free was intentional tortious conduct causing serious injuries to the plaintiff.[44] Under *Kathleen K. v. Robert B.*, the act of a person with AIDS exposing another without disclosing the disease may be considered an intentional harmful or even violent act, thus invoking the physician or therapist's *Tarasoff* duty to protect foreseeable victims. Post-*Tarasoff* decisions place on the psychotherapist the difficult (several commentators say impossible)[45] diagnostic responsibility of predicting violent behavior. Treatment of AIDS patients may place on the physician or psychotherapist the even more difficult task of predicting the patient's sexual behavior. Although no case has yet been reported of a person who has contracted AIDS suing a physician or psychotherapist for failure to disclose that a sexual partner, family member, or associate had AIDS, it is likely that in such cases, courts would find the legal issues to be analagous to the earlier tuberculosis and venereal disease cases. In an intentional tort situation, like that raised in *Kathleen K.*, the concepts raised in *Tarasoff* might also apply.

On the other hand, there is a strong public policy against disclosure to third parties. Recently, in *South Florida Blood Service Inc., v. Rasmussen*,[46] the administrator of an estate requested that the names of blood donors be disclosed to enable him to seek damages on behalf of the decedent who died of AIDS allegedly contracted through a blood transfusion. Over a strong dissent, the court refused to order disclosure. The court held that individual privacy interests and the state's interest in promoting the free distribution of blood outweighed the plaintiff's right to know the names of the donors. The dissent argued that there was no statutory or constitutional privilege protecting the donors, especially since the blood bank already knew their identities. Moreover, the dissent stated, however the interests against disclosure were characterized, "they fade into total insignificance in the face of the rights of a blood donee to be free of AIDS and those of his survivors to recover under the law when the horrendous result has occurred."[47]

Several courts have held that the confidentiality of information gathered for purposes of epidemiological research should be safeguarded. In *Farnsworth v. Procter & Gamble Co.*,[48] a federal court of appeals balanced the Centers for Disease Control interest in maintaining confidential records against the litigation interests of a tampon manufacturer, Procter & Gamble, which was being sued for injuries from toxic shock syndrome. Procter & Gamble attempted to procure records from the CDC containing names of participants in the study that linked the use of tampons to toxic shock syndrome. The court of appeals refused to order the CDC to disclose the names because such disclosure would undermine the CDC's ability to conduct research.

Similarly, in *In re District 27 Community School Board v. Board of Education of the City of New York*,[49] a New York court, relying on the New York City Health Code, which protects the confidentiality of reports gathered for epidemiological studies, held that the New York Commissioner of Health could not use such reports to identify children with AIDS in the school system.[50] In *District 27*, the plaintiffs sought to have children with AIDS excluded from school and to have their identities disclosed. Without even considering what interests the plaintiffs might have had in the disclosure of the identity of children with AIDS, the court stated point-blank: "The use of surveillance data [to identify individuals with AIDS] is not a permitted vehicle."[51]

Farnsworth and *District 27* reflect a crucial medical interest in safeguarding confidentiality. The progress of medical research depends on the availability of individuals willing to participate in studies. Such participation often hinges on the preservation of confidentiality. This concern is particularly weighty in the context of the current ongoing medical struggle against AIDS.

The effects on a patient of disclosure of the existence of AIDS can be catastrophic. At least one commentator has considered the need for confidentiality to increase as the potential harm from disclosure increases. Since the repercussions of disclosure of AIDS are so great, the need for confidentiality arguably outweighs even the potential death of a third party, who might contract AIDS as a result of the failure to disclose.[52] Nonetheless, courts will likely view AIDS as part of the continuum of the contagious or infectious disease cases. Just as venereal disease cases were resolved identically to the earlier tuberculosis cases, so can we expect that the duty to disclose AIDS will be viewed as comparable to the duty to disclose venereal diseases.

Known Sexual Partners

Under either a contagious disease or a *Tarasoff* analysis, it is likely courts will find that physicians and therapists have a duty to inform their patients' known sexual partners if the patient has AIDS. The accepted knowledge that AIDS is communicable through sexual intercourse, the possibility that exposure will lead to contracting the disease (even if only by a consensual sexual act), and the foreseeability of known sexual partners as "identifiable victims" fulfill the requirements necessary to overcome the presumption of confidentiality and establish a duty to disclose.

The question is more difficult when the patient states an intention to have "safe sex," i.e., using medically accepted techniques that are believed to prevent transmission during intercourse. The duty to disclose will depend on an assessment of the patient's reliability, knowledge, and consistency in adhering to "safe sex" practices. If the physician believes that sex will be practiced safely, we believe, the presumption should be in favor of confidentiality. However, in a case where the physician's judgment is wrong and transmission occurs because the patient did not engage in safe sex, the physician may be held liable.

Intravenous Needle Sharers

While the likelihood than an intravenous drug user will inform his or her physician or therapist of third persons with whom the patient shares needles is not great, the legal analysis concerning liability for failure to disclose is identical to that of known sexual partners.

Family Members

As noted, a number of courts have imposed a duty on physicians to disclose their patients' contagious diseases to family members. However, the holdings were based uniformly on the foreseeability of a family member contracting the disease, such as in the case of tuberculosis, where returning a patient to his home would subject household members to airborne bacteria.[53] Courts have not imposed a duty on physicians to warn family members other than spouses of a patient's venereal disease.[54] Because the accepted medical conclusion is that AIDS is not transmitted by casual contact, the duty to disclose the disease should not generally extend beyond spouses or other known sexual partners.

However, some patients with AIDS develop serious neuropsychiatric complications, including organic brain syndromes.[55] The manifestations of these conditions might include disorganized, agitated, confused, belligerent, impulsive, and erratic behavior, which could be hypersexual or even violent and assaultive.[56] The patient might not be able to cooperate with reasonable infection-control guidelines. While this requires a case-by-case approach, in those cases in which family members are foreseeable victims of such behavior, disclosure may be mandated.

Employers, Schoolmates, and the Rest of the World

While the analysis here is similar to that for family members, the general population is farther removed, militating even more strongly against disclosure. Foreseeability is problematic at best.[57] In *Tarasoff*, the patient's threats were directed toward an identifiable victim, but in *Lipari*, the victims were unknown shoppers in a store. If a patient with AIDS advises his physician/ therapist of his intention to remain sexually active and promiscuous, it is not clear whether the physician has a responsibility to protect the public beyond meeting state reporting requirements. If the physician believes that this intention reflects impaired judgment based on mental illness, the physician may have an obligation to seek hospitalization in accordance with state civil commitment standards.

The Psychiatric Inpatient Unit

The psychiatric inpatient unit presents unique problems. As noted previously, neuropsychiatric complications, both organic and psychogenic, are common and important clinical features of AIDS. Indeed, AIDS patients can exhibit neurological disease including meningitis, encephalitis, and dementia, as well as major psychiatric disorders including affective disorders, psychosis, anxiety, adjustment disorders, and stress response syndromes. Psychiatric evaluation and treatment are frequently necessary, and at times the severity of symptomatology will require inpatient psychiatric treatment.[58]

In general, the details of a patient's history and condition are confidential on a psychiatric unit, and it is up to the patient to decide how much he will disclose to other patients in the therapeutic milieu. For the AIDS patient, because of the potential for contagion and the need for special precautions and cooperation (i.e., avoiding sexual activity), ignorance of the diagnosis on the part of other patients could jeopardize their safety. To receive support and understanding from the patient community, to be able to work on related issues in groups and community meetings, and to ensure the cooperation of others regarding precautions, the AIDS patient should be encouraged to share his diagnosis with others.

Should the AIDS patient refuse to disclose the diagnosis, however, as might occur because of fear of isolation and stigmatization, the physician must look at the specific circumstances. If the AIDS patient is cooperative and careful regarding precautions, there might not be a need to disclose his or her diagnosis. However, the AIDS patient may be uncooperative and irresponsible with precautions, perhaps because of a wish to deny his illness. Because of his psychiatric illness—such as psychosis, organicity, and impaired judgment—he may lack the capacity and understanding necessary to cooperate (i.e., an intrusive, hypersexual manic patient or a biting, spitting aggressive patient). In the latter cases, unless the patient can be safely discharged or transferred to another facility, the need to protect the patient community will outweigh the patient's right to confidentiality. In the case of transfer, the accepting facility must be informed of the patient's AIDS diagnosis.

The psychiatric hospital can also have a critical responsibility in helping plan the disposition for the AIDS patient once he or she is ready to leave the hospital. Where the patient is returning to live with others, they may not know about his or her AIDS diagnosis. The patient may refuse to disclose the diagnosis to family members, perhaps even a lover or spouse, with whom he or she will live. In such an instance, the analysis above as to known sexual partners or family members applies.

15

Physicians versus Lawyers:
A Conflict of Cultures

DANIEL M. FOX

The AIDS epidemic raises problems of public health policy that require physicians and lawyers to work together as never before. They must collaborate, for example, in safeguarding the privacy of persons with AIDS when their names are reported to public health agencies. Together, the two professions must assess what information is needed to monitor the epidemic, to assist science, and to protect people who have not become seropositive, and then develop strategies to preserve some privacy for persons with the disease.[1]

Working collaboratively is no easy task for professions that have fundamentally different conceptions of their roles and their prerogatives and that increasingly regard each other as antagonists. Thus, even as the AIDS epidemic provides an opportunity for cooperation, it provides new occasions for conflict between members of the legal and medical professions. If we are to move in the direction of cooperation rather than conflict, we must understand the roots of the antagonism between the professions and the contemporary forces that threaten to deepen it.

I have observed the antagonism of physicians toward lawyers during fourteen years as a faculty member and senior manager of an academic health center—a teaching hospital and five professional schools—that is a unit of a large state university. This experience has no doubt given me a limited view of both professions. The lawyers I have observed are either public employees or private counsel retained to assist them. The physicians I work with are clinicians and scientists who are full-time faculty members at a medical school. I have recently observed physicians and lawyers concerned about AIDS while doing research on issues of public policy raised by the disease and coediting a special issue of a journal addressing the public context of the epidemic.

In this chapter, I oversimplify the relationship between physicians and lawyers in order to examine the conflict between them. In particular, I emphasize physicians' antagonism to lawyers, rather than lawyers' role in the conflict. In part I do this because I have little first-hand knowledge concerning lawyers' unguarded opinions about physicians. But it is also because—the negligence bar aside—I suspect that most lawyers are not normally antagonistic toward physicians. Physicians, on the other hand, believe they are being taken advantage of by lawyers who do not understand medicine or value it properly. They are, moreover, mortified because the conflict is usually displayed in public settings controlled by lawyers—court proceedings and legislative hearings. To be sure, not all physicians fall within the terms of my analysis. Some of them enjoy a role analogous to barracks or jailhouse lawyers. A few even study the law. Others relish it: I know an eminent physician, for example, who is fond of quoting in his administrative work aphorisms about the law he learned from his late father. Moreover, as I will describe at the end of the chapter, some physicians and lawyers are in fact collaborating on issues pertaining to AIDS.

The conflict between physicians and lawyers, though it is rooted in the modern history of the two professions, has become more intense in recent years as the authority most people accord to physicians has diminished. Some physicians accuse lawyers of helping to undermine public confidence in them by mindlessly pursuing malpractice litigation. Many attribute their rising premiums for malpractice insurance to the work of greedy and unscrupulous lawyers. Others assert that so-called "defensive medicine," ordering marginally useful tests and therapies to avoid being sued, has helped to increase the cost of medical care. Physicians often blame lawyers for the mass of regulations that burden them. In an astonishing display of professional bigotry, the new president of the Association of American Medical Colleges told a medical school graduating class in June 1986, "We're swimming in shark-infested waters where the sharks are lawyers."[2]

Events during the AIDS epidemic have reinforced physicians' irritation with lawyers. Many physicians are offended that decisions about whether particular children with AIDS can attend school are made by judges after argument by lawyers. They are dismayed when an official of the U.S. Department of Justice issues a ruling about discrimination against persons with AIDS in the workplace that ignores medical opinion. Even though physicians disagree among themselves about precisely who is at risk of getting AIDS, they condemn lawyers who argue on behalf of their clients that any conceivable risk is intolerable. They routinely curse the politicians and even the public health officials who debate laws or issue regulations that, in their view, interfere with the practice of medicine; an instance in point is the guidelines for AIDS treatment centers in New York State, which require hospitals to designate a unit for AIDS patients.

Physicians are often grateful to the lawyers who defend them against lay intruders into the practice of medicine. For instance, I heard no complaints about the lawyers who defended the State University of New York, my employer, against the Right-to-Life movement and the federal government in the Baby Jane Doe case in 1983 and 1984. Occasionally, however, physicians would recall, in vexed tones, that lawyers had caused the problem in the first place—notably A. Lawrence Washburn, a free-lance Right-to-Lifer, and the attorneys who advised the Department of Health and Human Services that Section 504 of the Rehabilitation Act of 1973 applied to disabled newborns.

The antagonism many physicians feel toward lawyers is the result of fundamental disagreement about five issues: the nature of authority, how conflict should be resolved, the relative importance of procedure and substance, the nature and significance of risk, and the legitimacy of politics as a method of solving problems.

This disagreement began in the early nineteenth century, when physicians and lawyers began to make very different assumptions about the sources of useful knowledge and the nature of authority. Until then, elite lawyers, physicians, and clergy shared knowledge and values derived from a common education in classical languages and history and in moral and natural philosophy. As knowledge became more specialized in the nineteenth century, the basis of physicians' expertise became the experimental sciences that had emerged from *natural* philosophy—anatomy, biochemistry, microbiology, pharmacology, physiology, and experimental pathology. Lawyers, in contrast, derived their expertise from the disciplines that emerged from the old *moral* philosophy—notably history, philosophy, economics, and politics—as well as from the traditions of the law itself.[3]

This difference in the sources of knowledge of the two professions became, by the middle of the nineteenth century, the basis of divergent views of authority. Lawyers held that authority derived from the law and its institutions; that is, from texts and how they were interpreted by opposing counsel and by judges. Authority, like knowledge, was, for lawyers, cumulative and as contingent on the interplay of people and events as it was constrained by logic, precedent, and values. Lawyers *made* law—as litigators, judges, and legislators. The law was what lawyers, following the rules of their profession and conscious of the dominant values of their society, said it was.

Physicians, on the other hand, derived authority from their command of increasingly effective technologies for diagnosis and treatment that were based on science. Unlike lawyers, who made law, scientists *discovered* the laws that, they presumed, governed nature. To most scientists, arguments about the relationship between laws of nature and social arrangements interfered with experiment and observation. For them, the old tests of discredited science were impediments to progress. Although some aspects of physicians' clinical acumen were cumulative, their command of science and the technology derived from it was the antithesis of reliance on precedent.

Authority reposed in individual physicians, armed with the latest knowledge, and not in precedent or in institutions. Lawyers were officers of the court. In sharp contrast, physicians were formally aloof from hospitals; they were accorded the privilege of practicing in them by lay trustees. These contrasting views of authority have persisted to the present.

To most physicians, adversarial proceedings are an ineffective and irrational method for resolving conflict. Where Anglo-American lawyers presume that a person accused of a crime is innocent until proven guilty in a court of law, physicians believe it is dangerous to make any presumption before examining evidence. Similarly, most physicians do not understand the history or the logic of lawyers' claim that formalized conflict between plaintiffs and defendants in a courtroom or around a table resolves disagreements with reasonable equity and preserves social peace.

Physicians are trained to rely on two methods of addressing conflicts about data and their interpretation. The first method is the assertion of authority from the top of a hierarchy in which power is derived from knowledge. The second method is peer review—discussion to consensus among experts of roughly equal standing and attainment. Both methods, the hierarchical and the consensual, rest on the assumption that truth is best determined by experts.

Hierarchical authority characterizes medical education, clinical decision-making in teaching hospitals, and the presumed relationship between the authors of papers in the most prestigious journals and their readers. A principal goal of medical education is to inculcate lifelong habits of deference to superior knowledge and experience. On the other hand, most academic physicians use consensus to resolve conflicts about scientific findings and the appropriateness of particular methods of diagnosis and treatment. Moreover, outside academic medicine, consensus is more important than deference to authority. According to recent studies, for example, physicians' decisions about the indications for particular surgical procedures and appropriate lengths of hospital stays vary from one geographic area to another.[4]

Courtroom procedure violates what most physicians believe about how conflicts ought to be resolved. The role of juries particularly appalls them. It is difficult for anyone trained in medicine to comprehend how people without expertise can determine guilt or innocence, fault, or liability—especially when a professional is accused of negligence. Physicians are also bewildered by judges' behavior. They are amazed that the person with the authority to interpret the law asks questions of witnesses and makes comments that seem to reveal personal opinions, and they are confused when the personal opinions and the result don't match. For example, during the recent suit brought by parents in Queens, New York, to prevent a child with AIDS from attending school, some physicians, like some journalists, were surprised by the apparent contradiction between the judges' comments during the proceeding and his decision. In addition, the notion that one set of rules governs the character and admissibility of evidence and another the interpretation of law is foreign to people who are unfamiliar with legal institutions.

Least comprehensible of all to physicians is the role of counsel. Most physicians do not believe that an individual's interest can be served by making the best possible legal case on his or her behalf. Like lawyers, physicians have a privileged, confidential relationship with the individuals who engage their services. Unlike lawyers, however, they diagnose and treat, rather than defend, these people, whom they call patients. Physicians disdain the use of the word *client* by lawyers, or social workers, or by some nurse practitioners because it connotes advocacy rather than an obligation to act honorably. Many physicians assert that lawyers are often too willing to distort evidence, or just take it out of context, to make the best case for their clients. Moreover, they accuse lawyers of being too willing to meddle in physicians' areas of expertise for the sake of a fee.

I have observed this aspect of the conflict between physicians and lawyers whenever allegations are made of cheating by medical students or of erratic or unethical behavior by physicians. Those who are accused almost always retain a lawyer, which incenses the members of the faculty or the medical staff of the hospital who are obligated to address the incident. To them, peer review is the proper way to determine facts and remedy errors. Moreover, the best remedies are, they believe, either exoneration, expulsion from the institution, or medical treatment. The concept of a settlement violates their values. As one of my colleagues once said with some disgust, "This is not a legal case; it is the case of an impaired physician."

Efforts to explain the purpose of adversarial proceedings to physicians rarely succeed. Yet physicians are no more ignorant of the law than most other Americans. They may know even more about legal institutions than most people as a result of their general education and personal experience. Like most nonlawyers, however, they do not truly comprehend what the rules of evidence are meant to accomplish. Nor do physicians understand the role of such central legal ideas as precedent, procedure, and legislative intent.

The convention that law, like history, is written in words rather than in unfamiliar symbols, formulae, or diagrams creates an illusion of communicability, but the law is just as difficult for outsiders to comprehend as medical science or mathematics. That is because the words—the letter of the law— represent only a fraction of what lawyers mean by "the law." The words derive much of their meaning from such considerations as: what those who enacted the provision (in which the words appear) meant to convey by the words; more broadly, what they were seeking to accomplish; the presence or absence of conflicting goals that need to be harmonized; how the words to be interpreted fit within the overall structure of the enactment; lessons drawn from earlier attempts to interpret the same or similar language used in the same or a similar context; the doctrinal consequences that flow from each plausible intepretation; the practical consequences; the existence or nonexistence of stable business or social arrangements based on a particular interpretation; and the imperatives of the institutions through which the law operates.

Even more incomprehensible to physicians than the vagaries of textual interpretation is the fact that law, lawyers, and legal institutions are every bit as much committed to employing the right process as to arriving at the right outcome. Lawyers' attachment to procedure, sometimes to the seeming detriment of substance, is the third issue that fundamentally divides the medical and legal professions.

Physicians find it difficult to appreciate, even after detailed explanation, why a case has been dismissed because a defendant's rights were violated or why a verdict was overturned because of a violation of procedure. Physicians value results over process. Even if they are admirably attentive to their patients as persons they are often irritated by fervent advocates of patients' rights. For many of them the central question is not whether a patient's autonomy was respected but whether the best possible medical care was provided. Due process is, at best, a vague memory from high school about the Fourteenth Amendment to the Constitution. Physicians usually associate the phrase with legal interference with proper treatment; with, for instance, cases in which consent must be obtained for blood transfusions for minor children of Jehovah's Witnesses or for surgery on long-term patients in state mental hospitals.

Equally incomprehensible to physicians is the approach lawyers sometimes take to risk assessment. Physicians contrast their own sophisticated view of risk to what they consider the simplistic definition used by lawyers. For physicians, risk is inherent in every activity, including every medical procedure. Their primary concern is relative risk; that is, the balancing of risk and benefit in the best interests of patients or (in environmental cases) of people who come in contact with the environmental hazard. Physicians often accuse lawyers—who, they insist, should know better—of advocating, on behalf of clients, concepts of risk held by the most frightened or uneducated members of the lay public. Just as physicians generally uphold the law, many of them argue, lawyers have an obligation to insist that because risks are inherent in life they must always be compared to other risks, not to the impossible ideal of certainty.

To be sure, there are competing views of risk within medicine. For ex' ample, at the trial in Queens, New York, in which parents sought to exclude a child with AIDS from attending school with their children, three distinct medical views of risk were displayed: the epidemiological, the clinical, and the laboratory-based. The epidemiologists testified that a low level of risk was not sufficient cause to exclude the child from school and that according to current knowledge, the plaintiff's children were at greater risk of accidents on the way to school than they were of acquiring antibodies to the AIDS virus, much less the disease itself. However, a witness who was a laboratory scientist testified very differently: a risk that had not been ruled out by scientists could not be dismissed. The views of most of the clinicians fell in between: patients should guard against any demonstrated risk, no matter how low.

The physicians, unlike the lawyers for either the plaintiffs or the city, testified to their professional opinions. The lawyers for each side, in contrast, represented their clients' standards for how much risk was tolerable. Lawyers for the city advocated the epidemiological view of risk. The plaintiff's lawyers insisted that the Board of Education should keep children with AIDS out of school as long as any other children might be at risk of harm. A recent analysis of the testimony in the case concluded that, "The school board and the judge proceeded as if a single counterexample to the usual transmission patterns would destroy the city's case."[5]

Statements outside the courtroom also exemplified the different roles of physicians and lawyers. Physicians are troubled by conflicts between their personal anxieties and professional opinion. When interviewed by reporters, at least two of them, witnesses for the city, acknowledged that, as parents, they would worry about sending their children to a classroom attended by a child with AIDS. Some lawyers may have similar anxieties but they are not a source of conflict; their professional obligation is to represent their clients. A few weeks after the trial in Queens, the counsel for the plaintiffs irritated many participants in a conference of health professionals when he said that he did not know whose definition of risk he personally supported. To physicians and other health professionals, it was unconscionable for him to advocate a definition of risk simply because it was his client's point of view. (Lawyers' personal opinions about risk may be influential in settings where they do not represent clients in litigation—when, for example, they work in regulatory agencies or legislatures. But that is beyond the scope of this chapter.)

The final area of profound disagreement between physicians and lawyers is the role and uses of politics. For lawyers, politics is a normal and essential aspect of professional life. Most physicians, in contrast, hold that politics is intrusive, a distraction from more important matters. Lawyers write or seek to influence laws and regulations as an extension of their other professional roles. Most physicians consider these activities to be so distasteful that, when they are unavoidably caught up in them, they behave petulantly. Even masters of medical politics often claim to be apolitical.

Most physicians are actually ambivalent about politics. On the one hand, they regard political activities as wasteful and undignified. On the other, they use politics, often successfully, to press their collective interests. This ambivalence has made them difficult allies in most of the public debates about health policy in this century. There is no reason to expect most of them to behave differently in issues relating to AIDS, even if what is at stake is protecting their patients' rights to insurance, employment, or housing.

The AIDS epidemic, then, will probably reinforce physicians' antagonism to lawyers, because it is rooted in fundamentally different assumptions about knowledge and authority. It has been reinforced by countless anecdotes and often by personal experience. Most physicians will continue to grumble about lawyers while they rely on them for defense against intrusions in medical practice.

But I have also observed a different relationship between some physicians and some lawyers during the AIDS epidemic. An unusual number of physicians are working collegially with lawyers. Physicians who treat substantial numbers of AIDS patients occasionally say they are impressed by lawyers' efforts to keep them in school or at work and to protect their entitlement to fringe benefits and public funds. Many physicians understand that this may be the first epidemic in this century in which lawyers can do as much for victims as doctors—and maybe more.

This collaboration of physicians and lawyers is certainly not occurring everywhere. Even within the federal government, there is conflict between the Public Health Service and the Department of Justice about the risk of transmitting AIDS in the workplace. Similar conflict, or at least mutual incomprehension, is most likely occurring in many states.[6]

A major reason for the collaboration, where it occurs, is that AIDS is the first major infectious disease in more than half a century that is beyond the reach of medical science. The present relative helplessness of physicians recalls epidemics of the past—during the centuries before there were antibiotics and reliable vaccines.

Another reason—and one that emphasizes the central argument of this essay—is that many of the physicians who are deeply involved in the AIDS epidemic were not particularly antagonistic to lawyers in the past. To describe the dominant medical attitude of antagonism to lawyers, I necessarily oversimplified the attitudes of the medical profession. However, within medicine there have always been people who understood perfectly well the purposes and practices of lawyers. Many of these physicians have been, in some significant way, marginal within medicine. These marginal physicians include those who chose careers in public health but also clinicians who pride themselves on being liberally educated intellectuals and, of course, those who are openly gay. Sadly, the collaboration of these physicians with lawyers on issues raised by the AIDS epidemic will most likely increase their marginality. For most physicians, encounters with lawyers remain occasions for impatience or anger.

PART FIVE
AIDS IN INSTITUTIONS

16

The Military

RHONDA R. RIVERA

Two characteristics of the AIDS epidemic in the United States present a special challenge to the U.S. military. First, AIDS is predominantly a disease of males, and it strikes them at the height of their physical powers; 90 percent of U.S. military forces are male and 50 percent are between seventeen and twenty-five years old.[1] Of people with AIDS, 93 percent are male and 21 percent fall within the ages twenty to twenty-nine.[2] Thus, military officials perceive the disease as a threat to the manpower requirements of the armed services. Second, the people most prone to infection fall into categories the military authorities have traditionally deemed unsuitable for military service. The group at highest risk for AIDS in the United States is gay and bisexual men, a category the Department of Defense (DOD) has always attempted, with great severity, to eliminate from its ranks. The second-highest risk group is intravenous drug users.[3] The use of drugs by military personnel is a punishable offense and a basis for separation from the service.

In response to the epidemic, the military has chosen a policy far more extreme than any policy suggested by the Centers for Disease Control (CDC). The military has ordered all military personnel and recruits to be tested for antibodies of the HIV virus, and has directed the services to reject any recruit who tests positively. This policy is controversial and is described by some critics as little more than a subterfuge to rid the services of gay personnel.[4] The military's unusual position in American law means that this program will not receive the same judicial scrutiny as civilian and government AIDS policies. Military policy in such areas as testing, discharges, confidentiality, and epidemiologic research—and the stories of individual service persons with AIDS—are the subjects of this chapter.

A SEPARATE SOCIETY

Deference describes the attitude courts take toward the military's conduct of its internal affairs. This deference is based on the doctrine, enunciated in *Parker v. Levy*, that the military is a "separate society."[5] The bases for considering it a "separate society" are that: (1) a clear body of social norms exists that is peculiar to the military and known to all reasonable personnel; and (2) of necessity, the organization of the military is hierarchical and based on response to command.[6] The need for hierarchy and immediate positive response to command justifies pervasive regulation of the individual within the military. This regulation of the individual is carried out through a separate judicial system[7] and a separate criminal code, the Uniform Code of Military Justice (UCMJ).[8]

The Supreme Court usually declines to intervene in military decisions and assumes that military courts will protect a serviceperson's rights.[9] As a consequence of this "healthy deference" to military decisions, federal courts usually rigorously insist that a serviceperson with a grievance exhaust all military remedies before turning to the federal court system.[10] Then the court will intervene only if "strong" considerations exist to "warrant intruding on the integrity of military court processes."[11] Thus, when the military establishment developed its policy concerning AIDS, it could expect judicial deference to its decisions and little interference, regardless of the effect on individual rights.

The Military and Homosexuality

Elimination of gay people from its ranks has been the official policy of the military since 1943.[12] In no other area of American life has discrimination against gays been so systematic and systemic.[13] Military attitudes toward gay service personnel contribute to AIDS policies that neither meet epidemiologic needs nor protect closeted, yet valuable, service personnel.

The strength of anti-gay policies and the level of enforcement have varied over the last 43 years. However, in January of 1981, the Department of Defense issued its most stringent regulation to date. The revised directive, DOD 1332.14, was designed to close all loopholes and provide a means to close the service to gay persons.[14] The directive states that the presence of homosexual

> members adversely affects the ability of the Military Services to maintain discipline, good order, and morale; to foster mutual trust and confidence among servicemembers; to ensure the integrity of the system of rank and command; to facilitate assignment and worldwide deployment of servicemembers who frequently must live and work under close conditions affording minimal privacy; to recruit and retain members of the Military Services; to maintain the public acceptability of military service; and to prevent breaches of security.[15]

The directive defines "homosexual" very broadly as a person "regardless of sex who engages in, or desires to engage in, or intends to engage in homosexual acts."[16] A "homosexual act" is also defined broadly as "bodily contact, actively undertaken or passively permitted, between members of the same sex for the purposes of satisfying sexual desires."[17] Taken at face value, the directive probably covers most of the American public. Nonetheless, federal courts, albeit in some cases with reluctance,[18] have upheld the power of the military to discriminate against gay people.[19]

Certain aspects of this anti-gay policy become crucial in relation to AIDS. How an individual is discharged from the military, for example, has consequences that reach far into civilian life. Any discharge less than Honorable carries with it a lifelong stigma for the recipient.[20] Moreover, the type of discharge also regulates subsequent access to veteran's benefits, including medical benefits. This latter result is particularly serious for gay servicepersons discharged for HIV seropositivity.

Gay people in the military are discharged through a variety of methods. If the military concludes that the serviceperson committed homosexual acts prior to his or her entrance into the service, that serviceperson can be separated for "fraudulent enlistment."[21] If the homosexual acts in question were undertaken with "aggravating circumstances," an Other Than Honorable discharge will be given. Understandably, aggravating circumstances can include such conduct as "force, coercion, intimidation or acts with a minor," but an aggravating circumstance also exists if the act takes place in a location "subject to military control so that an adverse impact occurs on discipline, good order, or morale."[22] The directive allows a court martial in appropriate circumstances. Sodomy is an offense under the UCMJ.[23] Homosexual behavior has also been characterized as "conduct unbecoming an officer and a gentleman," another offense under the UCMJ.[24] Gay persons separated from a U.S. military service may not only have discharges that follow them into civilian life, but they may end up in a military prison for acts that are not criminal in civilian life.[25]

In this severe environment, medical and clerical confidentiality is virtually nonexistent. Many servicepeople have revealed gay feelings or acts to military doctors and clergy only to have their admissions passed up the chain of command and used against them. The military encourages this behavior and offers immunity to persons who have admitted a gay act to induce them to reveal the names of other gay military personnel. Significant pressure often accompanies these situations. The revelations are then used to remove the named persons from the service. Often the climate of purge exists.[26]

The Military and Drugs

The military also seeks to separate service personnel who use drugs. Drug users may be court-martialed,[27] or they may be administratively separated.

Shortages of skilled manpower, however, prevent the military from adopting wholesale separation of drug users as a viable policy. The services maintain extensive drug rehabilitation programs in an attempt to reclaim drug users. The military may, however, treat continued use of drugs as misconduct, which generally results in an Other Than Honorable discharge.[28] The user may also be characterized as a "drug abuse rehabilitation failure," which can result in an Honorable or General discharge.[29]

The military drug program has screening procedures that share some features of the HIV testing program. Under a DOD directive, a military service can order a serviceperson to undergo mandatory urinalysis for drugs.[30] Disciplinary action may follow positive test results. However, when the urinalysis is ordered as part of a medical evaluation, military officials may not use the results for actions under the UCMJ or on the issue of characterization of service in separation hearings.[31]

These policies against homosexual service personnel and drug users have colored much of the institutional reaction to AIDS. The failure to distinguish HIV case identification and treatment from a program of punitive action against gays and drug abusers has compromised the creation of a public health plan well suited to the real medical needs of all service personnel.

INDIVIDUAL CASES

In June of 1983, a news report stated that the Navy was attempting to oust an officer who sought HIV testing.[32] Subsequently, a number of individual cases have made their appearance in the news media.[33] They show that the military's anti-gay bias has compromised the epidemiologic validity of the military's HIV screening program. They also reveal the terrible human cost to those discovered to carry HIV.

One of the first test cases involved Petty Officer John Baskin.[34] In July 1983, he was admitted to a naval hospital. During his stay, he was diagnosed as having AIDS. His doctors found him medically unfit for duty and recommended him for medical retirement. Before the medical retirement was granted, however, military authorities notified Baskin that they were giving him an administrative discharge for homosexuality. Baskin had discussed his sex life with Navy doctors after they assured him of confidentiality. Baskin's lawyer succeeded in convincing a naval review discharge board that insufficient evidence existed to discharge Baskin for homosexuality. In January of 1984, the board sent the case back for medical proceedings. Then, on February 1, 1984, Baskin was again notified by the Navy that he was being considered for administrative discharge, this time "in the best interest of the service" because homosexuality is "incompatible with Navy service." After a series of letters and the threat of an injunction by Baskin's lawyer, the Navy withdrew its proposal to dismiss Baskin for homosexuality. However, the victory was pyrrhic; Baskin died in a Veteran's Administration hospital shortly thereafter.[35]

The Broyhill case was similar.[36] Broyhill was a twenty-eight-year-old Navy corpsman who was diagnosed with AIDS by naval doctors in March 1985. Like Baskin, he discussed his sexual orientation with his doctor under promises of confidentiality. Shortly after these statements, the Naval Investigative Services told him that they were discharging him for homosexuality. About a month later, Broyhill was offered immunity if he would "cooperate in an investigation of homosexual activity involving U.S. Navy Personnel."[37] He refused. His appointed Navy counsel refused to meet in the same room with him. As had Baskin before him, Broyhill turned to lawyer Harvey Friedman of Washington, D.C. The Navy never discharged Broyhill for homosexuality. He died in November 1985.[38]

A third Navy man suffered similar treatment. While he lay ill with AIDS in a San Diego naval hospital, Bryon G. Kinney was threatened with a discharge for fraudulent enlistment based on alleged preservice homosexuality.[39] The discharge would have cut off all Kinney's medical benefits. With the help of the American Civil Liberties Union, Kinney sued.[40] The Navy immediately placed the case on "hold" and later agreed to give Kinney a medical retirement with full medical benefits.[41] Bryon Kinney died before the retirement process was completed.

The introduction of HIV testing of recruits brought more legal action on behalf of service personnel. The DOD ordered HIV screening of all recruits as they passed through Military Entrance Processing Stations (MEPS) beginning October 1, 1985.[42] At this stage in the process, persons with HIV antibodies would be screened before their formal induction into the military. Initially, however, some recruits were not tested until after they left MEPS and arrived at basic training. In late 1985, naval authorities abruptly removed five naval recruits from basic training and told them they were HIV positive.[43] At first, the Navy proposed to separate the men with "uncharacterized" entry-level discharges[44]—discharges that usually indicate poor performance.[45] The men asked to be retained. They claimed they were no longer recruits but personnel on active duty who had been sworn in and begun basic training. When the Navy refused, they sued.[46] A federal judge granted a temporary injunction. Simultaneous to the filing of the lawsuit, the Secretary of the Navy ordered the men discharged "honorably."[47] Subsequently, the federal judge dismissed the injunction saying that the "honorable discharges undercut the argument of irreparable harm,"[48] which is legally necessary to maintain an injunction.

The Army responded to the time problem by ordering[49] that all recruits be tested within 30 days of active duty. Persons tested after 30 days who were seropositive for HIV would be treated as personnel on active duty and retained, if not ill.[50]

In April 1986, Phillip J. Nolan, a Navy petty officer, refused to take the

HIV test. Nolan argued that being ordered to take the test violated his constitutional right to be free of unreasonable searches and seizures. Nolan was court martialed, sentenced to 45 days confinement, reduced to the lowest enlisted rank, and given an Other Than Honorable discharge.[51]

Had they been administratively discharged for homosexuality, any of these men would have lost his military medical benefits. Baskin, Broyhill, and Kinney spent the last precious moments of their lives fighting military attitudes and policies on homosexuality, having trusted their doctors to keep information confidential. Most gay rights lawyers familiar with such cases believe that only the combination of publicity and legal action forced the military into a position of relative fairness and humanity.[52] The National Lesbian and Gay Task Force, Lambda Legal Defense and Education Fund, and the National Gay Rights Advocates worked intensely. The treatment of seropositive servicepersons who have not marshaled such forces may not be known for years.

These cases are casualties of the military's decision to screen all personnel for HIV and of the military's minimal regard for confidentiality. The remainder of this chapter will discuss the military's screening and confidentiality policies and their negative impact upon epidemiological investigation and medical research.

TESTING

The military's first public foray into the controversial area of screening blood for HIV antibodies[53] came on March 13, 1985, when the Director of the Military Blood Program ordered program personnel to test all donated blood for HIV antibodies.[54] The same order required civilian blood agencies[55] collecting blood on military installations to report the names of military personnel who tested positive for HIV antibodies.[56] Seven months later, the military moved far beyond screening blood donors and adopted a testing policy to screen 2.1 million personnel on active duty, 300,000 yearly recruits, and 1.1 million reservists.

From the start, the military's testing policy has caused controversy. Critics have challenged the program's objectives, its broad scope, and its reliance on tests that are not always accurate. (For a discussion of the accuracy of antibody tests, see Chapter 9.)

Public debate began in response to the March 13 memorandum. The civilian blood banks balked at the reporting order, arguing that it violated their general policy of maintaining confidential donor records[57] and would make service personnel reluctant to donate blood.[58] Representatives of the national gay advocacy groups publicly expressed anxiety that the memorandum provided a method to find gay servicepersons in order to discriminate against them.[59]

Although the Military Blood Program modified this position, first delaying implementation and then adding screening provisions for hepatitis-B and syphilis, by August 14 screening and reporting orders were made final.[60] The DOD required both civilian and military blood facilities to begin screening blood from military donors as of September 1 and to report the results to military personnel. However, the DOD announced that it would not interfere with civilian blood bank policy of requiring military blood donors to sign a consent form authorizing notification of positive results to the military. The form included the information that donors could leave donor stations without explanation if they desired not to sign the form.[61] Blood bank officials accepted this policy with strong reservations. They described their choice as complying with DOD policy or terminating blood collection at military facilities altogether.[62]

As some military officials were debating these testing requirements for blood banks, others were considering broader applications of testing. The Armed Forces Epidemiological Board (AFEB), a group of civilians composed primarily of medical personnel, held a hearing on the question of testing on August 9, 1985, in response to a request by J. Jarrett Clinton, MD, Deputy Assistant Secretary of Defense.[63] At this hearing, Jeff Levi testified for the National Lesbian and Gay Task Force,[64] raising concerns that many gay and civil rights groups shared about testing programs.

Levi advised against confusing the test for HIV antibody with a test for AIDS. He pointed to the Food and Drug Administration's label for the antibody test, which reads that it is "inappropriate" to use the test "as a screen for AIDS or as a screen for members of groups at increased risk for AIDS in the general population."[65] Levi outlined the danger that HIV positivity could be used against gay service personnel and drug-using service personnel. To illustrate his point, Levi told of two Navy servicemen who were seriously ill with AIDS and threatened by the Navy with dishonorable discharges.[66] Levi also argued that testing would not prevent the spread of AIDS in the military and that DOD funds would be better spent on risk reduction education.[67]

The AFEB reported its findings on September 17, 1985, and recommended against testing all personnel on active duty. Mass screening, it found, was "unnecessary."[68] The board considered several factors, including the risk that individuals with positive test results would spread the disease or be unable to perform work responsibilities. It found that, given available information, these risks were too small to require a policy both difficult to implement and economically unsound.[69] The board did recommend testing for some individuals: personnel about to be deployed overseas who would be at high risk from exotic diseases and recruits who are at risk from the live viruses in vaccines routinely given upon induction. The board recommended that donated blood be screened and that service planning on contingency blood supplies "take HIV infection into account." Lastly, the board recommended education to reduce fears.[70]

By the time the AFEB made these recommendations, however, the DOD had already decided to test all persons seeking to join the armed services.[71] In a memorandum dated August 30, 1985, the DOD ordered tests on all recruits for the National Guard, the reserves, advanced ROTC programs, and military academies—some 25,000 persons, predominantly males, each month.[72] The DOD ordered tests to begin no later than October 1 at MEPS and ordered medical personnel to withhold required smallpox vaccinations until after a recruit tested negatively for HIV antibody.[73]

The DOD justified its recruit testing policy in the following way. Testing would protect recruits who are HIV positive from illnesses induced by live vaccines given at induction. It would prevent serious illnesses such as that of a nineteen-year-old Army recruit, later found to be HIV positive, who contracted meningitis after a smallpox innoculation. (The Army had used all of the nation's vaccinia immune globulin supply saving his life.[74]) The screening policy would also protect HIV-positive recruits, susceptible to infection, from being deployed in areas of the world with high incidence of threatening diseases.[75] Finally, the testing policy would prevent HIV-positive personnel from participating in person-to-person blood transfusions.[76] Such transfusions take place, according to Navy officials, on a regular basis aboard ship and were used during battle in Vietnam, Beirut, and Grenada.[77] The memorandum did not state the consequences to recruits of having HIV-positive test results.

As late as October 1985, the military had officially decided to screen only recruits and active duty personnel who were about to be deployed overseas. In late September, however, the *New York Times* reported that some defense officials were pushing for screening of all active duty personnel.[78] Speculation ended on October 24, 1985, when the secretary of defense ordered the screening of all active duty personnel. He issued a memorandum that provided the military's fullest articulation of its testing policy to date, with detailed provisions for handling those with positive test results.[79]

With regard to recruits, the DOD required disqualification from the service, offering as justification that: (1) HIV seropositivity was a condition that existed prior to their entry into the service;[80] (2) the department would avoid medical costs and the possibility that the recruit would not complete his or her service commitment;[81] and (3) no method existed to distinguish which recruits would progress into clinical disease.[82] Between the start of the program of testing recruits in October 1985 and September 30, 1986, 976 recruits were denied entry into the armed forces.[83]

The DOD also set priorities and policies for testing personnel on active duty. Testing was to start with personnel subject to deployment on short notice and proceed to "all remaining individuals in conjunction with routinely scheduled periodic physical examinations."[84] Personnel whose test results were positive would receive medical evaluations. If evaluators found that HIV-positive personnel showed no evidence of progressive clinical illness or immunological deficiency, they would be "retained"—i.e., they would not be discharged but might have the nature or location of their duty assignment restricted. Personnel with clinical symptoms would be medically retired.[85]

As part of the medical evaluation, evaluators would interview service personnel for epidemiological information on how the individual acquired the virus and who else was at risk (e.g., wife, lovers) of transmission. These interviews brought into conflict two stated goals of the military: preventing the spread of AIDS virus and discouraging practices of homosexuality and drug use. To serve an epidemiologic function, information gathered during these interviews needed to be truthful and complete, with interviewers promising strict confidentiality. To serve a disciplinary function, information had to be made available to a serviceperson's superiors, with no guarantees of confidentiality. The problem, simply put, was this: suppose a serviceman indicated he had had sex with another man or had used intravenous drugs. Who would receive this information and how would they use it?

Recognizing the inherent problem, DOD placed some restrictions on the use of information received during epidemiologic assessments. The information was not to be used for "punitive actions."[86] While this restriction suggests protection for individuals who provide medical evaluators with sensitive information, "punitive" has specific and limited meaning in military regulations. Such information may not be used in actions "under the UCMJ, in a line of duty determination, or on the issue of characterization in separation proceedings."[87] However, it may still be used to separate a serviceperson for reason of physical disability or "for the convenience of the government."[88] Under the new policy, a serviceperson *can* be administratively discharged based on a revelation of homosexuality or drug use. Military officials may use medical information in military legal proceedings to impeach or rebut testimony of the serviceperson. Also, the memorandum specifically permitted disciplinary actions against an HIV-positive serviceperson based on "independently derived evidence."[89]

In January 1986, the military issued a policy for testing civilian employees and family members of military personnel "on a voluntary basis."[90] Service personnel and recruits, it said in the January memo, were tested for "force-readiness reasons." Since civilian employee and family members of military persons do not contribute directly to "force readiness," they would not be subject to mandatory testing. In addition, DOD noted that the Public Health Service did not require HIV screening for civilians traveling abroad, and so no military family members needed to be tested.[91] This policy seems to undermine the rationale stated in earlier memoranda that an objective of the broad military testing policy was the protection of personnel on active duty in areas with exotic diseases or inadequate medical facilities.[92]

The military issued its policy regarding ROTC personnel and service academy students with positive test results in a memorandum signed by Deputy

Defense Secretary William H. Taft, IV, on August 25, 1986.[93] The policy distinguished between students enrolled in one of the three service academies or participating in an ROTC program at college (118,320 persons) and students who have completed their undergraduate education and are enrolled in officer candidate school (4,240 persons).[94] If members of the first group have positive test results, they may be disenrolled from ROTC or asked to leave a service academy. While the policy recommends that commanders exercise "compassion" in discharging students, it does not provide mechanisms to challenge the dismissals. If members of the second group test positively, they will be allowed to remain in their programs if they do not show signs of having AIDS. They may graduate, but they will not be made officers.

Exactly how often screening of personnel on active duty will take place is unclear. Policy documents use the word "periodic." Pentagon officials, however, are still pondering this complicated problem.[95] Since seropositivity occurs weeks or months after exposure to the virus, persons with the virus may initially test negatively.[96] They may also be exposed to the virus after being tested.

The cost of even one round of testing will be very high. Like many costs of the military, the cost of testing is difficult to assess accurately, and estimates vary. In November 1985, DOD was reported as estimating the total cost of initial testing to be $20 million.[97] The most recent congressional authorization for testing is $55 million.[98] Abbott Laboratories, which won a $400,000 contract to supply HIV antibody tests to the Army, has not estimated the final value of its contract publicly.[99] All of the reported figures seem based on an initial, one-time test. Already high, if multiplied by years of testing all personnel even once a year, costs become staggering. Separating servicepersons who in the course of testing procedures admit homosexuality or drug use increases these costs. Gay rights activists have urged that the money could better be spent on risk-reduction education for all service personnel.

CONFIDENTIALITY

The military's decision to screen both recruits and personnel on active duty brought into sharp relief the very problems forecast by civil libertarians and leading public health officials. The CDC has consistently opposed screening of the general population and has opposed mandatory testing even of high-risk groups.[100] The military, in direct contrast, has established mandatory screening of persons in the general population. Civil rights advocates know that any testing produces results, results are recorded, and lists are made. They fear such lists will be used to discriminate in employment situations or, in the extreme, to create isolation or quarantine camps. If the military screening program is a precursor of civilian policy, the worst fears of civil libertarians may prove well-founded.[101]

The decision to screen and to reject recruits creates two sorts of confidentiality issues: the "external" issue, of who—such as potential post-service employers—will have access to test data, and the "internal" issue. A DOD memorandum issued in October 1985 addressed the external confidentiality question.[102] The memorandum acknowledged that, according to media reports, some results were being shared with civilian authorities. DOD ordered that no data be released "except in response to a valid civilian health authority request" that had been approved by the Assistant Secretary of Defense of Health Affairs.[103] However, the same memorandum indicated that such results would be shared if state law made seropositivity a reportable communicable disease.[104]

At present only AIDS and, in a few states, AIDS-related complex (ARC) are reportable. Legislation is being considered in some states that would make HIV positivity reportable.[105] Presumably, the DOD would then report results to state health officials. The stigma of rejection by the military could follow the recruit back into civilian life, particularly since the decision to reject a recruit is, in one sense, a decision not to employ. In theory, however, the reason behind a medical discharge appears nowhere in a recruit's general file.[106]

The current policy regarding internal confidentiality is to retain military personnel who are seropositive but asymptomatic and send the test results to the individual's commander. For example, when the Navy retains a seropositive person, his or her commander receives a letter. The letter contains information on the HIV virus and instructions on what to do with the serviceperson. A key instruction reads: "Ensure the member is aware he is being retained on active duty despite statistics which indicate that 90% of all individuals having the HIV antibody are homosexual or drug abusers. He is not being labeled as such unless his actions reflect otherwise. If his actions reflect such behavior, he will be subject to disciplinary action and/or administrative separation."[107] Can one doubt how this information will influence the commander?

Other servicepersons can infer a colleague's test results even if they are not publicized. The military sends seropositive servicepersons to a military hospital for a two-week clinical evaluation. Michael Foster's tragic story illustrates how serious the consequences of this policy can be.[108] Foster, HIV positive, was sent to Walter Reed Hospital for evaluation. There, he was constantly harassed and called such names as "faggot." He hanged himself. Similar reports of harassment abound.[109]

The services all state in their procedures the need for strict confidence.[110] Regarding information obtained during epidemiologic assessments, each service issued its own rules and procedures to supplement DOD's limited instructions for confidentiality.[111] The Army required that the results for recruits go within twenty-four hours to the MEPS commander[112] and stated specifically: "patient confidentiality will not be a basis for not reporting confirmed positive results."[113] Navy regulations sent the results to "command personnel to the extent necessary to perform their duties."[114] The Air Force notified "unit commanders."[115]

In February 1986, the Army added another destination for test results and epidemiologic interview findings: they were to be reported to commanders for revocation of security clearances or suspension from surety programs.[116] For many years and today in some agencies, the government has denied or revoked security clearances for gay persons.[117] Gay men and women were considered to be inherent security risks. Unless considered a surrogate marker for homosexuality, why HIV positivity alone would render one a security risk is unclear.

Doctors are the source of much of the information military officials receive, but confidentiality between doctor and patient[118] has little respect in the military, as the cases of Kinney, Baskin, and Broyhill illustrate.[119] (For more information on doctor-patient confidentiality, see Chapter 14.) In the Kinney case, the doctor voiced anger at the way military officials used medical records against the serviceman. He signed an affidavit stating his position, and Kinney's attorney sought to introduce it as evidence in a discharge hearing. The military board rejected the affidavit as irrelevant to the issue.[120]

The confidentiality policy seems to vary somewhat from service to service and doctor to doctor. The Navy imposes an obligation on Navy doctors to report admissions of homosexuality.[121] Army doctors are not so specifically obligated, and the Army medical corps has a tradition of keeping sexually transmitted disease contacts confidential from commanders to encourage accurate reporting and treatment.[122] Reporting also varies depending on whether or not a particular doctor is "hard core"[123] military. A high Pentagon official has indicated that the general policy of most military doctors was not to report a homosexual admission.[124] Another Pentagon official, Robert L. Gilliat, said that the lack of confidentiality may cause the military to be working against its own interests.[125]

The publicity surrounding the Broyhill case prompted DOD to issue a statement saying that "military physicians will adhere to the ethics of the medical profession and honor the tradition of doctor-patient confidentiality to the absolute maximum extent *consistent with national security*."[126] This statement must be read with the knowledge that the phrase "consistent with national security" is the loophole through which confidentiality can be breached.

RESEARCH

In many ways, the military is an epidemiologist's dream for studying AIDS. With over two million people, predominantly men in their most sexually active years, the military offers regular medical evaluations and an opportunity to follow research subjects over a long period of time. The mandatory mass testing of these active duty personnel, coupled with the testing of recruits, provides a large and well-documented data bank. Aware of research opportunities, Congress has allocated $40 million to the Army Medical Corps for research.[127]

Recent research, however, has called into question the quality of studies performed on military personnel and points out how the lack of confidentiality in epidemiologic interviews may distort data. The most controversial research is that of Robert Redfield of Walter Reed Army Institute of Research. In 1985, Dr. Redfield reported his initial findings about military AIDS patients in the prestigious *Journal of the American Medical Association*.[128] He discussed forty-one AIDS patients who were or had been hospitalized at Walter Reed. He reported that 37 percent of these patients acquired AIDS by heterosexual transmission. This percentage is significantly higher than CDC figures, which attribute only 4 percent of AIDS cases to heterosexual transmission.[129] Redfield categorized most of his patients as heterosexual, based on their self-identification. He discounted the probability that military personnel might lie to prevent separation. Redfield claimed that the heterosexuality of the fifteen persons was confirmed by interviews with the patients' family and friends and by the patients' negative culture for rectal gonorrhea.[130] Redfield attributed the infection in most of the self-identified male heterosexuals to sexual contacts with prostitutes in Germany.[131]

Redfield's conclusions were attacked in a later issue of the same journal. Doctors from the New York City Health Department doubted the soundness of data with regard to self-identified heterosexuals, pointing out that admitting homosexuality would cause discharge from the service. Moreover, they questioned the validity of asking family members and friends who would be highly protective of the patient. The New York doctors also pointed out that a physical examination and a single culture for rectal gonorrhea were not "sensitive techniques to identify male homosexual behavior."[132] Lastly, the doctors pointed out that seropositivity in German prostitutes was very low and that German doctors had found no evidence of AIDS transmission by prostitutes.[133]

In a reply to the critique, Redfield argued that the military personnel were not lying.[134] To support his claims, he stated that 75 percent of his patients on active duty had admitted homosexuality or drug use "and none were subjected to military judicial proceedings."[135] That these persons were not subject to "military judicial proceedings" has a narrow meaning in military language. At most, it means only that they were not court-martialed or otherwise punished.

Data from recruit testing have also yielded unexpected results. From October 15, 1985 through June 30, 1986, the military tested 466,629 recruits and found a seropositivity of 1.5 per 1,000.[136] This level of seropositivity is much higher than the civilian blood donor rate during some of the same period, which was approximately 0.3 per 1,000.[137] A number of factors may explain the difference. Civilian blood banks have discouraged and screened out donors from high-risk groups and also take blood from women of all ages. Military recruits include a much higher proportion of younger males. As of June 30, 1986, 689 recruits were found to be seropositive. Of these recruits, 649 were male and 40 were female.

Another breakdown showed different rates of seropositivity for recruits based on age and geography.[138] Seropositivity was 4.4 per 1,000 for persons over twenty-six, 2.5 for persons twenty-one to twenty-five, and 0.5 per 1,000 for those seventeen to twenty years old. Geographically, 2.8 per 1,000 people from the mid-Atlantic area were seropositive, compared with 0.6 in the New England area.[139] Almost startling are the figures that show a 10.1 percent seropositivity rate in recruits over twenty-six years of age from the mid-Atlantic area.

Ironically, the military's research may contribute to the cure of a disease that strikes predominantly at gay men, the group rejected by the military.

At a recent AIDS conference in the Midwest, a public health official asked a gay rights activist why she did not support testing and contact tracing for high-risk individuals. Didn't she, he asked, think those procedures were sound medically and epidemiologically? The gay rights lawyer agreed "that in the best of all possible worlds," the procedures were sound. "If all public health officials will lobby their legislators and obtain an amendment to Title VII which adds sexual orientation to the protected groups of citizens, then I and probably every other gay rights leader will join you in urging testing and contact tracing." The analogy to the military speaks for itself. It is not the best of all possible worlds . . . yet.

17

Prisons

URVASHI VAID

The incidence of AIDS in prisons and correctional facilities throughout the United States is critically important. More than one thousand inmates have been diagnosed as having the disease, and many more are likely to carry Human Immunodeficiency Virus (HIV), the virus associated with AIDS. The responses of officials to AIDS prisoners have differed dramatically from their responses to AIDS in the community at large. For example, a number of states practice mandatory testing of inmates for antibodies to HIV, and others states may soon follow. Several states routinely segregate inmates with AIDS, ARC, or even HIV antibodies. However, comprehensive educational programs, including information about risk reduction, remain unavailable to many prisoners and staff members. Moreover, prison conditions are uniformly harsh and in most states seriously deficient. Prisons and jails in at least thirty-seven states are now under court order to improve conditions or are involved in litigation seeking such improvements.[1] In this context, the medical and therapeutic needs of prisoners with AIDS, ARC, or HIV antibodies will probably receive little attention from the outside.

This chapter discusses the problems presented by the incidence of AIDS among prisoners. The first part gives an overview of prison life and the effect the prisoners' rights movement has had on conditions of confinement; it also sets forth the demographics of AIDS among prisoners. The second part addresses the transmission of AIDS in prisons and the roles antibody testing, segregation, and education can play in preventing its spread. The third part discusses the potential liability of prison officials to inmates who contract the disease in prison. This section also evaluates the legal duties of prison officials to care for inmates who contract AIDS. Finally, the fourth part identifies five obstacles to a progressive and humane response to AIDS among prisoners.

PRISON LIFE AND AIDS

Prison Conditions and the Prisoners' Rights Movement

Prison riots and lawsuits challenging conditions of confinement have provoked judicial recognition of prisoners' legal rights. Over the last twenty years, litigation has sought to eradicate unsanitary and hazardous physical facilities, guard brutality, denial of medical care, and arbitrary and vindictive internal prison policies. In a series of decisions, the Supreme Court has held that prisoners are entitled under the Constitution to incarceration free from cruel and unusual punishment and to fairness and due process in the decisions that affect their lives.

Briefly, constitutionally adequate prisons must satisfy four criteria.[2] First, prisons must meet minimum living standards for their inhabitants; that is, they must provide nutritional and edible food, suitable clothing, clean shelter that is not overcrowded, and adequate medical, dental, and psychiatric care.[3] Second, prisons must respect inmates' rights to communicate and visit with loved ones, to observe their religions, to exercise, to receive publications, to protest conditions of confinement, and to have unobstructed access to the courts.[4] Third, prisons must maintain an adequate and competent staff to guard against violence.[5] Finally, prisons must demonstrate fundamental fairness in all aspects of their operation; decisions regarding institutional rules, staff members, discipline, and inmate classification must be made objectively, free of individual whims.[6]

Unfortunately, most American prisons and jails fall far short of the constitutional minimum, particularly regarding medical and mental-health care. Many prisons today have serious shortages of workers, poorly trained or incompetent providers of medical care, long delays in treatment, insufficient attention to ongoing medical problems, and inadequate health care facilities. Many of these substandard conditions can be traced to the failure of state and federal legislatures to allocate enough money for the operation of correctional facilities. Championing basic human rights for prisoners has never been a popular cause; the current get-tough-on-criminals mentality leaves even less incentive for politicians to seek increased funding for jails and prisons.

This same get-tough attitude contributes to the biggest single problem facing the American corrections system today: overcrowding. Mandatory sentencing, lengthy minimum terms, preventive detention, and a failure to explore alternatives to incarceration have produced the spiraling populations that burden nearly all state and federal prisons. At the end of 1986, the U.S. prison population exceeded 500,000 persons. During the first six months of 1986, the number of inmates in state and federal facilities jumped by 5,630, an increase of more than 5 percent.[7] The federal prison system is operating at nearly 140 percent of its capacity; the vast majority of state prisons frequently house two or more inmates in a cell designed for one.

Jails warehouse another enormous segment of the country's inmate population. Operated by counties and cities, they generally hold pretrial detainees and people sentenced for less than one year. A Department of Justice survey found that the jail population increased by 40 percent between 1978 and 1983 and that nearly eight million people were admitted to local jails in 1983 alone.[8] Overcrowded jails have resorted to placing bunk-beds in hallways and recreation rooms.

Overcrowding puts unmanageable burdens on all services in a prison. It leads to overextended and often unsanitary food services and to deficient medical care. It reduces the chance for recreation, education, and vocational training. It limits access to courts. It restricts the number of visitors, even the opportunity for correspondence. All this leads to pervasive idleness and to the increased tensions that can give way to violence.

Demographics of Prisoners with AIDS

During the winter of 1985, both the ACLU National Prison Project (NPP) and the National Institute of Justice (NIJ), in conjunction with the American Correctional Association (ACA), conducted nationwide surveys of the incidence of AIDS, ARC, and HIV seropositivity among prisoners in the United States. The NPP survey canvassed all state correctional systems to determine the prevalence of AIDS and to identify the policies being developed by states to address the problem.[9] The NIJACA survey examined federal and municipal correctional facilities as well as state prisons.[10]

The NIJACA study found that between 1981 and October 1986 there were 784 confirmed AIDS cases in thirty-one state and federal prisons and 448 cases in twenty-seven large city and county jail systems.[11] During the eleven-month period between November 1985 and October 1986, the total number of AIDS cases in all responding correctional systems increased from 766 to 1,232, a 61 percent increase.[12] Over 70 percent of the AIDS cases occurred in prisons in New York, New Jersey, and Pennsylvania.[13] The NPP study found that state prisons in New York, New Jersey, and Florida accounted for 85 percent of the 420 cases of AIDS recorded in the survey. The distribution of cases shows that the vast majority of prisoners with AIDS have been intravenous drug users. In a report issued in May 1986, the New York State Commission of Correction estimated that 92 percent of New York prisoners who had died of AIDS had a history of intravenous drug use.[14]

Transmission of AIDS in Prisons

The incidence of AIDS among prisoners raises the question of whether the virus is being spread inside correctional facilities. Given the high rates of intravenous drug abuse among inmates who have died of AIDS and the relatively short length of time such inmates have spent in prison before developing the disease, state and federal prison officials have attributed the cases of AIDS among inmates before 1986 to infection prior to incarceration. Among inmates who died of AIDS during 1986, however, the New York Commission of Corrections found seven inmates who had been in prison more than six years and one who had been in prison more than seven years.[15] Similarly, a study found 2 seropositive inmates among 137 Maryland prisoners who had been jailed continuously for at least seven years.[16] Since most people who develop AIDS have been infected with HIV within the previous four and one-half years, these findings suggest what common sense already tells us is true: the virus is being transmitted within prisons.

Seropositive prisoners spread the AIDS virus in the same ways as anyone else: through their semen, if male, and through blood. The virus is not spread through casual contact. None of the cases of AIDS among prisoners originated from contact with urine, feces, or spit. Nor have any correctional employees contracted AIDS, ARC, or the virus while carrying out their prison responsibilities.[17]

The most common means of transmission is the exchange of bodily fluids during sexual contact. (For more information on the transmission of AIDS, see Chapter 2.) Sex between inmates, a fact of prison life, takes three forms. According to the NPP, consensual sex is the most prevalent. Almost as common is coerced sex, in which sexual favors are traded for protection from assault or for other benefits. Finally, rape takes place in nearly every American prison and jail, although precise figures are difficult to obtain.[18]

Rape presents problems for administrators who want to control the spread of the virus in prisons. Rapists are not easily persuaded to refrain from violence; they need compelling incentives. The epidemiology of AIDS, unfortunately, gives rapists little reason to modify their behavior. The receptive partner in anal intercourse bears the higher risk of contracting the virus. This means that a rapist is less likely to become infected from a victim who carries HIV than is a victim from a seropositive rapist.

Two programs, however, can slow the spread of the virus through sexual contact. First, education about the transmission of AIDS—and about methods of safe sex—has proved effective outside prison, particularly in the gay community. Since inmates fear the disease as intensely as any other group, they will certainly pay attention to educational efforts and benefit from them. Rapists, too, might curtail their aggression if materials make clear that active partners in anal intercourse, although less likely to contract the virus, are also at risk for what is, after all, a fatal disease. Second, prison officials have developed tools to identify violent inmates and control their activities: objective classification, which tags potential assaultive inmates at sentencing and isolates them; the hiring of more guards to provide better supervision; harsh penalties for sexual assault; and the elimination of unsupervised dormitory housing.

There are two other ways that prisoners can transmit HIV to each other: sharing needles for intravenous drug use and sharing tattooing implements. No one appears to know how prevalent the former practice is in prisons. Because the vast majority of seropositive inmates contracted the virus through intravenous drug use before prison, it is logical to assume that they will continue to take intravenous drugs in jail, particularly if they have developed an addiction. No matter how vehemently prison officials deny the fact, drugs are available in prison.[19] And intravenous drug abusers probably continue to share needles as they did when they were free, particularly because needles are even scarcer in jail than outside.

Anecdotal information suggests that the shared use of tattooing needles can cause transmission of the virus, even though no documented cases of such transmission exist.[20] We know that tattooing has long been a ritual in prison, that implements are hard to find, and that inmates pass them around. We also know that if blood from an infected inmate is on a tattooing needle, the next person who uses the instrument could contract the virus, unless the instrument has been properly sterilized. Many facilities have banned tattooing, but they have so far been unable to stop it.

PRISON OFFICIALS' RESPONSES TO AIDS

HIV-Antibody Testing

Although the National Association of State Corrections Administrators voted in January 1986 against mandatory testing of all inmates for antibodies to the AIDS virus, most state correctional facilities use the HIV antibody test in some fashion. Three states, according to the NIJACA survey—Nevada, Colorado, and South Dakota—have implemented or plan to implement mass screening programs for all inmates.[21]

Antibody testing in prison is used for several purposes: to assist in a diagnosis of AIDS, to gather epidemiological information on HIV infection in a prison population, and to identify HIV carriers for isolation. Most state and federal institutions use antibody testing to confirm a diagnosis of AIDS or ARC in symptomatic inmates. Federal prisons run double-ELISA and confirmatory Western Blot antibody tests on all inmates who exhibit symptoms for AIDS or ARC as defined by the CDC.[22] The NPP study found that more than half of state prison systems either used or were in the process of adopting antibody testing for diagnostic purposes.

All prisons that use the test as a diagnostic tool should run both double-ELISA and confirmatory Western Blot tests to ensure accuracy. Early diagnosis may increase the likelihood that inmates will receive medical care that could postpone or prevent infection by opportunistic diseases. Indeed, early diagnosis may be the only hope for highly touted drugs such as AZT and DDC to be effective. However, testing should not be the substitute for thorough medical examination.

Antibody testing to generate information about the prevalence of HIV infection within a prison is justifiable if such testing is anonymous and voluntary. Proponents of such screening argue correctly that prison administrators can more accurately anticipate their needs for staffing, budgeting, AIDS education, and health care if they know how many seropositive inmates live in their prisons. Since informational testing seeks the total number of seropositive inmates, rather than their identities, it can be carried out anonymously and thereby avoid the greatest cost of testing—a potentially dangerous marker in a prisoner's file. Anonymous testing reduces the risk that a seropositive inmate will face stigmatization, discrimination, or violence from guards and other inmates due to a breach of the confidentiality of medical records, a common occurrence in prisons. While the cost of administering and readministering the ELISA and Western Blot tests to a large inmate population may prohibit mass screening,[23] studies of statistically significant samples would be a useful source of information to prison administrators.

Some proponents of mass antibody testing contend that states should screen prisoners to enable administrators to identify and segregate seropositive inmates in order to decrease the possibility of transmission in prison. For prison systems with a large number of intravenous drug abusers, mass testing and the use of test results to segregate seropositive prisoners is precluded by high costs and the lack of physical facilities to carry out such programs. Nonetheless, a growing number of prisons and jails are using the test to identify and segregate seropositive inmates.

This type of testing is the least justifiable, for several reasons. For one thing, a seropositive person is not always clinically ill; in fact, studies show that only between 20 and 50 percent of all seropositives are likely to develop AIDS or ARC. There is no treatment for people who test seropositive. Segregation, therefore, cannot be defended as an effort to provide better health care to a seropositive inmate. For another thing, people simply do not "catch" the virus from close, day-to-day contact. In a recent study of people who shared with AIDS patients homes, dishes, beds, meals, and toothbrushes, no one converted from antibody negative to positive.[24] It is thus difficult to justify a policy of testing and segregating on the basis of guards' or other inmates' fear of transmission through casual contact.

Mandatory testing and segregating, moreover, may not even halt the spread of AIDS in prison. People do not produce antibodies immediately after infection, and the screening test cannot identify inmates infected with the virus who have not yet generated detectable antibodies. These false negatives create a continuing risk that the virus may be passed along even if all confirmed seropositive inmates are separated from the general population, because seronegative persons who assume that they are "safe" may continue to transmit the virus through high-risk activities.

Segregation

Probably the strongest argument against mandatory testing is that testing exposes seropositive inmates to discriminatory and substandard conditions of confinement. Despite the absence of justifiable grounds, some prison systems segregate all seropositive inmates, including those who exhibit no symptoms of illness. The NPP has received numerous reports from inmates and their attorneys describing the deplorable treatment seropositive inmates have received in prison.[25] Sometimes prisons place such inmates in medical observation cells that are not suitable for long-term confinement. Seropositive inmates have been confined to segregated cells under twenty-three or twenty-four hour-a-day lockdown conditions and denied access to law libraries, outdoor exercise, and educational, vocational, and work-release programs.[26] Their inability to participate in such programs prevents them from earning good-time credits that reduce their period of incarceration.

As disturbing as these isolation policies themselves is the effect the fear of AIDS has had on the behavior of corrections staff responsible for the care of segregated inmates. Many inmates have reported that guards push food trays under cell doors and ignore inmates' requests for assistance such as basic hygiene supplies or access to medical personnel. Finally, segregation permanently brands a seropositive inmate. The lack of confidentiality inside prisons ensures that an inmate who is segregated as seropositive can never return to the general prison population without risking his life.

Prison systems, however, more commonly segregate prisoners who are diagnosed as having AIDS or ARC. The federal prison system, for instance, transfers male inmates who are diagnosed as having AIDS or ARC and who are healthy enough to travel. They are sent to an isolation unit at the Medical Center for Federal Prisoners in Springfield, Missouri. Until recently these inmates were assigned to this special unit for the remainder of their sentence. The Federal Bureau of Prisons, however, is currently revising this policy to permit inmates who are in remission to remain in the general population at Springfield.[27] Female inmates with AIDS or ARC are sent to the medical center at a Federal Correctional Institute in Lexington, Kentucky. The NPP survey indicates that approximately half of all state systems segregate inmates with AIDS or ARC, while the systems with the highest incidence of AIDS—California, Florida, New Jersey, and New York—segregate only prisoners with AIDS.

Prisons may segregate inmates with AIDS or ARC in different ways and for different purposes. Transfer to a prison infirmary or hospital can be justified when an inmate's medical condition warrants such isolation: if, for example, the inmate cannot control bodily secretions or is so weak that he needs intensive care. Because of both misinformation about AIDS transmission and breaches of the confidentiality of prison medical records, segregation of inmates with AIDS, ARC, or simply HIV may also be necessary to protect them from harassment and threats of violence by other prisoners.

A federal district court in New York recently upheld the constitutionality of segregating all inmates with AIDS. Unfortunately, the court failed to distinguish segregation for health care or protection from segregation intended to stop the spread of AIDS. In *Cordero v. Coughlin*,[28] a group of inmates with AIDS argued that the New York State Department of Corrections' policy of segregating all prisoners with AIDS deprived them of social, recreational, and rehabilitative opportunities in violation of the First, Eighth, and Fourteenth Amendments. The federal district court rejected the inmates' equal protection claim after finding that a state could legitimately "protect both the AIDS victims and other prisoners from the tensions and harm that could result from the fears of other inmates" and that "the separation of these inmates . . . bears a rational relation to this objective."[29] The court rejected their Fourteenth Amendment "liberty interest" claim on the basis of Supreme Court decisions holding that prisoners have a narrow range of liberties and that transfer of inmates to more restricted quarters for nonpunitive reasons does not abridge those liberties.[30] The court also rejected their Eighth Amendment claim that such segregation constituted cruel and unusual punishment, on the grounds that the plaintiffs had not asserted that they were denied adequate food, clothing, shelter, sanitation, medical care, and safety. Finally, the court dismissed the inmates' First Amendment claim on the basis of a Supreme Court decision stating that a prisoner's First Amendment rights to privacy, free expression, and free association are limited by the "fact of [a prisoner's] confinement and the needs of the penal institution."[31]

Cordero illustrates the tendency of courts today to constrict the civil liberties of inmates when they appear to conflict with prison officials' assertions of what is needed to preserve order in prisons. As long as guards, inmates, and administrators are misinformed about AIDS, courts will continue to uphold segregation on the grounds that it is required to maintain order and safety in prisons. *Cordero* leaves open, however, the possibility that segregated prisoners with AIDS could successfully challenge their segregation if the conditions under which they are held violate the Eighth Amendment.

The NPP has taken the position that if segregation is imposed for any reason, it must be similar to protective custody, not punitive or administrative detention.[32] Like inmates in protective custody, prisoners segregated because of AIDS, ARC, or the HIV infection should have access to programs, jobs, recreation, visits, and exercise.[33] Prison officials should remember that even when the decision to segregate is reasonable under the circumstances, conditions of confinement in segregation must be constitutionally adequate.

Education

Prison officials can best alleviate fear and hostility about AIDS and slow down its spread by educating inmates and guards about the disease, particularly its transmission. The NIJ/ACA study concluded that many correctional administrators feel strongly that education and training about AIDS should be the cornerstone of efforts to prevent transmission of the AIDS virus in prison.[34] When the NIJ/ACA conducted its survey, 96 percent of state correctional systems offered or were developing educational materials and programs for staff members, and 86 percent offered or were developing such programs for inmates.[35] Prisoners are most often educated by brochures from state health agencies and by inmate newspapers that explain how the AIDS virus is transmitted. Every federal correctional facility also has a videotape that discusses the basic medical facts of AIDS, including its transmission, and warns inmates about the potential danger of sharing razors and tattooing needles. The New York State Department of Correctional Services has recently completed a similar videotape on AIDS in prison to be shown to inmates at all state correctional facilities.[36] Produced by and for New York State inmates, "AIDS: A Bad Way to Die" presents a sobering view of AIDS from the perspective of inmates suffering from the disease.[37]

Problems in developing materials about AIDS, however, appear to be inhibiting an all-out effort to quell fears, insure prevention, and contain transmission.[38] Administrators contend that rapid population turnover in some prisons and most jails makes it difficult to organize educational and training programs that will attract and hold the attention of inmates passing through the system. Prison officials in a county in California have expressed fear that AIDS education would "most likely cause panic" among inmates and guards. Both staff members and inmates may be suspicious of materials prepared by local bureaucracies. Finally, educational efforts need to be ongoing, authoritative, and consistent. The absence of a nationwide curriculum or standard materials has slowed down educational efforts.

The largest single problem constraining the educational efforts is the reluctance of prison administrators to provide inmates with information about how to avoid the risks of transmission that stem from certain prohibited acts, namely, sexual contact and intravenous drug abuse. Thus, while educational materials in the federal prison system recommend precautions—such as using condoms—that lower the risk of infection from sexual activity once inmates leave prison, they do not address safe-sex practices for inmates to follow during their incarceration. Prison officials almost uniformly refuse to consider seriously the recommendation of leading prison experts that condoms be distributed to inmates.[39] Similarly, even though illicit intravenous drug abuse is common in prisons, inmates receive no information about sterilizing hypodermic needles, or "outfits," as they are called in prison.

To make education work in prisons, administrators will have to overcome their fear that straight talk about the spread of AIDS through prohibited practices will lead to an increase in those practices and disrupt order and security within prisons. Sexual activity and intravenous drug abuse in prison are unlikely to cease. Like educational efforts outside prisons, safe-sex and safe drug-use counseling within prisons can only slow the spread of the disease and improve living conditions for groups at a high risk of contracting HIV.

The NIJ/ACA survey recommended several ways for prison policy makers to improve their educational programs.[40] Prison administrators should supplement printed materials and videotapes with live training for inmates and workers. Question-and-answer sessions can effectively calm the specific and immediate concerns of correctional staff and inmates. Repeating and updating educational programs, moreover, is critical to their effectiveness.

Allowing health care professionals from outside prison to conduct training sessions may alleviate the political qualms some people have about AIDS education in prison; thus, prison officials can avoid the impression that they are fostering the behavior that they have criminalized. Outside speakers from a public health department or the private sector may also be more credible to inmates and staff members than speakers from within the prison hierarchy. Finally, the NIJ/ACA study counsels that, regardless of the medium, all materials and presentations should be in clear language that can be understood by lay people.

Education is a cost-effective and proven means of changing attitudes and behavior. It represents the best hope for prison administrators concerned with the spread of AIDS in the prison population and with violence. Outside prisons, education and counseling on risk reduction have significantly changed the behavior of many high-risk group members.[41] Likewise, the NIJ ACA study confirmed that prisons and jails with education and training programs about AIDS have mitigated the fear among workers and inmates.[42] A good education program can decrease the level of anxiety in a prison, thereby improving the quality of life and conditions of confinement for prisoners with AIDS. Education can reduce the liability of prisons sued by inmates or staff members who may claim that they developed AIDS because of the prison's negligence. Education can prevent violence triggered by a lack of awareness of how AIDS is transmitted. Finally, education allows officials to avoid draconian schemes for controlling transmission—antibody-status identity cards, mandatory testing, and quarantine.

LIABILITY ISSUES IN PRISONS

The incidence of AIDS in prisons requires an assessment of the legal responsibility of prison officials to protect inmates from infection and to care for those who develop the disease. State and federal prison authorities owe prisoners a duty of care that stems from the Eighth Amendment's prohibition on "cruel and unusual punishment." Deliberate neglect of a prisoner's important need for medical treatment breaches this duty, as does the failure of prison officials to protect inmates from a pervasive risk of harm from other inmates. Inmates have sued prison officials under federal civil rights statutes that impose liability on state officials who violate a complainant's rights.[43] Although these statutes do not apply to federal officials, the Supreme Court has held that federal inmates may pursue analogous claims against federal officials through a lawsuit that is popularly known as a "*Bivens*" action.[44] Federal prisoners may also sue under the Federal Tort Claims Act, which waives the federal government's sovereign immunity for claims under the law of the state where the violation occurred.[45]

Failure to Protect Inmates from Infection by Sexual Assault

Federal courts have held that "a prisoner has a right, secured by the Eighth and Fourteenth Amendments, to be reasonably protected from constant threat of violence and sexual assault by his fellow inmates, and he need not wait until he is actually assaulted to obtain relief."[46] A prisoner must prove that (1) "there is a pervasive risk of harm to inmates from other prisoners" and (2) officials are not "exercising reasonable care to prevent" such harm.[47] It is still unclear how courts will define "pervasive risk" and "reasonable care," although plaintiffs have previously had to show a pattern of assaults and an inadequate security staff. In a 1980 suit against officials at the Maryland House of Corrections, a federal court of appeals found that the officials had been negligent in placing the inmate in a cell with another inmate who had a history of violent, aggressive sexual assaults.[48] The court found that the officials' act violated the inmate's Eighth Amendment rights and awarded injunctive relief. It did not award damages, however, because the suit presented so novel a legal claim that the official could not be held to have knowingly abridged a constitutionally protected right. The publication of the court's decision presumably puts all state prison officials on notice that they may henceforth be responsible for damages in such constitutional violations.

Under this line of cases, a prison official may be held legally accountable for the transmission of AIDS. For instance, an administrator may be liable if (1) he puts in the general population an inmate who he knows is seropositive and sexually violent and (2) the prisoner rapes someone who contracts AIDS and becomes ill. Mass HIV-antibody testing, however, is rare in prisons with many inmates with AIDS, so the liability issue actually turns on the decisions of prison officials to return to the general population inmates who are in remission from AIDS. If such a prisoner has a history of sexual aggression, officials may have a duty to keep the inmate segregated. Prison administrators should be aware, however, that the inmate's violent behavior—and not infection with HIV or diagnosis of the disease alone—makes him a potentially dangerous transmittor of AIDS and therefore a reasonable candidate for segregation.

No inmate has yet sought damages for having contracted the AIDS virus while in a correctional facility, largely because it is difficult to establish causation.[49] In order to show that the correctional system provided inadequate protection, the inmate would have to prove that he became infected with the AIDS virus through activity that could reasonably be assumed to be under the control of prison officials. This, in turn, requires a prisoner to engage in the nearly impossible task of identifying the specific episode (or episodes) during which he became infected.[50]

In addition, an education program could work as the prison administration's best defense to liability suits. By providing inmates with detailed information about transmission and prevention, prisons may well be able to meet their duty to warn and can thereby raise affirmative defenses such as assumption of risk.

Failure to Provide Adequate Health Care to Infected Inmates

Prison officials will probably be most vulnerable to suits from AIDS patients over inadequate medical care. A decade ago the Supreme Court held that prisons have a duty to maintain a certain standard of health care for their inmates.[51] The Court defined that standard by concluding that "deliberate indifference to serious medical needs of prisoners constitutes the 'unnecessary and wanton infliction of pain'... proscribed by the Eighth Amendment."[52]

Since then federal and state courts, responding to suits from inmates, have reviewed conditions on a case-by-case basis and, in doing so, have begun to decide the kind and quality of medical services a prison must provide. Courts have held that prison officials do not breach their constitutional obligations if they treat a patient negligently: there must be "such *systemic* and gross deficiencies in staffing, facilities, equipment or procedures that the inmate population is effectively denied access to adequate medical care."[53] During the last decade courts have identified which deficiencies push prisons below acceptable levels, and they have fashioned remedies. They have ordered prisons, among other things, to increase the number of hours a week inmates can see doctors, to employ more nurses and doctors, to hire on-site psychiatrists, to provide twenty-four-hour emergency care, to make sure that prisoners can go to the infirmary whenever they become ill, to have transportation to civilian hospitals always available for inmates who cannot be treated in prison, and to make it easier for patients to discuss their ailments with the medical staff.[54]

Prisoners with AIDS and ARC are particularly susceptible to inadequate medical conditions. For one thing, poorly informed health care workers may be frightened of catching the virus and therefore unresponsive. For another, AIDS patients become sick very quickly and may not have the strength or presence of mind to force nurses and doctors, already overworked, to care for them properly. Moreover, disagreements within the medical establishment over the correct treatment make a pattern of negligence or malpractice difficult to prove. Finally, prison hospitals, already overcrowded, will be unable to cope with the influx of patients as the AIDS epidemic in prison approaches the level on the outside.

Some states have treated prisoners with AIDS harshly. In New Jersey, for instance, prisoners with AIDS were recently shackled to their infirmary beds for as long as six months and denied visits from their families and access to training programs.[55] In Texas, four prisoners with AIDS were hospitalized with prisoners who had infectious diseases; such an arrangement can kill an AIDS patient, whose destroyed immune system cannot shield his or her body from opportunistic infections.[56] The NPP reports that AIDS patients face similar indignities and dangers throughout the country.[57]

Most systems, however, have set up procedures to ensure that inmates with AIDS have access to proper care. The federal system's assignment of all male and female inmates with AIDS to the federal medical centers for prisoners is a mixed blessing, though. On the one hand, transfer to a medical center ensures an inmate correct medical care for his or her condition. On the other hand, most of these inmates are thereby separated from their families and loved ones, many of whom cannot visit them in another state.

Some state systems have also established special methods to treat prisoners with AIDS. In late 1985, Ohio opened an eight-bed ward in a hospice for the terminally ill at the Orient Correctional Institute. The unit included a lounge furnished with rocking chairs and plants, a small patio, and a yard. At the time, only three of the twenty thousand inmates in Ohio's prisons had contracted AIDS; the facility may soon be too small.[58]

The New York State system, the system with the largest number of inmates with AIDS, puts each of them in his prison's infirmary, where he stays until he becomes too sick for the prison to treat his infection properly. He is then transferred to the nearest of the AIDS centers located in large hospitals around the state. Created to relieve hospitals of the overwhelming burden that the disease has placed on them, the AIDS centers treat all patients, not just prisoners. An inmate returns to the prison infirmary only if his opportunistic infection clears up, and even then the center remains responsible for his continued care, including follow-up examinations. When he has a relapse, he goes back to the center. An inmate rarely returns to the general population of the prison, and when he does, the decision usually rests on four factors: the health of the prisoner, his popularity with his fellow prisoners, the disposition and knowledge of the prison administrator, and the level of hysteria in the prison regarding the disease's transmission.[59]

CONSTRAINTS ON THE CURRENT OFFICIAL RESPONSE TO AIDS IN PRISON

Several obstacles have blocked the efforts of many prison administrators to develop a balanced response to the problems presented by AIDS in prison. These include hysteria about the illness, the political unpopularity of sexual activity and drug use in prison, inadequate financial resources, overcrowding, and the fundamental paternalism and chauvinism of the criminal justice system.

Although hysteria about AIDS is not unique to prisons and jails, it is especially pernicious there because prisoners with AIDS-related illnesses are entirely dependent upon their keepers. When fear pervades the thinking of prison officials, prisoners with AIDS-related conditions suffer more than patients elsewhere.

Like most people, corrections officers and inmates fear "catching AIDS" from other inmates.[60] Even though AIDS is not casually transmitted, corrections officers assert that the intimate nature of their contact with inmates—guards routinely encounter prisoners' spit, urine, feces, and blood—places them in danger of contracting AIDS. This danger, however, is simply an illusion, as demonstrated by the experience of health care workers who also deal intimately with their patients' bodily fluids but who have not become seropositive.[61]

Nonetheless, hysteria among guards has provoked many unions, such as the Association of Federal, State, County and Municipal Employees, to press for mandatory antibody testing of all inmates and for segregation of all those who are seropositive. It has resulted in the development of a special "moon-suit" (so called because it resembles an astronaut's space suit) for guards fearful of inmates with AIDS. And it has led to guards using masks and gloves while escorting prisoners with AIDS, locking seropositive inmates in medical isolation cells without access to outdoor exercise, visits, prison jobs, or programming, and other unfair and irrational practices. Such fear has also caused inmates to threaten to riot if a seropositive inmate was placed in their ward, to torch the cell of a seropositive inmate to convince the administration that he had to be removed, and to file lawsuits seeking mandatory testing and isolation.[62]

A second obstacle to a progressive response to AIDS is the unpopularity and political vulnerability of the two groups of people who constitute the majority of AIDS patients: gay people and intravenous drug abusers. Politicians have been slow to allocate sufficient funds for AIDS programs and unwilling to oppose AIDS-related discrimination because they do not want to appear to be endorsing the "lifestyle" of gay men and intravenous drug abusers. The prevalence of sexual activity between inmates and of intravenous drug use in prisons forces a similar dilemma on prison officials. Many states have criminalized sexual activity among prisoners. In other states, sodomy itself is a crime, as is drug use. Thus, prison officials interested in disseminating risk-reduction or safe-sex information find themselves in the awkward position of educating inmates about the very practices their regulations proscribe.

Many prison systems have a vested interest in denying, or at least minimizing, the sexual activity that goes on in prison—consensual and forced. To admit that consensual homosexual activity is widespread would expose prison officials to condemnation from many social conservatives, while admitting that rape frequently occurs in prisons exposes the fallibility of a system that gives rise to such aggression. Consequently, prison officials simultaneously overstate the danger that consensual sexual activity poses to prison security and understate the extent of prison rape. The U.S. Department of Justice, for example, commissioned a study of the frequency of sexual activity and sexual assault in the federal system.[63] The report, whose methodology and premise have been strongly criticized by leading criminologists and prisoners' rights activists,[64] sought to substantiate the "central assumption"[65] that "consensual homosexual activity is dangerous, destructive, . . . [and] leads to violence among prison inmates" and must be controlled.[66] The authors of the study advocated "normalization" of prison society by strengthening "attitudes that do not favor homosexuality, but do include a commitment to traditional religious beliefs."[67] Despite methodological infirmities, the study continues to influence the corrections community.

The uncomfortable posture in which prison officials find themselves should not obstruct the dissemination of invaluable educational information. Creative solutions exist. As I have said, by allowing health educators from outside prisons to conduct training sessions, prison officials can mitigate the impression that they are directly undermining the public trust. Risk-reduction and safe-sex guidelines can be prefaced with a simply worded statement about the illegality of drug use and sex in prisons.

Sadly, these simple solutions are not politically acceptable to some officials. Instead, mass antibody testing is proposed as a "solution," although it is intrusive, unnecessary, expensive, and ineffective. Prison officials should be encouraged to tackle the behavior that actually causes transmission; lawsuits seeking more educational material will have to provide the missing impetus.

The paucity of funds allocated for prisons is a third factor that limits prison policies on AIDS. Poverty stops many prison systems from developing special wards for AIDS patients, and it diminishes the quality of medical care and the creativity and effectiveness of educational efforts. The need to reduce costs may lead in the future to the early release of prisoners with AIDS to hospices and other private medical care facilities.[68]

Overcrowding, a by-product of the lack of funds available to prisons, also constrains the decisions of prison officials, especially about antibody testing and segregating seropositive inmates. And finally, the paternalism of the criminal justice system inhibits the correctional response to AIDS. Proceeding upon the premise that prisoners have committed crimes for which they are condemned and punished by society, the prison system views itself as having a mandate to protect the general public. This sense of obligation has led to the implementation of intrusive measures that abridge prisoners' civil liberties. For example, 31 percent of state and federal prisons notify public-health authorities when an inmate with AIDS or ARC is released.[69] Most prison systems routinely inform the correctional staff of the names of inmates with AIDS-related diagnoses, and bills now under consideration in some state legislatures would require disclosure of such information to parole boards. Some proponents of greater disclosure measures even argue that inmates with AIDS-related illnesses should not be allowed parole.

AIDS in prison is likely to be a growing problem, given the numbers of incarcerated people who have been intravenous drug abusers. But policy makers and prisoners' rights advocates must not accept at face value the justifications for mandatory screening and wholesale segregation put forward by some in the corrections community. These policies will further stigmatize prisoners with AIDS-related conditions, heighten their sense of isolation, and perhaps subject them to unconstitutional and grotesque living conditions. Prison officials must develop alternative remedies that protect the health of inmates and staff members while also protecting prisoners' rights to privacy, due process, and freedom from cruel and unusual punishment.

PART SIX

CONFRONTING AIDS: THE PROBLEMS OF SPECIAL GROUPS

18

Intravenous Drug Abusers

CATHERINE O'NEILL

People who use drugs intravenously, or who have done so in recent years, are among the groups at highest risk for and hardest hit by AIDS in the United States. Intravenous (IV) drug users risk exposure to Human Immunodeficiency Virus (HIV) through sharing or reusing needles (and other "works" for injecting drugs) that have been contaminated with blood containing the virus. Those who use drugs intravenously also put their sexual partners and the children they bear at increased risk—so much so that IV-drug users now appear to be a primary link for the transmission of AIDS both to heterosexuals and to children.[1]

The numbers reveal the great risks that AIDS poses to people connected in one way or another with intravenous drug use. Individuals with histories of IV-drug use are, in the United States, the second largest group with AIDS— a quarter of the more than 28,098 cases reported nationally to the federal Centers for Disease Control (CDC) by December 8, 1986.[2] In New York and New Jersey, where about 80 percent of all cases of AIDS among IV-drug users have occurred, the proportion of cases linked to IV-drug use is higher than the national average. About a third of all AIDS cases in New York and more than half of those in New Jersey have involved people with histories of drug abuse or addiction.[3]

Most women and children who have AIDS in this country appear to have been infected, directly or indirectly, through intravenous drug use. More than half of the 1,870 cases of AIDS among women reported to the CDC by December 1986 involved women who themselves used drugs intravenously. A substantial proportion of the rest were apparently infected through heterosexual contacts with men in risk groups, most often IV-drug users.[4] And women who have been exposed to HIV are transmitting the virus to the children they bear, during pregnancy, at birth, or shortly thereafter.[5]

People with AIDS associated with IV-drug use are disadvantaged in ways

NOTE: As this book went to press, the federal confidentiality regulations discussed at pp. 266–76 were being renumbered and significantly revised, effective Aug. 10, 1987. The new regulations, which place fewer restrictions on the release of information, appear at 52 Fed. Reg. 21,796 (1987).

that distinguish them not only from the population at large but even from other people with AIDS. Though in the United States, most people with AIDS are white, 51 percent of those whose illness is attributed to IV-drug use are black and 30 percent are Hispanic.[6] They are poorer, have less access to basic support systems, and are less well organized politically than the gay men who form the largest risk group. Moreover, they are often subject to race discrimination in addition to suspicion and mistreatment based on their illness or drug use. Compared to others with AIDS, IV-drug users tend also to be less well insured (or completely uninsured) and sicker when first diagnosed.[7]

What the future bodes is a matter of increasing concern. Health authorities estimate that there are a half million or more addicts in the United States, with an estimated 250,000 in New York and 40,000 in New Jersey alone.[8] What proportion of these people have already been exposed to AIDS is not known. Recent surveys of IV-drug users admitted for medical care or drug-abuse treatment in and around New York City suggest that over half of those who use drugs intravenously in that metropolitan area have already been exposed to HIV, as indicated by positive results of tests for antibodies to the virus ("seropositivity"). Surveys of IV-drug users in other urban areas have shown lower rates of exposure. In Chicago and San Francisco, 10 percent tested seropositive. However, the potential for the spread of infection among these people and their sexual contacts concerns health authorities everywhere.[9]

What proportion of those who have already been exposed will ultimately develop AIDS or related conditions is unknown.[10] Nor is it known how many others may be infected or become ill through drug abuse. Since the latency period between infection and the development of AIDS apparently extends up to five years, the potential number of AIDS cases among those who have used intravenous drugs is large indeed.[11]

This chapter explores three issues raised by AIDS that create complex problems for past and present drug users and for those who work in the field of drug-abuse prevention and treatment:

The Threat of Discrimination. Those labeled with the stigma of drug abuse and AIDS face the prospect of discrimination from two directions at once. The first section of this chapter discusses laws that offer protection from discrimination based on drug abuse and AIDS-related conditions.

Drug-Abuse Treatment, Confidentiality, and Reporting Conflicts. Programs for drug-abuse treatment must confront and resolve many conflicts in deciding whether and how to test, treat, and tell others about their increasing population of patients infected or ill with AIDS. Among other problems, the double threat of discrimination against people who bear the burden of both drug abuse and AIDS makes the need for confidentiality about their backgrounds and treatment all the more profound. Over a decade ago, Congress passed laws protecting the privacy of people being treated for drug abuse and the confidentiality of all records relating to their treatment. As yet, however, no federal and few state confidentiality laws offer comparable protection to those tested or treated for AIDS. To further complicate matters, most states now mandate reporting of AIDS cases to public health authorities, some require reporting of AIDS-related conditions, and an increasing number have proposed mandatory testing of groups at risk for AIDS. The potential conflicts between these measures and the federal law protecting the confidentiality of drug-abuse treatment records are great.

   The "Clean Needles" Controversy. To reduce the risk of AIDS, health and drug-abuse professionals recommend that people who use drugs intravenously stop shooting-up or else stop sharing or reusing needles or "works."[12] Professionals recognize, however, that to stop using drugs is difficult for most IV users and impossible without treatment for some. Yet treatment programs lack the resources to help all who are in need.[13] Consequently, many addicts will probably continue to use drugs intravenously and to expose themselves to needles contaminated with HIV. This has led some health and drug-abuse experts to propose that sterile needles be made more freely available to IV-drug users.[14] The last section of this chapter considers the legal and other barriers that would have to be removed should "clean needle" proposals prevail.

LAWS PROTECTING PEOPLE FROM DISCRIMINATION BASED ON DRUG ABUSE, ADDICTION, AND AIDS

Both former and current drug abusers suffer widespread discrimination— including denials of medical care, jobs, housing, and other benefits and services—simply because they have histories of drug abuse or addiction. Hostility extends not only to those actively involved in illicit drug use, but also to those participating in treatment programs that enable them to lead responsible, functional lives, and to those who have long since recovered from drug abuse or dependency. Growing recognition of the links between IV-drug use and AIDS now subjects such individuals to discrimination arising from ignorance and fear of another widely misunderstood medical condition.

   Various means are commonly used to identify and exclude former and current drug abusers from jobs, benefits, and services. Questions about past or present drug abuse and treatment on application forms for employment, public housing, medical care, insurance, or other benefits are one method. In addition, injection "track marks" may be discovered in medical examinations that employers, insurers, or other service providers give to applicants. Growing numbers of employers also demand that both job applicants and employees undergo drug-screening urine tests, even without reason to believe the individuals tested are either using or impaired by drugs. Urine tests reveal not only the presence of drugs of abuse (including heroin and cocaine) that can be used intravenously, but also the presence of methadone, a medication prescribed for the treatment of heroin addiction. Thus, urinalysis can disclose that a person is in treatment for drug addiction even though that person no longer takes drugs of abuse. Finally, many employers, occupational licensing agencies, and other entities (including public housing authorities) investigate applicants' criminal records. Since drug abuse and addiction often result in drug-related arrests or convictions, such investigations can easily lead to discovery of an individual's history.

In short, people with histories of drug abuse or treatment are vulnerable in many ways to having their background or status in treatment discovered. Those who want to identify and screen out individuals who are linked to drugs, however remotely, have ample means for doing so.

Now, some employers and insurers are using or seeking the right to use still another screening tool: antibody tests to determine whether applicants have been exposed to HIV. Like the methods already used for identifying individuals' past or present involvement with drugs, these new screening tests have enormous potential for abuse.

Federal Antidiscrimination Laws

Two federal antidiscrimination laws offer some protection to persons who are, have been, or are perceived by others as being drug abusers. The Drug Abuse Office and Treatment Act of 1972 specifically forbids discrimination based on drug abuse or dependency.[15] The Rehabilitation Act of 1973 bars discrimination against individuals who are, have been, or are regarded as being handicapped.[16] Drug abuse or addiction, and treatment for those conditions, are considered handicaps within this law. AIDS and related conditions are beginning to be recognized as handicaps within the protection of this law as well.

The Drug Abuse Office and Treatment Act of 1972

Discrimination in Medical Care. Both drug abusers (even without AIDS) and people who have AIDS (even without links to IV-drug use) have frequently been denied access to medical care or have been victims of discriminatory treatment.[17] The combination of drug abuse and AIDS, and often poverty, is lethal in more ways than one since the critically ill and socially despised are hardly in a position to contend with discrimination in medical admissions and treatment, too.

Discrimination against drug abusers and addicts by providers of medical care was so severe that Congress enacted specific legislation to remedy the problem. The Drug Abuse Office and Treatment Act of 1972 provides that "[d]rug abusers who are suffering from medical conditions shall not be discriminated against in admission or treatment, solely because of their drug abuse or . . . dependence, by any private or public general hospital" that is in any way supported, whether directly or indirectly, by federal funds (including Medicaid and Medicare).[18] Hospitals violating this law face suspension or revocation of their federal funding.[19] Persons victimized by discriminatory health care in violation of this law may file complaints with the Office of Civil Rights of the U. S. Health and Human Services Department, which can threaten to cut off federal funds as a lever to achieve compliance. The Rehabilitation Act, discussed below, and the Veterans' Benefits Law have parallel or broader provisions.[20]

AIDS and related conditions fall within the scope of the "medical conditions" or "disabilities" for which drug abusers and addicts may seek treatment in hospitals and other health care facilities covered by these laws.[21] If such persons do seek treatment for AIDS or related conditions, their drug abuse or dependency may not legally be used to deny them the care they need. Nor, for reasons explained below, may AIDS itself be used to deny any person needed medical care.

Formal legal procedures, though, may not provide the fastest and most effective means of solving problems that present or former drug abusers with AIDS may encounter in seeking decent medical care. Immediate solutions can be found by working with patient advocates in medical care facilities, with organizations that have been established to help people with AIDS, and with the staffs of drug-abuse treatment programs, who can act effectively on behalf of drug-treatment clients in general medical care facilities. The New York State Division of Substance Abuse Services is working hard to educate not only those receiving treatment for drug abuse, but also treatment personnel, about AIDS. It has also encouraged treatment programs to designate special staff members as liaisons between the drug-treatment and general medical-care communities. New Jersey is promoting similar education efforts among workers in health care and drug-abuse treatment.

Employment Discrimination. Other purposes of the Drug Abuse Office and Treatment Act of 1972 were to establish drug-abuse prevention, treatment, and rehabilitation programs for federal civilian employees, to encourage state and local governments and industry to do the same,[22] and to ensure that those who successfully overcome drug problems receive fair federal employment opportunities. The law provides that "[no] person may be denied or deprived of federal civilian employment solely on the ground of prior drug abuse."[23] The law does not, however, prevent federal civilian employers from dismissing any individual who "cannot properly function in employment" because of a drug (or any other) problem.[24] The distinctions the law makes between individuals who can and cannot perform their jobs are similar in purpose and effect to those of the Rehabilitation Act of 1973 and will be addressed in the following section.

The Rehabilitation Act of 1973
The Rehabilitation Act of 1973 is the major federal civil rights law protecting disabled persons from discrimination in jobs, programs, and activities that

are federally run or assisted. The "handicapped individuals" protected from discrimination by the Rehabilitation Act are broadly defined to include anyone who "(i) has a physical or mental impairment that substantially limits one or more of such person's major life activities, (ii) has a record of such an impairment, or (iii) is regarded as having such an impairment."[25] (For a full discussion of the Rehabilitation Act and its application to AIDS, see Chapter 8.)

Since 1977, both federal agencies and courts have expressly ruled that people with histories of drug abuse or addiction, including those who participate in methadone maintenance treatment for former heroin addiction, are handicapped persons within the compass of the law. The U.S. Department of Health, Education and Welfare (HEW), was the first agency to recognize that the Rehabilitation Act covered drug users, and other federal agencies followed its lead.[26] The courts have also followed suit. In *Davis v. Bucher*, a federal district court ruled that a history of heroin addiction and current participation in methadone maintenance treatment for addiction are handicaps under the Rehabilitation Act.[27] Persons perceived as drug abusers when they are not have also successfully challenged adverse employment actions under the law.[28]

The Rehabilitation Act prohibits discrimination only against those "handicapped individuals" who are "otherwise qualified" for the jobs, services, or benefits they seek. But those who are so qualified may not be excluded from participating in, be denied the benefits of, or be subjected in any way to discrimination in any program or activity subject to the law "*solely* by reason of . . . handicap."[29] What do these basic principles mean with respect to people who are, who once were, or who are regarded as drug abusers or addicts? What do they mean with respect to people who have, who are at risk for, or who are perceived by others as having or being in risk groups for AIDS? Federal agencies, courts, and Congress have clarified the essential meaning of these principles in several respects.

First, in general, federal regulations state that a handicapped individual is "otherwise qualified" if that person "meets the essential eligibility requirements" of the program in question.[30] With respect to employment, the regulations define such an individual as "one who, with reasonable accommodation, can perform the essential functions of the job in question."[31]

Exclusionary policies and actions based merely on an individual's status as someone with a past, present, or perceived handicap—however stigmatizing that condition may be—are simply not permissible.[32] Under the Rehabilitation Act, policies and decisions concerning every individual (with any form of handicap) must be based on criteria that shed light on that particular person's actual ability successfully to participate in a program or to perform a particular job. The court emphasized this point in *Davis v. Bucher*,[33] when it ruled that a city flatly violated Section 504 by maintaining a policy of excluding drug-free former addicts and persons currently participating in methadone programs from all city jobs, without any regard to the "uncontested evidence that persons with a history of substance abuse, and in particular ex-heroin addicts, could be employed successfully," and without any consideration of the individual qualifications and abilities of any person in the excluded group.

Shortly after *Davis*, Congress amended the act's definition of "handicapped individuals" to provide clear protection to all people with histories or conditions of substance abuse *except* those "alcoholic[s] or drug abuser[s] whose current use of alcohol or drugs prevents [them] from performing the duties of the job in question or whose employment, by reason of such current alcohol or drug abuse, would constitute a direct threat to property or the safety of others."[34] In doing so, members of Congress emphasized that mere fear or disapproval of an individual's status as a past or present abuser of drugs cannot justify denying that person access to employment, benefits, or services. Nor may exclusionary policies stem from blanket assumptions that such individuals cannot responsibly perform the jobs or successfully participate in the programs in question, or from unsubstantiated fears about the "dangers" that such persons may pose to themselves or others.[35] Each individual must be considered on his or her current merits. The same is true for individuals with every other "handicap," actual or perceived.

Some persons argue that drug addicts or people with AIDS deserve to be shunned because they brought their disabilities on themselves. The Rehabilitation Act, however, forbids government agencies and employers who receive federal funds to discriminate against disabled individuals on the basis of any handicap; the law makes no distinctions based on how or why a particular handicap is acquired.[36] Personal merit, not personal morality, must rule policies and decisions that affect individuals with stigmatizing illnesses.·

Another rationale for discrimination against drug users or persons with AIDS-related conditions is fear of contagion: fear that those who use or once used drugs will corrupt and addict everyone around them; fear that those who have AIDS or have been exposed to HIV will expose and infect everyone around them. Although the Supreme Court has not yet settled this issue, it has responded to similar fears by finding that the Rehabilitation Act requires known facts and good sense—not panic—to prevail. Congressional and judicial explanations of the Act make clear that unfounded fear cannot justify discrimination against current or former drug addicts. Important court decisions dealing with discrimination against persons carrying infectious or contagious diseases reach the same conclusion. These cases should serve as precedents for cases involving the dual problem of addiction and AIDS-based discrimination.

In *New York State Ass'n for Retarded Children v. Carey*,[37] a school board's plan to isolate certain mentally retarded children who had been tested and found to be carriers of hepatitis B, placing them in separate classes within the public schools, was challenged as violating the Rehabilitation Act and other laws. The Court of Appeals invalidated the school board's quarantine plan because there was no evidence that it was necessary or even justifiable. The school board "was unable to demonstrate that the health hazard posed by the hepatitis B carrier children was anything more than a remote possibility."[38]

The Supreme Court ruled, in *School Board of Nassau County v. Arline*, that a contagious disease, recurrent tuberculosis, constitutes a handicap for purposes of the Rehabilitation Act. The Court emphasized that a decision to dismiss a worker with a contagious illness would be legally justifiable only if it were based on an individualized medical judgment that the person in question "poses a significant risk of communicating an infectious disease to others in the workplace."[39] Like the court in *Carey*, the *Arline* Court pointed out that an adverse employment decision about a particular individual based on nothing more than "the prejudiced attitudes or the ignorance of others" would contravene the federal law.[40]

The remoteness of the risk of transmission of either HIV or AIDS has already led a New York court to uphold a school board's policy not to automatically exclude children with AIDS from New York City public schools. In *In re District 27 Community School Board v. New York City Board of Education*, after considering both the medical realities and legal precedents established by the federal appellate courts in *Carey* and *Arline*, a state court determined that anything other than the policy the school board did adopt—individualized consideration of each child's case—would violate section 504 of the Rehabilitation Act.[41]

Many people see *any* risk of exposure to a potentially lethal disease as unacceptable and seek policies that will eliminate *all* risk. That sentiment impels those who talk of excluding, isolating, or quarantining people who have or who may have been exposed to AIDS. But, as medical experts, health authorities, and the court pointed out in *District 27*, no part of life can ever be made risk free.[42] Moreover, no policy could effectively identify and isolate all those who have been or may in the future be exposed to AIDS. The potential numbers are too large, and the potential risks are too minute, to justify such draconian action.

People with addiction histories and AIDS-related conditions also inspire doubt in employers due to their possible future incapacity to perform a job. Consequently, employers may seek to screen applicants with those characteristics. How does the Rehabilitation Act restrict the ability of covered employers to ferret out information about applicants' and employees' past or possible drug use, addiction, exposure to HIV, or diagnosis of AIDS?

To prevent handicapped people from being deprived of a fair opportunity to lead ordinary lives, the act demands that all selection criteria, screening tools, tests, and the like be directly related to the determination of an individual's qualifications for whatever he or she seeks to do. The law attempts to ensure that irrelevant information not even *enter* the marketplace by forbidding the use of inquiries or screening tools that elicit irrelevant information.[43]

The Rehabilitation Act should bar inquiries in job application forms and interviews as to whether the applicant has, has had, or has been treated for conditions related to drug abuse or AIDS, if such questions are not directly job-related. Moreover, the act's requirement that employment tests be job-related raises serious questions about whether an employer subject to the law may test applicants for such conditions. (For a complete discussion of the legality of HIV testing in the workplace under various antidiscrimination laws, see Chapter 9.)

Drug-screening urinalyses and HIV antibody tests are suspect for two reasons. First, both drug-screening and HIV tests produce false results too often to permit their use as divining rods for identification of disfavored groups.[44] Second, even if such tests accurately identify some individuals who have the disfavored characteristics, screening tests only confirm an individual's possible history or condition of drug use or of HIV infection. They provide no answer to the only permissible inquiry under law: can this person do this job? It is illegal for employers to assume that prior or even current use of drugs by itself shows present or future incapacity to perform a job. Nor may they conclude from a positive test for HIV that an applicant poses a present danger to himself or to others in the workplace or that he or she will develop AIDS or any related condition. The act's mandate that employers focus on job-related criteria is contravened when employers use tenuous tests with tenuous import. Such tests open the doors to the "unthinking and unnecessary discrimination" that the Rehabilitation Act proscribes.[45]

Cases that concern employers' fears of employees' future illnesses or disabilities clarify another point: what no one knows, no employer may presume. Only if there is a significant and well-substantiated risk of future incapacity on the part of a particular handicapped individual may an employer legally refuse training or employment opportunities. Once again, simple statistical possibilities do not suffice.[46]

State Antidiscrimination Laws, Addiction, and AIDS

The vast majority of states have their own laws forbidding discrimination against persons with handicaps or disabilities, and an increasing number are interpreting those laws to protect people who have histories of addiction or AIDS, as well as those perceived as at risk for AIDS. These laws typically forbid discrimination in jobs, housing, and public accommodations, as well as in the provision of other benefits and services.

Though many of the state laws on disability discrimination were modeled after or are being interpreted as parallel to the federal Rehabilitation Act, their coverage of specific conditions, including addiction and AIDS, varies considerably. Yet these laws are extremely important in two respects. First, while the federal law reaches only discrimination by federal agencies and recipients of federal contracts or funds (admittedly a broad sweep), state laws are likely to apply to virtually all public and private employers, to private as well as public housing, and to many other providers of benefits and services. Also, the agencies charged with enforcing these laws are able, at least in some instances, to move more quickly to investigate and resolve discrimination complaints than are the federal agencies responsible for monitoring compliance with the Rehabilitation Act.

All five of the states with the highest concentration of AIDS cases associated with intravenous drug use have handicap or disability discrimination laws. The speed with which they have applied those laws to AIDS (and, to a lesser degree, to addiction as well) reflects the degree to which AIDS in general, and AIDS linked to IV-drug use specifically, has become a major problem. By mid-March 1986, New York state had the highest number of cases of AIDS linked to IV-drug use (1,869), followed by New Jersey (490), Florida (165), California (88), and Connecticut (55).[47]

Of the five, New York is the only state that has explicitly recognized both addiction and AIDS as disabilities: New York's Human Rights Law prohibits discrimination in housing, public accommodations, employment, and other areas.[48] New Jersey's Division on Civil Rights has taken the position that the state's Law Against Discrimination encompasses AIDS and related conditions, whether actual or perceived.[49] Though neither the Civil Rights Division nor the state courts have ruled whether drug abuse is a "handicap" under New Jersey's law, other rulings of the Division indicate that this question will be answered affirmatively.[50] California, which has been at the forefront of the effort to combat AIDS-based discrimination, has both statewide laws prohibiting discrimination against persons with "physical handicaps" or "medical conditions"[51] and municipal ordinances in its two largest cities that specifically bar AIDS-based discrimination.[52] Although California's Fair Employment and Housing Practices Commission has for some time interpreted the antidiscrimination law to exclude "narcotics addiction,"[53] IV-drug users may nonetheless be covered as persons "perceived" as having or carrying AIDS.[54] The Florida Commission on Human Relations was the first state agency to rule formally that AIDS constituted a "handicap" under state law,[55] but the commission has not yet issued a decision on addiction. Although Connecticut has not faced a discrimination case involving drug abuse or AIDS, if it follows federal law or the laws of other states, it will probably find one or both of these conditions within the scope of its Human Rights and Opportunities Act. Thus state as well as federal law may provide grounds for action against persons or organizations that discriminate on the basis of drug abuse, AIDS, or both.

DRUG-ABUSE TREATMENT AND AIDS: TREATMENT AND CONFIDENTIALITY CONFLICTS

Drug-abuse treatment programs and the professionals who staff them are directly affected by the spread of HIV among people who use drugs intravenously or who have done so during the last decade. Most treatment programs already have many clients with AIDS or at risk of developing the disease, and must expect many more in the future, especially in New York City, northern New Jersey, and surrounding areas. The rate of exposure to the virus is so high that programs in those areas presume seropositivity is the norm, not the exception, in their client populations.

Thus, treatment programs must learn to deal with AIDS whether they want to or not. They must confront and resolve conflicting obligations and potential liabilities: responsibilities relating to AIDS prevention and risk reduction for their clients, their staff, and perhaps even for their clients' families and sexual contacts; responsibilities to report cases of AIDS to state public health authorities; and responsibilities under federal law and regulations to protect the privacy of both drug-abuse patients and their treatment records.

Treatment Issues

The answers to questions of law concerning the treatment of drug-abuse patients with AIDS or seropositivity (and conditions in between) are increasingly clear, though the conflicts they create are hardly resolved.

May Treatment Programs Legally Screen Prospective and Current Patients for AIDS and Seropositivity?

The response to this question depends on the purpose behind the proposed screening. Most if not all drug-abuse treatment programs are federally assisted in some way and are therefore obliged to comply with the nondiscrimination provisions of the Rehabilitation Act. Even if not covered by this law, treatment programs are either expressly defined as, or likely to be considered, "public accommodations" under state antidiscrimination laws. Therefore, treatment programs risk violating both federal and state laws if they discriminate against people with AIDS, related conditions, or seropositivity.

If a treatment program's only (or real) purpose in screening for seropositivity is to exclude people from treatment, then such screening is probably illegal. In light of what is known about AIDS and its modes of transmission, there is no rational—let alone substantial—justification from a medical, rehabilitative, or legal point of view for refusing to treat those people who, in addition to being addicted, may be infected with HIV. Treatment programs daily encounter in their patient populations the similarly transmitted but much hardier and more infectious virus that causes hepatitis

B. In most instances, however, the programs have neither refused to admit nor segregated clients who have or who are suspected of carrying hepatitis B.

Screening for AIDS or seropositivity is equally troublesome if it is used to separate those who have AIDS or related conditions from the rest of the clients (and staff) of a drug-abuse treatment program. Ambulatory detoxification programs, outpatient drug-free or methadone maintenance clinics, and other nonresidential treatment facilities would be hard put to justify any across-the-board segregation for the protection of either patients or program staff. The functions these programs perform—counseling, dispensing medication in methadone maintenance programs, and the like—ordinarily involve only nondangerous, casual contacts among patients and staff.

Studies of people with AIDS who have lived for long periods of time in close, nonsexual contact with their families have shown that people run no appreciable risk of being infected merely by working and living with AIDS patients.[56] Thus, even in residential programs, segregation of all AIDS patients for the protection of other residents and staff is uncalled for. There may, however, be instances in which an AIDS patient's suppressed immunity and susceptibility to infection call for protecting that person from the risk of exposure to *others'* illnesses or infections. But the occurrence of such individual instances does not support an across-the-board policy of sequestering all AIDS or seropositive patients in residential drug-abuse treatment programs.

Increasing numbers of drug abusers have already been exposed to and are presumably capable of transmitting the virus. Thus, given the potential numbers involved, any attempt to separate all patients who have been infected from the rest of the client population may well be practically impossible for treatment programs.

Treatment programs' legitimate concern for maintaining good hygiene and eliminating any risk of infection—with respect not just to AIDS but also to hepatitis—should be addressed by implementing the precautions that the CDC recommends to all health care facilities dealing with cases of AIDS, seropositivity, or hepatitis B. In addition, measures designed to prevent the particular activities that put people at risk of AIDS—having unsafe sex and sharing contaminated needles—are already in place in many treatment programs. None of these precautions requires the segregation of infected patients.

Programs can establish rules forbidding all patients to use drugs intravenously or forbidding those in residential treatment to have unsafe (or any) sex. Treatment programs should clearly inform prospective and present patients of those rules and may wish to have each client sign an agreement that he or she has been told, understands, and will abide by the risk-reduction rules while in treatment. Admission to, or continuation of, treatment may be conditioned on a patient's signing such an agreement. Those who refuse to abide by a treatment program's risk-reduction rules may then be legally discharged from treatment—not because they have or may have been exposed to AIDS, but because, by violating the rules, they have undermined their own and others' rights to receive effective treatment.

Should Treatment Programs Screen Patients for AIDS and Seropositivity for Purposes of AIDS Prevention, Counseling, and Care?

Some health authorities urge that treatment programs test patients to educate them about their antibody status and to counsel them about appropriate risk-reduction methods. But professionals have conflicting opinions about whether routine screening of patients in drug-abuse treatment would enhance or endanger effective treatment and preventive efforts. For example, the U. S. Public Health Service, which originally opposed widespread screening of any risk group, now urges that all people in risk groups for AIDS, including past and present users of IV drugs, be encouraged to undergo voluntary periodic screening for seropositivity.[57] Some officials at the National Institute on Drug Abuse (NIDA), the main federal agency charged with promoting research, prevention, and treatment efforts concerning drug abuse and addiction, agree with this recommendation.[58] Both agencies emphasize, however, that testing should be encouraged, not required, and that test results should be kept confidential. Drug-abuse prevention and treatment agencies in New York and New Jersey, the two states hardest hit by AIDS linked to IV-drug use, have not adopted the federal authorities' recommendations. The lack of consensus reflects the real dilemmas that routine screening of drug-abuse patients creates.

What Difference Should It Make? Some question the point of HIV testing because they believe that IV-drug users and drug-abuse treatment personnel should simply presume what already is, or may soon become, the case: IV-drug use itself means exposure to AIDS. Consequently, all drug users should (given the risks) simply assume that they already are infected or may become infected and should change their behavior accordingly. Similarly, many believe that drug-abuse treatment programs should act on the presumption that increasing numbers of their clients will be seropositive and should implement across-the-board policies that address the problems they and their clients will necessarily face. Periodic screening would not add to knowledge about the problem of drug abuse and AIDS; in fact, screening might send some treatment personnel into irrational panic about their clients, or (perhaps worse) give the staff a false sense of security about patients who, for the moment, test negative. After all, negative antibody tests today say nothing about results tomorrow—or even about exposure within the month or so before.

What Good Would It Do? Some are also concerned about the effect information about antibody status may have on patients. For example, AIDS specialists in the New York State Division of Substance Abuse report that drug abusers (both in treatment and not in treatment) have willingly submitted to HIV tests in connection with research projects. Many of those tested, however, not only did not want to know, but actively avoided finding out the test results. This reaction indicates that, at least for some drug abusers, the fear of having to know might actually deter them from entering or continuing in drug treatment. In that case, such testing—especially by treatment programs themselves—could defeat the purpose for which it has been urged.

What Harm Might Follow in Its Wake? Finally, there is the perpetual dilemma faced by those who are involved with drug-abuse treatment: having information opens a Pandora's box containing potential abuses of the information.

Drug abusers and addicts, and people in treatment for those conditions, often bear heavy burdens of anxiety, depression, and guilt. Positive test results, which remind addicts of the destructive legacy of their drug abuse, may only increase the burdens that they carry. In addition, treatment personnel may react negatively to knowing an individual patient's antibody status, or to knowing that some staff members in the program have that information. A general policy that identifies individual patients as seropositive will be counterproductive if it inspires fear and its usual companion, the impulse to discriminate, in the treatment staff. The reaction of the world at large is a final source of worry. Neither treatment programs nor their clients can afford more disapproval. And, if the programs have information on seropositivity, the external pressures to release it may be almost irresistible, making confidentiality a serious problem.

Treatment programs may wish to consider one practical alternative to conducting HIV testing themselves. "Alternative test sites" offer confidential testing (by code numbers rather than by names) and counseling. The states with the highest incidence of IV-drug-associated AIDS have already established alternative test sites.[59]

Liability Issues

Legal Duties

No law requires treatment programs to examine their clients for AIDS or test for seropositivity. Those programs that do will face several questions. Do treatment programs have a legal obligation to advise drug-abuse patients of the test results? Are the programs required to report the results to public health authorities? Do treatment programs have a legal duty to warn staff, other patients, family members, sexual contacts, or others, about the medical condition of patients whom they know to have AIDS, AIDS-Related Complex (ARC), or seropositivity? If so, how can treatment programs fulfill their obligation to inform others of patients' conditions without violating federal law and regulations governing confidentiality of drug-abuse treatment records?

Before addressing these questions, a brief overview of the federal law and regulations governing the confidentiality of records of drug-abuse patients is in order.

Federal Rules on the Confidentiality of Drug-Abuse Treatment Records

When Congress enacted Section 408 of the Drug Abuse Office and Treatment Act of 1972,[60] it stated:

> [T]he strictest adherence to the provisions of this section is absolutely essential to the success of all drug abuse prevention programs. Every patient and former patient must be assured that his or her right to privacy will be protected. Without that assurance, fear of public disclosure of drug abuse or of [drug abuse treatment] records that will attach for life will discourage thousands from seeking the treatment they must have if this tragic national problem is to be overcome.
>
> Every person having control over or access to patients' records must understand that disclosure is permitted only under the circumstances and conditions set forth in this section. Records are not to be made available to investigators for the purpose of law enforcement or for any other private or public purpose in any manner not specified by this section.[61]

All questions concerning the disclosure of drug-abuse treatment records—including those relating to AIDS—must be considered in light of the law's purposes. The law was enacted to protect the privacy of people who are in treatment for drug abuse or addiction. It also sought to enhance the quality and attractiveness of substance-abuse treatment by fostering a community-wide perception that it is safe to enter treatment.

Except under certain limited circumstances, the confidentiality law and regulations forbid treatment programs supported by or licensed by the federal government to disclose any patient records.[62] The prohibition on unauthorized disclosures applies whether or not the person seeking information already has the information, has other means of obtaining it, enjoys official status, or has obtained a subpoena or warrant for it.[63]

The "records" protected from unauthorized disclosure include any information acquired about a patient, whether written or not, such as the patient's identity, address, medical status or diagnoses, treatment information, and all communications from him or her to the staff of the treatment program. The nondisclosure provisions therefore cover AIDS-related diagnoses.[64]

The "patients" whose records are protected from disclosure include any person who has applied for, participated in, or received an interview, counseling, diagnostic test, evaluation, or any other service or activity related to drug-abuse education, training, treatment, rehabilitation, or research. An individual is considered a "patient" even if he or she is found not to have a drug-abuse problem. Former patients and deceased patients are also protected. "Diagnosis" or "treatment" is not limited to that rendered by members of the medical profession.[65]

A "disclosure" includes almost any communication of information about a patient, whether implicit or explicit.[66] Only three kinds of communications are *not* "disclosures" under the law and are therefore permissible: (1) internal communications among the staff member of treatment programs when they need the information to perform their duties; (2) communications that do not disclose any patient-identifying information, either directly or indirectly; and (3) certain communications to "qualified service organizations," which may enter an agreement with a treatment program to provide services (such as laboratory work or medical care) to the program and its patients.[67]

The limited exceptions to the general prohibition against disclosure of patient-identifying information are relevant to AIDS reporting. A program may disclose patient-identifying information if the patient voluntarily signs a written consent that complies with requirements set out in the regulations, and the program independently assures itself that the disclosure will not harm the patient.[68] The program must notify the recipient of a consensual disclosure that federal law protects the confidentiality of the information and prohibits its redisclosure except with the specific written consent of the patient or as otherwise authorized by the law.[69] Special circumstances justify the disclosure of patient-identifying information without the patient's consent. Programs may make unconsented-to disclosures (1) in bona fide medical emergencies; (2) to qualified private or governmental personnel for the purpose of conducting scientific research or evaluations concerning drug abuse patients or treatment programs; and (3) when a court issues a proper order authorizing a particular disclosure.[70] The penalties for disclosures in violation of the law include criminal fines and perhaps civil liability as well.[71]

Federal confidentiality law and regulations supersede all conflicting state or local requirements. Although treatment programs and staff must comply with other laws to the extent possible, "[n]o State law . . . may authorize or compel any disclosure prohibited by" the federal law and regulations.[72]

Testing and Telling Patients about Their AIDS or HIV Antibody Results

If a treatment program decides to offer AIDS tests to its clientele, the process of testing and telling each patient his or her results must be conducted in accordance with two basic rules. First: *never* test the patient without his or her prior, voluntary, informed consent. Second: *never* disclose to the patient his or her test results without obtaining from the patient a written consent to the disclosure that complies with the requirements of the federal confidentiality law. Even with such a consent, do not reveal the test results if doing so would be "harmful" to the patient.

First Obtain the Patient's Informed Consent to the Test Itself. AIDS-related diagnostic tests are medical procedures. An absolute prerequisite for such tests is the individual's informed consent. The federal confidentiality law and regulations make clear that patients receiving treatment for drug abuse, like others, have the right not to be tested without their consent.[73] Moreover, California, Florida, and selected other states have enacted special laws (and New York and others have comparable administrative rules) mandating that those who offer AIDS-related tests obtain prior informed consent.[74] States without such laws probably have other statutes or case law requiring informed consent to all medical procedures. The violation of these laws may, and in some states certainly will, subject those who test others thoughtlessly and without consent to both civil and criminal penalties.[75]

To give informed consent, patients must not only know what tests will be performed but also be aware of the risks (both psychic and physical) and of the possibilities for error in the test procedures.[76] At a minimum, a treatment program should offer AIDS tests only to patients who are mentally and physically stable enough to deal with the tests and their results. This may mean *not* testing everyone as a condition of treatment or immediately upon admission to a clinic, especially if some applicants or patients are suffering from withdrawal or experiencing other problems that impair mental or physical functioning.

Obtain the Patient's Proper Written Consent before Disclosing AIDS Test Results to the Patient. Advising a drug-abuse patient of the results of his or her own AIDS test constitutes a "disclosure" under the federal confidentiality law and regulations, as does revealing to a patient any other information from his or her treatment file. Thus, the patient must consent in writing to the disclosure of test results to him- or herself. Even with proper consent, disclosure should not be made if, in the treatment program's judgment, it would be "harmful to the patient."[77]

The question of possible "harm" to the patient is complicated by certain laws that impose on treatment personnel an obligation to tell the patient of test results if they perform medical tests at all. For example, medical professionals who assume responsibility for examining or treating individuals in their professional capacity may be under a duty to advise patients of diagnosed medical conditions. This duty is imposed to equip patients with the necessary knowledge to take care of themselves and, in cases of certain infectious illnesses, to take care not to expose others.[78]

In light of these confusing and conflicting obligations, alternative antibody test sites may offer an excellent solution for treatment programs, as well as patients, struggling to find responsible ways to deal with AIDS. Referring patients to such sites, or to other health professionals with special expertise in testing, counseling, and treating those who have, or are at risk for, AIDS makes sound legal, therapeutic, and medical sense. Documenting referrals may offer programs some security against possible complaints that they failed to fulfill their responsibility to make their patients aware of medical conditions linked to histories of drug abuse.

Ways to Comply with Both Reporting Requirements and Confidentiality Laws

Most states now mandate the reporting of cases of AIDS (and in some states, related conditions) to state public health authorities, who in turn report the epidemiological data they gather to the federal Centers for Disease Control (CDC). Reporting requirements vary from state to state. Under federal law and regulations protecting the confidentiality of records of drug-abuse patients, treatment programs that have a duty to report known cases of AIDS or related conditions to public health authorities have four basic options.

A treatment program may make a mandated AIDS report in an individual case (and may include patient-identifying information in that report) if it obtains voluntary, written consent from the patient involved.[79] As in the context of reporting to the patient, however, a program must first determine that the consented-to disclosure will "not cause substantial harm to the relationship between the patient and the program or to the program's capacity to provide services in general," and "will not be harmful to the patient."[80] For example, if program personnel believe that the patient involved, or other patients, will not enter or stay in treatment because they fear disclosures of AIDS-related diagnoses, seeking a patient's consent may not be wise or permissible.[81]

Treatment programs making consensual, harmless, and proper disclosures of AIDS cases must remember to notify the recipient of the report that federal law protects the confidentiality of the patient-identifying information and prohibits redisclosure of that information in any way that violates the confidentiality law.[82] For example, a state's public health policy concerning communicable diseases may authorize the use of AIDS reports to investigate or prosecute subjects of those reports who are suspected of engaging in such activities as prostitution or illegal drug use or sale. Public health authorities in such states must be made aware that the federal confidentiality law prohibits investigation or prosecution on the basis of patient-identifying information gleaned from AIDS reports made by treatment programs with their patients' consent.

The second and perhaps the simplest means of making required AIDS reports to state or local public health authorities is to use the "research or evaluation" exception to the federal law's general rule against nonconsensual or otherwise unauthorized disclosures.[83] The exception permits qualified personnel in governmental agencies to obtain treatment data (including patient-identifying information and AIDS-related diagnoses or test results) for the purpose of conducting "scientific research or long-term evaluation studies." A treatment program's release of data for this purpose requires no patient consent and may not require written agreement between the program and the governmental agencies. However, every person in those agencies who receives such information—including every staff member of public health departments—"is legally required to hold such information in confidence, is prohibited from taking any administrative, investigative, or other action with respect to any individual patient on the basis of such information, and is prohibited from identifying, directly or indirectly, any individual patient in any report of such research or evaluation, or otherwise disclosing patient identities in any manner."[84]

Unless a treatment program is assured that these restrictions will be obeyed, it need not, and indeed must not, turn over information to public health authorities. A treatment program must investigate potential problems with confidentiality before it hands over information to public health personnel. Programs are entitled to obtain a written legal opinion from their state attorney general confirming that the federal confidentiality law's requirements will be obeyed and that adequate measures to safeguard the data are in place before they disclose patient-identifying information for research purposes.[85]

Third, a treatment program may be able to make an AIDS report to public health authorities, even without a patient's consent, if the "disclosure" is made without divulging to unauthorized personnel any person's past or present participation in a drug-abuse treatment program.[86] This method of reporting is permissible only if the information reported does *not* include data about an individual's drug-use history or treatment, for that data is protected from disclosure by the confidentiality law.

There are two possible ways of making a mandated AIDS report without revealing a patient's involvement with drug use. The first is "anonymous" reporting that does not identify the individual as a patient in drug-abuse treatment. "Anonymous" AIDS reports do not require a patient's consent but may be made only if the patient's participation in treatment can be kept completely confidential. This may be more difficult for free-standing drug-treatment programs whose names reveal their purposes than for programs that are associated with general medical facilities.

Treatment programs may also communicate information about patients without those patients' consent and without revealing patient-identifying information, through "qualified service organizations" (QSO).[87] Programs may enter into agreements with QSOs providing medical care or operating laboratories to perform diagnostic services for the programs and their patients and to make mandated AIDS reports to the public health authorities. In the agreement, the QSO must acknowledge that it is bound by the federal confidentiality law and thus may not identify as a drug-abuse patient any individual who is the subject of an AIDS report. In addition, the QSO must agree to safeguard all data, especially patient-identifying information, from unauthorized disclosure and from the efforts of others to obtain access to the information.[88]

The last and least-simple option is for a treatment program to make an AIDS report in compliance with a court order authorizing disclosure.[89] Court orders may be issued at the program's own initiative or in response to the application of another person or agency, such as a public health department. A court may issue an authorizing order only after it follows certain special procedures and makes particular determinations required by the confidentiality regulations. A subpoena or search warrant, even when signed by a judge, is *not* sufficient, standing alone, to allow or require a program to make a disclosure.[90]

Before a court can issue an authorizing order, the program and the patient whose records are sought must receive notice of the application for the order and must be given some opportunity to make an oral or written statement to the court. The application and order must use fictitious names for any known patient, and all court proceedings in connection with the application must remain confidential unless the patient requests otherwise.[91] In addition, the court must find "good cause" for the disclosure. A court can find good cause only if it determines that the public need for disclosure outweighs any adverse effect on the patient, the program-patient relationship, the effectiveness of the program's treatment services, and the effectiveness of other programs similarly situated. If the information sought is available elsewhere, the court should ordinarily deny the application.[92]

There are also limits to the scope of disclosure that a court may authorize, even with good cause. The disclosure may include only information essential to fulfill the purpose of the order, and it must be restricted to those persons who need the information for that purpose. A court may authorize disclosure only of *objective* data, such as diagnosis and test results, where such information is necessary to confirm the reportable condition. Thus, not even a court may compel disclosure of communications by a patient to program personnel.[93] Finally, court orders authorizing AIDS reports should limit disclosures to those mandated by the state's public health law, and even mandated disclosures should be released only to designated public health authorities who are forbidden from redisclosing or using that information in violation of the federal confidentiality law.

Conflicts between the Duty to Inform Other People and Confidentiality Laws

Is a drug-abuse treatment program either required or forbidden to inform others—treatment staff, other patients in the program, patients' family members or sexual partners, or the world at large—about patients who are known to have AIDS or to be infected with the virus? The answer to this question will depend on the answers to two other basic inquiries. First, does the treatment program have a legal duty or legitimate need to inform others of a patient's condition? Second, if it does, how can the program make a disclosure in compliance with the federal confidentiality law and regulations governing drug-abuse treatment records?

The duty of particular treatment programs to inform others about patients with AIDS or related conditions has not yet been clearly defined and may differ from state to state. Analogous situations have, however, led to the articulation of a general duty of "reasonable care." Treatment programs, like other health care providers, may be required to take reasonable care to know about and to prevent foreseeable harm both to persons with whom they have a special relationship (including their employees and patients) and to others at risk for particular illnesses or injuries caused by persons in their care. (For a detailed discussion of this issue, see Chapter 14.)

Even if treatment professionals have a duty to protect others from uneasonable risks of harm through exposure to AIDS, it does *not* follow that treatment programs have either a responsibility or the right to inform all their staff, all their patients, all their patients' families, friends, or sexual contacts, or all the world, about patients who carry the virus. Programs should do only what is necessary and reasonable to protect those whose risk of infection with HIV is the foreseeable result of particular patients' behavior. Finally, several specific requirements of the federal confidentiality law and regulations will govern the manner in which treatment programs may legally inform others of patients' medical conditions.

Informing Staff Members about Particular Patients' Exposure to HIV. A policy of routinely informing all or even selected members of a treatment program's staff when a patient has AIDS or a related condition cannot be justified on the grounds that staff members have a general "need" to know such information to protect their health. (For a discussion of the extent of risk of transmission, see Chapter 2.) The medical conditions of particular staff members may, however, justify taking extra precautions. For example, pregnant health-care workers ought not to be exposed to certain infections associated with AIDS, including cytomegalovirus, which may cause birth defects.[94] A treatment program might implement special arrangements for workers who are pregnant or considering pregnancy, including changing their job duties to eliminate the possibility of exposure. Such changes could be made without disclosing the medical status of every patient who has or might develop AIDS.

The personnel of treatment programs may legitimately need to know about particular patients' AIDS-related conditions to carry out counseling, treatment, or related duties. Clearly, though, the need to know varies with the duties of the staff members in question and the nature of the treatment program. For example, a program's physician and clinic coordinator may well need to have information about specific patients' medical conditions in order to coordinate care in the program and elsewhere. A patient's counselor might also need to know. In addition, some residential therapeutic communities believe that staff and patients should communicate with each other freely about every aspect of each others' lives, since knowing and being known by others in the program are essential to becoming well. Therefore, psychological imperatives and treatment goals may justify open communications between patients and staff when medical or risk-reduction imperatives do not.

One final note: even if certain staff members have a legitimate need for AIDS-related information about their clients, that information may not be disclosed unless program administrators have some assurance that the employee(s) in question will not use the information in keeping the antidiscrimination and confidentiality laws.

Informing Other Patients. The Office of the General Counsel of the U.S. Department of Health and Human Services (HHS), which advises treatment programs of their obligations under the federal confidentiality law and regulations, has issued a legal opinion concluding that the law allows only two avenues for treatment programs to inform other patients about particular clients' medical conditions.[95] First, the program may disclose the identity of patients with AIDS to other patients if it obtains a proper, voluntary, written consent from each patient whose condition is to be disclosed. Second, the staff may try to persuade the patient with AIDS to tell other patients on his or her own. HHS's general counsel has also suggested that treatment programs may permissibly require that patients either consent to disclosures by the staff or agree to tell others on their own as a condition of receiving treatment.[96]

Informing Patients' Families or Sexual Contacts. Do treatment programs have either the duty or the right to tell the families, sexual contacts, or friends of a client that he or she has AIDS or carries the virus?

One point to consider is whether persons or organizations other than the staff of the treatment program are aware of a patient's AIDS-related condition, and also know about, are responsible for, and can be relied upon to inform those who may need to know about that condition. If a patient has a physician (not connected with the treatment program) who has diagnosed or is treating him or her for AIDS or a related condition, that doctor may be responsible for and capable of alerting the patient's family and sexual contacts about the person's condition without disclosing his or her participation in drug-abuse treatment. A program might also fulfill its duties to inform others by complying with state requirements for reporting communicable diseases to public health authorities, since those authorities often contact persons who may be exposed to communicable or infectious illnesses.

The staff of a treatment program may, however, occasionally feel obliged to assume direct responsibility for informing persons who risk exposure to AIDS by their contact with patients. The federal confidentiality rules once more specify the method for making such disclosures. A program may provide information about a person's status in treatment, including information about his or her medical condition, to that person's family and to "any person with whom the patient has a personal relationship" if that patient provides the program with a proper written consent and disclosure would not be "harmful" to the patient.[97]

The "medical emergency" exception to the federal confidentiality law, allowing programs to make disclosures without consent to the extent necessary to meet a bona fide medical emergency, allows disclosures only to medical personnel. Thus, emergencies do *not* ordinarily justify disclosures to a patient's family or friends. If, however, an individual becomes incapable of rational communication as a result of drug or alcohol abuse, *the treating physician* may disclose the patient's condition to the patient's family or to anyone with whom the patient has a personal relationship.[98]

Finally, though treatment programs may have no duty to inform patients' families and sexual contacts of those patients' AIDS-related diagnoses, patients themselves may have a responsibility to do so. In some states, for example, courts have held that persons who know they have herpes, another sexually transmissible illness, but fail to tell their sexual partners about that condition are liable for their partners medical expenses and other damages.[99] Consequently, treatment programs should consider counseling clients who are seropositive about their potential liability for failing to tell sexual partners of their condition. (For a fuller discussion of potential personal liability for transmission of HIV, see Chapter 11.)

Informing Prospective or Current Employers. Employers' efforts to obtain information about applicants' and current employees' treatment for drug abuse has so often led to the abuse of that information, and to job discrimination against those who had been or who were then in treatment, that federal confidentiality regulations establish strict standards and limitations on any disclosures about drug-abuse patients to employers and employment agencies. The prospect that employers will seek and then misuse information about drug-abuse patients' exposure to AIDS is also so great that treatment programs must rigorously comply with federal confidentiality requirements.

Those requirements permit disclosures to employers and employment agencies only when two conditions are met. Even with the patient's consent, a treatment program may make disclosure to an employer only if (1) it "has reason to believe, on the basis of past experience or other credible information . . . that [the information sought] will be used for the purpose of assisting in the rehabilitation of the patient and not for the purpose of identifying the individual as a patient in order to deny him employment or advancement because of his history of drug . . . abuse," and (2) it also determines that "the information sought appears to be reasonably necessary in view of the type of employment involved."[100] The confidentiality regulations also require that the scope of any consensual disclosure be limited to "a verification of the patient's status in treatment or a general evaluation of progress in treatment." More specific information may be given only "where there is a bona fide need for [it] to evaluate hazards which the employment may pose to the patient or others, or where such information is otherwise directly relevant to the employment situation."[101]

Informing Those Who Wish to Investigate or Prosecute Drug-Abuse Patients for Illegal Activities That Might Spread AIDS. Public health or law enforcement authorities may attempt to obtain information about patients exposed to AIDS in order to investigate or prosecute those suspected of engaging in illegal activities, such as prostitution or IV-drug use or sales, that the authorities deem dangerous to the public health. Only a court order can empower such authorities to obtain or redisclose patient-identifying records for this purpose.

Federal confidentiality law strictly limits the availability of court orders authorizing such disclosures. In addition to showing "good cause" for the order, an investigative, law enforcement, or prosecutorial agency must demonstrate to the court that (1) the crime involved is extremely serious, such as an act causing or threatening to cause death or serious injury; (2) the records sought are likely to contain information of significance to the investigation or prosecution; (3) there is no other practical way to obtain the information; and (4) the public interest in disclosure outweighs any actual or potential harm to the doctor-patient relationship in the program involved and in similar programs, as well as to those programs' ability to attract patients.[102] These criteria will rarely be satisfied.

THE "CLEAN NEEDLES" CONTROVERSY

Sharing or reuse of paraphernalia used for injecting drugs (including needles, syringes and other "works") is a major means for the transmission of the AIDS virus both directly to those involved in intravenous drug use and indirectly to their sexual partners and to children born of infected parents. Three possible approaches have been suggested for stemming the spread of AIDS through contaminated needles: stopping people from abusing drugs altogether; stopping them from using drugs intravenously; or stopping them from using contaminated needles when they do use drugs intravenously.

Proposals to End Drug Abuse

The first proposal—to end drug abuse itself—is obviously the most attractive. Preventing illicit drug use has long been the objective of both health and law enforcement authorities; this proposal would promote that objective and help prevent the spread of AIDS. It would also be the most effective way of reducing the risk of AIDS posed by IV-drug use because it would eliminate the use of potentially contaminated needles.

However attractive the idea, though, the proposal is fraught with practical difficulties. The intravenous use of heroin and cocaine—the form of drug abuse most likely to lead to AIDS exposure—is extremely addictive. Users may not be able to kick their habits without some form of treatment. Unfortunately, there are nowhere near enough resources or treatment facilities to help all addicted people. Shortages are worst in those states where most AIDS cases related to IV-drug use are occurring.[103] Researchers in New York estimate that there are approximately seven IV-drug users not in treatment for every one currently treated.[104]

Efforts aimed at reducing the transmission of HIV by providing IV-drug users with effective treatment "would require a massive expansion of the treatment system"[105] through a great increase of financial resources devoted to drug-abuse treatment. Although "the economics of treating AIDS (approximately $150,000 per case) versus providing drug abuse treatment (approximately $3,000 per patient per year) . . . argue for the expansion of the treatment network,"[106] the amount of money required to mount effective treatment efforts remains daunting.

In addition, even drug-abuse therapists disagree about how to use additional funds. For instance, methadone maintenance treatment is an effective method of treating narcotic addiction, and one of the methods most acceptable to heroin addicts themselves. But some therapists are philosophically opposed to any form of treatment that does not aim for total abstinence from drugs. Moreover, methadone maintenance is not appropriate for treating those who abuse only non-opiate drugs, such as cocaine. The rising awareness of cocaine and crack (a purified, smoked form of cocaine) abuse has increased demands that treatment dollars be devoted to those problems.[107] And even if all the necessary financial resources were available to treat both heroin and cocaine abuse, treatment programs would still face community resistance. Of all treatment facilities, methadone maintenance programs are often the least well-accepted and most misunderstood; accordingly, those programs are frequently opposed by the community at large.[108]

Finally, even when treatment is available, only a fraction of those abusing drugs may seek it. Although the fear of AIDS may well increase the numbers who do, recent studies suggest that many drug abusers will try to find ways to make their drug use safer, rather than stop using drugs completely.[109] So, though the goal of ending all drug abuse may be preferable to other proposals, it is unlikely to be achieved as a practical matter in the near future.

Proposals to Prevent or End the Intravenous Use of Drugs

Proposals more narrowly focused on reducing at least *intravenous* drug use raise both public policy and practical problems. Those who oppose and want to end all drug abuse will find no comfort in any proposal that accommodates (even if it does not endorse) the idea that drug abuse may well persist. Even beyond this objection, efforts to reduce intravenous use of drugs face the difficulty of bringing about significant changes in both the perceptions and the behavior of drug abusers.

Although researchers have found evidence that drug abusers are increasingly aware of AIDS and its association with needle use, they have also noted several factors that may impede addicts' full perception of the terrible risks they face. Those who use drugs intravenously are often alienated, difficult to reach, and distrustful of mainstream society. This situation makes educational efforts difficult. The years-long latency period between exposure to HIV and development of an AIDS-related illness dilutes the reality of the risk, making AIDS easier to ignore than other threats to addicts' life and health. The symptoms associated with AIDS-related conditions, such as fatigue, weight loss, and frequent sickness, are often similar to those that accompany addiction anyway. Finally, AIDS is only one among many causes of illness and death that persons involved in drug abuse commonly risk. These factors create barriers to drug abusers' concern about the lethal effects of AIDS exposure.[110]

In any case, mere awareness of the dangers that come with contaminated needles might not suffice to bring about so radical a change as widespread abandonment of the use of drugs intravenously. Needle using and sharing rituals are part and parcel of the drug-use subculture. Injection is the most efficient way to ingest heroin and speedballs (heroin and cocaine) and to ensure the immediacy and intensity of their effect. Thus the compulsion to use drugs as soon and as efficiently as possible creates intense pressures for continuing to use them intravenously.[111]

Proposals for "Clean" or "Free" Needles

Realistically, neither drug abuse nor the intravenous use of drugs will end soon. Consequently, some have proposed helping IV users avoid exposure (or repeated exposure) by making sterile needles and syringes more freely available by removing legal barriers to their purchase and use;[112] providing clean needles free of charge to those who use drugs intravenously;[113] and, last and perhaps least effective, teaching drug abusers how to clean their works so as to reduce their risk of exposure.[114]

Legal Barriers to "Clean" or "Free" Needles Proposals

At least eleven states, including the four with the highest incidence of AIDS cases linked to drug abuse (New York, New Jersey, California, and Connecticut), have outlawed sale or purchase of hypodermic needles and syringes without a prescription from a medical practitioner.[115] Some of these states impose criminal penalties for sale, purchase, or possession of unprescribed needles or syringes.[116] Many other states do not require a prescription, but make it a criminal offense to sell, use, or possess hypodermic needles, syringes, and other paraphernalia in order to inject controlled substances illicitly. Florida, another of the states with a high incidence of drug-related AIDS cases, is one such state.[117]

The obvious purpose of statutory efforts to restrict access to needles and other works is to deter illicit IV-drug use. Whether these laws have that effect is questionable; two of the states with the most severe restrictions on needles—New York and New Jersey—have between 200,000 and 300,000 active addicts.[118] And, although these legal restrictions and penalties may have reduced the supply of sterile needles in those states, plenty of needles—increasingly, contaminated ones—remain available.

Whether or not these statutory restrictions counteracted drug abuse, they made sense only so long as their effect (however minimal) was consistent with their intent—to protect the public health. Instead of safeguarding health and life by reducing drug abuse, however, these laws now contribute to drug abusers' increasing exposure to a lethal disease, the consequences of which are uniformly worse than addiction itself, and which may spread from drug abusers to the general public.

Policy Conflicts

Any proposal to make drug use safer creates an apparent conflict between two policies: preventing and ending drug abuse and stemming the spread of AIDS. This society must evaluate the merits of laws restricting the availability of needles in the light of reality as it has been altered by AIDS.

Families and children of drug abusers deserve protection from infection by AIDS. As for drug abusers themselves, punishing the sick is neither legal nor humane. The Supreme Court and many states have for years recognized that addiction is an illness; although the status of being addicted may warrant treatment, it may not constitutionally be punished as a crime.[119] To let people who are already addicted to drugs become infected or ill with a lethal disease seems extreme punishment indeed.

This is not to say that states have no power or right to prohibit or regulate instruments and activities that may facilitate drug abuse; indeed, they do. The laws restricting the availability of needles and punishing their illicit use came about through the legitimate exercise of states' power to police bad or unhealthy acts. But sterile needles and syringes have now become important prophylactic measures—in the literal sense of measures that guard against disease—in the battle against AIDS. In the final analysis, the harm that the "free" or "clean" needles proposals seek to avoid is greater than the harm some fear they might do.

Practical Barriers

Opponents of "clean" and "free" needles proposals have argued that making sterile needles more freely available to people who use drugs intravenously would do no good. They point out that needle sharing is an ingrained social ritual of the drug subculture; that it has continued in face of other health threats (such as hepatitis); that reusing needles is cheaper than using new ones; and that the compulsion of addicted people to use drugs as soon as they are obtained makes it likely that they will use whatever needles are at hand, whether they are clean or not.[120]

Preliminary research into intravenous drug users' responses to AIDS, however, indicates that increasing numbers understand the connection between contaminated needles and AIDS and are trying to obtain sterile needles or to clean their works, though usually ineffectively.[121] To assume that it would be futile to increase the supply of sterile needles, or try to teach people to clean them effectively, thus seems unwarranted.

To date, only the Netherlands and Australia have implemented AIDS-prevention programs in which addicts are permitted to trade used hypodermic needles and syringes for new ones or to receive sterile needles for free. The Dutch Health Minister has noted that no new cases of AIDS have been reported among IV-drug users since that country implemented its needle-trading program; Australian authorities working on AIDS have reported that addiction there has not increased.[122]

In this country, the head of AIDS research in the federal Centers for Disease Control has emphasized the urgent need for comprehensive efforts to combat the spread of AIDS through intravenous drug use. Despite initial misgivings, he has endorsed a proposal for a test program to give clean hypodermic needles and syringes to addicts as one part of the national effort to curtail the spread of AIDS.[123] The National Academy of Sciences has also concluded that "trials to provide easier access to sterile, disposable needles and syringes are warranted" in the battle against AIDS.[124]

AIDS so far has no known cure or vaccine. Although not a perfect or complete solution, clean needles may help to prevent some deaths from AIDS. Of course, clean-needle proposals alone cannot stop the spread of AIDS among those who use drugs intravenously or who have links to those who do. But these proposals may play a part in what must become a far more comprehensive effort to prevent unnecessary deaths from AIDS.

19

The Black Community

WAYNE L. GREAVES, M.D.

The person with AIDS as portrayed by the media is a white homosexual man. Data from the Centers for Disease Control show, however, that in approximately 25 percent of reported cases of AIDS, the patient is black. The disease has aggravated existing health care problems within the black community and underscored the racial inequalities and injustices of American society. The economic consequences of the disease have been staggering, especially for poor blacks who often have no medical or disability insurance. AIDS has strained and at times disrupted previously stable relationships in black families. The church, historically an important cultural institution in the black community, has not addressed the problem of AIDS and has failed to provide leadership and support traditionally offered during times of crisis. Professional groups and organizations have similarly ignored the problem of AIDS and few community networks or resources are geared to black patients or their families.

THE EPIDEMIOLOGY OF AIDS

There are marked racial differences in the distribution of AIDS cases. Whereas blacks account for only 11.5 percent of the U.S. population, black people represent 25 percent of reported AIDS cases overall, 51 percent of all women with AIDS, and 58 percent of all children with AIDS.[1] Whereas fewer than 12 percent of white adults with AIDS are strictly heterosexual, 46 percent of black adults with AIDS fall into that category.[2] The incidence of AIDS among black women in terms of cases per million women is over thirteen times the incidence among white women.[3]

These disparities are in large part due to the differential significance of drug use as a major risk factor for AIDS. Approximately 7.4 percent of white adults with AIDS reportedly used intravenous drugs; for black adults with

AIDS, the comparable figure is 43 percent.[4] These figures are not altogether surprising, given how deep and serious a problem drug use is for inner city black communities. While the prevalence of drug use is about the same for blacks and whites, black drug users are much more likely to use *intravenous* drugs—drugs that have been associated with serious health problems such as bacterial endocarditis, hepatitis B, and now AIDS.[5] Comprehensive statistics on racial distribution of intravenous drug abuse do not exist, but a 1982 survey of drug-abuse treatment clinics in the U.S. revealed that in the cities reporting two-thirds of all AIDS cases among IV drug abusers (New York City and Newark, New Jersey), 40 to 50 percent of abusers attending the clinics were black.[6] Moreover, there is evidence from New York City that black intravenous drug abusers are infected with the virus associated with AIDS, Human Immunodeficiency Virus (HIV,) at a higher rate (42 percent) than are white abusers (14 percent). Survey responses suggests that this disparity may reflect a higher incidence of needle sharing among blacks than among whites.[7] These findings undoubtedly reflect the high proportion of blacks living in inner-city areas where such drugs, and abandoned buildings in which they can be used, are readily accessible and where group use is prevalent.

Intravenous drug use also contributes significantly to the incidence of AIDS among black children. As previously noted, approximately 58 percent of reported pediatric AIDS cases involve black children. Fifty-eight percent of these children were born to a mother who is known to have been an intravenous drug abuser or to have had a sex partner who was.[8] The same is true for white children less than half as frequently.

Our experience with AIDS cases seen at Howard University Hospital suggests that in addition to marked racial differences in the distribution of AIDS cases, there are clinical differences in how the disease presents itself. Most of our patients come from the inner city and are black; 70 percent of them are gay. They have experienced a higher incidence of opportunistic infections and a lower incidence of Kaposi's sarcoma than is true for AIDS cases overall.[9] Although the difference might be attributable in part to a greater susceptibility by drug users to infection and a (thus far unexplained) greater resistance to Kaposi's sarcoma, the high percentage in our sample of gay men who do not use drugs suggests that race is an independent factor. During the same period, the median survival of black patients with AIDS admitted to our hospital was approximately seven months,[10] which is similar to the survival of patients with opportunistic infections reported in other studies[11] but much shorter than the national average of twenty-four months for all AIDS patients.[12]

We can only speculate about the reasons for our findings. Unique patterns of exposure to stressors and particular ways of dealing with stress and adversity in black populations may account for at least some of the differences. Black city dwellers may be exposed to a relatively large number of physical and environmental stressors, including pollution, traffic hazards, substandard and overcrowded housing, and crime. A higher proportion of blacks than whites may also be employed in positions that potentially present greater levels of exposure to toxic substances. Moreover, an increasing body of research suggests that the ways an individual copes with stress and the resources available to resolve stressful situations, rather than stress itself, are key determinants of health outcome.[13] Traditional and culturally specific family patterns may affect the ability of black people to withstand social, economic, and psychological stress. Whatever the reasons, statistics show that one primary stress-related condition, hypertension (high blood pressure), occurs significantly more frequently among blacks than among whites.[14]

Another possible explanation for our findings may be lack of knowledge about AIDS, coupled with recognized problems associated with access and utilization of health care facilities. Some data suggest that black populations have less knowledge or awareness of specific health problems than whites. For example, blacks tend to underestimate the risk and severity of cancer, give less attention to its warning signs, get fewer screening tests, and be diagnosed at later stages of the disease than is true of whites.[15] A similar phenomenon might explain the higher morbidity of black AIDS patients. For the reasons just outlined, they may tend to be first seen by a physician later in the course of their clinical disease. And because of their generally poorer health status, the disease probably progresses more quickly. There are no scientific data to suggest that there is any ethnic or genetic difference in susceptibility to the AIDS virus itself or any intrinsic difference in the immune systems of blacks and whites. The virus appears to be color blind, though not culture blind.

Even though we may never be able to explain our findings completely, the epidemiology of AIDS among blacks allows us to determine which groups are at greatest risk for AIDS, to develop targeted educational programs, and to disseminate relevant information in the black community. We can conclude that, overall, intravenous drug use is nearly as common a risk factor for AIDS among blacks as is sexual behavior and that the expression of the disease differs somewhat from the pattern shown by whites. Black patients are usually seen later in the course of their disease and are more likely to have serious infections and die sooner than their white counterparts.

THE PSYCHOSOCIAL IMPACT OF AIDS

Patients with AIDS, regardless of race, encounter all the feelings experienced by anyone approaching death. These include denial, fear, anger, ambivalence, and a search for the meaning of life. However, unlike many other seriously ill patients, those with AIDS have a special burden due to the limited knowledge about the origins, transmission, and treatment of the disease.

Because of the stigma attached to AIDS, patients fear rejection by society, loss of work, and abandonment by close friends and family. Patients often speak of feeling like a leper and most prefer to keep their diagnosis secret.[16]

Psychologically vulnerable AIDS patients have serious difficulties handling stress. They frequently have low frustration tolerance and high anxiety. Psychiatric problems are not uncommon. One study indicates that at least 30 percent of AIDS patients may have associated psychiatric disorders.[17] Severe depression, suicidal tendencies, and paranoia are occasionally the first signs of undiagnosed disease.[18] The psychological consequences of AIDS are not surprising when one considers the pervasive and catastrophic loss the victim suffers. In contrast to the usual sympathetic and caring response offered to others with serious illnesses, the patient with AIDS is often treated as deserving of his or her fate and as an inferior person whose loss is not particularly important. Although all persons with AIDS face these devastating psychological pressures, for a disproportionate number of blacks they are aggravated by the already demoralizing burdens of poverty, inner-city life, and racial discrimination. Moreover, as will be seen presently, cultural characteristics of the black community make blacks even more likely than whites to be left isolated, without moral support.

FINANCIAL IMPACT

The economic consequences of AIDS are staggering. The average health care cost per patient with AIDS is approximately $140,000.[19] For people of low income, again a group in which blacks are overrepresented by nearly three times their proportion in the general population,[20] the economic hardships of AIDS are especially heavy. The poor and near poor often have no medical or disability insurance, and if not unemployed, have jobs that offer very little security. At Howard University Hospital, 58 percent of AIDS patients either had no insurance or had insurance that was terminated when they were dismissed from their job because of their diagnosis.[21]

More often than not, the poor are unable to prepare adequately for future economic strain; when a problem or crisis arises, they are ill-equipped to respond. Medicaid and social security are potential sources of income, but patients must be virtually devoid of resources to qualify for benefits.[22] This often means that patients must give up familiar health care settings and providers at a time when they most need security. In addition, obtaining benefits requires time, during which patients may have no insurance and few resources. Many persons with AIDS are, therefore, faced with the challenge of applying for public assistance, if only as a stopgap measure. Even with the help of a social worker, this often proves to be yet another frustrating and unproductive experience, which is stressful to an already overstressed patient.[23]

SOCIOCULTURAL IMPACT

The black community's perception of AIDS has been shaped largely by the news media. The media, particularly radio and television, have done little to change the myth prevalent in the black community that AIDS is a disease of white gay men.[24] Almost every television special on AIDS has focused on the disease as experienced by white gay males while ignoring the statistics on AIDS among blacks. The few medical experts who draw attention to the fact that blacks are disproportionately affected by AIDS are often criticized by persons in the black community for spouting heresies and racist propaganda. Not surprisingly, then, many people within the black community still believe that AIDS is not a problem for blacks, or subscribe to the notion that it is a racist ploy or the result of germ warfare gone awry.

Even if press accounts of the scope of AIDS remain incomplete, the perception of the disease within the black community will change as more and more people die. But true progress in addressing the needs of black persons with AIDS is not likely until the black community comes to grips with two highly charged issues: drug use and homosexuality. I have already alluded to the breadth of the drug problem, especially in our inner cities. It is a sore subject for most black people, largely because of their well-founded fear that the larger society will see broad drug use as confirmation of its worst fears about blacks, will blame the victims rather than the victimizers from outside the inner city, and will use the evil of drug abuse to justify indiscriminate and highly intrusive police activity within the black community. The connection between AIDS and drug use simply ups the ante. Nevertheless, unless the black community takes responsibility for locating, educating, caring for, and protecting those within its midst who are most likely to contract AIDS and spread it to others, the community itself will suffer severe losses.

Similarly, the black community must face up to the fact that within its ranks are substantial numbers of gay people. While it is true that more virulent forms of homophobia (such as "queer bashing") are largely absent from the black community, the community has traditionally frowned upon homosexuality, scoffed at it, considered it taboo. At best, homosexuality is ignored, rendered invisible. For some black parents, it is more acceptable to pretend that a son with AIDS was an intravenous drug user than to admit that he is gay. Although many people manage to be openly gay and proudly black, gay blacks are largely closeted. Yet the fact that nearly half of all black people with AIDS are gay or bisexual is a clear, if poignant, testament to their existence.[25]

If the black community is to reach out to people with AIDS, it must work through its homophobia. The same can be said of the black family. Traditionally the family has been a source of strength and support to its members and has served as a shield from the abuses of an often hostile and racist society. AIDS, however, poses a unique challenge to this traditional role. Homosexuality is often viewed as an affront to family values. Families that do not accept the homosexual orientation of one of their members find it particularly difficult to be supportive throughout the AIDS ordeal.[26] The potential loss of family support looms especially large when one considers that there are few alternative sources of support for blacks with the disease. Around the country, special groups have been formed to provide an opportunity for persons with AIDS and their families to discuss their concerns and emotions, in a safe atmosphere, with understanding and empathetic people.[27] Unfortunately, few support groups exist in the black community, and few outside it reach out to black persons with AIDS. Those that do exist are primarily geared toward gay men, leaving unaddressed the plight of more than half of all black people with the disease.[28]

The *origin* of AIDS is also a sensitive and controversial issue within the black community. Despite conflicting theories and incomplete scientific data, many blacks, particularly Haitians and Africans, have been the victims of discrimination by those who believe the disease first started in black people. It is not clear from available scientific data when AIDS first occurred in Africa. However, most known cases have occurred since 1981, which is consistent with the simultaneous emergence of AIDS in North America and Haiti. One popular hypothesis advanced to explain the AIDS pandemic is that the AIDS virus or a similar virus existed initially in remote pockets of Africa in an animal reservoir (monkeys) that it spread to humans either through animal bites or through blood to blood contact during ritual animal sacrifices, and that recent population shifts introduced the virus into urban areas of Central Africa and then to Haiti, where gay Americans on vacation became infected.[29] While an African origin is plausible, many facts that would confirm or refute it are simply not yet available; it therefore must be considered a matter of speculation. For American blacks, however, the ultimate truth concerning the origin of AIDS is less important than the sense that blacks are unjustifiably associated with a disease every bit as foreign to them as to whites. Such unfounded association only promotes denial of AIDS as an urgent problem for the black community, thus hindering effective response.

A final trauma for the black community is the fact that AIDS poses a serious threat to the health and reproduction of black women. Though women account for only 6 percent of all reported cases of AIDS, 51 percent of them are black. In most cases, these women contracted the disease by sharing a drug needle with someone who was infected, by engaging in unsafe sex with someone who had himself shared a dirty needle, or by engaging in unsafe sex with an infected bisexual man. Most of these women, and the many others who harbor the virus even though they haven't developed AIDS, are of childbearing age and are at risk of giving birth to infected children. Thus, in the black community, AIDS threatens to decimate not one generation, but two. To prevent continued transmission from mother to child, the

Centers for Disease Control has recommended that women infected with the virus avoid or postpone pregnancy, and that all women considering pregnancy, especially those in high risk groups, be tested for evidence of infection by the virus.[30]

THE ROLE OF THE CHURCH

The church has been an important institution in the evolution of the black community. In the civil rights era and even today, many outreach programs for the ill and the disadvantaged have had their origins in the church and were effectively implemented by persons with ties to both the church and the community.[31] AIDS, however, has prompted a very different response; the black church has been sorely lacking in its support for persons with AIDS and their families.[32] The more liberal black clergy have avoided condemning individuals who have AIDS, particularly gay men, but at the same time have maintained enough distance from the problem to avoid alienating the more conservative members of their congregations. These clergy at times address the issue of AIDS, typically from the standpoint of prevention, by calling attention to scriptural passages that proscribe adultery, fornication, and promiscuity. The more conservative clergy usually do not even address the issue of AIDS when speaking to their congregations. Some confess the belief that AIDS is God's punishment and condemn both the disease and the patient.

Our data at Howard University suggest that many black patients with AIDS experience spiritual turmoil and some request the visit or prayers of clergy.[33] Unfortunately, very few black clergy have responded to these requests and, for the most part, black patients dying from AIDS have had to turn to white clergy when they needed spiritual solace and comfort. In fairness, some clergy have attempted to educate themselves and their more conservative parishioners.[34] But they are all too few, and the church has not played its traditional role of educating and supporting the black community during this time of crisis.

COMMUNITY RESPONSE

Professionals and lay persons alike have ignored the problem of AIDS in the black community.[35] Some physicians tacitly refuse to care for patients with AIDS or patients suspected of having AIDS and refer them to other physicians.[36] Homosexuality is still anathema to many professionals in and outside the health care field. The few conferences on AID have not been supported by many black professional or lay groups.[37]

Five years into the AIDS crisis, there are finally signs that the black community is mobilizing to combat further spread of the disease.[38] Black organizations doing educational and support work for black people at risk for AIDS have recently formed in several large urban centers. A common objective of these organizations is development and dissemination of new risk-reduction material geared toward the black community in general, women, intravenous drug users and their partners, and youth. An organization in Washington, D.C., is working to develop public service announcements for television and radio. Another organization in Chicago has been using the "house party," modeled on the "Tupperware party," to disseminate information about AIDS and risk reduction. The party format provides an effective setting for discovering what information participants already have, for distributing risk-reduction guidelines, lubricants, and condoms, and, finally, for informally discussing the materials and answering questions. While such programs have great potential, a lack of resources threatens the effectiveness of educational efforts targeted at minorities.

FUTURE STRATEGY CONSIDERATIONS

AIDS continues to have a devastating effect on the black community, causing high morbidity and mortality among young adults, and particularly among children. As AIDS forces the black community increasingly to face issues of homosexuality, bisexuality, and drug use, it strains and disrupts family relationships, alienates friends, and highlights the lack of organizational and community support for persons with AIDS and their families.

Although several promising drugs are now being tested for use in containing the development of AIDS, there is not yet a cure for the disease nor any effective treatment to reverse it. Therefore our most important defense is to prevent the continued spread of AIDS through education. (For more on the value of AIDS education, see Chapter 7.) The black community obviously needs more accurate information about AIDS. The media must be persuaded to present a balanced perspective on AIDS, and the black media in particular must be encouraged to emphasize those statistics of greatest relevance to the black community. Also, funds must be found to sustain the few fledgling grassroots organizations working to educate and counsel black people at risk for AIDS.

Information must be tailored to the target audience, and the mode of disseminating information must be thoughtfully chosen. Traditionally, information has been passed orally within the black community.[39] Black people today remain oriented toward oral communication. Therefore written materials, such as literature distributed by public health clinics and newspaper or magazine articles, are unlikely to reach or be read by a large portion of the black community. Even graphic presentations such as bus and subway posters should be culturally specific in order to capture the attention of blacks who ordinarily are apt not to notice such material. Overall, however, electronic media (radio and television) will prove more effective in reaching black people than written media. Underestimation of the difficulty of reaching blacks has led to failure in some educational programs.[40]

Another problem facing the black community is its continued lack of access to adequate health care. Blacks, because of their generally lower income level, are more likely to seek public medical care and to postpone seeking medical care until disease has progressed quite significantly. In addition, they are less likely to have a family physician as a regular source of medical care.[41] Access to health care might be improved by exerting political pressure on local and federal health agencies, but might also be improved if more black health care providers were to stand up and be counted as willing to offer care and counseling to both patients with AIDS and their families.

Unless professional and community groups become more involved, the response to AIDS within the black community will remain fragmentary, unorganized, and ineffectual. The inexorable spread of the disease, high morbidity and mortality among blacks, and poignant lack of information about AIDS in the black community demand that professional groups, lay organizations, and leaders in the black community develop a coherent and comprehensive strategy to address the problem of AIDS.

20

The Lesbian and Gay Community

MARK S. SENAK

More material about the rights of lesbians and gay men has appeared in the non-gay press since 1981 than in any other five-year period of American history. This unprecedented media coverage reflects the impact that AIDS has had on the lives and civil liberties of gay people. Because so many of the people hit by AIDS are homosexual men, AIDS has been popularly perceived as a gay disease or "gay plague."[1] Even though the demographics of AIDS have begun to shift within major cities, with the percentage of cases involving homosexual men decreasing,[2] this public perception has not changed.[3] Thus AIDS has acted as a catalyst for public discussion of issues involving gay people's rights, with both advances and setbacks for gay rights resulting from increased public debate. Importantly, AIDS has also brought about a cohesion of the gay community.

THE CONTEXT FOR CURRENT DEBATES ABOUT GAY RIGHTS

In the past, mainstream society concerned itself little with homosexuality. Gay Americans, however, have always suffered widespread discrimination—with the support of our legal system. Now the AIDS epidemic has riveted public attention on homosexuality and has moved some members of mainstream society finally to become concerned about the plight of lesbians and gay men. For others, AIDS has provoked an adamantly anti-gay stance. This polarization has emerged in a crisis involving sex, death, religion, politics, and homosexuality—a provocative combination.

Rarely is AIDS dealt with simply as a disease. Discussion of the issue of AIDS in the workplace, for example, has ranged far beyond simple questions of worker disability. It has fostered heated debate about the presence of homosexuals in the workplace and the acceptability of homosexuality in general.[4] The Vatican has used AIDS to reinforce church teachings on the immorality of homosexuality, invoking homosexuality as a synonym for the disease. A Vatican document issued in late 1986, severely criticized by civil rights groups, states that "homosexuality may seriously threaten the lives and well-being of a large number of people."[5]

Many, despite recent publicity and debate, still question the need for legally protecting lesbians and gay men against discrimination in such basic areas as employment and housing. To many Americans it is indeed news that lesbians and gay men suffer discrimination and that they are sometimes victims of physical assault because of their sexual orientation.[6] To gay men and women, the need for wide-reaching protection is obvious. It is *not* news to us that a man seen in front of a gay bar on a Saturday night by his boss, passing in a taxi, may be fired the following Monday, or that some landlords refuse to rent to lesbian couples because they erroneously believe that lesbians are at high risk for AIDS.

As awareness of AIDS has increased through media coverage, the number of complaints of gay- and lesbian-related discrimination has risen dramatically. The New York City Commission on Human Rights, for example, reports that from November 1983 through June 1984, it had approximately 32 cases of discrimination involving sexual orientation issues per quarter. During the first quarter of 1985, the Commission had 128 such cases.[7] Thus the need for legal protection is now especially strong.[8]

Blatant discrimination is not the only unequal treatment with which gay men and lesbians must cope. There are other forms of discrimination so ingrained in our system that even many lesbians and gay men are not conscious of them. For example, when a heterosexual couple marries, the state writes an instant marriage contract for them and also establishes rules for their possible separation or divorce. The couple's social security benefits and tax status are readjusted and their inheritance rights are affected to make provision for one another. If one spouse dies without a will, the laws of intestacy in virtually every state allow the surviving spouse to inherit all or part of the estate. In some states, the law recognizes heterosexual marriage by common law, not even requiring a formal wedding ceremony to secure these rights of marriage. Homosexual couples, however, cannot accomplish any of these ends without doing something considerably more complicated than uttering "I do." Gay couples cannot obtain marriage licenses for formal, legal marriage, and no matter how long they live together, they will not be considered married by the state.

Thus, even if two lesbians live together in a fully committed relationship for twenty-five years, when one dies the other will not automatically inherit her estate. The family of the deceased lover may have rights to the couple's common home. The surviving lover has little legal recourse unless she has entered into explicit, enforceable property arrangements. And the survivor, having lost her life partner, may not be able to ask her employer for time off to attend the funeral of a "close friend." The survivor must yield funeral arrangements to the deceased lover's blood relatives, who may not even permit her attendance at the funeral.[9]

Since the late 1960s gay groups have organized to fight for equal treatment in society through a political movement. Gay activists regard the Stonewall Riot, July 27, 1969, as the movement's birth date.[10] When police raided the Stonewall Inn, a gay bar in Greenwich Village, that night, a spontaneous protest erupted throughout the Village. After this show of strength, men and women in New York formed the Gay Liberation Front. Within a year, similar political groups had formed in other cities. Through the 1970s the gay rights movement was a grassroots political campaign, with charismatic leaders such as San Francisco Supervisor Harvey Milk asking all gay men and lesbians to "come out" and band together to accomplish change. Although openly gay candidates such as Milk were elected to public office, and the movement achieved other victories, many gay men and women remained apolitical.[11]

Historically there have often been divisions between lesbian activists and politically active gay men. Lesbians have had to combat sexism within the gay movement as well as discrimination from without. In addition, many gay women have felt that they have little in common with gay male sexuality, which to them connotes anonymous and promiscuous sex. Other lesbians, however, have always worked side by side with gay men in attempting to bring about equal rights. Lesbians as well as gay men are suffering from increased discrimination since the onset of AIDS because the public lumps all homosexuals together, not realizing that lesbians are actually a group at very low risk of contracting the disease. As explained below, gay men and women have now banded together against a problem that cannot be ignored while we resolve differences within the gay rights movement. It is important, however, to point out that differences remain and constitute part of the challenge facing gay activists.

In the early gay liberation movement, gay men and lesbians fought for important civil rights. In the 1980s, we are fighting for our lives as well. AIDS has brought the gay and lesbian community together as never before. Gay men and lesbians, joined by sympathetic heterosexuals, have established community care groups for persons with AIDS. In unprecedented numbers, gay professionals have donated their time to help deal with complicated new problems facing the gay community.[12] While public officials dragged their feet in responding to the health crisis because the disease was linked to homosexuality, lesbians and gay men cared for their own. Organizations founded by gay people continue to care for all persons with AIDS, regardless of their sexual orientation. The Gay Men's Health Crisis (GMHC) in New York City, the oldest and largest AIDS service organization in the world, has sponsored public forums on AIDS, has conducted other educational efforts, and has raised significant sums for AIDS care and AIDS research. GMHC also offers crisis counseling, a buddy system (linking support volunteers with persons with AIDS), and help in dealing with the welfare bureaucracy and with legal assistance. The Shanti Project, aided by the San Francisco city government, offers a housing program for people with AIDS. In smaller cities, gay activists have also mobilized to cope with AIDS: a hotline and support group have been established in Kansas City, for example, and the city's gay bars have raised money for medical costs.[13]

Lesbians and gay men now have more self-awareness and self-respect, more care and concern for one another, and a stronger, more sophisticated movement to safeguard their lives and rights. The term "Gay Pride," a rallying cry in the 1970's, has taken on new meaning. Understanding this development is essential for understanding the impact of AIDS on the lesbian and gay community. A long, complicated campaign undoubtedly still lies ahead, however, if gay men and gay women of all races and economic backgrounds are to become equal citizens in this society.

GAY CIVIL RIGHTS ISSUES IN THE ERA OF AIDS

The interactions between AIDS issues and gay civil rights issues are complex. Reporters looking for dramatic stories, public officials worried about re-election, insurance companies preoccupied with costs of medical care, doctors trying to solve the puzzle of AIDS, and gay men and lesbians working to save lives and preserve rights, all influence where struggles will take place and what their outcomes will be. Overall, the results in these struggles have been mixed for gay persons, and many controversies remain unresolved.

The Bathhouses Controversy

The clash on the issue of gay bathhouses in major cities provides a vivid example of the political maneuvering that surrounds AIDS, and of the destructive impact this maneuvering can have on gay civil rights, and on the fight against AIDS. Bathhouses, portrayed as dens of rampant AIDS contagion by some public officials, were closed in San Francisco in 1984 and New York in 1985—largely because politicians wanted to appear to be doing something about AIDS.[14] The bathhouses presented a visible target at a time when medical authorities knew little about how the disease spread and how to control it. Politicians in New York and San Francisco downplayed the fact that educational efforts based in the bathhouses were reaching members of gay society who might not otherwise receive information about safe sexual practices. As experts have learned more about the disease, they have focused on education as the best weapon against it. Thus, later moves to close baths in other cities have failed and government officials are at last pursuing more effective measures.

Crucial to any consideration of the closure issue is the symbolic importance of the bathhouses. To gay men who came of age during the Stonewall era of gay liberation, bathhouses represent newfound freedoms. For this reason, some members of the gay community reacted especially strongly to the assault on bathhouses. On a scale of the civil rights problems gay men and lesbians face, the freedom to enjoy bathhouses probably does not rank high, but its symbolic meaning for some made this freedom an important one to defend. Many gay men perceived the moves to close the baths as purposeful attacks on their "gay lifestyle."[15]

For others, including many lesbians, the baths symbolized a type of promiscuity and irresponsibility that they believed it was time to move beyond. Many gay people were willing to give up the bathhouses, at least temporarily, to improve the gay community's public image and thus stave off a severe backlash by the heterosexual majority in the wake of AIDS. In Los Angeles, for example, a prominent gay political organization in 1985 called for the voluntary closure of gay and heterosexual bathhouses for the duration of the AIDS epidemic. Although the group viewed baths as only a tiny part of the problem, it sought voluntary closure as a symbolic gesture to show that the gay community was doing all it could to deal responsibly with AIDS.[16]

The magnitude of the political debate surrounding the bathhouse issue clearly exceeded the practical importance of the baths as places where AIDS might spread. Only a small percentage of the gay male population frequented the baths in San Francisco and New York, as in other cities. While politicians pointed to these establishments as public health menaces, the New York City Health Commissioner, Dr. David Sencer, admitted that closure would contribute "little if anything to the control of AIDS."[17] Regulating places very seldom enables the government to regulate persons; those few gay men who still engage in compulsive unsafe sex will continue to do so whether or not bathhouses remain open.

Bathhouses do provide an ideal forum for educating members of the gay community about AIDS. At St. Mark's Baths in New York, now closed, patrons were required to sign a form stating that they had read the guidelines for safe sex formulated by New York Physicians for Human Rights. Along with literature on safe sex, each man at the baths received a condom. Free condoms were readily available at St. Mark's, contained in envelopes advising that the contents "could save your life."[18] Finally, in 1986, some health officials, such as Surgeon General C. Everett Koop, began to convince politicians that the best weapons against AIDS are those that gay leaders have advocated all along—education and condoms.[19]

The closure of gay bathhouses in San Francisco and later in New York constituted a small but important defeat for gay civil rights, with little or no off-setting benefit in the fight against AIDS. More broadly, these political moves signaled a renewed vigor in the regulation of sexual behavior, especially gay sexual behavior. Protesters in San Francisco anticipated the upholding of sodomy laws by the Supreme Court when, in 1984, they fought closure with signs saying "Today the tubs, tomorrow your bedrooms."[20]

Although supporters of the baths lost their fight in some cities, bathhouses in other cities continue to outlast repeated, often hysterical, attacks. In Los Angeles, officials recently attempted to impose severe restrictions on what they call "AIDS factories." Three bathhouse owners sued, and Judge John L. Cole refused to order the baths to comply with the regulations. The judge found no conclusive evidence that the restrictions would stop the spread of AIDS. On the contrary, the judge stated that he was impressed with bathhouse distribution of condoms and of information about safe sex, and that he felt removing the bathhouse environment would fuel the disease's spread.[21]

Quarantine Proposals

A more serious threat to gay civil rights is the specter of quarantine. (For a complete discussion of the quarantine issue, see Chapter 4.) Though so far there have been no proposals to quarantine homosexual persons merely for their sexual preference, there have been several vocal proponents of quarantine for persons with AIDS. In a recent *Newsweek* opinion poll, 54 percent of the respondents favored quarantining all those with AIDS.[22] While acknowledging the harshness of AIDS, it is important to remain mindful of the severity of quarantine and "the possibilities that prejudice and fear may combine to turn the quarantine power from an instrument of public health to one of public bigotry and hatred."[23]

One proposal for quarantine emerged in Texas during 1985. Dr. Robert Bernstein, the Texas State Health Commissioner, advocated quarantine to "control an individual who warrants it in the interest of protecting the public." He stated further that "[t]his does not deal with the average AIDS patient. This is not aimed at a disease, it is aimed at individuals who have the disease and might be incorrigible in a public health way."[24] These statements seem to indicate that quarantine would not be imposed unless an infected person continued to engage in unsafe sexual practices with uninfected individuals. Indeed, the Texas proposal came in response to a much publicized case of a male prostitute with AIDS who continued to engage in activities that could spread the disease.[25] The Texas proposal, however, allowed county health officials to impose quarantine at their discretion, requiring only the concurrence of the State Health Commission.[26] Thus, the proposal itself imposed few limits on the use of AIDS quarantine.

The danger behind any proposal for quarantine is that, once put into effect, a quarantine system could be abused to unjustifiably deprive persons with AIDS, and perhaps all homosexual persons, of their civil rights.[27] Misinformed or prejudiced officials might impose quarantine based solely on a person's AIDS diagnosis, rather than on a supportable finding that he or she presents a clear threat to public health. The only mass experience with quarantine in this country took place on the basis of just such misinformation and prejudice during World War II, when thousands of Japanese Americans were placed in camps because of a supposed national security threat. Only recently have we seen the error of that episode in American history; such hindsight cannot repair the damage done. This possibility of irreparable abuse makes quarantine such a serious issue. Fortunately, the Texas proposal has fallen, at least temporarily, by the wayside.

In California, a testing and quarantine proposal sponsored by Lyndon LaRouche appeared on the November 1986 ballot. The LaRouche Initiative, endorsed at the petition-signing stage by twice the number of voters necessary to put it on the ballot, posed a great threat to the civil liberties of all California residents, particularly seropositive individuals and persons with AIDS. California voters eventually rejected the LaRouche testing and quarantine plan by a large margin,[28] but LaRouche followers and others are still advocating such measures.

According to California's health director, the LaRouche Initiative would have required AIDS testing for all 27 million Californians. All persons with AIDS and all virus "carriers" would, under the proposal, have had to register with public health officials. Ten thousand people would have lost jobs in agriculture, restaurants, and schools; forty-seven thousand children could not attend school if the initiative were implemented. The proposal may have required—lawyers are not sure—the state to quarantine anyone who came into contact with the virus. Defeat of the proposal, as outlandish and destructive as its provisions may seem, was not certain. The gay community raised $3 million with which to fight the LaRouche Initiative.[29] Unfortunately, much time and money had to be spent to defeat a plan fueled by fear and by antipathy to gays, a plan with no relation to fighting AIDS successfully.

Two other quarantine proposals illustrate the importance of quick response by gay leaders and the reluctance of politicians to deal head-on with AIDS. In late 1983 California's Chief of Infectious Diseases proposed quarantine to handle "recalcitrant" AIDS patients. Once National Gay Rights Advocates (NGRA) obtained information about the proposal, the organization triggered adverse publicity that forced the official to drop the idea.[30] In 1984, the Connecticut legislature changed that state's quarantine law in response to fear generated by news of a New Haven prostitute rumored to have AIDS. The new legislation did not mention AIDS, however, and it was drafted so that it did not apply to the prostitute who had provoked the concern.[31] She was driven off the street by other prostitutes.[32]

Quarantine simply cannot be effective on a large scale because of financial and logistical difficulties. For the person willing to harm others, there are already social control mechanisms in place, such as criminal and tort law. (For a discussion of criminal and tort law in disease control, see Chapters 4 and 11.) Further laws, coupled with animosity toward persons with AIDS and toward gay people, would only open opportunities for significant abuse.

Insurance Discrimination

AIDS has provoked insurance companies to deny coverage on the basis of sexual orientation, a type of discrimination not seen before. (For a full discussion of insurance issues, see Chapter 13.) Much of the insurance industry has decided that because gay males are catagorized as at high-risk for AIDS, they are uninsurable. Companies either deny coverage because an application indicates a man may be gay, or they subject possibly gay applicants to testing for the antibody to Human Immunodeficiency Virus (HIV), and then deny coverage if the antibody is detected.[33] The insurance industry's business decision has provoked a major civil rights controversy. Several states, pressured by gay rights groups, have passed laws to counteract this discrimination, not merely for moral reasons, but for fiscal reasons as well.

Use, or rather abuse, of the HIV antibody test by insurance companies has become epidemic. Insurance companies request antibody testing whenever they suspect from the written application that a person may be gay; they do not otherwise request the test. The determination is made by analyzing the answers to simple background questions on the application, as well as through a look at the individual's medical history. For instance, an applicant's marital status, domicile, occupation, and zip code may provoke a company's suspicion about his sexual preference. Combine this suspicion with a medical history that includes sexually transmitted disease, parasites, or hepatitis B, and an HIV antibody test undoubtedly will be requested. Should an individual name an unrelated beneficiary of the same sex on a life insurance policy, the insurer may on that basis alone require a test.[34]

For those people forced to take the antibody test in order to secure insurance, the outcome may be devastating. A positive test result that is not kept confidential may result in ostracism and unemployment. A person who tests positive, and is therefore denied insurance, may be unable to obtain a mortgage since many mortgage lenders require that the life of the mortgagor be insured. Obviously, knowledge that one is infected is a tremendous psychological burden. A positive antibody test can be almost as severe in its effects as quarantine.

Insurance company requests abuse the test by singling out gay men for an intrusive procedure that can only roughly predict medical costs and life expectancy. The HIV antibody test was designed as a mechanism for screening blood, not people. Although it will reveal fairly accurately whether or not a person has been exposed to the virus, it will not reveal whether that person will develop AIDS.[35] (For a detailed discussion of the antibody test, see Chapter 9.) All seropositive applicants, however, suffer discrimination in attempts to purchase insurance.[36]

By creating a large group of individuals without insurance, HIV antibody testing also creates a social crisis in funding for medical care. If insurers are successful in weeding out seropositive people, health care providers and state and local governments will have to absorb the medical costs of an expensive course of treatment for approximately 270,000 people over the next few years.[37] In addition, the seropositive persons who do not develop AIDS or AIDS-related complex will still have their share of accidents, heart attacks, and other medical needs unrelated to AIDS, the costs of which ordinarily are covered by or offset by insurance. The victims of insurance discrimination, therefore, include the taxpayer. By discriminating against seropositive people, the private insurance industry shifts the financial burden of health care to the public sector.

Although insurance discrimination presents a new obstacle for gay civil rights, proponents of laws forbidding abuse of the antibody test have met with some success.[38] California and the District of Columbia have enacted legislation that forbids the use of the HIV antibody test for insurance purposes.

Employment Discrimination

Because laws prohibit employment discrimination against disabled persons, legal remedies are in many instances available when employment discrimination stems from fear of AIDS. (For a complete discussion of employment discrimination related to AIDS, see Chapter 8.) In most states, however, it is possible to discharge employees on the basis of their sexual orientation. The legislatures have not proven anxious to protect gay persons from job-related discrimination, nor have courts been zealous in rectifying the frequent episodes of employment discrimination against gay people.[39]

The number of gay people being fired has increased dramatically since the beginning of this health crisis. Out of misinformation and fear, some employers who formerly tolerated gay people suddenly fire them, perceiving them to be potential carriers of AIDS.[40] In professions where it was once even fashionable to be gay, employers and co-workers now want to be rid of this perceived potential threat.[41]

Although increased discrimination is grim news, new legal tools become available to gay persons to the extent that they are discharged based upon fear of AIDS. Courts may treat such discharges not as discrimination on the basis of sexual orientation but as discrimination related to a physical handicap.[42] Many states prohibit discrimination based upon perceived as well as actual disability. A growing number of states recognize AIDS as a disability that fits within the protection of their anti-discrimination laws.[43] Thus, in a tragic irony, a gay person who is ill with AIDS or who is perceived to be at risk for AIDS may have more protection from losing his or her job than almost any homosexual in America had during the pre-AIDS era.

Gay Rights Legislation

Even more important, however, is legal protection that *does* specifically prohibit discrimination based upon sexual preference, because this kind of protection extends to all lesbian and gay employees and can outlast AIDS. In a few areas of the country, local legislation now protects lesbians and gay men from discrimination in employment, housing, and other important aspects of their lives.[44] Control of AIDS has been a significant issue in recent debates concerning the desirability of these gay rights ordinances. In Houston, conservatives capitalized on the fear of AIDS to gain repeal of that city's anti-discrimination ordinance by a four-to-one margin in a special election.[45] One pamphlet attacking the ordinance began: "The medical problems associated with homosexuality impact upon us all. Since the diseases of one segment of society are often transmitted to others, it is in the collective interest to inhabit as disease-free a society as possible."[46]

On the other hand, in 1986, after fifteen years of considering such a measure, the New York City Council enacted a law making discrimination on the basis of sexual orientation illegal.[47] AIDS helped secure legal protection for gay people in New York City by increasing media coverage of discrimination against gay men and lesbians, and by spurring better political organization in the gay community. Another advance for gay rights occurred in November, 1986, when Minnesota Governor Rudy Perpich became the eighth governor in the country to ban discrimination based on sexual orientation in state government employment.[48]

Sodomy Statutes

A bitterly divided U.S. Supreme Court, on June 30, 1986, upheld the constitutionality of Georgia's sodomy statute.[49] According to a majority of the Court in *Bowers v. Hardwick*, the Constitution does not protect homosexual relations between consenting adults, even in the privacy of their own homes. The Georgia statute challenged in the case defines sodomy as "any act involving the sex organs of one person and the mouth or anus of another" and applies to heterosexual couples as well as gay couples, women as well as men.[50] Twenty-three other states and the District of Columbia also have statutes that criminalize sodomy.[51] Five of these laws apply only to homosexual sex; most cover heterosexual as well as homosexual sodomy.[52] The five-to-four majority opinion in *Hardwick*, however, concentrated on homosexuality as the issue and did not discuss whether the Constitution protects heterosexual couples engaged in these criminalized sex acts.

Justice White, writing for the majority, rejected as "facetious" the argument that the Georgia law invades the constitutional right to privacy.[53] In his vehement dissenting opinion, Justice Blackmun stated that the "right of an individual to conduct intimate relationships in the intimacy of his or her own home seems to me to be at the heart of the Constitution's protection of privacy."[54] Blackmun correctly concluded that although the Court "claims that its decision today merely refuses to recognize a fundamental right to engage in homosexual sodomy, what the court really has refused to recognize is the fundamental interest all individuals have in controlling the nature of their intimate associations with others."[55]

Gay activists view this decision as a significant setback in the fight for gay civil rights. The decision not only supports the states that make gay sex illegal; it also provides support for discrimination in every aspect of gay people's lives. If gay men and lesbians are criminals, the argument goes, they can rightfully be denied equal employment opportunities, equal housing, and the like.[56] Since *Hardwick*, for example, both sodomy laws and AIDS have been raised as issues in child custody cases by those seeking to deprive homosexuals of contact with their children.[57] The Supreme Court's biased decision in *Hardwick* has breathed new life into old arguments that gay people are unfit parents, despite overwhelming factual evidence to the contrary. In states without sodomy laws, a number of well-informed appellate state courts have rejected homosexuality of the mother or father as a factor in custody disputes.[58]

Unfortunately, the *Hardwick* decision may also contribute to the spread of AIDS. The decision could hinder the fight against AIDS because gay men at risk may now be less willing to come forward for counseling and, where necessary, treatment. In addition, by validating laws that criminalize homosexuality and drive gay people underground, the *Hardwick* decision undermines the formation of stable, monogamous relationships among gay men, relationships in which the risk of AIDS transmission is reduced dramatically.

The factors that contributed to the passage of a broad antidiscrimination ordinance in New York City in the midst of the AIDS epidemic highlight the many relevant issues in evaluating the impact of AIDS on gay civil rights. For example, when AIDS became a "hot" media topic, especially after the diagnosis of Rock Hudson, the New York press also began to discuss homosexuality, thereby presenting it seriously to many people for the first time. Furthermore, gays and lesbians formed groups to combat the epidemic. Since the gay community no longer can afford the price of apathy, more political organization has been accomplished during the AIDS era than would have been accomplished otherwise. And as a result of increased information about the lives of homosexuals, enlightened adults of all sexual orientations have come to realize that gay people need legal protection against discrimination. The battle for civil rights during the AIDS epidemic is no doubt bloodier and crueler than before, but the battle has not been without reward, as shown by passage of the New York City ordinance. Simply coping with the disease now consumes much of the gay community's energy. Nevertheless, it seems likely that the pride and strength that have emerged in the past five years will continue to bring about significant gains in our struggle for equal rights.

Notes

Chapter I

1. W. McNeill, Plagues and Peoples (1976).

2. Although the scope of this article, and this book, is confined to the United States, AIDS is a worldwide problem. In Africa, where the disease was first spotted in the late 1970s, the virus has already killed at least fifty thousand people and infected two to five million others. The virus is transmitted there primarily through heterosexual contact. As of the end of 1986, cases of AIDS have been reported in eighty-five countries, with particularly heavy concentration in Western Europe, Brazil, the Philippines, and Haiti. The World Health Organization has estimated that one hundred thousand people have come down with AIDS, one million have AIDS-related disorders, and ten million are infected with HIV and are therefore capable of spreading it. N.Y. Times, Nov. 20, 1986, at A1.

3. Szmuness, Stevens, Harley, Zang, Oleszko, William, Sadovsky, Morrison & Kellner, *Hepatitis B Vaccine: Demonstration of Efficacy in a Controlled Clinical Trial in a High-Risk Population in the United States*, 303 New Eng. J. Med. 833 (1980).

4. *Update: Acquired Immunodeficiency Syndrome—United States*, 35 MMWR 757 (1986).

5. *Id.* at 758.

6. *See* Chapter 2 in this volume.

7. *See id.* for CDC definitions of AIDS and ARC.

8. For an explanation of cell-mediated immunity, *see* Institute of Medicine, National Academy of Sciences, Mobilizing Against AIDS 74-88 (1986).

9. Barre-Sinoussi, Chermann, Rey, Nugeyre, Chamaret, Gruest, Dauguet, Axler-Blin, Vezinet-Brun, Rovziout, Rozenbaum & Montagnier, *Isolation of a T-Lymphotropic Retrovirus from a Patient at Risk for Acquired Immune-Deficiency Syndrome (AIDS)*, 220 Science 868-71 (1983).

10. Popovic, Sarngadharan, Read & Gallo, *Detection, Isolation and Continuous Production of Cytopathic Retroviruses (HTLV-III) from Patients with AIDS and Pre-AIDS*, 224 Science 497-500 (1984).

11. Levy, Hoffman, Kramer, Landis, Shimabukuro & Oshiro, *Isolation of Lymphocyto-pathic Retroviruses from San Francisco Patients With AIDS*, 225 Science 840-41 (1984).

12. Landesman, Ginzburg & Weiss, *The AIDS Epidemic*, 312 New Eng. J. Med. 521 (1985).

13. *See* Chapter 6 in this volume.

CHAPTER 2

1. N.Y. Times, Mar. 28, 1985, at B6.

2. N.Y. Times, Sept. 5, 1985, at B2.

3. N.Y. Times, Aug. 31, 1985, at A25.

4. N.Y. Times, Sept. 1, 1985, at A41.

5. N.Y. Times, Sept. 2, 1985, at A25. *See, e.g., id,* Sept. 9, 1985, at B3.

6. N.Y. Times, Nov. 17, 1984, at A8.

7. N.Y. Times, Jan. 6, 1986, at B10.

8. N.Y. Times, Oct. 4, 1985, at B10.

9. *Court Officers Wear Masks And Gloves At Trial Of A Defendant With AIDS,* N.Y. Times, Oct. 24, 1984, at A31.

10. Lieberson, *The Reality of AIDS,* The N.Y. Rev. Books, Jan. 16, 1986, at 43.

11. Jaret, *The Wars Within,* Nat. Geographic, June 1986, at 702.

12. *Update: Acquired Immunodeficiency Syndrome-United States,* 35 MMWR 757 (1986) [hereinafter *AIDS Update*].

13. Antibodies are proteins of a specific composition that are formed by the body to repel foreign proteins such as those found in bacteria and viruses.

14. A person is seropositive after testing positive in both the test used for screening large groups for possible infection (the Enzyme-Linked Immunosorbent Assay, or ELISA) and the more specific confirmatory test (Western Blot). Blattner, *et al., Epidemiology of Human T-Lymphotropic Virus Type III and the Risk of Acquired Immunodefiency Syndrome,* 103 Annals Internal Med. 665 (1985).

15. *Transfusion-Associated Human T-Lymphotropic Virus Type III/Lymphadenopathy-Associated Virus Infection From Seronegative Donor,* 35 MMWR 390 (1986).

16. *Epidemiology of AIDS: Current Status and Future Prospect,* 229 Science 1354 (1985).

17. *Id.*

18. Petermen, Drotman & Curran, *Epidemiology of the Acquired Immunodeficiency Syndrome (AIDS),* 7 Epidemiological Reviews 1 (1985).

19. *Revision of the Case Definition of Acquired Immunodeficiency Syndrome for National Reporting,* 34 MMWR 373, 373-75 (1985). More recently, the CDC has proposed a four group classification of infection, based on symptomology: 1) early acute, though transient, signs of disease; 2) asymptomatic infection; 3) persistent swollen lymph glands; and 4) presence of opportunistic disease and/or rare cancers, such as Kaposi's sarcoma. *See* CDC, *Classification System for Human T-Lymphotropic Virus Type III/Lymphadenopathy-Associated Virus Infection,* 105 Annals Internal Med. 234 (1986).

20. *See* Goedert, *HIV (AIDS Virus): Modes of Transmission and Natural History,* in AIDS: Legal Aspects of a Medical Crisis (1986).

21. T. Spira, *et al.,* An Analysis of Progression of Immunologic Abnormalities In A Cohort Of Homosexual Men With The Lymphadenopathy Syndrome (paper presented at the Second International Conference on the Acquired Immunodeficiency Syndrome, Paris, France, June, 1986 [hereinafter *Paris Conference*]).

22. J. Gold & D. Armstrong, Continuing High Risk for AIDS In A Cohort of Homosexual Men With Persistent Unexplained Lymphadenopathy (*Paris Conference* paper).

23. J. Kaplan, *et al.,* Lymphadenopathy Syndrome In Homosexual Men (*Paris Conference* paper). Nineteen eighty-seven data from a long-term San Francisco study of 104 seropositive gay and bisexual men indicate that the risk of developing AIDS may increase yearly. After seven years, 36 percent of the men had developed AIDS. Altman, *Data Suggest AIDS Risk Rises Yearly,* N.Y. Times, Mar. 3, 1987, at C1.

24. Levine, *The Acquired Immunodeficiency Syndrome In Persons With Hemophilia,* 103 Annals Internal Med. 723, 723-26 (1985).

25. See notes 42-45 below.

26. *Education and Foster Care of Children Infected With Human T-Lymphotropic Virus Type III/Lymphadenopathy-Associated Virus*, 34 MMWR 517, 517-21 (1985).

27. *AIDS Update*, note 12 above, at 758.

28. Lyman, *et al.*, *Minimal Risk of Transmission of AIDS-Associated Retrovirus Infection by Oral-Genital Contact*, 255 J.A.M.A. 1703 (1986). Oral-genital sex and kissing have not been documented as having resulted in AIDS transmission.

29. Jaffee, *et al.*, *Persistent Infections With Human T-Lymphotropic Virus Type III/Lymphadenopathy-Associated Virus in Apparently Healthy Homosexual Men*, 102 Annals Internal Med. 627 (1985).

30. *Update: Acquired Immunodeficiency Syndrome in the San Francisco Cohort Study, 1978-1985*, 34 MMWR 573 (1985).

31. *See* Goedert, *et al.*, *Determinants of Retrovirus (HTLV-III) Antibody and Immunodeficiency Conditions In Homosexual Men*, 1 Lancet 711 (1984); Goedert, *et al.*, *Three-Year Incidence of AIDS in Five Cohorts of HIV-Infected Risk Group Members*, 231 Science 992 (1986); Melbye, *et al.*, *Long-Term Seropositivity for Human T-Lymphotropic Virus Type III in Homosexual Men Without Acquired Immunodeficiency Syndrome*, 104 Annals Internal Med. 496 (1986).

32. Kreiss, *et al.*, *Antibody to Human T-Lymphotropic Virus Type III in Wives of Hemophiliacs*, 102 Annals Internal Med. 623 (1985); Redfield, *et al.*, *Frequent Transmission of HIV Among Spouses of Patients With AIDS-Related Complex and AIDS*, 253 J.A.M.A. 157 (1985).

33. N.Y. Times, Oct. 28, 1986, at C1; Kreiss, *et al.*, *AIDS Virus Infection in Nairobi Prostitutes*, 314 New Eng. J. Med. 414, 414-418 (1986).

34. Fischl, *et al.*, *Evaluation of Heterosexual Partners, Children, and Household Contacts of Adults with AIDS*, 257 J.A.M.A. 640 (1987).

35. *Heterosexual Transmission of Human T-Lymphotropic Virus Type III/Lymphadenopathy-Associated Virus*, 34 MMWR 561-3 (1985).

36. Weiss, *et al.*, *HIV Infection Among Health Care Workers*, 254 J.A.M.A. 2089 (1985); Calabrese & Gopakakrishna, *Transmission of HIV Infection From Man to Women to Man*, 314 New Eng. J. Med. 987 (1986). The 10-year old daughter of the married couple, both of whom died of AIDS, is seronegative. *Id.*

37. Wofsy, *et al.*, Isolation of AIDS-Associated Virus (ARV) From Vaginal and Cervical (V/C) Secretions of ARV Seropositive Women (*Paris Conference* paper). The virus was found in 4 of 8 women in one study and 4 of 14 in another.

38. A disproportionately high percentage of AIDS patients are black largely because disadvantaged groups are more likely to fall victim to the abuse of drugs. Almost a quarter of adult AIDS patients are black (more than double the proportion of United States blacks). Sixty percent of children with AIDS are black. Over half of all female patients with AIDS are black. Centers for Disease Control, Weekly Surveillance Report, July 28, 1986.

39. 1 AIDS Alert, June 1986, at 103.

40. The normal clotting of blood requires the presence of several blood factors. In hemophilia A, the most common form of hemophilia, there is a deficiency of Factor VIII. In hemophilia B, there is a deficiency of Factor IX. Other factors are deficient in the form known as Von Willebrands' disease and in other rarer forms. *Pneumucysitis Carinii Pneumonia Among Persons With Hemophilia A*, 31 MMWR 365-67 (1982).

41. Blattner, *et al.*, *Epidemiology of Human T-Lymphotropic Virus Type III and the Risk of Acquired Immunodeficiency Syndrome*, 103 Annals Internal Med. 665 (1985).

42. *Pneumocystis Carinii Pneumonia Among Persons With Hemophilia A*, note 40 above.

43. Kitchen, *et al.*, *Aetiology of AIDS-Antibodies to T-Cell Leukemia Virus (Type III) in Hemophiliacs*, 312 Nature 367 (1984).

44. Johnson, *et al.*, *AIDS and the Hemophiliac*, 121 Am. J. Epidemiology 797 (1985).

45. Koerper & Levy, Prevalence of Antibodies to AIDS-Associated Retrovirus (ARC) and Recovery of Infectious Virus From Hemophiliacs in San Francisco (*Paris Conference* paper);

see also Changing Patterns of Acquired Immunodeficiency Syndrome in Hemophilia Patients—United States, 34 MMWR 241 (1985).

46. *Provisional Public Health Service Inter-Agency Recommendations for Screening Donated Blood and Plasma for Antibody to the Virus Causing Acquired Immunodeficiency Syndrome*, 34 MMWR 1 (1985).

47. Scott, *et al.*, *Acquired Immunodeficiency Syndrome in Infants*, 310 New Eng. J. Med. 76 (1984); Oleske, *et al.*, *Immune Deficiency Syndrome in Children*, 249 J.A.M.A. 2345 (1983).

48. Grouse, *HTLV-III Transmission*, 254 J.A.M.A. 2130 (1985).

49. *Update: Prospective Evaluation of Health-Care Workers Exposed Via The Parenteral or Mucous-Membrane Route To Blood Or Body Fluids From Patients With Acquired Immunodeficiency Syndrome—United States*, 34 MMWR 101 (1985); *Update: Evaluation Of Human T-Lymphotropic Virus Type III/Lymphadenopathy-Associated Virus Infection in Health-Care Personnel—United States*, 34 MMWR 575 (1985).

50. *Recommendations for Preventing Transmission of Infections With Human T-Lymphotropic Virus Type III/Lymphadenopathy-Associated Virus in the Workplace*, 34 MMWR 68 (1985).

51. D. Henderson, *et al.*, *Risk of Nosocomial Infection With HTLV/LAV-III*, 104 Annals Internal Med. 644 (1986).

52. *Apparent Transmission of Human T-Lymphotropic Virus Type III/Lymphadenopathy-Associated Virus From a Child to a Mother Providing Health-Care*, 35 MMWR 76 (1986).

53. *Id.* at 78.

54. *Recommendations for Preventing Transmission of Infection With Human T-Lymphotropic Virus Type III/Lymphadenopathy-Associated Virus in the Workplace*, note 50 above, at 691-95.

55. *Innoculation of Cryptococcosis With Transmission of the Acquired Immunodeficiency Syndrome*, 313 New Eng. J. Med. 267 (1985).

56. Gerberding, *et al.*, *Transmission of Hepatitis B Without Transmission of AIDS By Accidental Needlestick*, 312 New Eng. J. Med. 56 (1985).

57. The CDC states: "routine serologic testing for evidence of HTLVLAVIII HIV) infection is not necessary for MCW's [medical care workers] who perform or assist in invasive procedures or for patients undergoing invasive procedures, since the risk of transmission in this setting is so low." *Recommendations for Preventing Transmission of Infection with Human T-Lymphotropic Virus Type III/Lymphodenopathy-Associated Virus During Invasive Procedures*, 35 MMWR 221 (1986).

58. Friedland, *et al.*, *Lack of Transmission of HTLV/LAV-III Infection to Household Contacts of Patients With AIDS or AIDS-Related Complex with Oral Candidiasis*, 314 New Eng. J. Med. 344 (1986); *see also* Fischl, note 34 above.

59. "[N]one of the family members of over 17,000 AIDS patients reported to CDC have been reported to have AIDS, except a small number of sexual partners of patients, children born to infected mothers, or family members who themselves had other established risk factors for AIDS. Seven studies involving over 350 family members of both adults and children infected with AIDS have not found serologic or virologic [isolation of the virus from the person] evidence of transmission of HTLVIIILAV HIV infection within families other than among sex partners, children born to infected mothers, or family members with risk factors for AIDS." *Apparent Transmission of Human T-Lymphotropic Virus Type III/Lymphadenopathy-Associated Virus From A Child To A Mother Providing Health Care*, note 52 above, at 78.

60. Melbye, *et al.*, *Anal Intercourse As A Possible Factor In Heterosexual Transmission of HTLV-III to Spouses of Hemophiliacs*, 312 New Eng. J. Med. 857 (1985).

61. There is also a case report of a woman who tested seropositive after her husband developed AIDS, but who then became seronegative after the couple began using condoms. Thus, it may be that repeated exposure to the virus for some persons is required for permanent infection. Moreover, some people exposed to the virus may ward off not only clinical illness but also the seropositive state as well. *Transient Antibody to Lymphadenopathy-Associated*

Virus/Human T-Lymphotropic Virus Type III and T-Lymphocyte Abnormalities in the Wife of a Man Who Developed Acquired Immunodeficiency Syndrome, 103 Annals Internal Med. 546 (1985).

62. Editorial, *Transmission of AIDS: The Case Against Casual Contagion*, 314 New Eng. J. Med. 380 (1986).

63. *Education and Foster Care of Children Infected With Human T-Lymphotropic Virus Type III/Lymphadenopathy-Associated Virus*, note 26 above.

64. Tsoukas, *et al.*, Risk of Transmission of HTLV/III-LAV From Human Bites (*Paris Conference* paper).

65. *Education and Foster Care of Children With Human T-Lymphadenopathy-Associated Virus*, note 26 above.

66. *Recommendations for Preventing Transmission of Infection with Human T-Lymphotropic Virus Type III/Lymphadenopathy-Associated Virus in the Workplace*, note 50 above, at 694. Employees who routinely handle food eaten by others have also been considered by the public to be a health risk. However, the CDC has concluded that food handlers with AIDS do not pose a risk. "Because AIDS is not transmitted through preparation or serving of food and beverages, . . . food service workers known to be infected with AIDS should not be restricted from work unless they have another infection or illness for which such restriction would be warranted." *Id.* at 681.

CHAPTER 3

1. One model has already been proposed in Susan Sontag's brilliant polemic, Illness as Metaphor (1978). In this work, Sontag assessed the important ways in which tuberculosis and cancer have been used as metaphors. Using techniques of literary analysis, she demonstrated prevailing cultural views of these diseases and their victims. But disease is more than a metaphor. These "social constructions" have very real sociopolitical implications.

2. The following discussion is abbreviated from A. Brandt, No Magic Bullet: A Social History of Venereal Disease in the United States since 1880 (1985).

3. On the problem of *opthalmia neonatorum*, see Wolbarst, *On the Occurrence of Syphilis and Gonorrhea in Children by Direct Infection*, 7 Am. Med. 494 (1912); Von Blarcum, *The Harm Done in Ascribing All Babies' Sore Eyes to Gonorrhea*, Am. J. Pub. Health, 926-31 (1916); Kerr, *Opthalmia Neonatorum: An Analysis of the Laws and Regulations in Relation thereto in Force in the United States*, Pub. Health Service Bull. No. 49 (1914).

4. *See* Burr, *The Guarantee of Safety in the Marriage Contract*, 47 J.A.M.A. 1887-88 (1906).

5. *See* E. Brieux, Damaged Goods, (J. Pollack trans. 1913). On the critical reception of the play, see *Demoralizing Plays*, Outlook, Sept. 20, 1913, at 110; Rockefeller, *The Awakening of a New Social Conscience*, 19 Med. Reviews of Reviews 281 (1913); *Damaged Goods*, Hearst's Mag., May 1913, at 806; *Brieux's New Sociological Sermon in Three Acts*, Current Opinion, Apr. 1913, at 296-97; *see also*, Rosenkrantz, *Damaged Goods: Dilemmas of Responsibility for Risk*, 57 Health and Soc'y. 1 (1979).

6. Kelly, *Social Diseases and their Prevention*, Soc. Diseases, July 1910, at 17; Kelly, *The Protection of the Innocent*, Am. J. Obstetrics, Apr. 1907, at 477-81.

7. On prostitution in Progressive America, see Boyer, Urban Masses and Moral Order (1978); R. Rosen, The Lost Sisterhood: Prostitution in America, 1900-1918 (1982); M. Connely, The Response to Prostitution in the Progressive Era (1980).

8. On nonvenereal transmission, see especially L. Bulkey, Syphilis of the Innocent (1894).

9. *What One Woman Has Had to Bear*, 68 Forum (1912); *see also*, *New Laws About Drinking Cups*, 58 Life 1152 (1911).

10. The wartime policy for the attack on the red-light districts and the testing and incarceration of prostitutes is described in greater detail in A. Brandt, note 2 above, at 80-95.

11. T.W. Gregory, Memorandum on Legal Aspects of the Proposed System of Medical Examination of Women Convicted under Section 13, Selective Service Act, National Archives,

Record Group 90, Box 223; *see also*, Dietzler, Detention Houses and Reformatories as Protective Social Agencies in the Campaign of the United States Government Against Venereal Diseases (United States Interdepartmental Social Hygiene Board, 1922).

12. Pierce, *The Value of Detention as a Reconstruction Measure*, Am. J. Obstetrics, Dec. 1919, at 629.

13. Henig, *AIDS: A New Disease's Deadly Odyssey*, N. Y. Times Magazine, Feb. 6, 1983, at 36.

CHAPTER 4

1. *Message from Secretary Heckler and Letter from Commissioner Young*, 15 FDA Drug Bull. 26 (1985); U.S. Public Health Service, Facts About AIDS 1 (1984).

2. *Update: Acquired Immunodeficiency Syndrome, United States*, 35 MMWR 757 (1986) [hereinafter *AIDS Update*]; Curran & Morgan, *Acquired Immunodeficiency Syndrome: The Beginning, the Present, and the Future*, in AIDS From The Beginning 23 (H. Cole & G. Lundberg eds. 1986).

3. *See generally* Morgenstern, *The Role of the Federal Government in Protecting Citizens From Communicable Disease*, 47 U. Cinn. L. Rev. 537 (1978).

4. 16A Corpus Juris Secundum §§432-433 (1979). The federal government's health authority is derived from its power to regulate commerce, and its taxing and spending powers. Morgenstern, note 3 above, at 545.

5. Jacobson v. Massachusetts, 197 U.S. 11, 37-38 (1905); *see, e.g.*, McCartney v. Austin, 31 A.D.2d 370, 371, 296 N.Y.S.2d 26, 27 (1969) ("That statutes of this nature . . . are within the police power and thus constitutional generally is too well established to require discussion.").

6. *See generally* Parmet, *AIDS and Quarantine: The Revival of an Archaic Doctrine*, 14 Hofstra L. Rev. 53 (1985).

7. U.S. Const. amends. I, IV, VI, V; *see, e.g.*, L. Tribe, American Constitutional Law §10-15 (1978).

8. *See, e.g.*, L. Tribe, note 7 above, §11-2. Whether various provisions of the Bill of Rights were "incorporated" wholesale by the Fourteenth Amendment or, instead, were made binding upon the states only insofar as they were necessary to "ordered liberty" was once a hotly debated topic. The distinction is of little contemporary significance.

9. *See, e.g.*, L. Tribe, note 7 above, §16-1.

10. U.S. Const. amend. I, states: "Congress shall make no law respecting an establishment of religion, or prohibiting the free exercise thereof; or abridging the freedom of speech, or of the press, or the right of the people peaceably to assemble, and to petition the Government for a redress of grievances."

11. *See, e.g.*, L. Tribe, note 7 above, §12-2, at p. 583 (discussing First Amendment).

12. *See id.* §16-2.

13. *See, e.g.*, Varholy v. Sweat, 15 So. 2d 267, 269-70 (Fla. 1943); State v. Rackowski, 86 A. 606, 608 (Conn. 1913) (and cases cited therein); Allison v. Cash, 137 S.W. 245 (Ky. 1911); Highland v. Schulte, 82 N.W. 62, 64 (Mich. 1900).

14. Jacobson v. Massachusetts, 197 U.S. 11, 25 (1905) (and cases cited therein).

15. *Ex parte* Martin, 188 P.2d 287 (Cal. App. 1948); State *ex rel.* Kennedy v. Head, 185 S.W.2d 530 (Tenn. 1945); *Varholy*, 153 Fla. 571, 15 So. 2d 267; City of Little Rock v. Smith, 204 P. 364 (Ark. 1922); *Ex parte* Company, 106 Ohio St. 50, 139 N.E. 204 (1922); *Ex parte* Arata, 52 Cal. App. 380, 198 P. 814 (1921); *Ex parte* Shepard, 52 Cal. App. 49, 195 P. 1077 (1921); *Ex parte* McGee, 105 Kan. 574, 184 P. 14 (1919); State *ex rel.* McBride v. Superior Court, 103 Wash. 409, 174 P. 973 (1918).

16. Greene v. Edwards, 265 S.E.2d 662 (W.Va. 1980); *In re* Halko, 54 Cal. Rptr. 661

(1966); Jones v. Czapkay, 6 Cal. Rptr. 182 (1960); White v. Seattle Local Union No. 81, 337 P.2d 289 (Wash. 1959).

17. Crayton v. Larrabee, 220 N.Y. 493, *aff'g*, 147 N.Y.S. 1105 (1917); Allison v. Cash, 137 S.W. 245 (Ky. 1911); Hengehold v. City of Covington, 108 Ky. 752, 57 S.W. 495 (1900); Henderson County Board of Health v. Ward, 107 Ky. 477, 54 S.W. 725 (1900); Highland v. Schulte, 123 Mich. 360, 82 N.W. 62 (1900); Smith v. Emery, 42 N.Y.S. 258, 11 App. Div. 10 (1896); *In re* Smith, 146 N.Y. 68, 40 N.E. 497 (1895); City of Richmond v. Henrico County Supervisors, 83 Va. 204, 2 S.E. 26 (1887); Spring v. Inhabitants of Hyde Park, 137 Mass. 554, 50 Am. Rep. 334 (1884); Beckwith v. Sturdevant, 42 Conn. 158 (1875); Harrison v. Mayor & City Council of Baltimore, 1 Gill. 264 (Md. 1843).

18. People v. Tait, 102 N.E. 750 (Ill. 1913); State v. Rackowski, 86 Conn. 677, 86 A. 606 (1913).

19. Kirk v. Wyman, 83 S.C. 372, 65 S.E. 387 (1909).

20. Rudolphe v. City of New Orleans, 11 La. Ann. 242 (1854).

21. Jew Ho v. Williamson, 102 F. 10 (N.D. Cal. 1900).

22. *See, e.g.*, State *ex rel.* McBride v. Superior Court, 103 Wash. 409, 174 P. 973 (1918).

23. *Kirk*, 83 S.C. 372, 65 S.E. at 392.

24. *See, e.g.*, *Ex parte* McGee, 105 Kan. 574, 185 P. 14 (1919).

25. *See, e.g.*, Mugler v. Kansas, 123 U.S. 623 (1887) (power to quarantine "so as to bind us all must exist somewhere; else, society will be at the mercy of the few, who, regarding only their appetites or passions, may be willing to imperil the security of the many, provided only they are permitted to do as they please"); Irwin v. Arrendale, 159 S.E. 2d 441 (Ga. Ct. App. 1967) (individuals must submit to reasonable public health measures for the common good); City of Little Rock v. Smith, 162 S.W. 2d 705 (Ark. 1942) ("private rights . . . must yield in the interest of security"; venereal disease "affects the public health so intimately and so insidiously that considerations of delicacy and privacy may not be permitted to thwart measures necessary to avert the public peril").

26. *See* Jacobson v. Massachusetts, 197 U.S. 11, 31 (1905); L. Tribe, note 7 above, §8-3.

27. *See* Parmet, note 6 above, at 76-77; L. Tribe, note 7 above, §8-4.

28. Viehmeister v. White, 179 N.Y. 235, 72 N.E. 97 (1904) (quoted in *Jacobson*, 197 U.S. at 34-35).

29. State v. Rackowski, 86 A. 606, 608 (Conn. 1913).

30. Kirk v. Wyman, 83 S.C. 372, 65 S.W. 387, 390 (1901).

31. *Id*.

32. *Ex parte* Company, 106 Ohio St. 50, 139 N.E. 204, 205 (1922); *see also Ex parte* Johnson, 40 Cal. App. 242, 180 P. 644 (1919).

33. 139 N.E. at 206.

34. People v. Strautz, 386 Ill. 360, 54 N.E.2d 441, 444 (1944); *see also* State *ex rel.* Kennedy v. Head, 185 S.W.2d 530 (Tenn. 1945); State v. Hutchinson, 18 So. 2d 723 (Ala. 1944); *Ex parte* Caselli, 204 P. 364 (1922).

35. Railroad Company v. Husen, 95 U.S. 465, 471-73 (1877); *see also Ex parte* Martin, 188 P.2d 287 (Ct. App. Cal. 1948); People v. Tait, 30 N.E. 750 (Ill. 1913).

36. *Ex parte* Shepard, 52 Cal. App. 49, 195 P. 1077 (1921).

37. *Ex parte* Arata, 198 P. 814, 816 (1921); *see also In re* Smith, 40 N.E. 497 (N.Y. 1895).

38. Smith v. Emery, 42 N.Y.S. 258, 260 (1896).

39. Jew Ho v. Williamson, 103 F. 10, 22 (N.D. Cal. 1900).

40. New York State Ass'n for Retarded Children v. Carey, 672 F.2d 644 (2d Cir. 1979).

41. Arline v. School Bd., 772 F.2d 759 (11th Cir. 1985). The Supreme Court employed similar language in affirming the decision of the court of appeals. 107 S. Ct. 1123 (1987)

42. *In re* District 27 Community School Bd. v. Board of Educ., 130 Misc. 2d 398, 413, 502 N.Y.S. 2d 325, 335 (N.Y. Sup. Ct. 1986).

43. For a discussion of the need for a scientific foundation for public health measures, see

Burris, *Fear Itself: AIDS, Herpes, and Public Health Decisions*, 3 Yale L. & Pol'y Rev. 479 (1984).

44. Roe v. Wade, 410 U.S. 113 (1973); Eisenstadt v. Baird, 405 U.S. 438 (1972); Griswold v. Connecticut, 381 U.S. 479 (1965).

45. *See generally* G. Gunther, Constitutional Law 586-92 (11th ed. 1985).

46. City of New Orleans v. Dukes, 427 U.S. 297 (1976).

47. Dunn v. Blumstein, 405 U.S. 330 (1972); Korematsu v. United States, 323 U.S. 214 (1944).

48. *See, e.g.*, Craig v. Boren, 429 U.S. 190, 197 (1976) (gender classification); Bell v. Burson, 402 U.S. 533 (1971) (right to driver's license).

49. *See, e.g.*, San Antonio Ind. School Dist. v. Rodriguez, 411 U.S. 1, 98 (1973) (Marshall, J., dissenting).

50. G. Gunther, note 45 above, at 589-92.

51. L. Tribe, note 7 above, §16-6, p. 1000.

52. L. Tribe, note 7 above, §16-2. *But see* City of Cleburne, Tex. v. Cleburne Living Center, 105 S. Ct. 3249, 3258-3260 (1985).

53. Education of the Handicapped Act, 20 U.S.C. §§1401-1461; Employment Opportunities for Handicapped Individuals Act, 27 U.S.C. §§701-796.

54. School Bd. v. Arline, 107 S. Ct. 1123 (1987).

55. Bayer, Levine & Wolf, *HIV Antibody Screening: An Ethical Framework for Evaluating Proposed Programs*, 256 J.A.M.A. 1768, 1768 (1986).

56. *Id.* at 1769.

57. Altman, *U.S. is Considering Much Wider Tests for AIDS Infection*, N.Y. Times, Feb. 4, 1987, at A1; *see also Mass Testing of High-Risk Groups Urged to Combat Spread of Infection*, 1 AIDS Policy & Law (BNA), Mar. 26, 1986, at 1 (discussing earlier proposal by U.S. Public Health Service). *But see* Altman, *Mandatory Tests for AIDS Opposed at Health Parley*, N.Y. Times, Feb. 25, 1987, at A1 (reporting on emerging consensus among public health officials against widespread mandatory testing).

58. For a thorough discussion of the ethics of testing, see Bayer, Levine & Wolf, note 55 above.

59. Institute of Medicine, National. Academy of Sciences, Confronting AIDS 45 (1986); Curran, *et al.*, The Epidemiology of AIDS: Current Status and Future Prospects, 229 Science 1352, 1354 (1985).

60. *See, e.g.*, Bayer, Levine & Wolf, note 55 above; *Mass Testing of High-Risk Groups Urged to Combat Spread of Infection*, note 57 above; Altman, *AIDS Poses a Classic Dilemma*, N.Y. Times, Feb. 10, 1987, at C3 (interview with Director of CDC).

61. Whalen v. Roe, 429 U.S. 589, 605 (1976).

62. *Leak of Health Records*, N.Y. Times, Aug. 30, 1986, at 6.

63. *In re* District 27 Community School Bd. v. Board of Educ., 130 Misc. 2d 398, 502 N.Y.S. 2d 325 (N.Y. Sup. Ct. 1986).

64. *See AIDS Update*, note 2 above.

65. *Id.*

66. *MacNeil-Lehrer News Hour* (PBS television broadcast, interview with Kristine Gebbie, chair of Association of State and Territorial Health Officials AIDS task force, Feb. 4, 1987); *see, e.g.*, Alaska Statutes §25.05.101 (Michie Supp., 1986), *repealed by* 1984 Alaska Sess. Laws ch. 134, §4; N.Y. Dom. Rel. Law §13-a (McKinney 1977 and Supp. 1986), *repealed by* 1985 N.Y. Laws 674 §1; Wis. Stat. Ann. §765.06 (West 1981 and Supp. 1986), *repealed by* 1981 Wis. Laws ch. 20, §1777r.

67. Altman, note 60 above.

68. Whalen v. Roe, 429 U.S. at 605.

69. National Treasury Employers Union v. Von Raab, 649 F. Supp. 380 (E.D. La. 1986).

70. *Requiring Physicians to Warn Contacts Seen as Misguided*, 1 AIDS Policy & Law (BNA), Nov. 5, 1986, at 8.

71. *Id.*

72. W. Curran, L. Gostin & M. Clark, Acquired Immunodeficiency Syndrome: Legal, Regulatory and Policy Analyses (U.S. Dep't H.H.S. No. 282-86-0032, 1986).

73. Whalen v. Roe, 429 U.S. 589, 606 (1977) (Brennan, J., concurring).

74. *See, e.g.,* U.S. Public Health Service, *Public Health Service Plan for the Prevention and Control of Acquired Immune Deficiency Syndrome (AIDS),* 100 Publ. Health Rpts. 453 (1985).

75. *Self-Reported Behavior Change Among Gay and Bisexual Men— San Francisco,* 34 MMWR 613 (1985); Schecter, Jeffries & Constance, *Changes in Sexual Behavior and Fear of AIDS,* 1 Lancet 1293 (1984); *Declining Rates of Rectal and Pharyngeal Gonorrhea Among Males—NYC,* 33 MMWR 295 (1984).

76. Cal. Health & Safety Code §§2520, 2525 (Communicable Disease Control) (West 1976).

77. W. Curran, L. Gostin & M. Clark, note 72 above, at 207.

78. *Id.* at i-ii.

79. *Id.* at ii.

80. *Texas Quarantine Plan Withdrawn by Official,* 1 AIDS Policy & Law (BNA), Jan. 29, 1986, at 5.

81. *Lack of Accord Kills Colorado Bill,* 1 AIDS Policy & Law (BNA), May 21, 1986, at 2.

82. Conn. Gen. Stat. Ann. §19a-221 (West 1986).

83. Leeson, *HTLV-III Antibody Tests and Health Education,* 1 Lancet 911 (1986).

84. Greene v. Edwards, 263 S.E.2d 661 (W. Va. 1980).

85. Kirk v. Wyman, 83 S.C. 272, 65 S.E. 387, 391 (1909).

86. *Ex parte* Martin, 188 P. 2d 287, 291 (Cal. Ct. App. 1948).

87. W. Curran, L. Gostin & M. Clark, note 72 above, at 346.

88. The charges were later dropped. N.Y. Times, Apr. 4, 1987 at 31.

89. W. Curran, L. Gostin & M. Clark, note 72 above, at 347.

90. Carne, Tedder & Smith, *Acute Encephalopathy Coincidence with Seroconversion for Anti-HTLV-III,* 2 Lancet 1706 (1985); Levy, Shimabukuro & Hollander, *Isolation of HTLV-III from Cerebrospinal Fluid and Brain of Patients with Neurologic Symptoms,* 2 Lancet 586 (1985); Goldstick, Mandybar & Bode, *Spinal Cord Degeneration in AIDS,* 35 Neurology 103 (1985).

91. *See, e.g.,* Conn. Gen. Stat. §19A-380 (1985); N.Y. Mental Hygiene Law §23.01 (McKinney 1978).

CHAPTER 5

1. *Roots of AIDS Boycott: Record of Independence,* N.Y. Times, Sept. 14, 1985, at B1.

2. *11,000 Pupils Out in Protest,* N.Y. Post, Sept. 10, 1985, at 4, 5.

3. *AIDS Update: Halting the "Epidemic of Fear,"* Infect. Rep. No. 2, at 1 (1985); *AIDS: A Growing 'Pandemic'?* Newsweek, April 29, 1985, at 71; *Now No One Is Safe From AIDS,* Life, July 1985.

4. *Education and Foster Care of Children Infected with Human T-Lymphotropic Virus Type III/Lymphadenopathy-associated Virus,* 34 MMWR 517 (1985) [hereinafter *CDC Guidelines*].

5. *Nomenclature: Human Immunodeficiency Virus,* 105 Annals Internal Med. 1345 (1986).

6. *Possible Transfusion-associated Acquired Immune Deficiency Syndrome (AIDS)—California,* 31 MMWR 652 (1982); *Unexplained Immunodeficiency and Opportunistic Infections in Infants—New York, New Jersey, California,* 31 MMWR 665 (1982); Rubinstein, Sicklick, Gupta, *et al., Acquired Immunodeficiency With Reversed T_4/T_8 Ratios in Infants Born to Promiscuous and Drug Addicted Mothers,* 249 J.A.M.A. 2350 (1983); Oleske, Minnefort, Cooper, *et al., Immune Deficiency Syndrome in Children,* 249 J.A.M.A. 2345 (1983).

7. *Update: Acquired Immunodeficiency Syndrome—United States,* 35 MMWR 757 (1986)

[hereinafter *AIDS Update*]; *see also Acquired Immunodeficiency Syndrome (AIDS) among Blacks and Hispanics—United States* 35 MMWR 655 (1986) [hereinafter *AIDS Among Blacks and Hispanics*]; *see also* Selwyn, *AIDS: What is Now Known II, Epidemiology*, 21 Hospital Practice 127-64 (1986).

8. *AIDS Among Blacks and Hispanics*, note 7 above; *Recommendations for Assisting in the Prevention of Perinatal Transmission of Human T-lymphotropic Virus Type III/lymphad-enopathy-associated Virus and Acquired Immunodeficiency Syndrome*, 34 MMWR 721 (1985) [hereinafter *1985 Perinatal Recommendations*].

9. *AIDS Update*, note 7 above; *AIDS among Blacks and Hispanics*, note 7 above; *see also 1985 Perinatal Recommendations*, note 8 above; Rubinstein, *Pediatric AIDS*, 1986 Current Problems in Pediatrics 364; Harris, Small, Klein, *et al.*, *Immunodeficiency in Female Sexual Partners of Men with the Acquired Immuno-deficiency Syndrome*, 308 New Eng. J. Med. 1181 (1983).

10. *AIDS Update*, note 7 above.

11. Hardy, Allen, Morgan, *et al.*, *The Incidence Rate of Acquired Immunodeficiency Syndrome in Selected Populations*, 253 J.A.M.A. 215 (1985).

12. *AIDS among Blacks and Hispanics*, note 7 above.

13. *Id.*; *see also* Pediatric AIDS Advisory Committee, Department of Public Health, City and County of San Francisco, Education of Children Infected with Human T-lymphotropic Virus-type III/lymphadenopathy-associated Virus (1986) [hereinafter San Francisco Guidelines].

14. *AIDS Update*, note 7 above.

15. *AIDS among Blacks and Hispanics*, note 7 above.

16. *See* Curran, *et al.*, *The Epidemiology of AIDS: Current Status and Future Prospects*, 229 Science 1352 (1985); Blatner, Biggar, Weiss, *et al.*, *Epidemiology of Human T-Lympho-tropic Virus III and the Risk of Acquired Immunodeficiency Syndrome*, 193 Annals Internal Med. 665 (1985). Approximately 30 percent of IV-drug-abuse related AIDS cases have been reported from three states: New York, New Jersey, and Connecticut. Spina, Des Jarlais, Marmor, *et al.*, *Prevalence of Antibody to Lymphadenopathy-associated Virus Among Drug-Detoxification Patients in New York*, 311 New Eng. J. Med. 467 (1984).

17. *1985 Perinatal Recommendations*, note 8 above.

18. Fauci, Macher, Longo, *et al.*, *Acquired Immunodeficiency Syndrome: Epidemiologic, Clinical, Immunologic, and Therapeutic Considerations*, 100 Annals Internal Med. 92 (1984); Blatner, note 16 above; Levy, Carlson, Hinrichs, *et al.*, *The Prevalence of HTLV-III/LAV Antibodies Among Intravenous Drug Abusers Attending Treatment Programs in California: A Preliminary Report*, 314 New Eng. J. Med. 446 (1986) (letter).

19. *CDC Guidelines*, note 4 above; *see also* San Francisco Guidelines, note 13 above.

20. Des Jarlais, Friedman & Hopkins, *Risk Reduction for the Acquired Immunodeficiency Syndrome Among Intravenous Drug Abusers*, 103 Annals Internal Med. 755 (1985); *New York Sets Pilot Program for Distribution of Clean Needles*, 1 AIDS Policy & Law (BNA), Nov. 19, 1986, at 1.

21. *Heterosexual Transmission of Human T-Lymphotropic Virus Type III/Lymphadenop-athy-associated Virus*, 34 MMWR 561 (1985); *Additional Recommendations to Reduce Sexual and Drug Abuse-Related Transmission of Human T-Lymphotropic Virus Type III/Lymph-adenopathy-Associated Virus*, 35 MMWR 152 (1986).

22. Hardy, Allen & Morgan, *The Incidence Rate of Acquired Immunodeficiency Syndrome in Selected Populations*, 253 J.A.M.A. 215 (1985); *Prevention of Acquired Immune Deficiency Syndrome (AIDS): Report of Inter-agency Recommendations*, 32 MMWR 101 (1983); *Provi-sional Public Health Service Inter-agency Recommendations for Screening Donated Blood and Plasma for Antibody to the Virus Causing Acquired Immunodeficiency Syndrome*, 34 MMWR 1 (1985).

23. Levin, *The Acquired Immunodeficiency Syndrome in Persons With Hemophilia*, 103

Annals Internal Med. 723 (1985); *Update: Acquired Immunodeficiency Syndrome (AIDS) in Persons with Hemophilia*, 33 MMWR 589 (1984).

24. *AIDS among Blacks and Hispanics*, note 7 above.

25. *AIDS Update*, note 7 above.

26. *Immunization of Children Infected with Human T-lymphotropic Virus Type III/Lymphadenopathy-associated Virus*, 106 Annals Internal Med. 75 (1987) [hereinafter *Immunization Guidelines*].

27. *Update: Acquired Immune Deficiency Syndrome (AIDS)—United States*, 31 MMWR 507 (1982); *Revision of Case Definition of Acquired Immunodeficiency Syndrome for National Reporting—United States*, 34 MMWR 378 (1985); Gottlieb, Groopman, Weinstein, *et al.*, *The Acquired Immunodeficiency Syndrome*, 99 Annals Internal Med. 208 (1983); Fauci, Macher, Longo, *et al.*, *Acquired Immunodeficiency Syndrome: Epidemiologic, Clinical, Immunologic, and Therapeutic Considerations*, 100 Annals Internal Med. 100 (1984).

28. Fauci, *et al.*, *The Acquired Immunodeficiency Syndrome: An Update*, 102 Annals Internal Med. 800 (1985); *Antibodies to a Retrovirus Etiologically Associated with Acquired Immunodeficiency Syndrome (AIDS) in Populations with Increased Incidences of the Syndrome*, 33 MMWR 377 (1984); *see also* Council on Scientific Affairs, *Status Report on the Acquired Immunodeficiency Syndrome: Human T-cell Lymphotropic Virus Type III Testing*, 254 J.A.M.A. 1242 (1985).

29. Pahwa, Kaplan, Fikrig, *et al.*, *Spectrum of Human T-cell Lymphotropic Virus Type III Infection in Children*, 255 J.A.M.A. 2299 (1986).

30. Chase, *AIDS is Causing Far More Illness Than the Official Figures Convey*, Wall Street Journal, May 30, 1986, at 23.

31. Melbye, Biggar, Ebbesen, *et al.*, *Long-term Seropositivity for Human T-lymphotropic Virus Type III in Homosexual Men Without Acquired Immunodeficiency Syndrome: Development of Immunologic and Clinical Abnormalities*, 104 Annals Internal Med. 496 (1986); *see also*, Curran, *et al.*, note 16 above.

32. *Classification System for Human T-Lymphotropic Virus Type III/Lymphadenopathy-associated Virus Infections*, 35 MMWR 334 (1986) [hereinafter *Classification System*].

33. Selik, Jaffe, Solomon & Curran, *CDC's Definition of AIDS*, 325 New Eng. J. Med. 315 (1986) (letter).

34. *Classification System*, note 32 above.

35. *Recommendations for Assisting in the Prevention of Perinatal Transmission of Human T-lymphotropic Virus Type III/Lymphadenopathy-associated Virus and Acquired Immunodeficiency Syndrome*, 34 MMWR 721 (1985).

36. Scott, Fischl, Klimas, *et al.*, *Mothers of Infants with the Acquired Immunodeficiency Syndrome; Evidence for Both Symptomatic and Asymptomatic Carriers*, 253 J.A.M.A. 363 (1985).

37. Thomas, Jaffe, Spina, *et al.*, *Unexplained Immunodeficiency in Children: A Surveillance Report*, 252 J.A.M.A. 363 (1984).

38. Rogers, *AIDS in Children: A Review of the Clinical, Epidemiologic, and Public Health Aspects*, 4 Pediatric Infectious Disease 230 (1985); Cowan, Hellmann, Chadwin, *et al.*, *Maternal Transmission of Acquired Immune Deficiency Syndrome*, 73 Pediatrics 382 (1984); Lapointe, Michaud, Pekovic, *et al.*, *Transplacental Transmission of HTLV-III Virus*, 312 New Eng. J. Med. 1325 (1985) (letter).

39. Pahwa, Kaplan, Fikrig, *et al.*, note 29 above; Zeigler, Cooper Johnson, & Gold, *Postnatal Transmission of AIDS-associated Retrovirus From Mother to Infant*, 1 Lancet 896 (1986); Thiny, Sprecher-Goldberger, Jonckheer, *et al.*, *Isolation of AIDS Virus From Cell-free Breast Milk of Those Healthy Virus Carriers*, 2 Lancet 891 (1985) (letter).

40. *AIDS Update*, note 7 above; Sande, *Transmission of AIDS: The Case Against Casual Contagion*, 314 New Eng. J. Med. 380 (1986); CDC, *Occupational Risk of the Acquired Immunodeficiency Syndrome Among Health Care Workers*, 314 New Eng. J. Med. 1127 (1986);

Henderson, Saah, Zak, *et al.*, *Risk of Nosocomial Infection with Human T-Lymphotropic Virus Type III/Lymphadenopathy-Associated Virus in a Large Cohort of Intensively Exposed Health Care Workers*, 104 Annals Internal Med. 644 (1986).

41. *CDC Guidelines*, note 4 above; *see also Recommendations for Assisting in the Prevention of Perinatal Transmission of Human T-Lymphotropic Virus Type III/Lymphadenopathy-associated Virus and Acquired Immunodeficiency Syndrome*, 34 MMWR 721 (1985).

42. *CDC Guidelines*, note 4 above.

43. *Id.*

44. *But see Immunization Guidelines*, note 26 above.

45. C. Koop, Surgeon General's Report on Acquired Immune Deficiency Syndrome (1986).

46. Perlez, *City Schools to Show New Videotape on AIDS*, N.Y. Times, Nov. 1, 1986, at 1, 34.

47. *In re* District 27 Community School Bd. v. Bd. of Educ., 502 N.Y.S.2d 325, 327 (Sup. Ct. 1986).

48. *Id.* at 328-29.

49. *2 Local Boards Call for a Delay on AIDS Pupils*, N.Y. Times, Sept. 5, 1985, at B5.

50. Statement of Panel Convened to Review the Cases of AIDS in School Aged Children (Sept. 7, 1985). Respondent's Verified Answer, Exhibit E, *District 27*, 502 N.Y.S.2d 325 (No. 14940/85).

51. 502 N.Y.S.2d 325.

52. N.Y. Sanitary Code, N.Y. Comp. Codes R. & Regs. tit. 10, §24.1 (1983) (emphasis added).

53. *District 27*, 502 N.Y.S.2d 325 at 329.

54. New York City Charter, ch. 22 (Health), §556(f); New York City Health Code, §3.01.

55. Respondent's Post-Trial Memorandum of Law at 69, *District 27*, 502 N.Y.S.2d 325 (No. 14940/85); New York City Health Code §49.15(d).

56. N.Y. Public Health Law §225(5)(h) (McKinney 1971).

57. N.Y. Public Health Law §228(2); New York City Charter, ch. 22 (Health), §558(b).

58. N.Y. Sanitary Code, N.Y. Comp. R. & Regs. tit. 10, §24.2 (1983); New York City Health Code, §11.07(a)(2); *see District 27*, 502 N.Y.S.2d at 33-36.

59. *District 27*, 502 N.Y.S.2d at 333.

60. San Antonio Indep. School Dist. v. Rodriguez, 411 U.S. 1, 35 (1973).

61. Brown v. Bd. of Educ., 347 U.S. 483, 493 (1953); Plyler v. Doe, 457 U.S. 202, 223 (1982).

62. *District 27*, 502 N.Y.S.2d at 337.

63. Immunization Practices Advisory Committee, *Recommendations for Protection Against Viral Hepatitis*, 34 MMWR 313 (1985).

64. New York State Assoc. for Retarded Children. v. Carey, 466 F. Supp. 479 (E.D.N.Y. 1978), *modified*, 466 F. Supp. 487 (E.D.N.Y.), *aff'd*, 612 F.2d 644 (2d Cir. 1979).

65. 29 U.S.C. §794.

66. *Id. See* regulations promulgated thereunder at 45 C.F.R. Part 84 (eff. June 3, 1977, rev. Oct. 1, 1985).

67. 107 S. Ct. 1123 (1987); *see also* Thomas v. Atascadero Unified School Dist., No. 886-609AHS (BY) (D.C.D. Cal. Nov. 17, 1986).

68. 107 S. Ct. at 1129.

69. *See, e.g., AIDS: A Growing Threat*, Time, Aug. 12, 1985, at 70.

70. Indiana State Board of Health, Guidelines for Children with AIDS/ARC Attending School (July 1985) [hereinafter Indiana Guidelines].

71. White v. Western School Corp. No. IP-85-1192-C (S.D. Ind. Aug. 16, 1985).

72. 20 U.S.C. §1400, *et seq.* (1982 & Supp. III 1986).

73. 20 U.S.C. §1400(c).

74. Bogart v. White, No. 49192 (Cir. Ct. Ind. Feb. 25, 1986).

75. Ind. Code §16-1-9-7 1983 reads: "Persons having custody of any child infected with a communicable disease shall not permit him to attend school or appear in public."

76. *Bogart*, No. 86-144.

77. New Jersey Commissioners of Health and Education, Admission to School of Children with AIDS/ARC or HTLV-III Antibody (Sept. 3, 1985, rev. Oct. 25, 1985).

78. Board of Educ. v. Cooperman, 209 N.J. Super. 174, 507 A.2d 253 (App. Div, 1986), *rev'd*, No. A–45/46 (N.J. Apr. 15, 1987).

79. N.J. Stat. Ann. §§52:14B-1, *et seq.* (West 1986).

80. N.Y. Public Health Law, §206(1)(j) (McKinney 1971); N.Y. Sanitary Code N.Y. Comp. R. & Regs. tit. 10, §24.2 (1983); *see also* N.Y.C. Health Code §11.07(a)(2).

81. *District 27*, 502 N.Y.S.2d at 339-42.

82. *See* Farnsworth v. Proctor & Gamble, 758 F.2d 1545, 1547 (11th Cir. 1985).

83. Fla. Admin. Code Ann. r. 10D-3.62(1)(a) (1982).

84. N.Y. Comp. R. & Regs. tit. §§10, 24.1-24.2 (1983).

85. N.J. Admin. Code §8:57-1.14 (1986).

86. Colo. Rules and Regs. Pertaining to Communicable Disease Control, Res. 3.

87. *6 AIDS Children to Attend Schools, City Officials Say*, N.Y. Times, Aug. 26, 1986, at B1.

88. *CDC Guidelines*, note 4 above; *see also* Indiana Guidelines, note 70 above.

89. Post-trial brief of Respondent-Intervenor John Doe at 54-60, Respondent's Post Trial Memorandum of Law at 61-64, *In re* District 27 Community School Bd. v. Bd. of Educ., 502 N.Y.S.2d 325 (Sup. Ct. 1986) (No. 14940/85).

90. Statement of Panel Convened to Review the Cases of AIDS in School Aged Children, note 50 above.

91. *6 AIDS Children to Attend Schools, City Officials Say*, note 87 above.

CHAPTER 6

1. *See* Chapter 1 in this volume; Kretchmer, *Can Sex Survive AIDS?* Playboy, Feb. 1986, at 48; Newsweek, Aug. 12, 1985, at 29; Time, Aug. 12, 1985, at 43; *id.*, Oct. 28, 1985, at 50; Van De Perre, *et al.*, *Female Prostitutes: A Risk Group for Infection With Human T-Cell Lymphotropic Virus Type III*, 2 Lancet 524 (1985).

2. Calabrese & Gopalakrishna, *Correspondence: Transmission of HTLV-III Infection From Man to Woman to Man*, 314 New Eng. J. Med. 987 (1986); Fischl, *et al.*, *Evaluation of Heterosexual Partners, Children, and Household Contacts of Adults with AIDS*, 257 J.A.M.A. 640 (1987); *see also* Weiss, *et al.*, *HTLV-III Infection Among Health Care Workers*, 254 J.A.M.A. 2089-92 (1985).

3. *See* J. Decker, Prostitution: Regulation and Control 27-78 (1979) (study of historical evolution of prostitution controls).

4. *Id.* at 38-49.

5. *See* Lynden, *The Oldest Profession Organizes At Last*, MS., Dec. 1973, at 17.

6. Krauthammer, *The Politics of a Plague*, New Republic, Aug. 1, 1983, at 18.

7. *See generally* D. Armstrong & P. Ma, The Acquired Immune Deficiency Syndrome and Infections of Homosexual Men (1983).

8. *See* J. Decker, note 3 above, at 181.

9. *Id.* at 5.

10. The so-called "marginal" prostitute is discussed in *id.* at 6-10.

11. *See id.* at 5.

12. *Update: Acquired Immunodeficiency Syndrome—United States*, 35 MMWR 757, 758 (1986).

13. *Id.*

14. *Id.* at 765; Curran, *The Epidemiology and Prevention of the Acquired Immunodeficiency Syndrome*, 103 Annals Internal Med. 658 (1985).

15. *See, e.g.*, Van De Perre, *et al.*, note 1 above.

16. Pape, Liantand, Thomas, *et al.*, AIDS in Haiti (paper presented at the International Conference on the Acquired Immunodeficiency Syndrome (AIDS), Atlanta, April 17, 1985).

17. *See* Redfield, *et al.*, *Heterosexually Acquired HTLV-III/LAV Disease (AIDS-Related Complex and AIDS): Epidemiologic Evidence for Female-to-Male Transmission*, 254 J.A.M.A. 2094, 2095-96 (1985). *But see* Chapter 16 in this volume.

18. Kretchmer, note 1 above, at 49.

19. Schultz, *et al.*, *Female-to-Male Transmission of HTLV-III*, 255 J.A.M.A. 1703, 1704 (1986) (letter).

20. Wykoff, *Female-to-Male Transmission of HTLV-III*, 255 J.A.M.A. 1703, 1704 (1986) (letter).

21. *Id.*

22. *Id.* A 1987 study suggests that genital ulcers may be an important factor in facilitating heterosexual transmission in Africa. Altman, *U.S. Study Examines Prostitutes and AIDS Virus*, N.Y. Times, Mar. 27, 1987, at A14.

23. Schultz, *et al.*, note 19 above.

24. *Id.*

25. Koch & L'age-Stehr, *Der Heutigestand unseres Wissens*, 82 Deutsches Artzeblatt 2560 (1985).

26. Schultz, *et al.*, note 19 above.

27. *Id.*

28. Altman, note 22 above.

29. J. Decker, note 3 above, at 11-15, 94.

30. *See* Fischl, *et al.*, note 2 above.

31. Decker, note 3 above, at 358; P. Wilson, The Sexual Dilemma: Abortion, Homosexuality, Prostitution and the Criminal Threshold 91 (1971); Newsweek, Aug. 12, 1985, at 29; Newsweek, Jan. 24, 1972, at 47.

32. *See* Fischl, *et al.*, note 2 above, at 644.

33. H. Greenwald, The Elegant Prostitute 223 (rev. ed. 1970); *see also* C. Winick & P. Kinsie, The Lively Commerce: Prostitution in the United States 206-07 (1971) (nine out of ten patrons request oral sex, whereas coitus is a "minority preference"); M. Stein, Lovers, Friends, Slaves . . . The Nine Male Sexual Types: Their Psychosexual Transactions with Call Girls 95 (1974) (83 percent, although the majority also request coitus). The Stein study is particularly noteworthy since it involved actual observation of 1,230 sexual encounters between female prostitutes and male patrons.

34. *See* Lyman, Winkelstein, Ascher & Levy, *Minimal Risk of Transmission of AIDS-Associated Retrovirus Infection by Oral-Genital Contact*, 255 J.A.M.A. 1703 (1986) (letter).

35. COYOTE, Policy on AIDS 3 (1985); Playboy, Sept. 1986, at 12 (letter).

36. M. Stein, note 33 above, at 95 (43 percent). It is doubtful that patrons of streetwalkers are as interested in cunnilingus as patrons of call girls.

37. Altman, *Fact, Theory and Myth on the Spread of AIDS*, N.Y. Times, Feb. 15, 1987, at 1, 32.

38. M. Stein, note 33 above, at 94 (1 percent).

39. *Id.* at 95 (36 percent). It is important to note that Stein's study involved contacts between call girls and patrons, where ongoing relationships between the parties is not uncommon. *Id.* at 89 (51 percent of the men observed had seen the same call girl at least five times within the previous year). On the other hand, my interviews of streetwalkers suggest that their transactions, in which anonymous relationships rarely survive the initial prostitute-patron encounter, involve kissing far less often.

40. Altman, note 37 above.

41. *See* note 2 and accompanying text above.

42. *Prostitutes Make Appeal for AIDS Prevention*, N.Y. Times, Oct. 5, 1986, at 8.

43. *See* J. Decker, note 3 above, at 181.

44. H. Miller, Whores, Streets & Cathouses 159 (rev. ed. 1973).

45. *See* J. Decker, note 3 above, at 213-14.

46. *See id*. at 81.

47. *See id*. at 89-92.

48. *See id*. at 94 (reporting that there may be over 300 million acts of prostitution in the United States annually, with only about 100,000 of those actually the subject of criminal prosecution).

49. *See* notes 76-78 and accompanying text below.

50. *See* J. Decker, note 3 above, at 82-83.

51. *See* Wachter, *The High Cost of Victimless Crime*, 28 Record N.Y. City Bar Assoc. 357, 358-60 (1973).

52. Lasky & Orrick, A Report on Non-Victim Crime in San Francisco: Part II—Sexual Conduct, Gambling, Pornography 20 (June 3, 1971) (S.F. Committee on Crime, 1971).

53. *See* Casper, *Determinate Sentencing and Prison Crowding in Illinois*, 1984 U. Ill. L. Rev. 231; Nardulli, *The Misalignment of Penal Responsibilities and State Prison Crises: Costs, Consequences, and Corrective Actions*, 1984 U. Ill. L. Rev. 365.

54. *See* J. Decker, note 3 above, at 175-76.

55. *See* note 48 above.

56. *See* J. Decker, note 3 above, at 94-95, 98-99, 106-07.

57. *See id*. at 107.

58. 370 U.S. 660, 666 (1962).

59. *Id*.

60. *See, e.g.*, Farber v. Rockford, 407 F.Supp. 529 (N.D. Ill. 1975) (loitering by "known prostitute").

61. *Id*. at 534.

62. *See, e.g.*, Fla. Stat. Ann. §384.02 (1983). Note that this statute only makes it unlawful for a person with venereal disease to have sex with a member of the opposite sex.

63. *See generally* 68 Am. Jur. 2d *Searches and Seizures* §§2, 10, 35, 60 (1973).

64. *See, e.g.*, Schmerber v. California, 384 U.S. 757, 766-72 (1966); Breithaupt v. Abram, 352 U.S. 432 (1957).

65. Winston v. Lee, 470 U.S. 753 (1985).

66. The warrant requirement might be avoided by invocation of the search incident to arrest doctrine. *Schmerber* upheld a warrantless blood test of a person arrested for drunken driving. This move, however, should fail, since the *Schmerber* decision was based in part on the ephemeral nature of the evidence: the driver had to be tested while the alcohol was still in his blood. Unfortunately, HIV infection is permanent. 384 U.S. at 766-72 (1966).

67. *See* J. Decker, note 3 above, at 87.

68. *See* Ala. Code §22-16-18 (1975).

69. *See, e.g.*, Idaho Code Ann. §39-603 (1985).

70. *See, e.g.*, W. Va. Code §§16-4-14 to 16-4-17 (1985).

71. *See, e.g.*, D.C. Code Enc. §22-2703 (1967); *Fulton Judge Offers AIDS Testing Deal for Sex Offenders*, Atlanta Jnl., Mar. 18, 1986; *Miami Testing Prostitutes for AIDS*, 1 AIDS Alert 1, 18 (1986).

72. *See* Bayer, Levine & Wolf, *HIV Antibody Screening: An Ethical Framework for Evaluating Proposed Programs*, 356 J.A.M.A. 1768, 1771 (1986).

73. H.B. 1290 (Colo. 1986) (sponsored by Representatives Erickson and Bath); *see also Bill to be Introduced in Colorado Legislature*, 1 AIDS Policy & Law (BNA), Jan. 14, 1987, at 4.

74. H.B. 5270 (Mich. 1986) (sponsored by Representatives Engler and Honigman).

75. H.B. 279 (Fla. 1986) (sponsored by Representative Lewis). (This bill "died" in the Committee on Appropriations.)

76. *Prostitute with AIDS Put Under Quarantine*, N.Y. Times, Feb. 13, 1987, at B4; *see also Dilemma for Southern Prosecutors: Infect Streets or Prison with AIDS?* N.Y. Times, Jan. 2, 1987, at A12.

77. *Prostitute with AIDS Put Under Quarantine*, note 76 above.

78. Mills, Wofsy & Mills, *The Acquired Immunodeficiency Syndrome: Infection Control and Public Health Law*, 314 New Eng. J. Med. 931, 934 (1986).

79. *See, e.g., In re* Bernardini, No. 86 P 3076 (Cir. Ct. Cook County Ill. 1986) (petition to have male with AIDS disorder severely affecting brain involuntarily committed given his incapacity to care for himself).

80. *See Ten-City Study Set on Prostitutes with HTLV-III*, 1 AIDS Policy & Law (BNA), Jan. 29, 1986, at 4 (study of 2,000 prostitutes to determine if they have AIDS and possible sources thereof); *see also* Playboy, note 35 above; Altman, note 22 above.

81. *See* J. Decker, note 3 above, at 449-68.

CHAPTER 7

1. Institute of Medicine, National Academy of Sciences, Confronting AIDS 110 (1986) [hereinafter *Confronting AIDS*].

2. C. Koop, Surgeon General's Report on Acquired Immune Deficiency Syndrome 5 (1986) [hereinafter *Surgeon General's Report*].

3. *Id*. at 31.

4. J. Jones, *et al.*, Assessment of Behavioral Recommendations made in AIDS Health Education Materials in Nine U.S. Cities 6 (undated CDC draft report) [hereinafter *Assessment of Behavioral Recommendations*].

5. Osborn, *The AIDS Epidemic: Multidisciplinary Trouble*, 314 New Eng. J. Med. 779, 781 (1986).

6. Stoddard, *The AIDS Crisis: What the ACLU Must Do To Guard Against Civil Liberties Abuses*, Civil Liberties, Fall 1985, at 1.

7. *See, e.g.*, N.Y. Times, Oct. 19, 1985, at A1.

8. *See* N.Y. Times, Feb. 22, 1986, at 6; *id*., Oct. 19, 1986, at A30.

9. *AIDS Beliefs Aired*, Phoenix Gazette, Nov. 12, 1985, at 7.

10. *Confronting AIDS*, note 1 above, at 98; *AIDS Overtakes Disease of Heart as No. 2 Worry*, N.Y. Times, Mar. 25, 1987, at B4 (27 percent).

11. *Surgeon General's Report*, note 2 above; *Confronting AIDS*, note 1 above; *see also $15 Million Federal Funds Tagged for States, Communities*, 1 AIDS Policy and Law (BNA), Jan. 29, 1986, at 2.

12. The Surgeon General states that compulsory testing is "unmanageable and cost prohibitive," that "quarantine has no role in the management of AIDS," and that "those who suggest the marking of AIDS carriers with some visible sign have not thought the matter through." *Surgeon General's Report*, note 3 above, at 33-34.

13. *See generally* Tavares & Lopez, *Response of the Gay Community to Acquired Immune Deficiency Syndrome*, in AIDS 106 (1984).

14. Mobilization Against AIDS/Phoenix, Safe Sex! Safe Sex is Fun! Safe Sex is Healthy! (1985) (pamphlet).

15. NIDA Capsule (pamphlet awaiting HHS approval and dissemination by National Institute on Drug Abuse) (reprinted in Seay, *AIDS Opens New Pandora's Box in Professional Drug Community*, 15 Drugs & Drug Abuse Educ. Newsletter 87 (1985)).

16. Califia, *Victims Without A Voice*, High Times, Dec. 1985, at 6.

17. *$15 Million Federal Funds Tagged for States, Communities*, note 11 above, at 2.

18. M. Kreuter, Health Promotion: The Public Health Role in the Community of Free Exchange (1984).

19. E. Rogers & F. Shoemaker, Communication of Innovations: A Cross-Cultural Approach (1971).

20. *See generally* J. Jones, *et al.*, The Nature and Scope of AIDS Health Education in Nine Cities 15 (CDC draft report, 1986) [hereinafter *Nature and Scope of AIDS Health Education*].

21. *AIDS Hotline is Expanding and Moving Site to New York*, N.Y. Times, Nov. 24, 1985, at B5; The National AIDS Hotline is 800-324-AIDS.

22. *See, e.g., Vermont Increases Education Effort on AIDS*, N.Y. Times, Nov. 30, 1986, at 60; *AIDS Week in Connecticut*, N.Y. Times, Nov. 17, 1986, at B4.

23. *Surgeon General's Report*, note 2 above, at 14.

24. *Women and AIDS: Discussing Precautions*, N.Y. Times, Nov. 3, 1986, at C15.

25. *Assessment of Behavior Recommendations*, note 4 above, at 6.

26. *See, e.g., City Schools to Show New Videotape on AIDS*, N.Y. Times, Nov. 1, 1986, at A1.

27. Osborn, note 5 above, at 781.

28. *Confronting AIDS*, note 1 above, at 101.

29. See the discussion of problems in assessing the effectiveness of risk-reduction education included *id.* at 104-05.

30. 34 MMWR 613 (1985).

31. *Study Finds AIDS Worries Affect Sex Habits*, N.Y. Times, Oct. 13, 1985, at B1.

32. L. McKusick, *et al.*, Reactions to the AIDS Epidemic in Four Groups of San Francisco Gay Men 27 (1984) (report prepared by San Francisco Dep't of Public Health) [hereinafter *Reactions of Gay Men*].

33. *Id.* at 29.

34. J. Newmeyer, AIDS and the San Francisco Intravenous Drug User 3 (Sept. 1983) (unpublished Haight-Ashbury Free Medical Clinic report).

35. Ginzburg, *Intravenous Drug Users and AIDS*, Pharm. Chem. Newsletter, Nov.-Dec. 1984, at 7; *see also* Des Jarlais, Friedman & Hopkins, *Risk Reduction for Acquired Immunodeficiency Syndrome Among Intravenous Drug Users*, 103 Annals Internal Med. 755 (1985); Mermor, Des Jarlais, Friedman, Lyden & El-Sadr, *The Epidemic of AIDS and Suggestions for its Control in Drug Abusers*, 1 J. Substance Abuse Treatment 237 (1984).

36. Des Jarlais & Hopkins, *'Free' Needles for Intravenous Drug Users at Risk for AIDS: Current Developments in New York City*, 313 New Eng. J. Med. 1476 (1985) (letter).

37. *Drug Abusers Try to Cut AIDS Risk*, N.Y. Times, Apr. 18, 1985, at B11.

38. *Surgeon General's Report*, note 2 above, at 4.

39. *Confronting AIDS*, note 1 above, at 101.

40. *Surgeon General's Report*, note 2 above, at 31.

41. *Education Allays Fears as New York Group Works Against AIDS*, Center, Mar. 1985, at 4.

42. Health and Public Policy Committee, American College of Physicians, *Position Paper*, 104 Annals of Internal Med. 575 (1986).

43. *Prejudice Against Gays May Keep AIDS Facts From Public, Poll Says*, Arizona Republic, Aug. 27, 1986, at A4.

44. *See* note 22 above.

45. *See Nature and Scope of AIDS Health Education*, note 20 above, at 7.

46. *Toronto's Proactive Approach, Begun in 1983, Uses Network of Medical and Community Groups*, Center, Mar. 1985, at 7.

47. H. McClosky & A. Brill, Dimensions of Tolerance: What Americans Believe About Civil Liberties 199-213 (1983).

48. *See, e.g., United Kingdom Advertisers Protest TV Education Campaign*, 1 AIDS Policy & Law (BNA), Jan. 14, 1987, at 7.

49. *Britain Begins Campaign to Educate Public*, N.Y. Times, Jan. 29, 1987, at B24.

50. 131 Cong. Rec. H7986 (daily ed. Oct. 1, 1985).

51. *See* Bayer, *AIDS and the Gay Community: Between the Specter and the Promise of Medicine*, 52 Soc. Research 581, 589 (1985).

52. Note, *Survey on the Constitutional Right to Privacy in the Context of Homosexual Activity*, 40 U. Miami L. Rev. 521, 524 n.9 (1986).

53. *See Assessment of Behavioral Recommendations*, note 4 above.

54. *City Schools to Show New Videotape on AIDS*, N.Y. Times, Nov. 1, 1986, at A1; *see also* N.Y. Times, Jan. 29, 1987, at B4.

55. 314 New Eng. J. Med. 779 (1986).

56. *More Ads to Reflect AIDS Peril*, N.Y. Times, Jan. 26, 1987, at D9; *Ads That Shatter an Old Taboo*, Time, Feb. 2, 1987, at 63.

57. *Campaigns Around the World*, Time, Feb. 2, 1986, at 63 (Scandinavian TV commercials contain animated sequence in which lower case letter "i" in the word AIDS becomes full size when covered with a prophylactic; broadcast in Italy included "sketches of couples engaged in various intimate acts.").

58. Seay, note 15 above, at 88.

59. Califia, note 16 above, at 6.

60. *Confronting AIDS*, note 1 above, at 105.

61. Califia, note 16 above, at 6.

62. *Confronting AIDS*, note 1 above, at 3. In Arizona, for example, there has been great resistance to the promulgation of materials that are explicit about safe sex for fear of offending the public. Health educators have been told not to use explicit material received from other states.

63. *Confronting AIDS*, note 1 above, at 130.

64. *$15 Million Federal Funds Tagged for States, Communities*, note 11 above. According to the Arizona Public Health Department, the funds available for education have been reduced to $9.2 million for 1986.

65. *Confronting AIDS*, note 1 above, at 112.

66. *Surgeon General's Report*, note 2 above, at 28.

67. *Interview with Dr. Ronald Bayer*, Center, Mar. 1985.

68. *Confronting AIDS*, note 1 above, at 104.

69. CDC, Program Announcement and Notice of Availability of Funds for Fiscal Year 1986, at 18.

70. *Id.* at 20.

71. *Id.* at 19.

72. *Assessment of Behavioral Recommendations*, note 4 above, at 6.

73. *Confronting AIDS*, note 1 above, at 111.

74. *Id.* at 99.

75. *Reactions of Gay Men*, note 32 above, at 29.

76. *Video Review*, Advocate Men, Sept. 1986, at 70.

77. Miller v. California, 413 U.S. 15, 24-25, (1973).

78. *Id.* at 30-34.

79. *Id.* at 26.

80. *See, e.g.,* Perry Educ. Ass'n v. Perry Local Educators' Ass'n, 460 U.S. 37, 46 (1983); Southeastern Promotions, Ltd. v. Conrad, 420 U.S. 546, 558 (1975).

81. *Id.*; Cornelius v. NAACP Legal Def. & Educ. Fund, 105 S.Ct. 3439, 3449 (1985).

82. American Council for the Blind v. Boorstin, 644 F. Supp. 811, 813 (D.D.C. 1986) (quoting Rep. Chalmers Wiley, 131 Cong. Rec. H5932 (July 18, 1985)).

83. *Id.* at 815-16 (applying forum analysis).

84. Board of Educ., Island Trees Free School Dist. No. 26 v. Pico, 457 U.S. 853, 856-57 (1982).

85. *Id.* at 870-76.

86. *Id.* at 867.

87. Bullfrog Films, Inc. v. Wick, 646 F. Supp. 492, 507 (1986).

88. *Id*. at 507-08.

89. Particularly 42 U.S.C. §243(b) and 247(c) as amended (1982).

90. 42 U.S.C. §247(c)-(d).

91. The caselaw suggests that standing could be conferred on parties if they are producers of AIDS literature (a state agency or a private group or individual), or on those at whom the material is aimed. *See Bullfrog Films*, 646 F. Supp. 492 (producers of educational material); *Boorstin*, 644 F. Supp. 811 (program beneficiaries).

92. For a complete discussion, *see* Chapter 4 in this volume; *see also* Note, *The Constitutional Rights of AIDS Carriers*, 99 Harv. L. Rev. 1274 (1986).

93. *See* Burris, *Fear Itself: AIDS, Herpes and Public Health Decisions*, 3 Yale L. & Pol'y Rev. 479, 504-16 (1985); Collier, *Preventing the Spread of AIDS by Restricting Sexual Conduct in Gay Bathhouses: A Constitutional Analysis*, 1985 Golden Gate L. Rev. 301.

94. *See* Burris, note 93 above, at 504-12.

95. Wis. Stat. §143.07(9) (1983).

96. Cal. Health and Safety Code §199.7(a) (West 1985).

97. *Id*. §199.71.

98. Washington State Human Rights Commission, Draft Statement of Policy: AIDS and Employment (1986). In challenging statutes that mandate an act on the part of a state agency, standing will be either conferred through the statute specifically or by implication so that a party harmed by the failure of state agency to act could sue for the enforcement of the statute.

CHAPTER 8

1. Leonard, *Employment Discrimination Against Persons With AIDS*, 10 U. Dayton L. Rev. 681, 689-96 (1985) [hereinafter Leonard, *Employment Discrimination*]; Leonard, *AIDS and Employment Law Revisited*, 14 Hofstra L. Rev. 11, 21 n.52 (1985).

2. Rehabilitation Act of 1973, §504, 29 U.S.C. §794.

3. 29 U.S.C. §§701 *et seq*.

4. 29 U.S.C. §791(b).

5. *See* Smith v. Christian, 763 F.2d 1322 (11th Cir. 1985).

6. 29 U.S.C. §793(a).

7. The Office of Civil Rights in each of the federal departments is involved in the administration of these affirmative action programs. The Office of Federal Contract Compliance Programs (OFCCP) in the Department of Labor has primary responsibility for enforcement of §503.

8. 29 U.S.C. §794.

9. Consolidated Rail Corp. v. Darrone, 465 U.S. 624 (1984).

10. Jones v. Metropolitan Atlanta Rapid Transit Auth., 681 F.2d 1376, 1377 n.1 (11th Cir. 1982), *cert. denied*, 465 U.S. 1099 (1984); Prewitt v. United States Postal Serv., 662 F.2d 292, 302 (5th Cir. 1981); Miener v. Missouri, 673 F.2d 969, 973 (8th Cir.), *cert. denied*, 459 U.S. 909 (1982). Under Executive Order 12250 of 1981, the Department of Justice is authorized to coordinate enforcement of §504 by federal agencies.

11. U.S. Dep't of Transp. v. Paralyzed Veterans of America, 106 S.Ct. 2705 (1986).

12. Leonard, *Employment Discrimination*, note 1 above, at 690-96. This is an area of continuing legislative action, so the statutory compilations by commercial labor law services should be checked for the latest information on laws in particular jurisdictions.

13. *Id*.

14. Delaware Executive Order 81, Jan. 31, 1980, 3 Empl. Prac. Guide (CCH) ¶21,503.

15. *See, e.g.*, New York City (NY) Admin. Code, §§B1-7.0 to 7.1 (Supp. 1985-86). These protections normally extend to employees of the locality or its contractors. Unfortunately, there is no conveniently available cumulation of municipal laws affecting employment rights.

16. 29 U.S.C. §706(7)(B) (1982).

17. 45 C.F.R. §84.3(2)(i) (1986).

18. 45 C.F.R. §84.3(2)(ii) (1986).

19. In a June 20, 1986, memorandum, the Office of Legal Counsel, Department of Justice, ruled that AIDS and disabling symptoms of ARC were "handicaps" under §504. Daily Labor Report (BNA) No. 122, June 25, 1986, at D-1.

20. The Justice Department memorandum of June 20, 1986, disputes this assertion. *Id.*

21. *Id.*

22. Charlotte Mem. Hosp., Complaint No. 04-84-3096 (Office for Civil Rights, Region IV, HHS, Aug. 5, 1986).

23. Thomas v. Atascadero Unified School Dist., No. 886-609AHS(BY)(D.C.D. Cal. Nov. 17, 1986)(Stotler, J.)

24. 107 S. Ct. 1123 (1987).

25. *Id.* at 1129.

26. *Id.* at 1128 n. 7.

27. *Id.* at 1131.

28. *Id.* at 1128-29 & n. 10 (citing with approval 45 C.F.R. §84.3).

29. *Id.* at 1129.

30. *Id* at 1131.

31. *Summary: Recommendations for Preventing Transmission of Infection with Human T-Lymphotropic Virus Type III/Lymphadenopathy-Associated Virus in the Workplace,* 34 MMWR 681 (1985).

32. New York Executive Law §292(21) (McKinney 1982 & Supp. 1987)

33. Wash. Rev. Code §166-22-040.

34. In one such state, Florida, the administrative agency held AIDS to be a covered handicap, relying on *Arline* as persuasive precedent, and noting definitions of handicap in other statutes. *See* Shuttleworth v. Broward County Office of Budget & Management Policy, FCHR No. 85-9624 (Dec. 11, 1985) (published in 1985 Daily Labor Report (BNA) No. 242, Dec. 17, 1985, at E-1). The complainant also filed a federal suit alleging violation of §504 of the Rehabilitation Act. The suit survived a motion to dismiss, 41 Fair Emp. Prac. Cases (BNA) 406 (S.D.Fla. 1986), but was settled prior to trial in December 1986. *See Settlement Reached in Landmark Bias Suit,* 1 AIDS Policy & Law (BNA), Dec. 17, 1986, at 1.

35. The California statute specifies loss of particular physical capacities, and was construed by an administrative law judge not to cover AIDS in a decision which is under appeal. Department of Fair Employment and Housing v. Raytheon Company, No. FEP 83-84 L1-031p (Aug. 4, 1986) (Lopez, ALJ). This ruling was reversed on appeal. *See* note 36 below; *Panel Protects AIDS Victims Against Job Discrimination,* N.Y. Times, Feb. 2, 1987, at B16.

36. Racine Educ. Ass'n v. Racine Unified School Dist., ERD Case No. 8650279 (Equal Rights Division, Apr. 30, 1986) (published in 1986 Daily Labor Report (BNA) No. 98, May 21, 1986, at E-1) (policy excluding persons with AIDS from the workplace unlawful under Wisconsin handicap discrimination law, as well as under Wisconsin sexual orientation discrimination law due to disparate impact on gay male employees); People v. 49 West 12 Tenants Corp., No. 43604/83 (Sup. Ct. Oct. 17, 1983) (unpublished decision holding AIDS is handicap in context of public accommodations discrimination complaint under New York Human Rights Law); Department of Fair Employment & Housing v. Raytheon Co., No. FEP83-84 L1-031p L-33676 87-04 (Calif. Fair Emp. & Housing Comm., Feb. 5, 1987) (published in 1987 Daily Labor Report (BNA) No. 29, Feb. 13, 1987, at E-1 (policy excluding persons with AIDS from workplace unlawful under California handicap discrimination law).

37. National Gay Rights Advocates, AIDS and Handicap Discrimination: A Survey of the 50 States and the District of Columbia (September 1986) (this publication will be updated from time to time as new developments occur); *see also States AIDS Discrimination Laws Reject Justice Department's Stand,* N.Y. Times, Sept. 17, 1986, at A20; *Most States Will Pursue Complaints,* 1 AIDS Policy & Law (BNA), Sept. 24, 1986, at 5.

38. The Justice Department's June 20, 1986, memorandum may diminish the helpfulness of federal agency offices of civil rights in combating such discrimination, although its reasoning is repudiated by the Supreme Court in *Arline*.

39. *See* note 36 above.

40. *See* 29 U.S.C. §794 (emphasis added).

41. *See* Southeastern Community College v. Davis, 442 U.S. 397, 410-11 (1979).

42. Leonard, *Employment Discrimination*, note 1 above, at 694-95.

43. 45 C.F.R. §84.12(a) (1986).

44. School Bd. v. Arline, 107 S. Ct. 1123, 1131 n. 19 (1987).

45. State Division of Human Rights v. Xerox Corporation, 65 N.Y.2d 213, 491 N.Y.S.2d 106, 480 N.E.2d 695 (1985).

46. This is particularly relevant given the insurance industry's desire to screen out "AIDS risks." Group policies covering most workplaces do not involve such individual screening. If an employee loses coverage under a group policy and then tries to qualify as an individual, the employee will be identified as an "AIDS risk" and denied private insurance coverage, unless he can afford to take advantage of "conversion" privileges that may exist at the time of discharge.

47. Rucker v. Higher Educ. Aids Bd., 669 F.2d 1179 (7th Cir. 1982). The court emphasized that Title VII omits race from the list of factors which might be considered a bona fide occupational qualification.

48. Diaz v. Pan American World Airways, Inc., 442 F.2d 385 (5th Cir.), *cert. denied*, 404 U.S. 950 (1971), *on remand*, 346 F. Supp. 1301 (D. Fla. 1972). Even though sex may be a bona fide occupational qualification under Title VII, this exception to the general rule against sex discrimination must be construed narrowly. *Accord Sprogis v. United Air Lines, Inc.*, 444 F.2d 1194 (7th Cir.), *cert. denied*, 404 U.S. 991 (1971) (customer preference not a valid defense of company rule against employment of married female flight attendants).

49. *See* 45 C.F.R. §§84.13-14 (1986).

50. To date: California, Wisconsin, Massachusetts, and arguably, Florida.

51. Such testing by public employers may raise constitutional issues beyond the scope of this chapter. Employers should check whether state or local agencies in their area have adopted regulations restricting testing. The District of Columbia and New York City human rights agencies have reportedly construed those cities' handicap discrimination laws to forbid testing, according to attorneys who have dealt with those agencies.

52. *Guidelines on AIDS in the Workplace*, 34 MMWR 681 (1985).

53. Courts have begun to recognize a civil privacy right under the common law, based on an expansive interpretation of §652B of the American Law Institute's Second Restatement of Torts, which suggests that certain unwarranted intrusions on personal autonomy would create compensable injuries. For example, in Cordle v. General Hugh Mercer Corp., 325 S.E.2d 111 (W. Va. Sup.Ct. App. 1984), a common law privacy right was held to justify an employee's refusal to submit to a polygraph examination. The employer's justification for requiring a test would be the central issue in such litigation. As to the emotional impact of learning of a positive test result, there have been some reports of suicides in connection with positive HIV results communicated in unsupportive circumstances.

54. Philipson & Wood, AIDS, Testing and Privacy: An Analysis of Case Histories (1987) (available from BALIF AIDS Legal Referral Panel, 1663 Mission St., Suite 400, San Francisco, CA 94103).

55. 29 U.S.C. §§1001 *et seq.*

56. *See id.* §1003.

57. *See id.* §§1002(1), (3).

58. 29 U.S.C. §1140.

59. *See* 29 U.S.C. §1132.

60. *See* Folz v. Marriott Corp., 594 F. Supp. 1007 (W.D. Mo. 1984) (employee with multiple sclerosis); Kross v. Western Electric Co., 701 F.2d 1238 (7th Cir. 1983) (§510 claim involving

prevention of attaining pension benefits); Zipf v. American Tel. & Tel. Co., 799 F.2d 889 (3d Cir. 1986) (§510 claim of discharged employee with rheumatoid arthritis).

61. 29 U.S.C. §§1161-1168. This requirement becomes effective for each employer's medical benefits plan in the first plan year beginning on or after July 1, 1986.

62. *In re* John Doe, No. SF-24774 (Cal. Unempl. Ins. App. Bd., Sept. 13, 1985). The employee had sought to extend an unpaid leave, but was forced to resign when additional leave was denied by the employer.

63. 50 Fed.Reg. 5573; 53 U.S.L.W 2414 (1985).

64. Elkouri & Elkouri, How Arbitration Works 650-707 (4th ed., 1985); Koven & Smith, Just Cause: The Seven Tests (1985).

65. Koven & Smith, note 64 above, at 72-138.

66. Leonard, *Employment Discrimination*, note 1 above, at 688 n. 32.

67. Some of these have been published in 3 Empl. Prac. Guide (CCH), at ¶¶20,950A, 20,950B. A California state law banning AIDS-related discrimination (AB 3667) was vetoed by Governor George Deukmejian on July 27, 1986. who also vetoed a second enactment banning discrimination against persons with a wide range of ills not casually communicable (AB 3407) on September 30, 1986. *See California Governor Vetoes Bill Defining AIDS As Physical Handicap*, 1 AIDS Policy & Law (BNA), July 30, 1986, at 1; *Deukmejian Vetoes Handicap Law as "Unnecessary" and "Inappropriate,"* 1 AIDS Policy & Law (BNA), Oct. 8, 1986, at 1.

68. Cal. Health & Safety Code, §§199.20-199.40 (West. Supp. 1986); Fla. Stat. §381.606, 3 Emp. Prac. Guide (CCH) ¶21,880 (May 30, 1985); Mass. Gen. Laws Ch. 11, §70F (July 15, 1986); Wis. Stat. §103.15, 3 Emp. Prac. Guide (CCH) ¶29,130 (July 30, 1985).

69. 1986 Daily Labor Report (BNA) No. 48, Mar. 12, 1986, at A-7.

70. *California Offers Lessons on Handling AIDS, Attorney Says*, 1 AIDS Policy and Law (BNA), Aug. 27, 1986, at 8; Curiale, *State Tort, Wrongful Discharge and Privacy Claims*, in Communicable Diseases in the Workplace ch. 6 (Practising Law Institute 1986).

71. Cronan v. New England Tel. Co., 41 Fair Empl. Prac. Cas. (BNA) 1273 (Mass. Super. Ct. Aug. 15, 1986) (Rouse, J.). The court also upheld a claim under the state's handicap discrimination law.

72. Labor Management Relations Act of 1947, as amended, 29 U.S.C. §§141 *et seq.*

73. 29 U.S.C. §157.

74. §8(a)(1), 29 U.S.C. §158(a)(1).

75. 370 U.S. 9 (1962).

76. *See, e.g.*, Quality CATV, 278 N.L.R.B. No. 156, 121 Lab. Rel. Ref. Man. (BNA) 1297 (1986). Some relatively recent cases suggest that "reasonableness" of the employees' fears may be relevant under some circumstances. *See* Johnson-Stewart-Johnson Mining Co., 263 N.L.R.B. 123 (1982).

77. Labor Management Relations Act of 1947, §502, 29 U.S.C. §143.

78. Gateway Coal Co. v. United Mine Workers of America, 414 U.S. 368, 385-87 (1974).

79. 85 Lab. Arb. (BNA) 1185, 86-1 Arb. (CCH) ¶8202 (Arb. Gallagher, 1985).

80. 29 C.F.R. §1977.12 (1986).

81. Bernales v. City and County of San Francisco, 1985 Daily Labor Report (BNA) No. 184, Sept. 23, 1985, at A-6.

82. Of related interest is a recent arbitration decision holding that a prison was required by its collective bargaining agreement to reveal to union-represented guards the names of prisoners who had tested positive for HIV. The decision is being appealed in a state court. Delaware Dep't of Correction v. Delaware Public Employees, Council 81, AFSCME, No. 8462 (Del. Ct. Chancery) (reported in 1 AIDS Law & Policy (BNA), May 21, 1986, at 8). The arbitration award is published in 86 Lab. Arb. (BNA) 849 (Gill, Arb., 1986).

83. *See, e.g.*, Prokesch, *Levi's Broad AIDS Program*, N.Y. Times, Mar. 12, 1987, at D1.

CHAPTER 9

1. M. Rothstein, Medical Screening of Workers 9 (1984).

2. *AIDS Antibody Screening Test*, 57 Analytical Chemistry 773A (1985).

3. 32 MMWR 101 (1983).

4. Petricciani, *Licensed Tests for Antibody to Human T-Lymphotropic Virus Type III*, 103 Annals Internal Med. 726, 727 (1985).

5. 34 MMWR 477 (1985).

6. For a technical discussion of how the ELISA test works, see Council on Scientific Affairs, American Medical Association, *Status Report on the Acquired Immunodeficiency Syndrome— Human T-Cell Lymphotropic Virus Type III Testing*, 254 J.A.M.A. 1342 (1985).

7. Levine & Bayer, *Screening Blood: Public Health and Medical Uncertainty*, Hastings Center Rep., Aug. 1985, at 8, 9.

8. *Id.*; Council on Scientific Affairs, note 6 above, at 1343; *see Puzzling Western Blot Results Worry Nation's Blood Bankers*, Med. World News, Dec. 22, 1986, at 69.

9. *AIDS Antibody Screening Test*, note 2 above, at 774A.

10. *See Acquired Immune Deficiency Syndrome (AIDS) Update—United States*, 32 MMWR 309 (1983) (AIDS diagnosis requires underlying immunodeficiency and presence of unexplained opportunistic infection or Kaposi's sarcoma in patient under sixty years of age); *AIDS Antibody Screening Test*, note 2 above ("Because the ELISA screening test detects only antibodies to the AIDS virus, it is not a test for AIDS virus and is not intended to diagnose AIDS").

11. Institute of Medicine, National Academy of Sciences, Confronting AIDS 91 (1986) [hereinafter *Confronting AIDS*]; *see also* Goedert, Biggar, Weiss, *et al.*, *Three Year Incidence of AIDS in Five Cohorts of HTLV-III Infected Risk Group Members*, 231 Science 992 (1986).

12. Landesman, Ginzburg & Weiss, *Special Report-The AIDS Epidemic*, 312 New Eng. J. Med. 521, 522 (1985).

13. *Confronting AIDS*, note 11 above, at 45; Curran, *et al.*, *The Epidemiology of AIDS: Current Status and Future Prospects*, 229 Science 1352, 1354 (1985); *see also* Marlink, *et al.*, 315 New Eng. J. Med. 1549 (1987) (letter) (low sensitivity of ELISA testing in early HIV infection).

14. Leeson, *HTLV-III Antibody Tests and Health Education*, 1 Lancet 911 (1986).

15. *See, e.g.*, Biggar, 315 New Eng. J. Med. 457 (1986) (letter) (possible nonspecific associations between malaria and HTLVIIILAV); Hunter, 2 Lancet 397 (1985) (letter) (persons with HLADR and HLADQW may test positive on ELISA; follow-up with Western Blot eliminates problem); Merianon, 1 Lancet 678 (1986) (letter) (persons with thalassemia may test positive on ELISA); Mortimer, Parry & Mortimer, *Which Anti-HTLV-III/LAV Assays for Screening and Confirmatory Testing?* 2 Lancet 873 (1985) (persons with malaria may test positive on Western Blot); Mendenhal, *et al.*, 313 New Eng. J. Med. 921 (1986) (letter) (persons with hepatitis may test positive on ELISA).

16. For a general discussion of the biostatistical concepts in test assessment, see R. Galen & S. Gambino, Beyond Normality: The Predictive Value and Efficiency of Medical Diagnosis (1975); Statland, Winkel, Burke, *et al.*, *Quantitative Approaches Used in Evaluating Laboratory Measurements and Other Clinical Data*, in Clinical Diagnosis and Management By Laboratory Methods (J. Henry ed. 1979).

17. *See generally* Council on Scientific Affairs, note 6 above (analyzing ELISA tests).

18. *See, e.g.*, *AIDS and Testing for AIDS*, 255 J.A.M.A. 743 (1986) (letters); *AIDS Blood Test: Qualified Success*, Science News, Aug. 10, 1985, at 84; Council on Scientific Affairs, note 6 above; Mortimer, Parry & Mortimer, note 15 above; Petricciani, note 4 above.

19. *AIDS and Testing for AIDS*, note 18 above; Council on Scientific Affairs, note 6 above; Petricciani, note 4 above.

20. Curran, *et al.*, note 13 above, at 1353; Hardy, Allen, Morgan & Curran, *The Incidence Rate of Acquired Immunodeficiency Syndrome in Selected Populations*, 253 J.A.M.A. 215 (1985).

21. *Confronting AIDS*, note 11 above, at 69; Curran, *et al.*, note 13 above.

22. *Confronting AIDS*, note 11 above, at 310-11.

23. *Id*.

24. It has been estimated that only fifty of 3.5 million blood recipients each year will become infected with HIV as a result of the transfusion. *Id*. at 54.

25. *See New Viral Antigen Assays Spot Early HIV Infection*, Med. World News, Dec. 22, 1986, at 69.

26. Bayer & Oppenheimer, *AIDS in the Workplace: The Ethical Ramifications*, Business & Health, Jan.-Feb. 1986, at 30; Levine & Bayer, note 7 above.

27. *See, e.g.*, Blaine, Iuculano & Clifford, Insurance Issues Related to AIDS (1986); Health Insurance Association of America, The Acquired Immunodeficiency Syndrome & HTLV-III Antibody Testing (Draft Position Statement, 1985); Kristof, *More Insurers Screen Applicants for AIDS*, N.Y. Times, Dec. 22, 1985, at 5.

28. *See, e.g.*, Companies Taking Low-Key Approach to AIDS in Workplace, Survey Finds, 4 Empl. Rel. Weekly (BNA) 291 (1986); Lewin, *AIDS and Job Discrimination*, N.Y. Times, Apr. 15, 1986, at 30. But at least one private employer has been screening workers for HIV since spring 1986. *Newspaper Gives AIDS Tests*, N.Y. Times, Oct. 31, 1986, at A17.

29. *See, e.g.*, McCormack, *AIDS-Phobia Creates Discrimination in the Workplace*, Houston Post, Feb. 7, 1986, at 18E; Roth, *Many Firms Fire AIDS Victims Citing Health Risk to Co-Workers*, Wall St. J., Aug. 12, 1985, at 19.

30. *Guidelines on AIDS in the Workplace*, 34 MMWR 682 (1985).

31. *Id*. (emphasis in original).

32. Altman, *U.S. Urges Blood Test for Millions With High Risk of AIDS Infection*, N.Y. Times, Mar. 14, 1986, at 1.

33. *See* Bayer & Levine, *Risks of Federal Screening*, N.Y. Times, Jan. 12, 1987, at A21; Bayer, Levine & Wolf, *HIV Antibody Screening: An Ethical Framework for Evaluating Proposed Programs*, 256 J.A.M.A. 1768 (1986). The testing of foreign service employees has been challenged. Local 1812, American Fed. of Gov. Employees v. United States Dep't of State, No. 87-0121 (D.D.C., filed Jan. 20, 1987) (reported in 2 AIDS Policy & Law (BNA), Jan. 28, 1987, at 1).

34. Wis. Stat. Ann. §103.15(2)(a), (2)(b), (3) (West Supp. 1985).

35. Cal. Health & Safety Code §§199.21(f), 199.38 (West Supp. 1987).

36. Fla. Stat. §381.606(5) (1985).

37. 1986 Mass. Legis. Serv. ch. 241 (West) (to be codified at Mass. Gen. Laws ch. 111, §70f).

38. Los Angeles Code art. 5.8, §§45.80-45.93 (1985).

39. San Francisco Police Code §§3801-3816 (1985).

40. Austin Ord. No. 861211-V (Dec. 11, 1986).

41. Phila. Exec. Order No. 4-86 (Apr. 15, 1986).

42. 107 S. Ct. 1123, 1128 n.7, 1129 (1987).

43. 29 C.F.R. §1613.706 (1986); 41 C.F.R. §60-741.6 (1986); 45 C.F.R. §84.14 (1986).

44. 45 C.F.R. §84.14(c) (1986).

45. *Id*. §84.13(a).

46. 29 C.F.R. §§1613.705-.706 (1986).

47. 41 C.F.R. §60-741.6 (1986).

48. *See, e.g.*, Cecere, *AIDS Presents Many Legal Issues for Workplace*, Legal Times, Dec. 2, 1985; Leonard, *AIDS and Employment Law Revisited*, 14 Hofstra L. Rev. 11 (1985); Leonard, *Employment Discrimination Against Persons with AIDS*, 10 U. Dayton L. Rev. 681 (1985).

49. Cal. Admin. Code §§7293.5-7294.2 (1985).

50. *See, e.g.*, E.E. Black, Ltd. v. Donovan, 497 F. Supp. 1088 (D. Hawaii 1980).

51. *See, e.g.*, Bentivegna v. United States, 694 F. 2d 619 (9th Cir. 1982); Bucyrus-Erie Co. v. Department of Industry, Labor & Human Relations, 90 Wis.2d 408, 280 N.W.2d 142 (1979).

52. *See Donovan*, 497 F.Supp. 1088; *In re* State Div. of Human Rights, 118 A.D. 2d 3, 504 N.Y.S. 2d 92 (App. Div. 1986); *see also* Cal. Lab. Code §7293.8(d) (West Supp. 1986).

53. *See* M. Rothstein, note 1 above, at 121-29.

54. Wis. Stat. Ann. §111.36 (West Supp. 1985).

55. D.C. Human Rights Act §1-2512 (1986).

56. N.Y. (City) Admin. Code §§8-107-108.1 (1986).

57. Philadelphia Code §9-1103a(1) (1985).

58. In jurisdictions without sexual-orientation discrimination laws it would not be illegal to refuse to employ a homosexual because of animosity toward homosexuals. It may violate a handicap discrimination law, however, to refuse to employ a homosexual because of a belief that this person is more likely to contract AIDS.

59. *See* 35 MMWR 757, 758 (1986).

60. Testing only former drug users might violate the 1978 amendment to the Rehabilitation Act, which protects current and former drug abusers whose current abuse does not constitute a direct threat to the safety or property of others. 29 U.S.C. §706(7)(B) (1982).

61. 548 S.W. 2d 743 (Tex. App.), *cert. denied*, 434 U.S. 962 (1977).

62. Eddy v. Brown, 715 P.2d 74 (Ok. 1986).

63. *Id.* at 78 (emphasis in original).

64. Saxton v. Vanzant, No. 86-CIV-59 (Fayette Cty., Ohio Ct. C.P., filed Mar. 7, 1986) (reported in 1 AIDS Policy & Law (BNA), Apr. 23, 1986, at 3).

65. Cronan v. New England Tel. Co., 41 Fair Emp. Prac. Cas. (BNA) 1273 (Mass. Super. Ct. Aug. 15, 1986).

66. *See* Council on Scientific Affairs, note 6 above, at 1344.

67. *See* Bayer, Levine & Wolf, note 33 above.

68. *See generally* M. Rothstein, note 1 above, at 191-207.

CHAPTER 10

1. Substantial protection is given tenants who apply for or who are evicted from federally assisted housing. *See* R. Schoshinski, American Law of Landlord and Tenant ch. 13 (1980). But sharp curtailment of federal housing subsidies and a shortage of federally assisted housing in most cities limit public housing opportunities for persons with AIDS.

2. *See id.*; Cunningham, *The New Implied and Statutory Warranty of Habitability in Residential Leases: From Contract to Status*, 16 Urb. L. Ann. 3 (1979); Glendon, *The Transformation of American Landlord-Tenant Law*, 23 B.C.L. Rev. 503, 539-40 (1982); Rabin, *The Revolution in Residential Landlord Tenant Law: Causes and Consequences*, 69 Cornell L. Rev. 517 (1984).

3. Glendon, note 2 above, at 539-40.

4. This section is based on Salzberg & Zibelman, *Good Cause Eviction*, 21 Willamette L.J. 61 (1985).

5. The leading case is Javins v. First Nat'l Realty Corp., 428 F.2d 1070 (D.C. Cir.), *cert. denied*, 400 U.S. 925 (1970).

6. Salzberg & Zibelman, note 4 above, at 71.

7. *E.g.*, N.Y. Unconsol. Laws ch. 249, §5 (Lawyers Coop 1984). Several municipalities in some states, particularly California and New Jersey, have adopted rent control ordinances.

8. *E.g.*, Fla. Stat. Ann. §723.061 (West Supp. 1986) (upheld in Palm Beach Mobile Homes v. Strong, 300 So. 2d 881 (Fla. 1974)).

9. D.C. Code Ann. §45-1561 (1981); N.J. Stat. Ann. §2A:18-61.1 (West Supp. 1986) (upheld in Stamboulas v. McKee, 134 N.J. Super. 567, 342 A.2d 529 (App. Div. 1975)).

10. *See* Uniform Residential Landlord & Tenant Act (URLTA) §1.302, 73 U.L.A. 443 (1985) (imposing "an obligation of good faith" in the performance of "[e]very duty under this Act"). This provision was adapted from §1-203 of the Uniform Commercial Code. *Id.* comment. Thirteen states have adopted the act. 73 U.L.A. at 427. For criticism of the Act and a suggestion that it include a "good cause" eviction limitation, see Blumberg & Robbins, *Beyond URLTA: A Program for Achieving Real Tenant Goals*, 11 Harv. C.R.-C.L. L. Rev. 1, 39-41 (1976).

11. *E.g.*, D.C. Code Ann. §45-1561(f)(4) (1981) (eviction for purposes of rehabilitation).

12. *See generally* Note, Reed v. King: *Fraudulent Nondisclosure of a Multiple Murder in a Real Estate Transaction*, 45 U. Pitt. L. Rev. 877 (1984).

13. Reed v. King, 145 Cal. App. 3d 261, 193 Cal. Rptr. 130 (1983).

14. 42 U.S.C. §3604 (1982).

15. *Id.* at §3604(a) ("[unlawful] to . . . otherwise make [housing] unavailable"); *see* Betsy v. Turtle Creek Assocs., 736 F.2d 983 (7th Cir. 1984) (application to eviction assumed).

16. *See In re* Cox, 3 Cal. 3d 205, 212, 474 P.2d 992, 995, 90 Cal. Rptr. 24, 27 (1970) (state Unruh Act prohibits all forms of arbitrary action by business enterprises).

17. Los Angeles, West Hollywood, and Berkeley, California, as well as Austin, Texas also have ordinances banning AIDS-based discrimination in housing. 1 AIDS Policy & Law (BNA), Dec. 31, 1986, at 1; *id.*, Mar. 26, 1986, at 6. Local ordinances provide first for the mediation of complaints by the agency charged with administering the law. The ordinances also authorize actions for injunctive relief. Court actions to remedy violations of the ordinance may be necessary because administrative agencies do not always enforce the law effectively.

18. 42 U.S.C. §3604. *But see* S. 2040, 99th Cong., 2d Sess. §6 (1986) (proposing amendment to prohibit discrimination against the handicapped).

19. *E.g.*, Wis. Stat. Ann. §101.22(2)(f) (West Supp. 1985).

20. *States' AIDS Discrimination Laws Reject Justice Department's Stand*, N.Y. Times, Sept. 17, 1986, at A20; *see also* letter from David E. Clarenbach, Speaker Pro Tem of the Wisconsin Assembly to the author (Mar. 19, 1986).

21. Anderson v. City of Olivette, 518 S.W.2d 34 (Mo. 1975).

22. *E.g.*, State v. Hutchinson, 624 P.2d 1116 (Utah 1981).

23. Inganamort v. Borough of Fort Lee, 62 N.J. 521, 303 A.2d 298 (1973).

24. For discussion of home rule, see D. Mandelker, D. Netsch & P. Salsich, State and Local Government in a Federal System 101-30 (2d ed. 1983).

25. *See* Birkenfeld v. City of Berkeley, 19 Cal. 3d 129, 550 P.2d 1001, 130 Cal. Rptr. 465 (1976) (upholding authority to adopt local rent control ordinance). California is a leading example of a home rule state in which the charter is only a limitation on the constitutional home rule power.

26. *See* Midwest Employers Council v. City of Omaha, 177 Neb. 877, 131 N.W.2d 609 (1964); Marshall v. Kansas City, 355 S.W.2d 877 (Mo. 1962); *see also* Hutchinson Human Relations Comm'n v. Midland Credit Management, 213 Kan. 308, 517 P.2d 158 (1973) (municipal human relations ordinance authorized by constitutional home rule provision). *See generally*, Note, *Municipal Civil Rights Legislation—Is the Power Conferred by the Grant of Home Rule?* 53 Minn. L. Rev. 342 (1968).

27. *Cf.* City of Miami Beach v. Forte Towers, Inc., 305 So. 2d 764 (Fla. 1975) (rent control ordinance authorized by home-rule statute granting municipalities authority to "exercise any power for municipal purposes, except when expressly prohibited by law").

28. *See generally*, Note, *Conflicts Between State Statutes and Local Ordinances*, 72 Harv. L. Rev. 737 (1959).

29. J.F. Cavanaugh & Co. v. City of Detroit, 126 Mich. App. 672, 337 N.W.2d 605 (1983); *see also* National Asphalt Pavement Ass'n v. Prince George's County, 292 Md. 75, 437 A.2d 651 (1981) (local employment discrimination ordinance may cover businesses with fewer than fifteen employees although state law limited to businesses with more than fifteen employees).

30. Dunlap, *For Homeless With AIDS, A New Home*, N.Y. Times, Jan. 5, 1987, at B1.

31. Hospices also have been established for persons with AIDS who are terminally ill. They are usually permitted under zoning ordinances in appropriate zoning districts or as an accessory use in residential districts.

32. D. Mandelker, Land Use Law §6.49 (1982). A special use is called a "special exception," in most state zoning laws, and also is referred to as a "conditional use." The zoning board of adjustment is the agency usually delegated the authority to approve special uses in most state zoning laws.

33. G. Gunther, Constitutional Law, 671-75, 889-90 (10th ed. 1980).

34. 416 U.S. 1 (1974).

35. *E.g.*, Rademan v. City & County of Denver, 186 Colo. 225, 526 P.2d 1325 (1974).

36. 27 Cal. 3d 123, 610 P.2d 436, 164 Cal. Rptr. 539, (1980).

37. *E.g.*, Charter Township of Delta v. Dinolfo, 419 Mich. 253, 351 N.W.2d 831 (1984); State v. Baker, 81 N.J. 99, 405 A.2d 368 (1979).

38. The Supreme Court affirmed *Belle Terre* in City of Cleburne v. Cleburne Living Center, 105 S. Ct. 3249, 3254 n.8 (1985).

39. *E.g.*, State *ex rel.* Ellis v. Liddle, 520 S.W. 2d 644 (Mo. Ct. App. 1975) (group home for juvenile delinquents); Group House of Port Washington, Inc. v. Board of Zoning & Appeals, 45 N.Y.2d 266, 380 N.E.2d 207, 408 N.Y.S.2d 377 (1978) (allowing group home for disturbed children but deferring consideration of group homes for adults such as the mentally disturbed); *see also* D. Mandelker, note 32 above, §5.5.

40. *E.g.*, Penobscot Area Hous. Dev. Corp. v. City of Brewer, 434 A.2d 14 (Me. 1981); Macon Ass'n for Retarded Children v. Macon-Bibb County Planning & Zoning Comm'n, 252 Ga. 484, 314 S.E.2d 218 (Ga. 1984), *appeal dismissed for want of a substantial federal question*, 105 S. Ct. 57 (1985).

41. *E.g.*, Awahnee Hills School v. County of Madera, 158 Cal. App.3d 348, 204 Cal. Rptr. 628 (1984) (opinion withdrawn).

42. 105 S. Ct. 3249 (1985). For discussion of *Cleburne* see Mandelker, *Group Homes: The Supreme Court Revives the Equal Protection Clause in Land Use Cases*, in 1986 Institute on Planning, Zoning, and Eminent Domain ch. 3.

43. The permit also was denied because the group home would be overcrowded and would be located in a floodplain. The Court held these objections also applied to similar group homes allowed in the zoning district without a special-use permit.

44. One problem in interpreting *Cleburne* is that two of the six Justices who signed the majority opinion also wrote a concurring opinion. The concurring opinion adopted a somewhat different standard of judicial review of equal protection cases, so there is no majority of the Court indicating what judicial review standard is applicable in such cases. Three Justices joined in an opinion concurring in part and dissenting in part. They would have invalidated the special permit denial and the special permit requirement by applying the middle tier standard of equal protection review.

45. *E.g.*, Cal. Welf. & Inst. Code §§5115-5116 (West 1984) (designated group homes to be considered residential use for zoning purposes); N.J. Stat. Ann. §30:4C-26(d) (West 1981) (prohibiting discrimination against homes for foster children). For a table describing a number of these statutes, see *Homes for the Developmentally Disabled*, Am. Plan. Ass'n, Zoning News, Jan. 1986, at 1, 2. For discussion of the state legislation and the text of a model law, see Hopperton, *A State Legislation Strategy for Ending Exclusionary Zoning of Community Homes*, 19 Urb. L. Ann. 47 (1980).

46. *See* Jaffe, *Coping with Cleburne*, 38 Land Use L. & Zoning Dig., No. 2, at 5 (1986).

47. Group homes protected from zoning discrimination in state legislation usually are licensed by a state agency. State licensing of group homes for persons with AIDS also should be considered.

CHAPTER 11

1. *See, e.g.*, Cal. Civ. Proc. Code §340 (Deering 1973).

2. *See, e.g.*, Ill. Rev. Stat. ch. 83 §15 (1966).

3. Prosser & Keeton, The Law of Torts §30, at 165-68 (1984).

4. *See, e.g.*, Wager v. Pro, 603 F.2d 1005, 1008 (D.C. Cir. 1979); Mettes v. Quinn, 89 Ill. App. 3d 77, 411 N.E.2d 549 (1980).

5. Note, *Survey on the Constitutional Right to Privacy in the Context of Homosexual Activity*, 40 U. Miami L. Rev. 521 (1986).

6. *Id.*

7. *See, e.g.*, Alice D. v. William M., 113 Misc. 2d 940, 450 N.Y.S.2d 350 (Civ. Ct. 1982).

8. De Vall v. Strunk, 96 S.W.2d 245, 247 (Tex. Civ. App. 1936).

9. Barbara A. v. John G., 145 Cal. App. 3d 369, 193 Cal. Rptr. 422 (1983).

10. Kathleen R. v. Robert B., 150 Cal. App. 3d 992, 198 Cal. Rptr. 273 (1984)

11. State v. Bateman, 113 Ariz. 107, 547 P.2d 6 (1976) (en banc).

12. Kathleen R. v. Robert B., 150 Cal. App. 3d 992.

13. *Id.* at 994.

14. *Id.* at 996-97 n.3.

15. Restatement (Second) of Torts §4.

16. Kathleen R. v. Robert B., 150 Cal. App. 3d at 994, 996.

17. Prosser & Keeton, note 3 above, §54, at 361-65.

18. Restatement (Second) of Torts §463.

19. *See, e.g.*, Li v. Yellow Cab, 13 Cal. 3d 804, 532 P.2d 1226, 119 Cal. Rptr. 858 (1975) (en banc) (abrogating doctrine of contributory negligence and adopting scheme of comparative negligence).

20. Prosser & Keeton, note 3 above, §68, at 480.

21. Restatement (Second) of Torts §§496B-C.

22. Prosser & Keeton, note 3 above, §68, at 482.

23. *Id.* at 481.

24. *See* Annotation, 91 A.L.R.3d 24 (1979).

25. Restatement (Second) of Torts §§13, 18.

26. State v. Lankford, 29 Del. (6 Boyce) 594, 594, 102 A. 63, 64 (1917).

27. Note, *Liability in Tort for the Sexual Transmission of Disease: Genital Herpes and the Law*, 70 Cornell L. Rev. 101, 125 (1984).

28. Restatement (Second) of Torts §525.

29. Barbara A. v. John G., 145 Cal. App. 3d 369, 193 Cal. Rptr. 422 (1983).

30. Prosser & Keeton, note 3 above, §106, at 737-38.

31. *Id.* at 738.

32. Note, *Kathleen K. v. Robert B.: A Cause of Action for Genital Herpes Transmission*, 34 Case West. Reserve L. Rev. 488, 522 (1984).

33. *See, e.g.*, Ala. Code §22-16-17 (1977) (misdemeanor); Colo. Rev. Stat. §§25-4-401(2), 25-4-407 (1982) (misdemeanor); Del. Code Ann., tit. 16 §§384.01, 03 (1973) (misdemeanor); Idaho Code §39-601, 607 (1977) (misdemeanor); Nev. Rev. Stat. §§441.220, 441.290 (1981) (misdemeanor); N.Y. Pub. Health Law §2307 (McKinney 1977) (misdemeanor); Okla. Stat. Ann. tit. 63, §1-519 (1984) (felony); Utah Code Ann. §26-6-5 (Supp. 1983) (misdemeanor).

34. *See, e.g.*, Panther v. McKnight, 125 Okla. 134, 256 P. 916 (1926) (court recognized limited private right of action for money damages for conduct in violation of criminal statute proscribing transmission of venereal disease).

35. *See, e.g.*, Azure v. City of Billings, 182 Mont. 234, 240, 596 P.2d 460, 464 (1979); Bayne v. Todd Shipyards Corp., 88 Wash. 2d 917, 918, 568 P.2d 771, 772 (1977).

36. *See, e.g.,* Gill v. Whiteside - Hemby Drug Co., 197 Ark. 425, 431, 122 S.W.2d 597, 601 (1938) (violation of state law merely evidence of negligence).

37. *See, e.g.*, Nev. Rev. Stat. §441.050 (1981); ("or any other disease which can be sexually transmitted"); Tenn. Code Ann. §68-10-101 (1983) ("other venereal diseases"); Okla. Stat. Ann. tit. 63, §1-517 (West 1984) ("any other disease which may be transmitted from any person to another by sexual intercourse and found and declared by medical science or accredited school of medicine to be infectious or contagious").

38. Kathleen K. v. Robert B., 150 Cal. App. 3d 992, 997 n.3 (1984).

39. *See, e.g.*, Cal. Health and Safety Code, §3353 (West 1979).

40. *See, e.g.*, H.B. 1685 (Hawaii) (1-16-86) (includes AIDS among infectious and communicable diseases); S.B.N. 825 (Maine) (2-28-86) (classifies AIDS as a dangerous commu-

nicable disease); H.B.N. 1922 (Washington) (1-24-86) (classifies AIDS as communicable or contagious disease).

41. *Update: Acquired Immunodeficiency Syndrome—United States*, 35 MMWR 757, 758 (1986).

42. Annotation, 24 A.L.R.4th 508, §4[b] (1983).

43. Comment, *Strict Liability for Blood Derivative Manufacturers: Statutory Shield Incompatible with Public Health Responsibility*, 28 St. Louis U. L.J. 443 (1984).

44. Prosser & Keeton, note 3 above, §98.

45. Cunningham v. MacNeal Memorial Hospital, 47 Ill. 2d 443, 266 N.E.2d 897 (1970).

46. *See. e.g.*, Community Blood Bank Inc. v. Russell, 196 So. 2d 115 (Fla. 1967).

47. *See, e.g.*, Hoder v. Sayet, 196 So. 2d 205 (Fla. App. 1967); Jackson v. Muhlenberg Hospital, 53 N.J. 138, 249 A.2d 65 (1969); Samuels v. Health & Hospital Corp., 432 F. Supp. 1283 (S.D.N.Y. 1977); Villareal v. Santa Rosa Medical Center, 443 S.W. 2d 622 (Tex. Civ. App. 1969).

48. 31 MMWR 652, 664 (1982).

49. Office of Biologics, National Center for Drugs and Biologics, Food and Drug Administration, Recommendations to Decrease the Risk of Transmitting Acquired Immune Deficiency Syndrome (AIDS) from Plasma Donors (1983).

50. *See, e.g.*, Cal. Health & Safety Code §1603.5 (West 1979); Ga. Code Ann. §31-24-4 (1985); Ill. Ann. Stat. Ch. 111 1/2 §620-4 (West Supp. 1986).

51. 31 MMWR 104 (1982).

52. Roberts, *Treatment of Opportunistic Infections in Patients with Acquired Immune Deficiency Syndrome (AIDS)*, in The Acquired Immune Deficiency Syndrome and Infections of Homosexual Men 314-15 (P. Ma & D. Armstrong eds. 1984).

53. *See, e.g.*, Chester v. United States, 403 F. Supp. 458 (W.D.Pa. 1975) (physician's negligence in failure to order cancer tests permitted metastasis and death); Trapp v. Metz, 28 N.Y.2d. 913, 323 N.Y.S.2d. 166, 271 N.E.2d. 697 (1971) (negligent diagnosis caused two-year delay in surgery for cancer).

54. *See, e.g.*, Kaplan v. Haines, 96 N.J. Super 242, 232 A.2d 840 (1967) (alleged erroneous diagnosis of spinal problem resulted in unnecessary operation); Willard v. Hutson, 234 Ore. 148, 378 P.2d. 966 (1963) (en banc) (misdiagnosis caused erroneous treatment of child known to be suffering from hemophilia).

55. The seeming inevitability of death from AIDS might, however, be a factor in a "wrongful death" action brought by a deceased patient's survivors.

56. *See, e.g.*, MacMahon v. Nelson, 568 P.2d 90 (Colo. 1977) (emotional distress of cancer victim actionable upon learning that removal of growth had been delayed for eight months due to misdiagnosis).

57. *See* Kraus v. Spielberg, 37 Misc. 2d 29, 236 N.Y.S.2d 143 (1962).

58. *See generally AIDS Anxiety in the "Worried Well,"* in Psychiatric Implications of Acquired Immune Deficiency Syndrome 49-60 (S. Nichols and D. Ostrow eds., 1984).

59. Beadling v. Sirotta, 176 A.2d 546 (N.J. 1961).

60. *See, e.g.*, Dowling v. Mutual Life Ins. Co., 168 So. 2d 107 (La. App. 1964) (liability for failure to notify plaintiff that he had tuberculosis); Hoover v. Williamson, 236 Md. 250, 203 A.2d 861 (1964) (failure to notify patient that he had silicosis).

61. James v. United States, 483 F. Supp. 581 (N.D. Cal. 1980).

The tort law is also concerned with overzealous or unauthorized medical treatment as a form of malpractice. The requirement of informed consent to medical treatment is premised on a patient's right to exercise control over her own body. The patient's reliance on the doctor's expertise creates an obligation on the part of the doctor to disclose relevant information to a patient faced with a decision to accept or reject treatment.

This duty could be particularly important on the issue of HIV antibody testing. A positive test may entail serious emotional, social, and economic damage. A patient cannot reasonably judge whether to submit to an antibody test without understanding the nature of the test, the significance of its results, and the possible effects of a record of a positive test. A physician who does not obtain the informed consent of her patient before administering an antibody test may be liable for damages which cause some kind of injury to the patient.

CHAPTER 12

1. *AIDS: A Time Bomb at Hospitals' Door*, 60 Hospitals 54, 60 (1986); *Attitudes That Shape the Fight Against AIDS: Even Among Doctors, An Epidemic of Fear*, N.Y. Times, June 2, 1985, at 6E; *Labor Letter: A Special News Report on People and Their Jobs in Offices, Fields and Factories*, Wall St. J., Dec. 17, 1985, at 1 (reducing AIDS anxiety among hospital staff by training session); *AIDS Risk Troubles MDs, Dr. Volberding Reports*, 28 Amer. Med. News, Oct. 18, 1985, at 3; *AIDS 'Unknowns' Have Paramedics Fearing On-the-Job Infection Risk*, 1 AIDS/Alert, March, 1986, at 61; Boodman, *As AIDS Spreads, So Does Discrimination*, Wash. Post Nat'l Weekly, Dec. 8, 1986, at 10 (nurses in New Orleans).

2. *See Treatment Refusal Legalities 'Muddied'*, 28 Amer. Med. News, Oct. 4, 1985, at 42; *Tips on Technology: AIDS Precautions*, 18 M.L.O. 11 (1986) (hospital pathologist); Flaherty, *A Legal Emergency Brewing Over AIDS*, Nat'l L.J., July 9, 1984, at 1, 45; *Citing Fears of AIDS Transmission, MD Stops Performing Artificial Insemination*, 28 Amer. Med. News, Nov. 8, 1985, at 19; Weiss, *et al.*, *HTLV-III Infection Among Health Care Workers: Association With Needle-Stick Injuries*, 254 J.A.M.A. 2089 (1985); *AIDS Risk to Health Workers Minimized*, 28 Amer. Med. News, Dec. 6, 1985 at 2.

No evidence exists that caring for AIDS and other HIV infected patients imposes any particular risk. *See Summary: Recommendations for Preventing Transmission of Infection With HTLV-III/LAV in the Workplace*, 254 J.A.M.A. 3023 (1985); Advisory Committee on Infections Within Hospitals, Management of HTLV-III/LAV Infection in the Hospital 10-15 (Jan. 1986).

3. Law Group Notes, Nov. 1983, at 4 (gay patient at NYU Dental Clinic); *AIDS and the Law*, 69 A.B.A. L.J. 1014 (1983).

4. The cities with the most AIDS cases are New York (8,681), San Francisco (2,912), Los Angeles (2,387), Houston (938), and Miami (857). *New York City AIDS Deaths Were Highest in 1986*, 30 Amer. Med. News, Jan 16, 1987, at 41.

5. *See* Volberding & Abrams, *Clinical Care and Research in AIDS*, 15 Hastings Center Report, Special Supp., Aug. 1985, at 16.

6. Flaherty, note 2 above, at 44; *Surgeon Won't Operate on Victims of AIDS*, N.Y. Times, Mar. 13, 1987, at A21.

7. Volberding & Abrams, note 5 above.

8. *Id.* If a physician reluctantly treats a patient with AIDS, the care may be of questionable quality. However, this issue is beyond the scope of this chapter.

9. Davis v. Weiskopf, 108 Ill. App. 3d 505, 439 N.E.2d 60 (1982); Lyons v. Grether, 239 S.E.2d 103 (Va. 1977); Childs v. Weis, 440 S.W.2d 104 (Tex. Civ. App. 1969). The Hippocratic Oath assumes a preexisting relationship between patient and physician. Agnew v. Parks, 172 Cal. App. 2d 756, 343 P.2d 118, 123 (1959); *see also*, Berg & Hirsch, *The Physician's Duty to Treat*, 11 Legal Aspects of Med. Prac. 4 (1983); Annot., 17 A.L.R.4th 132 (1982).

10. American Medical Association, Code of Ethics, §5. This passage was cited with approval in Hiser v. Randolph, 617 P.2d 774, 776 (Ariz. App. 1980); *see also Childs*, 440 S.W.2d 104; Agnew v. Parks, 343 P.2d 118, 123 (Cal. 1959). *See generally*, Note *Emergency Care: Physician Should be Placed Under an Affirmative Duty to Render Essential Medical Care in Emergency Circumstances*, 7 U.C. Davis L. Rev. 246 (1974).

11. Berg & Hirsch, note 11 above, at 4.

12. Lyons v. Grether, 239 S.E.2d 103 (Va. 1977); Osbourne v. Frazor, 425 S.W.2d 768 (Tenn. App. 1968).

13. Hurley v. Eddingfield, 59 N.E. 1058 (Ind. 1901).

14. Childer v. Frye, 158 S.E. 744, 746 (N.C. 1931) (refusal to treat injured man who had been drinking).

15. The term health maintenance organization is used here to refer to prepaid medical services that are: (1) created by independent groups, (2) organized by individual physicians (group practice), or (3) established by local medical associations. All three types of organization provide comprehensive health care to patients/members who contract in advance with the HMO for their health care needs. J. Ludlam, *Health Maintenance Organizations: Do They Really Work?* 10 Forum 405 (1974).

16. *Lyons*, 239 S.E.2d 103 (patient made appointment for treatment of vaginal infection but was ejected from waiting room because she would not remove her seeing eye dog).

17. Davis v. Weiskopf, 108 Ill. App. 3d 505, 439 N.E.2d 60 (1982).

18. Buckroyd v. Bunten, 237 N.W.2d 808 (Iowa 1976); *see also* Oliver v. Brock, 342 So. 2d 1 (Ala. 1977); Rainer v. Grossman, 31 Cal. App. 3d 539 (1973).

19. *See generally*, Note, *Good Samaritans and Liability for Medical Malpractice*, 64 Colum. L. Rev. 1301 (1964).

20. Note, note 10 above, at 247.

21. Cities with local ordinances prohibiting discrimination based on AIDS include Berkeley, Cal., 1 AIDS Policy & Law (BNA), Mar. 26, 1986, at 6, Los Angeles, Los Angeles Code art. §5.8 §45.80 (1985), San Francisco, San Francisco Police Code §3801 (1985), West Hollywood, Cal., West Hollywood Mun. Code, Ch. 2, art. IV §4270 (1985), and Philadelphia, Pa, Executive Order No. 4-86 (Apr. 15, 1986).

22. Minnesota's governor issued an executive order prohibiting AIDS-based discrimination. *Governor Prohibits State from AIDS Discrimination*, 30 Amer. Med. News, Jan. 9, 1987, at 39. Ten states—Arizona, California, Connecticut, Maine, Massachusetts, Minnesota, New Jersey, North Dakota, South Dakota, and Wisconsin prohibit insurance companies from asking questions about one's antibody status. *Insurance Companies are Charged with Discrimination in 11 States*, 1 AIDS Alert 223 (1986).

23. These laws generally cover discrimination in employment, although many cover discrimination in other areas, such as housing and public services, too. *See* Leonard, *Employment Discrimination Against Persons With AIDS*, 10 U. Dayton L. Rev. 681, 690 (1985).

24. *Most States Will Pursue Complaints*, 1 AIDS Policy & Law (BNA), Sept. 24, 1986, at 5; *see also* Leonard, note 23 above, at 692; Parry, *AIDS as a Handicapping Condition—Part II*, 10 Mental & Physical Disability L. Rep. 2, 3-4 (1986).

25. Parry, note 24, above, at 4. Generally, the offices of private physicians and dentists are not considered public accommodations. Rice v. Rinaldo, 119 N.E.2d 657 (Ohio App. 1951). *But cf.* Lyons v. Grether, 239 S.E.2d 103, 106 (Va. 1977). Note also that the refusal to provide professional services due to race has been viewed in some states as professional misconduct. N.Y. Educ. Law §6509 (McKinney 1985).

26. Washington State Human Rights Commission, Statement of Policy: AIDS and Public Accommodation 2, (draft 1986) [hereinafter *Washington State Human Rights Policy*].

27. "It is the policy of the City and County of San Francisco to eliminate discrimination based on the fact that a person has AIDS or any medical signs or symptoms related thereto." San Francisco Police Code §3801 (1985); *see also Prohibition Against Discrimination Based on a Person Suffering From the Medical Condition AIDS, Or any Medical Signs or Symptoms Related Thereto, Or any Perception that a Person is Suffering From the Medical Condition AIDS Whether Real or Imaginary*, Los Angeles Code art. 5.8, §45.80 (1985). Other states prohibit discrimination based on sexual orientation in particular circumstances. Still other states interpret laws not mentioning sexual orientation to cover such discrimination. But note that twenty-four states and the District of Columbia have sodomy statutes criminalizing consensual homosexual activity. Note, *Survey on the Constitutional Right to Privacy in the Context of Homosexuality*, 40 U. Miami L. Rev. 521, 524 n.9 (1986).

28. Wis. Stat. Ann. §§66.395, 66.4325, 101.22 *et seq.*, 111.31-.32, 111.36, 111.70, 942.04 (West Supp. 1983-84). Michigan has a law prohibiting discrimination in health care facilities, Mich. Comp. Laws Ann. §333.20201 (West Supp. 1986).

29. *See, e.g.,* D.C. Code Encycl. §§6-2201 *et seq.* (West Supp. 1978-79).

30. *But see Washington State Human Rights Policy*, note 26 above §VI (c) (discrimination based on sexual orientation allowed where "AIDS issue" not "primary focus" of such discrimination).

31. Norton v. Hamilton, 89 S.E.2d 809, 812 (Ga. 1955).

32. Vann v. Harden, 47 S.E.2d 314 (Va. 1948).

33. Ricks v. Budge, 64 P.2d 208 (Utah 1937).

34. Buttersworth v. Swint, 186 S.E.2d 770 (Ga. App. 1936).

35. Hiser v. Randolph, 617 P.2d 774, 778 (Ariz. App. 1980).

36. *See* Volberding & Abrams, note 5 above, at 17; Cameron, *Acquired Immunodeficiency Syndrome: Review of Epidemiology*, 79 J. Okla. St. Med. Ass'n 55, 57 (1986).

37. *See AIDS: A Time Bomb at Hospitals' Door*, note 1 above, at 57.

38. 29 U.S.C. 651 *et seq.*

39. *See, e.g.,* Bernales v. City and County of San Francisco, 1985 Daily Labor Report (BNA) No. 184, Sept. 23, 1985, at A-6 (city hospital did not violate statutory rights of nurses by ordering them to attend persons with AIDS without wearing gowns, gloves, and masks pursuant to Centers for Disease Control guidelines).

40. *AIDS: A Time Bomb at Hospitals' Door*, note 1 above, at 57.

41. Hardy, *et al., The Economic Impact of the First 10,000 Cases of Acquired Immunodeficiency Syndrome in the United States*, 255 J.A.M.A. 209 (1986).

42. *Cost of AIDS Worrying Hospitals*, N.Y. Times, Jan. 1, 1986, at A18 (national average cost per day of AIDS patients is $830, nearly double daily average cost for other patients); Seage, *et al., Medical Costs of AIDS in Massachusetts*, 256 J.A.M.A. 3107 (1986); Scitovsky, *Medical Care Costs of Patients with AIDS in San Francisco*, 256 J.A.M.A. 3103 (1986).

43. *AIDS Costs Battering Hospitals*, 28 Amer. Med. News, Nov. 15, 1985, at 2, 27:

> Public hospitals, the traditional 'safety net' for AIDS patients, could be forced to close their doors unless the government offers financial support.... Long lengths of stay, high treatment costs, and a large number of uncollectible debts make AIDS victims particularly expensive patients....
>
> It is clear that the current payment system is counter-productive.... Hospitals will either have to reduce the level of service provided to all patients to fund AIDS patient care, or transfer AIDS patients into the already overburdened governmental facilities.
>
> The economic burden also could be eased by broadening Medicare coverage to AIDS patients....
>
> Reform of the diagnosis-related groups (DRG) payment system is essential.... Hospitals now receive too little money for the AIDS cases because the DRG categories ... are designed for relatively healthy people with short term lengths of stay. *Id.*

44. *U.S. Must Deal With AIDS as Public Policy*, 29 Amer. Med. News, Feb. 7, 1986, at 22.

45. *AIDS: A Time Bomb at Hospitals' Door*, note 1 above, at 55-56.

46. Fabian v. Matzko, 344 A.2d 569 (Pa. Super. 1975); Le Juene Road Hosp. v. Watson, 171 So. 2d 202 (Dist. Ct. App. Fla. 1965);

47. Doe v. Bellin Mem. Hosp., 479 F.2d 756 (7th Cir. 1973); Stanturf v. Sipes, 224 F. Supp. 883 (W.D. Mo. 1963);

48. Guerrero v. Copper Queen Hosp., 537 P.2d 1329 (Ariz. 1975); Wilmington Gen. Hosp. v. Manlove, 174 A.2d 135 (Del. 1961);

49. *See, e.g.,* Cal. Health & Safety Code §1317 (West 1979).

50. Harper v. Baptist Med. Center, 341 So. 2d 133 (Ala. 1976). Private hospitals have, in the past, refused to admit patients with certain highly contagious diseases. *See e.g.,* Birmingham

Baptist Hosp. v. Crews, 157 So. 224 (Ala. 1934) (refusal under hospital policy to admit patient with diptheria).

51. *Washington State Human Rights Policy*, note 26 above (hospitals included in list of public accommodations); San Francisco Police Code §3801 (1985) (covers hospitals).

52. *See, e.g.*, Los Angeles Code art 5.8, §45-80 (1985).

53. I.R.C. §501(c)(3) (1982).

54. Rev. Rul. 69-545, 1969-2 C.B. 117; *id.* 56-185, 1956-1 C.B. 202. Two subsequent revenue rulings concluded that activities reasonably classified as contrary to established federal policy could not be designated charitable organizations under §501(c)(3). Rev. Rul. 71-447, 1976-2 C.B. 230; *id.* 75-231, 1975-1 C.B. 158. While these rulings pertained to hospitals that discriminated on the basis of race, an analogy to AIDS may be made.

55. *Cf.* Eastern Ky. Welfare Rights Org. v. Simon, 426 U.S. 26 (1976) (denying standing to organization challenging validity of revenue ruling granting tax exempt status to nonprofit hospital that denied all but emergency care to indigents).

56. Williams v. Hospital Auth., 168 S.E.2d 336, 337 (Ct. App. Ga. 1969).

57. The Centers for Disease Control has issued specific guidelines for health care providers who come in contact with persons with AIDS. If these guidelines are followed, the risk of transmission of HIV is negligible. *Acquired Immunodeficiency Syndrome (AIDS): Precautions for Health-Care Workers and Allied Professionals*, 32 MMWR 450 (1985); *see also, Human T-Lymphotropic Virus Type III/Lymphadenopathy-Associated Virus: Agent Summary*, 256 J.A.M.A. 1857 (1986).

58. *See generally*, Annotation 21 A.L.R.2d 910 (1950).

59. Bergman v. City of Los Angeles, C497793 (Los Angeles Co. Super. Ct.) (cited in Flaherty, note 2 above, at 45).

60. Advocate, Oct. 1, 1985, at 20.

61. Hollander v. Smith & Smith, 76 A.2d 697, 700 (N.J. Super. 1950).

62. *See, e.g.*, Kan. Stat. Ann. §§44-1002 (1986) (defining public accommodation as "any person . . . who caters or offers his goods, facilities, and accommodations to the public" and including public transportation as covered accommodation).

63. *See, e.g.*, N.Y. Gen. Mun. Law §122 (McKinney 1986) (misdemeanor for an ambulance service supported in whole or in part by public monies or managed or controlled by a public authority to refuse to take a person to or from the hospital).

64. *Nursing Care is Closed to AIDS Victims*, N.Y. Times, Feb. 1, 1987, Section 11 (Connecticut Weekly), at 1; *Nursing Homes Turning Away AIDS Victims*, Houston Post, July 29, 1984, at A20; *Incentives Encourage Nursing Homes to Open Doors to AIDS Patients*, 2 AIDS/ Alert, Jan., 1987, at 6.

65. Le Juene Road Hosp. v. Watson, 171 So. 2d 202, at 204 (Dist. Ct. App. Fla. 1965).

66. *Funerals for AIDS Victims*, N.Y. Times, Feb. 13, 1987, at B1 (seventy-six of New York City's five hundred funeral homes acceptable to AIDS organization); *The 'But They Seemed Like Such Nice Undertakers' Award*, Advocate, Dec. 24, 1985, at 45 (Philadelphia funeral home refused to handle the remains of deceased AIDS patient and city's Director of Disease Control claimed it responded legally); *AIDS: A Growing Threat*, Time, Aug. 12, 1985, at 45 (funeral home directors in St. Louis and New York have refused to embalm the remains of persons with AIDS).

67. *Acquired Immunodeficiency Syndrome (AIDS): Precautions for Health-Care Workers and Allied Professionals*, note 57 above.

68. *Funerals for AIDS Victims*, note 66 above, at B4.

69. *But cf.*, Scott v. Eversole Mortuary, 522 F.2d 1110 (9th Cir. 1975). A private mortuary refused to provide funeral services or sell caskets to persons because they were Native Americans. The appellate court found a violation of 42 U.S.C. §§1981-1982 which prohibit racial discrimination in making contracts and selling property even in the absence of government involvement. *Id.* at 1113.

70. *See* note 62 above and accompanying text.

71. N.Y. Times, Jan. 15, 1987, at B2; *see also, City Panel May Review AIDS Bias Cases*, 30 Amer. Med. News, Feb. 6, 1987, at 43.

72. Holland v. Metalious, 198 A.2d 654, 656 (N.H. 1964) (decent burial); People v. Bloomington Cemetery Ass'n, 187 N.E. 455 (Ill. 1933) (neighborhood custom); Kitchen v. Wilkinson, 26 Pa. Super. 75, 80-81 (1904).

73. The most common example is the Roman Catholic Church's prohibition on burying suicides in "hallowed ground." *See* Terry v. Elmwood Cemetery, 307 F. Supp. 369 (N.D. Ala. 1969) (public cemetery); Spencer v. Flint Memorial Park Association, 4 Mich. App. 157, 144 N.W.2d 622 (1966) (nonprofit corporation with a restrictive covenant); Erickson v. Sunset Memorial Park Association, 108 N.W.2d 434 (Minn. 1961) (covenant in deed to lot in public cemetery); In the Matter of George Washington Memorial Park Cemetery Association, 52 N.J. Super. 519, 145 A.2d 665 (1958) (nonprofit corporation with a restrictive covenant).

74. *Terry*, 307 F. Supp. at 371 (citing 42 U.S.C. §1982 requiring that blacks and other nonwhites be extended equal rights to purchase property); *Erickson*, 108 N.W.2d at 436-37; *Spencer*, 4 Mich. App. 157, 144 N.W.2d at 628-29.

75. 14 Am. Jur. 2d *Cemeteries* §31; *Bloomington Cemetery Ass'n*, 187 N.E. at 457.

76. *See, e.g., Holland* 198 A.2d at 656. *See generally*, Annot., 54 A.L.R.3d 1037 (1973).

77. *See, e.g., Washington State Human Rights Policy*, note 26 above.

CHAPTER 13

1. A fourth major type, liability insurance, also plays a role in the AIDS crisis. Pharmaceutical companies may be cautious in developing treatments for AIDS out of fear that administration of experimental regimens could lead to liability claims by the subjects. Since this area has not been a focus of the public debate on AIDS and insurance, it will not be discussed in this chapter.

2. *See, e.g.*, Conn. Gen. Stat. §38-61 (1986) (listing proscribed unfair trade practices); *id.* §38-68 (providing for hearings on practices not specifically proscribed).

3. By 1984, twenty-five jurisdictions had legislation addressed to insurance discrimination based upon specific physical disabilities. *See* Congressional Research Service, State Statutes Prohibiting Discrimination in Insurance on the Basis of Handicapping Conditions (1984); *see, e.g.*, Conn. Gen. Stat. §38-61 (defining as unfair insurance practice refusal of coverage or charging of different premiums to the blind, physically disabled, or mentally retarded except where based on sound actuarial principles or related to actual or reasonable anticipated experience); *id.* §38-174k (extending coverage by mandating home health care coverage in hospital or medical expense insurance policies); *id.* §38-262d (requiring extensions of coverage, at group insurance rates, to members of health insurance groups who become ineligible for continued participation in plan). Such short term extensions of group coverage at relatively low premiums are particularly important for persons with AIDS, and will become broadly available to employees at companies with twenty or more employees as a result of recent amendments to the Internal Revenue Code, 26 U.S.C. §162(i). Pub. Law 99-272, 100 Stat. 223 (1986).

4. N.Y. Ins. Law §§2403-2404 (McKinney 1985); *see also* N.Y. Comp. Codes R. & Regs. tit. 11, §217.1 (prohibiting sex discrimination).

5. Breen v. Cunard Lines S.S. Co., 33 N.Y.2d 508 (1974).

6. Halpin v. Prudential Ins. Co., 48 N.Y.2d 906 (1979); Hubbell v. Trans World Life Ins. Co., 50 N.Y.2d 899 (1980); Dano v. Royal Globe Ins. Co., 59 N.Y.2d 827 (1983).

7. K. Abraham, Distributing Risk 71-74 (1986).

8. Committee on Risk Classification, American Academy of Actuaries, Statement: Risk Classification and AIDS (1986).

9. The $28,000 estimate comes from a study of San Francisco, whose model treatment program emphasizes less expensive, out-patient care. *See* Scitovsky, Cline & Less, Medical Care Costs of AIDS Patients Treated in San Francisco (paper presented at the Annual Meeting of the American Public Health Association, Nov. 19, 1985). More recent studies have suggested that San Francisco patients incur costs of hospitalization more in the range of $60,000 to $75,000,

still about half of the $147,000 per patient which was projected by the Centers for Disease Control in 1985. *Cost of AIDS Care is Half What was Projected, Economist Reports*, N.Y. Times, June 8, 1986, at 30 (reporting study by Anne Scitovsky, Palo Alto Medical Foundation). In June 1986 the Public Health Service, abandoning the earlier cdc estimate of $147,000 in costs, estimated annual costs of $46,000 per year per patient by 1991. Although this was a substantially lower estimate than the cdc's, which the insurance industry continues to quote, it is still high relative to the Scitovsky surveys. *See generally* Fox, *The Cost of AIDS From Conjecture to Research*, 2 AIDS & Pub. Pol'y J. 25 (Winter, 1987).

10. *Indiana Blues Studying Cuts in AIDS Cover*, Bus. Ins., Feb. 24, 1986, at 4.

11. *Id.*

12. N.Y. Ins. Law §§3217(a)(4)-(a)(5).

13. N.J. Dep't of Insurance, Bulletin No. 85-3.

14. Gallo, Salahuddin, Popovic, *et al.*, *Frequent Detection and Isolation of Cytopathic Retroviruses from Patients with AIDS or Risk of AIDS*, 224 Science 500 (1984).

15. American Council of Life Insurance, Health Insurance Association of America, White Paper: The Acquired Immunodeficiency Syndrome & HTLV-III Antibody Testing 3 (1986) [hereinafter White Paper].

16. *Id.* at 4.

17. The differential between seropositive and seronegative people diminishes greatly with age. The figures used by the insurance industry for purposes of debate are those for thirty year olds. The ability to offer insurance merely by increasing the premiums would increase significantly for seropositive fifty-five year olds. It is also important to remember that the aids mortality projections used by the insurance companies are based upon small-sample studies of what may be atypical populations with an unusually high number of risk factors.

18. While the General Reassurance Company may have indeed received these high death claims, it may also be misleading to compare them to the overall average. The gay men who have died of aids have tended to be young men from major metropolitan areas, who may typically be insured for higher amounts than, for example, rural people who may have bought their insurance a number of years ago.

19. Cal. Health & Safety Code §199.20 *et seq.* (Deering 1986); District of Columbia Prohibition of Discrimination in the Provision of Insurance Act of 1986, D.C. Law 6-132 (effective Aug. 7, 1986); 1986 Maine Laws 711; Wis. Stat. Ann. §631.90. (West Supp. 1986).

By the terms of the Wisconsin statute, the antibody test could be used for purposes of individual life, accident, and health insurance policies when the state epidemiologist certified the test as medically significant and sufficiently reliable for detecting the presence of the antibody, and the insurance commissioner found and designated by rule that the test is sufficiently reliable for use in underwriting of individual policies. The state epidemiologist made the necessary certification in July 1986. Davis, Serological Tests for the Presence of Antibody to Human T-Lymphotropic Virus Type III: Information Pursuant to the Purposes of Wisconsin Statute S.631.90 Regarding Their Use in Underwriting Individual Life, Accident and Health Insurance Policies (July 28, 1986). In late 1986 the Wisconsin insurance commissioner formulated a rule permitting the use of antibody tests, which must be approved by the state legislature. The rule is expected to come before the Assembly Health Committee in March, 1987. Telephone interview with Mary Haffenbredl, Legislative Assistant to Representative John Robinson (Feb. 18, 1987); *see also* 1 AIDS Policy & Law, Dec. 3, 1986, at 1.

20. *Hearings on AIDS Bills*, N. Y. Native, Mar. 31, 1986, at 13.

21. New York: Cornet v. Bankers Sec. Life Ins. Co.; California: Miller v. North American Life and Casualty; New Jersey: Ehlert v. Aid Ass'n for Lutherans, No. 83246 (N.J. Dep't of Insurance); Ohio: complaint filed anonymously against Minnesota Life Insurance Company.

22. Interview with Michael Zinicola, Zinicola & Fischman, Columbus, Ohio, attorney for complainant (May 8, 1986).

23. Letter from Department of Insurance to Lambda Legal Defense and Education Fund, Inc., attorneys for complainant (Nov. 13, 1986).

24. Interview with Edward Reeves, attorney for complainant (Nov. 21, 1986).

25. The first complaint to the New York Insurance Department was brought by Lambda Legal Defense and Education Fund, Inc. Information regarding the second pending complaint is from Mark Senak, of Gay Men's Health Crisis, Inc., who represents the complainant.

26. The department's position against the test has been taken in informal letters to insurers of which the writer has become aware.

27. N. Y. Native, Aug. 11, 1986, at 6.

28. P. Hiam (Massachusetts Commissioner of Insurance), Policy Statement Regarding Application Form Questions Inquiring About Acquired Immune Deficiency Syndrome (AIDS) and AIDS-Related Complex (ARC) (Dec. 12, 1986).

29. N. J. Dep't of Insurance, Bulletin No. 86-1 (Apr. 28, 1986); Wash. Admin. Code §284-90 (1986).

30. Lambda Legal Defense and Education Fund, Inc., AIDS Update, Dec. 1986, at 5.

31. 132 Cong. Rec. S10104-12 (daily ed. Aug. 1, 1986).

32. *Id.* H4873-75 (daily ed. July 24, 1986).

33. *Gay Leaders, Insurers Meet on D.C. AIDS Law*, Washington Post, Aug. 23, 1986, at B-1.

34. American Council of Life Ins. v. District of Columbia, 645 F.Supp. 84 (D.D.C. 1986).

35. 1 AIDS Policy & Law (BNA), Dec. 17, 1986, at 7.

36. Blood and other laboratory tests have rarely been used in the past for smaller life and disability policies. The antibody tests may be likened to tests for genetic markers for predisposition to alcoholism, heart disease, and the like, of which the insurance industry has not availed itself. Actuarially, unjustified conclusions may be drawn from HIV testing. Seropositive thirty year olds may present extraordinarily high risks compared to their seronegative peers, but the relative risks of seropositive and seronegative fifty-five year olds are much less different. An insurance company should be able to write insurance for the seropositive fifty-five year old, but it is unlikely to do so.

37. *See, e.g.*, N.Y. Ins. Law §2606 (McKinney 1985).

38. N.Y. Ins. Law §3225; Mass. Gen. L. Anno. ch. 175, §108C (West 1986); Ill. Anno. Stat. ch. 73, ¶968f (West 1986) (Ill. Ins. Code §356f); Me. Rev. Stat. Ann. tit. 24-A, §2450 (West 1986).

39. Ala. Code §27-5-13 (1986); La. Rev. Stat. Ann. §22:652.1 (West 1986).

40. White Paper, note 15 above, at 8.

41. For the formulation of these proposed restrictions, I am indebted to Carol Levine and her colleagues at the Hastings Center, who have articulated many of the ethical guidelines which should apply to use of the HIV antibody test. *See, e.g.*, Bayer, Levine & Wolf, *HIV Antibody Screening: An Ethical Framework for Evaluating Proposed Programs*, 256 J.A.M.A. 1768 (1986).

42. New Jersey has these first two protections in part by regulation. N.J. Dep't of Insurance, note 29 above.

43. Conn. Gen. Stat. Ann. §38-500 *et seq.* (1986).

44. Bayer & Levine, *Screening Blood: Public Health and Medical Uncertainty*, Hastings Center Report, Special Supp., Aug. 1985, at 8, 10.

45. *Cost of AIDS Care is Half What was Projected, Economist Reports*, note 9 above, at 30.

46. Eight states currently have such pools. *See* D. Meyer & K. Zellner, Insuring Against the Cost of AIDS (unpublished paper presented at DePaul University College of Law Conference on AIDS, Apr. 10-11, 1986).

47. Waldman, *The Other AIDS Crisis*, Washington Monthly, Jan. 1986, at 27.

48. Jaffe, *et al.*, *The Acquired Immunodeficiency Syndrome in a Cohort of Homosexual Men, A Six-Year Follow Up Study*, 103 Annals Internal Med., 210 (1985).

49. District of Columbia Human Rights Act. D.C. Code Ann. §1-2501 *et seq.* (1981).

50. At a September, 1985 hearing before the Subcommittee on Intergovernmental Relations and Human Resources, James P. Corcoran, New York's Superintendent of Insurance, testified

that inquiries regarding sexual orientation would constitute unfair discrimination under New York's Insurance Law. Any state where persons of the same risk must be treated equally should have a similar determination.

51. 1 AIDS Policy & Law (BNA), Dec. 17, 1986, at 7.

52. Exhibit to Complaint, National Gay Rights Advocates and David Hurlbert v. Great Republic Life Ins. Co., No. 857323 (Cal. Super. Ct. 1986). A motion to dismiss the complaint in this case has been denied. 1 AIDS Policy & Law (BNA), Sept. 10, 1986, at 1.

53. *Gay Legal Organization Fights AIDS Insurance Bias*, N.Y. Native, May 19, 1986, at 12.

54. *Insurer Screening Unmarried Males*, N.Y. Times, Oct. 7, 1985, at 28.

55. Zachary Trading, Inc. v. Northwestern Mutual Life Ins. Co., No. 85 Civ. 1290 (JES) (S.D.N.Y. 1985); Northwestern Mutual Life Ins. Co. v. Barth, No. 85 Civ. 8360 (GLG) (S.D.N.Y.); Northwestern Mutual Life Ins. Co. v. Barth, No. 85 Civ. 5805 (SWK) (S.D.N.Y.); Young v. Manhattan Life Ins. Co., No. 28774/85 (Sup. Ct. N.Y.); Equitable Life Assurance Soc'y v. Wagner (no index number assigned) (Sup. Ct. N.Y.).

56. *Survey: Cost of AIDS to Health Plan: $200,000*, Nat'l Underwriter, Jan. 11, 1986.

CHAPTER 14

1. Fleming & Maximov, *The Patient or His Victim: The Therapists Dilemma*, 62 Cal. L. Rev. 1025, 1031-33 (1974). Fleming and Maximov note that California law states explicitly that psychotherapy is "dependent upon the fullest revelations of the most intimate and embarrassing details of the patient's life." *Id.* at 1032 (quoting Cal. Evid. Code §1014, legislative comment (West 1966)).

2. Modern statutes extend well beyond the doctor-patient privileges. For example, Connecticut has separate statutes protecting communications between battered women's or sexual assault counselors and victims, Conn. Gen. Stat. §52-146k (1985), and psychiatrists and patients, *id.* §52-146d.

3. Watts v. Cumberland County Hosp. Sys., Inc., 75 N.C. App. 1, 330 S.E. 2d 242 (1985); Vassiliades v. Garfinckel's, Brooks Brothers, 492 A.2d 580 (D.C. 1985); Alberts v. Devine, 395 Mass. 59, 479 N.E. 2d 113 (1985); Humphers v. First Interstate Bank, 298 Ore. 706, 696 P.2d 527 (1985); MacDonald v. Clinger, 84 A.D.2d 482, 446 N.Y.S.2d 801 (1982); Horne v. Patton, 291 Ala. 701, 287 So. 2d 824 (1974); Simonsen v. Swenson, 104 Neb. 224, 177 N.W. 831 (1920); Schaffer v. Spicer, 88 S.D. 36, 215 N.W. 2d 134 (1974); Hague v. Williams, 37 N.J. 328, 181 A.2d 345 (1962); Hammond v. Aetna Casualty and Surety Co., 243 F. Supp. 793 (N.D. Ohio 1965).

4. Quarles v. Sutherland, 215 Tenn. 651, 389 S.W.2d 249 (1965); Collins v. Howard, 156 F. Supp. 322 (S.D. Ga. 1957).

5. Farnsworth v. Procter & Gamble Co., 758 F.2d 1545 (11th Cir. 1985); *In re* District 27 Community School Bd. v. Board of Educ., 130 Misc.2d 398, 502 N.Y.S.2d 325 (Sup. Ct. 1986).

6. *See, e.g.*, Conn. Gen. Stat. §19a-215 (1985), which requires physicians to report communicable diseases to local health officials. While statutes may vary from jurisdiction to jurisdiction, venereal diseases are generally mentioned specifically, and their diagnosis often imposes additional reporting requirements. Furthermore, Conn. Gen. Stat. §52-146f(2) (1985) permits disclosure when the psychiatrist determines there is "substantial risk of imminent physical injury by the patient to himself or others" or when necessary for purposes of placement or commitment.

7. Statutes have been amended in recent years to conform to court-established limits on civil commitment standards. *See, e.g., id.* §§17-176-183.

8. *See, e.g.*, Tarasoff v. Regents of the University of California, 17 Cal.3d 425, 551 P.2d 334, 131 Cal. Rptr. 14 (1976).

9. McIntosh v. Milano, 168 N.J. Super. 466, 489, 403 A.2d 500, 511-12 (1979). In *McIntosh*, the New Jersey Supreme Court noted "the obligation a practitioner may have to protect the

welfare of the community." Courts have viewed the threat of spreading tuberculosis and other contagious diseases similarly. *See* cases cited in note 27 below; *see also*, Fleming & Maximov, note 1 above (proposing accommodation of competing concerns of confidentiality and public safety); George, Korin, Quattrone & Mandel, *The Therapist's Duty to Protect Third Parties: A Guide for the Perplexed*, 14 Rutgers L.J. 637, 645 (1983) (*McIntosh* echoes medical profession's ethical standards that probable danger to public overrides duty of confidentiality).

10. *See* cases cited note 3 above.

11. *See, e.g.*, Leonard, *Employment Discrimination Against Persons With AIDS*, 19 Clearinghouse Rev. (1986); Comment, *AIDS—A New Reason to Regulate Homosexuality?* 11 J. Contemp. L. 315, 316 (1984); Specter & Engel, *AIDS Curbs Sought in Prisons*, Washington Post, Nov. 4, 1985 at D4; *AIDS as a Handicapping Condition*, 9 Mental & Physical Disability Law Rep. 402 (1985).

12. Gallo, Salahuddin, Popovic, *et al.*, *Frequent Detection and Isolation of Cytopathic Retroviruses (HTLV-III) from Patients with AIDS and at Risk for AIDS*, 224 Science 500 (1984).

13. Barin, Goudeau, Romet-Lemonnes, *et al.*, *Virus Carriage in Symptom-Free Blood Donor Positive for HTLV-III Antibody*, 2 Lancet 981 (1985); *AIDS: Interim Guidelines*, 1 Lancet 234 (1985); Sande, *Transmission of AIDS, the Case Against Casual Contagion*, 314 New Eng. J. Med. 380 (1986); American Hospital Association, Management of HTLV-III/LAV Infection in the Hospital. The Recommendations of the Advisory Committee on Infections Within Hospitals (rev. 1986).

14. Acheson, *AIDS: A Challenge for the Public Health*, 1 Lancet 662 (1986); *AIDS: Interim Guidelines*, note 13 above; Sande, note 13 above.

15. Groopman, Salahuddin, Sarngadharan, *et al.*, *HTLV-III in Saliva of People with AIDS-Related Complex and Healthy Homosexual Men at Risk for AIDS*, 226 Science 447 (1984).

16. Fujikawa, Salahuddin, Palestine, *et al.*, *Isolation of Human T-Lymphotropic Virus Type-III from the Tears of a Patient with Acquired Immunodeficiency Syndrome*, 2 Lancet 529 (1985).

17. Friedland, Saltzman, Rogers, *et al.*, *Lack of Transmission of HTLV-III/LAV Infection to Household Contacts of Patients with AIDS or AIDS-Related Complex with Oral Candidiasis*, 314 New Eng. J. Med. 344 (1986).

18. McCray, *Occupational Risk of the Acquired Immunodeficiency Syndrome Among Health Care Workers*, 314 New Eng. J. Med. 1127 (1986).

19. Weiss, Saxinger, Rechtman, *et al.*, *HTLV-III Infection Among Health Care Workers: Association with Needlestick Injuries*, 254 J.A.M.A. 2089 (1985); Stricoff & Morse, *HTLV-III/ LAV Seroconversion Following a Deep Intramuscular Needlestick Injury*, 314 New Eng. J. Med. 1115 (1986).

20. Conte, Hadley & Sande, *Infection Control Guidelines for Patients with Acquired Immunodeficiency Syndrome (AIDS)*, 309 New Eng. J. Med. 740 (1983); *AIDS: Interim Guidelines*, note 13 above; American Hospital Association, note 13 above.

21. Friedland, Harris, Butkus-Small, *et al.*, *Intravenous Drug Abusers and the Acquired Immunodeficiency Syndrome (AIDS): Demographic, Drug Use and Needle Sharing Patterns*, 145 Arch. Intern. Med. 1413 (1985);

22. Ammann, *The Acquired Immunodeficiency Syndrome in Infants and Children*, 103 Annals Intern. Med. 734 (1985); Scott, Buck, Letterman, *et al.*, *Acquired Immunodeficiency Syndrome in Infants*, 310 New Eng. J. Med. 76 (1984); Sande, note 13 above; Acheson, note 14 above.

23. Thiry, Sprecher-Goldberger, Jonckheer, *et al.*, *Isolation of AIDS Virus from Cell-Free Breast Milk from Three Healthy Virus Carriers*, 2 Lancet 891 (1985).

24. *See* cases cited in notes 26-27 below.

25. American Medical Association, Principles of Medical Ethics §9.

26. *See, e.g.*, Edwards v. Lamb, 69 N.H. 599, 45 A. 480 (1899). This is a specific instance of the more general rule that a person negligently exposing another to a contagious disease may be liable. *See, e.g.*, Earle v. Kuklo, 26 N.J. Super. 471, 98 A.2d 107 (1953) (landlord

exposing tenants to tuberculosis); Kliegel v. Aitken, 94 Wis. 432, 60 N.W.67 (1896) (employer exposing employee to typhoid fever).

27. Davis v. Rodman, 147 Ark. 385, 227 S.W. 612 (1921) (typhoid fever); Skillings v. Allen, 143 Minn. 323, 173 N.W. 663 (1919) (scarlet fever); *Edwards*, 69 N.H. 599, 45 A.480 (infectious sore); Fosgate v. Corona, 66 N.J. 268, 330 A.2d 355 (1974) (tuberculosis); *see also* Wojick v. Aluminum Company of America, 18 Misc. 2d 740, 183 N.Y.S.2d 351 (Sup. Ct. 1959) (employer who administers regular x-rays to employee liable for failure to disclose tuberculosis).

28. Hofmann v. Blackmon, 241 So. 2d 752, *cert. denied*, 245 So. 2d 257 (Fla. 1970).

29. Earle v. Kuklo, 26 N.J. Super. at 974-75, 98 A.2d at 108. *But see* Gammill v. United States, 727 F.2d 950, 953-54 (10th Cir. 1984).

30. Most publicized is the Colorado proposal to track people exposed to the AIDS virus. Russell, *Colorado to Track Those Exposed to Virus*, Washington Post, Aug. 23, 1985, at A1; 9 Mental and Physical Disability Rep. 402, 405 (1985).

31. McIntosh v. Milano, 168 N.J. Super. 466, 484-87, 403 A.2d 500, 509-10; Peck v. Counseling Service, 499 A.2d 422, 425 (Vt. 1985). *But see Gammill*, 727 F.2d at 953-54 (reporting statute creates no duty to warn third parties under Colorado law).

32. 17 Cal.3d 425, 551 P.2d 334, 131 Cal. Rptr. 14 (1976).

33. *McIntosh*, 168 NJ Super. at 489, 403 A.2d at 511-12 (emphasis added).

34. *Id.* at 489-90, 403 A.2d at 512. In Hedlund v. Superior Court, 34 Cal.3d 695, 669 P.2d 41, 154 Cal. Rptr. 805 (1983), the California Supreme Court further extended the psychotherapist's duty. There, the patient informed the therapist of his intent to harm the plaintiff. The therapist failed to warn the plaintiff, who was subsequently shot by the patient. The plaintiff sued not only for her own injuries, but on behalf of her three year old son, who was present at the shooting and suffered serious emotional injuries and psychological trauma. The court upheld both claims, holding it is not unreasonable to recognize a duty to persons in close relationship to the object of the threat. Given the young age of the son, he was foreseeable and identifiable as a person who might be injured if the patient assaulted the plaintiff.

35. 497 F.Supp. 185 (D. Neb. 1980).

36. *Id.* at 193.

37. Peck v. Counseling Service, 499 A.2d 422 (Vt. 1985).

38. New Jersey, in McIntosh v. Milano; Indiana, in Estate of Mather v. Ireland, 419 N.E.2d 782 (Ind. App. 1981); Georgia, in The Bradley Center v. Wessner, 161 Ga. App. 576, 287 S.E.2d 716 (1982); Michigan, in Davis v. Lhim, 124 Mich. App. 291, 335 N.W.2d 481 (1983); Washington, in Peterson v. State, 150 Wash.2d 421, 671 P.2d 230 (1983); Kansas, in Durflinger v. Artiles, 234 Kan. 484, 673 P.2d 86 (1983).

39. *See Peck*, 499 A.2d at 425; *McIntosh*, 168 N.J. Super. at 484-87, 403 A.3d at 509-10.

40. *Tarasoff*, 17 Cal.3d 425, 551 P.2d 334, 131 Cal. Rptr. 14; *Hedlund*, 34 Cal.3d 695, 669 P.2d 41, 154 Cal. Rptr. 805; *McIntosh*, 168 N.J. Super. 466, 403 A.2d 500.

41. In defending against an action for failure reasonably to protect a third party from exposure to AIDS transmitted through homosexual intercourse, a doctor may argue that he or she is not liable because the third party, by engaging in homosexual activity, assumed the risk of infection. (*See* chapter 11 in this volume.) Whether courts will treat assumption of risk as a defense against liability is open to question. In states in which sodomy laws prohibit homosexual sexual acts, courts are more likely to find that participation in a homosexual sexual act is against the public policy of the state and that, consequently, a participant who contracts AIDS may not recover civilly. In at least one state, physicians have organized to reinstate sodomy laws, which still exist in twenty-four other states. Cassens, *Social Consequences of the Acquired Immunodeficiency Syndrome*, 103 Annals of Internal Med. 768 (1985). The Supreme Court has recently held that such laws do not violate the Constitution. Bowers v. Hardwick, 106 S. Ct. 2841 (1986).

42. *See e.g.*, Duke v. Housen, 589 P.2d 334 (Wyo. 1979) (dismissing action as barred by applicable statute of limitations).

43. 150 Cal.App.3d 992, 198 Cal. Rptr. 273 (1983).

44. *Id.* at 996, 198 Cal. Rptr. at 276.

45. *See* Fleming & Maximov, note 1 above, at 1044-45; George, Korin, Quattrone & Mandel, note 9 above, at 642-43; Roth & Meisel, *Dangerousness, Confidentiality, and the Duty to Warn*, 134 Am. J. Psych. 508, 509 (1977).

46. 467 So.2d 798 (Fla. App. 1985).

47. *Id.* at 807.

48. 758 F.2d 1545 (11th Cir. 1985).

49. 130 Misc.2d 398, 502 N.Y.S.2d 325 (Sup. Ct. 1986).

50. *Id.* at 54.

51. *Id.* at 56.

52. Address by Dean Guido Calabresi, Yale Law School AIDS Conference (Feb. 1, 1986).

53. *See* cases cited in note 27 above.

54. *See* notes 43-44 and accompanying text above.

55. Belitsky & Lieberman, *The Psychiatric Patient with AIDS: New Issues and Challenges for the Inpatient Unit*, 8 Yale Psychiatric Q. 4 (1985); Rundell, Wise & Ursano, *Three Cases of AIDS-Related Psychiatric Disorders*, 143 Am. J. Psych. 777 (1986); Perry & Jacobsen, *Neuropsychiatric Manifestations of AIDS-Spectrum Disorders*, 37 Hosp. & Community Psychiatry 135 (1986); Karmani, Drob & Alpert, *Organic Brain Syndrome in Three Cases of Acquired Immune Deficiency Syndrome*, 25 Comp. Psychiatry 294 (1984).

56. Cohen & Weisman, *A Biopsychosocial Approach to AIDS*, 27 Psychosomatics 245 (1986); Navia & Price, *Dementia Complicating AIDS*, 16 Psychiatric Annals 158 (1986).

57. *See* Gammill v. United States, 727 F.2d 950, 954 (10th Cir. 1984) (doctor has no special relationship with and cannot foresee harm to third parties).

58. Belitsky & Lieberman note 55 above.

CHAPTER 15

1. Gostin, *The Future of Communicable Disease Control: Toward a New Concept of Public Health Law*, 64 Milbank Quarterly, Supplement I, at 79 (1986).

2. *196 New Doctors Are Told of Problems Awaiting Solutions*, N.Y. Times, June 3, 1986, at A2 (quoting Dr. Robert G. Petersdorf).

3. For sources about the impact of the divergence between natural and moral philosophy on medicine and the social sciences, see D. Fox, Economists and Health Care (1979).

4. For physicians' views of hierarchy and peers and their relationship to public policy, see D. Fox, Health Policies Health Politics: The Experience of Britain and America, 1911-1965 (1986). For small area variation in medical practice, see the many papers of John Wennberg, in the New England Journal of Medicine and other publications.

5. Nelkin & Hilgartner, *Disputed Areas of Risk: A Public School Controversy Over AIDS*, 64 Milbank Quarterly, Supplement I, at 117 (1986).

6. For a review of the history of policy for AIDS, see Fox, *AIDS and the American Health Polity: The History and Prospects of a Crisis of Authority*, 64 Milbank Quarterly, Supplement I, at 7 (1986).

CHAPTER 16

1. J. Herbold (Senior Policy Analyst Preventive Medicine and Health Promotion, Office of the Assistant Secretary of Defense, Health Affairs), AIDS Policy Development Within the Department of Defense 7 (manuscript cleared for open publication Feb. 3, 1986).

2. *See Additional Recommendations to Reduce Sexual and Drug Abuse-Related Transmission of Human T-Lymphotropic Virus Type III/Lymphadenopathy-Associated Virus*, 35 MMWR 152 (1986); *Update: Acquired Immunodeficiency Syndrome—United States*, 35 MMWR 757 (1986) [hereinafter *AIDS Update*]; *see also* Gay Community News, May 24, 1986, at 1.

3. Twenty-five percent of adult AIDS patients have a history of IV-drug abuse. *AIDS Update*, note 2 above, 758.

4. *See* Letter from Jeffrey Levi, Director of Governmental and Political Affairs, National Gay Task Force, to William Mayer, M.D., Assistant Secretary of Defense for Health Affairs (Aug. 13, 1985); Gilberd, *DOD Policy Sparks Opposition*, National Lawyers Guild Notes, Spring 1986, at 1; Keller, *Military Reclarifies Discharge Policy on AIDS Test*, N.Y. Times, Oct. 29, 1985, at 1.

5. Parker v. Levy, 417 U.S. 733, 743 (1974).

6. *Id.* at 743-44, 746-49, 759.

7. *See* Burns v. Wilson, 346 U.S. 137, 140 (1953).

8. The Uniform Code of Military Justice, 10 U.S.C. §§801-940, is the direct descendant of the Articles of War approved by the Continental Congress on September 20, 1776. The Uniform Code, passed May 5, 1950 and in full force and effect by May 31, 1951, superseded the Articles of War and replaced separate disciplinary laws of each branch with a single statute encompassing both substantive and procedural law for all the armed services. The UCMJ, amended by the Military Justice Act of 1968, expanded the right of the accused to the services of a certified military lawyer, and expanded the role of the military judge. Some offenses punishable under the UCMJ are peculiar to the military, for example, "Conduct Unbecoming an Officer and a Gentleman."

9. Schlesinger v. Councilman, 420 U.S. 738, 761 (1975).

10. Rostker v. Goldberg, 453 U.S. 57, 66 (1981); *Schlesinger*, 420 U.S. at 758, 761.

11. *Schlesinger*, 420 U.S. at 761.

12. *See* Berube, *Coming Out Under Fire*, Mother Jones, Feb.-Mar. 1983, at 24.

13. Rivera, *Queer Law: Sexual Orientation in the Mid-Eighties—Part II*, 11 U. Dayton L. Rev. 275, 287 (1986) [hereinafter Rivera, Part II]; *see* Rivera, *Recent Developments in Sexual Preference Law*, 30 Drake L. Rev. 311, 319-24 (1980-82); Rivera, *Our Straight-Laced Judges: The Legal Position of Homosexual Persons in the United States*, 30 Hastings L.J. 799, 837-55 (1979) [hereinafter *Our Straight-Laced Judges*]; *see also* Heilman, *The Constitutionality of Discharging Homosexual Military Personnel*, 12 Colum. Hum. Rts. L. Rev. 191 (1980-81); Comment, *Homosexual Conduct in the Military: No Faggots in Military Woodpiles*, 1983 Ariz. State L.J. 79; Comment, *Employment Discrimination in the Armed Services—An Analysis of Recent Decisions Affecting Sexual Preference Discrimination in the Military*, 27 Vill. L. Rev. 351 (1981-82); Diamond, *Homosexuals in the Military: They Would Rather Fight Than Switch*, 18 J. Mar. 937 (1985).

14. Dept. Def. Directive No. 1332.14 (1982) (Enlisted Administrative Separations); *see* Rivera, Part II, note 13 above, at 296.

15. Dept. Def. Directive No. 1332.14, encl. 3, §H.1.a (1982) (Enlisted Administrative Separations).

16. *Id.* No. 1332.14, encl. 3, §H.1.b.1. (1982).

17. *Id.* §H.1.b.3.

18. "[T]he Court, individually, for what it is worth, has reached the conclusion that it is desirable for the military to reexamine the homosexual problem, to approach it in perhaps a more sensitive and precise way." Matlovich v. Secretary of the Air Force, Civ. No. 75-1750 (D.D.C. July 16, 1976) (oral opinion of Judge Gesell); *see also* benShalom v. Secretary of the Army, 489 F.Supp. 964, 973-74 (E.D. Wis. 1980) (opinion of Judge Evans ordering benShalom's reinstatement); Beller v. Middendorf, 632 F.2d 788, 812 (1980); Miller v. Rumsfeld, 647 F.2d 80, 88 (Norris, J., dissenting) (9th Cir.), *cert. denied*, 454 U.S. 855 (1981).

19. *See Beller*, 632 F.2d at 812; Dronenberg v. Zech, 741 F.2d 1388 (D.C. Cir. 1984); Matthews v. Marsh, 755 F.2d 182 (1st Cir. 1985).

20. C. Williams & M. Weinberg, Homosexuals and the Military 34-35 (1971).

21. Rich v. Secretary of the Army, 516 F.Supp. 621 (D. Colo. 1981), *aff'd*, 735 F.2d 1220 (10th Cir. 1984).

22. Dept. Def. Directive No. 1332.14, encl. 3, §H.2 (1982).

23. 10 U.S.C. §925 (1982).

24. *Id.* §933.

25. *See* United States v. Newak, 15 M.J. 541 (A.F.C.M.R. 1982); *see also* Rivera, Part II note 13 above, at 306-09.

26. *See* Rivera, Part II, note 13 above, at 301-03.

27. Court martials for drug offenses are under Article 134, General Article (10 U.S.C. §934).

28. Dept. Def. Directive No. 1332.14 §K (1982) (Enlisted Administrative Separations).

29. *Id.* No. 1332.14, §I.

30. Dept. Def. Directive No. 1010.1 (Dec. 28, 1984).

31. *Id.* §E.2.a.

32. News of the Columbus Gay and Lesbian Community, June, 1983, at 186.

33. Interview with attorney John Heilman (June 27, 1986).

34. Ryan, *Gay Man With AIDS Wins Discharge Battle*, Gay Community News, Mar. 10, 1984, at 1.

35. Telephone interview with Harvey Friedman, John Baskin's attorney (June 12, 1986).

36. Boffey, *Of AIDS and the Lack of Confidentiality*, N.Y. Times, Aug. 10, 1985, at 7; *see* Walter, *AIDS Confidentiality in the Military*, Advocate, Nov. 26, 1985, at 12.

37. *Id.*

38. Advocate, Jan. 7, 1986, at 23.

39. National Lawyers Guild Notes, Fall 1985, at 5.

40. Kinney v. Lehman, No. 851836 (S.D. Cal. Aug. 15, 1985).

41. National Lawyers Guild Anti-Sexism Newsletter, March, 1986, at 6.

42. W. Taft (Deputy Secretary of Defense), Memorandum: HTLV-III Testing (Aug. 30, 1985).

43. Washington Blade, Dec. 16, 1985, at 7.

44. *See* N.Y. Times, Jan. 19, 1986, at 19; Chibbaro, *Judge Won't Stop Navy Discharges*, Washington Blade, Jan. 24, 1986, at 1.

45. *See* Dept. Def. Directive No. 1332.14, pt. 2.C.3a(1)(b).

46. Batten v. Department of the Navy, No. CA 85-4108 (D.D.C. Jan. 18, 1986).

47. Walter, *Navy Ousts Eleven Sailors*, Advocate, Mar. 4, 1986, at 3; Chibarro, note 44 above.

48. Chibbaro, note 44 above, also contains a similar case of recruits in San Diego, who were separated with "general" discharges; *see also* National Lawyers Guild Anti-Sexism Newsletter, note 41 above.

49. R. Sparacino (Chief, Classification and Standards Branch, Dept. of Army, Office of Deputy Chief of Staff for Personnel), Memorandum: Department of Army Accession Testing Program (Feb. 18, 1986).

50. *Id.*

51. Nolan was also found guilty of failing to deploy with his ship. Nolan refused to board his ship after his commanding officer told him, "We'll take care of you as soon as you get on that boat." N.Y. Times, June 24, 1986, at 8; Columbus Dispatch, June 24, 1986, at 4A; Walter, *Sailor Refuses To Take Antibody Test*, Advocate, June 10, 1986, at 20.

52. *See* Gilberd, *Military Policy on A.I.D.S. and H.T.L.V.-III Testing*, National Lawyers Guild On Watch, Apr. 1986, at 5; telephone interview with Thomas Homann, attorney for Bryon Kinney (June 12, 1986).

53. Little information is available on the subject of AIDS and the military prior to 1985. *See* News of the Columbus Gay and Lesbian Community, June 1983, at 186 (Navy seeks to discharge Navy Petty Officer who asks to be tested for AIDS); Columbus Dispatch, Oct. 19, 1985, at 2A (estimating that between 1981 and August of 1985 roughly 100 active duty military personnel were diagnosed with AIDS).

54. A. Polk (Director, Dept. Def. Military Blood Program Office) Memorandum: Military

Implementation of Public Health Service Provisional Recommendations Concerning Testing Blood and Plasma for Antibodies to HTLV-III (Mar. 13, 1985).

55. Columbus Citizen-Journal, Mar. 30, 1985, at 5. Civilian blood banks began large scale screening of blood products for the HIV antibody on March 22, 1985.

56. A. Polk, note 54 above, at (1)(b).

57. G. Neitzer (American Association of Blood Banks), Memorandum: Joint Statement on Blood Collections on Military Installations (Sept. 4, 1985); *see* Scott, *DOD Wants Lists of Military Personnel Who Test Positive for HTLV-III Antibody*, Washington Blade, Apr. 26, 1985, at 1, 23.

58. Chibbaro, *Defense Department 'Delays' Plan to Collect HTLV Lists*, Washington Blade, July 12, 1985, at 1.

59. *See* Scott, note 57 above, at 1; Chibbaro, *Red Cross Says DOD's Rethinking HTLV Lists*, Washington Blade, May 3, 1985, at 1.

60. W. Mayer (Assistant Secretary of Defense), Memorandum: Military Implementation of Public Health Service Provisional Recommendations Concerning Testing Blood and Plasma for Antibodies to HTLV-III (July 17, 1985).

61. W. Mayer (Assistant Secretary of Defense), Memorandum: Standardization of Reporting Requirements for Blood Collection Agencies on Military Installations (Aug. 14, 1985).

62. *See* American Association of Blood Banks, American Red Cross, & Council of Community Blood Centers, Joint Statement on Blood Collections on Military Installations (Sept. 3, 1985); G. Neitzer, note 57 above. For compliance, see Columbus Dispatch, Oct. 27, 1985, at 2.

63. J. Clinton (Deputy Assistant Secretary of Defense), Memorandum: HTLV-III Antibody Positivity (June 15, 1985).

64. HTLV-III Screening in the Military and AIDS as a Health Issue Within the Armed Forces: Hearing Before the Armed Forces Epidemiological Board (Aug. 9, 1985) (statement of Jeffrey Levi, Director of Governmental and Political Affairs, National Gay Task Force).

65. *Id.*

66. *Id.* These cases are discussed in text accompanying notes 34-38 above.

67. *Id.*

68. T. Woodward (President, DOD Armed Forces Epidemiological Board), Memorandum: Human T-Lymphotrophic Virus Type III (HTLV-III) Antibody Positivity §(4) (Sept. 17, 1985).

69. *Id.*

70. *Id.* §§(5)(a)-(c), (6), (7)(a)-(c).

71. W. Taft, note 42 above. The DOD directed that one positive ELISA should be confirmed by the Western Blot test.

72. Chibbaro, *Pentagon Announces Go-Ahead on Blood Tests*, Washington Blade, Sept. 6, 1985, at 1; *see* Boffey, *Military Services Will Be Screened For AIDS Evidence*, N.Y. Times, Oct. 18, 1985, at 1; Columbus Dispatch, May 29, 1986, at 9A (indicating these academy classes were the first to be screened for HIV antibodies).

73. W. Taft, note 42 above. Some recruits were only tested after leaving MEPS. The problems created are discussed in text accompanying notes 42-50 above.

74. Telephone interview with Dr. E. Takafugi, Disease Control Consultant to Army Surgeon General (June 26, 1986); telephone interview with John Herbold, Senior Policy Analyst Preventive Medicine and Health Promotion, Office of the Assistant Secretary of Defense, Health Affairs (June 13 and 24, 1986)[hereinafter Herbold Interview]; *see also* Robert R. Redfield (Walter Reed Army Institute of Research), Disseminated Vaccinia in a Military Recruit With HTLV-III Disease (unpublished manuscript 1984); J. Herbold, note 1 above, at 17.

75. *See* L. Mass, Medical Answers About AIDS 2 (1985) (available from Gay Men's Health Crisis); *see also* Curran, *The Epidemiology of AIDS: Current Status and Future Prospects*, 229 Science 1335 (Sept. 27, 1985).

76. Poggi, *Military to Screen Recruits for HTLV-III*, Gay Community News, Sept. 14, 1985, at 1; *see* Columbus Dispatch, Aug. 31, 1985, at B7; *see also* Chibbaro, note 72 above.

77. Herbold Interview, note 74 above.

78. Keller, *More Military AIDS Tests Proposed*, N.Y. Times, Sept. 27, 1985, at 11; Boffey, note 72 above, at 1; *see also* Chibbaro, *DOD Considers Giving Blood Tests to All GIs and Recruits*, Washington Blade, July 19, 1985, at 1. For an early indication of complete screening policy, see H. Kruger, Information Packet For Commanders on HTLV-III, at enc. 1 (DOD release Sept. 26, 1985).

79. C. Weinberger, Memorandum: Policy on Identification, Surveillance, and Disposition of Military Personnel Infected With Human T-Lymphotropic Virus Type III (HTLV-III) (Oct. 24, 1985).

80. If recruits are tested at the MEPS, the presumption is that infection with HIV preceded their induction. *See Hepatitis B Associated with Jet Gun Injection—California*, 35 MMWR 373 (1986) (suggesting a virus might be transmitted by vaccination guns like those used by military).

81. C. Weinberger, note 79 above, §A. *See generally* Smith, *AIDS Seen Bankrupting Military Medical System*, Navy Times, Aug. 26, 1985, at 4.

82. DeGruttola, Mayer & Bennett, *AIDS: Has the Problem Been Adequately Assessed?* 8 Rev. Infectious Diseases 295-97 (1986).

83. *Recruits Exposure Rate Stable*, 1 AIDS Policy & Law (BNA), Dec. 3, 1986, at 8.

84. C. Weinberger, note 79 above, §B.

85. *Id*; *see also Top Pentagon Health Official Backs AIDS Policy*, N.Y. Times, Dec. 18, 1986, at A32.

86. C. Weinberger, note 79 above, §B

87. An action under the UCMJ would be a court martial for an alleged violation of one of the Punitive Articles, Articles 77 through 134 (10 U.S.C. §§877-934) (*e.g.*, a charge of sodomy, Article 125, a charge of "conduct unbecoming an officer and a gentleman," Article 133 or a drug charge under Article 134, General Article). "A line of duty determination" is required when personal injuries or diseases are incurred by service personnel. An injury or disease which is either intentionally incurred or was the proximate result of negligence so gross that it demonstrated a reckless disregard of consequences is the result of misconduct. If misconduct is present, the result is never in the line of duty. An individual who contracts a venereal disease will not be subject to a misconduct finding if he has complied with regulations governing the reporting and treatment of such a disease. E. Byrne, Military Law 450-55 (3d ed. 1981). "Characterization in separation proceedings" refers to whether a discharge is Honorable, General, or Other Than Honorable.

88. Dept. Def. Directive No. 1332.14, pt. 1.C describes "[a] separation for the convenience of the government." Such a separation may be for a variety of reasons unrelated to this article. However, such a separation may be for "[o]ther designated physical or mental conditions," 1332.14, pt. 1.C.4.h, or for "[a]dditional conditions," 1332.14, pt. 1.C.4.i. A separation for the convenience of the government is usually Honorable unless an Entry level separation is required or characterization of service as General (under honorable conditions) is warranted. 1332.14, pts. 1.C.2.(a)-(b). Characterization of service as General (under honorable conditions) is warranted when significant negative aspects of the member's conduct or performance of duty outweigh positive aspects of the member's military record. 1332.14, pt. 2.C.b.(2).

89. C. Weinberger, note 79 above, §(F)(2)(b).

90. C. Weinberger, Memorandum: Policy for Human T-Lymphotropic Virus Type III (HTLV-III) Testing for Family Members of Military Personnel and for DOD Civilian Employees (Jan. 22, 1986); *see DOD Declines to Require Civilians to Undergo Test for AIDS Exposure*, 24 Gov't Empl. Rel. Rep. (BNA), No. 1180, at 172 (Feb. 10, 1986).

91. *Id*.

92. "'I think you ought to tell the secretary (of defense) that he should block the deployment of active-duty (personnel), civilians or dependents overseas if they test positively,' Stevens,

chairman of the Senate Defense Appropriations Subcommittee, told Pentagon officials." Columbus Dispatch, May 16, 1986, at 6B.

93. W. Taft (Deputy Secretary of Defense), Memorandum, (Aug. 25, 1986); *see Pentagon Extending Its AIDS Curb to ROTC's*, N.Y. Times, Sept. 14, 1986, at 37.

94. *Id.*

95. Herbold Interview, note 74 above.

96. *See* Salahuddin, *et al.*, *HTLV-III in Symptom-Free Seronegative Persons*, 2 Lancet 1418 (1984); 254 J.A.M.A. 2865, 2866 (1985); Washington Post, Jan. 6, 1985, at A14; Cleveland Plain Dealer, Jan. 1, 1985, at C1.

97. Columbus Citizen-Journal, Nov. 4, 1985, at 18.

98. *Further Continuing Appropriations for Fiscal Year 1986*, H.R.J. Res. 465, 99th Cong., 1st Sess. (1985).

99. Gay Community News, March 22, 1986, at 2.

100. The U.S. Public Health Service recommended that members of high risk groups for AIDS voluntarily submit to periodic HIV antibody testing. The report stressed the crucial need for health departments to protect confidentiality. *Additional Recommendations*, note 2 above, at 152-55. In February, 1987, the CDC prepared, for discussion, a number of proposals for broad population screening. See Chapter 4 in this volume.

101. *See* Friedman, *Testing Military Personnel for AIDS*, N.Y. Native, Oct. 14-20, 1985, at 25; Walter, note 36 above, at 12; Byron, *This Is Not Only A Test*, Village Voice, May 27, 1986, at 29.

The Job Corps is planning to test 100,000 mostly minority youths who train in its program each year. *Job Corps Planning to Screen Its Trainees for AIDS Virus*, N.Y. Times, Dec. 17, 1986 at A23. The occupational relevance of this plan is baffling. Perhaps the estimated $1 million needed to test these youths might better be spent educating them about prevention of AIDS, *i.e.*, safe sexual practices and the danger of sharing needles.

102. W. Mayer (Assistant Secretary of Defense), Memorandum: Reporting of HTLV-III Antibody Status of Pre-Accession Individuals Determined at the Military Entrance Processing Stations (Oct. 11, 1985).

103. *Id.*

104. *Id.*

105. Currently, six states—Arizona, Colorado, Georgia, Minnesota, Nevada, and South Carolina—require the reporting of antibody-positive results. *The Initial Impact of AIDS on Public Health Law in the United States—1986*, 257 J.A.M.A. 344 (1987).

106. Telephone interview with Lt. Colonel Peter Wyro, Pentagon spokesperson (Mar. 31, 1986). Also, the Navy has enjoined its personnel to treat test results with "the highest degree of confidentiality," noting discrimination in employment, health and life insurance, and school attendance. SECNAVIST 5300.30, Dec. 4, 1985, §§3(c), 6(a).

107. COMNAVMILPERSCOM LETTER, From: Commander, Naval Military Personnel Command, 1300 Ser. N453/, at (2)(d).

108. Chibbaro, *Soldier Tested for AIDS Hangs Himself*, Washington Blade, Jan. 24, 1986, at 1.

109. Advocate, Mar. 18, 1986, at 14. "Harassment and abusive treatment have been reported at a number of commands and hospitals. We've been called the 'A' team and 'faggots.' " Gilberd, *John Does 1 to 9 v. Lehman, et al.*, National Lawyers Guild On Watch, April 1986, at 6.

110. Navy: SECNAVINST 5300.30 §(6)(a)(b) (Dec. 4, 1985); Air Force: T. McCoy (Assistant Secretary of the Air Force), Policy on Identification, Surveillance, and Disposition of Military Personnel Infected With Human T-Lymphotropic Virus Type III (HTLV-III) §(4)(a) (Jan. 24, 1985); Army: Dept. of the Army, Office of the Adjutant General, Policy for Identification, Surveillance, and Disposition of Personnel Infected With Human T-Lymphotrophic Virus Type III (HTLV-III), HQDA LTR 40-86-1, at encl. 3 (Feb. 1, 1986); *see also* R. Elton (Deputy

Chief of Staff for Personnel), Department of the Army Accession Testing Program (Nov. 4, 1985); R. Sparacino (Dept. of the Army, Office of the Deputy Chief of Staff for Personnel), HTLV-III Antibody Screening Policies for Direct Appointment Applications (Jan. 2, 1985).

111. C. Weinberger, note 79 above, §(B)(3).

112. R. Elton, note 110 above, at 6.

113. *Id.*

114. SECNAVINST 5300.30, note 110 above, §(4)(c).

115. T. McCoy, note 110 above, §(D)(2).

116. Dept. of the Army, Office of the Adjutant General, note 110 above, at 9.

117. *See Our Straight-Laced Judges,* note 13 above, at 829-37; Rivera, Part II, note 13 above, at 275-87.

118. American Medical Association, Principles of Medical Ethics, §9 says:

A Physician may not reveal the confidence entrusted to him in the course of medical attendance, or the deficiencies he may observe in the character of patients, unless he is required to do so by law or unless it becomes necessary in order to protect the welfare of the individual or of the community.

119. *See* text accompanying notes 34-53 above.

120. "The information contained in the [medical] board was obtained from Bryon *with the understanding it would be used purely* for purposes of medical diagnosis and treatment. *Any attempt to use this information for other purposes without Bryon's permission represents an unconscionable breach of the prinicple of confidentiality between patient and caregiver. This principle is an ethical standard which exists above and beyond any attempt by courts of law to invalidate it.*" The italicized portions of Dr. Millard's statement were excised by the court. Exhibit F, Administrative Discharge Board Proceedings in the case of HM3 Bryon G. Kinney, USN (June 24, 1985).

121. *See* Smith, *Navy Forces Out Victims Who Admit Homosexual Contact,* Navy Times, Aug. 26, 1985, at 4; *see also* Boffey, note 36 above.

122. *See* Boffey, note 36 above.

123. Lt. Colonel Anthony Polk, head of the DOD Military Blood Program was quoted saying "[W]hile generally he believes patient-doctor confidentiality will be maintained, if you say that [you're gay] to a physician, and he's hardcore, it may not be maintained. I'm not naive enough to think it's not in the back of the minds of some of these hardcore guys." Poggi, note 76 above.

124. Telephone interview with a high Pentagon official who asked to remain anonymous.

125. Boffey, note 36 above, at 7.

126. *See id.* (emphasis added).

127. *Officials See Research Opportunity in Testing Program,* 1 AIDS Policy and Law (BNA), May 21, 1986, at 4.

128. Redfield, *Heterosexually Acquired HTLV-III/LAV Disease (AIDS-Related Complex and AIDS),* 254 J.A.M.A. 2094 (1985).

129. *AIDS Update,* note 2 above, at 758.

130. Redfield, note 128 above, at 2094.

131. *Id.* at 2095.

132. Schultz, *et al.,* 255 J.A.M.A. 1703-04 (1986) (letter).

133. *Id.* at 1704.

134. Redfield, *et al.,* 255 J.A.M.A. 1705 (1986) (letter).

135. *Id.*

136. *New Pentagon Report on Screening for AIDS,* N.Y. Times, Sept. 7, 1986, at 7; *see also Human T-Lymphotropic Virus Type III/Lymphadenopathy-Associated Virus Antibody Prevalence in U.S. Military Recruit Applicants,* 35 MMWR 421 (1986) (statistics through March 1986).

137. A. Polk (Director, Dept. of Defense, Military Blood Program Office), Memorandum: DOD Blood Programs HTLV-III Results 2 Qtr. Fy 96 (May 21, 1986).

138. W. Mayer (Assistant Secretary of Defense), Memorandum: Prevalence of HTLV-III Antibody in DOD Recruit Applicants-Information Memorandum (May 14, 1986).

139. *Id*; *see* Advocate, May 13, 1986, at 20.

CHAPTER 17

1. ACLU National Prison Project, Status Report on Prisons (Feb. 20, 1986).

2. This discussion paraphrases an excellent analysis by Vince Nathan, the Special Master in four major prison conditions cases in Texas, New Mexico, Ohio, and Georgia. *See* Nathan, *Guest Editorial*, J. Prison & Jail Health, Spring/Summer 1985, at 3.

3. *See, e.g.*, Rhodes v. Chapman, 452 U.S. 337 (1981); Bell v. Wolfish, 441 U.S. 520 (1979); Hutto v. Finney, 437 U.S. 678 (1978); Estelle v. Gamble, 429 U.S. 97 (1976).

4. *See, e.g.*, Bounds v. Smith, 430 U.S. 817 (1977); Pell v. Procunier, 417 U.S. 817 (1974); Procunier v. Martinez, 416 U.S. 396 (1974); Cruz v. Beto, 405 U.S. 319 (1972).

5. *See, e.g.*, Whitley v. Albers, 106 S. Ct. 1078 (1986); Smith v. Wade, 461 U.S. 30 (1983).

6. Hewitt v. Helms, 459 U.S. 460 (1983); Wolff v. McDonnell, 418 U.S. 539 (1974).

7. N.Y. Times, Sept. 16, 1986, at A23.

8. Bureau of Justice Statistics, U.S. Dep't of Justice, Jail Inmates 1983 (1985).

9. Vaid, *NPP Gathers the Facts on AIDS in Prison*, Nat'l Prison Project J., Winter 1985, at 1. The NPP sent a four-page questionnaire to the medical directors of all state departments of corrections. The survey sought information in five general areas: epidemiological data, screening and medical care, institutional questions, and staff and inmate education. Twenty-six written surveys were returned. Follow-up phone calls to obtain basic statistical and factual information yielded twenty-two additional responses.

10. *See* T. Hammett, AIDS in Correctional Facilities: Issues and Options (1986) and Update: AIDS in Correctional Facilities (Jan. 1987) (sponsored by the National Institute of Justice and the American Correctional Association [hereinafter *NIJ/ACA Study* and *NIJ/ACA Update*, respectively]. The *NIJ/ACA Study* was based on responses to a questionnaire from all fifty state correctional departments, the Federal Bureau of Prisons, and thirty-three large city and county jail systems.

11. *NIJ/ACA Update*, note 10 above, at 6.

12. *Id*.

13. *Id*. at 10.

14. N.Y. State Commission of Correction, Acquired Immune Deficiency Syndrome: A Demographic Profile of New York State Inmate Mortalities 1981-1985, at 2 (March 1986). A significant number of prisoners with AIDS are black or Hispanic. Although the data collected by the NPP and NIJACA surveys are incomplete on the issue of race, people of color account for 39 percent of all adult cases of AIDS in the United States. In New York State, for instance, 46 percent of inmates who have died of AIDS were Hispanic, 39 percent black, and 15 percent white. *Id*. at 15.

15. Telephone interview with Dr. Rosemary Gida of the New York State Commission of Correction (Oct. 5, 1986).

16. *NIJ/ACA Study*, note 10 above, at 23.

17. *NIJ/ACA Update*, note 10 above, at 12.

18. The lack of data results from several factors. First, prisoners adhere to an ethic of silence, keeping artificially low the number of rapes reported to prison officials and researchers. Second, many victims feel humiliated and refuse to discuss their traumas. Third, the few studies of sexual assault in prison have yielded conflicting results. *See generally* Robertson, *Surviving Incarceration: Constitutional Protection from Inmate Violence*, 35 Drake L. Rev. 101, 104-106 (1985-1986); Comment, *Rape: The Unstated Sentence*, 15 Pac. L.J. 899, 901-902 (1984).

19. N.Y. Times, Aug. 11, 1985, at A12.

20. Vaid, note 9 above, at 2.

21. *NIJ/ACA Update*, note 10 above, at 16. Missouri has decided that mass screening is unnecessary but still plans to screen risk-group members. Iowa discontinued mass screening after a prevalence study of about eight hundred inmates identified no seropositives.

22. *See* Federal Bureau of Prisons, Memorandum on AIDS Medical Procedures (Oct. 25, 1985) (addressed to regional medical administrators).

23. *NIJ/ACA Study*, note 10 above, at 36. Each ELISA test costs about $5. The cost of the confirmatory Western Blot averages about $75 per test, ranging from $25 to $100.

24. Friedland, Saltzman, Roger, Kahl, Lesser, Mayers & Klein, *Lack of Transmission of HTLV-III/LAV Infection to Household Contacts of Patients with AIDS or AIDS Related Complex with Oral Candidiasis*, 314 New Eng. J. Med. 344 (1986); *see also* Sande, *Transmission of AIDS: The Case Against Casual Contagion*, 314 New Eng. J. of Med. 380 (1986).

25. The following summary of prison conditions for segregated seropostive inmates is based upon letters on file at the offices of NPP. For a horrifying description of conditions in the AIDS unit of New York City's Riker's Island jail, see Sullivan, *Surge in AIDS Cases Leading to Crisis in Prisons*, N.Y. Times, Mar. 5, 1987, at B1.

26. Recently, an asymptomatic, or otherwise healthy, seropositive inmate filed a lawsuit challenging his segregation on constitutional grounds. *See* Farmer v. Levine, C.A. No. HM 85-4284 (D. Md. amended complaint filed Mar. 6, 1986).

27. Telephone interview with Dan Kelly, Deputy Director, Medical Services Division of the Federal Bureau of Prisons (Oct. 6, 1986).

28. 607 F. Supp. 9 (S.D.N.Y. 1984).

29. *Id*. at 10.

30. *See, e.g.*, Hewitt v. Helms, 459 U.S. 460 (1983).

31. 607 F. Supp. at 11 (quoting Jones v. North Carolina Prisoners' Labor Union, 433 U.S. 119, 125 (1977)). A federal district court in Oklahoma recently dismissed a suit by a seropositive inmate who had challenged his segregation on constitutional grounds. Without citing *Cordero*, the court found that the segregation policy furthered legitimate correctional objectives of preventing the spread of disease and protecting the seropositive inmate from other inmates. *See* Powell v. Dep't of Corrections, Nos. 85-C-820-C and 85-C-816-B (N.D. Okla. dismissed Feb. 20, 1986).

32. Vaid, *Balanced Response Needed to AIDS in Prison*, Nat'l Prison Project J., Spring 1986, at 5.

33. *See, e.g.*, Cody v. Hillard, 599 F. Supp. 1025 (D.S.D. 1984); French v. Owens, 538 F. Supp. 910 (S.D. Ind. 1982); Wojtzak v. Cuyler, 480 F. Supp. 1288 (E.D. Pa. 1979); Laaman v. Helgemoe, 561 F.2d 411 (1st Cir. 1977).

34. *NIJ/ACA Study*, note 10 above, at 21.

35. *NIJ/ACA Update*, note 10 above, at 12.

36. Telephone interview with William Gaunay, forensic investigator, New York State Commission of Corrections (Oct. 7, 1986). As the state with the largest number of inmates with AIDS, New York provides a range of educational materials to inmates including a report, *AIDS: 100 Questions and Answers*, produced by the state's Department of Health. On July 15, 1986, the Commission of Corrections adopted Policy #86-MRB-01 setting forth the commission's minimum standards regarding the distribution and disinfection of shaving equipment used by inmates in local correctional facilities.

37. Copies of the videotape are available without charge by sending a blank VHS cassette with a self-addressed mailer to Charles Hernandez, Superintendent, Taconic Correctional Facility, 250 Harris Road, Bedford Hills, New York 10507. Telephone (914) 241-3010.

38. *See generally NIJ/ACA Study*, note 10 above, at 21-25.

39. The National Prison Project supports the distribution of condoms in prisons. One state, Vermont, decided in early 1987 to provide inmates with condoms. N.Y. Times, Mar. 8, 1987, at 50; N.Y. Times, Apr. 14, 1987, at B6 (experimental distribution in N.Y. City jail).

40. *NIJ/ACA Study*, note 10 above, at 25; *see also NIJ/ACA Update*, note 10 above, at 12-13 (strongly reiterating recommendation that correctional facilities provide live training—lectures, discussion groups, and seminars—on AIDS for inmates and staff members).

41. *See, e.g.*, Research and Decisions Corporation, Designing an Effective AIDS Prevention Strategy for San Francisco: Results from the Second Probability Sample of an Urban Gay Male from the Second Probability Sample of an Urban Male Community (prepared for the San Francisco AIDS Foundation, June 1985).

42. *NIJ/ACA Study*, note 10 above, at 21-22.

43. 42 U.S.C. §1983 (1982).

44. *E.g.*, Carlson v. Green, 446 U.S. 14 (1980).

45. United States v. Muniz, 374 U.S. 50 (1963).

46. Woodhaus v. Virginia, 487 F.2d 889, 890 (4th Cir. 1973).

47. *Id.*

48. Withers v. Levine, 615 F.2d 158 (4th Cir. 1980).

49. *NIJ/ACA Study*, note 10 above, at 62.

50. *Id.*

51. Estelle v. Gamble, 429 U.S. 97 (1976).

52. *Id.* at 104.

53. Ramos v. Lamm, 639 F.2d 559, 575 (10th Cir. 1980); *see also* Goff v. Bechtold, 632 F. Supp. 698 (S.D. W.Va. 1986) (mere negligence does not give rise to Eighth Amendment violation under guidelines established by Supreme Court in *Estelle* v. *Gamble*); West v. Keve, 571 F.2d 158, 161-63 (3d Cir. 1978) (under *Estelle* standard, prison breaches its constitutional duty only when it ignores "serious" medical need—a condition that has been diagnosed as serious by doctor or was so obvious that even a lay person would understand that condition required doctor's care).

54. *See, e.g.*, *Ramos*, 639 F.2d 559; Todaro v. Ward, 565 F.2d 48 (2d Cir. 1977); *see also* Balla v. Idaho State Bd. of Corrections, 595 F. Supp. 1558 (D. Idaho 1984).

55. Outlook on Justice, Mar.-Apr. 1986, at 1-2.

56. *Id.*

57. Vaid, note 32 above, at 4-5.

58. Columbus Citizen-Journal, Dec. 2, 1985, at 26.

59. Telephone interview with William Gaunay, forensic investigator, New York State Commission of Corrections (Oct. 9, 1986).

60. *NIJ/ACA Study*, note 10 above, at 21 (93 percent of correctional systems reported staff concerns about casual contacts; 83 percent reported inmate concerns).

61. Weiss, *et al.*, *HTLV-III Investigation Among Health-Care Workers: Association with Needlestick Injuries*, 254 J.A.M.A. 289 (1985).

62. In an early case brought before the discovery of an HIV antibody test, a New York court held that prison officials did not have a duty to screen and segregate inmates infected with the AIDS virus. *See* LaRocca v. Dalsheim, 467 N.Y.S.2d 302 (Sup. Ct. 1983). Recently, however, several lawsuits have been filed by inmates seeking antibody screening and other policies for the systematic identification and segregation of infected inmates. *See, e.g.*, Maberry v. Martin, No. 86-341-CRT (E.D.N.C. 1986); Herring v. Keeney (D. Or., filed Sept. 17, 1985); Potter v. Wainwright, No. 85-1616-CIV-T15 (M.D. Fla. 1985).

63. Nacci & Kane, Executive Summary: Inmate Sexual Aggression (1984).

64. Wolfgang & Durham, Sex and Sexual Aggression in Prison: A Review, (unpublished paper, Dec. 15, 1982); Letter from Ed Koren, NPP, to John Conrad, National Institute of Corrections (Nov. 15, 1982).

65. Nacci & Kane, note 63 above, at 7.

66. *Id.* at 13.

67. *Id.* at 11.

68. *See, e.g.*, N.Y. Times, Jan. 7, 1986, at B3 (3 inmates with AIDS in New York prisons

released into care of hospice operated by Mother Teresa and the Roman Catholic Archdiocese of New York).

69. *NIJ/ACA Study*, note 10 above, at 58.

CHAPTER 18

1. Institute of Medicine, National Academy of Sciences, Confronting AIDS: Directions for Public Health, Health Care and Research 12 (1986) [hereinafter *Confronting AIDS*]; Des Jarlais, Friedman & Strug, *AIDS and Needle Sharing Within the IV Drug Use Subculture*, in The Social Dimensions of AIDS: Methods & Theory 111 (Feldman & Johnson eds. 1986) [hereinafter *AIDS and Needle Sharing*]; Des Jarlais, Friedman & Hopkins, *Risk Reduction for the Acquired Immunodeficiency Syndrome Among Intravenous Drug Users*, 103 Annals of Internal Medicine 755 (1985) [hereinafter *Risk Reduction*]; Marmor, Des Jarlais, Friedman, Lyden & El-Sadr, *The Epidemic of Acquired Immunodeficiency Syndrome (AIDS) and Suggestions For its Control in Drug Abusers*, 1 J. Substance Abuse Treatment 237, 238-239 (1984) [hereinafter *Drug Abuse and AIDS*]; Altman, *New Fear on Drug Use and AIDS*, N.Y. Times, April 6, 1986 at A1.

2. *Update: Acquired Immunodeficiency Syndrome—United States*, 35 MMWR 757, 758 (1986) [hereinafter *AIDS Update*].

3. Peterman, Drotman & Curran, *Epidemiology of The Acquired Immunodeficiency Syndrome (AIDS)*, 7 Epidemiologic Reviews 10-11 (1985) (available from Dr. Thomas A. Peterman, AIDS Branch, Centers for Disease Control, 1600 Clifton Road, Atlanta, Ga. 30333) [hereinafter *Epidemiology of AIDS*]; *Risk Reduction*, note 1 above, at 755; Wallace, *Jersey Aims AIDS Education Drive At Drug Users*, N.Y. Times, Feb. 16, 1986, at 51.

4. *AIDS Update*, note 2 above, at 758-59; *see also AIDS and Needle Sharing*, note 1 above, at 111; Des Jarlais & Friedman, Prevention Policy Questions for AIDS among Intravenous Drug Users, at 3 (Paper presented at the Annual Convention of the American Public Health Association, Washington, D.C., Nov. 18, 1985) (available from Don C. Des Jarlais, State of N.Y., Division of Substance Abuse Services, 55 West 125 Street, N.Y., N.Y. 10027) [hereinafter Prevention Policy Questions].

5. *Recommendations for Assisting in the Prevention Of Perinatal Transmission of Human T-Lymphotropic Virus Type III/Lymphadenopathy-Associated Virus and Acquired Immunodeficiency Syndrome*, 34 MMWR 721-722 (1985); Altman, note 1 above, at A30; Centers for Disease Control, AIDS Program, *AIDS Weekly Surveillance Report*, Nov. 17, 1986, at 1 [hereinafter *CDC AIDS Surveillance Report*]; New York City Department of Health, *AIDS-Surveillance Update* 6 (Nov. 26, 1986) (available from N.Y.C. Dept. of Health Surveillance Office, 125 Worth Street, N.Y., N.Y. 10013); *see also* Prevention Policy Questions, note 4 above, at 2-3; *AIDS and Needle Sharing*, note 1 above, at 111.

6. Telephone interview with Don C. Des Jarlais, State of N.Y., Division of Substance Abuse Services (Mar. 28, 1986); *see also CDC AIDS Surveillance Report*, note 5 above; *AIDS-Surveillance Update*, note 5 above.

7. IV-drug users are likely to have more severe opportunistic infections than are other people with AIDS and to have a lower median survival time after diagnosis, in the range of only ten months. *Epidemiology of AIDS*, note 3 above, at 8; Prevention Policy Questions, note 4 above, at 4-5; *Drug Abuse and AIDS*, note 1 above, at 239; Friedland, *Hospitals Say AIDS Strains Resources*, N.Y. Times, Feb. 16, 1986, at A1; Sullivan, *AIDS: Bellevue Tries to Cope with Disease it Cannot Cure*, N.Y. Times, Dec. 23, 1985, at A1.

8. *Confronting AIDS*, note 1 above, at 59; telephone interview with Don C. Des Jarlais, State of N.Y., Division of Substance Abuse Services (Mar. 28, 1986); Wallace, note 3 above, at 51.

9. *Confronting AIDS*, note 1 above, at 106-07; *Risk Reduction*, note 1 above, at 755; U.S. Public Health Service, U.S. Dept. of Health & Human Services, *AIDS Indices/Facts*,

Feb. 2, 1986, at 2 (summarizing and citing studies of seroprevalence in IV-drug user populations); Altman, note 1 above, at A1, A30.

10. *See* Chapter 2 in this volume.

11. *Risk Reduction*, note 1 above, at 756; Prevention Policy Questions, note 4 above, at 3.

12. *Confronting AIDS*, note 1 above, at 12-13, 108-12; *AIDS and Needle Sharing*, note 1 above, at 120-23; *Drug Abuse and AIDS*, note 1 above, at 245-46; Bird, *Little Success in Curbing Spread of AIDS by Addicts is Seen*, N.Y. Times, Dec. 1, 1985, at 64; Nix, *More and More AIDS Cases Found Among IV Drug Abusers*, N.Y. Times, Oct. 20, 1985, at 51.

13. The New York State Division of Substance Abuse Services has estimated that there are 250,000 addicts in New York, with 30,000 in treatment and up to 1,500 on waiting lists (as of December 1985). Barbanel, *Koch Seeks a State Rise in Drug Abuse Treatment Aid*, N.Y. Times, Dec. 17, 1985, at B7. According to New Jersey Health Department and drug-abuse treatment officials, treatment programs in New Jersey were operating at 120 percent of capacity, with up to two thousand addicts awaiting but unable to obtain treatment, as of December 1986. Telephone interview with Joyce Jackson, N.J. Health Dept. Div. of Narcotic and Drug Abuse Control, East Orange, N.J. (Dec. 16, 1986).

14. *Confronting AIDS*, note 1 above, at 109-10, 112; Prevention Policy Questions, note 4 above, at 7-8; Des Jarlais & Hopkins, *"Free" Needles For Intravenous Drug Users at Risk for AIDS: Current Developments in New York City*, 313 New Eng. J. Med. 1476 (1985) (letter).

15. Pub. L. 92-255, Title IV, §§407, 413, 86 Stat. 78, 84 (1972). The 1972 Act's antidiscrimination provisions, originally codified as 21 U.S.C. §1174 (now 42 U.S.C. §290ee-2 (Supp. III 1985)) and 21 U.S.C. §1180 (now 42 U.S.C. §290ee-1 (Supp. III 1985)), were transferred and made a part of the Public Health Service Act by Pub. L. 98-24, §§2(b)(16)(A) and (B), 97 Stat. 182 (1983).

16. Pub. L. 93-112, Title V, §§501-505, 87 Stat. 390-394 (1973) (codified as amended at 29 U.S.C. §§791-794a (1982 & Supp. III 1985)).

17. *See* note 20 below; Perkins & Boyle, *AIDS and Poverty: Dual Barriers to Health Care*, 19 Clearinghouse Rev. 1283 (1986); *see also* Chapter 12 in this volume.

18. 42 U.S.C. §290ee-2(a) (Supp. III 1985).

19. 42 U.S.C. §290ee-2(b) (Supp. III 1985).

20. 29 U.S.C. §794; 45 C.F.R. §84.53 (1985) (HEW (now HHS) regulations implementing nondiscrimination requirements of 1972 Drug Abuse and Rehabilitation Acts among medical care providers receiving federal financial assistance); 42 Fed. Reg. 22,676, 22,685 and App. A, Subpt. F, para. 37, at 22,694 (1977) (explaining both 1972 Drug Abuse and Rehabilitation Acts' coverage of drug abusers and addicts); *see also* 43 Fed. Reg. 2132, 2137 (1978) (HEW regulations establishing government-wide standards for enforcing §504 of the Rehabilitation Act); 38 §U.S.C. 4133 (1982); 38 C.F.R. Part 18, §18.453 (1980) (VA regulations implementing this nondiscrimination provision and §504 of the Rehabilitation Act); 45 Fed. Reg. 63,264, 63,265 (1980) (explaining laws "requiring hospitals not to discriminate against alcoholics and addicts who need medical services"); *cf.* Alexander v. Choate, 105 S. Ct. 712, 722-23 (1985); United States v. Baylor Univ. Medical Center, 736 F.2d 1039 (5th Cir. 1984), *cert. denied*, 105 S. Ct. 958 (1985) (holding Medicaid and Medicare to constitute federal financial assistance for purposes of §504 of the Rehabilitation Act).

21. For example, the Veterans Benefit Law defines "disability" for purposes of veterans medical care benefits as meaning "a disease, injury or other physical or mental defect." 38 U.S.C. §601(1) (1982).

22. 42 U.S.C. §290ee-1(a) and (b) (Supp. III 1985).

23. 42 U.S.C. §290ee-1(c) (Supp.III 1985).

24. 42 U.S.C. §290ee-1(d) (Supp. III 1985).

25. 29 U.S.C. §706(7)(B) (1982).

26. HEW (now HHS) explained the act's coverage of persons with histories or conditions of drug abuse or addiction in regulations it issued to implement §504 of the act. *See* 42 Fed. Reg.

22,676, 22,685-22,686 (1977) (discussing regulations now codified at 45 C.F.R. Part 84 (1985)); 43 Fed. Reg. 2132, 2134, 2137 (1978) (discussing government-wide standards for implementing §504, formerly codified at 45 C.F.R. Part 85). And see the Justice Department's explanation of this issue in its §504 regulations, 44 Fed. Reg. 54,951, 54,957 (1979) (codified at 28 C.F.R. Part 42 (1986); 28 C.F.R. Part 32 (1986) (Dept. of Labor §504 regulations); 38 C.F.R. Part §18, 18.403(j)(2)(i)(C) (1985) (VA §504 regulations).

27. 451 F.Supp. 791 (E.D. Pa. 1978).

28. Rodriguez v. New York City Police Department, No. 80 Civ. 4784, slip op. at 5-6, 23-24 (S.D.N.Y., Jan. 19, 1981) (order approving settlement of class action brought under §504 of the Act by applicants for jobs as police officers who had been disqualified from employment on the basis of pre-employment urine tests, the results of which erroneously indicated their involvement in illicit use of prescription drugs); Keyes v. New York City Department of Personnel, No. 79-5786 (S.D.N.Y. Aug. 18, 1980) (awarding plaintiff attorney's fees after settlement of case brought under Rehabilitation Act on behalf of individual who was fired from his job as the result of a urine test that mistakenly indicated he used methadone). *But cf.* McCleod v. City of Detroit, 39 Fair Emp. Prac. Cas. (BNA) 225 (E.D. Mich. 1985) (holding that a city's termination of firefighters labeled as marijuana users on the basis of tests did not violate the Rehabilitation Act).

29. 29 U.S.C. §794 (1982).

30. *E.g.*, 45 C.F.R. §84.3(k)(4) (1985).

31. *E.g.*, 45 C.F.R. §84.3(k)(1). The Supreme Court endorsed these basic principles in Alexander v. Choate, 105 S. Ct. 712, 722 n.24 (1985).

32. A 1977 opinion of the Attorney General makes this point nicely:

[T]he statute does not require the impossible. It does not unrealistically require that recipients of Federal contracts and grants ignore all the behavioral or other problems that may accompany a person's alcoholism or drug addiction if they interfere with the performance of his job or his effective participation in a federally assisted program. At the same time, the statute requires that contractors and grantees covered by the act not automatically deny employment or benefits to persons solely because they might find their status as alcoholics or drug addicts personally offensive, any more than contractors or grantees could discriminate against an individual who had some other condition or disease—such as cancer, multiple sclerosis, amputation, or blindness—unless its manifestations or his conduct rendered him ineligible.

43 Op. Att'y Gen. No. 12 at 16-17 (April 12, 1977).

33. 451 F. Supp. at 796-97 (E.D. Pa. 1978).

34. 29 U.S.C. §706(7)(B) (1982).

35. *See, e.g.*, 124 Cong. Rec. S19001-19002 (daily ed. Oct. 14, 1978), and Op. Att'y Gen., note 32 above.

36. Tinch v. Walters, 573 F. Supp. 346 (E.D. Tenn. 1983) (Veteran's Administration ruling denying benefits to primary alcoholics violates Rehabilitation Act), *aff'd*, 765 F.2d 599 (6th Cir. 1985); McKelvey v. Walters, 596 F. Supp. 1317 (D.D.C. 1984), *rev'd sub nom.* McKelvey v. Turnage, 792 F.2d 194 (D.C. Cir. 1986); Traynor v. Walters, 606 F. Supp. 391 (S.D.N.Y. 1985), *rev'd on jurisdictional grounds*, 791 F.2d 226 (2nd Cir. 1986). The regulation in question is 38 C.F.R. 3.301(c)(2).

37. 612 F.2d 644 (2d Cir. 1979).

38. *Id.* at 650.

39. School Bd. v. Arline, 107 S. Ct. 1123, 1131 & n.16 (1987). An employee may also be dismissed if he or she cannot, with reasonable accommodation, do the job.

40. *Id.* at 1129.

41. 502 N.Y.S.2d 325 (Sup. Ct. 1986).

42. *Id.* at 335.

43. *See, e.g.*, 28 C.F.R. Part 41, §41.55 (1986), and Part 42, §§42.512, 42.513 (1986) (Dept.

of Justice regulations coordinating implementation of §504); 45 C.F.R. Part 84, §84.13, 84.14 (1985) (HEW (now HHS) §504 regulations); 41 C.F.R. §60-741.5(c) (1985) (Rehabilitation Act regulations governing federal contractors).

44. *See* note 28 above. HIV tests are unreliable when used on the general population unless repeated and confirmed with a Western blot test. Many employers may be unwilling to incur the expense of triple testing. See Chapter 9 in this volume.

45. School Bd. v. Arline, 772 F.2d 764 (11th Cir. 1985), *aff'd*, 107 S. Ct. 1123 (1987).

46. *See, e.g.*, Mantolete v. Bolger, 767 F.2d 1416, 1422 (9th Cir. 1985) (condition must be shown to create reasonable probability of substantial harm in future to justify job denial); Pushkin v. Dept. of Transp., 658 F.2d 1372, 1387-90 (10th Cir. 1981). *Cf.* Doe v. New York University, 666 F.2d 761 (2nd Cir. 1981) (where there is significant risk of relapse of serious psychiatric condition that repeatedly caused applicant to behave self-destructively in past, it was not illegal to refuse her admission to stressful setting of medical school).

47. Telephone interview with Don C. Des Jarlais, State of N.Y. Division of Substance Abuse Services (Mar. 28, 1986).

48. N.Y. Human Rights Law, N.Y. Exec. L. §§290 *et seq.* (McKinney 1982 & Supp. 1986); *id.* §292.21 (definition of covered disabilities).

49. N.J. Stat. Ann. §§10:5-4.1, 10:5-5q (West Supp. 1986); N.J. Civil Rights Division, AIDS Discrimination and Mandatory Testing (undated announcement 1986) (available from the N.J. Civil Rights Division, 1100 Raymond Blvd., Newark, N.J. 07102).

50. *Cf.* Clowes v. Terminix Int'l., Inc., OAL Dkt No. CRT 6584-83, Agency Dkt No. EL11HB-18516-C (N.J. Dept. of Law & Public Safety, Division on Civil Rights, June 18, 1984) (ruling parallel condition of alcoholism is a handicap under law), *rev'd*, No. A-3886-84T-1 (Sup. Ct. App. Div. May 30, 1986) (leaving undisturbed Civil Rights Division ruling on law's coverage of alcoholism, but reversing on the facts), *cert. granted*, Dkt. No. 25,972 (N.J. Sup. Ct. Nov. 10, 1986).

51. California Fair Employment and Housing Act, Cal. Gov't. Code §§12900 *et seq.*, 12926(f), (h) (West 1980 & Supp. 1986). The state Fair Employment and Housing Commission held the law to cover AIDS in Department of Fair Employment and Housing v. Raytheon Corp.; Estate of John Chadbourne, Complainant, P83-84, L10310o, L-33676, *reported in* N.Y. Times, Feb. 12, 1987, at B1.

52. Los Angeles Ordinance No. 160289, L.A. Municipal Code §§45.80-49.93 (1985); San Francisco Ordinance No. 49985, S.F. Municipal Code, §§3801-16 (1985).

53. California Fair Employment and Housing Commission Rules and Regulations, 2 Cal. Admin. Code, Div. 4, §7293.6(a)(4).

54. *See* notes 51-52 above.

55. Shuttleworth v. Broward County Office of Budget and Management Policy, No. 85-0624 (Fla. Comm. on Human Rel'ns Dec. 11, 1985), *reprinted in* Daily Labor Report (BNA), Dec. 17, 1985, at E1-6.

56. Fischl, *et. al.*, *Evaluation of Heterosexual Partners, Children, and Household Contacts of Adults with AIDS*, 257 J.A.M.A. 640 (1987); Friedland, *et. al.*, *Lack of Transmission of HTLV-III/LAV Infection to Household Contacts of Patients with AIDS or AIDS-Related Complex With Oral Candidiasis*, 314 N. Eng. J. Med. 344 (1986).

57. *Additional Recommendations to Reduce Sexual and Drug Abuse-Related Transmission of Human T-Lymphotropic Virus Type III/ Lymphadenopathy-Associated Virus*, 35 MMWR 154 (1986).

58. Substance Abuse Report, March 1986, at 8.

59. *See* McQuiston, *AIDS Test Centers are Set for City*, N.Y. Times, Mar. 30, 1986, at 29; N.J. Stat. Ann. §26:5C-3 (West Supp. 1986); Cal. Health & Safety Code, §§1630-32 (West Supp. 1986) (establishing alternative test sites); (Supp. 1986); Fla. Stat. §381.606 (1985); Fla. Admin. Code §§10D-93.61 to 10D-93.67 (1985) (establishing alternative test sites and protecting confidentiality of test results).

60. This law, originally codified as 21 U.S.C. §1175, was transferred and made a part of

the Public Health Services Act in 1983, and is now codified at 42 U.S.C. §290ee-3 (Supp. III 1985).

61. H.R. Rep. No. 920, 92d Cong., 2d Sess. 33 (1972).

62. 42 U.S.C. §290ee-3(a) (Supp. III 1985); 42 C.F.R. §§2.12, 2.13(a) (1985).

63. 42 C.F.R. §2.13(b) (1985).

64. 42 C.F.R. §§2.11(o), 2.13(c) (1985); *see* Office of General Counsel, U.S. Dept. of Health and Human Services, Legal Opinion No. 83-6: Reporting AIDS to Fellow Patients Under the Alcohol and Drug Abuse Confidentiality Regulations, 42 C.F.R. §§2.31, 2.40 (Nov. 1, 1983) (advising that AIDS data in patients' records is protected by confidentiality law) (available from Office of the General Counsel, U.S. Dept. of Health & Human Services, Public Health Division, 5600 Fishers Lane, Room 4A-53, Rockville, MD 20857).

65. 42 C.F.R. §§2.11(e), 2.11(i), 2.11(k), 2.16 (1985).

66. 42 C.F.R. §2.13(e) (1985).

67. 42 C.F.R. §2.13(p) (1985).

68. 42 U.S.C. §290ee-3(b)(1) (Supp. III 1985); 42 C.F.R. §§2.31, 2.40 (1985).

69. 42 C.F.R. §2.32 (1985).

70. 42 U.S.C. §290ee-3(b)(2) (Supp. III 1985); 42 C.F.R. §2.51 (1985) (medical emergencies); 42 C.F.R. §2.52 (1985) (research by nongovernmental personnel); 42 C.F.R. §2.53 (1985) (research or evaluation by governmental personnel); 42 C.F.R. §§2.61-2.65 (1985) (court orders authorizing disclosure).

71. 42 U.S.C. §290ee-3(f) (Supp. III 1985); 42 C.F.R. §2.14 (1985); *cf.* Logan v. District of Columbia, 447 F. Supp. 1328 (D.D.C. 1978).

72. 42 C.F.R. §2.23 (1985).

73. 42 C.F.R. §2.52-1(h) (1985).

74. *E.g.*, Cal. Health & Safety Code, §1632(a) (West Supp. 1986) (requiring information about validity and accuracy of antibody tests to be given to individuals tested at alternative test sites); *id.* §199.22 (requiring written consent of every person given antibody test); Fla. Admin. Code §§10D-93.62(8), 10D-93.65(2)(b)(1) (1986) (providing for pre- and post-test counseling of persons tested at Florida's alternative test sites); N.Y.S. Dept. of Health, Emergency Rule on HTLV-III Testing, N.Y. Comp. Codes R. & Regs. tit. 10, §§58-1.1(b)(12), 58-1.11(b)(2) (incorporating New York requirements for informed consent to HIV testing and pre- and post-test counseling).

75. *Id.*

76. *Id.*

77. 42 C.F.R. §§2.31, 2.40(a)(3) (1985).

78. *See* Chapter 14 in this volume.

79. 42 C.F.R. §2.31 (1985).

80. 42 C.F.R. §§2.40(a)(2)-(3) (1985).

81. *See* Comm'r of Social Services v. David R. S., 55 N.Y.2d 588, 594-97, 451 N.Y.S.2d 1, 4-6 (1982) (refusing to order disclosure of drug abuse treatment records in paternity proceeding).

82. 42 C.F.R. §2.32 (1985).

83. 42 C.F.R. §§2.52-.53 (1985).

84. 42 C.F.R. §2.53(c) (1985).

85. 42 C.F.R. §2.53(d)-(e) (1985).

86. 42 C.F.R. §§2.11(p)(2)-(3), 2.11(n) (1985).

87. 42 C.F.R. §§2.11(n), 2.11(p)(2) (1985).

88. 42 C.F.R. §2.11(n) (1985).

89. 42 U.S.C. §290ee-3(b)(2)(C) (Supp. III 1985); 42 C.F.R. Subpart E, §§2.61-2.65 (1985).

90. 42 C.F.R. §2.61 (1985).

91. 42 C.F.R. §§2.64(a)-(b) (1985).

92. 42 C.F.R. §§2.64(d)-(f) (1985).

93. 42 C.F.R. §§2.63, 2.64(g) (1985).

94. *See, e.g., AFSCME Fact Sheet on AIDS and Guidelines for Workers Employed in Health Care Institutions and Correctional Facilities*, in Daily Labor Report (BNA), Feb. 3, 1986, at D-1, D-3 (advising that pregnant women be excused from direct care of AIDS patients); *cf. Summary: Recommendations for Preventing Transmission of Infection with Human T-Lymphotropic Virus Type III/Lymphadenopathy-Associated Virus in the Workplace*, 34 MMWR 681, 684 (1985) (pregnant health care workers "should be especially familiar with precautions for preventing transmission").

95. Office of General Counsel, note 64 above.

96. *Id.*

97. 42 C.F.R. §2.36 (1985).

98. 42 C.F.R. §2.51 (1985).

99. *E.g.*, Kathleen K. v. Robert B., 150 Cal. App. 3d 992, 198 Cal. Rptr. 273 (Cal. Ct. App. 1984); *see also*, Chapter 11 in this volume.

100. 42 C.F.R. §§2.38(a), (d) (1985).

101. 42 C.F.R. §2.38(c) (1985).

102. 42 C.F.R. §2.65; *see also* a series of legal opinions elucidating the requirements of this section, issued by the Office of the General Counsel, U. S. Health and Human Services Department, including Legal Opinons No. 78-18A (July 18, 1978), in HHS Legal Opinions on Confidentiality at 50-58; No. 78-19 (Sept. 5, 1978), *id.* at 61-62; No. 77-2 (Feb. 1, 1977), *id.* at 87-92; No. 77-12 (June 7, 1977), *id.* at 122-23; No. 77-15 (June 15, 1977), *id.* at 136-44; No. 77-22 (Oct. 3, 1977); No. 76-53 (Aug. 25, 1976), *id.* at 321-22; No. 76-79 (Nov. 29, 1976), *id.* at 378; and No. 75-9(A) (Oct. 2, 1975), *id.* at 409-13.

103. *See* note 13 above; Fuerst, *"Clean Needles" Idea Still Alive*, U.S. J. Drug & Alcohol Dependence, May 1986, at 1, 10 (reporting on shortage of funding and facilities in New York for providing addicts with treatment); Kerr, *Drug Treatment in City Is Strained By Crack, a Potent New Cocaine*, N.Y. Times, May 16, 1986, at A1, A18.

104. Prevention Policy Questions, note 4 above, at 7.

105. *Id.*

106. *Id.; see also Confronting AIDS*, note 1 above, at 12-13, 108-09.

107. *See, e.g., Confronting AIDS*, note 1 above, at 109; Kerr, note 103 above at A1, A18; Fuerst, note 103 above, at 1, 10; Altman, note 1 above, at A30.

108. Prevention Policy Questions, note 4 above, at 7.

109. *AIDS and Needle Sharing*, note 1 above, at 121. An unpublished study by researchers at the Montefiore Medical Center in New York City found that of 261 IV-drug users, 40 percent reported a decrease in needle sharing because of fear of AIDS, and 51 percent who continued to share needles said they did so because of the unavailability of sterile needles. Only 11 percent of addicts surveyed said that they had stopped injecting drugs; and many of them (primarily cocaine addicts) remained addicted but used a different method of ingestion (smoking or snorting). Thus, though the awareness of AIDS may result in risk reduction efforts, it may not drive addicts into treatment. Committee on Medicine and Law, Ass'n of the Bar of the City of New York, *Legalization of Non-Prescription Sale of Hypodermic Needles: A Response to the AIDS Crisis*, in 41 Record of the Assn. of the Bar of the City of New York 809, 813-14 (1986) [hereinafter *NYC Bar Ass'n Report on Legalization of Needles*] (available from Ass'n of the Bar of the City of New York, 42 W. 44th Street, New York, N.Y. 10035-6690). The Montefiore study was reported in P. Selwyn, C. Cox, C. Feiner, C. Lipshutz & R. Cohen, Knowledge About AIDS and High-Risk Behavior Among Intravenous Drug Abusers in New York City (Jan. 1986) (unpublished manuscript).

110. Prevention Policy Questions, note 4 above, at 3-6, 8; *Risk Reduction*, note 1 above, at 756-57.

111. *NYC Bar Ass'n Report on Legalization of Needles*, note 109 above, at 812-15; *Risk Reduction*, note 1 above, at 757-59; Prevention Policy Questions, note 4 above, at 6-8; *AIDS and Needle Sharing*, note 1 above, at 112-21.

112. *E.g.*, *Confronting AIDS*, note 1 above, at 112; *NYC Bar Ass'n Report on Legalization of Needles*, note 109 above; Des Jarlais & Hopkins, note 14 above, at 1476.

113. Sullivan, *Health Commissioner Considers Distribution of Needles to Addicts*, N.Y. Times, Nov. 8, 1986, at A8; *Jersey "Willing" to Give Addicts Clean Needles*, N.Y. Times, July 24, 1986, at A12; Fuerst, note 103 above, at 10; Korcok, *More Concern About Needles Expressed*, U.S. J. Drug & Alcohol Dependence May 1986 at 10; Altman, note 1 above, at A30.

114. These educational efforts are described in Wallace, note 3 above, at 51; Fuerst, note 103 above, at 11.

115. N.Y. Pub. Health L. §3381 (McKinney 1985); N.J. Stat. Ann. §24:21-51 (West Supp. 1986); Cal. Bus. and Prof. Code, §§4140, 4149, 4151 (West Supp. 1986); and Conn. Consumer Protection L., Conn. Gen. Stat. Ann. §21a-65 (West 1985); *see also NYC Bar Ass'n Report on Legalization of Needles*, note 109 above, at 811-12 & n.15 (listing states with such laws).

116. *E.g.*, N.Y. Penal L. §220.45 (McKinney 1980); N.J. Stat. Ann. §24:21-51(c)(d) (West Supp. 1986); Cal. Bus. and Prof. Code §4151 (West Supp. 1986); Conn. Gen. Stat. Ann. §21a-65(d) (West 1985).

117. Fla. Stat. §§893.145, 893.147 (1985).

118. *See* note 13 above.

119. Robinson v. California, 370 U.S. 661, 666-68 (1962).

120. *See e.g.*, *NYC Bar Ass'n Report on Legalization of Needles*, note 109 above, at 811-12, 817. Korcok, note 113 above, at 11.

121. *See* note 109 above; Des Jarlais & Hopkins, note 14 above, at 1476; *Risk Reduction*, note 1 above, at 758-59.

122. *AIDS Policy and Law* (BNA), May 21, 1986, at 7.

123. Sullivan, *Official Favors a Test Program to Curb AIDS—Calls For Giving Addicts Syringes and Needles*, N.Y. Times, May 30, 1986, at B36.

124. *Confronting AIDS*, note 1 above, at 13, 109-10, 112; *see also* Sullivan, note 113 above, at A8; N.Y. Times, July 24, 1986, at A12.

CHAPTER 19

Editor's note: Although this chapter focuses on aspects of AIDS that are particularly poignant for the black community, many of the effects discussed are felt within other racial and ethnic minority communities or are pervasive. Effects related to poverty and inner-city living, for example, are special hardships for a disproportionate number of Latinos as well as for all others in like circumstances. In some cases statistics indicating high incidence of specific conditions within the Latino community are included in the notes.

1. *Acquired Immunodeficiency Syndrome (AIDS) Among Blacks and Hispanics—United States*, 35 MMWR 655 (1986) [hereinafter *AIDS Among Blacks and Hispanics*]. Though only six percent of the U.S. population, Latinos represent 14 percent of reported cases. Latino women and children account for 21 percent and 22 percent of reported cases respectively. *Id.*

2. Calculated from data in *id.* Among Latino adult cases, 54 percent are heterosexual. *Id.*

3. *Id.*

4. Forty-four percent of Latino adults with AIDS report intravenous drug use. Calculated from data in *id.*; *see also* Bakeman, Lumb, Jackson & Smith, *AIDS Risk-Group Profiles in Whites and Members of Minority Groups*, 315 New Eng. J. Med. 191 (1986).

5. Secretary's Task Force on Black and Minority Health, U.S. Dept. Health & Human Serv., 1 Report of the Secretary's Task Force on Black and Minority Health 135 (Aug. 1985).

6. Nat. Inst. on Drug Abuse, Main Findings for Drug Abuse Treatment Units, National Drug Abuse Treatment Utilization Survey: Statistical Series, No. 10 (Sept. 1982).

7. Schenbaum, Schoyn, Klein, *et al.*, Prevalence of and Risk Factors Associated with HTLV-III/LAV Antibodies Among Intravenous Drug Abusers in Methadone Program in New York City (paper presented at the International Conference on AIDS, Paris, France, June 1986).

8. Calculated from data in *AIDS Among Blacks and Hispanics*, note 1 above. Of the 22 percent of children with AIDS that are Latino, 82 percent of them were born to a woman who was an intravenous drug abuser or who had had an abuser as a sex partner.

9. Greaves, Tankerson & Page, *Impact of AIDS on the Black Community: A Hospital Based Study*, 79 J. Nat. Med. A. (forthcoming, summer 1987).

10. *Id.*

11. *See* Mayan, Wormser, Hewlett, et al., *Acquired Immunodeficiency Syndrome (AIDS) in an Economically Disadvantaged Population*, 254 J.A.M.A. 1607 (1985).

12. *See* Chapter 2 in this volume.

13. *See* Secretary's Task Force on Black and Minority Health, note 5 above, at 47-53.

14. *See* Prineas & Gillum, *U.S. Epidemiology of Hypertension in Blacks*, in Hypertension in Blacks 7-31 (H. Hall, E. Saunders & N. Shulman eds. 1985); *see also* Duh & Willingham, *An Ecological View of Hypertension in Blacks*, 78 J. Nat. Med. A. 617 (1986).

15. *See* Secretary's Task Force on Black and Minority Health, note 5 above, at 9.

16. Morin, Maylon, Epstein, *et al.*, *Psychosocial Aspects of AIDS,* in Living With AIDS (J. Lang, J. Spiegal & S. Strigle eds. 1986) (publication of AIDS Project Los Angeles).

17. *See* Norman, *Behind the Mental Symptoms of AIDS*, Psychology Today, Dec. 1984, at 12 (reporting study by Deane Wolcott of the University of California Los Angeles Neuropsychiatric Institute).

18. *See* Nichols, *Psychiatric Aspects of AIDS*, 24 Psychosomatics 1083 (1983).

19. Hardy, Rauch, Echenberg, Morgan & Curran, *The Economic Impact of the First 10,000 Cases of Acquired Immunodeficiency Syndrome in the United States*, 155 J.A.M.A. 209 (1986).

20. *See* Bureau of the Census, U.S. Dep't Commerce Series P-60, No. 154, Money, Income & Poverty Status of Families and Persons in the United States: 1985, at 21 (1986). Latinos are represented among persons below the poverty line at a rate nearly five times their proportion in the population.

21. *See* Greaves, Tankerson & Page, note 9 above.

22. *See* Morin, Maylon, Epstein, *et al.*, note 16 above.

23. *Id.*

24. *See* Williams, *AIDS Among Black People*, Philadelphia Inquirer, Mar. 11, 1986 at 1E.

25. Approximately 46 percent of black adults with AIDS are known to be homosexual. Calculated from data in *AIDS Among Blacks and Hispanics*, note 1 above, at 664.

26. Christ & Weiner, *Psychosocial Issues in AIDS*, in AIDS: Etiology, Diagnosis, Treatment and Prevention (V. DeVita, S. Hellman & S. Rosenberg eds. 1985) [hereinafter *AIDS*].

27. *Id.*

28. *See* Poggi, *The Black Community Organizes to Fight AIDS*, Gay Community News, Sept. 23, 1986, at 3.

29. Steis & Broder, *AIDS: A General Overview*, in *AIDS*, note 26 above; *see also* Gallo, *The AIDS Virus*, Scientific American, Jan. 1987, at 47, 55, 56; *cf.* Piot, Quinn, Taelman, *et al.*, *Acquired Immunodeficiency Syndrome in Heterosexual Population in Zaire*, 2 Lancet 65 (1984).

30. *See Recommendations for Assisting in the Prevention of Perinatal Transmission of Human T-lymphotropic Virus Type III/Lymphadenopathy-associated Virus and Immunodeficiency Syndrome*, 34 MMWR 721 (1986).

31. *See* A. Morris, The Origins of the Civil Rights Movement: Black Communities Organizing for Change (1984).

32. Latinos with AIDS may face analogous cultural homophobia and lack of support from the Catholic church. Containing the spread of AIDS may be doubly problematic due to Catholic orthodoxy disapproving the use of condoms, perhaps the single most important tool in preventing the spread of AIDS.

33. *See* Greaves, Tankerson & Page, note 9 above.

34. *See., e.g.*, Poggi, note 28 above (noting efforts of the Rev. Carl Bean, founder of AIDS Minority Project in Los Angeles).

35. Greaves, *AIDS: No Time for Apathy*, 78 J. Nat. Med. A. 97 (1986) (editorial).

36. *See* Chapter 12 in this volume.

37. *See Efforts on AIDS Often Ignore Minorities, Officials Say*, 1 AIDS Policy & Law (BNA), May 7, 1986, at 7; *cf.* Poggi, note 28 above (discussing black community focus on developing autonomous programs).

38. For a review of the various minority AIDS education efforts discussed in this paragraph, see Poggi, note 28 above; *see also D.C. Program Targets Minority Groups*, 1 AIDS Policy & Law (BNA), July 30, 1986, at 7.

39. *See* Williams, note 24 above.

40. *Id.*

41. Neighbors, *Ambulatory Medical Care Among Adult Black Americans: The Hospital Emergency Room*, 78 J. Nat. Med. A. 275 (1986).

CHAPTER 20

1. *See, e.g.*, Petrucelli, *Gay Plague*, Us, Aug. 31, 1982; *Gay Plague Baffling Medical Detectives*, Philadelphia Daily News, Aug. 9, 1982 (cited in D. Altman, AIDS in the Mind of America 16-17 (1986)).

2. In New York City, for example, the bulk of new AIDS cases arise among IV-drug users and their sexual partners. *See* Chapter 18 in this volume. Experts predict that by 1991, 9 percent of AIDS cases will come from heterosexual transmission. *Future Shock*, Newsweek, Nov. 24, 1986, at 30-31.

3. Much of the mainstream media continues to paint AIDS as a disease that afflicts gay men and IV-drug users, a disease "the general public" need not worry about. *See, e.g., Don't Panic, Yet, Over AIDS*, N.Y. Times, Nov. 7, 1986, at A34 (editorial). While heterosexual transmission of the disease is increasingly being publicized, many Americans still view AIDS as an act of God directed against gay people. *See* Leishman, *Heterosexuals and AIDS*, Atlantic, Feb. 1987, at 39.

4. *See, e.g., AIDS Victim's Colleagues Walk Out*, N.Y. Times, Oct. 23, 1986, at A24 (medical literature about AIDS, posted in the workplace, defaced by anti-gay graffiti after AIDS patient returned to work).

5. Suro, *Vatican Reproaches Homosexuals With a Pointed Allusion to AIDS*, N.Y. Times, Oct. 31, 1986, at A17.

6. For surveys documenting violence against gay persons, see S. Aurand, R. Addessa & C. Bush, Violence and Discrimination Against Philadelphia Lesbian and Gay People 31 (Dec. 1985) (available from Philadelphia Lesbian and Gay Task Force) (citing studies by Philadelphia Lesbian and Gay Task Force, National Gay Task Force, Wisconsin Governor's Council on Lesbian and Gay Issues, and Maine Lesbian/Gay Political Alliance).

7. Gay and Lesbian Discrimination Documentation Project, New York City Commission on Human Rights, Two Year Report on Complaints of Sexual Orientation Discrimination 7 (1985).

8. *See* Greer, *Violence Against Homosexuals Rising, Groups Seeking Wider Protection Say*, N.Y. Times, Nov. 23, 1986, at 36; Nordheimer, *Campuses Press Efforts on Awareness of AIDS*, N.Y. Times, Sept. 22, 1986, at A14 ("growing AIDS awareness has apparently caused a backlash against homosexuals on many campuses").

9. *See AIDS Victims' Wills Under Attack*, N.Y. Times, Feb. 19, 1987, at B1. For detailed discussions of discrimination against same-sex couples see Ingram, *A Constitutional Critique of Restrictions on the Right to Marry—Why Can't Fred Marry George—or Mary and Alice at the Same Time?* 10 J. Contemp. L. 33 (1984); Rivera, *Our Straight-Laced Judges: The Legal Position of Homosexual Persons in the United States*, 30 Hastings L.J. 799 (1979); Rivera, *Recent Developments in Sexual Preference Law*, 30 Drake L. Rev. 311 (1980-81).

10. *See* J. D'Emilio, Sexual Politics, Sexual Communities 1, 231-33 (1983).

11. For an excellent account of the gay liberation movement in the 1970s, see R. Shilts, The Mayor of Castro Street: The Life and Times of Harvey Milk (1982).

12. *See* D. Altman, note 1 above, at 103-04.

13. *See id.* at 82-90.

14. *See* Purniek, *AIDS and the State*, N.Y. Times, Oct. 30, 1985, at B4. Some San Francisco baths reopened during a court challenge to closure, but these establishments remained a prime target for politicians such as Mayor Dianne Feinstein. *See Mayor of San Francisco Plans to Shut Bathhouses*, N.Y. Times, Nov. 11, 1985, at A12.

15. *See 2 Cities Consider a Bathhouse Ban*, N.Y. Times, Nov. 22, 1985, at B13; D. Altman, note 1 above, at 151-52, 168.

16. *2 Cities Consider a Bathhouse Ban*, note 15 above.

17. *State Permits Closing of Bathhouses to Cut AIDS*, N.Y. Times, Oct. 26, 1985, at 1.

18. *See* Blumenthal, *At Homosexual Establishments, A New Climate of Caution*, N.Y. Times, Nov. 9, 1985, at A29; Mailman, *The Battle for Safe Sex in the Baths*, N.Y. Times, Dec. 5, 1985, at A31, col. 1.

19. C. Koop, Surgeon General's Report on Acquired Immune Deficiency Syndrome (1986); *see* Boffey, *Surgeon General Urges Frank Talk to Young on AIDS*, N.Y. Times, Oct. 23, 1986, at A24.

20. D. Altman, note 1 above, at 152. The Supreme Court rejected a gay man's challenge to Georgia's sodomy law in *Bowers v. Hardwick*, discussed at text accompanying notes 49-58 below.

21. *Bathhouse Ban Nixed in L.A. By Court Order*, Au Courant, Sept. 22, 1986, at 3; *Judge Rules on Bathhouses*, N.Y. Times, Aug. 30, 1986, at A27.

22. *Growing Concern, Greater Precautions*, Newsweek, Nov. 24, 1986, at 32, 33; *see also Poll Indicates Majority Favor Quarantine for AIDS Victims*, N.Y. Times, Dec. 20, 1985, at A24.

23. Parmet, *AIDS and Quarantine: The Revival of an Archaic Doctrine*, 14 Hofstra L. Rev. 53, 90 (1985).

24. *AIDS Quarantine Proposed in Texas*, Newsday, Dec. 16, 1985, at 7C.

25. *Texas Health Chief Seeks Quarantine in AIDS Cases*, Washington Post, Oct. 23, 1985, at A2.

26. *Id.*

27. Americans increasingly view homosexual persons as pariahs. *See Growing Concerns, Greater Precautions*, note 22 above, at 33 (because of AIDS, more people are avoiding those thought to be gay, and more people are avoiding "certain places where homosexuals may be present").

28. Lindsey, *Deukmejian and Cranston Win as 3 Judges Are Ousted*, N.Y. Times, Nov. 6, 1986, at A30.

29. Kirp, *LaRouche Turns to AIDS Politics*, N.Y. Times, Sept. 11, 1986, at A27.

30. Hyde, *AIDS Quarantine, the Government, and Us*, Gay Community News, Mar. 24, 1984, at 3.

31. *See* Conn. Gen. Stat. §19a-221 (1985 Supp.).

32. Miller, *Public Health and Civil Rights in the Age of AIDS*, Boston Phoenix, Mar. 26, 1985.

33. *See* Shipp, *Insurance Concerns Press for AIDS Test*, N.Y. Times, Feb. 1, 1987, at 24.

34. National Gay Rights Advocates has filed a $10 million suit against Great Republic Insurance Co. for segregating applications of single males with no dependents working in certain occupations and for seeking additional information from that group. 1 AIDS Policy and Law (BNA), May 21, 1986, at 4.

35. It is now projected that only 25 to 50 percent of serpositive persons will develop AIDS. Institute of Medicine, National Academy of Sciences, Confronting AIDS 91 (1986); *see also* Chapter 1 in this volume.

36. Insurers argue that categorizing individuals according to group traits is justifiable; they

analogize HIV antibody tests to tests routinely given for high blood pressure or coronary disease. *See* 55 U.S.L.W. 2185 (Oct. 7, 1986) (discussing district court case upholding constitutionality of District of Columbia statute that prohibits insurers from denying, canceling, or modifying rates or coverage based on the results of an HIV antibody test).

37. *See Future Shock*, note 2 above, at 30.

38. There is precedent for protecting classes of persons against uninsurability. During the 1940s and 1950s many women took the drug DES to increase fertility. Children born to those women now stand a higher than average chance of developing cancer of the cervix or testicle. Yet in New York it is illegal to deny or cancel any application or policy, whether for individual, group, health, or accident, because the insured person has been exposed to DES. N.Y. Ins. Law §3225 (McKinney 1985).

39. *See* Rivera, *Our Straight-Laced Judges: The Legal Position of Homosexual Persons in the United States*, and *Recent Developments in Sexual Preference Law*, note 9 above (discussing employment discrimination against gay persons).

40. *See, e.g., Nurse's Suit Cites Friend's AIDS Death*, Philadelphia Inquirer, Oct. 1, 1986, at 13A (male nurse has sued employer for reinstatement, alleging discrimination because employer fired him days after his roommate died of AIDS).

41. *See* D. Altman, note 1 above, at 65.

42. *See AIDS Victim's Colleagues Walk Out*, note 4 above (discussing court rulings on employment rights of persons with AIDS).

43. Ward, *33 States Say AIDS is Protected Handicap*, Philadelphia Gay News, Sept. 12, 1986, at 1, col. 2.

44. Forty-eight municipalities, eleven counties, and seven states currently have gay rights ordinances. *See* United States v. City of Philadelphia, 789 F.2d 81, 88 n.9 (3d Cir. 1986).

45. *Houston Divided by Gay Rights Ordinance*, Washington Post, Jan. 19, 1985, §1, at 3.

46. Baker, *Houston to Vote on Gay Rights Issues*, Advocate, Sept. 4, 1984 at 17.

47. N.Y. Times, Mar. 21, 1986, at 1.

48. *Gov. Signs Pro-Gay Executive Order*, Au Courant, Dec. 29, 1986, at 3.

49. Bowers v. Hardwick, 106 S. Ct. 2841 (1986).

50. *Id.* at 2842.

51. N.Y. Times, July 1, 1986, at 19.

52. *Id.*

53. *Hardwick*, 106 S. Ct. at 2846.

54. *Id.* at 2853.

55. *Id.* at 2852.

56. *See, e.g.*, 55 U.S.L.W. 2191 (Oct. 7, 1986) (discussing recent decision upholding consideration of bisexuality as factor in adoption proceeding; the decision emphasizes that because homosexual conduct is illegal in the state, it would be anomalous to permit one who practices such conduct to head a state-created family).

57. *See* Gutis, *Homosexual Parents Winning Some Custody Cases*, N.Y. Times, Jan. 21, 1987, at C1; *AIDS Looms as an Issue in Visits by Fathers*, N.Y. Times, Oct. 5, 1986, at 33.

58. *See* Gutis, note 57 above.

Glossary

Acquired Immune Deficiency Syndrome (AIDS): A severe manifestation of infection
 with the HIV. First recognized in 1981, the condition is characterized by impaired
 immune function resulting in one of a number of rare infections or certain types
 of cancer.

AIDS: See Acquired Immune Deficiency Syndrome.

Antibody: A blood protein produced by the immune system in response to exposure
 to specific foreign molecules. Detection of the presence of antibody to the AIDS
 virus indicates that a person's immune system has been exposed to the virus.

Asymptomatic: Without symptoms. Persons exposed to the HIV may manifest laboratory evidence of infection without suffering from any symptoms of HIV-related
 disease.

Aziothymidine (AZT): An antiviral agent believed to inhibit the enzyme reverse
 transcriptase, an enzyme required for the replication of the HIV. It is now being
 used by many AIDS patients in the United States.

AZT: See Aziothymidine.

B-Lymphocytes: White blood cells involved in the production of antibodies.

CDC: See Centers for Disease Control.

Centers for Disease Control (CDC): A division of the U.S. Public Health Services
 located in Atlanta, Georgia. The CDC investigates and designs measures to control
 diseases which have epidemic potential.

Dementia: Deterioration of mental state with reduction of intellectual facilities due
 to infection or cancer or other organic brain disease.

ELISA: See Enzyme-Linked Immunosorbent Assay.

Enzyme-Linked Immunosorbent Assay (ELISA): A technique for detecting the presence in blood of antibody to the HIV.

Epidemiology: The study of disease frequency and distribution, and the factors that
 account for them.

Etiology: The study of the causes and mechanisms of disease.

HBV: See Hepatitus B Virus.

Hemophilia: A hereditary bleeding disorder occurring almost exclusively in males.

It is characterized by a deficiency of a blood factor (Factor VIII) which is necessary for clotting. Hemophiliacs are treated with intravenous injections of Factor VIII prepared from donated blood.

Hepatitis B Virus (HBV): A virus which causes inflammation of the liver. Like the HIV, the virus can be transmitted by transfusion of infected blood products, by intravenous injection with an infected needle, and by intimate sexual contact.

HIV: See Human Immunodeficiency Virus.

HTLV-III: See Human T-Cell Lymphotropic Virus Type III.

Human Immunodeficiency Virus (HIV): The name recently agreed upon for the virus which causes AIDS.

Human T-Cell Lymphotropic Virus Type III (HTLVIII): The name given by researchers at the National Institutes of Health (NIH) to the virus which causes AIDS.

Incubation Period: The interval between exposure to infection and the appearance of the first symptom.

Intravenous: Within or into a vein. Intravenous drug abuse involves injection of substances with needles directly into a vein.

Kaposi's sarcoma: A rare cancer of blood vessel walls. It often appears as pink to purple painless skin bumps, but can cause disease in lungs and other organs. Before the recognition of AIDS, it was seen primarily in elderly men of Mediterranean origin.

LAV: See Lymphadenopathy-associated Virus.

Lymphadenopathy: Swollen lymph nodes. When this condition is persistent (more than 3 months) and generalized (located diffusely in places like the neck, armpits, and groin) in a person exposed to the HIV, it is known as Lymphadenopathy Syndrome.

Lymphadenopathy-associated Virus (LAV): The name given by researchers at the Institut Pasteur in Paris to the virus which causes AIDS.

Lymph Nodes: Rounded bodies found at intervals along the body's lymphatic drainage system. The nodes filter bacteria and other foreign matter from the lymph fluid which is formed in the tissues and eventually transported to large central veins. The lymph nodes may become enlarged as a result of an infection or cancer.

Mortality Rate: The death rate. The ratio of the number of deaths to a given population. For example, the number of deaths from AIDS represents about sixty percent of the total number of cases reported.

Opportunistic Infections: Infections seen in patients with severe immune deficiency.

Pathogen: An organism which is capable of causing disease.

Parenteral: This denotes a route of administration other than oral ingestion. It may be intravenous (directly into a vein), subcutaneous (injected just under the skin), intramuscular (injected deep into a muscle), or mucosal (absorbed through a mucous membrane).

Perinatal Period: The period beginning after the 28th week of pregnancy and ending 28 days following birth.

Platelets: Blood cells playing an important role in clotting.

Pneumocystis Pneumonia: An unusual form of pneumonia caused by a protozoan parasite, *Pneumocystis carinii*.

Red Blood Cells: The oxygen-carrying cells of the blood.

Retrovirus: A virus whose genetic material consists of RNA (ribonucleic acid). This genetic material can be transcribed into DNA (deoxyribonucleic acid) by the enzyme reverse transcriptase and incorporated into a human cell's DNA. The HIV is a retrovirus.

Safe Sex: Sexual practices designed to prevent the exchange of body fluids and thereby limit the opportunity for HIV transmission.

Seropositive: A condition in which the presence of HIV antibody has been confirmed by ELISA or other test. Persons seropositive for the AIDS virus have been exposed to the virus and are presumed to carry active viral particles.

T4 Lymphocytes ("Helper/Inducer cells"): A type of white blood cell which is essential to the proper function of the immune system. The HIV apparently multiples in and ultimately kills these cells.

T8 Lymphocytes ("Suppressor cells"): A type of white blood cells which "turns off" antibody production.

T4:T8 Ratio: The ratio of helper/inducer lymphocytes to suppressor lymphocytes. The normal ratio is about 2:1. By killing T4 cells, the HIV decreases the T4:T8 ratio.

Toxoplasmosis: An infection caused by a protozoan parasite *Toxoplasma gondii*. In AIDS patients, this agent frequently infects the brain.

Transfusion: The injection of blood or blood products directly into the bloodstream.

Vaccine: A preparation consisting of an infectious agent or some portion of an infectious agent which is administered to stimulate the development of defense mechanisms by the body's immune system.

Virus: A minute organism which consists solely of a strand of genetic material—either DNA or RNA—surrounded by a protein capsule.

Western Blot: A technique for identifying the presence of antibodies. It is more difficult and expensive to perform than the ELISA; but it is also more specific and can be used to confirm the accuracy of a positive test by ELISA.

White Blood Cells (Leukocytes): The blood cells which make up the immune system.

A Selected Bibliography

(Compiled by Arthur S. Leonard as of March 6, 1987)

Abramovsky, *Criminal Law and Procedure: Issues Involving AIDS*, New York Law Journal, December 2, 1985 and January 15, 1986 (two-part review of special problems presented by AIDS in the criminal justice system).

Aiken, *AIDS—Pushing the Limits of Scientific and Legal Thought*, 27 Jurimetrics Journal 1 (Fall 1986) (broad overview of frontier legal questions presented by AIDS epidemic).

American Law Institute-American Bar Association, AIDS and the Law (study materials published February 1986).

American Management Association, AIDS: The Workplace Issues (1985) (summary of legal issues and survey of corporate policies and responses to AIDS in the workplace).

Association of the Bar of the City of New York, Committee on Medicine and Law, *Legalization of Non-Prescription Sale of Hypodermic Needles: A Response to the AIDS Crisis*, 41 Record of the Association 809 (November 1986) (advocating legalization of sale of clean hypodermic needles as a means of reducing spread of HIV infection in addict community).

At Issue: Is AIDS a Handicap?, American Bar Association Journal, February 1, 1987, 38 (contrasting views expressed by Congressman William Dannemeyer, Hellar Ann Hancock, and Nan Hunter, Esq., ACLU).

Bayer, Levine & Wolf, *HIV Antibody Screening: An Ethical Framework for Evaluating Proposed Programs*, 256 Journal of the American Medical Association 1768 (October 3, 1986).

Bayer & Oppenheimer, *AIDS in the Workplace: The Ethical Ramifications*, Business & Health, January/February 1986 (consideration of ethical problems of business coping with AIDS).

Beauchamp, *Morality and the Health of the Body Politic*, 16 Hastings Center Report No. 6, Special Supplement 30 (December 1986).

Bittle, *Private Rights v. Public Protection: AIDS in the Classroom*, 3 Complete Lawyer No. 3, 6 (American Bar Association, 1986).

Blodgett, Nancy, *et al.*, Student Lawyer, January 1984 (summary of early AIDS discrimination problems).

Bompey, *AIDS: An Employment Issue for the '80s*, The Digest (February 1986).

Breen, *AIDS — An Acquired Community Problem*, 32 Medical Trial Technique Quarterly 249 (Winter 1986).

Bureau of National Affairs, AIDS in the Workplace (study materials published March 1986).

Burris, *Fear Itself: AIDS, Herpes and Public Health Decisions*, 3 Yale Law & Policy Review 479 (1985) (review of public health law responses to infectious disease epidemics).

Case Law Developments, *Miscellaneous: Veterans' Benefits, AIDS, Attorneys' Fees and Program Administration*, 10 Mental & Physical Disability Law Reporter 395 (September/October 1986).

Cassel, *Advising Employers Who Have Persons with AIDS in Their Work Force*, 7 California Business Law Reporter 213 (Calif. CEB, May 1986).

Cecere, Payson & Kaynard, *AIDS in the Workplace*, 22 Trial No. 12, 40 (December 1986).

Check, *Public Education on AIDS: Not Only the Media's Responsibility*, 15 Hastings Center Report No. 4, Special Supplement 27 (August 1985).

Collier, *Preventing the Spread of AIDS by Restricting Sexual Conduct in Gay Bathhouses: A Constitutional Analysis*, 15 Golden Gate Univ. Law Review 301 (Summer 1985) (criticism of San Francisco bathhouse closure case from a constitutional perspective).

Comment, *AIDS: A Legal Epidemic*, 17 Akron Law Review 717 (Spring 1984) (focus on torts issues surrounding transmission of AIDS-related virus).

Comment, *AIDS—A New Reason to Regulate Homosexuality?*, 11 Journal of Contemporary Law 67 (1984) (exploration of AIDS as a justification for criminalizing consensual adult sodomy).

Comment, *AIDS and Employment: An Epidemic Strikes the Workplace and the Law*, 8 Whittier Law Review 651 (1986).

Comment, *AIDS and Employment Discrimination under the Federal Rehabilitation Act of 1973 and Virginia's Rights of Persons With Disabilities Act*, 20 Univ. of Richmond Law Review 425 (1986).

Comment, *AIDS: Does It Qualify as a "Handicap" under the Rehabilitation Act of 1973?*, 61 Notre Dame Law Review 572 (1986).

Comment, *Educating through the Law: The Los Angeles AIDS Discrimination Ordinance*, 33 UCLA Law Review 1410 (June 1986).

Comment, *Opening the Schoolhouse Door for Children With AIDS: The Education for All Handicapped Children Act*, 13 Boston College Environmental Affairs Law Review 583 (1986).

Comment, *Protecting the Public from AIDS: A New Challenge to Traditional Forms of Epidemic Control*, 2 Journal of Contemporary Health Law & Policy 191 (spring 1986) (discussion of ways in which AIDS differs from historical epidemics, raising new public health law issues).

Comment, *Quarantine: An Unreasonable Solution to the AIDS Dilemma*, 55 Cincinnati Law Review 217 (1986).

Committee on Government Operations, U.S. House of Representatives, 99th Congress, 2nd Session, *Oversight of the Office for Civil Rights at the Department of*

Health and Human Services: Hearings before a Subcommittee of the Committee, August 6 and 7, 1986. (Testimony and documents about enforcement of Rehabilitation Act 504 in connection with AIDS discrimination complaints.)

Committee on State Labor Law, Section on Labor and Employment Law, American Bar Association, *State Regulation of Employment Relationships: Highly Communicable Diseases*, 2 The Labor Lawyer 382 (1986).

Curran, Gostin & Clark, AIDS: Legal and Regulatory Policy (Harvard School of Public Health, Department of Health Policy Management Report, 1986).

Dolgin, *AIDS: Social Meanings and Legal Ramifications*, 14 Hofstra Law Review 193 (1985).

Douglas, *et al.*, *Homophobia Among Physicians and Nurses: An Empirical Study*, 36 Hospital & Community Psychiatry 1309 (December 1985) (study of attitudes of health care personnel dealing with AIDS patients).

Druhot, *Immigration Laws Excluding Aliens on the Basis of Health: Reassessment After AIDS*, 7 Journal of Legal Medicine 85 (March 1986) (review of medical exclusions under immigration law and applicability to AIDS).

Duncan, *Commentary: Public Policy and the AIDS Epidemic*, 2 Journal of Contemporary Health Law & Policy 169 (spring 1986) (proposal for mass testing and counseling as a means of containing spread of the epidemic).

Eckert, *AIDS and the Blood Bankers*, Regulation, September/October 1986, 15.

Feerick, *AIDS in the Workplace*, New York Law Journal, May 2, 1986, 1 (brief summary of some workplace legal issues).

Flaherty, *A Legal Emergency Brewing Over AIDS*, 6 National Law Journal No. 44, 1 (July 9, 1984) (summary of early AIDS legal issues).

Fox, *From TB to AIDS: Value Conflicts in Reporting Disease*, 16 Hastings Center Report No. 6, Special Supplement 11 (December 1986).

Frank, *AIDS Data-Sharing: Help Sought to Combat Bias*, American Bar Association Journal, January 1986, 22 (report on public interest law firms responding to the AIDS crisis).

Frank, *AIDS Victims Are Wary of Discrimination*, American Bar Association Journal, November 1985, 19.

Frank, *Alarm on AIDS*, American Bar Association Journal, December 1985, 22.

Freedman, *Wrong without Remedy*, American Bar Association Journal, June 1986, 36.

Freiberg, *AIDS and Legal Problems*, The Advocate, April 3, 1984 (summary of AIDS-related legal problems).

Fuchsberg, *Introduction: Law, Social Policy, and Contagious Disease: A Symposium on AIDS*, 14 Hofstra Law Review 1 (1985).

Goldberg, *The Meaning of "Handicapped"*, American Bar Association Journal, March 1, 1987, 56.

Gostin & Curran, *The Limits of Compulsion in Controlling AIDS*, 16 Hastings Center Report No. 6, Special Supplement 24 (December 1986).

Gray & Melton, *The Law and Ethics of Psychosocial Research on AIDS*, 64 Nebraska Law Review 637 (1985) (consideration of special problems posed by social science research among minority groups afflicted with AIDS).

Halper, *AIDS Court Case Raises Many Serious Right of Privacy Questions*, 3 Business and Health 51-52 (May 1986).

Hammett, AIDS in Correctional Facilities: Issues and Options (U.S. Department of Justice, National Institute of Justice, Office of Communication and Research Utilization, January 1986).

Harness, *AIDS: An Emerging Crisis*, Labor Law Journal, August 1986, 559.

Hartstein, *EEO Issues in the Health-Care Field: A Roundup of Recent Developments*, 12 Employment Relations Law Journal 241 (Autumn 1986) (section on health care employees with AIDS at 253-54).

Heilman, *AIDS Discrimination*, Los Angeles Lawyer, June 1986, 26 (anecdotal account of AIDS discrimination cases and legal protections in Los Angeles area).

Jones, *The Education for All Handicapped Children Act: Coverage of Children with Acquired Immune Deficiency Syndrome*, 15 Journal of Law & Education 195 (Spring 1986) (consideration of impact of federal education law on right of children with AIDS to classroom instruction).

Kandel, *Current Developments in EEO—AIDS in the Workplace*, 11 Employee Relations Law Journal 678 (Spring 1986).

Kilberg, *From the Editor: AIDS*, 12 Employee Relations Law Journal 1 (Summer 1986).

Kirby, *AIDS Legislation—Turning Up the Heat?*, 60 Australian Law Journal 324 (June 1986) (discussion of public health responses to AIDS compared to prior epidemics in Australia).

Kramer & Freger, AIDS and the Workplace: Employment Law Issues, 39th Annual National Conference on Labor (New York University, 1986).

Krim, *AIDS: The Challenge to Science and Medicine*, 15 Hastings Center Report No. 4, Special Supplement 2 (August 1985).

Lambda Legal Defense & Education Fund, Inc., AIDS Legal Guide (1984) (early effort to provide information for litigators coping with the problems of persons with AIDS).

Larson, *What Disabilities Are Protected Under the Rehabilitation Act of 1973?*, 16 Memphis State Univ. Law Review 229 (Winter 1986).

Law Journal Seminars-Press, AIDS: Legal Aspects of a Medical Crisis (New York, 1985) (coursebook for what may have been the first legal program on AIDS, held in October 1985 in New York City).

Leonard, *AIDS and Employment Law Revisited*, 14 Hofstra Law Review 11 (1985) (updating and expanding the author's 1985 article, *Employment Discrimination against Persons with AIDS*).

Leonard, *Employment Discrimination Against Persons With AIDS*, 10 University of Dayton Law Review 681 (Spring 1985) (consideration of handicap discrimination law as a source of legal protection for persons with AIDS).

Leonard & Tanenbaum, *AIDS and Employment Law*, in Employment Problems in the Workplace (Practising Law Institute, 1986) revised and reprinted in 7 Legal Notes & Viewpoints Quarterly No. 1, 45 (Nov. 1986).

Levine & Bayer, *Screening Blood: Public Health and Medical Uncertainty*, 15 Hastings Center Report No. 4, Special Supplement 8 (August 1985).

Lewin, *AIDS and Job Discrimination*, New York Times, April 15, 1986, D2.

Lipner, *Legal Aspects of AIDS: Preparing for the Worst*, New York Native, April 23, 1984 (focus on estate-planning and other legal issues for persons with AIDS and their partners).

Lipton, *Blood Donor Services and Liability Issues Relating to AIDS*, 7 Journal of Legal Medicine 131 (1986).

Macklin, *Predicting Dangerousness and the Public Health Response to AIDS*, 16 Hastings Center Report No. 6, Special Supplement 16 (December 1986).

Marcotte, *AIDS Questions Grow*, American Bar Association Journal, November 1, 1986, 28.

Margolick, D., *Legal Help Tailored to Victims of AIDS*, New York Times, January 3, 1986 (report on legal assistance efforts for persons with AIDS in New York).

Matthews & Neslund, *The Initial Impact of AIDS on Public Health Law in the United States—1986*, 257 Journal of the American Medical Association 344 (1987).

Mayer, *The Epidemiological Investigation of AIDS*, 15 Hastings Center Report No. 4, Special Supplement 12 (December 1986).

McDougall, *AIDS: A Plague Upon Your Civil Liberties*, 5 In the Public Interest (State University of New York at Buffalo Law School) 35 (1986).

McGuirl & Gee, *AIDS: An Overview of the British, Australian and American Responses*, 14 Hofstra Law Review 107 (1985).

Merritt, *The Constitutional Balance Between Health and Liberty*, 16 Hastings Center Report No. 6, Special Supplement 2 (December 1986).

Mohr, *AIDS, Gay Life, State Coercion*, 6 Raritan 38 (1986).

Mohr, *AIDS: What to Do—And What Not to Do*, 5 Philosophy & Public Policy (Univ. of Maryland) No. 4, 6 (Fall 1985) (philosophical argument on appropriate governmental response to AIDS epidemic).

National Gay Rights Advocates, AIDS and Handicap Discrimination: A Survey of the 50 States and the District of Columbia, September, 1986 (results of mail and telephone survey of all state human rights agencies on their approach to AIDS discrimination charges).

National Lawyers Guild Military Law Task Force, *The Military and AIDS*, 9 On Watch No. 1 (April 1986) (detailed treatment of issues raised by military screening for HIV infection).

National Lawyers Guild AIDS Network & National Gay Rights Advocates, AIDS Practice Manual: A Legal and Educational Guide (1986) (practical advice for attorneys representing persons with AIDS).

New York Business Group on Health, AIDS and the Employer: Guidelines on the Management of AIDS in the Workplace (1986) (summary of proceedings of a conference on AIDS and the workplace held in New York City in 1985).

Note, *AIDS-Related Litigation: The Competing Interests Surrounding Discovery of Blood Donors' Identities*, 19 Indiana Law Review 561 (1986) (casenote on South Florida Blood Service v. Rasmussen).

Note, *Hepatitis, AIDS and the Blood Product Exemption from Strict Products Liability in California: A Reassessment*, 37 Hastings Law Journal 1101 (July 1986).

Note, *Recent Developments: Public Health and Employment Issues Generated by the AIDS Crisis*, 25 Washburn Law Journal 505 (1986).

Note, *Reportability of Exposure to the AIDS Virus: An Equal Protection Analysis*, 7 Cardozo Law Review 1103 (summer 1986).

Note, *The Constitutional Rights of AIDS Carriers*, 99 Harvard Law Review 1274 (April 1986) (discussion of constitutional issues raised by proposals to restrict civil liberties in connection with attempts to curb spread of the epidemic).

Oppenheimer & Padgug, *AIDS: The Risk to Insurers, the Threat to Equity*, 16 Hastings Center Report No. 5, 18 (October 1986).

Orland & Wise, *The AIDS Epidemic: A Constitutional Conundrum*, 14 Hofstra Law Review 137 (1985).

Panem, *AIDS: Public Policy and Biomedical Research*, 15 Hastings Center Report No. 4, Special Supplement 23 (August 1985).

Parmet, *AIDS and Quarantine: The Revival of an Archaic Doctrine*, 14 Hofstra Law Review 53 (1985).

Parry, *AIDS as a Handicapping Condition: Part I*, 9 Mental & Physical Disability Law Reporter 402 (November/December 1985) (consideration of applicability of handicap discrimination law in a wide variety of AIDS contexts).

Parry, *AIDS as a Handicapping Condition: Part II*, 10 Mental & Physical Disability Law Reporter 2 (January/February 1986).

Partida, *AIDS: Do Children with AIDS Have a Right to Attend School?*, 13 Pepperdine Law Review 1041 (1986).

Pear, *States' AIDS Discrimination Laws Reject Justice Department's Stand*, New York Times, September 17, 1986, A20.

Perkins & Boyle, *AIDS and Poverty: Dual Barriers to Health Care*, 19 Clearinghouse Review 1283 (March 1986).

Philipson & Wood, AIDS, Testing, and Privacy: An Analysis of Case Histories (1987) (available from AIDS Legal Referral Panel, 1663 Mission Street, Suite 400, San Francisco, CA 94103) (case studies of failure to keep HIV antibody test results confidential in violation of California law.)

Practising Law Institute, Communicable Diseases in the Workplace: Legal, Medical, Economic, and Human Resource Issues (1986) (Litigation Course Handbook Series No. 309).

Rabin, *The AIDS Epidemic and Gay Bathhouses: A Constitutional Analysis*, 10 Journal of Health Politics, Policy & Law 729 (Winter 1986).

Randal, *Too Little Aid for AIDS*, Technology Review, August/September 1984, 1 (report on charges of inadequate government support for AIDS research and treatment).

Recent Developments, *Employment Discrimination: AIDS Victims—Shuttleworth v. Broward County Office of Budget and Management Policy*, 9 Harvard Journal of Law & Public Policy 739 (1986) (casenote).

Reidinger, *Communicable Diseases and Civil Rights: LawPoll*, American Bar Association Journal, March 1, 1987, 14.

Robinson, *AIDS and the Criminal Law: Traditional Approaches and a New Statutory Proposal*, 14 Hofstra Law Review 91 (1985).

Rothstein, *Medical Screening of Workers: Genetics, AIDS, and Beyond*, 2 The Labor Lawyer 675 (Fall 1986).

Rothstein, *Section 504 of the Rehabilitation Act: Emerging Issues for Colleges and Universities*, 13 Journal of College and University Law 229 (Winter 1986) (includes discussion of AIDS issues, including accommodation of students with AIDS).

Rowe *et al.*, *The Fear of AIDS*, 64 Harvard Business Review No. 4, 28 (1986).

Rubenfeld, *Legal Aspects of AIDS*, AIDS: Facts and Issues (Gong & Rudnick rev. ed. 1986).

Saad, *AIDS—Legal Implications for the Employer*, 66 Michigan Bar Journal 164 (February 1987).

Sand, *Current Developments in OSHA—AIDS According to the Justice Department*, 12 Employee Relations Law Journal 515 (Winter 1986/87).

Sand, *Current Developments in OSHA—AIDS: Some of the Smoke Is Blown Away*, 12 Employee Relations Law Journal 148 (Summer 1986).

SantaVicca, *AIDS in the Minds of Librarians: Opinion, Perception, and Misperception*, Library Journal, February 15, 1987, 133 (poll of librarians on adequacy of AIDS information reveals misperception about possible roles libraries can play in helping to fight the epidemic).

Schacter & Seeburg, AIDS: A Manager's Guide (Executive Enterprises, Inc., 1986).

Schram, *AIDS 1991: What Could America Be Like in Five Years?*, Los Angeles Times Magazine, August 10, 1986.

Schwarz & Schaffer, *AIDS in the Classroom*, 14 Hofstra Law Review 163 (1985).

Sencer & Botnick, Report to the Mayor: New York City's Response to the AIDS Crisis (December 1985) (detailed discussion of steps taken by City of New York through 1985 to respond to the AIDS epidemic).

Sicklick & Rubinstein, *A Medical Review of AIDS*, 14 Hofstra Law Review 5 (1985).

Silas, *AIDS on the Job,* American Bar Association Journal, January 1986, 22 (report on current employment discrimination disputes).

Silverman & Silverman, *AIDS and the Threat to Public Health*, 15 Hastings Center Report No. 4, Special Supplement 19 (August 1985).

Simpson, *The Living Will: A Matter of Life and Death*, 125 Trusts and Estates No. 4, April 1986, 10.

Stein, *AIDS—An Employer's Dilemma*, Florida Bar Journal, July-August 1986, 55.

Stein, The Settlement of AIDS Disputes: A Report for the National Center for Health Services Research, Environmental Mediation International (September 1986; revised, January 1987).

Stromberg, *AIDS Poses Significant Legal Considerations for the Work Place*, Business & Health, January/February 1986 (summary of workplace legal issues with respect to AIDS).

Symposium on Law and Health Care: Legal Aspects of AIDS (panel discussion), 8 Whittier Law Review 503 (1986).

Tarr, *AIDS: The Legal Issues Widen*, National Law Journal, November 25, 1985, 29 (overview/report on AIDS legal issues).

TB Case as AIDS Precedent? 44 Congressional Quarterly 2993 (November 29, 1986).

Triantafillou & Withers, *AIDS and the Law: Blaming the Victim*, 30 Boston Bar Journal No. 3, 6 (May/June 1986) (argument for compassionate respect for human rights of persons with AIDS).

United State Conference of Mayors, Local Policies in Response to AIDS and HTLV-III/LAV Infection (July 1986) (useful compilation of local regulations and policy statements).

Volberding & Abrams, *Clinical Care and Research in AIDS*, 15 Hastings Center Report No. 4, Special Supplement 16 (August 1985).

Weeks & Lowry, *AIDS and the Campus*, 10 Lex Colleqii No. 2 (Fall 1986).

Williams, *Blood Transfusions and AIDS: A Legal Perspective*, 32 Medical Trial Technique Quarterly 267 (Winter 1986).

Wilson, *From AIDS to Z: A Primer for Legal Issues Concerning AIDS, Drugs, and Alcohol in the Workplace*, 2 The Labor Lawyer 631 (Fall 1986).

Wing, *AIDS in the Workplace: The Emerging Legal Issues*, 42 Journal of the Missouri
    Bar 163 (April/May 1986).
Yale Lesbian/Gay Law Students' Association, AIDS Legal Conference (Feb. 1, 1986;
    transcript, $17.50, from AIDS Conference/LGLSA, %Brown, 39 Grumman Hill
    Rd., Wilton, Ct. 06897).

Contributors

EDITORS-IN-CHIEF

Scott Burris, a recent graduate of the Yale Law School, is the author of *Fear Itself: AIDS, Herpes, and Public Health Decisions*, published in the Yale Law and Policy Review, 1985. Mr. Burris is presently a law clerk to Judge Dolores K. Sloviter of the U.S. Court of Appeals for the Third Circuit.

Harlon L. Dalton is Associate Professor of Law at Yale Law School and serves on the editorial boards of the Journal of Legal Education and the Archives of Sexual Behavior. Professor Dalton serves on the boards of directors of the Connecticut Civil Liberties Union and the Legal Action Center in New York City and is also a member of the board of governors of the Society of American Law Teachers.

CONTRIBUTING AUTHORS

Jane Harris Aiken holds a graduate degree in law and is Associate Professor of Law at Arizona State University College of Law. Professor Aiken has served as a director of the Arizona Civil Liberties Union and is presently a member of the American Civil Liberties Union's National AIDS Task Force. Among her writings is *AIDS: Pushing the Limits of Scientific and Legal Theory*, published in Jurimetrics Journal, 1986.

Taunya Lovell Banks is Professor of Law at the University of Tulsa College of Law. Professor Banks serves as a director of the American Civil Liberties Union of Oklahoma and chairs the Law and Ethics Subcommittee of the Oklahoma Department of Public Health's AIDS Advisory Committee.

Richard Belitsky, M.D., is Assistant Professor of Psychiatry at the Yale University School of Medicine. Dr. Belitsky is a Diplomat in Psychiatry certified by the American Board of Psychiatry and Neurology, and is a member of the American Psychiatric Association and of the American Academy of Psychiatry and the Law. Dr. Belitsky is author of *The Psychiatric Patient with AIDS: New Issues and Challenges for the Inpatient Clinic*, published in Yale Psychiatric Quarterly, 1986.

Allan M. Brandt holds two master's degrees as well as a doctorate in American history and is Assistant Professor of the History of Medicine and Science at Harvard Medical School, Department of Social Medicine and Health Policy, and at the Harvard University Department of the History of Science. Professor Brandt serves on the board of the Hastings Center Study Group on AIDS and Civil Liberties and is author of *No Magic Bullet: A Social History of Venereal Disease in the United States since 1880*, published by Oxford University Press, 1985; revised edition including material on AIDS, 1987.

John F. Decker holds two graduate degrees in law and is Professor of Law at DePaul University College of Law. Professor Decker serves as a Professor/Reporter to the Illinois Judicial Conference, lecturing judges on recent developments in the law, and is author of *Prostitution: Regulation and Control*, published by Fred B. Rothman & Co, 1979.

Daniel M. Fox holds a doctorate in history and is both Professor of Humanities in Medicine and Assistant Vice President for Health Science Academic Affairs at the State University of New York at Stony Brook. Dr. Fox serves as Director of the New York State Center for Assessing Health Services and is author of *Health Policies, Health Politics: The Experience of Britain and America, 1911-1965*, published by Princeton University Press, 1986. Dr. Fox is also author of *AIDS and the American Health Polity: The History and Prospects of a Crisis of Authority*, published in Milbank Quarterly Supplement, 1986.

Larry Gostin is Executive Director of the American Society of Law and Medicine and Editor-in-Chief of its publication, Medicine and Health Care. Mr. Gostin is also Lecturer in Health Law at the Harvard University School of Public Health, and an attorney of counsel to Warner and Stackpole, a Boston law firm. Currently conducting a world-wide survey of AIDS legislation for the World Health Organization, Mr. Gostin is author of *Legal Control Measures for AIDS: Reporting Requirements, Surveillance, Quarantine and Regulation of Public Meeting Places*, published in the American Journal of Public Health, 1987, and is co-author, with William Curran, of *The First Line of Defense in Controlling AIDS: Casefinding— Testing, Screening and Reporting*, published in the American Journal of Law and Medicine, 1986.

Wayne L. Greaves, M.D., a Fellow of the American College of Physicians, is Assistant Professor of Medicine at the Howard University College of Medicine, and Chief of the Division of Infectious Diseases at Howard University Hospital. Dr. Greaves is co-author of *Impact of AIDS on the Black Community: A Hospital Based Study*, forthcoming in the Journal of the National Medical Association, 1987, and is author of *AIDS: No time for Apathy*, an editorial in that journal, 1986.

Richard Green, M.D., is Professor of Psychiatry and Director of the Program in Psychiatry, Law, and Human Sexuality at the University of California, Los Angeles, as well as a member of the Yale Law School Class of 1987. Dr. Green is author or editor of over one hundred scientific publications, including *Homosexuality: A Health Practitioners Text*, published by Williams & Wilkins, 1975, 2d edition, 1979, and also published internationally in several translations. Dr.

Green's recent works include *The "Sissy Boy" Syndrome and the Development of Homosexuality*, published by Yale University Press, 1987.

Donald H. J. Hermann holds a doctorate in philosophy as well as a graduate degree in law. He is Professor of Law and Philosophy and Director of the Health Law Institute at the DePaul University College of Law. Professor Hermann is a member of the American Academy of Hospital Attorneys, serving as Editor of its monthly publication, Health Law, and was program coordinator for a conference entitled "AIDS: Legal, Medical and Social Dimensions of a Health Crisis," Chicago, 1986.

Frederic C. Kass, M.D., holds degrees in public administration and law in addition to his medical degree, and is a Fellow in the Section of Medical Oncology of the Department of Internal Medicine at the Yale University School of Medicine. Dr. Kass has served as an advisor to U.S. Representative Thomas J. Downey and has published a number of papers and articles concerning legal and policy implications of disease.

Arthur S. Leonard is Associate Professor of Law at New York Law School and member of the Section on Labor and Employment Law of the American Bar Association. Professor Leonard serves on the national board of directors of the Lambda Legal Defense and Education Fund and is co-founder and chairman of the Section on Gay and Lesbian Legal Issues of the Association of American Law Schools. A frequent lecturer on issues involving AIDS at legal seminars for practicing attorneys, Professor Leonard is author of *Employment Discrimination Against Persons with AIDS*, published in the University of Dayton Law Review, 1985, and *AIDS and Employment Law Revisited*, published in the Hofstra Law Review, 1985.

Daniel R. Mandelker, holder of two graduate degrees in law, is Stamper Professor of Law at Washington University Law School, as well as frequently a consultant on municipal planning and zoning issues to cities across the United States. He is a member of the Development Policies and Regulations Council of the Urban Land Institute, and serves on the Advisory Commission on Intergovernmental Relations of the Local Government Advisory Board. Professor Mandelker is author or co-author of nearly twenty books and dozens of articles and book-chapters on housing, zoning, and land use.

Catherine O'Neill is Senior Staff Attorney at the Legal Action Center in New York City, and serves on the board of the Association of Drug Abuse Prevention & Treatment. She edits Of Substance, a newsletter of legal issues affecting persons with present addictions and past histories of substance abuse, and is particularly active in outreach, education about AIDS, and support services to drug users and their families.

June E. Osborn, M.D., is Dean of the School of Public Health at the University of Michigan, where she also holds professorships in epidemiology and in pediatrics and communicable diseases. Dean Osborn serves on the Executive Committee: Working Group on AIDS of the National Institutes of Health and is chairperson of the Ad Hoc Working Group on AIDS and the Nation's Blood Supply of the National Heart Lung & Blood Institute. Dean Osborn's writings concerning AIDS include *The AIDS Epidemic: An Overview of the Science*, in Issues in Science and Technology, 1986, *Sounding Board: The AIDS Epidemic: Multidisciplinary Trouble* in the New England Journal of Medicine, 1986, and *AIDS, Social Sci-*

ences, and Health Education: A Personal Perspective, in Health Education Quarterly, 1986.

Rhonda R. Rivera holds an graduate degree in public administration as well as a degree in law and is Associate Dean and Professor of Law at the Ohio State University College of Law. Past president of the Society of American Law Teachers, Dean Rivera is co-founder of the Section on Gay and Lesbian Legal Issues of the Association of American Law Schools and is a member of the AIDS Task Force of the Episcopal Diocese of Southern Ohio, the AIDS Task Force of the Ohio State University, and the AIDS Task Force of Columbus Ohio. Dean Rivera has written widely on legal issues pertaining to homosexuals including, most recently, a three-part article entitled *Queer Law: Sexual Orientation Law in the Mid-Eighties*, appearing in the University of Dayton Law Review, 1985-1987.

Mark A. Rothstein is Professor of Law and Director of the Health Law Institute at the University of Houston Law Center and is a member of the Genetic Monitoring in the Workplace Advisory Panel of the National Academy of Sciences. Professor Rothstein's treatise, *Occupational Safety and Health Law*, published by West Publishing Co., 1978, 2d ed. 1983, is a standard reference on such law. More recently, he has written a chapter entitled *Assessing the Capacity of the Impaired Worker* for the book *Legal Issues in Assessing Vocational Capacity*, edited by S. Scheer and published by Aspen Press, 1987.

Mark Scherzer is a partner in Scherzer and Palella, a New York City law firm, with a practice concentrating on insurance law. Mr. Scherzer is a volunteer attorney for Gay Men's Health Crisis and a cooperating attorney with the Lambda Legal Defense and Education Fund, and is author of a chapter about insurance issues for that organization's *AIDS Legal Guide*. Most recently, Mr. Scherzer has written an article entitled *Insurance: The Case Against HIV Antibody Testing*, published in AIDS & Public Policy Journal, 1987.

Mark S. Senak is Director of Legal Services at Gay Men's Health Crisis and an attorney in private practice in New York City. Mr. Senak is a former chairperson of the AIDS Resource Center, the first housing project for persons with AIDS in New York.

Robert A. Solomon is Supervising Attorney and Fellow at the Jerome N. Frank Legal Services Organization at Yale Law School, and a partner in Sheehan & Solomon, a New Haven law firm.

Urvashi Vaid is an attorney and Director of the AIDS Education Program of the National Prison Project of the American Civil Liberties Union, as well as Public Information Director for the National Gay and Lesbian Task Force. She is author of articles in the National Prison Project Journal concerning issues raised by AIDS in prisons.

Index

Acquired Immune Deficiency Syndrome (AIDS), 1, 22; history of, 18–19, 20–21, 286; symptoms of, 19–20, 30; risk-groups, 23–24, 31; public fear of, 28–29, 116–17, 121–23, 123–24, 175–76, 247, 259, 298; neurologic and psychiatric disorders associated with, 64–65, 201, 208–09, 284; in children, 68–69, 253; and malpractice, 169–72; costs of treating, 189, 284; in prison, 237–39; characteristics of, in blacks as opposed to whites, 281–83; psychosocial impact of, 283–84; perception of, in black community, 285; in the media, 291

AIDS carriers. *See* Seropositive state

AIDS-related complex (ARC), 20–21, 22, 23, 55, 68, 109, 175, 239; symptoms of, 30; as handicap, 111; and the ELISA test, 131

AIDS-related virus (ARV). *See* Human Immunodeficiency Virus (HIV)

Ambulance services: duty to public, 181; and antidiscrimination laws, 182

Antibody positive. *See* Seropositive state

Arline v. School Board of Nassau County. See *School Board of Nassau County v. Arline*

AZT (experimental drug), 26, 55, 239

Bathhouses: and the least restrictive alternative analysis, 103; and image of homosexuality, 294; as locus for education, 295

Bivens action, 245

Blacks: epidemiology of AIDS in, 47–48, 254, 281–83; psychosocial impact of AIDS on, 283–84; financial impact of AIDS on, 284; attitudes toward homosexuality among, 285–86; sociocultural impact of AIDS on, 285–87; and origin of AIDS, 286; women and AIDS, 286–87; and the church, 287; community response to AIDS, 287–88; and AIDS-related education, 288–89; and health care, 289

Bowers v. Hardwick, 299–300

Buchanan, Patrick, 96

Casual contact, 33–36, 66, 69, 75, 124, 181, 202–03, 238, 240, 264

Centers for Disease Control (CDC): statistics on AIDS, 2, 19, 29, 47, 67, 68, 82, 221, 253, 270, 280, 281, 287; definition of AIDS by, 30, 130–31; and screening proposals, 55; guidelines on HIV-infected schoolchildren, 69–72, 78–80; modification of sexual behavior advocated by, 90; guidelines on AIDS in the workplace, 117–18, 129; guidelines on blood and plasma screening, 168; guidelines on funeral homes, 183

Children, AIDS in, 67–69, 253, 282

Civil Rights Act of *1964*, Title VII, and HIV antibody testing, 139

Condoms: use of among prostitutes, 84; and male prostitution, 85; as part of AIDS education program, 96–97, 288;